Leaving God for God

Leaving God for God

The Daughters of Charity of St Vincent de Paul in Britain 1847-2017

Susan O'Brien

Susan O'Brien

DARTON · LONGMAN + TODD

First published in 2017 by
Darton, Longman and Todd Ltd
1 Spencer Court
140 – 142 Wandsworth High Street
London SW18 4JJ

ISBN: 978-0-232-53288-3
A catalogue record for this book is available from the British Library

Phototypeset by Kerrypress, St Albans AL3 8JL
Printed and bound in Great Britain by Bell and Bain, Glasgow

Remember that when you leave meditation and Holy Mass to serve poor persons, you lose nothing, Sisters, because to serve those who are poor is to go to God.

Explanation of the Regulation of the Company of the Daughters of Charity, 1634

Contents

APPENDICES

GRAPHS AND TABLES

3.3   Graph: Comparison of foundations in Ireland,
      England and Scotland 1880-1920

4.1   Table: Five generations of Sisters

4.2   Table: Service in Europe by generation

4.3   Table: Stages of admission and commitment

4.4   Table: Social class of Sisters entering before 1885

4.5   Table: Birth country of Sisters entering before 1885

4.6   Table: Age at entry in the first generation

4.7   Table: Sister Servants in Britain by class and nativity in
      1884

6.1   Table: Horarium before the Second World War

6.2   Table: Provincial office-holders, 1885-1919

6.3   Graph: Number of Sisters in the Province 1860-1920

6.4   Graph: Yearly entrant numbers, 1885-1930

6.5   Table: Total number of entrants and age profiles,
      1880-1929

7.1   Table: Institution-based welfare provisions for
      children and young adults in Britain 1885-1925

7.2   Table: Residential care by sex 1915

7.3   Table: Parish- and community-based ministries
      1885-1925

MAPS

Foreword

It is entirely fitting that this book is being published during the 400th year of the birth of the Vincentian charism.

It was in 1617, while preaching in the parish church of Chatillon in Northern France that the young Vincent de Paul inspired his congregation to take responsibility for a poor family from the parish who had taken seriously ill and were in need of food and comfort. The family was saved by the overwhelming response to this call to action and Vincent, seeing the response, realised that great charity must be organised if it were to be effective. These were the first moments of what is now a vast worldwide movement of Vincentian service to the vulnerable of the world. In 1633 this movement gave rise to the foundation of the Daughters of Charity of St Vincent de Paul, co-founded by St Louise de Marillac who had by this time become St Vincent's greatest collaborator in the organisation of their charitable works.

The story of the Daughters of Charity of St Vincent de Paul in Great Britain drops into this historic and growing scene in the year 1847 when the international Company of the Daughters of Charity was expanding rapidly, having reached out across Europe to the shores of other continents. This book helps us to take our place in this distinctive global movement and in so doing we honour all those Sisters on whose shoulders we stand today. We pay tribute to all those with whom we have lived, worked and collaborated over so many years and especially we honour those who, experiencing poverty for a time, have allowed us to accompany them.

Our author, Susan O'Brien, skilfully traces the intricacies of the story, interweaving the charism and vocation of the Daughters of Charity and the socio-ecclesiastical content with precision, care, reverence, sensitivity and attention to detail underpinned by extensive research. We offer her our respect and admiration as we turn over these pages in gratitude and appreciation.

Undoubtedly, as with any history, we notice both the opportunities undertaken and the mistakes made, sensing the inevitable darkness juxtaposed with light in the story. The events and the human lives touched in giving and receiving make a colourful mosaic of experience as the charism of the Founders is expressed increasingly in the passage of time.

The title Leaving God for God has significant resonance for the Daughters of Charity, characterising as it does the unique missionary emphasis of our vocation. The phrase was used by Vincent de Paul in his customary talks to the Sisters. The following instance dates back to 1655:

'...if the good pleasure of God were that you should go on a Sunday to nurse a sick person instead of going to Mass, even though that's a matter of obligation, you should do it. That's called leaving God for God.'[i]

And Louise de Marillac used a similar phrase in 1656 in a letter to Sister Laurence Dubois:

'We are leaving God for God if we leave one of our spiritual exercises for the service of the poor'[ii]

Put simply it means that a Sister can leave the chapel and her prayer if the cries of the poor demand it, for there – 'in the heart and life of those who are poor'[iii] – she finds the same God.

While in this current generation we are experiencing a fall in vocations and facing the diminishment of our work in this part of the world, our trust in the marvellous Providence of God, one of St Vincent's major themes, gives us confidence that innovative and collaborative ways of serving will renew the energy and spirit of the Daughters of Charity in Great Britain in the years to come.

Sister Ellen Flynn
Provincial
March 2017

i Vincent de Paul *Correspondence Conferences Documents*, Pierre Coste, edited by Marie Poole DC et al, 2006, Vol. 10, No. 68, p.76.

ii *Spiritual Writings of Louise de Marillac*, translated and edited by Louise Sullivan DC, 1991, p.510/511

iii *Constitutions and Statutes of the Daughters of Charity of St Vincent de Paul*, 2004, C10a, p.31

Acknowledgements

Over the years of researching and writing this book I have incurred many debts of hospitality, kindness and intellectual collaboration. It is a great pleasure to acknowledge the individuals and communities who have provided me with sustenance of many kinds.

This book owes its origins to the determination of a small number of Daughters of Charity in Britain to have their story told and their courage in allowing me to tell it my own way, that is as integral to a larger and changing social and Church history. My first debt is, therefore, to successive provincials and provincial council members of the British Province of the Daughters of Charity and, in particular, to Sister Judith Greville, first provincial archivist, who provided the inspiration for this book, and to Provincial Sarah King-Turner who commissioned the study. We gladly acknowledge the financial support of the Jerusalem Trust in support of the commission.

My researches were supported by more members of the Province than can be mentioned here: through conversations over meals, practical help of many kinds, in laughter and in prayer. Sisters Joan Conroy and Bernadette Ryder as successive archivists were always ready to answer my questions and seek out material, regularly digging out fresh sources from the piles that came into the archive as houses closed. With Sisters Margaret Donnelly, Joan Moriarty and Maria Parcher they formed a reading group to check the visual essays and the Gazetteer – a significant undertaking - while Sister Maria Parcher read the whole text on behalf of the Province. I am particularly grateful for the insights she shared about the spirituality of St Louise and St Vincent.

The understanding shown by provincial Marie Raw when the project faltered during my term as principal of the Margaret Beaufort Institute of Theology was remarkable. I am pleased to have this opportunity to thank her publicly. The exercise of extreme patience must have been testing for one so committed to the research and so knowledgeable about the Daughters in Britain. That knowledge, and Sister Marie's willingness to share her own journal reflections on recent events, has enriched the work greatly. She and Sister Ellen Flynn have worked together to see the project to completion and I am grateful to Sister Ellen for so cheerfully adding me and the book to an already overfull in-tray.

Appreciative thanks go to Daughters further afield; to superioress general Evelyne Franc for her encouragement and to archivists in the Company's Paris and Dublin archives. Archivists of Catholic diocesan collections went beyond the call of duty to find rare sightings of Daughters of Charity in their collections: Reverend Dr David Lannon in Salford, Dr Meg Whittle in Liverpool, Dr Mary McHugh at the Catholic Scottish Archives in Edinburgh and archive staff at Birmingham and Westminster.

Members of the transnational community of scholars responded generously to my enquiries and requests for help. Special thanks to Alana Harris, Matthieu Brejon de Lavergnée, Betty Ann McNeill DC, Anselm Nye, Jacinta Prunty CHF, John Rybolt CM, Margaret Susan Thompson and Edward Udovic CM for their learned companionship. Stephen Lown, graphic designer, engaged wholeheartedly with the Daughters' history to create the series of visual essays.

Chapter 6 describes the 'trinity' of Sisters Eugenie Marcellus, Etheldreda Howard and Mary Langdale who undergirded the Daughters' fledgling British Province during the 1890s. I had my own undergirding 'trinity': fellow historian of women religious and friend, Carmen Mangion; editor and friend Mari Shullaw; historian and precious husband, Peter O'Brien. Only I know what this book owes to their contributions.

The thousands of guests of the Cambridge City Foodbank over the past five years have kept me close to the reality of poverty – and to the continuing importance of kindness and *caritas*. My personal dedication of the book is to them and to all who live with the injustice of poverty.

Part I
Introduction

1

Introduction

Modern public relations experts define a brand as a 'public promise' whose values
and attributes are instantly recalled by its logo or key symbol.[1] If ever a community
of women had a powerful brand linked to a compelling visual language it was
the Company of the Daughters of Charity of St Vincent de Paul whose history
in Britain from 1847 to the early twenty-first century is the subject of this study.
By the end of the nineteenth century their highly visible and unique winged
white head-covering - the cornette - had become an international signifier of
womanly Christian ministry to the sick and destitute. European and American
artists depicted Daughters in city streets, in sick-rooms and on the battlefield in
scenes of self-sacrificing dedication. Daughters embodied 'Charity' in paintings
of that name by Bonvin (1850) and Picasso (1897).[2] Popularly associated with
herbal dispensaries and home nursing, their image was appropriated by canny
commercial producers in France and Britain to advertise the wonders of Thé de la
Soeur Borel and Beecham's pills.[3] More poetically, the Daughters inspired bird
metaphors such as 'God's geese' and 'swallows of Allah', originating in places as
far apart as Nevada and Smyrna.[4] Even after the cornette had been replaced with
a more practical head-covering in 1964, a version of the original had a starring
role in the American TV sit-com series *The Flying Nun* (1967-70). It even made
an appearance in an affectionate parody of skating sisters during the closing
ceremony of the 2012 London Olympics as part of a pageant of an inclusive Britain
presented to millions of viewers worldwide. It seems safe to conclude that the
brand values of the Daughters of Charity have been absorbed by many different
cultures across time.

---

1 See Debbie Millman ed., *Brand Thinking and Other Noble Pursuits* (New York: Allworth Press, 2011),
Introduction.

2 The best-known representation is Picasso's sickroom painting of a mother, doctor and a Daughter of Charity,
'Science and Charity' but see also Armand Gautier (1825-94); Henriette Browne (Sophie de Bouteiller 1829-1901)
whose painting 'Sisters of Mercy' was in fact the Daughters of Charity; the Italian Giulio Bagnoli (b.1927) 'Nuns
by the Sea' and American artists such as S. Seymour Thomas (1868-1952) whose battle-field paintings of Sisters of
Charity form another important genre strand. Also see works by the artists Lepine and Jourdain. More recently
see the works of the artist Robert Vickrey.

3 Beecham's Pills in the 1880s in England and Thé de la Soeur Borel in France over a much longer period.

4 Part of the tradition of the Company. External sources are not clearly identified. An Irish Catholic priest and
writer, the Very Reverend Patrick Augustine Sheehan, authored a poem 'Swallows of Allah', published in *The
Irish Monthly*, Vol. XXVI (November 1898), pp. 601–602.

The Company of the Daughters of Charity was founded in Paris in 1633 by Vincent de Paul and Louise de Marillac who were both later canonised for their works of organised charity. Working collaboratively they created a new type of organisation that gave Roman Catholic women from humble backgrounds a way 'to imitate the life of Jesus Christ on earth'.[5] In the opening words of the community's seventeenth-century Rule, Daughters of Charity were

> called and assembled to honour and venerate Our Lord Jesus Christ as the source and model of all charity; serving him corporally and spiritually in the person of the poor.[6]

Like Jesus, who 'worked constantly for His neighbour, visiting and healing the sick and instructing the ignorant for their salvation', their purpose was to respond to people in spiritual and material poverty.[7] The original name, Servants of the Sick Poor, signified clearly that those most in need were to have priority and were to be served.[8] As disciples of Jesus they were to welcome 'the poor [as] our Masters'.[9] With this challenging commitment as its foundation stone the Company attracted many women, continuing to grow steadily even after both founders died within a short time of one another in 1660.

For the first 170 years, with the exception of houses opened in Poland and a single house opened in Spain, the Company was concentrated in France.[10] By 1790 it had founded more than 400 houses in its native land. Almost all of them were forced to close during the French Revolution, but the Company gradually re-established itself across France during the first quarter of the nineteenth century. Then, between 1830 and 1860, in a vigorous movement of outward expansion, Sisters were sent on mission to make new foundations in other parts of Europe and in Latin America, in

---

5 Maria Poole et al. eds., *Saint Vincent de Paul: Correspondence, Conferences, Documents* newly translated, edited and annotated from the 1920 edition of Pierre Coste (Brooklyn, New York: 2004) Volumes 1-14 [hereafter *CCD*], Vol. IX. p. 52. Conference given 16 March 1642.

6 'Common Rules of the Daughters of Charity: Servants of the Sick Poor' reprinted in Frances Ryan and John E. Rybolt eds., *Vincent de Paul and Louise de Marillac: Rules, Conferences and Writings* (New York: Paulist Press, 1995), p. 167 ff. This was the Common Rule amended by Father René Alméras who succeeded Vincent de Paul as head of the Vincentian double family.

7 *CCD*, Vol. IX. p. 14.

8 Elizabeth Rapley, *The Dévotes: Women and Church in Seventeenth-Century France* (Buffalo, N.Y: McGill-Queen's University Press, 1990), p. 84.

9 See Chapter 2 for a more developed discussion of the Vincentian vocation.

10 Daughters went to Poland initially at the request of Queen Marie de Gonzague. In 1790, on the eve of the Revolution, the Company had 420 Houses in France, 20 in Poland and 1 in Spain. *Genesis of the Company* Vol. 2 (Emmitsburgh, Maryland: Saint Joseph's Provincial House Press, 1973), p. 4. Archives of the Daughters of Charity, Mill Hill 1-7-2 [hereafter DCMH].

China and in the Middle East.[11] Between 1839 and 1900 more than 2,500 Daughters of Charity left their own homeland for a mission elsewhere in the world.[12] As part of this intense international missionary drive Sisters were sent to England in 1847 and Ireland in 1855. The Company's global reach was further extended in 1850 when foundations of the Emmitsburg Sisters of Charity in the United States, established independently in 1809 by Elizabeth Ann Seton using the Company's Rule and Statutes, were formally affiliated to the French mother house as the first American Province of the Company.[13] After 1890 the Company's missionary drive reduced because the leadership was forced to focus its energy on ensuring survival in France against the political pressure for the laicisation of education and welfare. By that time, however, more than half of the Company's 2,000 houses of charity were already outside France - including the small but growing number in the United Kingdom.[14] The Company resumed a modest expansionary drive in the post-World War I political era; the impulse this time shaped largely by the colonial connections of the nations to which it had spread during the nineteenth century.[15] When this remarkable transnational organisation reached its maximum size in 1960 it had some 45,000 Sisters across the globe.

Yet, paradoxically, both the power of the Daughters' symbolic presence and the scale and nature of their activities have served to reinforce a fundamental misunderstanding about some aspects of their identity. Despite their being thought of as nuns by Catholics and the frequency with which they are represented as archetypal apostolic or active nuns by scholars,[16] the Daughters of Charity of St Vincent de Paul are not religious sisters or nuns.[17] Properly speaking these are categories defined by canon law and particular conditions apply to any

---

11 An upper case 'S' will be used for Sisters who are Daughters and a lower case 's' for all other sisters. A mission was made to Switzerland in 1810 and another to the Canary Islands in 1829. For discussion of the French missionary drive see Owen White and J.P. Daughter, eds., *In God's Empire: French Missionaries and the Modern World* (Oxford: Oxford University Press, 2012) in general and the essay by Sarah A. Curtis, 'Charity Begins Abroad: The Filles de la Charité in the Ottoman Empire', in particular, pp. 89-107.

12 *Vincentian Calendar* (published as a Supplement to *The Echo of the Mother House*, privately circulated), p. 8. 1-5 DCMH.

13 See Daniel Hannefin, *Daughters of the Church: A Popular History of the Daughters of Charity in the United States 1809-1987* (New York: New City Press, 1989), p. 90.

14 *Genesis of the Company* Vol. 1 (Privately Printed, 1968), p. 105 and Vol. 2, p. 2. 1-7-2 DCMH

15 For example, The Congo via Belgium in 1925, Australia via Britain in 1926, Viet Nam via France in 1928 and Indonesia via Holland in 1931.

16 See, for example, the use of their image on the cover of Elizabeth Kuhns, *The Habit: A History of the Clothing of Catholic Nuns* (New York: Doubleday, 2003) and the cover of Sarah Curtis, *Civilising Habits: Women Missionaries and the Revival of French Empire,* which focuses on women from three congregations of apostolic nuns, and other places too numerous to list.

17 Canonically speaking the term 'nun' refers only to women who make permanent vows of poverty, chastity and obedience and live an enclosed life in community. Apostolic religious sisters are women who make simple vows of poverty, chastity and obedience and live in an unenclosed community undertaking a range of works and ministries outside of the convent. In popular and common parlance the terms nun, sister and religious sister are used interchangeably with the term 'women religious' used by Church insiders since Vatican II. The terms order and congregation do not apply to the Daughters of Charity and are replaced here by 'institute' and 'community' and the word 'nun' is never applied to them unless in a direct quotation.

organisation and any person whose canon law status is 'religious' rather than 'lay'. The Daughters of Charity are lay women living in community who have never sought to be approved as religious: on the contrary the Company has always safeguarded its canonical lay status with tenacity. The Daughters' little-understood status as consecrated Catholic lay women called to live in community is fundamental to any account of their history. In turn, this history has a wider significance for the ecclesiology of Catholic women's ministry that has not yet been sufficiently appreciated. This is partly because historians have interpreted the Sisters' lay status as a matter of historical expediency and have not recognised that it became constitutive of their identity,[18] partly because in certain periods the behaviours and norms governing the Daughters and active women religious have converged, and partly because, as one recent scholar put it, 'the Daughters of Charity have a quite extraordinary history that has been almost wholly neglected'.[19]

Historiography

Despite its reputation, its geographical reach and its size, it is only in recent years that the Company's nineteenth- and twentieth-century history has been researched by scholars. Still less of that history has been absorbed into broader social and cultural histories of the modern era.[20] This gap is the more surprising given a considerable advance in writing the history of nineteenth-century Roman Catholic women religious in North America, Europe and Australia since 1990 (with whom their history certainly belongs), and in the history of Anglican, Lutheran and Methodist sisters and deacons, much of it written in the context of women's and gender history. Although there have been a number of excellent thematic and local histories of seventeenth-century and eighteenth-century Daughters based on public sources in the Archives Nationales and on regional archives,[21] it is only since 2011 with the publication of Matthieu Brejon de Lavergnée's *Histoire des Filles de la Charité XVIIe-XVIIIe: La rue pour cloître* that a comprehensive study of the pre-Revolution Company, based on full access to the mother house archives, has been available. Restricted access to archives also inhibited the study of its global work in the modern era until recently.[22] A collection of essays edited by

18 See, for example, Sarah Curtis, 'Charity Begins Abroad: The Filles de la Charité in the Ottoman Empire', in White and Daughton, *In God's Empire*, p. 104 n.

19 Book review of Matthieu Brejon de Lavergnée, *Histoire des Filles de la Charité XVIIe-XVIIIe: La rue pour cloître* (Paris: Fayard, 2011) *Catholic Historical Review*, Vol. 98, 4 (October, 2012), pp. 816-7.

20 See the point made by Brejon de Lavergnée, *Histoire des Filles de la Charité* , p. 18 and the Introduction.

21 Outstanding histories of the Daughters before the French Revolution using public archives include Barbara Diefendorf, *From Penitence to Charity: Pious Women and the Catholic Reformation in Paris* (New York: Oxford University Press, 2004); Susan E. Dinan, *Women and Poor Relief in Seventeenth-Century France: The Early History of the Daughters of Charity* (Woodbridge: Ashgate, 2006); Colin Jones, *The Charitable Impulse: Hospitals and Nursing in Ancien Régime and Revolutionary France* (New York: Routledge, 1989) and Elizabeth Rapley, *The Dévotes*.

22 In his review of Brejon de Lavergnée's *Histoire des Filles*, Colin Jones notes that 'The Daughters of Charity have a quite extraordinary history that has been almost wholly neglected...' *The Catholic Historical Review*, Vol.98, 4 (October, 2012), pp. 816-7.

Brejon de Lavergnée and published in 2016 now provides a study of the history of the Daughters in France and across the world from the seventeenth to twentieth century.[23] To these developments and to the opening of the mother house archives we must add the important role of the Vincentian Studies Institute of the United States in promoting academic research and study. The Institute owes its origins to the Congregation of the Mission in the United States in the late 1970s, the American Vincentians being joined in the enterprise by the American Daughters in 1992.[24] Since 1995, when the Institute made a home in DePaul University in Minnesota, it has created a major digitised text and visual archive and has sponsored international research collaboration.[25] Supported by the superiors general of the Company and the Congregation of the Mission, The Daughters of Charity are now being given the attention their historical and ecclesial significance warrants.

It is only since the turn of the new century too that the history of Catholic nuns and sisters in modern Britain has been the subject of book-length scholarly works.[26] A turning point for scholars of nineteenth-century Catholic history everywhere came in 1984 with the publication of Claude Langlois' seminal study *Le catholicisme au féminine: Les congrégations françaises à supérieure générale au XIX siècle*.[27] The number of recent monographs on individual institutes and about sisters as nurses, hospital founders, teachers, evangelisers and welfare innovators is testimony to the vigour of research in Belgium, the Netherlands and the United States, Australia and Canada.[28] The first history of nineteenth-century nuns in Ireland was published

---

23 Brejon de Lavergnée, ed., *Des Filles de la Charité aux Soeurs de Saint-Vincent-de-Paul: Quatre siècles de cornettes (XVIIᵉ – XX ᵉsiècle)* (Paris: Honoré Chapman, 2016). This is the fruit of a symposium sponsored by the general council of the Daughters of Charity, the Sorbonne and De Paul University, Minnesota in 2011.

24 Edward Udovic, 'The First Twenty-Five Years of the Vincentian Studies Institute of the United States,1974-2005', *Vincentian Historical Journal* (hereafter *VHJ*) (2005), Vol.25, Issue 1, Article 4.

25 At http://via.library.depaul.edu/vhc/

26 For primary and secondary sources which show the important but unacknowledged presence of religious sisters in Britain see: J.N. Murphy *Terra Incognita: or, The Convents of the United Kingdom* (London: Longmans, 1873); F.M. Steele, *The Convents of Great Britain and Ireland* (London, 1923); G.A. Beck, ed., *The English Catholics, 1850-1950* (London: Burns and Oates, 1950); Susan O'Brien, 'Terra Incognita: The Nun in Nineteenth Century England', *Past and Present* No.121 (November, 1988), pp. 110-14) and O'Brien, 'A Survey of Research and Writing about Roman Catholic Women's Congregations in Great Britain and Ireland 1800-1950', in Jan de Maeyer, Sofie Leplae and Joachim Schmeidl, eds., *Religious Institutes in Western Europe in the 19ᵗʰ and 20ᵗʰ Centuries* Leuven: Leuven University Press, 2004, pp. 91-116.

27 (Paris:Éditions du Cerf, 1984).

28 For a survey of the historiography in European countries see the individual essays in Jan de Maeyer, et al., *Religious Institutes in Western Europe*. For the USA see Carol K. Coburn, 'An Overview of the Historiography of Women Religious: A Twenty-Five-Year Retrospective,' *U.S.Catholic Historian*, 22 (Winter,2004), pp. 1-26. New studies include Anne M. Butler, *Across God's Frontiers: Catholic Sisters in the American West, 1850-1920* (Chapel Hill: University of North Carolina Press, 2012); Maureen Fitzgerald, *Habits of Compassion: Irish Catholic Nuns and the Origins of New York's Welfare System, 1830-1920* (Urbana and Chicago: University of Illinois Press, 2006); Suellen Hoy, *Good Hearts: Catholic Sisters in Chicago's Past* (Urbana and Chicago: University of Illinois Press, 2006); Barbra Mann Wall, *Unlikely Entrepreneurs: Catholic Sisters and the Hospital Marketplace, 1865-1925* (Columbus: Ohio State University Press, 2005). Some insight into research developments can be gained from the website of the United States Conference on the History of Women Religious, https://www.chwr.org/

in 1988.[29] In the case of Britain, however, to borrow Carmen Mangion's words, Catholic religious sisters continue to be 'an enigma of nineteenth-century social history'.[30] Since 2000 two comparative histories of nineteenth-century sisters have been published for England and Wales and one for Scotland, together with several scholarly institutional and biographical studies.[31] These works have enriched my own interpretation and made some comparisons between religious sisters and Daughters of Charity in Britain possible, at least for the long nineteenth century that ended with the First World War.

When it comes to the decades since 1920, historical research on Catholic sisters is still in its infancy. At the same time a particular narrative of the history of religious sisters in the twentieth century has become fairly entrenched in Catholic circles. In it the decades between 1920 and the present day are usually divided into two distinct eras with a hinge around 1965, that is, at the end of the Second Vatican Council. The period from 1920 to around 1965 is regarded as something of a 'golden age'[32] characterised by esteem, growth and stability in religious communities while the years after 1965, with waning numbers, organisational changes and an apparent loss of direction, are understood as a drawn-out era of decline and diminution caused by the Council itself. Interpreting the story of Catholic sisters in this way parallels what Alana Harris has described as the 'caesura or rupture' framework for constructing modern Catholic history in general; from vigour and security to discontinuity and decline.[33] Its outline is apparently so compelling when applied to Catholic sisters in western societies that any challenge to it may seem perverse.

Yet the few histories of religious institutes in Britain that have explored more carefully the nature of consecrated life in the twentieth century suggest new ways of understanding these seventy or eighty years. It has proved fruitful, for example, to examine the impact that the 1917 Code of Canon Law had on the practice of female religious life in a more critical way and to recognise its cramping effects on the daily life of sisters, particularly when implemented in the

---

29 Catriona Clear, *Nuns in Nineteenth-Century Ireland* (Dublin: Gill and MacMillan, 1988).

30 Carmen Mangion, *Contested Identities: Catholic women religious in nineteenth-century England and Wales* (Manchester: Manchester University Press, 2008), p. 1. This is so despite an active network and website bringing together interested researchers from the medieval to modern periods (History of Women Religious in Britain and Ireland). Mangion provides a survey of the literature in the Introduction to her book.

31 Barbara Walsh, *Roman Catholic Nuns in England and Wales, 1800-1935* (Dublin: Irish Academic Press, 2002); Mangion, *Contested Identities*; Karly Kehoe, *Creating a Scottish Church : Catholicism, gender and ethnicity in nineteenth-century Scotland* (Manchester: Manchester University Press, 2010). For individual orders and congregations, Judith Lancaster, *Cornelia Connelly and Her Interpreters* (Oxford: Way Books, 2004); Anselm Nye, *A Peculiar Kind of Mission: The English Dominican Sisters 1845-2010* (Leominster: Gracewing, 2011) and Teresa White, *A Vista of Years: History of the Society of the Sisters of the Faithful Companions of Jesus 1820-1993* (Privately printed, 2013).

32 Michael Hornsby-Smith, *Roman Catholics in England* (Cambridge: Cambridge University Press, 1987), pp. 26-30.

33 See Alana Harris, 'Undying devotions' *The Tablet* 15 December 2012, p. 11 and her full-length study, *Faith in the Family: a lived religious history of English Catholicism before and after Vatican II* (Manchester: Manchester University Press, 2013) for a critique of the change-without-continuity interpretations.

anxious post-war decades of the 1920s and 1930s.[34] Conversely, the description of post-conciliar communities as 'diminished' can be questioned in the light of the activities undertaken by many sisters during the 1980s and 1990s, despite their reduction in numbers. The dynamism of some Catholic female communities since the 1980s demands to be taken seriously.[35] In these decades, for example, a numerically much smaller group of Daughters than had comprised the Province in the 1930s undertook a series of large-scale and high-impact activities that include 'The Passage', London's largest voluntary day centre for homeless people, and the Depaul Trust, a national charity for homeless young people that has extended from Britain to Ireland. And since the beginning of the twenty-first century an even smaller group have undertaken strategic initiatives to widen the reach of Vincentian values and practices.

As already noted, the archival sources for the interwar period and beyond are often not available to scholars. Community archives are private and there are understandable concerns about confidentiality when it comes to the very recent past. At the same time other sources outside the archive concerning the Second Vatican Council and the years since have grown rapidly with the publication of biographies of former and continuing sisters, surveys conducted by national bodies of major superiors, works of sociology and oral interviews. Yet it will not be possible to understand fully the response of communities of sisters to the post-Vatican II ecclesial and wider social climate without examining their lives in the era from the 1920s to 1950s.[36] What is emerging from research in the British context suggests that the 1950s were pivotal and transitional and that there was more evolutionary change and more continuity than is usually portrayed.[37] Greater knowledge about the interwar period is providing explanations for some patterns of renewal. What is needed is for the modern era to be historicised, and with the passage of time this becomes increasingly possible. With the generous collaboration of the Daughters of Charity of the British Province, this study aims to make a contribution to the re-assessment of the modern history of Catholic sisters. Their willingness to grant archival access has allowed me to interpret the post-Vatican II years in the light of those that preceded them. While no amount of inspired research can conjure numbers of young Daughters of Charity who do not exist, new sources and fresh perspectives can reveal much more about the twentieth century than

---

34 Nye, *Peculiar Kind of Mission*, pp. 104-5, 136-41; White, *Vista of the Years*, pp. 185-202.

35 My own thoughts about this matter have been developed in discussions with Sister Gemma Simmonds CJ and Catherine Sexton who are undertaking 'The Religious Life Vitality Project', a research project focused on Britain and sponsored by the Conrad Hilton Foundation. For a report on the project's findings see http://www.margaretbeaufort.cam.ac.uk/assets/documents/research%20key%20findings%20report.pdf

36 But see the work of Yvonne McKenna who has interviewed Irish sisters born between the 1910s and 1940s: 'Embodied Ideals and Realities: Irish Nuns and Irish Womanhood, 1930s-1960s', Éire-Ireland 41: 1 & 2 (Spr/Sum 2016); *Made Holy: Irish Women Religious at Home and Abroad* (Dublin: Irish Academic Press, 2006); and 'Entering Religious Life; Claiming Subjectivity: Irish Nuns, 1930s-1960s', *Women's History Review*, 15:2 (2006).

37 See Harris, *Faith in the Family*, p. 38.

is suggested either by the narrative of pre-Vatican II 'golden age' or that of post-conciliar 'decline and diminishment'.

The prospect of extending the history of Catholic sisters into the interwar and post-war eras has become more urgent because a re-interpretation of 'the place of religion in Britain's social and cultural landscape' in these decades is already underway.[38] Catholic women should be integral to this contemporary re-interpretation. Having been declared almost extinct as a consequence of secularisation, religion has become central to debates about social change in the twentieth century and about who 'we' are in twenty-first century Britain. This is partly because globalisation has made it difficult to avoid the knowledge, as Peter Berger put it, that 'the greater part of the world (both developed and developing) is 'as furiously religious as ever',[39] partly because of Britain's increasing religious plurality and partly because of increasing tensions between secular and religious world views. But it is also, according to the contributors to *Redefining Christian Britain: Post-1945 Perspectives*, because 'Christianity has neither disappeared nor even declined' as was predicted in the 1960s and 1970s,[40] but 'rather has been transformed'.[41]

If Christianity can be understood as a faith once again in transformation,[42] there is general agreement that women's religious identities and the nature of their commitment to churches are central to that process.[43] How religious leaders have engaged with matters vital to women, including questions of pastoral priorities, teaching about sexuality and gendered forms of authority, is a defining matter for most churches. No less is true for the Roman Catholic Church in the later twentieth and twenty-first centuries.[44] Consecrated sisters, as the Church's full-time dedicated women 'professionals' or 'virtuosi', to apply a Weberian term,[45] have been the touchstone for some of the issues at stake.[46]

---

38 Sue Morgan and Jacqueline de Vries, eds., *Women, Gender and Religious Cultures in Britain, 1800-1914* (Abingdon: Routledge, 2010), p. 231.

39 Peter Berger quoted in Jane Garnett, Matthew Grimley, Alana Harris, William Whyte and Sarah Williams, eds., *Redefining Christian Britain: Post-1945 Perspectives* (London: SCM, 2006), p. 6. See also C.A. Bayley, *The Birth of the Modern World 1780-1914* (Oxford: Blackwell, 2004), p. 329.

40 See the Introduction of Garnett, *Redefining Christian Britain* for a thorough discussion of the secularisation debate.

41 Ibid., p. 289.

42 See Harris's discussion in *Faith in the Family*, pp. 41-7.

43 See the discussion in Morgan and de Vries, eds., *Women, Gender and Religious Culture*, pp. 232-4.

44 See, for example, Catholic Women Speak Network, *Catholic Women Speak: Bringing Our Gifts to the Table* (New York: Paulist Press, 2105)

45 Patricia Wittberg uses Weber's term 'virtuosi' for consecrated sisters, Patrica Wittberg, *From Piety to Professionalism – and back?:Transformations of organized religious virtuosity* (Oxford: Lexington Books, 2006), pp. 4-12.

46 See, as a prime example, the entire story of the Vatican's engagement with the U.S. Leadership Conference of Women Religious, widely discussed across national, international and Catholic media between 2008 and 2015. Margaret Cain McCarthy and Mary Ann Zollman, eds., *The Power of Sisterhood: Women Religious Tell the Story of the Apostolic Visitation* (Lanham MD: University Press of American, 2014).

Approaches, scope and themes

This is an institutional history written at the request of the British Province of the Daughters of Charity to record its work over 170 years as definitively as possible. Beyond fulfilment of this purpose, my intention is to connect the Sisters' past to other histories within and beyond the Catholic community in England, Scotland and Wales. The production of institutional histories of individual Catholic religious institutes that has already taken place in other countries has been criticised for being 'introverted' and leading to 'an under-appreciation of the social and cultural role played by orders and congregations both in the Catholic past and in the national past'.[47] By integrating the Daughters' history as a dimension of Catholic experience in Britain and arguing that this experience was woven into British religious and social culture, I hope to avoid both the pitfall of introversion and the danger of 'contribution' history.

Institutional history has the potential to ask 'large questions in small places' and to take the long view, 'of groups, collective destinies and general movements', to adopt Ferdinand Braudel's terms.[48] For example, it becomes possible to investigate whether the Catholic theology of poverty, particularly a Vincentian theology, made Catholic charity any different from mainstream philanthropy in Victorian and Edwardian Britain. Recent scholarship has emphasised the long-standing part and changing role played by voluntary organisations, many of them motivated by their faith, in the provision of welfare and care in Britain. Other studies have brought out the centrality of Protestantism to the construction of civil society in Britain and to the emergence of welfare policies and new social work professions.[49] With the Daughters as a case study, I will argue that active involvement in British civil society was part of the process by which Catholics were incorporated within the state and through which Catholic sisters were (not always easily) accepted by their Protestant neighbours. The ready assumption that Catholic organisations simply paralleled Protestant ones on a small scale and for their own community can be interrogated through the Daughters' history. Likewise, the development of a working relationship between the Catholic Church and the British state to construct Catholic welfare can be viewed through the eyes of the women who provided the care on a day-to-day basis. It widens our angle of vision to understand this religious work as engagement in civil society through participation in the voluntary sector. New questions are provoked if the Daughters

47 Jan Roes and Hans de Valk, 'A World Apart?: Religious Orders and Congregations in the Netherlands', in Jan de Maeyer et al., *Religious Institutes in Western Europe*, p. 152 and p. 158.

48 Ferdinand Braudel, *La Méditerranée et le monde méditerranéen à l'époque de Philippe II. Vol 2. Destins collectifs et mouvements d'ensemble* (Paris: Armand Colin, 1949).

49 See for example any of the works by leading scholars in this field: Frank Prochaska, *Women and Philanthropy in Nineteenth Century England* (Oxford: Clarendon, 1980) and *Christianity and Social Service in Modern Britain: The Disinherited Spirit* (Oxford: Oxford University Press, 2008); G. Finlayson, *Citizens, State and Social Welfare in Britain 1830-1990* (Oxford: Oxford University Press, 1994); Colin Jones, 'Some recent trends in the history of charity', in Martin Daunton, ed., *Charity, self-interest and welfare in the English past* (London: UCL Press, 1996), pp. 51-63.

are seen as an integral part of Britain's 'mixed economy of welfare', albeit a part shaped by their particular Catholic and Vincentian ethos.[50] A recognition of their place in this welfare economy leads naturally into an assessment of the impact that policy changes in the field of welfare and social care have had on the extent and the nature of their involvement over a timespan of more than a century. How, for example, did they respond to legislation in the 1850s that established provision for children in need of care and protection and for young offenders, or to the Curtis and Clyde Committee Reports of 1946, criticising large-scale institutional living? Was their practice influenced by the development of the 'science' of social work in the late nineteenth century and its professionalisation in the 1960s? Did they innovate outside the state's welfare framework, and how have they managed the emergence of partnership and competition between agencies since the 1980s? These questions sit at what Ninna Edgardh has called 'the specific intersections between gender, welfare and religion in Europe' that have been little explored, despite the growing evidence about the impact that gender has on the agency of churches.[51]

Ideas about care are, indeed, closely connected to questions about gender and welfare. Edgardh underlines the impossibility of understanding 'the form and nature of contemporary welfare without a concept like "care" although, as she observes, 'sociological models of welfare have often disregarded care altogether'.[52] Vincent de Paul and Louise de Marillac articulated a particular ethic of care derived from their understanding of the example set by Jesus Christ on earth and from their understanding of what was proper for women. As we will see, it was developed in the conferences Vincent de Paul gave to the early Daughters about how they should act towards those they served. Although this book is not a specialist study in the history of care, the question of how the Vincentian vision of care was lived out at different times in Britain is too central to the Daughters' story to be set aside. To study the way that care was practised in the changing 'normative, economic and social frameworks' operating in the Company and in Britain over 150 years, however, presents serious challenges.[53] These arise from the nature of the sources and from the methods available to study care practices but are further complicated by society's current concerns about almost all aspects of social care. Since the 1990s, largely as a consequence of revelations of abuse and the cover-up of abuse, society has developed a set of assumptions which are grounded in suspicion about a wide range of past and present institutional care and about

50 Jane Lewis, 'The Voluntary Sector in the Mixed Economy of Welfare', in David Gladstone ed., *Before Beveridge: Welfare Before the Welfare State* (London: Civitas, 1999), pp. 10-17.

51 Ninna Edgardh, 'A Gendered Perspective on Welfare and Religion in Europe', in Anders Bäckström, Grace Davie, Ninna Edgardh and Per Petterson, eds., *Welfare and Religion in 21st Century Europe: Gendered, Religious and Social Change* Vol. 2 (Farnham: Ashgate Publishing, 2011), p. 61.

52 Ibid., p. 66 quoting M.Daly and J. Lewis, 'The concept of social care and the analysis of contemporary welfare states', *British Journal of Sociology* 51 (2), pp. 281-298.

53 Ibid.

unsupervised relationships between carers and vulnerable adults and children. Mark Smith, practitioner and theorist of residential child care, notes that 'it has become fashionable to focus on negative images of care'.[54] Society no longer makes positive assumptions about unknown and unknowable care practices, including historic ones, and it has become a matter of justice for governments to instigate a series of investigations into historic abuse allegations in childcare institutions and in specific localities. Indeed, as this book is being written, two major independent enquiries into historic child abuse, one for England and Wales and the other for Scotland, are in progress.[55] In this context it is vital to acknowledge the difficulty of the subject matter in relation to the historic work of sisters. In a pioneering study of Dutch sisters and care, ethicist and historian Annelies van Heijst developed an approach precisely to explore 'the historical care practice of women religious'.[56] Allowing for the limitations of the available evidence and the broader purpose of this study, van Heijst's work indicates how it is possible to make some contribution to a more historicised understanding about the nature of social care from the perspective of a single community of sisters.

In an ecclesial sense all aspects of the Daughters' pastoral and social care can now be understood to have been ministry, a term that until recently was reserved to the priesthood by Catholics. Its deliberate use in this study serves to draw attention to the Daughters' participation in the mission of the Church and to their purposes of evangelisation and salvation of souls. In this respect sisters have not necessarily been well-served by the way they have been represented. American Benedictine sister and author, Joan Chittister, has repeatedly called attention to the fact that consecrated life was never meant to be 'the labour force in the church ... a kind of church machine designed simply to provide a base for social service. It was intended, rather, to be "a catalyst".[57] And St Teresa of Calcutta, who dedicated her life to service, pleaded in some anguish that 'We are misunderstood, we are misrepresented. We are not nurses, we are not doctors, we are not teachers, we are not social workers ... we do this for Jesus'.[58] There is, then, a challenge coming from today's religious sisters to re-assess and re-present the ontology of consecrated life as missionary, spiritual, prophetic and ministerial: to retrieve it from perspectives

---

54 Mark Smith, *Rethinking Residential Child Care: Positive Perspectives* (Bristol: The Policy Press, 2009), p. 25 and Mark Smith, Leon Fulcher and Peter Doran, eds., *Residential Child Care in Practice: Making a difference* (Bristol: The Policy Press, 2013).

55 See https://www.iicsa.org.uk/about-us and http://www.gov.scot/Topics/People/Young-People/protecting/child-protection/historical-child-abuse (accessed 16 June 2016).

56 Annelies van Heijst, *Models of Charitable Care: Catholic Nuns and Children in their Care in Amsterdam, 1852-2002* (Leiden and Boston: Brill, 2008), p. 3.

57 Joan Chittister, *The Fire in these Ashes* (Leominster: Gracewing, 1996), p. 71, pp. 90-91. See also Sandra Schneiders, 'Discerning ministerial religious life today', *National Catholic Reporter*, 11 September 2009 and her other extensive work on the subject.

58 Quoted in Angelo Devananda, *Daily Prayers with Mother Teresa* (Fount Press, 1987), p. 91

both religious and secular that tend to narrow that vision.[59] As a history of a single community, this study aims to show what it meant to the Daughters to 'do this for Jesus' while acknowledging the reality of their often being regarded as 'the labour force in the church' and even as 'a kind of church machine'. In this historic context it becomes particularly important to assess the ways the Daughters have chosen to work in recent decades when they have developed their own community analysis of needs and order of priorities to respond with limited resources.

Finally, an organisational approach affords a well-grounded basis for discussing the women who became Sisters and their experiences of everyday life. As members of communities made up of individuals who come together for a defined purpose, Sisters' experiences of life differ in specific ways from lives in relational families or lived alone.[60] The primary relationship of all Roman Catholic sisters is with God in Jesus Christ. Commitment to their vows is the path to deepen that relationship. Life in community and relationships between members have always been intended to form part of the journey, but their place has been understood differently in succeeding generations. As a way of understanding change over time I have used an historical method called prosopography to construct a collective profile of the Sisters' community in Britain and Ireland.[61] This 'biography of a community' is divided into generations for analysis and comparison, each generation being distinguished from the one before and the one after by significant break-points in the community's own history.[62] The generations are not even in size or length but the women who belong to each have a shared community history and, through their upbringing before entry, generally have much in common. Using this definition I have identified five generations of Daughters in Britain from the making of the first foundation to the present day. The first, or *foundation,* generation was active before there was a British Province (those who entered 1840-85); the *expansion* generation, was the period of greatest absolute growth in houses and Sisters and it began with the establishment of a Province of Great Britain and Ireland (entered 1885-1919); the third, or *conserving,* generation entered in a period affected by European wars, economic depression and, for consecrated women, the anti-Modernist Code of Canon Law of the Catholic Church (entered 1920-1945); the fourth, or *renewal,* generation experienced the Second Vatican Council when they were at their most vigorous (entered 1946-64); and the last and smallest group, the *transformation* generation, was a post-conciliar generation influenced by new attitudes towards authority, poverty and gender roles and the imperative

---

59 Pope Francis has identified clericalism as a narrowing perspective. See cronline.org/blogs/ncr-today/new-pope-s-real-target-clericalism and https://cruxnow.com/church/2016/04/27/pope-blasts-clericalism-says-clock-has-stopped-on-hour-of-laity/ (accessed 21 June 2016).

60 See http://www.ic.org/wiki/exploration-intentional-community-means/ (accessed 10 January 2015)

61 Lawrence Stone, *The Past and the Present Revisited* (London: Routledge & Kegan Paul, 1979), p. 45.

62 This is an adaptation of Karl Mannheim's idea of generational units formed by generational contexts. See Jane Pilcher, 'Mannheim's sociology of generations: an undervalued legacy', *British Journal of Sociology,* Vol 45, Issue 3. (September 1994), pp. 481-95.

of sustaining the community's charism (entered since 1965). Because the group approach to narrative inevitably concerns itself with averages and generalisation, it is complemented by short pen portraits of a small number of Sisters in the main text and in the illustrated sections, to suggest something of the individuality that existed in reality. Shaped by forms of behaviour and thinking that became normative within the community, their way of life has also been subject to changes that have come from outside. Just as I argue that the Daughters in Scotland, England and Wales were engaged in the mainstream of British history, so I will suggest that their community identity was shaped by the particular social and religious context of Britain as well as by Vincentian influences.

Much about this identity emerges from the way that the national context worked within the international or, more accurately, the transnational nature of the Company. Since the early 1990s historians have been interested in transnational groups and movements as an alternative focus to that of political territories. This approach brings attention to groups of people, above all migrants, whose lives and purposes cross national boundaries. Other particular groups suggested by historians have included pirates, artists, and academics[63] and 'networks of merchants, working-class radicals or neoliberal economists'.[64] Neither includes Catholic sisters - but perhaps they might have done since religion has so often been transnational in its nature, as Anne O'Brien has convincingly shown in a recent essay.[65] Other scholars have identified the religious origins of what they call 'global service movements', providing aid to people across political and geographic boundaries.[66] Stimulated by an appreciation that both social transformation and meaning-making in individual lives can take place outside the nation-state, transnational history is the study of how this actually happens through networks, beliefs and practices that work across boundaries. It is a helpful lens for understanding the Company of Daughters. Few women's organisations in 1900 had the global reach and presence of the Company and few women at this time worked across boundaries with the same confidence as did Daughters of Charity. The interplay between the British context and the Company as a French-originated transnational community runs through the Daughters' history at every phase. Daughters of Charity had a shared foundation story and a common mission that crossed borders. Whatever their country of origin or wherever they were sent,

---

63 Alex Korner, 'Five Thoughts on Transnational History' 2008 UCL Home Centre for Transnational History at www.ucl.ac.uk/cth (accessed 3 February 2015).

64 *AHR* Conversation: On Transnational History', *American Historical Review*, 111 (5), p. 1446. See also Breda Gray, 'Thinking Through Transnational Studies: Diaspora studies and gender', in D.A.J. MacPherson, Mary J. Hickman eds., *Women and Irish Diaspora Identities: Theories, Concepts and new perspectives* (Manchester: Manchester University Press, 1997), pp. 34-54.

65 Anne O'Brien, 'Catholic nuns in transnational mission, 1528-2015', *Journal of Global History*, (2016), 11, pp. 387-408. Because this wide-ranging and important essay was published just as this study was going to press its analysis and arguments have not been integrated here.

66 Stephen M. Cherry and Helen Rose Ebaugh, eds., *Global Religious Movements Across Borders: Sacred Service* (Farnham, Surrey: Ashgate, 2014).

members had a powerful sense of belonging both to the Company and to the people among whom they worked: the Company was a main source of their adult identity, a second 'family' they had elected to join as Sister-companions (a term they often used). This strong and self-consciously constructed international network enabled a small group of companions in, say, inner city Liverpool or Kingussie in the Scottish Highlands to imagine themselves at one with companions in other parts of Britain and Ireland or in France – and even in China, Brazil or Ethiopia.

Yet their shared world was not nationality neutral: it existed inside national cultures. The Company was rooted in the charismatic inspiration of its French founders and in the specific ways the founding inspiration had been lived out in France since 1633. Directed from the Paris mother house by a superioress general and a superior general, their vocation of public ministry and community life evolved to become, in the words of historian Colin Jones, 'a vocation generally known and widely esteemed in its native France'.[67] The *filles de la charité* became deeply embedded in French popular culture taking, on the status of a French 'cultural archetype'.[68] When it came to expansion in the nineteenth century it was undertaken quite overtly by the Company's leaders as an extension of French religious and political culture. The missionary drive that brought the Company to Britain was an expression of both French nationalism *and* of transnational Catholic revivalism; these two major historical forces were not mutually exclusive.[69]

But what did this French archetypal status mean for Daughters who were not French-born, and how did the nationalist aspirations of the Company's leaders affect its operation in other countries? What, for example, has it meant for English and Welsh, Scottish and Irish Daughters in Britain that the mother house is in Paris, that the administrative and devotional language of the Company was for many years French and that all its cultural and administrative norms had developed out of its experience of working in France? When the Company crossed borders so did its spiritual, symbolic, and discursive world. What meanings were given to its French-originated symbols and spirituality as they were lived out and adapted in Britain during the nineteenth and twentieth centuries? Salient for the Company's mission across cultures, for example, was the responsibility it accepted for spreading devotion to the Immaculate Conception of the Blessed Virgin Mary through distribution of the Miraculous Medal. As a consequence of an apparition of the Blessed Virgin in 1830 to Sister Catherine Labouré in the chapel of the mother house, the first of the French nineteenth-century Marian apparitions, the Company became the centre of a growing global Catholic devotional movement.[70] It might be anticipated that there would be little cultural support for this devotion

---

67 Jones, *The Charitable Impulse*, p. 89.

68 Ibid.

69 For a discussion of the relationship between nationalism and transnationalism see, '*AHR* Conversation: On Transnational History,' *American Historical Review*, 111 (5): 1441-64. See also Curtis, *Civilising Habits*.

70 See René Laurentin, *The Life of Catherine Labouré 1806-1876* (trans. Paul Inwood, Collins: London, 1982).

in Victorian and Edwardian Britain or for the causes to canonise Catherine Labouré and the Company's co-founder Louise de Marillac. But these were important concerns for the Company, and management of their reception in Britain became part of the story of resurgent public Marian devotions in Scotland and England.

The transnational lens may also be reversed, this time to explore any impact the British Province has had on the Company, starting with the significance its leaders attached to this mission. The driving force behind expansion into Britain might be explained in several ways: as a Catholic evangelical mission to an heretical Protestant nation; as a pastoral response to human misery created by industrialisation, urbanisation and migration, particularly for the impoverished Catholic minority in Britain; or as a pathway to other new Catholic missions through the British empire of trade and colonisation whose sphere of influence differed from that of France. None of these are mutually exclusive and each had a different implication for the Company; working in Britain meant that converts from Anglicanism or Presbyterianism became Daughters, for example. But for the Company to be effective in Britain there had to be an understanding among its leadership of the nature of the British state and the place of voluntary organisations involved in poverty relief and provision of welfare. This is the strand of its history that belongs to what Peggy Levitt named 'transnational civil society creation'.[71] Exploring it enables us to see what opportunities a British Province offered the Company and the extent to which its leaders were more or less open at different times to ideas and practices from outside France. Questions of cultural transfer and of reception, of cultural exchange and adaptation - along with cultural divergence and incongruity - shaped some of the central realities of institutional daily life for Daughters in Britain.

Within this set of relationships lies, often deeply buried, the matter of how 'Britishness' and 'Irishness' sat together in the Province of Great Britain and Ireland, and how they were understood by the community's superiors in France. The Company's decision to follow the geo-political contours of the United Kingdom of Great Britain and Ireland as it existed at the time of their expansion in the mid-nineteenth century was of immense strategic and practical significance. At the request of the Irish Province, which has already published a history of the houses and experience of the Daughters in Ireland, this study focuses on the houses and work in Britain only.[72] It is nonetheless attentive to the Irish dimension within the history of the Company's work in Britain, whether that be in terms of personnel, expertise, networks of communication or in acknowledging the important role played by Vincentian priest-directors of the British Province – all of whom were Irish men from the Vincentian Irish Province. Just as no sensible

---

71   For a discussion of the social theory that underpins the framework adopted here see Peggy Levitt, 'Conceptualizing Simultaneity: A transnational social field perspective on society', *International Migration Review*, 38 (145) Fall 2004, pp. 595-629.

72   Jacinta Prunty and Louise Sullivan, eds., *The Daughters of Charity of St Vincent de Paul in Ireland: The Early Years* (Dublin: Columba Press, 2014).

history of modern Catholicism in Scotland or England and Wales can be written without understanding the centrality of Ireland, Irish migration and the presence of the Irish diaspora in Britain, so too for the history of the Company in Britain.[73] While most of the island of Ireland separated politically from the United Kingdom in 1922 after the Irish War for Independence and the creation of the Irish Free State, the Company did not create two separate Provinces of Ireland and Britain, one for each of the two islands, until 1970.[74] The administrative unity of the British and Irish Province before 1970 and the separation of the Provinces mark very distinctive phases in the life of the Daughters in Britain. Both phases are integral to the analysis here. The relationship between Britain and Ireland may make the question of cultural identity and exchange within the Company more complex but this simply reflects a reality of British and Irish history.[75]

Sources

In telling the story of this one organisation, its own archives – in London and in Paris – provide the main sources, textual and visual. It is a privilege to have been allowed unrestricted access to almost all the materials in the Provincial archives.[76] The Company established sound and consistent administrative methods and record-keeping in the seventeenth century under the leadership of Louise de Marillac. Its centralised systems were subsequently developed with the zeal and expertise that characterises modern French bureaucracy, although it has to be noted the early provincial leaders in Britain were seen to fall short of those exacting standards.[77] Yet despite local gaps and inconsistencies, the willingness of the Company to systematise and collect records has left an impressive legacy that includes the following types of content: formal minutes taken at the regular and frequent provincial and general council meetings; regular visitation reports made by senior Sisters or directors that assess the well-being of a house against Company criteria; individual notes on each Sister's passage through the stages of community life and about her piety, health, education, and capacity for responsibility - and her death notice; lists of houses, their Sister Servants and Sister companions; house records including correspondence and building plans; and annual statistical provincial summaries of the number of Sisters, houses, works, and finances (of which a small number have survived). Formal records

---

73 See for example Mo Moulton, *Ireland and the Irish in Interwar England* (Cambridge: Cambridge University Press, 2014), a study of the interdependence of Irish and English identities in the 1920s and 1930s.

74 The Province of Ireland encompasses the island of Ireland.

75 See the work of Bronwen Walter, for example, *Outsiders Inside: Whiteness, Place and Irish Women* (London: Routledge, 2001).

76 The exception has been personal records of Sisters who are still alive. Parts of the archive that relate exclusively to the Daughters' work in Ireland were transferred to the Irish Province archive in Dunmanway and I was kindly given permission to work in these archives too.

77 This point is discussed in Chapter 5. On French bureaucracy as an expression of modernity see Clive H. Church, *Revolution and Red Tape: French Ministerial Bureaucracy, 1770-1850* (Oxford: Clarendon Press, 1981).

such as these and collections of printed circulars, calendars, books of customs, spiritual conferences, prayer books, in-house journals and newsletters are the greatest strengths of the provincial and mother house written archives.

In addition Sisters in Britain have, at different times, gathered materials on the more than 160 houses that have been opened and closed on the island, often adding items gained from local sources such as newspaper clippings or local memorabilia. Individual house archives form a significant part of the provincial archive. Where the house was responsible for an institution the archive may (or may not) include some of its records, such as admission registers for a Poor Law School or annual reports for one of the residential special schools. Where these records exist they are carefully preserved and are in regular use by the provincial archivist in response to requests for information from individuals who were resident in children's homes managed by the Province, or from members of their families researching family history.[78]

In 1985, to mark the Province's centenary, a major initiative was undertaken to compile an illustrated album of the history of each house open at that date. Varying in size and detail the albums supplement the archival house-based materials with more modern data and with personal reflections. A team of Sisters compiled a chronology for the centenary, highlighting key events in the Province's history. All these sources became available to the Sisters in a Heritage Room which has held a significant place in the life of all members, many of whom, inspired by its contents, have added to them. One outcome of the centenary was the appointment of a Sister-archivist who was given professional training. She established the archive's architecture, sorted and catalogued the documents and began the considerable task of identifying the large collection of photographs and artefacts, many of which are now displayed in the Heritage Room. Archival cataloguing has been continued by two subsequent Sister-archivists, also trained for the archive role, who have also conserved visual sources and material objects from paintings and reliquaries to community crockery and habits. This material culture has been vital to my interpretations, revealing aspects of everyday life that would have been otherwise inaccessible to an outsider.

Some of the limitations of these internal records would apply to most organisational sources, but others particular to the Company and its record-keeping culture are worth highlighting. With rare exceptions, such as letters from missionary Sisters, the subjective thoughts of the first generations are only rarely encountered. But the archive speaks through these gaps and silences too. They corroborate other evidence indicating that daily life was structured so that work and activity absorbed all time not spent in prayer and show how the community's collective discourse shaped an ideal of collective service. As one outside biographer

---

78 Judith Greville DC, 'Records of the Children's Homes of the Daughters of Charity', *Catholic Archives: The Journal of the Catholic Archive Society*, No. 15, pp. 3-12 lists the location of the surviving archives of the Province's children's homes and notes the nature of the holding.

attested, the culture of the community did not encourage rumination.[79] Such discouragement was intended, among other things, to dissolve any human urge for 'singularity'. Writing, particularly about oneself, fell into this category. Moreover, since the Company was an 'exempt institute' whose clerical oversight, including visitations, was provided by the Congregation of the Mission, there are far fewer revealing exchanges with other priests and with bishops. Searches in several diocesan archives yielded some valuable material but, of course, no visitation or permission records and little correspondence. To learn more about individual Sisters we must largely rely on accounts *about* them such the 'Notices of Deceased Sisters'. A number of Sisters who entered in the 1930s and 1940s have written their own life stories, adding their own voices to the archive. More evidence of this reflective kind was gathered in 2005 when eighty Sisters responded to my invitation to complete a short questionnaire about their reasons for entering the Company, their experience of the Second Vatican Council and their current thoughts about its significance in their lives. Finally, over years of working in the provincial archive I have benefited from many conversations with Sisters and Vincentian priests which have clarified and deepened my understanding of their spirit and mission. It proved possible to conduct a number of structured and unstructured individual and group interviews about particular topics which are under-represented in the archive, such as the practice of home visiting and the role of the provincial director.

The perceptions and experiences of those who received the Daughters' ministries are given voice occasionally in the archives in correspondence or through the organised activities of associations run by former residents of children's homes. A very small number of former residents have published memoirs which include reflections on their time in the Daughters' care and some recollections are available on internet sites, including family history sites. Because literally thousands of children and adults had encounters with the Daughters in a range of settings from 1857 onwards it is not possible to generalise or make claims on the basis of the small number of voices recorded in these ways or represented here, but they are nonetheless important for the perspectives they offer and are vital to the approach to the history of care proposed by van Heijst.

Church teaching about religious and consecrated life from the late nineteenth century to the present day has served both to deepen my understanding of the differences between the vocation of a Daughter of Charity and that of religious sisters, and the ways in which differences have been eroded or re-emphasised in particular historical periods, as has my research in the archives of multiple other women's religious communities, Roman Catholic and Anglican.[80] Internal

---

79 Lady Cecil Kerr, *Edith Feilding: Sister of Charity* (London: Sands and Co., 1933), p. 25.

80 Archives of the Benedictines of Stanbrook, the Congregation of Jesus, the Society of the Holy Child Jesus, the Faithful Companions of Jesus, the Religious of the Sacred Heart, the Franciscan Missionaries of St Joseph, the Sisters of the Cross and Passion, the All Saints' Sisterhood, Sisters of the Holy Union of the Hearts of Jesus and Mary and the Poor Servants of the Mother of God.

Company sources have been supplemented by a number of external records: government inspectors' reports on various institutions; diocesan archives in Westminster, Liverpool, Salford, Edinburgh and Birmingham; census data; accounts in Catholic newspapers and magazines such as *The Month* and *The Tablet* of the work of the Daughters, and reports in local newspapers and weeklies. Family and local history records have added to the depth of analysis for case studies of particular houses. By mining the Daughters' own archive and illuminating its content with a wide range of primary and secondary sources this book seeks to tell the story of five generations of Catholic sisters in Britain as part of the nation's less-known history.

Structure

The study opens with a thematic study of the nature and evolution of the Daughters' Vincentian vocation over more than three hundred years, its juridical status and its 'double family' relationship to the Congregation of the Mission (Vincentian priests and brothers, known as Lazaristes in France). The Company's origins in seventeenth-century France and its defence of the Daughters' distinctive vocation in later centuries, particularly in the second half of the nineteenth century, need to be explored in some detail if their history in Britain and the post-conciliar Company history is to be fully understood. Issues and debates opened out here act as a reference point for the Daughters' history in Britain more than two hundred years after the Company's foundation and they continue to have relevance to the present day.

The 170-year history of the Daughters in Britain is structured into three chronological eras. A case is made that each has an identifiable historical coherence, although this case is never made at the expense of the importance of continuity. The narrative divisions gain some of their salience from internal organisational dynamics and some from the external environment – with the dynamic between internal and external always present: for example, the importance of support from prominent Catholic families, the prevalence of anti-Catholicism and the poverty of the Catholic community characterise the first era and the first two generations of Sisters; the impact of two World Wars on political and social life and the centrality of devotional life help to define the third generation and the second era; and the impact of the Welfare State and the Second Vatican Council, the division of the Province and major shifts in gender roles, the third era and fourth generation. Themes identified in this introduction, such as the lay identity of the Daughters, the care for people in poverty and transnational organisation, are explored in each era.

In total the Sisters opened more than 160 houses in Britain during these years (the term convent was never used). There were always Sisters on the move and the process of packing and unpacking was taking place somewhere in the community every year. The challenge of identifying the many places where Daughters lived and worked without overwhelming the text has been met through the compilation of a descriptive Gazetteer (Appendix I). This geographically organised listing gives a miniature history of each house. Maps and tables created from the data are embedded in the relevant chapters for ease of use. The combination of these different ways of presenting information is intended to give clear information about the scale of the Daughters' operation, its geographical spread and concentrations, and the nature of the activities in different places at various times. Finally, a sample of places, people and ministries are illustrated in the visual essays that accompany the chapters. These visual essays reinforce the book's themes through images and are also the best way to document the material, devotional and symbolic culture that is so central to the Company's way of life.

2

The vocation of a Daughter of Charity: spirit and history

> For eight hundred years or so, women have had no public role in the Church; in the past there were some who were called Deaconesses... About the time of Charlemagne, however, by a discreet working of Divine Providence, this practice came to an end; persons of your sex were deprived of any role and have not had any since then.
>
> (Vincent de Paul, 1657)[1]

When the Company of the Daughters of Charity sent a first group of Sisters to the United Kingdom in 1847 it already had more than two hundred years' organisational history behind it. There was a strong ready-made vocational identity for British and Irish women to inhabit when they joined the Daughters' mission in Britain in the middle nineteenth century.[2] Even before those first Sisters arrived a small but steady stream of women from Britain and Ireland had entered the community to serve in France and elsewhere as 'Sisters of Charity' (as the *filles de la charité* were known in Britain until 1970).[3] As a result of the Crimean War (1853-56), when Daughters received a good deal of publicity in Britain as battlefield nurses, the nature of their practical service became more widely understood. It would seem there were few questions about the nature of the vocation either for the women who became Daughters or for the sponsors and patrons who invited them to work in parishes and institutions. Yet, although this was so in relation to purpose and values, the historical development of the Company had not only shaped the organisation that arrived in Britain, but underlay the unresolved questions it would face in the nineteenth and twentieth centuries.

Part of the strength of the Company in its earliest years had been its ability to sustain ambiguities about such important matters as canonical status, the nature

---

1 *CCD*, Vol.XIIIb, p. 432. 'Report on the State of the Works', 11 July 1657.

2 See, for example, the writings of Anna Brownell Jameson, 'Sisters of Charity' (1855) and 'The Communion of Labour' (1857), which were influential, and the excellent discussion in Sheridan Gilley, 'Heretic London, Holy Poverty and the Irish Poor, 1830-1870', *Downside Review,* Vol.89, No. 294 (January, 1971), pp. 64-89.

3 Registers Daughters of Charity Archives Paris (hereafter DCP)

of the vows made by its members, the authority exercised by the superior general of the Congregation of the Mission, and the Sisters' membership of the double Vincentian family alongside the confrères of the Congregation of the Mission. A degree of ambiguity had helped the Company to establish itself and flourish during the seventeenth and eighteenth centuries. Increasingly, however, these same ambiguities led to misunderstandings about its canonical identity and its place in the order of the Catholic Church, as the leadership and organisation of the Church became progressively more centralised after the second half of the nineteenth century. In addition to questions of identity as seen from the perspective of the clerical Church there was also the impact on the internal dynamic of the Company of what had happened to it during the Napoleonic era (1800-1815). There was, understandably, no problem about assimilating the story of the Company's disbandment during the Revolution; the suffering of its members and the execution of some Sisters became heroic strands of its past. But for more than a century the Company found it impossible to incorporate the history of internal disunity and factionalism between groups of Sisters that had taken place between 1802 when it had been restored by Napoleon and 1814. The events of this period, discussed in detail below, were glossed over in internal accounts and were not known by most Sisters until relatively recently.[4] Beneath the surface and unacknowledged, these events played a part in creating a strong culture of uniformity and discipline in the Company in reaction to what had gone before. At the same time a powerful narrative emphasising unity through uniformity and strong attachment to the mother house was developed by leaders who described themselves as 're-founding' the Company and returning it to the 'purity' or 'l'esprit primitive' of the founders' intentions.[5]

It was not until the 1950s and 1960s that the Company's superiors began to re-evaluate the norms and practices they had inherited, seeing many of them as the product of a particular past rather than as immutable or essential. After 1960 a fresh appropriation of the foundation story and of the later history was developed in the light of three fresh impulses: firstly, new historical research into the original sources was required of all religious institutes by the Second Vatican Council's Decree 'Appropriate Renewal of Religious Life' (1965); secondly, the theology and ecclesiology of the Second Vatican Council (1962-1965), with its emphasis on community, the 'pilgrim Church' and the 'people of God', rather than on hierarchy and uniformity, created a shift in attitudes: and thirdly, an appreciation of the role of gender in the life of the Company and of the Church eventually enabled a more comprehensive recovery of the part that Louise de Marillac had played in the spiritual and organisational foundation of the Company. All three impulses helped

---

4 See Elisabeth Charpy DC 'A Challenge to Napoleon: The Defiance of the Daughters of Charity', *VHJ*, (2011), Vol.30: Iss. 2, Article 3.

5 Edward R. Udovic, *Jean-Baptiste Étienne and the Vincentian Revival* (Chicago: Vincentian Studies Institute, 2001) and 'Jean-Baptise Étienne C.M.: Refondateur des Filles de la Charité', in Brejon de Lavergneé, ed., *Des Filles de la Charité aux soeurs de Saint-Vincent-de-Paul*, pp. 53-64.

to promote an exploration of the nature of the charismatic friendship between the two founders. Whereas it had previously been thought that a Vincentian vocation had originated exclusively with Vincent de Paul, it gradually came to be understood as stemming from the dynamic co-operation and collaboration between the two founders and the early Sisters.[6]

We can see from the foregoing summary that the concept of a Vincentian vocation has comprised both a primary spirit (often known as 'charism') – 'the unique gift of grace to the founder or founders' - and interpretations of that spirit shaped by context and by historical layers of renewal, ossification, disruption and reconstruction.[7] This chapter is concerned with the distinctive identity and internal culture of the Daughters of Charity as it was initially established and as it subsequently developed from the seventeenth century. Continuity and change were both always present, but not always in the same measure. It is in this light that the ideal of a Vincentian vocation handed on to the Daughters in Britain in the second half of the nineteenth century and the re-assessment of that Vincentian vocation undertaken by the whole body of Sisters in the second half of the twentieth century can be seen. The Vincentian theology and practice of charity that underpinned the Daughters' vocation, the 'double family' relationship with the Congregation of the Mission, and the relationship that developed between the Company and the French state were all elements of this distinctiveness. So too was the lay status of the Daughters within the wider Catholic Church. The initial establishment and later defence of their lay status with all its ambiguities and gendered dynamics is as important a strand in the overall history of active ministry for Roman Catholic women as it is within the Daughters' own history.

Vincentian vocation: the poor are our masters

There was never any question in the minds of the founders about the vocation of a Daughter of Charity. She was an evangeliser who was to serve the poorest of the poor in merciful ways through direct personal encounters that would be salvific for her and for the people she encountered. 'To be true Daughters of Charity you must do what the Son of God did when He was on earth', Vincent de Paul told them, 'And what did he chiefly do? After submitting His will by obeying the Blessed Virgin and St Joseph, he laboured unceasingly for His neighbour, visiting and healing the

---

6 See, for example, Louise Sullivan, 'God wants first the heart and then the work: Louise de Marillac and leadership in the Vincentian tradition', *VHJ*, (1998) Vol.19. Issue 1. Article 11 and Gertrude Foley, 'Saint Louise de Marillac: Woman of Substance; Woman of God', *VHJ*, (2000), Vol.21, Issue 2, Article 2. Matthieu Brejon de Lavergnée, 'Du mythe des origines les Filles de la Charité et leurs fondateurs, XVIIᵉ-XXᵉ siècle', in Brejon de Lavergnée ed, *Quatre siècles de cornettes*, pp. 27-35.

7 The somewhat vexed question of the meaning of charism in the context of consecrated life, and whether all communities have a founding charism, is discussed by Margaret Susan Thompson in 'Charism or Deep Story? Toward a Clearer Understanding of the Growth of Women's Religious Life in Nineteenth-Century America', Paper given to the History of Women Religious Conference, Chicago 1998.

sick and instructing the ignorant unto their salvation'.[8] The Daughters shared the vocation of the priests and brothers of the Congregation of the Mission (founded by Vincent de Paul in 1625) to be active disciples of Jesus Christ. 'Evangelising by word and action' was as much the vocation of the *filles* as it was of the *confrères*, even though the way they were to fulfil it differed.

The majority of early Sisters were countrywomen with little formal education.[9] De Paul believed it to be 'the Providence of God' that willed 'that your Company should be made up of poor girls, either by birth or by the choice they would make of poverty'.[10] The community made no social distinctions between companions in its structures and customs. In the light of what is known about the humble social origins of the early Daughters several scholars have explored the founders' methods of forming the Daughters so that they internalised the nature of their vocation and could act without needing detailed instructions.[11] Louise de Marillac formed the Sisters through personal relationships, visits, art and symbolism, and through the extensive and detailed correspondence she conducted with them. De Paul developed the Conference as a key instrument for the formation of as many Sisters as possible.[12] Literally 'a conferring', the conference comprised, in varying proportions, short lectures by Vincent de Paul, a question and answer dialogue between himself and the Sisters, and peer education through the sharing of experiences and personal responses to questions.[13] Sisters spoke from their experience of ministry in the field and the dialogue encouraged companions to draw out the theological and spiritual meaning of their care practices through reflection.

Using this pedagogy Sisters were to learn that the manner of giving charity mattered as much as the practical help itself.[14] Values, principles and the foundation of personal conversion were reinforced: 'God demands first the heart and then the work'.[15] They were to act 'with compassion, gentleness, cordial respect and devotedness' towards people in their care; their companions were to be 'like Sisters whom Jesus Christ has bound together by the bond of His love'. Injunctions about behaviour and attitudes were intended to become meaningful at a deep level, forming and transforming the actions of each individual from a focus on the practical task into a loving service. 'The poor are our masters,' was the concept Vincent de Paul returned to repeatedly, 'They are our kings, and they must be

---

8 *CCD*, Vol. IX, p. 14. For Vincent de Paul on 'the poor are our Masters' see *CCD*, Vol. IX p. 97; Vol. X, pp. 267-68.

9 *CCD*, Vol. IX, pp. 74-75.

10 Ibid., p. 193 'On the love of our vocation and on helping the poor,' 13 February 1646.

11 Brejon de Lavergnée, *Histoire des Filles*, p. 173ff and Jones, *Charitable Impulse*, p. 107.

12 See Alison Forrestal, 'Vincent de Paul as Mentor,' *Vincentian Historical Journal* (2007), Vol.27. Iss. 2, Article 1. and Colin Lucas, *The Charitable Impulse*, p. 106ff.

13 '...whenever she learned something, she taught her companions'. *CCD*, Vol.9, p. 194.

14 See, for example, *CCD*, Vol. 9 Conf. 3, pp. 16-23 and Conf. 85. Vol 10, pp. 267-79.

15 Leonard, *Conférences* Conf.71 18 October 1655, 'On the End of the Company', p. 746.

obeyed. It is not an exaggeration to speak of them like this, since Our Lord is in the poor.'[16] Because these precepts were central, they were even built into the contracts the Company made with hospitals and local authorities who asked for Sisters:

> [the Sisters] will be obliged to interrupt the order of their spiritual exercises and even to leave them promptly when necessity and the service of the poor requires it; they are already obliged to this by their rules, since this is their first and principal obligation.[17]

Louise de Marillac used her voluminous correspondence with the Sisters to encourage and reinforce the same vocation and to instruct.[18] 'I beg you', she wrote to Sister Geneviève Doinel in 1659, 'to be...an example of a true Daughter of Charity who is given to God for the service of the poor and who, therefore, must be more with the poor than with the rich'.[19] To another she wrote that the Blessed Virgin Mary 'is the saint who must show us our work, since she was fortunate to serve the poor in the person of Our Lord, just as we serve Our Lord in the person of the poor'.[20] As a gifted artist, in 1643 she designed the Company's seal to express symbolically the theology and spirituality that underpinned it: a burning heart surmounted by Christ on the cross and encircled by words adapted from St Paul's Second Letter to the Corinthians, 'the love of Christ crucified urges us'.[21] In other words 'the heart of the crucified Lord is the font of the Company's works of love'.[22] According to Robert Malone, Louise's full-size execution of Jesus as 'The Lord of Charity', an image of Christ favoured by both founders, 'is one of the first such representations of the Heart of Jesus that we know of'.[23]

Other men and women were similarly inspired at this time of Catholic Reformation but the Vincentian 'spiritual way' was unique in making the personal practice of care its central plank and in creating institutional structures to enable its own practice of holy living. Inspired in 1617 by an individual instance of poverty and need when he became pastor in the village of Châtillon-les-Daubes in the

---

16 Elizabeth Rapley, *The Dévotes*, p. 92. See also *Conference SVP,* IX, p. 252 and *Conference, SVP* X, p. 123.

17 John E. Rybolt, 'From Life to the Rules,' *VHJ* (1991) Vol.12: Iss.2, Article 6 p. 183

18 Over time more than 700 of her letters have been discovered and preserved, 374 of which were to Daughters. See Carmen Urrizburu, 'Letters of Louise de Marillac', available at famvin.org/wiki/Letters_of_Louise_de_Marillac_to_the_Daughters_of_Charity_(I) for a description of how and when the letters were discovered and published. (Consulted 22 September 2015.) See Sullivan, ed., *Spiritual Writings of Louise de Marillac* and Louise Sullivan, 'God wants first the heart and then the work' *VHJ,* (1998), Vol.19. Issue 1. Article 11.

19 Sullivan, *Spiritual Writings* L.627, September 1659, p. 645.

20 Ibid., L276 January 1650, p. 314.

21 2 Corinthians 5:14-15.

22 Robert P. Maloney, 'The Heart of Jesus in the Spirituality of Vincent de Paul and Louise de Marillac', *VHJ,* (2014), Vol. 32. Issue 1. Article 8.

23 Ibid.

Lyons district, Vincent de Paul established his first confraternity of charity there.[24] After founding many other such local confraternities he went on to establish the Confraternity of the Ladies of Charity for wealthy women, directed after 1625 by Louise de Marillac. The Company of the Daughters of Charity in 1633 was a later development of the original impulse. Each was a realisation of what de Paul saw as the imperative of active love. He reinforced its message by constant reference to the human actions of Jesus but also by a theological understanding of the poor as Christ himself. This theology was not new; it had strong medieval roots.[25] But, as Suzanne Roberts has shown, it had fallen from favour in the late fourteenth century in the face of new anxieties about social instability stemming from the widespread impoverishment of the time.[26] All de Paul's confraternities reinvigorated this earlier strand in Catholic theology, affirming that Christ is in the poor and is at one with them, but it was through the public ministry of the Daughters that praxis was developed and brought to a new point of respecting the dignity of those in poverty. [27] The clearest expression of 'Christ in the poor' came through the understanding, shared across the Company, that any Daughter interrupted in 'meditation and Holy Mass to serve poor persons' was simply leaving God 'to go to God'.[28] Her own salvation lay in doing so and her action embodied the theology. It was in the lives of the *filles de la charité,* too, that the theology of holy poverty was most effectively combined with 'modern' administrative and welfare practices to transform what might otherwise have been a pious and well-meaning charitable association into an effective instrument of the Catholic Reformation. 'There is great charity', Vincent de Paul observed of other efforts at the time, 'but it is badly organised'.[29] The Company, working with Ladies of Charity, proved capable of responding in a more systemic manner to the extreme material want and spiritual neglect of people in poverty in France at this time than most existing organisations, enabling de Paul to 'ret[ie] the knot between religion and action'.[30]

The unswerving vocational purpose of personal and practical care-giving outlined here was accompanied by flexibility about forms of service. Initially it seems the *filles de la charité* were envisioned as 'parish sisters', working practically in twos, employed by a Confraternity of Charity and sponsored by a benefactor

---

24 José María Román, *St Vincent de Paul: A Biography* trans. Joyce Howard, (London: Melisande, 1999), Chapter IX. His arrival at Châtillon provides the opening to Maurice Cloche's award winning 1947 film, *Monsieur Vincent* starring Paul Fresnay.

25 Gilley, 'Heretic London, Holy Poverty', pp. 64-89.

26 Suzanne Roberts, 'Contexts of Charity in the Middle Ages: religious, social and civic', in J.B. Schneewind ed., *Giving – Western Ideas about Philanthropy* (Bloomington: Indiana University Press, 1996), pp. 14-53.

27 Michel Mollat, *The Poor in the Middle Ages: An Essay in Social History* trans. Arthur Goldhammer (New Haven, CT: Yale University Press, 1986).

28 *CCD,* Conference 1 'Explanation of the Regulations, 31 July 1634' , Vol. IX, p. 5.

29 Quoted in Thomas G. Fuechtmann, 'There is Great Charity, But...': Vincent de Paul and the Organization of Charity', *VHJ* (2005), Vol.26: Iss. 1, Article 5.

30 André Dodin, *Saint Vincent de Paul et la Charité* (Paris, 1974. 3rd edition), p. 50.

from the Ladies of Charity.[31] The early *filles* visited people at home, taking food and medicines and ensuring the comfort of the sick, praying with them, accompanying those who were dying and attending to the dead.[32] As word of the Company's effectiveness travelled, however, benefactors asked for *filles* to undertake other services. During the 1630s and 1640s members of elite families, bishops and town authorities asked for Daughters to take over the running of existing and new *hôtels Dieu* which had responsibility for the welfare of the indigent poor and unemployed. Elizabeth Rapley has argued that the institutionalisation and professionalisation of the Daughters' ministries that took place when they began to run large-scale organisations was a 'deviation from the original purpose' of home visiting.[33] Home visiting was undoubtedly the first ministry of the Daughters. It remained an important dimension of their work, emphasised at some times and in some places more than others, but always practised. Two considerations to emerge from Rapley's own research and that of others, suggest that the term 'deviation' might be too strong to describe the advent of institution-based ministries. First, there is clear evidence that Vincent de Paul turned down proposals that went against anything he regarded as fundamental to his vision for service of the poor. Management of any institutions that forcibly detained individuals was one such.[34] Second, his way of acting demonstrated a consistent preference for flexibility and for 'waiting on God' to see how the vision might unfold.[35] As Rapley says, the Company's development was organic, experimental and sometimes seemingly uncontrolled. What is certain is that the founders pursued a twin track of ministries from an early stage.

Even though the Company of Daughters challenged some aspects of the Church's gender norms (such as activity in the public realm), the roles and services it carried out were readily accepted by benefactors and beneficiaries because they were traditionally feminine.[36] The founders did not extend female activism into new areas but rather, as Colin Jones has suggested, undertook a 'revalorization of manual work [that] strove to make nursing drudgery divine'.[37] In their appreciation of personal charity and acts of kindness as Christ-centred ministry, the founders accorded what was regarded as 'feminine work' the dignity of discipleship. De Paul refused to allow critics of a public role for women to stereotype them: 'Our Lord

---

31 Rapley, *The Dévotes*, p. 88.

32 Ibid., pp. 79-94.

33 Ibid., p. 90.

34 Alison Forrestal, 'Vincent de Paul: The Principles and Practices of Government, 1625-60', *VHJ* (2009), Vol.29: Iss. 2. Article 3, p. 58.

35 Ibid., p. 57.

36 Rapley, *The Dévotes*, p. 83; Susan Dinan, 'Restriction, Circumvention, Innovation: The Daughters of Charity and the French Catholic Reformation Church,' in *Collide: Styles, Structures, and Ideas in Disciplinary Writing* Richard McNabb and Belinda Kremer eds, (New York: Pearson, 2005), p. 131.

37 Jones, *Charitable Impulse*, p. 105.

is as much glorified in the ministry of women as in that of men,' he wrote, 'and there is no fault to find in their administration, so careful and accurate are they'.[38]

What emerged, gradually and experimentally through thirty years of collaboration between Vincent de Paul, Louise de Marillac and the Sisters themselves, was a new vocation. Other groups of *filles séculières* developed, but they were always under obedience to a bishop as a diocesan group. Detailed calculations made by Matthieu Brejon de Lavergnée have led him to conclude that about 8,200-8,300 women took up the vocation of Daughter of Charity from the time of foundation to the end of the Ancien Régime, making the Company by far the largest single organisation of women in the French Church at the time of the French Revolution.[39] Just before its dissolution in 1792 the community is estimated to have had over 3,000 members working in more than 400 hospitals, institutions and parishes in France and comprising one in three of all *filles séculières* across the country.[40]

The outcome was a vocation that made sense to French society within an organisation that was robust. It proved strong enough to survive the deaths of both the founders within months of one another in 1660, the year also when the first Vincentian Director of the Company also died - a circumstance that might have caused a faltering or even demise of any relatively new organisation. In subsequent decades the Company was sustained by spiritual fidelity and by an elaboration of the foundational structures.[41] Its practices of care continued to expand in the eighteenth century in the changed religious climate of the Enlightenment, undergoing and surviving some dilution of discipline and spirit of service before the Revolution,[42] the dissolution brought about by the French Revolution and restoration of the Company in the post-Revolutionary era. The continuity of focus on ministry to people in poverty through so many changes of circumstance is striking. In the 1890s, the elderly Florence Nightingale recalled the impression the Daughters in Paris and Alexandria had made on her during the late 1840s and early 1850s: 'The Misericorde under the Sisters of Charity,' she reminisced, 'did all the minor surgery of the out-door patients, District Nursing, but more than that...They were besides, the Relieving Officers – and *we* have nothing like it. They and they alone *knew* the Poor'[43] [original emphasis]. Despite the disruption, disunity and re-configuration that had been experienced in the Company, Nightingale's observation is evidence that the primary vocational

---

38 Rapley, *The Dévotes*, p. 83.

39 Brejon de Lavergnée, *Histoire des Filles*, pp. 302-303.

40 Ibid., p. 299.

41 Ibid., p. 231ff.

42 Ibid., p. 259.

43 Letter of Florence Nightingale to unknown female, 4 August 1896 Nightingale MSS 45813 f219, British Library. However, Nightingale was also very critical of the Daughters as hospital nurses. See Lynn McDonald ed., *Florence Nightingale's European Travels vol 7 Collected Works of Florence Nightingale* (Waterloo, Ontario:Wilfrid Laurier University Press, 2004), pp. 748-758.

identity and Vincentian character of the Daughters as women serving the poorest in society had been sustained. It was this vocation which was transferred and transmitted to the United Kingdom mission along with the unresolved questions about status in the Church and authority for action.

Juridical Status: secular or religious?

If the essence of the Daughters' vocation was clear to the founders it was much less obvious how they could put it into practice with the blessing of the Church. They believed what they were advocating - women's ministry - was novel: 'Since the time of the women who ministered to the Son of God and the Apostles,' according to Vincent de Paul, 'there has been no community established in God's Church with this end in view'.[44] Through the recent work of historians we now know that an active life of practical female ministry was widespread during the Middle Ages but, with few exceptions, was repressed or reconfigured by church or civic authorities sooner or later.[45] Both founders, moreover, were close to other communities of women founded in their own day which had been forced to accept enclosure, even when their initiatives had been relatively modest.[46]

Only a well-organised community could sustain a coherent and effective practice of charity on a large-scale. Only by living in a community could the *filles de la charité* gain the respect and protection they needed as single women who had no juridical independence. And, perhaps, only the discipline of community life could provide the stability, communication and good order to deepen their own life in God as they sought. But a residential community model immediately raised questions about the ecclesial and civic status of the women. The only permitted religious communities of women were those of enclosed orders of nuns under solemn vows. The decree of the Council of Trent (1563) on religious life for women left no room for negotiation about enclosure or *clausura*: 'for no nun, after her profession, shall it be lawful to go out of her convent, even for a brief period, under any pretext whatever ...'[47] Following this decree all remaining Third Order Franciscan or Dominican women had to choose 'either the wall or the husband'

---

44 *CCD*, Vol. IX, p. 14.

45 See for example: Craig Harline, 'Actives and Contemplatives: The Female Religious of the Low Countries Before and After Trent,' *Catholic Historical Review* 81/4 (1995), pp. 541-67; Joanna Kay McNamara, *Sisters in Arms: Catholic Nuns through Two Millennia* (Cambridge Mass.: Yale University Press, 1996); Walter Simons, *Cities of Ladies: Beguine Communities in the Medieval Low Countries, 1200-1565* (Philadelphia: University of Pennsylvania Press, 2001).

46 Both enjoyed personal friendships with Francis de Sales and Jane de Chantal who in 1610 had set out to establish a community of women to visit other women, the Visitation, on the model of Mary's visit to her cousin Elizabeth as 'an experiment...a community of prayer without solemn vows and *clausura*'. It was forced to accept *clausura*. Vincent de Paul had been their official Visitor.

47 Decree of Council of Trent Session XXV. With this decree the Council consciously referred to and reinstated the Papal Bull of 1298 *Periculoso* that required all women in religious orders to live within a convent and its grounds, behind walls.

('aut murus aut maritus').[48] There was to be no 'in-between' state. If women were to follow Jesus's model of compassionate action in the world, and if the most complete and effective way to do so was to live and work in a community, what canonical and social status could women have in a Church that would not permit them to be solemnly-vowed nuns and permitted no other model?

The challenge was, therefore, to devise a formula that would bring together three categories so far kept apart: female gender, consecration within a permanent community, and an active charitable and missionary purpose. It had to be a formula acceptable to Church and civic authorities. Whatever organisation was devised must not prevent the Sisters being 'women who come and go like seculars'.[49] Only gradually through a process of trial, experiment, review, and a degree of tactical ambiguity did a workable compromise evolve. It was also the consequence of de Paul's skill as a canon lawyer and de Marillac's absolute insistence on certain pre-conditions.

Initially brought together as an informal community under the guidance of Louise de Marillac, the first members were closely linked to de Paul's Confraternities of Charity. Confraternity was an elastic nomenclature, not used precisely even in pontifical statements; terms such as 'pious union', 'sodality', and 'confraternity' were interchangeable. All signified 'an association of the faithful joining together with the recognition or approval of the competent ecclesiastical authority with the intention of achieving a pious or charitable purpose'.[50] Regulations or Statutes to govern a confraternity and provide it with clear aims were usually approved by the local bishop. In the case of the *filles de la charité* the founders waited thirteen years, until there were about a hundred women in the association, before asking Cardinal de Retz (de Gondi), Archbishop of Paris, to approve the 'articles according to which they have been living as a confraternity'. In 1646 the community and its statutes received formal approbation by decree when the Cardinal 'erected...the conference of the unmarried women and widows in this diocese into a separate Confraternity under the title of the Servants of the Poor of the Charity'.[51]

De Gondi conferred approval on an organisation that did not, however, *behave* like a regular confraternity. The Daughters combined the juridical status of a confraternity with a 'unique mode of behaviour' which historian Susan Dinan has concluded 'separated them from laywomen and from nuns' in practice if

---

48 Constitution *Circa pastoralis* of Pius V (1566).

49 Sullivan, *Spiritual Writings*, A2. p. 1.

50 Miguel P. Flores, 'The Superior General of the Congregation of the Mission and the Daughters of Charity,' *VHJ* (1984), Vol. 5. Iss.2. Art.1., p. 2. note 2.

51 Ibid, p. 2. quoting from *CCD*, XIIIb, pp. 132-3.

not in law.[52] Because the interests of clergy, the French authorities and leading members of powerful lay spiritual movements committed to religious renewal in France (*les dévotes*) coincided sufficiently with those of women who wanted to pursue this new vocation, a more open situation was created for the Daughters and for communities of women committed to active ministry under their bishop's guidance with no canonical status outside his approbation. Historians have placed the Daughters among these diocesan groups and described them all as being in '"an intermediate state" between religious and secular ...[that] was here in fact if not in canon law.'[53] Unsurprisingly, historians are able to point to texts which state the founders' determination that the Daughters should not be mistaken for 'religious' because they were lay and others that state how they were to behave in ways that marked them out from other laywomen and were as 'perfect' as religious.

The Rules and Statutes of the Company developed gradually, being put together by the founders only in 1645, extended and codified in 1672, twelve years after the founders' deaths.[54] These juridical texts reinforced the secular status of the Company and its members, while in practice the Company was increasingly seen as a new category of religious community. But, according to Vincentian canonical expert Miguel Flores, de Gondi's decree of approval brought into existence 'an apostolic community of women in the juridical form of a confraternity' which was insistent on formal *lay* [secular] status.[55] It was not 'a new form of religious life'.[56] Flores contends that de Paul chose confraternalism because it safeguarded the vision and purpose of the community. Here lay the first of several unresolved questions of status.

A second concerned the vows taken by Daughters. During the life of the founders 'a certain pluralism obtained in the Community on the matter of vows'[57]: some Sisters made no vows, a very few made permanent vows but most made annual private vows.[58] It is important to note that private vows were made to God by many other religiously devout individuals. Louise de Marillac described

---

52 Susan Dinan, 'Restriction, Circumvention, Innovation', p. 131. See also by Dinan: *Women and Poor Relief in Seventeenth-Century France: The Early History of the Daughters of Charity.* (Aldershot: Ashgate, 2006); 'Compliance and Defiance: The Daughters of Charity and the Council of Trent,' in *Reforming the Church before Modernity,* Christopher Bellitto and Louis Hamilton. eds. (Aldershot: Ashgate, 2005), pp. 199-217.

53 Rapley, *The Dévotes,* p. 193. For a thorough examination of the various rules of the Company (general and particular) and their relationship to one another see John Rybolt, 'From Life to the Rules', *VHJ,* Vol. 12, Iss. 2, Article 6.

54 Miguel Flores, 'The Common Rules of the Daughters of Charity', *VHJ* (1987) Vol.8. Iss. 1 Article 1.

55 Flores, 'The Superior General of the Congregation of the Mission', p. 3.

56 See the history as it was explained to the Sisters in 1969 by James Jamet CM, Director of the Company , 'The End or Vocation of the Company', *The Echo of the Mother House,* January 1969, pp. 15-25. DCMH

57 Richard McCullen, Superior General of the Company, in a talk given to the British Province on 11 October 2003. He also noted that 'When our two communities set out to look at the sources of our vows, we found ourselves, with St Vincent and St Louise, in rather marshy ground.' http://www.daughtersofcharity.ie/join-us/ features/589-the-vows-of-the-daughters-of-charity-1 (accessed 15 April 2013).

58 Román, *St Vincent de Paul,* pp. 464-67.

the Daughters' vows as even less public than those taken by many confraternity members. This was true, but the wording composed by de Marillac included not only a fourth vow to serve the poor but also the distinctive vow of obedience to the superior general of the Congregation of the Mission:

> I, the undersigned, in the presence of God, renew the promises of my baptism, and I vow poverty, chastity and obedience to the Venerable Superior General of the Priests of the Mission in the Company of the Daughters of Charity in order to give myself, for the whole of this year, to the corporal and spiritual service of the sick poor, our true Masters.[59]

A practice of annual vow re-commitment emerged during the lifetime of the founders, although not undertaken by all members. Superior René Almeras (1660-1672) established the distinctive practice of renovation of the vows and community-wide annual individual vow renewal, then became normative. The date chosen was the Feast of the Annunciation of the Blessed Virgin (25 March) which memorialised the date of Louise de Marillac's own perpetual vows in 1542.[60] It was she who had given vow renewal a spiritual purpose as a way of deepening the Sisters' sense of consecration, not least in the context of their secular status.[61] Over time this spiritual purpose was articulated more overtly, particularly through the preparations that preceded renewal which included a formal request made ultimately to the superior general and a retreat.[62] Before long Daughters came to experience vow renewal as a powerful and binding annual ritual at an individual and community level rather than as second-best to perpetual vows.[63] At the same time, compared to what was normative in both religious life and parish life, the Daughters' vow continued to be anomalous and ambiguous. In the nineteenth century many other new communities of apostolic sisters made annual vows until and unless they received papal approval. But as apostolic sisters began to be seen as religious in all but law the Daughters' lay vowed lay status re-emerged as a 'problematic' form of distinctiveness in the eyes of the Church.

Given its close identification with the emergence of female ministry we might expect that the Company of the Daughters would slip into the mainstream and associate itself with the pressure for canonical religious status as simple-vowed sisters in an apostolic institute. Instead, under the leadership of the Superior General of the Congregation of the Mission, the Company continued to assert its identity as a lay community and to resist any attempt by others at re-categorisation. In 1855, for example, Superior General Étienne sent a Memorandum to Pope Pius

---

59 Sullivan, *Spiritual Writings*, A.44.B, 'Formula of the Vows', p. 782.

60 Brejon de Lavergnée, *Histoire des Filles*, p. 195ff

61 Sullivan, *Spiritual Writings*, A.44.B, 'Formula of the Vows', p. 782.

62 *Genesis of the Company*, p. 45. 1-7-2 DCMH

63 The significance and experience of annual vow renewal is discussed in Chapter 4.

IX asserting the historical status of the Daughters as 'not members of a religious order'. Bishops continued to raise questions. Shortly before the First Vatican Council met in Rome, Archbishop Manning of Westminster submitted a request to the Pope that the Daughters of Charity 'be considered religious'.[64] Étienne felt compelled to draft a detailed memorandum to all the bishops, circulated to them during the Council, to remind them of the Company's secular nature.[65] Evidently - and somewhat ironically given previous positions on religious status - bishops did not accept this situation very readily. In 1883, following an appeal from Superior General Fiat invoking Vincent de Paul's insistence that the 'said Institute be absolutely lay', the Sacred Congregation of Religious once again notified all bishops that 'The character of this Association has always been, by the consent of the Sovereign Pontiffs, lay and secular. The conditions of other religious Institutes do not apply to it'.[66]

While this concern by the nineteenth-century superiors for the Company's secular status and distinctive identity was consistent and unequivocal, the same leaders nonetheless seemed to promote some behavioural norms associated with the new apostolic religious congregations. These included an increased sense of hierarchy and deference to Sister Servants (local superiors), a greater separation from 'externs' (other lay people), a plethora of regulations governing every aspect of personal conduct, and adaptations to clothing, particularly the cornette, that removed it further and further from the original idea of the everyday dress of working women and aligned it with religious dress. The construction of 'a true Daughter' was changing even while the discourse of continuity was maintained. Practices borrowed from the newer congregations were braided together with the older Company ways which still served to mark Daughters out from apostolic religious, such as giving priority to the urgent needs of people in crisis rather than to community regimes, moving about easily in the streets, and being able to leave altogether without dispensation from a bishop or Pope and then to marry. On the one hand, the Company's superiors resisted the new normative ideas about active religious sisters, but on the other they were influenced by dominant ideas of female 'religious' behaviour and wider gender precepts.

When canon law eventually extended religious status to apostolic sisters the Company became a more obvious anomaly. The apostolic constitution *Conditae a Christo* promulgated by Pope Leo XIII in 1900 gave the status of 'religious' in general to women making simple vows in approved congregations and institutes. Many who had been making these vows annually now made them in perpetuity. As a result of their new status, fresh Church norms and requirements were articulated

---

64 Flores, 'The Superior General of the Congregation of the Mission', p. 32.

65 *Genesis of the Company*, Vol. 1. p. 81 1-7-2 DCMH. John E. Rybolt, *The Vincentians: A General History of the Congregation of the Mission Vol. 4 Expansions and Reactions (1843-1878)* (New York: New York City Press, 2014), p. 124. 1-7-2 DCMH.

66 Rybolt, *The Vincentians Vol 4.*, pp. 100-105.

and there were greater pressures for conformity from diocesan clergy involved in canonical governance. There was a price in freedom of action and autonomy paid for canonical status. Each new regulation applied to apostolic religious became an occasion of difficulty for the Company which had to prove that it was exempted. In 1913, for example, when the Sacred Congregation of Religious issued a 'Decree on the Confession of Nuns and Religious Sisters' to ensure liberty of conscience for sisters in the selection of confessors, the Company sought clarification about its own exemption in order to ensure that bishops did not apply these norms to Daughters in their dioceses.[67] Similarly it had to insist that the Daughters' houses were exempt from canonical visitation by local bishops because ever since the seventeenth century this responsibility had been granted to Directors and Superiors of the Congregation of the Mission. Such challenges only increased after 1917 with the promulgation of the first Code of Canon Law.

The Code of Canon Law of 1917 has been described as the first 'systematization of the vast corpus of church law, with its countless exceptions and scope for local discretion, into a Napoleonic-style single Code of Canon Law'.[68] It represented a 'reforming' impulse to override localism and differentiation and 'clearly expressed the Papal tendency towards centralisation'.[69] For the active religious life it was also a moment of great significance because simple vows were described as *public* and were accepted *in the name of the Church* (C.488,1).[70] In the Code's typology the Company of Daughters was now placed in the new category of 'simple-vow active congregation' because, as a Dean of the School of Canon Law at the Gregorian University remarked to the Sisters in 1968 'yours is a unique case and a 'unique case' cannot be catalogued'.[71] The nature of this uniqueness was, however, simply not grasped at the time of the new Code. The Sacred Congregation's puzzlement in the face of the Company's insistence on its lay and secular status and on the private nature of the Sisters' vows is not difficult to understand. Why would any group wish to retain lay status in a Church that emphatically taught the spiritual superiority of the 'religious state' over the 'lay state'? It is an important question that can only be answered by understanding the strength of the Daughters' identification with their foundation story, as they knew it. In this 'deep story', a term Bernard Lee has advocated as more helpful than 'charism', the Daughters' understood their own spirituality and its relationship to their service of people

67 *Decree of the Sacred Congregation of Religious on the Confessions of Nuns and Religious Sisters* (London: Burns and Oates, 1913). A circular letter to all Daughters from Superior General Fiat noted that before the Decree had been promulgated he had written to Rome 'to recall the special nature of your Institute, mentioning the Papal documents relative to your canonical position in the Church'. Circular Letters DCMH.

68 John Cornwell, reviewing two new books on Pius XII in *The Times Literary Supplement* 12 June 2013.

69 Georg Schwaiger, 'Benedikt XV,' in Martin Greschat, ed., *Das Papstum* Vol II (1993), p. 252, quoted in Jan de Maeyer, *Religious Institutes*, p. 23.

70 Discussed in Council of Major Superiors of Women Religious ed., *The Foundations of Religious Life: Revisiting the Vision* (Notre Dame IND: Ave Maria Press, 2009), pp. 6-7.

71 J. Beyer, 'Conference' to the General Assembly of the Daughters of Charity, 11 June 1968, reprinted in *The Echo* January 1969, p. 99. DCMH

in poverty to be inextricably connected to their relationship with the Superior General of the Congregation of the Mission and their membership of the double family.[72]

Superior General Verdier's Circular Letter addressed to the whole Company in June 1918 tackled head-on any internal doubts or confusions that the new Code might have created about status or place in the Church: 'without any possible hesitation', he wrote,'your Community is regulated by Title XVII of the section concerning religious...Societies either of men or of women, "living in common without vows"'.[73] They belonged here because 'these societies are not properly speaking"Religious".[74] Despite Verdier's calmness of tone, in reality the Code had created a new context requiring superiors to make the case for further exemptions while at the same time sustaining all members in their sense of formally 'belonging' to the Church - something they themselves had never actually doubted. This task was made more difficult because the insistence on lay status and on the clerical authority of the superior general of the Company continued to be contested by bishops during the 1930s, leading to yet a further restatement of the privileges by Rome in 1946.[75]

The Sacred Congregation for Religious expected the Congregation and the Company to propose revised Constitutions which would conform with the canons of the 1917 Code. One attempt was rejected by the Sacred Congregation and the double family remained in a state of canonical limbo until 1954 while continuing to grow.[76] At this point there were more than 40,000 Sisters in the Company worldwide. Following lengthy discussions between 1947 and 1953 the Company presented Constitutions to the Holy See for approval in 1954.[77] For the first time the Company and the Congregation had a place within the Church's canonical order that had been mutually agreed with the juridical authorities. It was, however, a compromise. A new canonical category - 'Society of Pontifical Right with privileged vows' - was created for the Company (and the Congregation of the Mission) which declared that the Company is not a religious congregation

---

72 Bernard Lee, 'A Socio-Historical Theology of Charism,' *Review for Religious* 48 (January-February 1989): 124-135. See Margaret Susan Thompson's discussion ' 'Charism' or 'Deep Story'? from which the reference to Lee's work comes.

73 For an example of the correspondence and discussion that ensued the 1917 Code see Circular Letter from Superior General Verdier dated 29 June 1918 on the impact of the new Code and another of 1927 from the same announcing that the Holy See had decided that the Company was subject to the regulations of Canon 505 of the 1917 Code i.e. triennial changes of superiors. 4-26-21-1 #2 DCMH

74 *Genesis of the Company* Vol 1. p. 116 1-7-2 DCMH

75 The requirement that house superiors be changed every three years was one such anomaly. The Company had no rules of this kind and asked for an exemption in certain circumstances which was granted as an experiment with restrictions in 1927. *Genesis of the Company* Vol 1. p. 120 and p. 131 for contested status. 1-7-2 DCMH

76 See John F. Zimmerman, 'Recollections of Father Slattery: The Years of his Generalship, 1947-1968', *VHJ* (1983), Vol. 4: Issue 1 Article 5.

77 Ibid.

and that it is exempt from episcopal oversight.[78] The status of 'privileged vows' was adopted to recognise that the vows were 'neither entirely private nor entirely public'.[79] Crucially, the structural character of the Company was retained within the double family. It had taken much patience and perseverance to reach this point but even so ground had continually been lost to norms drawn more from religious life.[80]

Only in the wake of the Second Vatican Council (1962-65), as we will see in Chapter 11, was the Company able to negotiate a canonical status that corresponded fully to its spirit and historical self-understanding. If the question is asked, 'what was at stake?' in the focus on status at a time of Catholic renewal, Vincentian Miguel Flores believes it was about 'freeing the vows of the sisters from an excessive canonical weight, for the purpose of reinforcing theological and Vincentian values'.[81] From a wider Church perspective the same question might be answered in terms of the challenge that the Daughters' existence made to the idea that lay people (women in this case) could not act as apostolic ecclesial agents or ministers. Their position as lay ecclesial agents leads on to the question, always present, of their authority to act in this capacity.

Authority in the Double Family

The locus and exercise of authority in any apostolic community of women was a matter of concern for the Church during the entire period from the thirteenth to the nineteenth century. It was not so much the active life *per se* that created the 'problem' over authority, since it was always assumed that the local bishop had authority, but rather the tendency for apostolic communities to grow and expand geographically beyond a single diocese. Angela Merici's 'Society of the Virgins of St Ursula' (1535) was one such, spreading rapidly beyond its origins in the Diocese of Brescia.[82] In the case of the Institute of Mary (1609), Mary Ward's founding vision was for a female religious order that would be missionary and mobile. Where institutes crossed Church and state boundaries either by design or through unplanned expansion, their founders were drawn to create structures of central governance to preserve union of spirit and purpose between widely separated members.

Any proposal for women to oversee such centralised governance in emerging trans-diocesan institutes was consistently rejected by Church authorities, long

78 See cmglobal.org/.../1-7-instruction-on-stabilities-chastity-poverty-and-obedience (accessed October 2013).

79 Supplement to *The Echo*, February 1968. 1-5 DCMH

80 Miguel P. Flores, 'The Common Rules of the Daughters of Charity,' *VHJ* (1987),Vol. 8. Iss. 1. Article 1., p. 21. See also Flores, 'Father Richardson and the Daughters of Charity' (1996), Vol. 17: Iss.2, Article 7, p. 95. Joseph Jamet, "What Are We?", Extract from *The Echo*, April 1968 15-4-1-1968 1-3 #14 DCMH

81 Flores, 'Father Richardson', p. 96.

82 Rapley, *The Dévotes*, pp. 48-50.

after the foundation of the Daughters of Charity.[83] Tridentine law, clerical territorial protectiveness and gender expectations about the exercise of authority worked in harness to make a female superior general of a trans-diocesan, let alone transnational, institute out of the question in the seventeenth and eighteenth centuries and still pioneering in the early nineteenth. Knowledge about the barriers that had been faced by others informed the approach taken by Vincent de Paul and Louise de Marillac. Given the clear missionary and universal vocation de Paul believed God had given to the Company, the issue of authority was one that would inevitably have to be faced when the time was right.[84]

The Company's sources of authority appeared to be laid out clearly in the Archbishop of Paris's 1646 decree of approval. It stated that the Daughters of Charity would 'always be under the authority and dependence of the Archbishop and his successors', who could appoint an ecclesiastic delegate in his place. De Gondi named Vincent de Paul as his delegate, 'for so long as God gave him life'. Furthermore, in the Statutes of the Association, it was stated that an elected superioress 'will have the whole direction of the said confraternity together with the said ecclesiastic' thus creating a tri-partite arrangement between bishop, clerical delegate and superioress that was quite normal for confraternities. According to Flores, 'the question is to know exactly what authority is really hidden behind this common stereotyped formula'.[85] His answer is that during the experimental period from 1634 to 1646, before the decree of approval, authority had been exercised charismatically by Vincent de Paul with the consent of Louise de Marillac, the members and the Archbishop. Another answer, one that recognises that only someone actually living the life can exercise certain kinds of community authority if it is to be authentic, would be that it was exercised by Louise de Marillac who looked to Vincent de Paul as clerical collaborator for particular aspects of authority. In either case the arrangements of the 1646 decree were insecure since they made no provision for the future beyond the life of Vincent de Paul: the Archbishop of Paris and his successors retained the right to nominate any ecclesiastic as delegated authority.

The initiative to ensure that the delegated authority would always be the superior general of the Congregation of the Mission was taken by Louise de Marillac. In November 1646, just after the decree of approval was given by Archbishop de Gondi, in a move that was an exercise of her own charismatic authority, she wrote to Vincent de Paul:

> Will these absolute terms concerning *the dependence on the Bishop* [original emphasis] not be able to do us harm in the future, since they

---

83 Jones, *Charitable Impulse*, p. 96.

84 On de Paul's way of proceeding see Alison Forrestal, ''Vincent de Paul: the Principles and Practice of Government, 1625-60', *VHJ* (2009) Vol.29; Iss.2. Article 3, p. 52ff.

85 Flores, 'The Superior General of the Congregation of the Mission and the Daughters of Charity'.

give him the freedom to separate us from the direction of the Superior General of the Congregation of the Mission?...In the name of God do not permit anything should happen which could one day make it possible that the Company be separated from the direction which God has given it. Be sure...the poor sick would no longer be taken care of...[86]

Authority had to be clerical to be ecclesial. Louise de Marillac's conviction that the God-given spiritual originality and apostolic mission of the Daughters required them to be connected to the Congregation of the Mission through the ecclesiastical authority of the single superior general was coherent but challenging, given the thinking of the day. Her goal was achieved somewhat providentially in 1655. The original decree of approval was mislaid before it had received the King's assent and ratification by the Parlement of Paris (both of which were necessary to make it valid). In the task of repeating the entire process Louise de Marillac was able to bring powerful voices, including that of the Queen of France, to bear on the question of authority over the Company. The replacement document of 1655 specified Vincent de Paul and his successors as the delegated ecclesiastical authority.

With this crucial change and with growing public support for the Daughters, it became easier to secure an autonomous authority structure. But there was still a real risk that future bishops would seek to 'colonise' the houses in their dioceses once the revered Vincent de Paul was no longer alive. Only approval as a pontifical institute could mitigate this potential threat. De Paul began the process for pontifical approval before his death and it was pursued by the founders' successors, being granted in 1668 by Cardinal Vendôme, Legate *a latere* to Paris of Pope Clement IX. With this step the Company 'ceased to be a confraternity' and was acknowledged as a community of women dedicated to the service of the poor 'without', in the words of the official text 'putting away their secular dress'.[87] It had become a *secular* community under pontifical law, depending on the Pope and no longer on the bishop. At the same time the Company had a clear hierarchical and clerical structure of authority that belonged firmly in the modern world of the Catholic Reformation rather than in the world of medieval confraternities with their 'horizontal orientation'.[88]

From this time until the early 1800s there were no further questions about the pontifical status of the Company nor about the authority of the superior general of the Congregation. The model of the double family had achieved several of the goals identified by other female founders of new religious institutes – an active apostolate, pontifical institutional status, a superioress general and autonomy as

---

86 Ibid., p. 8. quoting Sullivan, *Spiritual Writings*, p. 187.

87 Ibid., p16.

88 See the work of Nicholas Terpstra on this important shift, for example 'Afterword: Confraternities, social capital and civil society: comparisons, contexts and questions' in Colm Lenonn ed., *Confraternities and Sodalities in Ireland* (Dublin: Columba Press, 2012), pp. 196-98.

a distinct institute closely connected to a parallel male apostolic community in a family of kindred spirits. It had achieved the goal closest to Louise de Marillac's heart in keeping the Daughters 'Vincentian', by which she meant close to the poor. It had not achieved, nor did it ever set out to do so, primary authority for a female superior general under the Supreme Pontiff as sought by Mary Ward and realised (with great difficulty) in the early nineteenth century by founders such as Sophie Barat of the Religious of the Sacred Heart and Julie Billiart of the Sisters of Notre Dame de Namur. The Company's superioress general was clearly subordinate to the superior general within a construct of complementary gender roles, yet at ground level, so to speak, the consequence was an increase of freedom of local action for women.[89]

After the death of the founders the nature of the relationship between the superior and superioress general became more distant as the Company's organisational double family model became less charismatic and more obviously hierarchical.[90] In the words of the saint's most recent biographer 'Missioners and Daughters of Charity were to be the two arms of Vincent's vocation and so he regarded them as dependent on each other,'[91] an interpretation reinforced by Alison Forrestal's conclusion that the founder 'did not tend to emphasise the subsidiary aspects of [the Company's] liaison with the Congregation [but] to emphasise the particular charisms'.[92] In reality, however, this was not simply a co-equal and mutually dependent relationship.

Evolution of an organisational model

The double family model was sustained in part through its own sound practical administrative systems. The administrative adroitness of both Vincent de Paul and Louise de Marillac has already been noted for its importance in creating a stable yet adaptable organisation.[93] Each founder had a flair for organisation which showed itself in the governance and management structures they created, such as the Company's officer roles - first assistant to the superioress general, second assistant, treasurer and économe (bursar), who met together as the General Council of the Company. These were the Company's only elected posts and the terms of election were strictly limited: any vowed Sister present in the mother house took part and chose from two Sisters proposed by the General Council. The system of visitation that had traditionally served monastic communities well was adopted to check that each house was well managed, the Sisters were looked after, and the true spirit was being practised. Written records were devised

89 Brejon de Lavergnée, *Histoire des Filles de la Charité*, Chapter 6.

90 Ibid. p. 242.

91 Román, *St Vincent de Paul*, p. 455.

92 Forrestal, "Vincent de Paul: the Principles and Practice of Government, p. 57.

93 See Sullivan, "God Wants First the Heart and then the Work', on Louise de Marillac's leadership.

and meticulously kept by Louise de Marillac, providing a counterweight to any potential charge of disorder or irresponsibility that might be made against such a highly mobile community of women. It was for the sake of good order too that Vincent de Paul insisted on every *maison de charité*, even one with only two Sisters, having a named superior. Her title, Sister Servant, signified that her conduct 'must be to give an example of virtue and humility to the others'.[94] The office of Sister Servant proved so critical to the organisational effectiveness of the Company that it was gradually developed by superiors general, serving them well in maintaining uniformity and *esprit de corps*.[95]

After 1660 the Company's governance and administrative practices were strengthened under superior general Father Edmund Jolly (1672-98) and superioress general Mathurine Guerin (1667-73, 1676-82, 1685-91, 1694-97 and 1703-09). In her study of the poor relief activity of seventeenth-century Daughters, Susan Dinan has argued that the Company underwent a process of bureaucratisation in response to its own growth.[96] The role of director of the seminary responsible for the formation of new Sisters (taken by Louise de Marillac before 1660) was added at the level of officer in the Company with a seat on the Council, as was the role of director of the Company, giving a senior level of responsibility for a second Vincentian priest officer who undertook canonical visitations.

The Rule and Statutes drawn together by the founders at various times from 1646 onwards were further reorganised and elaborated during the eighteenth century, particularly in the time of superior general Bonnet (1711-36). Bonnet divided the Company's now extensive work in France into Provinces each having its own visitatrice (provincial), director and officers with defined delegated authority in relation to the central Council in Paris. Processes for the conduct of a visitation and systems for reporting and recording them were developed. Communication also continued to evolve: annual letters (Circulars) were disseminated, such as the 1 January Circular from the superioress general, and printed spiritual reflections were institutionalised, for example at the time of preparation for renovation of the vow. In time the development of these communications, together with special feast days (including, after 1737, the Feast of St Vincent de Paul), created a Company calendar of events that, in turn, added a distinctive community dimension to the Church's liturgical year and gave the Daughters' life its rhythm and annual cycle. By 1780 the outcome of such attention to models and systems of organisation was, in the words of one historian of the Daughters' health and hospital work, 'An organisational framework staffed by a cadre of capable administrators drawn from their own ranks...a strict admissions policy; a rigorous and highly centralized

94 *Genesis of the Company*, p. 30. 1-7-2 DCMH

95 Ibid., p. 48.

96 See Dinan, *Women and Poor Relief*, Chapter 5 for a detailed discussion of the bureaucratic development of the Company.

training in which the spiritual and the material were amalgamated into a potent critical mass...'[97]

The impact of Revolution and Restoration

Although the Sisters were perceived to be providing 'the highest levels of patient care and institutional control',[98] the Company was nonetheless dissolved by the Revolutionary regime along with all French religious communities in 1792. The Sisters had numbered more than 3,000 in 1790. Now each had to decide how to act on the basis of conscience and in the context of local circumstances. The profundity of what happened cannot be overstated. Many Sisters returned to their families while others went into exile, some were imprisoned and died there, and a small number were executed. Many simply changed their clothing and continued to do what they could to support their neighbours clandestinely in the spirit of their vows.

When Napoleon Bonaparte assumed power in 1799 the Sisters still living in the mother house were allowed, with his agreement, to receive and form new members for work in the hospitals and schools. Seminary Sisters began to arrive once again; more than 200 of them between 1801 and 1803. By 1804 there were around 1,600 Daughters in the restored Company, making it once again the largest community of consecrated women in France. Napoleon approached the restoration of active sisters in general in a practical and pragmatic way, regarding social welfare for poor as a responsibility of a civilised state and Catholic sisters as the most effective, efficient and respected means to discharge that responsibility. This did not mean he had any sympathy for their religious motivations. For Napoleon, therefore, a well-functioning state permitted religious sisters to conduct their work and even provided them with financial support – on condition that they subscribed to his own philosophy that religion was an arm of the state and therefore subject to state regulation and rationalisation.

The Emperor, who wanted every religious institute to accept a single Rule or a Rule template allowing for minor approved individual interpretations, and could see no reason why they would object to this condition. The template, moreover, required all sisters to come under the jurisdiction of their local bishop. Since this form of governance was contrary to the entire tradition and norms of the Company its leaders petitioned Pope Pius VII (1800-1823) to issue a papal brief to this effect. *Quum uti accepimus* (October 1804) stated that the 'care and government' of the Daughters of Charity belonged to the superior general of the Congregation of the Mission. Given the bishops' determination to prevent any such arrangement and Napoleon's own philosophy the scene was set for a 'conflict of ideologies'.[99]

---

97 Jones, *Charitable Impulse*, p. 109.

98 Ibid.

99 Rybolt, *The Vincentians. Revolution and Restoration*, p. 171.

Disputes over authority only served to underline the political, ecclesial, social and cultural importance of deciding who had control over the Daughters of Charity. For more than a decade the Emperor, Pope Pius VII and the bishops and vicars-general of Paris were involved in a conflict which also engaged the most senior members of the Congregation of the Mission and almost the entire membership of the Daughters of Charity. The issues for Napoleon were the efficient running of the French welfare system and the rule of the state over the Church, above all in the making of appointments. The Papacy's chief concern was to assert its authority over a Gallicanising church which aspired to autonomy from Rome. At the level of the bishops, themselves appointed by the state, what mattered was the primacy of episcopal authority over that of the superior general of the Congregation of the Mission. Finally, and with least power to influence, was the interest of the Daughters themselves. At stake for them was the question of their identity: a new identity as a female religious congregation separate from the Congregation of the Mission or their traditional lay identity in the Vincentian double family under the authority of its superior general?

These disputes await further historical analysis but, thanks largely to the work of American Vincentians and Daughters, a detailed narrative of events between 1801 and 1816 is now in the public domain.[100] As these recent studies conclude, because the episode was suppressed after 1816 in the interests of restoring internal peace, 'the whole period has been largely ignored in the history of the Daughters of Charity as well as that of the Congregation of the Mission'.[101] This is not the place to rehearse the often tortuous details with the many personalities involved, but because these events tell us so much about the Company's identity and because they had significant longer-term consequences in the Company as it expanded and globalised, some broad understanding of what happened is essential.

Played out without pause between 1804 and 1814 the conflict was nuanced only by the fluctuations in states of enmity and rapprochement between the various male parties and their rise and fall in power at different stages. For example, the concordat between the Emperor and the Pope in 1801 was broken in 1809 by the invasion of the Papal States by Napoleon. The papal riposte was to excommunicate the Emperor (1809). The Emperor lifted the ban on the Congregation of the Mission in 1801, but rescinded it in 1804 – a move which led to the imprisonment of its most senior officer and the theoretical superior of the Daughters, Father Dominique Hanon. In the midst of this turmoil the Company continued to renew itself and carry on its work, holding elections for superioress general in 1804, 1807 and 1809. Each superioress general faced political and Gallican Church pressure to present a new conforming Rule for approval, and counter-pressures from within

---

100 The most recent and thorough discussion is to be found in Rybolt, *The Vincentians. Revolution and Restoration*, pp. 170-88. I am indebted to this work and the work of Elisabeth Charpy for this section.

101 Ibid.,188.

the Company, the disbanded Congregation and the papacy to resist taking such action.[102]

By 1810 a number of Daughters had reached the conclusion that they should conform: some because it would protect their work for the poor and others because they had come round to thinking that the proposed governance structures represented a modernising and liberalising spirit in keeping with the intellectual and cultural developments of the day. The newly elected superioress general, Judith Mousteyro, and her officers were of this persuasion, and church authorities in Paris had hopes that their will would prevail.[103] But in April 1810, when Sister Mousteyro was presented with the new vow formula requiring the Sisters to vow obedience to the Archbishop of Paris the reality of the change struck her so forcibly that she resigned saying, 'my conscience would reproach me for the rest of my life if I accepted such a formula'. Divisions in the Company deepened when her successor, Sister Dominique Durgueilh, was appointed by the new Vincentian director and assistant director (themselves appointed by the Parisian vicars general) rather than elected, and proceeded to accept the new formula on behalf of the Sisters. A schism developed that pitted Daughter against Daughter. More than one hundred Sisters left rather than serve under Durgueilh and a further five or six hundred Sisters were expelled during 1811 and 1812 for refusing to submit to the new vow formula. In total a third of all the Sisters who had entered after 1801 left or were expelled. When this figure is added to the 'lost generation' of the 1790s it can be seen that the Company experienced a significant generational deficit.

At the same time younger women continued to enter in significant numbers indicating either that the internal conflict was not widely known or, if it was, was not a complete deterrent. In 1812 Sister Dominique was elected superioress general by the Sisters of the mother house. But even this did not signal a new consensus: many Sisters made their vows using the original Company formula, a smaller number adopted the new formula – and a third group substituted Durgueilh's name to the vow of obedience.

Only with Napoleon's abdication in April 1814 did a clear re-assertion of the traditional double family system of governance take place. With the return of Louis XVIII to Paris in April 1814 Father Hanon was released from prison and began to reassert his authority as superior general in the Company. He made it clear that anything other than this would forfeit the Sisters the name of Daughters of Charity (of St Vincent de Paul). It took a further nine months of open dispute between Hanon and Sisters Mousteyro and Durgueilh about who was the legitimate superioress general and who the legitimate clerical authority before the Company accepted in March 1815 that Hanon would preside over the election of a new superioress general. Elizabeth Baudet was elected. In August 1815 Hanon took the opportunity of blessing the chapel of the Daughters' newly acquired rue

---

102 See Elisabeth Charpy, 'A Challenge to Napoleon', pp. 47-89.

103 Elected 10 December 1809.

du Bac mother house to give a lengthy conference on tradition. 'Let us be careful,' he warned, 'of allowing any break or change in the precious chain of ancient observances, pious usages, holy rules, or of bringing in novelties or relaxations'.[104] By January 1816 the superioress general and her council were ready to agree to a set of statements which included acknowledgement that supreme authority in the Company was vested in the superior general of the Congregation of the Mission while the authority of the superioress general came from him as well as from the vote of the Sisters. The Statues and Rules were confirmed to be those devised by Vincent de Paul and Louise de Marillac. After a period of great disturbance the identity of a Daughter of Charity was reasserted through its historical lineage and traditions. Even so, it was not until 1834, the time of superioress general Boulet, that uniformity of habit and daily timetables were re-established.[105]

One of the few commentators on this entire episode has observed that, 'the majority of the houses of the Company in France would bear the wounds of this discord for decades'.[106] Even as late as 1870 some Sisters in Toulouse resisted the authority of the restored mother house in favour of the Bishop of Toulouse. What is remarkable, therefore, is the fact that the Company underwent massive expansion and became a transnational organisation only twenty years after this trauma. Its imprint can be seen, however, in the self-conscious and remorseless concentration on what the then superior general Jean-Baptiste Étienne called 'l'esprit primitif' of the Company and in his concern for uniformity, order and central control as the Company expanded and globalised under his leadership. The Company culture created by Étienne was to shape the way the Daughters were established in Britain and provided part of the context for the encounter between British and Irish Sisters and their French superiors and companions.

'Re-birth' of the Company in the nineteenth century

The impact and legacy of Jean-Baptiste Étienne, superior general between 1843 and 1874, is best understood against the background of the Company's experience of disunity already outlined and the even more durable and bitter disunity of the Congregation of the Mission which he entered in 1825. His recent biographer, Edward Udovic, has argued that Étienne 'deserves his title of "Second Founder".' Certainly, his claim for Étienne as 'the most important figure in the modern histories of both communities until the Second Vatican Council'[107] is unlikely to be contested, even though Étienne's influence has been reassessed by Udovic and others and its controlling, hierarchical and patriarchal characteristics acknowledged.[108] It was

---

104 Rybolt, *The Vincentians. Revolution and Restoration*, p. 187

105 Laurentin, *The Life of Catherine Labouré*, p. 129.

106 Rybolt, *The Vincentians. Revolution and Restoration*, p. 187

107 Edward Udovic, 'Jean-Baptiste Étienne, C.M. and the Restoration of the Daughters of Charity,' *VHJ* (2012), Vol.31: Iss. 2. p. 10.

108 See Father General Robert P. Maloney's Introduction to Udovic's biography of Étienne.

only when Vincentian scholars undertook research into both the founding era and the Étienne era that they came to appreciate both the latter's contribution to sustaining Vincentian unity and core values *and* the extent to which he rewrote and reinterpreted the Company's history, creating a narrative of decline and rebirth to achieve this end.[109]

It was Étienne himself who coined the term 're-birth' to describe what he believed was taking place in the Company under divine Providence during his superior generalship. But re-birth was also his prescription to cure the ills of the Company. Étienne interpreted the Restoration era, and even the final decades of the pre-Revolutionary period, as a time of moral decay and spiritual decline in the double family away from *'l'esprit primitif'* of Vincent de Paul.[110] *'L'esprit primitif'* was the leitmotiv of his period in office. It 'obsessed' him according to Udovic who sees it as 'the organizing principle which guided *all* of his rhetoric, policies, and actions as superior general to restore the community and make it successful in the…new world'.[111] In Étienne's idealised and simplified view of the past all the early Daughters were humble, obedient and imbued with the spirit of Vincent de Paul. Sisters were to use 'every means, every effort, every sacrifice in order to reproduce in [themselves] the first Daughters of Charity'.[112] At the same time Étienne's understanding of *'l'esprit primitif'* emphasised a Christo-centric discipleship formed in prayer as essential to the personal service Daughters gave to the poorest in society. This grasp of the fundamentals and his success in overseeing 'an explosive increase in numbers and vitality' left both Vincentian companies as 'vibrant apostolic societies' at his death. It made him, in the words of a twentieth-century superior general, 'a hero in the Vincentian Family'.[113] Yet, it is now clear that this was achieved at the expense of the place of Louise de Marillac in the Company's self-understanding and by a distortion of the lived experience of the early Sisters as flesh and blood women. The striking – and essential - collaboration between the co-founders and the relationships Louise de Marillac had with the early Sisters were of no interest to Étienne. It was only in the 1880s, after Étienne's death, that Louise de Marillac, whose memory had been kept by many of the Sisters themselves, was recovered to the Company's official memory.[114] Under Superior General Antoine Fiat, as Matthieu Brejon de Lavergnée has argued, in the context of the 'feminisation of religion', when it was

---

109 I have drawn extensively on the work of Edward Udovic for the conclusions in this section and likewise on John E. Rybolt, *The Vincentians. Revolution and Restoration*.

110 Udovic, 'Étienne and the Restoration of the Daughters of Charity', p. 15.

111 Ibid., p. 10.

112 Ibid, p. 20, quoting Étienne.

113 Ibid., Introduction by Father General Robert P. Malone.

114 Ibid., p. 16. See Louise Sullivan preface to *Louise de Marillac: A Spiritual Portrait*, p. 39.

clear that women wanted and expected female role models and leaders, the cause for the canonisation of Louise was introduced.[115]

Étienne's complex personality, methods and legacy have only very recently been explored in any nuanced and historicised way.[116] Unlike Vincent de Paul, Étienne insisted that authentic obedience to spiritual authority was total and unquestioning. Personal interpretations were 'illusions' and no competing narratives were permitted. His attention to the details of administration and community life in both communities was acute and his observations of failings and potential failings led him to supervise the production of what his first biographer (and nephew) described as 'numerous mind-numbing directories and rules of office'.[117] The Company's printing presses were soon busy issuing detailed rules of office for each office holder and regular circular letters promulgating Étienne's unswerving messages about uniformity, conformity and *'l'esprit primitif'*. Warnings were strongly worded. The houses in Poland, for example, were held up to all as 'no longer based on the firm foundation laid by St Vincent in your Constitutions'. Rather they had 'become a relaxed and degenerative Community, which retains your holy Habit...but which no longer possesses its spirit, and can no longer perform its works'.[118] Those in Spain were denounced in similar terms. Being 'fruitful' and 'generative', terms he used time and again, was not possible without total conformity to an understanding of the Vincentian spirit as approved by himself.

The 'problem' of the Polish and Spanish Sisters in the eyes of French superiors lay in the local adaptations they had made. In Étienne's eyes they failed to replicate the essence of the Company, in which a good deal of French culture was inevitably embedded. Setting aside the rights and wrongs of these adaptations, it was impossible for Étienne to imagine the Company and the double family as anything other than essentially French. Moreover, he could not envisage anyone other than a Frenchman leading the Congregation or a Frenchwoman leading the Company. 'L'esprit primitif' was French and Vincent de Paul's charism was a French charism. At 'one point he even went so far as to tell the Holy See that it would be better for the communities to be suppressed than to change anything of their constitutive French identity as bequeathed by St Vincent'.[119] As an ardent nationalist (who was little concerned with whether the nation was a republic or a monarchy) Étienne believed in France's destiny to be great on the world stage through empire, culture, and political vision. But what made greatness possible in Étienne's eyes was

---

115 Matthieu Brejon de Lavergnée, 'Du mythe des origines les Filles de la Charité et leurs fondateurs, XVIIe-XXe siècle', in Brejon de Lavergnée ed,, *Quatre siècles de cornettes*, pp. 27-35. For details of the process see Urrizburu, 'Letters of Louise de Marillac' and Betty A. McNeil, 'Spes Unica – Path to Glory: The Canonization of Louise de Marillac', *VHJ* (1992), Vol.13: Iss.2, pp. 113-26.

116 Udovic, *Jean-Baptise Étienne*, p.xi and Rybolt, *The Vincentians* Vol 4, pp. 139-141.

117 Auguste Devin quoted by Udovic, *Jean-Baptiste Étienne*, p. 311.

118 Udovic, *Jean-Baptiste Étienne*, p. 18.

119 Udovic, 'Étienne and the Restoration', p. 16.

French Catholicism, a Gallican Catholicism that held together state and Church under God's Providence and within which the Vincentian family, supported by the state, was a major actor for the work of Providence. Fittingly Étienne was 'one of the last Catholic leaders of the nineteenth century who resisted the ultramontanism ...[of] Pope Pius IX'.[120]

The Company's expansionist policies under Étienne were an enactment of his own form of Gallicanism and nationalism at a time of renewed French imperial power and of 'French universalism'.[121] At times the Company moved with the French empire and the Daughters were its official agents, on other occasions it moved into areas of the globe beyond the empire.[122] But as French Daughters were increasingly sent on mission outside France and as the numbers of Daughters born in other countries grew steadily there was to be no dilution of the French identity of the Company. All Daughters, no matter where they lived and worked, must act in exact conformity of behaviour with the Daughters of the mother house. Étienne was keen to praise 'those Sisters whom nature has made natives of a foreign land' in whom he saw 'the same spirit, the same regularity, the same sentiments, the same habits which make true Daughters of Charity in France!' It was only to be expected that they would express 'their desire of coming some day to drink at that pure fount of the spirit of their Vocation' that could only be found in the rue du Bac.[123] Sister Servants were the key to ensuring uniformity, hence the issuing of lengthy 'Advice' manuals for them in 1843 and 1854, the latter with a section of 'particular advices for Sister Servants outside France'. In 1862 'Regulations for the Provinces outside of France' were issued with detailed rules for governance.

It is well known that large-scale organisations in the nineteenth-century underwent processes of rationalisation, bureaucratisation and centralisation (although the continuing importance of family-based networks needs also to be borne in mind as not necessarily incompatible with centralisation).[124] In the case of the Company such processes built on the administrative innovations of the founders and on the bureaucratisation of the post-founder eras. They were probably inevitable if the Company's mission was to flourish in a transnational community. The connection between global mission and a centralised model was apparent to Étienne: 'The more your Company extends', he wrote, 'the more necessary does it become to preserve unity of purpose and of means of administration, and that all of those who are the depositaries of my authority,

---

120 Ibid, p. 15.

121 Adam J. Davis and Bertrand Taithe, 'From the Purse and the Heart: Exploring Charity, Humanitarianism and Human Rights in France,' *French Historical Studies*, Vol. 3 (Summer 2011), pp. 413-32.

122 Sarah Curtis, *Civilizing Habits*, pp128-9.

123 Udovic, 'Restoration,' p. 16. Circular 118.

124 See, for example: 'Professionalization, Bureaucratization and Rationalization: The Views of Max Weber', *Social Forces* (1975) 53 (4), pp. 627-634.

should follow one same line of conduct in the government of your Houses'.[125] It is clear from the roll call of international expansion during the 1840s and 1850s (Mexico and Egypt 1844; Cuba, Lebanon and England 1847; China 1848; Puerto Rico and Brazil 1849 and so on)[126] that his approach was, as Udovic concludes, 'wildly successful'.[127]

When Étienne commissioned a new work in London in 1867, his advice to the Sister Servant was consistent with all that Udovic has emphasised about his approach: 'A beautiful mission is offered to you in Great Britain', he wrote to Henriette Chatelain, 'where the Company is destined to work on a large scale; but this depends on moving with caution and wisdom, and establishing everything well and above all seeing that everything is done in accordance with the spirit of St Vincent'.[128] The extent to which his prophecy for Britain was fulfilled will be explored in our next chapter.

---

125 Udovic, 'Restoration', p. 17 Circular 129.

126 *Genesis of the Company*, p. 75. 1-7-2 DCMH

127 Udovic, 'Restoration', p. 22.

128 *Annals of the Congregation of the Mission*, Vol. 63, 1903, p. 405. 1-4 DCMH Father Étienne's only remaining letter to Sister Chatelain (she had her correspondence destroyed).

The origins, spirit and history of the Company in France

Vincent de Paul 1581-1660
Canonised 1737
Universal Patron of Charity 1883

Louise de Marillac 1591-1660
Canonised 1934
Patron of Christian Social Workers 1960

Vincent de Paul and Louise de Marillac gain the support of noble-born women for the work of caring for foundlings. The women are shown offering their jewels.

(André Jean OP 1662-1753 Musée de l'Assistance Publique Hôpitaux de Paris)

Many infants were left with the Daughters by women working in prostitution or by parents unable to provide for their care because of poverty.

The Rules governing the way of life and purpose of the Daughters of Charity

Despite the use of the term 'Constitution' the Company had no canonical Constitution until 1954 and operated through application of the Rule and Customs drawn up by the co-founders.

Seal of the Company of the Daughters of Charity designed by Louise de Marillac (original left) and still in use today.

Christ crucified at the centre of the Heart on fire with love and surrounded by the text 'The charity of Christ crucified urges us' from St Paul's Second Letter to the Corinthians 5:14.

'The charity of Christ crucified urges us'

Soeur de la Charité.

One of the earliest drawings of a Fille de la Charité – they were popularly known either as daughters or sisters of charity. Most were what the founders called 'village girls': capable country women were thought to be best suited for the mission and ministry.

She is represented in the street to indicate that she is not a nun (her status was lay) and that her work of charity was to visit people at home. The soup pot she carries signifies her practical care for people in need.

The head covering was everyday wear for many women in rural France at this time – sometimes starched and folded upwards. The upturned head covering became known as the 'cornette'. The Daughters did not fold it upwards to any great degree until the late eighteenth century, by which time other women had largely ceased to wear it.

Preparation of herbal remedies. The Daughters operated as apothecaries and ran dispensaries. (18c. engraving)

Les Sœurs de la Charité visitent et soulagent les Prisonniers.

Prison visiting was undertaken from the earliest years. (mid-18c. engraving)

French Revolutionary era and beyond

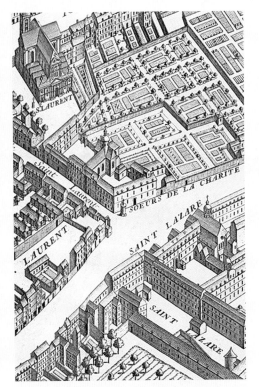

Pre-Revolutionary Motherhouse on the corner of rue Saint Laurent and rue Saint Lazare (opposite the Motherhouse of the Congregation of the Mission).
Detail from Plate 13 of Turgot's 1739 map of Paris.

On the eve of the Revolution the Company had more than 3,000 Sisters in 426 Houses in France. De-Christianisation of France by the revolutionary National Assembly included legislation forbidding religious vows and religious dress and confiscating the property of religious houses. Despite presenting the case that they were lay not religious, in October 1792 the Daughters were forced to leave their Motherhouse and in 1793 the Company was formally disbanded.

Some Daughters changed their clothing and continued with their work in hospitals and dispensaries supported by alms, some had their Houses confiscated and had to return to their families, some were imprisoned. There were executions of Daughters in Angers, Arras and Dax.

Marguerite Rutan Sister Servant (Superior) of the Hospital at Dax, guillotined 1794, beatified 2011.

Four sisters of Arras guillotined for sedition in June 1794, beatified 1920.
(Artist Auguste Moreau-Deschanvres 1838-1913)

The new Maison Mère

In 1801 Emperor Napoleon agreed to restore the Daughters to meet nursing and welfare needs in the Republic. An Imperial Decree in 1813 gave the Daughters use of the former Hôtel de Châtillon at 140 rue du Bac in Paris as their Maison Mère.

Seminary Sister at the Sisters' entrance (wearing the seminary Sister habit).

Interior courtyard with Sisters and seminary Sisters. More than 500 Sisters lived at the rue du Bac by the 1860s.

The Chapel of the Apparition of Our Lady of the Miraculous Medal (the Sisters' chapel at the Motherhouse) as it looked in the late 1880s. Although it was open to the public in 1880 the opening hours were very restricted and it was not yet a place of pilgrimage.

The nineteenth century at home and abroad

Apparition of the Blessed Virgin to Sister Catherine Labouré (1806-1876) in the chapel of rue du Bac in 1830. The Virgin showed herself to Catherine on three occasions to give her a mission to petition for a medal to be struck.

This painting by the artist Le Cerf (1836) was approved by Sister Catherine as a true representation and has always hung in the seminary.

Sister Catherine lived the remainder of her life quietly in service of the poor as a Sister of the House in Reuilly, a few miles from the centre of Paris.

Back and front of the medal, soon known as the Miraculous Medal, first struck by Parisian goldsmith Adrien Vachette in June 1832.

One million medals had been distributed by 1835 and one billion by the time of Catherine's death in 1876.

Crimean War, Battle of Inkerman (1854)
In 1853 Napoleon III confided the nursing care of the wounded to the Daughters of Charity. The Daughters nursed on the battlefield; those needing treatment were taken to Constantinople and other locations. Knowledge of this nursing provision for the French army led to debate in Britain about the lack of similar provision for British soldiers and opened the way for the work undertaken by Florence Nightingale in the Crimea. Nightingale had already visited the Daughters' hospitals in Paris and in Alexandria to study their techniques and approach to patient care.

(Reproduced with kind permission of the Wellcome Library)

Surp Agop Armenian Hospital in Pera, Istanbul (1854).

(Reproduced with kind permission of the Wellcome Library)

Mission in empire and beyond

French imperial expansion played a part in shaping the Company's missionary direction but did not determine it. The missionary outreach of the Congregation of the Mission and the Company was one of the hallmarks of the history of the 'double family' after 1830. The Daughters became the first women missionaries to China when a group arrived in 1848. They were also very active in the Middle East, in North Africa and in Latin America.

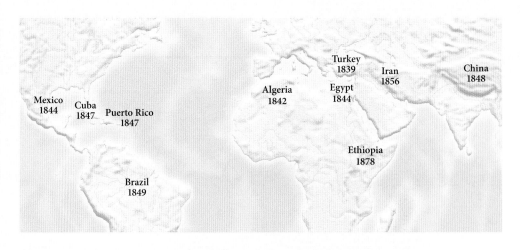

Part II

1847 – 1925 Experiment and Expansion

3
Finding a place in Britain

The first Daughters to leave Paris for Britain arrived in the north-west cotton manufacturing district of Salford and Manchester in June 1847. They were one of six groups of Sisters sent by the Company to different territories that year as part of a conscious drive to globalise 'the Vincentian charitable and evangelistic mission', the others being Libya, Syria, Lebanon, Cuba, the West Indies and Puerto Rico.[1] But where other missions flourished - the Daughters' clinic in Beirut, for example, recorded 20,000 patient visits by 1850 - the group in England experienced such sustained verbal and physical harassment that they were withdrawn after less than two years.[2] Thirty years later, when Bishop Vaughan of Salford welcomed Daughters back to inner city Manchester, he rightly observed that they had been better received in Turkey than in his own district of England.[3] For several years after the 1849 withdrawal, despite requests from priests and leading members of the laity in different parts of Britain, the Company's general council was not prepared to risk sending Sisters to the nation described by its superior general as a 'sterile land'.[4]

But in 1857 there was a change of heart at the top of the Company in response to new circumstances. Sisters were sent from Paris to the steel town of Sheffield in Yorkshire and this time they were able to establish an effective local and parish ministry of home visiting, night schools and sodalities for working-class girls and women. Encouraged by this success the Company made other foundations in England and in 1860 opened its first house in Scotland. By 1900, with thirty-seven canonically erected houses in England and six in Scotland[5], the Daughters had not only made a place for themselves in Britain but had taken part in a process of

---

1 See Udovic, *Jean-Baptiste Étienne*, p. 87.

2 See 'Sarah Curtis, 'Charity begins Abroad: the Filles de la Charité in the Ottoman Empire,' in White and Daughton eds, *In God's Empire*, p. 95.

3 *Manchester Evening News*, 22 March 1877, p. 2.

4 Letter from Superior General Étienne to Fr Philip Dowley, Superior of the Irish Vincentians on the news of their Sheffield mission in 1853: Jerome Twomey, 'The Vincentians in Britain', *Colloque: Journal of the Irish Province of the Congregation of the Mission* (1980), Vol.3.p. 54.

5 A canonically erected house has the formal approval of the local bishop. A house at a distance to an erected house could have the status of an annexe of that house on a temporary basis. Houses needed to be formally licensed and could not be opened and closed without the local bishop's permission: permission from the Curia also being needed for closure of a house. The Company's own definition of a house was a group of sisters having a Sister Servant and specific works. A work or house could be extended and new activities added without permission needing to be applied for provided they all continued under the same Sister Servant.

cultural change taking place in the nation.[6] 'When I see the way our good Sisters of Charity can move about now-a-days (sic),' one Mancunian Catholic reflected in the 1890s, 'the good they are doing and how they are respected, I often say to myself, "what changes from forty years ago for the better".[7]

The Daughters' history in Britain was one strand in a much larger religious and cultural phenomenon. In the second half of the nineteenth century, as a result of many separate community and diocesan decisions, a network of convents was built across England and Scotland and, more tentatively, reached into Wales. By 1910 no fewer than 80 different Catholic congregations or institutes of apostolic sisters had made foundations in England and 22 had done the same in Scotland, establishing more than 550 convents between them – a larger number even than in Catholic Ireland (although often on a smaller scale).[8] Just as they became an integral part of the Catholic Church in Britain, Catholic sisters also became a constitutive part of the nation's civil society.[9] Their presence in the religious, charitable and physical landscapes of Britain has been mapped during the past twenty years by scholars who have begun to study its meaning, but much remains to be explored, including the cultural encounters and exchanges involved in creating such a network. Like the Daughters of Charity, two-thirds of the orders and congregations present in Britain by 1910 were originally Francophone, congregations founded in France or Belgium, either making a mission in England or opening a 'safe' house because of political difficulties at home.[10] This historical phenomenon has received relatively little notice by social historians, leaving unanswered questions about the cultural transactions which took place when Francophone communities worked *across* the national boundaries of France, Britain and Ireland and *within* the ethnic and social class mix of the Catholic community in Britain. What did it mean to find or create a place in this context? The Daughters' early history in the British Isles illustrates the complicated cultural processes that took place when missionary Catholic sisters, lay or religious, made foundations and sought to establish roles for themselves in the Church and wider society.

6 They were third largest whether measured by the number of Sisters or houses. The largest women's congregation in terms of the number of houses and sisters was the Sisters of Mercy but this was a decentralised institute where each house was autonomous. The Sisters of Notre Dame de Namur and the Faithful Companions of Jesus had more professed sisters (more than 800) than the Daughters (more than 700) while the Sisters of Charity of St Paul the Apostle had slightly more convents (54) than the Daughters. Mangion, *Contested Identities*, p. 191 and p. 196.

7 *The Harvest* (June, 1898), p. 142. Salford Diocesan Archives (SDA).

8 There were 61 convents in Scotland. See Mark Dilworth 'Religious Orders in Scotland, 1878-1978' in David McRoberts ed., *Modern Scottish Catholicism 1878-1978* (Glasgow: Burns, 1979), pp. 92-109 and the annual *Catholic Directory for Scotland* (1829). For England see Barbara Walsh, *Roman Catholic Nuns in England and Wales 1800-1937* and Mangion, *Contested Identities*. See also Susan O'Brien, 'Religious Life for Women', in V. Alan McLelland and Michael Hodgetts eds., *From Without the Flaminian Gate: 150 Years of Roman Catholicism in England and Wales, 1850-2000* (London: Darton, Longman and Todd, 1999), pp. 108-143.

9 Civil society defined here as 'the sphere of institutions, organisations and individuals located among the family, the state and the market, in which people associate voluntarily to advance common interests.' Helmut K. Anheier, 'How to Measure Civil Society', http://fathom.lse.ac.uk/features/122552/ (accessed 11 December 2013).

10 Susan O'Brien, 'French Nuns in Nineteenth Century England,' *Past and Present* Number 154, February 1997, pp. 142-180 and Walsh, *Roman Catholic Nuns*, Appendix II.

The historical context for convent expansion

From the time of the Elizabethan Act of Uniformity of 1559 to the 1790s, with one clandestine exception, there were no convents, nuns, or sisters in England, Scotland or Wales.[11] By the early seventeenth century the Catholic community in Britain had been reduced to a tiny minority, concentrated in less accessible pockets of the country such as the East Riding of Yorkshire, West Lancashire and the Scottish Highlands as well as more prominently in the West Midlands and London. Some Catholic families went into permanent or temporary exile in northern Europe and the institutions they established provided spiritual nourishment to their co-religionists in Britain.[12] Twenty-six convents for contemplative religious life were founded by and for exiled Catholics in the Low Countries or northern France in the seventeenth century and some 3,500 women from the British Isles spent their lives in one of them in the seventeenth and eighteenth centuries. Enclosed English convents were an important element in the cross-Channel web of 'British' Catholic life for two hundred years, but Catholic women from Britain tended not to experience the new apostolic developments in religious life at this time.[13]

Anti-popery sentiment, a strong element in the Protestant Reformation in England and Scotland from the time of Henry VIII, broadened in the later sixteenth and seventeenth centuries into antipathy to all things Catholic, not least because of the need for constant political vigilance against Catholic enemies at home and abroad. Penal laws, which prohibited the practice of the faith and the presence of priests, created martyrs among the resistant, or recusant, Catholic community. At the same time, as Alexandra Walsham has shown, Catholics who conformed outwardly to the Church of England were able to sustain their faith less dramatically in ways hidden from view.[14] On the one hand, a rich tradition of Catholicism as 'devious other' evolved through time from the real and the imagined presence of Catholics, but on the other hand actual Catholics were often left alone to worship as they chose, provided they did so quietly.[15] Anti-Catholicism became a core component of the new 'British' identity successfully forged between Scots, Welsh and English; hostile feelings could be ignited if Protestant hegemony was at all threatened and Catholics were not equal before the law, but by the early

---

11 The exception was Mary Ward's Institute of the Blessed Virgin Mary with bases in London and York.

12 Sarah L. Bastow, *The English Catholic Gentry of Yorkshire 1536-1642: Resistance and Accommodation* (New York: Edwin Mellen Press, 2008); John Bossy, *The English Catholic Community, 1570-1850* (London: Darton, Longman and Todd, 1976). On the role of printed material see Alexandra Walsham, *Catholic Reformation in Protestant Britain* (London: Ashgate, 2014).

13 Caroline Bowden and James Kelly eds., *The English Convents in Exile, 1600-1800: Communities, Culture and Identity* (Farnham: Ashgate, 2013); Caroline Bowden, gen. ed. *English Convents in Exile, 1600-1800* a six-volume study published in two sets each of three volumes (London: Pickering and Chatto, 2012 and 2013). I am indebted to Dr Caroline Bowden for the figures. Again, the exception was Mary Ward's community.

14 Walsham, *Catholic Reformation*.

15 Arthur F. Marotti, *Religious Ideology and Cultural Fantasy: Catholic and Anti-Catholic Discourses in Early Modern England* (Notre Dame, Ind: University of Notre Dame Press, 2005);Michael Touks, *Romanticism and The Catholic Question: Religion, History and National Identity, 1778-1829* (Basingstoke and New York: Palgrave Macmillan, 2011).

eighteenth century many Catholic families lived peaceably side by side with their neighbours.[16]

At the end of the eighteenth century the French Revolution's frontal attack on Christianity created a climate of some sympathy among British elites for the persecuted Catholics of France. With the advent of the Terror in 1793 and war between France and Britain, the British government was willing to receive the exiled nuns of the English convents as victims of religious persecution. By 1800 most had returned from France and were discreetly accommodated in the country houses of the English Catholic gentry. Although they were received as 'creatures of a new species, very proper objects of curiosity',[17] neither their presence nor that of a large number of refugee French priests aroused much public anxiety. The government went so far as to grant each of them, and the large number of émigré French priests to whom it also offered refuge, a pension of ten pounds a year for a period.

In 1801 the union of the kingdoms of Great Britain and Ireland increased the long-standing pressure for relief from discriminatory legislation against Catholics in both islands. Political and religious campaigners achieved the goal of Catholic Emancipation in 1829 and it seemed that an era of tolerance would accompany this acknowledgement of Christian plurality in the two islands. However, rather than heralding a steady increase in acceptance of Roman Catholicism, Emancipation was followed by an increase in virulent anti-Catholic sentiment in England and Scotland.[18] Carol Herringer has described the anti-Catholicism 'revived in the mid-nineteenth century' as 'in some ways more significant than earlier manifestations of the prejudice'.[19] Heightened nationalism was a significant element and large-scale migration from Ireland to Britain during the 1840s and 1850s certainly played

---

16 Linda Colley, *Britons: Forging the Nation 1707–1837*(New Haven and London: Yale University Press, 1992) but for a more nuanced view see Liesbeth Corens, 'Catholic Nuns and English Identities. English Protestant Travellers and the English Convents in the Low Countries, 1660-1730,' *Recusant History*, Vol 30, No.3 (May, 2001), pp. 441-59 and John Bossy, 'English Catholics after 1688,' in O.P. Grell, J.I. Israel, and N. Tyack eds., *From Persecution to Toleration: The Glorious Revolution and Religion in England* (Oxford: Oxford University Press, 1991).

17 *The Tablet*, 23 February 1850, p. 123 quoted in Carmen Mangion, *Contested Identities*, p. 31.

18 John Wolffe, *The Protestant Crusade in Great Britain, 1829-1860* (Oxford: Clarendon Press, 1991), p. 2.

19 Carol Engelhardt Herringer, *Victorians and the Virgin Mary: Religion and Gender in England, 1830-85* (Manchester: Manchester University Press, 2008), p. 7.

a crucial role in stirring the emotions of prejudice.[20] But the causes of popular anti-Catholicism were more complex even than this, and they had particular consequences for the new communities of active Catholic sisters.[21]

Early Victorian Britain was a society in transformation, changed in part by significant movements of people to the cities from the British countryside and from Ireland, but even more by new technologies and forms of employment accompanied by reconfigured labour and class relations. It was no coincidence that the tone of religious culture changed at the same time. By 1840 a powerful evangelical Protestant movement had developed within the Church of England and across all the Protestant nonconformist denominations. An emancipated and expanding Roman Catholic Church (and the catholicising Oxford Movement within the Church of England) increased tensions and provided a focus for anxieties. The invigoration of Roman Catholicism which occurred during the 1840s and 1850s aroused a fresh phase of prejudice that drew on historic antipathies.[22]

Even this picture of contemporary religious tensions is insufficient to explain the particular intensity of feeling against nuns. According to one historian 'it was the nuns, rather than the Irish who were…the most unpopular single group in Victorian England'.[23] Whether this statement is accurate or not (and it does elide the fact that many sisters in Britain *were* Irish), religious sisters were almost invariably treated with suspicion or misguided pity.[24] In 1839, at a time when there were few convents in England and only one in Scotland, the popular women's writer Sarah Lewis warned that religious houses were the 'prison of involuntary victims' and 'a withering atmosphere in which to place warm young hearts and expect them to expand and flourish'.[25] Despite some influential voices raised

---

20 See, Walter L. Arnstein, *Protestant versus Catholic in Mid-Victorian England: Mr Newdegate and the Nuns* (New York and London, University of Missouri Press, 1982); Tom Gallagher, *The Uneasy Peace: Religious Tensions in Modern Scotland 1819-1914* (Manchester University Press, 1987); Marjule Anne Drury, 'Anti-Catholicism in Germany, Britain, and the United States: A Review and Critique of Recent Scholarship', *Church History* (2001), Vol. 70, pp. 98-131; D.G. Paz, 'Anti-Catholicism, Anti-Irish Stereotyping, and Anti-Celtic Racism in Mid-Victorian Working-Class Periodicals', *Albion* (1986), Vol. 18. pp. 601-16; Roger Swift and Sheridan Gilley, eds., *The Irish in the Victorian City* ((London: Croom Helm, 1985); Wolffe, *The Protestant Crusade* and, for an interdisciplinary perspective on prejudice that deploys behavioural psychology see Frank Wallis, 'Anti-Catholicism in Mid-Victorian Britain', *Journal of Religion and Society* (2005), Vol. 7., pp. 1-17.
The numbers of Irish-born migrants in England and Wales (not all of whom were Catholics) increased from 291,000 in 1841 to 520,000 in 1851. In England and Wales it peaked in 1861 at 602,000 (or three per cent of the population), and in Scotland from 128,000 in 1841 to 207,000 (or just under seven per cent of the population in 1851) with concentrations in the north-west of England, the west of Scotland and East End of London. Statistics taken from Swift and Gilley, *The Irish in the Victorian City*, p. 1.

21 Marotti, *Religious Ideology and Cultural Fantasy.*

22 Michael Wheeler, *Catholic and Protestant in Nineteenth-Century English Culture* (Cambridge: Cambridge University Press, 2006).

23 Swift and Gilley, *The Irish in the Victorian City*, p. 8 referring to the work of William Arnstein.

24 For the hostility directed at the new Anglican sisterhoods see Susan Mumm, "Lady Guerrillas of Philanthropy": Anglican Sisterhoods in Victorian England' (PhD thesis, University of Sussex, 1992) and *Stolen Daughters, Virgin Mothers;* see also Carmen Mangion, 'Women, religious ministry and female-institution building'.

25 [Sarah Lewis], *Woman's Mission* (London 1839), pp. 69-70 quoted by Mangion, *Contested Identities*, p. 57. See Sue Morgan, *Women, Religion and Feminism in Britain, 1750-1900* (Basingstoke,: Palgrave Macmillan 2002), p. 14 and the excellent discussion in Mumm, *Stolen Daughters*, pp172-206.

in favour of the social good that active sisters did, Lewis's views were widely endorsed. In 1852, for example, at the height of fresh 'No Popery' riots which followed the establishment of the Catholic hierarchy in England in 1850, the city of Edinburgh sent one of the many contemporary petitions to the Queen against convents. Theirs bore 'the signatures of 15,000 Scottish women, protesting that the blessings of civil and religious liberty enjoyed by Her Majesty's loyal subjects were denied to the"inmates' of nunneries".[26] Between 1851 and the early 1870s the campaign for government inspection of convents remained active and the issue was debated in Parliament on a number of occasions.

All consecrated religious life, male or female, was regarded as 'un-British', but the attack on 'sisterhoods' had a gendered character that focused on the defence of family life and motherhood against the practices of female celibacy and living independently of families. Celibacy was perceived as undermining the idealised domesticity that had emerged between the 1790s and 1830s 'as a reaction to the fears of revolution and a consolatory response to the transformation of industrialisation'.[27] In Britain the strongest and most consistently promoted female role model was an Evangelical Christian mother. Although a new form of domesticity was emerging in Catholic countries too, Catholic women were also forging an alternative feminine ideal at this time. It took the form of Christian service as a religious sister in one of the new or restored post-Revolution institutes founded for active ministry and mission. Concepts such as 'spiritual motherhood' ensured that religious consecration and activities which were often quite radical were thought about in reassuringly gendered ways, but nonetheless religious life offered women a genuine alternative. The high esteem in which the life was soon held was reflected in the numbers attracted to it. One calculation of female religious in France, Belgium, Prussia and Ireland around 1900 puts their number at 193,554.[28]In France the nursing, teaching and poor relief undertaken by religious sisters and their prominent role in the re-Christianisation of the nation were widely appreciated, and in Ireland active religious sisters were respected for their contribution to Catholic reform and national identity-formation as well as to poverty relief.[29]

---

26 Moses Creighton, 'Anti-Catholicism in Mid-Victorian Britain,' p. 9.

27 Leonore Davidoff and Catherine Hall, *Family Fortune: Men and Women of the English Middle Class, 1780-1850* (London: 1987), pp. 107-118; Joanne Bailey, *Parenting in England 1760-1830: Emotion, Identity and Gender* (Oxford: Oxford University Press, 2012), p. 9.

28 Maarten Van Dijck, Jan de Maeyer, et al. eds., *The Economics of Providence: Management, Finances and Patrimony of Religious Orders and Congregations in Europe, 1773-c1930* (Leuven: Leuven University Press, 2012), p. 14. The classic study is Claude Langlois, *Le Catholicisme au feminins*. Clear, *Nuns in Nineteenth-Century Ireland* and Maria Luddy, *Women and Philanthropy in nineteenth-century Ireland* (Cambridge: Cambridge University Press, 1995).

29 See Hazel Mills, "La Charité est une Mère': Catholic Women and Poor Relief in France, 1690-1850', in H. Cunningham and J. Innes eds., *Charity, Philanthropy and Reform from the 1690s to 1850* (Basingstoke: St Martin's Press, 1998), pp. 168-192 and ' 'Saintes soeurs and 'femmes fortes': Alternative Accounts of the Route to Womanly Civic Virtue, and the History of French Feminism,' in Clarissa Campbell Orr ed., *Wollstonecraft's Daughters: Womanhood in England and France 1780-1920* (Manchester: Manchester University Press, 1996), pp. 135-150.

This movement had been underway for more than thirty years on the other side of the Irish Sea and the English Channel respectively, before there were any developments in Britain. Following Emancipation a handful of French and Irish congregations sent small groups of missionary sisters to England and Scotland between 1830 and 1845.[30] Two new native foundations were made in England in the mid-1840s.[31] Just as the movement was gathering some momentum in the Roman Catholic community the first Anglican sisterhood was founded in 1845 and was quickly followed by others.[32] In the context of wider societal changes this modest increase in active women's communities, already underway when the first Daughters arrived, challenged British society in ways that the discreet enclosed convents some thirty years earlier had not done. Given what has been said about their differing ideals of Christian womanhood it is unsurprising that religious sisters were perceived in starkly different terms by Protestants and Catholics.

Anti-convent sentiment in Britain has attracted a significant degree of scholarly research, most of which has focused on the motivations and discourses discussed above. Less attention has been paid to the sisters' own experiences or to the impact of intimidation. Threats against their persons were a frightening reality that inhibited behaviour in public and reduced their scope for action in the 1840s and 1850s, and even later. Any Catholic sisters who ventured onto the streets of Britain during this time were at risk. The Sisters of Notre Dame de Namur, for example, who had been offered a first base in Penryn in Cornwall, faced regular public resistance between 1845 and 1848 and did not wear their habit outdoors 'without there being an incident'.[33] In Glasgow, the Franciscan Sisters of the Immaculate Conception 'dressed down' in 'a straw bonnet and cloak' from the time of their arrival in 1847 to 1896 when their Chapter finally decided they could switch to 'a long circular cloak and no bonnet'. Even disguised they were 'easily recognized, struck at, mobbed, insulted and [had] offensive things thrown at them'.[34] All unenclosed Catholic sisters worked in a climate of resistance and harassment during the 1840s and 1850s but, for a number of reasons discussed below, the Daughters of Charity who went to Salford in 1847 experienced a particularly intense form of hostility.

---

30 The Good Shepherd nuns of Angers in France went to west London (1841), the Religious of the Sacred Heart arrived from Paris in Berrymead in the south-west outskirts of London (1842), the Italian Providence Sisters settled a group in Loughborough in Leicestershire (1843), and the Sisters of Notre Dame de Namur went to Penryn, Cornwall (1845) before moving to Clapham, London in 1848. In 1847 the Sisters of Charity of St Paul the Apostle from Chartres arrived in Banbury in Oxfordshire, and the Franciscan Sisters of the Immaculate Conception of Tourcoing in France sent a group to Glasgow.

31 Two English foundations of active Catholic sisters, a Third Order Dominican house in Stone, Staffordshire and the Society of the Holy Child Jesus in Derby, were founded in 1844 and 1846 respectively. See Susan O'Brien, 'Terra Incognita: The Nun in Nineteenth Century England' and Walsh, *Roman Catholic Nuns in England and Wales*.

32 See Mumm, *Stolen Daughters, Virgin Mothers*.

33 *Jubilee: Sisters of Notre Dame de Namur Celebrate 150 years in Britain, 1885-1995* (Privately printed, 1995), p. 23.

34 S. Kehoe, 'Special Daughters of Rome: Glasgow and its Roman Catholic Sisters, 1847-1910' (PhD thesis, University of Glasgow, 2005), Chapter III.

Daughters of Charity in Salford 1847-1849

The Salford-Manchester conurbation of the 1840s was 'probably the most economically and socially dynamic city in the world'; the very 'symbol of the new age'.[35] As such it was a magnet for rural migrants from northern England and from Ireland. By 1840 the central area had one of the highest Irish population concentrations in the country and some of its worst housing conditions.[36] Although many of the Irish were Protestant, far more were Catholic. Manchester's Catholic population grew from just under three hundred in 1767 to about 80,000 by 1852, of whom more than 50,000 were Irish-born.[37] As John Bossy has noted there were few, if any, 'old' Catholics in the Manchester-Salford area, making the community dynamic quite different from Preston some thirty miles away, with its long-standing and accepted English Catholic community.[38]

Catholic provision became more visible as it tried to keep up with the demographic expansion. St John the Evangelist Church in Chapel Street close to the centre of Manchester (the future Salford cathedral), was the first cruciform Catholic church to be built in Britain since the Reformation. Its foundation stone was laid in 1844 in an impressive ceremony that incorporated an unprecedented Catholic procession of 6,000 children from the Catholic Sunday Schools of Manchester and Salford, an initiative which began the tradition of Manchester Whit-week "walks". Completed in 1848 and consecrated by Cardinal Wiseman, St John's expressed in bricks and mortar the desire of the Catholic community to live its faith fully and visibly.[39] But bricks and mortar were not enough for St John's main patron, millionaire cotton merchant Daniel Lee, whose vision included an extensive social outreach and spiritual mission. Lee had heard accounts of the Daughters of Charity from two Salford priests trained at St Sulpice, the Paris seminary strongly influenced by Vincentian spirituality and only a few minutes' walk from the Daughters' mother house.[40] One of these priests, Father James Boardman, a local man from Ashton-in-Makerfield, was appointed to St John's in 1845.[41] Sisters of Charity were Boardman and Lee's preferred pastoral workers for the working-class and predominantly Irish Catholic population of Salford. When they asked for Sisters they found they were pushing at an open door because by

---

35 A. Briggs, *Victorian Cities* (London: Penguin Books, 1963), the latter phrase is the heading for the chapter on Manchester.

36 On Irish migrants in Manchester see Donald M. MacRaild, *Irish Migrants in Modern Britain, 1750-1922* (London, 1999), Chapter 2.

37 Figures quoted in Edna Hamer, *Elizabeth Prout 1820-1864: A Religious Life for Industrial England* (Bath: Downside Abbey, 1994), p. 46 and MacRaild, *Irish Migrants*, p. 55.

38 Bossy, *The English Catholic Community*, p. 303.

39 See Hamer, *Elizabeth Prout 1820-1864*, 'Manchester's Catholic Revival' who argues that Manchester's Irish Catholics became Anglo-Roman Catholics, pp. 46-56.

40 J. Gillow, ed., *Biographical Dictionary of English Catholics* Vol. 4 (London: Burns and Oates, 1885-1902), p. 179.

41 I am indebted to Father David Lannon, Salford Diocesan Archivist, for this and other information about Catholicism in Salford and Manchester in the middle decades and for copies of *The Harvest*.

the mid-1840s superior general Étienne had already identified Britain as potential missionary territory for both Vincentian priests and Daughters of Charity. In April 1847 the council agreed that four Sisters could be authorised for Salford.

If Lee had a vision, so did Étienne. It was his fervent hope that Vincentians of the Irish Province of the Congregation of the Mission would work with Daughters for the Catholic regeneration of Great Britain.[42] It was not usual practice for Daughters to work in a country where there were no Vincentian priests, hence his expectation of collaboration. There is nothing to indicate that he understood the history of hostility that lay between Irish Catholics and the English, or that he anticipated how this quasi-colonial relationship might complicate his plan for collaboration. From Étienne's perspective it was straightforward, but according to one commentator from the Irish Vincentian Province 'the [Vincentian] missionary outreach to England suffered from confusion and fudging and conflicting goals' from the outset.[43]

The Irish Vincentian Province owed its origins to a small group of priests at Maynooth College who had begun following the rule of St Vincent. In 1841 they affiliated to the Congregation of the Mission and began to give parish missions in keeping with the Congregation's core vocation. In 1849, in a somewhat rapid development, they were recognised as the Irish Province and the Reverend Philip Dowley was appointed as first provincial. Their numbers were small, the needs in Ireland were great and the community had more requests for missions than it could meet. Even without taking account of his antipathy towards British authority, it is not difficult to understand why Philip Dowley showed no enthusiasm for Étienne's project to establish a permanent base for Irish confrères in England or for collaboration with Daughters of Charity there.[44] Dowley's reluctance meant that the Sisters in Salford worked on their own apart from occasional visits when confrères travelled over to give missions in the north of England.

Responsibility for the Salford house belonged to its Sister Servant, Clemence de Missy, a thirty-eight year old London-born and French-educated Sister with an English mother and French father. Her companions were one English and two French Sisters.[45] Relatively little is known about them, including the level of spoken English by the French Sisters, although we are told that Sister de Missy 'spoke English with a perfect accent'.[46] The group is only fleetingly referred to in local Catholic studies[47] and, while it was noted, the episode in Salford was not made much of in the overall narrative of the Daughters' history in Britain until

---

42 McCrohan, 'The Future of the Irish Vincentians in Britain,' *Colloque*, Spring 1988, No.17, p. 370.

43 Ibid., p. 369.

44 Ibid.

45 General Council Minutes Book 8, 28 April 1847, p. 954 DCParis.

46 Ibid.

47 See, for example, John O'Dea, *The Story of the Old Faith in Manchester* (London: R & T Washbourne, 1910) whose chronological listing omits the Daughters.

relatively recently.[48] Yet the Sisters' experiences in Salford reveal a good deal about the conditions under which Catholic women's communities worked in some parts of Britain at this time and about the way the Daughters' particular and distinctive characteristics exacerbated those difficulties.

The community lived in a small rented house close to St John's and their initial work was home welfare visits to families and to the sick poor in the neighbourhood where fever was rife in 1847.[49] In a matter of weeks the Sisters were teaching at St John's elementary school, had started evening classes for young female factory workers and organised catechetical sessions for adults and children to prepare them for the sacraments of baptism, first communion, confirmation, and confession.[50] It was standard work for parish Daughters but one member of the community later recorded that:

> Ma Soeur de Missy had a special gift for giving religious instructions... These evening instructions were a source of great good. Many elderly persons came to see us, when we first came to Manchester who never tired telling us of how these instructions were appreciated. Hundreds were prepared for the Sacraments....[51]

The Sisters went about their business, moving openly in the neighbourhood between house, school, church and market. The only other community of sisters in Manchester at this time was the semi-enclosed Presentation Sisters who lived in a purpose-built convent, school and orphanage surrounded by a wall and gardens in the grounds of St Patrick's church, just north of Manchester city centre. Compared to them the Daughters were both highly visible and unprotected.[52] Although they did not wear a conventional nun's habit - the blue-grey skirt, apron and black outdoor shawl being similar to what was worn by local working-class women - their large set of rosary beads and white cornette marked them out. All other sisters in Britain at this time avoided religious dress in public as a matter of prudence as well as conformity with the law, and in any case they did not move freely about in their local communities.[53]

It seems likely that a degree of negative reaction to the Daughters' presence would have occurred almost anywhere in Britain at this time but in Salford it was intentionally directed and orchestrated. One of their near neighbours was Canon

48 In 1955, for example, the Province celebrated the centenary of the Drogheda foundation as the centenary of the Daughters' presence in Great Britain and Ireland. See *Pioneer Sisters of Charity of Saint Vincent de Paul in Great Britain and Ireland* (Privately printed, Mill Hill, 1955), pp. x and xi. DCMH

49 http://www.manchestereveningnews.co.uk/news/greater-manchester-news/chapel-street-regeneration-site-in-salford-698496. (accessed 27 January 2014) and O'Dea, *Old Faith in Manchester* , p. 217.

50 'Manchester Mission' Handwritten undated account in French by one of the sisters. 11-1 DCMH.

51 Ibid.

52 See http://manchesterhistory.net/manchester/outside/stpatricks.html (accessed 24 February 2014).

53 See Mumm, *Stolen Daughters, Virgin* Mothers, p. 78 as well as the archival examples cited above.

Hugh Stowell, rector of Christ Church, widely known as the 'Protestant Watchman' for his energetic anti-popery campaigns.[54] By the late 1840s Stowell was at the peak of his reputation as a defender of the established church in Ireland against Catholicism. He had built a national reputation among Anglican Evangelicals for his ability to take on Dissenters, liberal churchmen and Tractarians. Historian of Salford, R.L. Greenall, describes him as 'paranoid about popery'[55] and particularly outspoken against the 'unnatural practices' of celibate priesthood and 'nunneries'.[56] Using familiar tropes Stowell urged Protestant women to work for the salvation of Catholic sisters who breathed 'the sighs of broken-hearted women...immured within walls where English law had no entrance'.[57] An active supporter of the British Reformation Society and of the Salford Operative Protestant Association, Stowell also had a platform among working-class men.[58]

Stowell's campaign against the Sisters began before they had arrived. 'When they commenced to build St John's, our present Cathedral', one local man remembered,' he was always crying out about the Popish Mass house, and protesting that the Protestant Alliance would never allow it to be opened':

> But when he heard that the Sisters of Charity were coming it seemed
> to set him off altogether. He held a special meeting in his school, Hope
> Street, and warned the people against letting them into their houses,
> and said many harsh things against them...[59]

Although this witness was careful to add that no one could be sure whether talk actually led to action, he recounted how, as a boy, he had seen the 'mass of a rabble, armed with clods and missiles to throw' so that the Sisters 'almost had to run the gauntlet through...as they passed along'.[60] From the start 'they had a very uncomfortable time of it' and the hostility was sustained. On one occasion a Sister was thrown to the ground and went home covered in blood.[61] Their house became a target: it was broken into and burgled on one occasion and set fire to another time.[62] Stowell had challenged Catholics to 'Let the poor Nuns walk abroad', arguing that 'if [convent life] would not stand contact with ordinary intercourse, and the ordinary scenes and sights of social life...It was not fit for the

---

54 R.L. Greenall, *The Making of Victorian Salford* (Lancaster: Carnegie Publishing, 2000), Chapter 4, pp. 84-107.

55 Greenall, *Victorian Salford*, p. 96.

56 Ibid., p. 97 Hamer, *Elizabeth Prout*, pp. 57-61.

57 *Protestant Witness*, p. 666 quoted in Hamer, *Elizabeth Prout*, p. 144.

58 Greenall, *Victorian Salford*, p. 99.

59 'Reminiscences of Catholicity in Manchester in the early part of this century', *The Harvest* (June, 1898), p. 142. SDA

60 'Reminiscences of Catholicity' *The Harvest* (June, 1898), p. 142 Ibid. SDA.

61 'Manchester mission' 11-1 DCMH

62 'Reminiscences' and 'Manchester mission' 11-1 DCMH

soil of England'.[63] When the Daughters did 'walk abroad' to conduct house visits, however, their public presence was a cause for outrage.

Clemence de Missy reported regularly on the situation and reports were also sent to Paris from time to time by the Irish Vincentians who visited when on mission in England.[64] After leaving the Sisters for almost two years the general council decided to withdraw them. It had come as something of a surprise to them to find that English attitudes towards the Sisters differed so markedly from those of the French.[65] Salford had proved a testing environment in other ways too: the expectation that school inspectors would examine the Sisters in front of pupils had challenged their sense of propriety. And there had initially been tensions in their relationship with Dr William Turner, Vicar General of the Lancashire District, because he had not been fully consulted by Lee and Boardman in the negotiations that brought them to Salford.[66] The situation was more complex than had been anticipated.

As a transnational organisation the Company had the option to remove the Sisters and deploy them elsewhere.[67] Its superiors concluded that England was not ready for their particular way of working and that they should wait for God to indicate when the time was ripe. Not everyone thought they were right to give up. William Turner, who believed the situation would have improved with time, was as exasperated at the Sisters' departure as he had been at their arrival.[68] Certainly, the initiative had strong lay backing and good financial support.[69] But the context in Salford at the end of the 1840s could also be seen as justifying the Sister Servant's fears and the less sanguine view taken by superioress general Mazin and superior general Étienne. Only one year later, at the time of the controversial establishment of the Catholic hierarchy in England and Wales, Chartist and anti-Catholic riots in the area around Manchester, provoked by 'local Anglican clergymen and electorally vulnerable Tory politicians', were the fiercest in Britain.[70]

When the Company made its second attempt at a United Kingdom mission, unsurprisingly, it was in Ireland. A foundation was made in Drogheda in 1855 with the support of the Irish Vincentians, a local benefactor and Dr Joseph Dixon,

---

63 *Protestant Witness,* p. 666 quoted Hamer, *Elizabeth Prout,* p. 145.

64 Twomey, 'Vincentians in Britain,' p. 48.

65 General Council Minutes Book 8 2 May 1849, p. 955 DCParis.

66 Ibid.

67 A pertinent example here would be the Manchester based congregation Sisters of the Cross and Passion founded in 1852 by Elizabeth Prout who had no option but to remain when they met opposition. See Hamer, *Elizabeth Prout.*

68 'Manchester mission' 11-1 DCMH and General Council Minutes Book 8 2 May 1849 p. 955 DCParis.

69 Lee was estimated to have donated more than £60,000 to support the development of the local Church and its welfare and educational infrastructure. See J. Gillow, *Biographical Dictionary* Vol. 4. It was a further thirty years before the Daughters returned to Manchester, arriving, according to oral tradition, just in time for Daniel Lee to know they had returned before he died. *Notes on Deceased Sisters,* Anne Gunning (1919) 10-3-1 DCMH

70 Swift and Gilley, *Irish in the Victorian City,* p. 6. See E. Hamer, *Elizabeth Prout,* p. 97, pp. 156-58

Archbishop of Armagh and Primate of All Ireland.[71] The Sisters received the warmest of welcomes from the local people. Two more houses were founded in 1857, this time in Dublin.[72] There seemed a good prospect of expanding the work considerably in Ireland. Events led superiors to believe they had received a providential sign to make a fresh start in England. There was no thought of forming the new houses into a province - all the houses of the Company were administered centrally from Paris - but a strategic decision was made to administer them as a single mission mirroring the geo-political composition of the United Kingdom. This administrative device meant that any Sister could be moved between houses on either side of the Irish Sea, a situation that was to be of great importance to the mission in Britain.

The double family in Sheffield

Sheffield was the location chosen for re-foundation in Britain because a community of Vincentian priests and brothers had taken on a mission there a few years earlier. This unexpected reversal of the Irish Province's earlier position had come about in response to an appeal from the parish priest of St Marie's church in the city, Edmund Scully and his Bishop, Dr John Briggs. Scully was not only a fellow Irishman but he had tried his vocation with the Irish Vincentians some time previously. He set before the Province the urgent case of Irish men and women living in Sheffield and the need for Irish missioners for the sake of their souls. The context for Scully's invitation was the marginalisation of Irish Catholics by English co-religionists and this, along with the known wishes of their superior general for a mission in England, persuaded Philip Dowley to accept the Sheffield mission.[73]

The heart of Catholic conflict in Sheffield was access to St Marie's, the only Catholic church in Sheffield. This large and noble new church had been designed by local Catholic architect Matthew Ellison Hadfield with much of the £10,000 construction cost being borne by Henry Fitzalan Howard, 14th Duke of Norfolk, premier earl of the realm and lay leader of the Roman Catholic community in England.[74] Although the Duke and his family lived for most of the year either at the castle in Arundel in Sussex or at Norfolk House in St James's Square, London, they also owned extensive estates in Derbyshire and in Sheffield which they visited frequently. Over time the family's protection and the employment opportunities afforded by a series of entrepreneurial Dukes of Norfolk had helped to build up an

---

71 Olive Sherlock et al., 'The Arrival of the Daughters of Charity of St Vincent de Paul to Drogheda, Ireland, November 1855', in Prunty and Sullivan eds., *Daughters of Charity in Ireland*, pp. 55-62.

72 Mary Purcell, *The Story of the Vincentians* (Dublin: All Hallows College: 1973), Chapters 5 and 6; Prunty and Sullivan eds., *Daughters of Charity in Ireland*, Chapters 3 and 5.

73 See, Derek Cullen, *St Vincent's: A History of a Parish 1853-2002* (Sheffield: St. Vincent's Parish Council, 2nd ed. 2003),p. 2 and p. 4 and *History of St Vincent's in Sheffield*© by Ted Cummings http://www.sheffieldindexers.com/ Memories/CherishedMemories_HistoryofStVincentsSheffield (accessed January 2014).

74 'Fitz', 14th Duke of Norfolk died 1860 described by his friend Montalembert as 'the most pious layman of our time'. See Mark Bence-Jones, *The Catholic Families* (London: Constable, 1992), p. 191.

indigenous Catholic community of workers, craftsmen, traders and professionals in Sheffield. From the early nineteenth century their number had been steadily added to by Irish migrants who arrived to work in the metal trades. After famine hit Ireland this community expanded rapidly. The 1851 Census identified 3.3 per cent of the city's population of 135,000 as Irish. Many were concentrated in the Croft districts close to the city centre, soon known locally as 'Little Ireland'.[75] Here iron and steel workshops were intermixed with housing in a densely packed maze of courts, back-to-backs and tenements. St Marie's was close by and some of its Irish worshippers had contributed to the cost of its construction.

Even before St Marie's was consecrated in 1850 the flock had become divided. Despite its capacity for fifteen hundred worshippers the building was too small, but more serious was the unwelcoming attitude shown by some towards Irish worshippers. In the face of exclusion and discrimination the latter took action.[76]Without clerical sanction they rented a building in Queen Street and employed an architect to adapt it as their own church of St Patrick's. While it is not clear how they intended to secure sacramental provision, the situation presented Dr Briggs with a challenge. Briggs moved Edmund Scully from his parish in Leeds to manage the conflict and supported his proposal to create a separate mission in Sheffield for the Irish community, particularly if it were to involve the Irish Vincentians. This was to be a school-chapel, preferably served by Irish missionary priests. Seeing it as likely to solve several 'problems' from their perspective, the wealthier parishioners of St Marie's backed the project financially and a site was bought in White Croft. It was argued that a dedicated mission would meet the spiritual needs of the Irish in ways that were familiar and consoling. At the same time this school-chapel model, deployed in so many other places in England at this time, would educate immigrant children, teach them a fully sacramental 'modern' practice of their faith and so help their assimilation into English culture.[77] At the opening, speaking to a gathering of 700, Scully described the school-chapel as 'a manufactory for souls', trusting 'that under the blessing of God, it would be the means of training up the rising generation to become good members of society'.[78]

Scully used his contacts to press the urgency of the cause on provincial Dowley, who twice agreed and twice rescinded before accepting what he described to Étienne as 'a very difficult Mission...forced on us by a chain of events, which I cannot but regard as the divine will'.[79] In reluctantly seeking the consent from Étienne which he knew would be granted, Dowley paid homage to Étienne's wish

---

75 Cullen, *St Vincent's*, p. 1.

76 See, Derek Cullen, *St Vincent's: A History of a Parish 1853-2002* (Sheffield: St. Vincent's Parish Council, 2ⁿᵈ ed. 2003),p. 2 and p. 4 and *History of St Vincent's in Sheffield*© by Ted Cummings http://www.sheffieldindexers.com/Memories/CherishedMemories_HistoryofStVincentsSheffield (accessed January 2014).

77 What happened in Sheffield exemplifies the argument made by Mary Hickman in her *Religion, Class and Identity: the State, the Catholic Church and the Education of the Irish in Britain* (Aldershot: Avebury Press, 1995).

78 *Sheffield Independent* 27 August 1853.

79 Twomey, 'Vincentians in Britain', p. 54 and Mary Purcell, *The Story of the Vincentians*, p. 143.

'to see his sons established in England'[80] and to the 'project so dear to your heart'.[81] They were willing, he said, to go to Sheffield to give 'that heretical country – one of the most important in the world – a branch of our little Irish mission'.[82] Three priests and a lay brother were sent from Dublin in November 1853 to the new school-chapel which, in anticipation of their arrival, had already been named for St Vincent rather than St Patrick.[83]

Michael Burke, superior of St Vincent's, described the group's first reaction to living conditions in the Crofts:

> The dirty, squalid and miserable conditions of their homes, or rather hovels, in back lanes and dark courts (we counted a hundred residents in one small dark court in White Croft) was such as made us come to the saddening conclusion that their pale and wretched looking children must die out in one or two generations.[84]

In the ten years he spent in Sheffield Burke proved to be an energetic social reformer and community organiser. Much of his work was innovative. In 1854 he collaborated with the founder of the Catholic Young Men's Society (CYMS) in Ireland to establish the first English branch of the Society. Its members had put aside enough savings by 1861 for Burke to establish St Vincent's Co-operative Society in a former local pub, 'The Ship', which had been driven out of business by his temperance campaigns. In three months almost £3,000 of goods had been sold providing items at a lower cost and giving a sound dividend return on shares which carried the harp as their symbol. St Vincent's drum and fife band flourished and men's sodalities were set up in an effort to combat the attractions of the public house and of Protestant evangelical missions. A conference of the St Vincent de Paul Society was founded in 1856 to assist the most needy members of the community. In 1862, mainly with the financial support of local Irish benefactors, Burke bought land in nearby Rivelin Valley Road to create Sheffield's first Catholic cemetery with its own chapel-of-ease, St Michael's.[85]

Most of this activism and outreach was centred on the men of the community. St Vincent's was supported by a group of very active lay women from St Marie's who provided funding and founded the Altar Sodality, but there was little engagement with the working-class women of the Crofts themselves. From the start Burke and his benefactors had wanted Daughters of Charity at St Vincent's but superiors were

---

80 McCrohan, 'The Future of the Irish Vincentians in Britain,' p. 370.

81 This is a reference to the fact that St Vincent had sent Missioners to both Ireland and Scotland and established his Congregation in both nations but, despite wishing to do so, had been unable to send any to England.

82 Twomey,'Vincentians in Britain', p. 53.

83 See Purcell, *The Story of the Vincentian* and Twomey, 'Vincentians in Britain,'

84 Michael Burke's diary for 1853 in Cullen, *St Vincent's*, p. 4.

85 See http://www.saintmichaelscemetery.org/. (accessed 23 October 2013). Around 20,000 parishioners are buried at St Michael's. In the first forty years most of them were Irish-born.

still reluctant to take the risk. Burke's opportunity came in 1857 when Étienne and other Council members, who had travelled from Paris to install the Daughters in Dublin, then crossed over to Sheffield to make a visitation. Étienne was shown round the Crofts and Burke talked to him about the difference the Daughters could make, particularly through home visiting. The outcome was that the General Council agreed to send Sisters on condition that a house was found for them. The top floor of a terraced house was rented in Solly Street on the boundary of White Croft: it could scarcely have looked less like the convent of popular imagination (see illustrated section).

Clemence de Missy once more found herself back in England as Sister Servant to a missionary community. In the eight years since she had left Salford not only had the Catholic hierarchy of bishops and dioceses been established in England and Wales but around 60 more convents had been founded by a number of other communities, making a total of around 100 active and contemplative houses.[86] This was a significant increase but the number of sisters across the country remained small (585 nuns across Roman Catholic and Church of England communities according to the 1861 census).[87] More than half of the convents were in London while Scotland had fewer than ten in total. Few people would encounter a Catholic sister. Accompanying de Missy were a French Sister, Marie Mervé, and two Irish Sisters, Bridget Clarke and Anne Farrell, the latter being the niece of the Reverend Thomas McNamara, assistant provincial of the Irish Vincentians. Theirs was a French-Irish mission to a predominantly Irish community in the heart of industrial England.

Important though the presence of the Vincentians was the Sisters could not rely on them financially. The confrères were always begging for their own works and had nothing to spare for the Sisters' upkeep. Within a few days of their arrival, however, the Duke and Duchess of Norfolk, Henry and Minna Fitzalan-Howard, visited the Solly Street Sisters and became their benefactors. They agreed to pay the annual rent of £25 and to provide a sum of money to be used to support families with food, fuel, clothing, rent and medicines.[88] Beyond solving their immediate financial difficulties this initial encounter between the Sisters and the Fitzalan-Howard family proved to be of long-standing importance for both parties. The Duchess and her girls became regular visitors to the *maison de charité*, a practice that continued when the Duke died in 1860 and was succeeded by his son Henry. When Etheldreda, the fourth daughter, declared a wish to become a Daughter of Charity, although a most unusual choice for a member of the British nobility, it was

86 Walsh, *Roman Catholic Nuns,* Tables 3, 16, and 17. Including the enclosed convents returned from France, there were around 40 female religious houses open in 1849 and 100 in 1857.

87 For an analysis of the 1861 census see www.visionofbritain.org.uk/census. (accessed 5 July 2015). In addition to the 585 nuns a further 236 'young sisters of charity or mercy' were noted who seem to be novices.

88 This list represents the usual range of support that the Sisters tried to offer.

unlikely to have been a surprise to the family.[89] Ardently committed to their faith and to charitable action they did not attempt to dissuade her, despite what they knew of the physical and psychological demands of a Daughter's life or what they could anticipate of the shock her choice would create in their social circle. Lady Etheldreda Fitzalan-Howard entered the Company in 1868 at the age of eighteen. It was a step that cemented the relationship between the Daughters in Britain and the extensive Fitzalan-Howard kinship network in England and Scotland and, as we will see, was a significant influence on the community's development in many ways during the next fifty years.

At the other end of the social scale the first Sisters owed much to the support of Irish working-class Catholics and that of the wider working-class community in the Crofts, particularly when the prejudices shown in Salford started to make themselves felt in Sheffield. 'Their first excursions abroad in the parish', according to the house history, 'met with sometimes almost violent bigotry...[and] often they had to be accompanied, for sheer physical protection, by some of the men of the parish'.[90] This time it was a Sheffield City councillor, Philip Ashberry, who attempted to whip up feelings against the Sisters, using the council chamber to do so. He had, he told fellow councillors in February 1858, recently seen 'a large coarse-looking person in female attire' who 'daily perambulated the streets bedizened with crosses and other trumpery' and wanted to know 'whether the attention of the Watch Committee had been called'. Speaking for himself, he was 'so disgusted with the exhibition' that he was ready to take action and would 'have great pleasure in rolling the person in the gutters' or in seeing 'some of our Sheffield grinders in their jocular humour do so'.[91] It was an incitement to harassment on grounds of gender and religious transgression. But Ashberry's presumption caused deep offence in the debating chamber and in the working-class community to which he had appealed. One grinder responded that 'if it were possible for men, whether grinders or otherwise, to be so depraved as to perpetrate such a detestable outrage upon any of these females, they ought to be served in the same manner and after that be sent to prison for an indefinite period'.[92]

Perhaps this stronger defence of the Sisters reflected some easing of religious intolerance nationally from the position ten years earlier. Certainly it owed something to the patronage of the Fitzalan-Howards and the middle-class Catholic presence in the community, with its respected members such as the architect and city councillor Ellison Hadfield. But explanatory weight should also be given to the reputation the Sisters had gained during the Crimean War (1853-56), still fresh

---

89 Family tradition has it that at the age of four Etheldreda had pointed to a china candle flame extinguisher decoratively shaped like a 'fille de la charité' and stated that she wanted to be one of those when she grew up. Cecil Kerr, *Memoir of a Sister of Charity*, (London:Burns Oates & Washbourne, 1928), p. 19.

90 Typescript note of the early history 11-72-1 1-1 #4a DCMH.

91 *Sheffield Independent* 13 February 1858.

92 Ibid.

in the national memory. Readers of *The Times* had been regularly informed of the bravery of the French Sisters of Charity.[93] Their battlefield service was known to returning soldiers, most of whom were working-class, and their support of the Sisters seems to have marked a significant turning-point in popular public opinion in several locations.[94] Six months before Ashberry's outburst the *Sheffield Independent* had carried an item about the Sisters, noting that two of them 'have borne their part in the severe campaigns of the Crimea...'[95] News that Solly Street was home to Sisters of Charity who had served in the Crimea is likely to have travelled quickly through the courts, alleyways and pubs in the Crofts. Sister Bridget Clarke had only just returned from the war front and in 1858 she was joined by Henriette Chatelain who travelled to Sheffield directly from Turkey.[96] A week after reporting Councillor Ashberry's intervention, *The Sheffield Independent* carried a reader's letter invoking the emotionally charged image of the 'white marble cross, twenty feet high' standing 'on a high rock in the neighbourhood of Sebastopol...inscribed "To the memory of the brave soldiers and the Sisters of Charity".'[97] After the Crimean War the cornette was a more complex symbol for the British, no longer suggesting only papist superstition and unnatural celibacy but also courage, self-sacrifice and compassion. The respect in which they were held by some gave something of a breathing space within which the Sisters could build a local reputation.

Within a month of arriving the Sisters had begun daily rounds of regular visits to private dwellings, later extended to the Sheffield Union Workhouse and the General Infirmary. They received several women into the Church almost

---

93 *The Times,* 14 October 1854. On the whole question of the impact of nursing in the Crimean War see Mary C. Sullivan, ed., *The Friendship of Florence Nightingale and Mary Clare Moore* (Philadelphia: University of Pennsylvania Press, 1999); Anne Summers, *Angels and Citizens: British Women as Military Nurses, 1854-1914* (London and New York: Routledge and Kegan Paul, 1988); Maria Luddy ed., *The Crimean Journals of the Sisters of Mercy, 1854-56* (Dublin:Four Courts Press, 2004) and Fanny M. Taylor, *Eastern Hospitals and English Nurses* (London: Hurst and Blackett, 1856).

94 David Murphy, *Ireland and the Crimean War* (Dublin: Four Courts Press, 2002). When Sisters arrived in Dunfermline in 1898 just two years after the opening of the first permanent post-Reformation Catholic church there, the *Dunfermline Press* reported the local pastor asking 'the Protestants of Dunfermline whether they are going to tolerate the blood-thirsty anti-Christ setting up a prison house in this land of ours.' But the same newspaper printed a response from a fellow Protestant who was shocked by such ignorance and wrote '...I like to see justice and being an old soldier serving abroad for years, I know what these sisters of mercy are. They are the first to help the wounded on the battle field, they have no fear to go among the worst cases of infectious disease, they are the bravest women ever I saw in my life...' 'Centenary History of Dunfermline' (typescript) 11-89-2 DCMH. See also *Pioneer Sisters of Charity*, p16 . The same happened when the Sisters arrived in London and rented a house in York Street, Marylebone in 1859: they were attacked in the streets but defended by soldiers who had returned from the Crimea. See *Memoir of a Sister of Charity*, pp. 29-30, 'it was by no means unusual to see the sisters walking along with a soldier on one side of them and a policeman on the other'.

95 *Sheffield Independent* , 29 August 1857, p. 7.

96 Sister Chatelain was well-acquainted with Florence Nightingale. See *Sister Chatelain* , pp. 15-21 and *Pioneer Sisters*, p. 13. At least three other first generation sisters nursed in the Crimea, Sisters Boylan, Clarke and Farrell. Nightingale herself was scathing about the nursing skills of the Daughters in the Crimean War. See McDonald ed., *Florence Nightingale's European Travels vol 7 Collected Works*, pp. 748-758.

97 *Sheffield Independent,* 20 February 1858.

immediately.[98] In an environment of deprivation such as this the practice of home visiting was the bedrock of the Daughters' work. In the large tie-on pockets they wore beneath their working apron and in their black cloth bags the Sisters discreetly carried food and clothing to distribute according to their own judgement of need. Oral tradition has it that they spent part of Friday evening visiting local public houses where a Sister's presence in the doorway signalled an invitation for men to 'offer' their wages for waiting wives.[99] They were called out to nurse the sick and attended the dying, to pray for them and to assist in the laying out in the manner expected by Irish and Catholic families; but their practical and spiritual resources were offered and accepted on a non-sectarian basis, an approach, it was claimed, that led 'many non-Catholics in and around the Crofts [to] come of their own wishes, to seek and receive instruction and to send their children to the school'.[100]

The Solly Street community also established night classes for working girls and soon 200 were attending classes in literacy and arithmetic as well as catechesis. On Sundays there were more than 300 children for religious instruction.[101] They did not undertake elementary school teaching because this was in the hands of the Sisters of Notre Dame de Namur who, unlike the unqualified Daughters, were trained and certificated teachers.[102] To match the sodalities for men already in place, the Daughters set up and ran four associations for girls and women of different ages and marital status. For their mainly Irish members the meetings were weekly occasions when sociability and piety combined. In the process of developing these organisations and creating Catholic spaces in the city, the Sisters and the confrères did, as Scully had hoped, encourage their community towards greater sacramental practice, a transformation in popular Catholicism already underway in many countries at this time, including in Ireland itself.[103] Five thousand people received Holy Communion at the various Easter Sunday Masses at St Vincent's in 1860.[104]

The Sisters' work in Sheffield expanded in new directions under the energetic leadership of Elizabeth Crawford (Sister Stephanie) who arrived in 1861 with three companions to manage the newly-founded St Joseph's Reformatory School for Roman Catholic Girls. The Catholic bishops of England and Wales had agreed to prioritise the provision of Catholic reformatories following the passage of the Act relating to Reformatories (1855) that aimed to remove children with a custodial

---

98 11-72-1 DCMH

99 Oral tradition.

100 *History of St Vincent's in Sheffield*© by Ted Cummings http://www.sheffieldindexers.com/Memories/CherishedMemories_HistoryofStVincentsSheffield (accessed January 2014).

101 St Vincent's Schools Sheffield 1877 Box X DCParis.

102 It was not until 1865 that there were certificated Daughters of Charity able to undertake running the schools in St Vincent's.

103 The seminal work on this subject was Emmet Larkin's 'The devotional revolution in Ireland, 1850-1875,' *American Historical Review*, 77 (1972).

104 http://www.sheffieldindexers.com/CherishedMemoriesIndex.html, p. 34. (accessed January 2014).

sentence from the prison system and give them training in a secure setting.[105] A northern bishops' committee chaired by Charles Langdale, a leading Catholic MP, was convened to establish a girls' reformatory for the north. A successful fundraising drive enabled the committee to buy Howard Hill House, a former private boys' school at Walkley in Sheffield, and they invited the Daughters of Charity to take charge of St Joseph's as the new institution was to be called.[106]

St Joseph's was the Company's first institutional foundation in Britain and its establishment marked the beginning of their work within the framework of the British state. Étienne appointed Irish-born Sister Elizabeth Crawford who had just completed seven years' service in institutional child care in Italy, urging her to 'do all that you can to make this work a success', because 'it is the first that the English Government has confided to your Community and you must do credit to it'.[107] As a certified Reformatory (re-registered as an Industrial School in 1887) St Joseph's was in receipt of government funding and was inspected regularly, resulting in public reports written against national accountability criteria. The stakes were high because the authorities were hostile to the idea of religious sisters and brothers being responsible for the upbringing of children. This view was much in evidence, for example, when James Nugent, the priest responsible for Catholic children's homes in Liverpool, accompanied Archbishop Henry Manning to a meeting in 1866 with Sir George Grey, the Home Secretary, in an attempt to change Grey's 'very decided stand against religious having the management of Reformatory and Industrial Schools'. Nugent and Manning were informed that 'the only nuns [sic] he considered qualified for the work were the Sisters of Charity'.[108] Grey's opinion had been formed by Sydney Turner, an Anglican clergyman who was the first Inspector of the Reformatory and Industrial Schools. Turner's Reports to Parliament made clear his views that 'religious orders...have little practical experience of the common working life of the world'.[109] Although Turner did not know the Daughters were not actually nuns he sensed that they were different from other sisters he came across in his work, noting the 'great advantage that the rules of the Order of Charity [sic] ... allow of so much more freedom and intercourse with everyday life of the world'.[110] Turner reported that 'the management' of St Joseph's 'is at once kind and judicious'.[111] 'The girls looking well,' he recorded, '...no absconding... discipline firmly kept up without resort to extreme measures...the girls passed my

105 David Lannon, 'Bishop Turner, the Salford Diocese and Reformatory Provision 1854-1872' *Recusant History* Vol. 23. No 3. 1997. See also, Murphy, *Terra Incognita*, pp. 201-251.

106 Typescript history written in 1921 and Sister Langdale's Account. 11-71-1 #3a and #4 DCMH

107 *Pioneer Sisters*, p. 90.

108 John Bennett, 'The Care of the Poor', in G.A. Beck ed., *English Catholics 1850-1950* (London, 1950), p. 566.

109 Eighteenth Report of the Inspector of Reformatory and Industrial Schools in Great Britain (1874), p. 17. Parliamentary Papers. He also notes in this Report that 'the greater number of relapses and reconvictions...among those who belong to the lower class of Irish families' who are less 'orderly and settled' than Protestants.

110 Fifteenth Report of the Inspector of Reformatory and Industrial Schools in Great Britain' (1871), p. 81.

111 Ibid.

examination satisfactorily and were all making progress…'[112] He praised the 'after-care' cottage established by Elizabeth Crawford so that young women could have somewhere safe to live when they left St Joseph's and started work. Turner was reported as saying that he would 'willingly give [Mrs Crawford's nuns] charge of all the industrial schools in the country'. Although society has learned to be cautious about the ability of inspectors to know all that takes place in the care of vulnerable children and adults, Turner's judgement was made in the context of comparisons drawn from his many visits to a large number of institutions managed by different charities and agencies.[113] Satisfactory arrangements between the Sisters, the state authorities and the board of management of St Joseph's inaugurated the strand of state-funded residential care work that was to become such an important part of the Company's activities in Britain, predominantly in the form of Catholic Poor Law Schools and Industrial Schools.

It was also in Sheffield that the community began the care and education of deaf children, taking the first step in what proved to be an enduring commitment to deaf and hearing impaired children and adults in the British Province, and a specialist skill for many Sisters. In 1869 Sister Crawford was invited by Canon Pierre Antoine de Haerne (1804-1890), Belgian deaf educationalist and founder of the Brussels Institute, to take on the management of the Catholic Institute for the Deaf recently founded in Sheffield on his initiative as a response to the lack of Catholic deaf provision in Britain. St John's Institute moved to Boston Spa in West Yorkshire in 1875 where it developed as the only Catholic residential school for deaf children in England and was the forerunner for the community's provision in Scotland.

Specific conditions made Sheffield a favourable environment for refounding the Company in Britain. The presence of Vincentian priests provided a secure starting point for the Sisters to learn about the potential for their ministry and the nature of the Church in Britain. Sheffield's mix of English and Irish poor was a sound testing ground for the Sisters' parish and community ministry, while at St Joseph's they learned how to engage with the civic authorities and explored the potential for the Company's traditions of charity to operate within the framework of the British state. The patronage of England's pre-eminent Catholic aristocrat and of established professionals in the local Catholic community made it possible to build networks in the city but also beyond it. It was here that Sister Henriette Chatelain, senior Sister and co-ordinator of the works in Britain before 1885, was sent to learn English and to receive an orientation to her adopted land before moving to London to open the Company's first house in the capital in 1859. This London foundation was soon to be followed by one in Liverpool, where Yorkshire-born cousins, Sisters Middleton and Maxwell, were sent by the superior general in 1862 to manage a diocesan boys' orphanage. But before this move into Liverpool,

---

112 Fourteenth Report of the Inspector of Reformatory and Industrial Schools in Great Britain (1870), p. 71.

113 *Pioneer Sisters*, p. 90

which was to become one of the Sisters' most important centres in Britain, they made their first foundation in Scotland.

The double family in Lanark

After Sheffield only one other collaboration with the Vincentians occurred before the 1960s,[114] but because the second joint initiative took place in Scotland and at the early date of 1860, the foundation in Lanark played a significant part in spreading the Sisters' activities, giving them the potential for a genuinely British mission. Scotland was a particularly challenging religious environment for Catholic sisters but being able to work with the Vincentians in north Lanarkshire, where there was a strong Irish presence, gave the Daughters a strong foothold. They developed a solid base from which to expand gradually into other parts of Scotland after the establishment of the Scottish Catholic hierarchy in 1878, at a time when relatively few Catholic women's communities had a presence in the nation.[115]

As in Sheffield, the Lanark mission had the support of a small number of wealthy benefactors who wanted to insert the service of Vincentian Missioners and Daughters into their parochial, educational, welfare and evangelising activities. Robert Monteith of Carstairs and Thomas Bowie - both converts - supported the parish in Lanark extensively, building the large new church of St Mary's and paying stipends.[116] In 1859 the Irish Province agreed to accept responsibility for St Mary's church, doing so in honour of St Vincent's appointment of Irish Vincentians as missionaries to Scotland in the seventeenth century.[117] A group of Sisters arrived in 1860. In addition to visiting, managing the school and starting sodalities they opened a small free hospital in a row of houses adjacent to the church. Under the leadership of English Sister Servant Mary (Alice) Blundell, in 1872 the hospital moved into a new building for which she paid. The initial work soon extended beyond the parish as it had in Sheffield, this time with the addition of a second foundation to manage the newly founded Smyllum orphanage. Smyllum grew rapidly to become the largest Catholic orphanage in Scotland as a result of the Scottish hierarchy's policy to bring many of the children referred by boards of guardians and workhouses across the country, together in one institution. Monteith and another convert, James Robert Hope-Scott (brother-in-law to Sister

---

114 In the nineteenth century there were two unsuccessful attempts at Vincentian foundations made by a French Missioner, Jean-Étienne Ginouvié, who joined the Irish province. The first was in 1865 at Bullingham in Herefordshire where the Sisters already had a developing project. The second in 1872 was to be based at Everingham Park, family home of the Middletons, two of whose daughters were Sisters of Charity: this also failed. Rybolt comments: 'It is worth noting that the superior general chose to negotiate [both] on his own rather than work through the Irish province'. Rybolt. *The Vincentians Vol.4*, p. 485

115 Dilworth, 'Religious orders in Scotland', pp. 92-109.

116 See B. Aspinwall, 'The Scottish dimension: Robert Monteith and the origins of modern British Catholic social thought', *Downside Review*, (1978), Vol. 97, pp. 46-68.

117 *Centenary: A Souvenir of St Mary's Lanark 1959* (Glasgow: John S Burns & Sons, 1959), pp. 19-25 and see also 'Early Days of St Mary's Lanark,' *Colloque* No. 2 (Spring,1980), pp. 36ff.

Etheldreda Howard), paid for the extensive building and land for Smyllum which they put in trust with the Archbishops of Glasgow and Edinburgh. The Sisters at Smyllum developed a wing for the care of deaf children and blind children, of whom there were significant numbers, which was to be the forerunner of the later specialist institute in Tollcross, east Glasgow, run by the Province.

Emerging patterns of work

The Sheffield and Lanark houses, the *maison de charité* established in London and the boys' industrial school (residential home) in Liverpool were the mainspring of this second Daughters' mission to Britain.[118] Four strands of ministry, discernible as early 1870, were to form the work of the Province. A parish–based strand comprised visiting, elementary schooling, and sacramental preparation in working-class or rural districts; a second strand was the residential provision for children referred by the criminal justice system and from the workhouses, including single-sex boys' homes; specialist Catholic residential provision for deaf and blind children made up a distinctive third element. Dispensary work, sick nursing in the home and to a lesser degree in hospitals was a fourth and minor strand. Other activities such as crèches, soup kitchens and night-shelters were usually attached to parish ministries but were undertaken flexibly in response to circumstances.

Broadly speaking, these activities took place in three different types of Sisters' house. The first type was a *maison de charité*, a small community of between three and six Sisters whose primary purpose was home visiting in the district, possibly, teaching in the parochial elementary school, and developing parish life through societies and associations. *Maisons de charité* could be found in either urban or rural settings. In the second type the Sisters lived in or adjacent to an institution they were managing, their number rising to more than twenty in the case of the largest institutions. The third category, of which there were only a small number in Britain, was the large multi-purpose urban complex known in France as *miséricordes*, managed by ten or more Sisters. In this category of house Sisters might undertake any blend of their parish, welfare, health and institutional ministries: visiting in the local workhouse, hospital and prison and family homes; management of several small-scale welfare and educational ventures such as a crèche, dispensary, night shelter, hostel, or a small orphanage and school alongside evening classes, confraternities, clubs and societies and, invariably, a soup kitchen. There were few early examples of this type of house but two developed in London, in Westminster and in Marylebone, from smaller houses established in 1859 and 1868 respectively.

The breadth of their welfare activities was what distinguished the Daughters from many other communities of sisters: it characterised their place within the spectrum of women's religious communities in Britain. Historians of women religious have rightly warned against classifying and quantifying any sisters' works

---

118 After Sheffield and Lanark the Vincentians adopted only one further work in Britain during the nineteenth century; the management of St Mary's College for teacher training in Hammersmith in 1899.

as watertight categories. In practice one activity often opened into another: schools for the poor, for example, were inseparable from social welfare interventions such as the provision of free meals at school or knowledge about which families were in greatest need. However, taking account of this important caveat, what has emerged in studies of Catholic sisters in Victorian Britain is just how dominant teaching became. In 1897 seventy-four out of 90 female religious congregations in England and Wales had education as their primary focus, often combining the management of elementary schools with running fee-paying convent schools.[119] A similar pattern evolved on a smaller scale in Scotland.[120] This concentration of effort had come about because 'the bishops took the issue of education and pursued it as their most important goal'.[121] Congregations from France and Belgium, from Ireland and Italy were invited into dioceses solely to teach. Communities for whom education was not their purpose were persuaded into teaching because of the significant pressure exerted by clergy and lay sponsors for this single cause in Britain.[122] The emphasis on schools was a challenge for the Daughters because, as Vincentian historian John Rybolt states, 'this was a work St Vincent had never fostered'.[123] Although the Daughters did take on a small number of parochial elementary schools in Britain before 1900 they sustained their focus on the Company's traditional priorities, even refusing to become certificated as teachers.[124] As will be explored further in Chapter 7, the core of their charitable practice was home visiting and the management of institutions providing shelter, food and training for the poorest children and young people. A determined concentration on providing these services enabled them to expand because there was both great need and little competition from other communities.

A developing geography

Convent geography in the middle decades of the century (and beyond) owed little to strategic planning or, in many cases, even to Catholic demographics. Expansion through networks, invitation and sponsorship marked this first phase. We have already seen how Daughters went to Sheffield and Lanark through the Vincentian network and the backing of local patrons. Family connections lay behind their opening a house of charity in Little Crosby in 1859, the Catholic village north of Liverpool in the patronage of the recusant Blundell family which had several female members already in the Company. Similarly, they arrived in London's Marylebone

---

119 Walsh, *Roman Catholic Sisters*, pp. 35-44.

120 Kehoe, *Creating a Scottish Church*.

121 Eric G. Tenbus, *English Catholics and the Education of the Poor, 1847-1902* (London: Pickering and Chatto, 2010), p. 9.

122 O'Brien, 'Religious Life for Women', p. 120.

123 Rybolt. *The Vincentians, Vol.4*, p. 169.

124 Their response is discussed in more detail in Chapter 4.

in response to a proposal made by Lady Mary Petre of Thorndon Hall in Essex, one of whose daughters had also entered the community, and they went to Westminster at the invitation of a number of eminent Catholic lay women, including the writer Lady Georgiana Fullerton, a central figure in this Catholic female network.

Invitations from senior priests or bishops originated foundations made in Liverpool, Newcastle, Plymouth and Darlington before 1885, and in 1877 the Sisters had returned to Manchester at the request of Bishop (later Cardinal) Herbert Vaughan whose sister Teresa was a member of the community. A more strategic development took place when Archbishop Henry Manning asked them to manage the orphanage at Leyton and encouraged them to work closely with him in the 'rescue' of London's Catholic children from the London Poor Law Schools, Barnardo's and other Protestant homes. Finally, language and ethnic cultural connections lay behind requests for the Sisters to take on the French Hospital in Leicester Square, the Italian Hospital in Bloomsbury and the Italian-Irish parish in Clerkenwell, all in London.

In each instance a definite work was proposed, vetted and accepted as matching the purpose of Daughters of Charity. It was not the projects but the resulting geography that had an air of randomness about it. Responding to specific calls gave the community a widespread reach across the country and across dioceses, with important concentrations in the North-West, North-East and in London north of the river (Westminster Archdiocese), as well as a presence in the west country and in Scotland. The major area of Catholic population not served by the Sisters in this early phase, apart from London south of the river (Southwark Diocese), was in Birmingham and the Midlands. Here the Sisters of Charity of St Paul the Apostle and the Sisters of Mercy, both of which had established themselves during the 1840s and 1850s, were the main congregations sought by local clergy. Both were at the flexible end of the spectrum of apostolic congregations and between them they were able to cover schooling of all kinds and a diverse range of welfare activities, Apart from Birmingham itself, the Daughters never developed a presence in this region. Distribution in this first phase was particularly important because of the part it played a part in shaping the Daughters' longer-term pattern of expansion in Britain, as we will see.

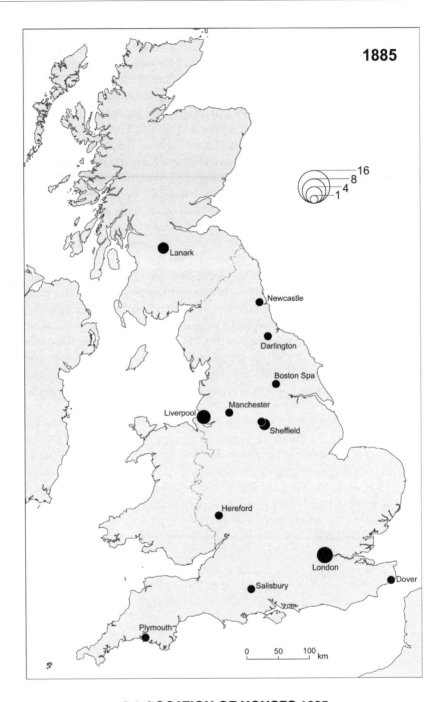

3.1: LOCATION OF HOUSES 1885

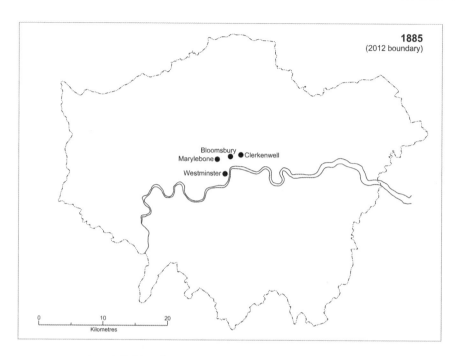

3.2: LOCATION OF LONDON HOUSES IN 1885

The Company in Britain and Ireland

By the end of 1885 the Company had twenty-four houses across England and Scotland, making it the third largest Catholic women's community in Britain. The scale of this British operation has to be understood, however, in relation to the relative lack of growth in Ireland. The brisk pace of expansion in Ireland between 1855 and 1857 came to an abrupt end almost as soon as it had begun: between 1857 and 1885 only one further Irish house was added to the initial three. After 1860 the balance of the Company's activities tilted towards England as shown in the graph (3.3) below. By 1880 a ratio of 1:5 Irish to British houses had developed that persisted until 1940. Entrants to the community arrived in the proportion of approximately 60:40 Irish-born to British-born throughout this time.

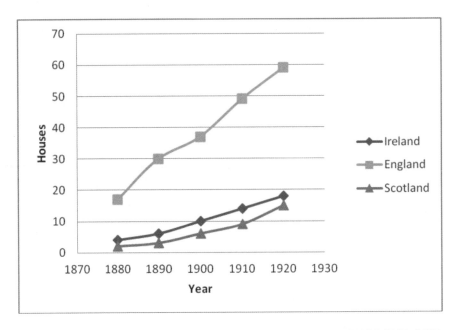

3.3: COMPARISON OF FOUNDATIONS IN IRELAND, ENGLAND AND SCOTLAND 1880-1920

Even taking into account the larger scale of some individual projects in Ireland, it was the minority mission. Several factors, such as the initial commitment of the general council to Ireland, the potential for partnership with the Irish Vincentian Province, the tremendous public welcome accorded the Sisters in Drogheda,[125] and the innovative nature of several of the Daughters' hospitals and other institutions in Ireland, indicate that this was not simply another instance of Ireland being seen primarily as a source of vocations to support a community in Britain, rather than as a place for service, as so often happened. How, then, might we explain the imbalance that developed so strongly?

Evidence suggests that in the 1860s, a critical time in the development of their work in Britain and Ireland, the Company's superiors in Paris encountered a number of serious difficulties in Ireland. First among these was the reluctance, even opposition, of Cardinal Archbishop Paul Cullen of Dublin (1852-1878), to see their work develop. A prelate of enormous personal and official power and a firm upholder of episcopal control in ecclesial matters, he disapproved of any religious congregations operating under pontifical rather than diocesan authority. Under Cullen's leadership, for example, the Plenary Council of Cashel of 1857 enacted that 'institutes of women with simple vows were to be generally subject

---

125 Discussed in detail in Sherlock et al., 'The Arrival of the Daughters', in Prunty and Sullivan, *The Daughters of Charity in Ireland*, pp. 55-62.

to the local bishop'.[126] And as a firm supporter of Irish nationalism he was not in favour of foreign authorities having powers of decision over Church matters in Ireland.[127] Spiritual colonisers were as much to be opposed as political ones. Cullen allowed the Daughters to work in Dublin in 1857 and even made a legacy available to them for their orphanage despite his own preference for the boarding-out system of childcare but, as Jacinta Prunty has shown, it later became clear he had not understood the nature of authority and obedience in the Company.[128] Vincentian Thomas McNamara had to explain to him that 'the Sisters of Charity have a government of their own distinct from us and they are not required to consult us in their projects or the conduct of their works'.[129] Their French mother house gave the Daughters an operational space separate from what Maria Luddy has described as the 'obsequiousness to bishops and members of the clergy' regularly practised as a 'strategy of compromise' by religious sisters in Ireland to allow them to get on with their work.[130] Moreover, Cullen was not impressed by the unwillingness of the Daughters to adapt their customary approaches and to take on new ideas he favoured, such as the boarding-out system for orphans. In 1860 he wrote to the Vincentian provincial to inform him that 'after a good deal of deliberation' he had 'come to the conclusion that the French Sisters of Charity are not suited to this country'. Persisting in believing that Dowley had authority over the Sisters in Ireland he instructed him to 'give the necessary notice to the Superior and Superioress'.[131] Charlotte de Virieu, Sister Servant of the North William Street house in Dublin, the senior Sister in Ireland, conveyed to Cullen that they accepted his decision 'as children of St Vincent, with true resignation to the holy will of God'.[132] But behind the scenes she and Dowley worked hard with the superiors general to ensure the Daughters did not have to leave the archdiocese. Virieu was retained in Dublin until her death in 1890 to manage this taxing situation and to keep the diocesan door open for the Company. Her Company obituary was explicit about the problems she had faced:

> What contributed most to the difficulty of her task was that the clergy did not approve of the establishment in Dublin of a foreign Community

---

126 MacGinley, *A Dynamic of Hope*, p. 69.

127 Dáire Keogh and Albert McDonnell eds., *Cardinal Paul Cullen and His World* (Dublin: Four Courts, 2011).

128 Jacinta Prunty *Lady of Charity, Sister of the Faith: Margaret Aylward 1810-1889* (Dublin: 1999). Jacinta Prunty's discovery of the true origins of the invitation to the Daughters of Charity to Ireland, which came from Margaret Aylward, and not Cullen, makes fascinating reading, revealing the extent to which Aylward's role as a Lady of Charity and reformer has not been told within the official history of the Company. I owe all the detail in this section to Prunty: the generalisations about the Irish ecclesial situation are my own.

129 Quoted in Prunty *Lady of Charity*, p. 86.

130 Luddy, *Women and Philanthropy in nineteenth-century Ireland*, pp. 27-29.

131 Cullen to Dowley, 22 December 1860, draft. Cullen Correspondence, Dublin Diocesan Archives, quoted in Jim McCormack, 'John Gowan: A Vincentian Vocation in Crisis,' *Colloque*, Winter 2011, No.44, p. 121.

132 Virieu to Cullen 31 December 1860. Dublin Diocesan Archives Nuns 1860, 333/6.

which received its direction from Superiors located in Paris. They mistrusted a house which did not depend on the Bishop for its interior government as well as for its works and in which everything was so different from what was customary in Irish communities.[133]

More unexpectedly, and not openly discussed, the Daughters found they were not able to count on the wholehearted support of all their Vincentian confrères either. McNamara remarked that some Vincentians showed 'a remarkable antipathy towards the Sisters of Charity on the grounds that they were introduced into this country [Ireland] by the direct authority of the Superior General, who thus undermined the immediate authority of the Visitor of the Province'.[134] Some even preferred to support the Sisters of the Faith, a new native Irish foundation made in the spirit of St Vincent.[135]

By contrast clergy in Britain were favourably disposed towards continental congregations; some even preferred them to new locally founded institutes.[136] The Church in England and Scotland was expanding rapidly with little infrastructure to serve its impoverished community and was eager to accept assistance. There were undoubtedly difficulties, some of which arose from cultural differences and others from a disagreement about authority,[137] but these seemed to have been offset by appreciation of the confident Catholicism that was expressed in the devotional and religious life of sisters formed in congregations from continental Europe. The Daughters soon established very good working relationships with some of the most energetic socially-minded clergy of the day among whom Henry Manning, later Cardinal Archbishop of Westminster, was the most notable, Canon Rooney in Doncaster being another and Monsignor James Nugent in Liverpool a third. After the initial partnership with the Congregation of the Mission in Sheffield and in Lanark, the Daughters in Britain were able to found new houses independently of the Vincentian confrères across many dioceses. It seems fair to conclude that the particular context of the Catholic Church in England and Scotland in the middle to later nineteenth century enabled international and transnational congregations

---

133 *Notices of Deceased Sisters* Charlotte de Virieu (1890). Typescript of translation from the French, Box N.William Street, DCIreland.

134 Quoted in Patrick McCrohan, 'The Future of the Irish Vincentians', p. 372. See also John Rybolt's discussion of the conflicts and tensions among the Irish Vincentians at this time, Rybolt, *The Vincentians Vol 4 Expansion and Reactions*, pp. 482-89.

135 See Prunty *Lady of Charity*.

136 See O'Brien, 'French Nuns', p. 154ff.

137 Karly Kehoe has shown that in the case of one of the earliest French congregations in Scotland, the Archbishop of Glasgow in 1847 was able to insist that they sever the links between Glasgow and the motherhouse in Tourcoing, *Creating a Scottish Church*, p. 83.

to flourish.[138] For a time at least it was an ecclesial environment that gave Catholic sisters, Irish and British-born, relatively more agency and initiative.[139]

It would not be too crude to suggest that whereas in Ireland the Sisters were given a warm welcome by the people but ran into difficulties with the hierarchy, in England the position was reversed. The Sheffield Catholic who complained that England was 'said to be an Elysium of freedom' but that Catholics were 'in fact surrounded by many of the inconveniences of intolerance and persecution' and 'popular prejudice, in its practical application throughout the relations of life, places [us] under many disadvantages...'was reflecting the situation at mid-century.[140] Even so, and without underestimating the presence of persistent anti-Catholic feeling, revived at particular moments,[141] the Daughters' subsequent story supports Carmen Mangion's suggestion that 'antagonism...dissipated once [the Sisters'] 'works of mercy' were shown to be useful to the community'.[142] Late nineteenth-century Daughters in Sheffield concluded that it was the 'undiscriminating application of practical help that 'gradually tempered the animosity of their original reception' there.[143] In Manchester, scene of the earlier trials, a well-attended public meeting was held in the Lord Mayor's Parlour of Manchester Town Hall in 1877 in support of establishing a non-denominational night shelter for girls under the Daughters' supervision.[144]

There were exceptions to this pattern of civic incorporation – particularly in Scotland[145] - but through processes of adaptation and engagement across religious, ethnic and social class divisions, the Daughters became embedded in local communities.[146] As early as 1865, when Sister Elizabeth Crawford organised a two-day bazaar in Sheffield to raise funds to build the after-care home for St Joseph's, the *Sheffield and Rotherham Independent* praised her and 'the good Sisters'

---

138 See O'Brien, 'Religious Sisters and Revival', pp. 143-64.

139 This is not to overlook the conflicts and tensions that took place and have been discussed in Mangion, *Contested Identities* and in my own work.

140 *Sheffield Independent* 27 August 1853.

141 Such as the promulgation of Papal Infallibility in 1870 and the International Eucharistic Congress held in London in 1908.

142 Mangion, *Contested Identities*, p. 100 .

143 Typescript note of the early history from annals Sheffield 11-72-1 DCMH

144 *The Manchester Courier and Lancashire General Advertiser*, 16 January 1894, p. 7.

145 In its centenary publication *Pioneer Sisters* the province narrated the story of their arrival in Dunfermline in 1898 as follows, 'Large posters were displayed about the town: 'Protestants of Dunfermline, will you allow your children to be taught by blood-thirsty Popish nuns?' [which] caused the Sisters no small amusement.', p. 99 – and notes how people were won over by their actions to the extent that they were able to hold a procession of the Blessed Sacrament.

146 See, for example, Geraldine Vaughan's discussion of 'sectarianism' and anti-Catholicism in the Edwardian era, *The 'Local' Irish in the West of Scotland 1851-1921*(Basingstoke: Palgrave Macmillan, 2013), pp. 40-50 and Alana Harris's discussion of the interwar period in 'Astonishing Scenes at the Scottish Lourdes: masculinity, the miraculous, and sectarian strife at Carfin, 1922-1945', *The Innes Review*, 66.1 (2015), pp. 102-129.

for their 'untiring zeal and earnest devotion'.[147] Such was the support for the Sisters' work that the bazaar was held in the Cutlers' Hall, Livery home of the Cutlers' Company, one of the city's most important civic buildings. Prizes donated by city notables included 'a phaeton and a pair of ponies with silver-mounted harness' and 'two very fine engravings of the Queen and the late Prince Consort'.[148] Elizabeth Crawford herself stayed in Sheffield long enough to become something of a local figure. At her death in 1897 she was honoured. An obituary in the local press summarised her life history from birth in Westmeath through service in Italy to her work in Sheffield overseeing the Daughters' many activities there for almost forty years. She would be remembered by people 'scattered in all parts of the world... who have a lively remembrance of her loving care and attention...' and by 'philanthropists of all denominations who have known and appreciated the Sister's Christian labours whilst in Sheffield'.[149] By 1900 the Daughters had made a place for themselves within the Catholic Church and community in Britain and in doing so they had, in their own way, become participants in British civil society.

---

147 I am indebted to Sister Joan Conroy DC for this reference. *Sheffield and Rotherham Independent*, 2 August 2,1865.

148 Ibid.

149 *Sheffield Telegraph* quoted in full in *Manchester Evening News*, 15 December 1897, p. 5.

4

First-generation Sisters

> I can only desire to serve God if his love draws me
>
> (Louise de Marillac)

> What is Vocation?.....
> Is vocation an inflamed desire
> To great and lofty duties to aspire…?
> O strange mistake!...
> Vocation is God's secret – none may say
> Why one is called to come while others stay.[1]
>
> (Sister Mary (Etheldreda) Howard)

Elizabeth Crawford experienced the desire to become a Daughter of Charity when she was at school. She was twenty-three before she had her mother's permission to make the journey, in the summer of 1850, from the small rural settlement of Finea, Westmeath in Ireland where her parents were landowners, to the mother house in Paris. At a time when there were no Daughters of Charity in either Britain or Ireland, she started as an aspirant in the Company's house in Notre Dame in Paris and was then missioned to Italy for seven years. We are told she had been a 'turbulent, self-willed child', who 'hardly knew what fear meant' and that she 'loved the freedom and independence' that country living gave her.[2] Later she admitted it had been very difficult to leave her parents and large family of siblings; the distance had actually made it easier to sustain her vocation.[3] Sister Crawford returned to Ireland only once, making a brief visit in 1857 at the time when she was being transferred from Naples to Sheffield.

The pace of the Company's development in the British Isles and the quality of its work were determined by the number and personal character of the women who answered the 'call to come'. It has been rare for Catholic women's communities to

---

1 Lines written by Sister Mary [Etheldreda] Howard, DC (1868) quoted in Kerr, *A Memoir of a Sister of Charity*, frontispiece.

2 *Pioneer Sisters*, p. 88. The source for these details are found in *Notices of Deceased Sisters*, 1898, Elizabeth Crawford. 10-3-1 DCMH.

3 Ibid.

provide a collective or group study of their members - the preference having been for individual biographies of 'notable' sisters - but there is considerable historical value in doing so.[4] Historian Lawrence Stone coined the term 'prosopography' to describe 'an investigation of the common background characteristics of a group of actors in history by means of collective study of their lives'.[5] Such an investigation allows us to answer a number of questions about the nature of the vocation call and about the community's internal composition at different times. In this chapter four such questions are explored: what attracted British and Irish women to the Daughters of Charity in the first generation; what were superiors looking for in an aspirant to their life; how did an aspirant pass through the stages to become a Daughter of Charity; and which Sisters of the first generation were the leaders who laid the foundations for what became the British and Irish Province.

Defining the first generation

Generation	Birth	Entry	Number*
1st *foundation*	1830–1864	**1840–1884**	281
2nd *expansion*	1865–1899	**1885–1919**	815
3rd *conservation*	1900–1924	**1920–1944**	663
4th *renewal*	1925–1944	**1945–1964**	331
5th *revisioning*	1945–	**1965–**	117

* Only those who made first vows are included

4.1: FIVE GENERATIONS OF SISTERS

The first generation comprised the 281 Sisters who were born before 1866 and who started their service in Britain and Ireland before 1885.[6] It includes 19 British and Irish Sisters who had entered before any foundations were made in the United Kingdom and whose experience in France and elsewhere now made them valuable seed-corn for the mission, and the 25 French and Italian Sisters commissioned by Paris to support the new initiative for varying lengths of time. Among the British and Irish Sisters of this generation were many who had grown up in families that had personal memories of religious marginalisation and civic

---

4 Carmen Mangion's work in *Contested Identities* has been ground-breaking in this respect. I would like to acknowledge the importance of her work on ten religious communities for what follows in this chapter and her generosity in allowing me access to the databases she constructed about the Daughters of Charity before 1900. I have also made extensive use of Barbara Walsh's *Roman Catholic Nuns in England and Wales, 1800–1937*.

5 Lawrence Stone, 'Prosopography', *Daedalus*, Volume 100, p. 46.

6 For purposes of comparison between the generations only those who entered and stayed will be included in the analysis. Women who left during the stages of formation and those who left later are accounted for and acknowledged in other ways, not least because changing rates of attrition invite explanation and interpretation.

discrimination. Within that living memory the practice of the faith had been family-centred rather than parochially based. This group expected that lay men and women would provide active faith leadership. In Britain at least, it required a high level of personal commitment to uphold a faith regarded by many as foreign and regressive, particularly in political life. Even those born towards the end of this generation, in the later 1850s and first half of the 1860s, experienced this older Catholic culture. Some aspects of the faith of observant Catholics did change after the middle of the nineteenth century in both Ireland and Britain to combine a more regularised sacramental life with a wider range of devotional practices (further discussed in Chapter 8).[7] This newer Catholic culture, with priest, parish and school at its centre, was only just beginning as the younger members of the first generation came to maturity.

This generation's experience of Company life was distinctive in a number of ways. The oldest among them had applied directly to a French house or to the mother house in Paris for admission: many completed their three-month postulancy in a French foundation and all undertook seminary formation in the rue du Bac for around nine months under the guidance of the French seminary directresses. In the seminary they were members of a small English-speaking minority in the company of hundreds of seminary Sisters from France and from other European countries.[8] The seminary itself was run as a distinct entity within the mother house. All that lay beyond its corridors and teaching rooms was quite separate. Conversing with habit Sisters was prohibited, but seminary Sisters still developed an awareness of the large secretariat administering the global Company, of the infirmary with its Sisters who came to the mother house for rest and nursing, and of the comings and goings of Sisters involved in the overseas missions to China, the Levant, North Africa and Latin America. In 1881 there were more than 600 Sisters across these different categories in the mother house, most of whom were in the seminary.[9]

A year-long socialising experience, with its immersion in the way things were done in the mother house, and the opportunity to see how experienced French Sisters comported themselves, helped to form a woman's subjectivity as a Daughter of Charity at this time. British and Irish Sisters were required to learn some French (with very different degrees of success), to adapt to the French housewifery that was normative practice in the mother house (in food, drink, housework and personal hygiene for example) and to participate in a prayer and devotional life that had evolved out of French Catholic culture, particularly in its modern Marian aspects. There was daily Mass and several appointed times of prayer in the mother

---

7 Larkin, 'The Devotional Revolution in Ireland, 1850–75'. For a more recent review of this thesis and one that encompasses England see, Sheridan Gilley's vivid evocation and sharp discussion of the changes in 'Devotions and the old rite', in Henning Laugerud and Salvador Ryan eds., *Devotional Cultures of European Christianity 1790– 1960* (Dublin: Four Courts Press, 2012), pp. 34–47.

8 See Laurentin, *Catherine Labouré*, p. 134.

9 *Genesis of the Company*, p. 105. 1-7-2 DCMH.

house chapel of Our Lady of the Miraculous Medal, site of the Blessed Virgin's appearances to Sister Catherine Labouré in 1830. This generation was very directly exposed to the foundation story and key incidents in the Company's history as they were interpreted and expressed through the iconography with which they were surrounded. At the same time they were also immersed in the signs of its modern and global reach. After seminary it was highly likely, as Table 4.2 shows, for formation purposes and for the purpose of acquiring skills such as nursing or in deaf education, that first-generation Sisters from Britain and Ireland would also spend several years on placement in France.

Destination	1st gen	2nd gen	3rd gen	4th gen	Total*
France	128	97	35	26	289
Italy	15	8	4	2	29
Spain	4	3	1	2	10
Greece	1				1
Totals	148	108	40	30	326

4.2: SERVICE IN EUROPE BY GENERATION

When they returned to Britain these Sisters were responsible for establishing houses and works, conscious that they were the foundation stones for the Company's way of life in the British Isles. Many of the houses they established were to make up the core of the Province's work for the next hundred years and more (see Appendix I).

Becoming a Daughter of Charity

Few of those who applied for admission were aware that the Sisters of Charity were not nuns or that they would never make perpetual vows.[10] It became part of their initiation process to learn about these differences and to test their vocation in the light of this knowledge. During and just after the lifetime of the founders the Company had developed structures and symbols for the formal admission and progression of a Sister that corresponded to her lay status, her personal consecration and her community commitment. They paralleled the novitiate and profession stages for enclosed nuns (and later for active Sisters), but were clearly distinctive. It is possible to identify five separate stages in the process of initial formation and

---

10 In many of the new communities of active Sisters, members made annual simple vows because they did not have approval to make perpetual vows. Papal approbation was sought to gain this distinction and became a major goal for many congregations but non-canonical status was not unusual for women called to ministry in community.

admission, although these were not described by the community itself as stages
in the way they are set out in Table 4.3. The evidence used to create this schema is
drawn from the experience in Britain and Ireland in the second half of the nineteenth
century, but the pattern was established by the end of the seventeenth century and
later became common throughout the Company across the world.

STAGE	TITLE	FEATURES	END POINT
Stage 1	Aspirant	Application to a Sister Servant in any House. References taken up.	Accepted by the Sister Servant for a trial.
Stage 2	Postulant	Around three months living in a Sisters' House undertaking selected work and some aspects of prayer life. Wears simple dark clothes.	Recommended by Sister Servant to superiors for acceptance or rejection.
Stage 3	Seminary Sister	Vocation date (entry to the community) is date of 'Little Retreat' before entering the seminary. Nine to twelve months seminary formation. Wears seminary Sister habit.	*Prise d'habit*; taking the habit of a Daughter of Charity.
Stage 4	Young Sister or Little Cornette	Given first *'placement'* i.e. a House and a specific role in that House. Could have a change of *placement* during this stage which lasts about four years.	Accepted by superiors to prepare for her Vow Catechism.
Stage 5	Habit Sister	Learns the Vow Catechism by heart. Continues daily life. Makes retreat and is tested on Vow Catechism.	Accepted to make vows for the first time.
Stage 6	Vow Sister	Continues as before. Makes annual renovation of the vows on 25 March.	Annual vow taking for life.

4.3: STAGES OF ADMISSION AND COMMITMENT

The initial enquiry was followed up by an interview with a Sister Servant (superior
of a local foundation) who was responsible for making the first judgement about a
woman's suitability (Stage 1). Any aspirant who was accepted for a trial became a
postulant (Stage 2), a period of about three months spent in one of the Sisters' houses
following elements of the daily timetable and undertaking simple tasks: a stage

described as 'role rehearsal' by sociologists.[11] At the end of this time, if the woman was going forward, the Sister Servant presented her to superiors through a written note. If judged suitable she was admitted to the seminary (Stage 3). Admission to the seminary (the Daughters never used the term novitiate) marked a very significant moment and before starting the aspirant undertook a preparatory three-day retreat known as the 'Little Retreat'. The date of the third day was noted in her record as her Entry or Vocation date. At this point she was admitted to the Company of Daughters with rights and obligations. Henceforth she would keep this date as the anniversary of her membership, marked by particular celebrations if she attained 50 years of vocation.[12] In the seminary she wore a seminary habit (very like the original dress of a *fille de la charité*) and undertook a programme of formation that lasted about nine months. At completion, in a *'prise d'habit'* ceremony at the mother house, she received the Daughters' cornette and habit and became known as a 'Young Sister' or 'Little Cornette' (Stage 4). She would be 'missioned' to her first 'placement', a specific role in a particular house suited to this stage (for example overseeing the children's dining room in an orphanage or accompanying an experienced visiting Sister on her rounds). She was given a name from the limited range used in the Company (Louise, Vincent, Mary, Joseph, Catherine, etc), which might be changed when she moved to another house if it was already in use there. In other words, about a year after application she had become a Daughter of Charity, living and working the full life of a Sister companion.

At this point, however, she had not yet made any vows. She continued as a 'Young Sister' for about four more years before the time came to ask permission of her Sister Servant to prepare to make vows for the first time. If approved by her Sister Servant she would learn the Vow Catechism of the Company by heart in French (Stage 5) in readiness for an oral examination (a type of catechism question and answer) on the meaning of the vows. This final hurdle was very demanding for some Sisters because of its use of French, the rote learning and individual oral examination. With the examination behind her she made vows for the first time (Stage 6), an important personal and community occasion but not the serious canonical and public event that it was in a religious order or congregation. There was no new name, no clothing ceremony or different habit, no special music and afterwards there was no new role or duties. Instead she received a letter of permission to make the vows together with a Vow cross to be worn beneath the habit in the habit sleeve, a copy of *The Manual of the Daughters of Charity* and a new habit to add to the used one she had been wearing. The Sister would pronounce her vows privately and 'in a low voice' during Mass (after the elevation of the chalice).[13] After Mass she would be embraced by her companions and might be

---

11 Lucinda San Giovanni, *Ex-Nuns: a Study of Emergent Role Passage* (Norwood, N.J.: Ablex, 1978), p. 41.

12 If, for example, she became mortally ill she would be permitted to make her vows prematurely.

13 *Book of Customs for the Private Houses of the Company of the Daughters of Charity* first published in 1862 and revised in 1938 (London: Salesian Press, 1940), p. 42. 3-1-7 DCMH.

given a card or other token. Each year thereafter she would request from superiors the privilege of renewing her annual vows and, if approved, would 'renovate' or renew those vows on 25 March at the same time as all other Daughters across the world. It was the Company's expectation, shared by every member, that once she had made her vows for the first time a Sister intended to renew them annually for the rest of her life. The stages or phases in admission to the life of a Daughter of Charity have many similarities to those of admission to religious life but the differences are also clear, not least the reality that a Daughter could leave at any time after vows without canonical dispensation or episcopal process and be free in the eyes of the Church to marry. In this context electing to remain for life has its own significance.

The attractions of a Vincentian vocation

It was relatively difficult for women in the United Kingdom in the middle decades of the nineteenth century to know about the ministries of a Daughter of Charity. Convent schools and teacher training colleges increasingly became pathways into a religious life centred round teaching, but there was no parallel vantage point in Britain from which to observe and experience the Daughters' way of life and work with the poor.[14] Women who applied at this time were more likely to be drawn by the power of an ideal than by anything they had been able to see for themselves, unless they had visited the continent. In a compellingly argued essay focused on London, Sheridan Gilley has shown how the concept of 'Holy Poverty' caught the imagination and the hearts of some Christians in the middle nineteenth century, determining their choices and actions.[15] Lady Georgiana Fullerton's vow to 'practise poverty in every way in my power' was representative of Catholic men and women who made personal commitments or joined tertiary orders as a way to live radically different lives.[16] Like other aspects of Christian life in the 1840s to 1860s the resurgence of interest in holy poverty (voluntary and involuntary) marked a reconnection with medieval Christianity. Poverty was romanticised and idealised in this contemporary discourse but it was nonetheless remarkable in its counter-cultural stance against mainstream contemporary utilitarian and philanthropic thinking; 'holy poverty' predisposed Catholics 'to suspend judgement upon even the apparently undeserving poor'.[17] Gilley notes that 'the single most important influence of this sort was the cult of the seventeenth-century Vincent de Paul'.[18] Vincentian praxis, for example, had inspired Mary Aikenhead's foundation of the Irish Sisters of Charity in 1815. Aikenhead decided against affiliation to the

---

14 On recruitment through convent schools see Walsh, *Roman Catholic Nuns,* pp. 139–141 and Mangion, *Contested Identities,* pp. 80–87.

15 Gilley, 'Heretic London, Holy Poverty', pp. 64–89.

16 F.M. Taylor, *The Inner Life of Lady Georgiana Fullerton* (London: Burns and Oates, 1899), p. 43–4.

17 Gilley, 'Heretic London', p. 66.

18 Ibid, p. 72.

Company of the Daughters once she learned that the Sisters took annual vows and were not religious sisters,[19] but she named Ireland's first hospital for Catholics St Vincent's (1832).[20] Helen Chadwick was drawn to the Company (1880) by reading 'a simple brochure in which the story of a homeless child was depicted and the works of the Daughters explained'.[21] Agnes Moser's 'attraction to our Community dated from her sojourn in Boulogne where she saw the Sisters and admired their work'. Later she came across a picture of St Vincent in her father's prayer book.[22] Access to such pictures and stories increased in the 1850s and 1860s when historical, promotional and devotional books in the Vincentian tradition began to be translated from the French by 'a small circle of cultivated Englishwomen', including Lady Georgiana Fullerton, who played an important part in establishing active female religious life in England and became involved with the Daughters.[23] Thus, when John Murphy compiled his comprehensive and lengthy study, *Terra Incognita or The Convents of the United Kingdom* (1873) he devoted an entire chapter to Vincent de Paul, remarking that 'of late, we frequently hear the name'.[24]

By the third quarter of the nineteenth century such ideas were increasingly reinforced by practical examples of Vincentian charity. The Society of St Vincent de Paul (SVP) was established in England in 1844 and in Scotland a year later. By the 1880s the SVP was represented in every diocese in England and Scotland and was particularly well developed in Ireland.[25] At this time, too, the most widely used English prayer book, *Garden of the Soul*, introduced 'Prayers for the Conference of St Vincent de Paul'.[26] In the mid 1850s second-generation Oxford Movement clergymen, Charles Lowder and J.M. Neale, made three foundations, two for women and one for men, that drew explicitly on the Daughters' Common Rules and the Rules of the Congregation of the Mission, Lowder having undergone a form of conversion by reading Abelly's life of St Vincent and Neale had visited the Daughters in Paris.[27] As we have seen the Daughters' nursing service in the Crimean War played its part in increasing knowledge about the Sisters. According to Murphy writing of the early 1870s, '[Now] we see the same Sisters occasionally

---

19 MacGinley, *A Dynamic of Hope*, p. 66.

20 *The Life and Work of Mary Aikenhead* (New York: Longmans, Green and Co., 1924), pp. 34–36.

21 *Notices of Deceased Sisters* (1964), p. 170. 10-3-1 DCMH

22 *Notices of Deceased Sisters* (1933), p. 31 10-3-1 DCMH.

23 Ibid. See also Susan O'Brien, 'Terra Incognita' pp. 128–131. See also anon., *The Inner Life of Lady Georgiana Fullerton* (London, 1899), pp. 56—7 where her 1866 letter to Lady Herbert of Lea is quoted: 'It gave me great pleasure to hear that you were affiliated to the Sisters of St Vincent de Paul. So have I been for the last three years, and I am happy to think we shall have a common object of interest.'

24 Murphy, *Terra Incognita*, p. 75.

25 See Mary Heimann, *Catholic Devotion in Victorian England* (Oxford: Clarendon Press, 1995), p. 127.

26 Ibid.

27 Nicholas Groves, 'Vincent de Paul in Nineteenth-Century England', *VHJ*, (1988), Vol. 9, Issue 1, Article 1, pp. 1–67.

in London and some of our other cities'.[28] Branches of the Ladies of Charity, the confraternity of comfortably-off women Vincent de Paul had founded, were established in London and in Edinburgh and a few other cities from the 1860s onwards, and earlier in Dublin.[29] In all these ways, knowledge of Vincentian spirituality and practice increased.

When members of the founding generation later reflected on their choice of the Company what they recalled was a desire to be of direct service, practical and spiritual, to the poor; they described the sense of a definite calling. To a considerable degree its attractions lay in the high demands it made on their ardour and practical energy. Jesuit Peter Gallwey had advised Eleanor Maxwell (1862), daughter of Lord Herries, that she would be suited to 'enter the Order of the Good Shepherd' only for her to inform him that she was set on the Daughters of Charity because for her the 'attraction was already centred on the poor' rather than 'fallen and endangered women'.[30] Her hopes were fulfilled: she was placed in the boys' orphanage in Liverpool where hers was 'the office of the kitchen: she baked bread for the boys; carried coals from the cellar; cleaned the ovens and boilers; made the fires; scrubbed tables and floors'.[31] Clarissa Reeves (1880) came back from school in France at the age of eighteen to prepare herself for a life with the Daughters, throwing herself for four years 'into the work of the parish of St Lawrence' in her home town of Birkenhead, visiting 'on a Saturday night into places where the police dared not go'.[32] Several dismayed parents demonstrated just how well they understood a Daughter's vocation even as they expressed bewilderment at what might draw their daughter to it.[33] 'This is no convent' remarked Anne Gunning's mother on seeing the working-class surroundings and poor internal fittings of the Sheffield house of charity.[34] Agnes Moser (1874) prayed that her mother's 13th child would be a daughter to take her place at home and 'leave her free to follow her vocation'. She was rewarded when a sister was born, only to discover her father opposed her becoming a Daughter of Charity because she would have to 'work hard, scrub floors, rise at an unearthly hour'.[35] Agnes went on to work for more than 50 years at St John's Institute, Boston Spa where she did have to rise at 4.00 a.m. and spent many hours cleaning and mending, but also became an acknowledged teacher of deaf children and headmistress of a large specialist

---

28 Murphy, *Terra Incognita*, p. 75.

29 *Handbook of Catholic Charitable and Social Works* (London: Catholic Truth Society, 1905), pp. 12–14.

30 *Notices of Deceased Sisters* (1924), p. 1. 10-3-1 DCMH.

31 Ibid.

32 *Notices of Deceased Sisters* (1922), p. 69 10-3-1 DCMH.

33 Mary Burns, (1864) whose father resisted her vocation, held out for two years until he reluctantly agreed: 'If Mary still wants to go to the Sisters of Charity' he told Mrs Burns, 'tell her to go, but do not let me see her, it is more than I can bear.' *Notices of Deceased Sisters* (1914), p. 86 10-3-1 DCMH.

34 *Pioneer Sisters*, p. 22.

35 *Pioneer Sisters*, p. 84

institution. At the end of it she 'owed so much gratitude to God'.[36] Reflections of this kind recur repeatedly in the obituary notices of the founding generation. And while it could reasonably be argued that obituaries, intended as they were solely for internal community consumption, would never offer an alternative message, it is still worth noting that Sisters chose to write narratives of desire about their deceased companion's passion for a specifically Vincentian vocation.

Social class and nationality in the first generation

Like every Catholic religious community in nineteenth-century Britain the Daughters of Charity had its own social composition. Community social profiles evolved through the subtle interaction of three elements: reputation, institutional structure and the ministry opportunities offered.[37] A community's reputation was influenced by the founder's story, the institute's subsequent history and the social classes historically associated with it. Older congregations which had a well-known founder, particularly a canonised saint such as St Dominic, St Angela Merici or St Teresa of Ávila, had a particular cachet within Catholic culture. Anselm Nye has remarked of the Third Order Dominicans founded in England by Margaret Hallahan that 'the register of clothings and professions during this period [1850s] reads something like a contemporary Catholic *Who's Who*'.[38] Congregations with no such pedigree might be seen as more risky by entrants and their families. But, like the Society of the Holy Child Jesus founded in England by Cornelia Connelly, they could also be highly attractive if the founder was alive and charismatic and the candidate open to risk-taking.[39]

Two institutional structures – the requirement of a dowry (or not) and the internal division of the community into two classes (or not) – either reinforced or mitigated the importance of social class. Little analysis has been made of the actual range of dowries accepted by congregations working in Britain as distinct from the requirement stated on paper.[40] Carmen Mangion has calculated that just over one-third of entrants to the Poor Servants of the Mother of God (an English foundation) had no dowry, about one-third were known to bring a dowry of which half brought less than £50, and the remaining third were unknown – suggesting that they too brought nothing.[41] By contrast, in her study of sisters in Scotland,

36 *Notices of Deceased Sisters* (1933), p. 33 10-3-1 DCMH.

37 See Mangion, *Contested Identities*, Chapter 7; Karly Kehoe, *Creating a Scottish Church*, Chapter 3; Susan O'Brien, 'Terra Incognita,' pp. 134–35 and Susan O'Brien, 'Lay Sisters and Good Mothers: Working-Class Women in English Convents, 1840-1910,' in W.J.Sheils and D. Wood, eds., *Women in the Church* (Oxford: Ecclesiastical History Society, 1990), pp. 453–65.

38 Nye, *A Peculiar Kind of Mission*, p. 28.

39 O'Brien, 'Terra Incognita', pp. 120–123 and pp. 135–6.

40 See for example, Rev H. Hohn, *'Vocations': Conditions of Admissions etc to convents, congregations, societies, religious institutes etc* (London, Manchester, Glasgow, Birmingham: R & T Washbourne:, 1912).

41 Mangion, *Contested Identities*, fn. 38, p. 194.

Karly Kehoe notes that 'many of the choir sisters' of the Ursulines of Jesus, 'entered with large dowries of £1,000' and Anselm Nye found similar amounts brought by a group of women entering the English Dominican Sisters.[42] In the middle of these two extremes, the Sisters of the Sacred Hearts of Jesus and Mary brought dowries of around £120.[43] Much of the evidence for Britain points to a lower dowry average than has been shown for Ireland in the second half of the century where £500 was required by the Presentation and Ursuline nuns and the average for the Sisters of Mercy was around £300.[44]

Most institutes were divided into two classes; a choir or teaching class and a class known variously as lay, house or auxiliatrix sisters.[45] Such a division affected the social class profile of the community in obvious ways. It offered a respectable environment to upper- and middle-class women in which they would associate with their own sort and have most domestic work performed by others. In many active congregations there were real differences between the lives of choir sisters and lay sisters, as there had always been in enclosed orders: the women who entered knew their place in the hierarchy.[46] But the picture was also more complex than appears at first sight. Divided congregations could be an aspirational destiny for less well-off but talented and qualified women and, conversely, subtle class dynamics could be at play in congregations that were structurally undivided and apparently egalitarian.[47] In a new community the social class of the founder could play a part in determining the social class of the members. Those founded by working-class women (there are several English examples) were more definitely working-class, attracting few women from elite social groups. Those with upper- or middle-class founders usually had more complex social profiles drawn from across the social classes.

The part played by an institute's work or primary ministry in shaping its social profile was important but not predictable. Clearly there was an association between education in a fee-paying convent school and well-to-do social class, just as there was between domestic work and a lower social class. But lower-class women with talent and gifts became teaching sisters in elementary schools, while upper-class women could desire to serve in roles regarded as demeaning in any other context but a religious vocation. What emerges clearly is the extent to which women from the highest social classes had the greatest choice while women at the very bottom of the social scale were less likely to find a place anywhere in religious life.

---

42 Nye, *A Peculiar Kind of Mission*, p. 27

43 Walsh, *Roman Catholic Nuns*, p. 105.

44 See Maria Luddy, 'Possessed of Fine Properties': Power, Authority and the Funding of Convents in Ireland, 1780–1900', in Maarten Van Dijck et al, eds., *The Economics of Providence*, pp. 227–246; M.R. MacGinley, *A Dynamic of Hope*, p. 64 and fn. 66, p. 367;Mary Peckham Magray, *The Transforming Power of Nuns: Women, Religion and Cultural Change in Ireland, 1750-1900* (Oxford: Oxford University Press, 1998), pp. 36-7.

45 O'Brien, 'Lay-sisters and Good Mothers', p. 457.

46 Nye, *A Peculiar Kind of Mission*, p. 46ff.

47 See O'Brien, 'Lay Sisters and Good Mothers', pp. 453–465.

There had never been an internal class division in the Company, nor was a dowry required. An aspirant was asked to pay a contribution towards costs during the stages prior to her first placement. In the second half of the nineteenth century the cost of postulancy was £2 or £3 ('no money may be taken from postulants for their board').[48] About £30 was needed for travel to Paris and for living expenses in the seminary.[49] Some entrants gave more as a gift to the community, most brought £50 or £60 and others were accepted with £20, which did not cover costs.[50] The costs of 'good' applicants without funds were frequently paid by a Sister Servant or other sponsor.[51] These modest financial requirements were out of the reach of the poorest but they were not dissimilar in value to the 'bottom drawer' many women would put together for their wedding day. In these ways the requirements of the Company continued to favour the 'village girls' so valued by the founders. Yet, from the early nineteenth century, for reasons that have already been explored, the Company in France began to attract women from across the social classes, even including the daughters of noble families. Although the Company was known to be a working and even a working-class community, during the nineteenth century women from other social classes were increasingly attracted to the life. At the other end of the social scale working-class membership was curtailed by the Company's historical prohibition on accepting former domestic servants. This restriction was made on the grounds that domestic service so systematically exposed women to predatory males that former servants' moral and sexual integrity could not be guaranteed, a striking perspective not shared by other congregations and institutes working in Britain.[52] Given the importance of domestic work in the second half of the nineteenth century in Britain this was a significant curb on the vocational aspirations of a large proportion of working women and a significant limitation on the potential pool for recruitment.

First-generation entrants from Britain and Ireland were more likely to be from better-off families simply because of the necessity to apply directly to French houses for admission to the Company. By the 1860s, when aspirants began to apply to the newly founded houses in Great Britain, it was already known that some elite

---

48 *Directions to the Sister Servants of the Daughters of Charity given by Our Most Honoured Father, J.B. Étienne 1854.* Translated into English. 13-7-1-1 DCMH.

49 http://safalra.com/other/historical-uk-inflation-price-conversion, consulted January 2014.

50 Exercise Book 'List of postulants sent from Drogheda to Mill Hill (and before that to Paris) and the amount of money they brought. Drogheda Box'. DCI and 13-4-1 Seminary Records, DCMH.

51 Conclusion drawn from study of all the available registers and lists in the archives in London and Paris.

52 'Note for the Admission of Postulants (Article Second of the Constitutions), Étienne, *Directions to the Sister Servants*, p. 29: 'although the same Constitutions do not speak of excluding postulants who have been servants, or who have been brought up in hospitals, the constant practice of the Company from its beginning, and the records in its possession, show that persons of this condition have never been admitted, and that, for serious considerations, tending to the honour of the Community…' This prohibition was not shared by other communities, including French originated ones. See O'Brien, 'Lay Sisters', p. 458 which shows that a high proportion of auxiliatrix sisters in the Society of the Sacred Heart had been in domestic service.

Catholic women were members and this encouraged others to follow.[53] Women from the upper and upper middle classes formed a significant proportion of first-generation Sisters. Conversely, at around one-tenth of the total membership, women of the working classes were unrepresentatively few. Table 4.4 shows how the community's social profile deviated markedly from the social stratification of high-Victorian Britain.

CLASS	DESCRIPTOR	FATHER'S OCCUPATION	No.	AS % OF TOTAL
I	Upper class and upper middle class	Owners of capital and land and upper professionals: landowner, proprietor, senior military, barrister, architect	68	24.2%
I/II	Middle class	Professional and intermediate: medic, clergy, banker, professor, publisher.	20	7.1%
I and I/II		*All owners of capital, land and upper professionals*	*88*	*31.4%*
II	Middle class to working class	Intermediate occupations: farmer, wholesaler, tradesman, shop-keeper, teacher, civil servant	148	53.0%
		Farmers within this total	*92*	*32.8%*
III	Working class	Skilled occupations: bookbinder, hatter, miller, foreman, superintendent	13	4.6%
IV	Working class	Partly skilled occupations: cooper, mechanic	12	4.3%
V	Working class	Unskilled occupations: labourer, carter	3	1.1%
III/IV/V	*Working class*	*All working class*	*28*	*10.0%*

4.4: SOCIAL CLASS OF SISTERS ENTERING BEFORE 1885

Total number of Sisters in group = 280
Total whose fathers had no known occupation = 26

---

53 Mary Oates points out the lack of such entrants in the USA: 'Relative to their working-class contemporaries, wealthy women did not find the active sisterhoods appealing.' Oates, *The Catholic Philanthropic Tradition in America* ((Bloomington, Ind: Indiana University Press, 1995), p. 15.

In part this profile was a reflection of the particular composition and history of the Catholic communities of England and Scotland, in part a consequence of having to train in France, and in part it was the product of the high level of Irish membership among the Daughters. Looking across religious communities in England and Scotland we can see that in every decade from the 1870s to the 1960s Ireland was a major net contributor, with communities having very varied proportions of Irish to British members.[54] In some the proportion was as high as 70 per cent by the late nineteenth century.[55] At around 60 per cent the ratio of Irish-born Daughters to British-born was at the higher end of the range and had an impact on the community's social profile, illustrated in Table 4.5.

Dates	Total	Irish	English	French	Scots	Welsh	Other
Before 1855	23	14 (61%)	4 (17.3%)	3 (13%)	1 (4.3%)	1 (4.3%)	-
1855–18	50	30 (60%)	19 (38%)	1 (2%)	-	-	-
1865–18	86	48 (55%)	29 (33.3%)	3	4 (4.5%)		2 (2.2%)
1875–	119	75 (62.5%)	36 (30%)	2 (1.6%)	1 (0.8%)	4 (3.3%)	1 (0.8%)
Total	280	167 (60%)	88 (31%)	9 (3%)	6 (2%)	5 (2%)	3 (1%)

4.5: BIRTH COUNTRY OF SISTERS ENTERING BEFORE 1885

Irish-born Sisters came from a range of social backgrounds, but they entirely dominated in the largest single group of all, that of 'farmer', as Table 4.4 shows.[56] Ninety-seven per cent of Daughters with fathers described as 'farmer' were from Ireland.[57]

The category of farmer can never be assumed to be homogeneous but, according to Barbara Walsh, who has studied the subject extensively in relation to the Irish backgrounds of religious sisters working in Britain, the majority of this category

54 See Mangion, *Contested Identities*, p. 192. In his study in 1996 Donal Harman Akenson noted that the group of Irish most in need of researching were 'religious women' i.e. sisters: *The Irish Diaspora: A Primer* (Toronto: P.D. Meany with Queen's University Belfast, 1996), p. 271.

55 For example, the Poor Servants of the Mother of God. See Mangion, *Contested Identities*, p. 191.

56 Mangion, *Contested Identities*, Chapter 7.

57 Ibid., p. 164

among the Daughters could be described as 'comfortably off'.[58] Most came from the counties lying south of a line drawn from County Louth in the north-east to County Limerick in the south-west and more especially from the 'strata of "strong farmer" communities in the rich cattle and dairy counties of Munster and south-east Leinster, particularly Cork, Limerick and Tipperary'.[59] Many of their daughters would have had a convent education, but they brought more than this to the Company. With their knowledge of dairying, poultry-keeping, kitchen gardens and experience of budgeting and marketing, these farmers' daughters could be seen as a modern incarnation of the 'country women' preferred by the founders.[60] Anne Farrell (1852), first Sister Servant of Smyllum Orphanage in Lanark in 1864, is a vigorous representative of the group. Writing about her achievements at Smyllum a contemporary paid tribute to the

> marvellous powers of organisation that enabled her to develop the works... she saw the necessity of adding to the property... and she sought the advice of her own relatives who were successful farmers in Ireland... she negotiated the purchase of Caldwellside Farm adjacent to the original property and further land [46 acres] was acquired as years went on. [She] appointed a bailiff who... improved the land and reared cattle and sheep. 40 cows were milked daily on the farm.[61]

Sister Farrell added a large poultry yard, known by the children as 'Chucky Lodge', which gave the home its eggs and fowl. Two acres of land were walled off for a vegetable and fruit garden with grapes grown in a hothouse, again for the children. A local spring provided their water supply and she commissioned the construction of a reservoir to collect water. As the number of children increased, buildings were developed to accommodate them: four dormitories; kitchens; schools; a chapel; a hospital and an isolation unit; a nursery and a school for the blind. By 1910 there were 25 Sisters on site at Smyllum, the majority of them Irish women. Honora Finucane from County Cork (1868), daughter of a market inspector, was not only head of the girls' school but designed many of the buildings; Ellen Doyle established workshops for the boys and set up brass bands using money given by her relatives in Dublin.[62] Although no more than one-third of the membership of the community in the British Isles before 1885, these Irish women can justly be

---

58 Walsh's use of farm land valuations and local directories to analyse in detail the backgrounds of the sisters from Limerick is a small sample, but taken with other evidence seems to be indicative of a broader pattern. See also Tony Fahey 'Nuns in the Catholic Church in Ireland in the Nineteenth Century' in *Girls Don't Do Honours: Irish Women in Education in the 19th and 20th Centuries* Mary Cullen, ed. (Dublin, 1987).

59 Walsh, *Roman Catholic Nuns*, p. 145.

60 Seminary notes 'knows all about poultry and butter making and helped out at the farm at home with her sisters'. 13-4-1 Box 1 # 6 p. 12. DCMH.

61   Sister Langdale typescript history of Smyllum. 11-67-11-1 #3a DCMH.

62 Finucane, *Deceased Sisters Lives* (1914). 10-3-1 DCMH.

described as its mainstay. They contributed a set of skills, attitudes and experiences that would have been scarce among British-born entrants.

Just as striking, if different, was the impact of the women from the English landowning and upper professional classes. Many came from strongly committed 'old' Catholic families. Their presence in the community, discussed below, was significant because of their education and childhood formation, their moral and spiritual seriousness, and the money and networks of influence within clerical and social circles they could access. Such families were accustomed to their daughters entering the Benedictines, Carmelites, Dominicans and Franciscans but any daughter who chose the Daughters of Charity was breaking with accepted social norms. At the same time women's quest for a purposeful and active Christ-centred life was part of a phenomenon of its time in Britain; a Catholic form of the historically more familiar search undertaken by supposedly 'leisured' Anglican and nonconformist Victorian women for a morally purposeful life.[63] Although 32 per cent of Vow Sisters who entered in the 1870s came from the upper and upper middle classes, this can be seen as a specific phase in the community's development. Women from this same social group comprised only 3 per cent of those who tried their vocation in the 1890s.[64]

Faith histories

Fulfilling work and personal purpose were strong attractions for the Victorian women who entered active religious communities. From her study of the accounts given by Anglican sisters Susan Mumm has concluded that work rather than spiritual life exerted the greatest motivational pull for the first generation (defined by her as the whole of the nineteenth century).[65] After exploring the self-accounts given by women in ten Roman Catholic congregations in England Carmen Mangion acknowledged the powerful attraction of the work but remained convinced that 'this life was not for any woman whose main motivation was not religious'.[66] She and other historians of Catholic sisters have rightly argued for a historical account that anchors motivation within a theology of the salvific and sanctifying purpose of works of mercy and charity while taking account of the context of women's lives and recognising the particular life of active ministry that attracted them. In the wider world of nineteenth-century philanthropy and social action Anne Summers has argued for the centrality of a 'spiritual framing' to women's social initiatives, an approach that is confirmed in the lives of first-generation Daughters.[67]

63 See, for example, Morgan and deVries, *Women, Gender and Religious Cultures* and Anne Summers, *Female Lives, Moral States: Women, Religion and Public Life in Britain 1800–1930* (Newbury: Threshold Press, 2000).

64 Calculated from the Sisters' database and Register using the Booth-Banks classification.

65 Mumm, *Stolen Daughters, Virgin Mothers*, Introduction and Chapter 2.

66 Mangion, *Contested Identities*, p. 61 and Chapter 3.

67 Summers, *Female Lives, Moral States*, p. 4.

The challenge of assessing an applicant's faith and motivation was one the Company took very seriously.[68] Superiors expected an applicant to give strong evidence of religious fidelity because, in the words of Vincent de Paul repeated so often down the decades, 'if you do not gather strength from prayer it will be very difficult, nay, impossible for you to persevere'.[69] The Church taught that a consecrated life was a reserved and special grace granted to the few chosen by God. Because each Daughter consecrated herself annually to God the Company understood her to be encompassed within the same grace.[70] Girded with such a theology of vocation it is unsurprising that the entry bar was at its highest when it came to spiritual 'evidence'. Although it is likely to strike a twenty-first-century Western sensibility as odd (given contemporary emphasis on individuals making their own identities), in the nineteenth century great weight was given to the faith of the aspirant's parents. Her personal spiritual merits were tested through the religious fidelity of her family and the benefits of validly administered sacraments. Louise de Marillac's view that it was best for aspirants to be known 'even from the cradle' neatly summarises this outlook.[71] Each had to demonstrate that she *and* her parents had received the sacraments of baptism, first communion and confirmation. Her parents were asked to provide evidence of their church marriage certificate and a careful check was made against its date and that of the baptismal certificate of the aspirant.[72] A priest was asked to confirm that they and the aspirant had led 'blameless' lives – a judgement that had little to do with perfection since it was accepted that all were sinners. Some were refused because superiors had received 'negative information' about one parent or both.[73] The terse marginal note, 'unsuitable family', referred to religious or moral shortcomings not social inferiority.

First-generation Daughters presented a high degree of Catholic fidelity, attested in a number of ways that went beyond the basic markers. A significant proportion had close relatives in the priesthood or religious life – or both.[74] The Company's

---

68 Walsh, *Roman Catholic Nuns*, p. 125.

69 Vincent de Paul, quoted in M.L.H., *Sister Xavier Berkeley: Fifty-Four Years a Missionary in China* (London: Burns & Oates, 1949), p. 12. 2-1-10 DCMH.

70 An analysis of the contemporary annual Vow Retreat Conferences written by the Superior General and printed and circulated across the Company each year underlines the centrality of this understanding to the Company. *Conferences* of Eugene Bore and Antoine Fiat 4-22 and 4-33 DCMH.

71 1 January 1915 Circular Letter from General Superioress Marie Maurice to Visitatrices, 'We cannot too earnestly recommend to you, my dearest Sisters, to secure from reliable sources, information relative to the family and reputation of the young girls for whom you ask admission to the community...bearing in mind that our Venerable Mother expressed the wish that aspirants be known 'even from the cradle''. Circular Letters from Superiors 6-43 DCMH.

72 Ibid.

73 MS Letter Book, letter to Sister Chatelaine, 9 August 1874. Box X DCParis.

74 This phenomenon has been widely noted. Maria Luddy, for example, confirms the work of other scholars that in Ireland kinship and friendship were at the heart of philanthropic networks. Luddy, *Women and Philanthropy*, p. 26.

record-keepers were understandably keen to note where a Sister had a relative in the Congregation of the Mission,[75] but the wide range and the sheer number of family members who were ordained or consecrated was more characteristic. Mary Boyle (1883) had one sister in the Cross and Passion congregation in England, a cousin in the Armagh convent of the Sisters of Loreto, and two of her brothers and four of her cousins were priests.[76] Helen Chadwick (1880), from an Anglo-Irish family, had a younger sister who was a Poor Clare in Darlington and two step-sisters who were Sacred Heart nuns; two of her brothers became canons in the Catholic Hexham and Newcastle Diocese where their uncle, James Chadwick, composer of the carol 'Angels we have heard on High', was Bishop from 1866 to 1882. Mary Burns' (1864) five sisters all became Ursuline nuns (three of them being sent to America together to found a new convent in Pittsburgh) and her brother was a priest in the Westminster Diocese. But perhaps no one could quite match Teresa Vaughan's (1861) family for its dedication to the Church. Her six brothers all became priests: Herbert founded the Mill Hill Missionary College and ended his life as Cardinal Archbishop of Westminster, another brother founded Fort Augustus Benedictine Abbey in Scotland and a third became a Jesuit missionary, while three of her sisters were nuns in the enclosed Visitation, Poor Clare and Benedictine orders respectively.[77]

Teresa Vaughan represented a group of Sisters who had passed childhoods in an environment described by her obituarist as 'a centre of elevated piety'.[78] Vaughan's home, Courtfield in Monmouthshire, had a private chapel where the Blessed Sacrament was reserved and Mass was celebrated by the family chaplain. Understood as creating the opportunity for daily intimacy with God, access to the Blessed Sacrament placed aspirants from such homes in a special category as to what might be hoped from their religious formation.[79] Frances Arundel (1864), Agnes Berkeley (1882), Anna Marie Blundell (1856), Helen Chadwick (1880), Catherine Eyston (1861), Etheldreda Howard (1868), Mary Langdale (1881), Marianne Middleton (1847) and her sister Frances (1855), Edith Noel (1878), Mary Petre (1881) and her cousins Emma (1884) and Edith (1884), Sybilla Plowden (1872), Frances Stainforth (1864), Monica Weld (1882), and the two Anglo-Scottish Constable Maxwell sisters, Eleanor (1862) and Everilda (1881), all entered the Company before 1885 from family homes whose domestic chapels had for

---

75 Alice O'Sullivan had a brother who was a Vincentian priest; Margaret Hogan (1877) was niece of Reverend Hickey, the Vincentian priest in charge at St Vincent's Sheffield, while Anne Farrell (1852), Anne Boylan (1854) and Rose Austin (1864) were all nieces of the well-known Reverend Thomas McNamara, Vincentian Provincial.

76 *Notices of Deceased Sisters* (1929), p. 2 10-3-1 DCMH.

77 A. McCormack MHM, *Cardinal Vaughan: the life of the third Archbishop of Westminster, Founder of St Joseph's Missionary Society Mill Hill* (London, 1966), pp. 11–12.

78 Notices of *Deceased Sisters* (1924), p. 2, writing about Monica Weld. 10-3-1 DCMH.

79 Almost half of the Catholic missions in England (locations where Mass was celebrated) were domestic chapels under family patronage in 1825 and in rural areas about 100 families retained this role throughout the century. Lynda Pearce, 'Catholic Philanthropy in Mid-Nineteenth Century Britain: The Reformatory Work of the Female Congregations' (PhD thesis, University of Kent, 2003), p. 87.

centuries been the only places of Catholic worship in their localities. It hardly needs to be said that the privilege of a private chapel was extremely rare and was only possible for upper-class or upper-middle-class Catholic families; but it *was* the childhood experience of 18 per cent of English-born Daughters in this generation. The potency of their Catholic identity and upbringing and the way it prepared them for the life they chose is another indicator of the strength of a particularly English strain of Catholicism in the middle nineteenth century.[80] Their vigorous faith, together with their social status, played a part in shaping the tenor of the Company in Britain in its early decades, giving the Sisters confidence to experiment and hold their own in times of difficulty.

A family of families

The community's social composition was reinforced through the effect of family influence. Having a relative in the community was a reliable way for some young woman to learn about life as a Daughter and the presence of a relative was reassuring. Consanguinity among members, always a feature of religious life in earlier centuries, continued to be so everywhere in the nineteenth and early twentieth centuries.[81] Kinship reinforced the family nature of community life in a quite literal way, but this was not a phenomenon peculiar to religious life at this time. According to one recent study 'kin networks intertwined with what was going on beyond the front door' across all the realms of public and economic life in Victorian Britain.[82] Even as they modernised and became more bureaucratic almost all companies and institutions continued to function through familial networks and family relationships.[83] Among the Daughters the potential for kin connections increased with each decade that passed, adding nieces, great-nieces, aunts and great-aunts to sisters and cousins. But even in the founding generation the rate of kin connectivity was high: 24 per cent, virtually one in every four Sisters of this generation, had a relative in the community. When Mary Ann Middleton, for example, was asked by the Superior General to take on the management of the Beacon Lane boys' home in Liverpool in 1862 she agreed provided that her cousin Eleanor Maxwell was also missioned there (a laying down of conditions that would have astonished later generations). The cousins worked together for the next 20 years – and theirs was by no means an isolated example of kin working together.

---

80 Heimann, *Catholic Devotion*.

81 For Ireland see Clear, *Nuns in Nineteenth Century Ireland*, p. 144; for Canada Marta Danylewycz, *Taking the Veil: An Alternative to Marriage, Motherhood and Spinsterhood in Quebec 1840–1920* (Toronto: McClelland and Stewart, 1987), pp. 112–113. For USA see Fitzgerald, *Habits of Compassion*, p. 32. Mangion, *Contested Identities*, pp. 67–75 provides excellent evidence of kinship connections in English convents.

82 Leonore Davidoff, *Thicker than Water: Siblings and their Relations, 1780-1920* (Oxford: Oxford University Press, 2012), p. 4.

83 Maria Luddy, *Women and Philanthropy*, p. 26 notes that in Ireland 'close personal friendships and family relationships lay at the heart of female philanthropic networks throughout the century...'

If it were possible to map friendship links the personal connectivity between the women of the Province in this era would be seen to extend even further.[84] A web of family and friendship relationships lay beneath the community's surface as was noted by Sister Louisa Blundell's biographer, herself an old friend as well as companion. She described Boulogne, the scene of Louisa's childhood, as the home of a 'somewhat large contingent of Catholic families at that time; besides the Blundells, there were the Cliffords, the Langdales, the Neaves and the Eystons, all of whom had either members or relatives among St Vincent's daughters'.[85]

Age and health

The age at which women entered religious life has generated a good deal of interest among historians, partly because of the high quality of information available and partly because analysis can be used to test powerful stereotypes about nuns.[86] Popular Victorian literature liked to portray women going into convents either as too young to know their own minds or as 'old maids' whom no man had chosen.[87] The Company's Rule stated that no one under the age of eighteen could be accepted and that a dispensation from the general council had to be granted for applicants over the age of thirty. No upper age limit was set and, keeping faith with Louise de Marillac's history, widows were accepted.[88] The normative age bracket of eighteen to twenty-nine, very common across women's religious communities, was intended to ensure cohorts of fit and energetic members who were not so young as to be underdeveloped in personality and judgement and yet not so settled in their ways as to be unresponsive to formation of habits and mentality.[89]

It is perhaps unsurprising, therefore, that the average age for aspirants to religious life across most religious communities in the nineteenth century was between twenty-three and twenty-five, depending on decade and congregation.[90] Historical research has shown that the average age for women to marry in mid-Victorian Britain was twenty-five to twenty-six,[91] that of women who became Protestant missionaries was twenty-four, which was also the average age of women

---

84 Teresa Butti (1856) from Somerset, for example, had been advised to enter with the Irish Sisters of Charity but 'was determined to follow the example of Miss Blundell who had an aunt in Taunton [at the Franciscan convent where she went to school] and who had recently entered our community.' She was later to be placed under Sister Blundell at Lanark. *Notices of Deceased Sisters* 10-3-1. See Fitzgerald, *Habits of Compassion*, p. 32.

85 *Life of Louisa Blundell*, p. 11.

86 Walsh, *Roman Catholic Nuns*, p. 134.

87 See Mumm, *Stolen Daughters*, p. 178.

88 Hohn, 'Vocations', p. 259.

89 A number of the communities listed by Hohn had a lower age limit of sixteen.

90 Walsh, *Roman Catholic Nuns*, p. 134 cites the work of Luddy, Clear and Peckham on Ireland. She herself states that 'the average age of all aspirants...was between 23 and 24.' p. 154.

91 Robert Woods, *The Population of Britain in the Nineteenth Century* (Cambridge University Press, 1995) and L. A. Clarkson, 'Marriage and Fertility in Nineteenth-Century Ireland' in R. B. Outhwaite ed., *Marriage and Society: Studies in the Social History of Marriage* (New York: St Martin's Press, 1982), pp. 237 - 55.

who emigrated from Ireland.[92] In other words, the decision to enter religious life was taken at the same age as women made other critical life-decisions. Table 4.6 sets out the data for the Daughters of Charity in Britain and Ireland between 1855 and 1884.

DATES	TOTAL	<20	20–24	25–29	30–34	35+
Before 1855	23	6 (26%)	11 (48%)	5 (22%)	1 (4%)	0
1855–1864	50	9 (18%)	22 (44%)	13 (26%)	4 (8%)	2 (4%)
1865–1874	86	7 (8%)	42 (47%)	29 (33%)	8 (9%)	0
1875–1884	120	7 (6%)	58 (48%)	45 (37.5%)	9 (7.5%)	1 (1%)

4.6: AGE AT ENTRY IN THE FIRST GENERATION

And, just as the average age for women marrying increased during the 1890s, 1910s and 1920s, so the median age for entry to the Company moved steadily upwards. The proportions of women entering below the age of twenty reduced and those aged over twenty-five increased. 'We prefer not to receive young people under the age of 20,' one Sister Servant in this era explained, 'because their health does not hold up when they enter too young.'[93] But there was discretion in the decision-making. Clarissa Reeves had known from the age of eighteen that her 'call' was to the Daughters but her younger sister Marian was forty-eight before she applied. In weighing up whether to recommend Marian for a dispensation on the grounds of her age it was noted that 'she has always wished to become a Sister of Charity but has given herself to looking after her aged mother and left her sister free to enter the community'. Now their mother was dead she had asked to be received and even though they 'know well how difficult it is to form someone for the community at this kind of age', Marian was admitted.[94]

Good health was another important consideration: indeed, it was something of a preoccupation for superiors because of the stress and burden created when a Sister's health failed. Over time the Company became more explicit about physical and health requirements. In 1876, for example, it was decided to refuse any applicant who was less than four feet and ten inches tall because it was believed that the lifting and portering involved in a Daughter's work was too demanding

---

92 See Walsh, *Roman Catholic Nuns*, especially re emigration age. See Rhonda Semple, *Missionary Women: Gender, Professionalism and the Victorian Idea of Christian Mission* (Woodbridge, Suffolk, 2003), p. 27 on missionaries who were 'considered to be in their prime between twenty-one and twenty-eight'.

93 To Paris superiors, 13 June 1876, Letter Book, Dublin, Box X DCParis. Over half of the 20 vowed sisters who left between 1900 and 1920 were aged 20 or under at entry which is some indication, but this is not a sufficiently large number to be of major concern. Calculated from '*Statistiques de la Province 1847–1970*' 10-1 DCMH.

94 Register DCMH and Proces Verbaux des Conseils Années 1896–1900, 2 June 1896. DCParis.

for smaller women.[95] By the turn of the century a formal medical was established; at first primarily to detect signs of tuberculosis, it was extended in range over the following 30 years. But the health of family members continued to be used as a major indicator. Any hint of inheritable disease or of mental instability in close relatives was sufficient for a woman to be refused outright.[96] Conditions were also laid down about physical appearance and health. No woman with obvious impairment or disfigurement was admitted. Deafness and bad facial scarring from smallpox were both grounds for rejection because the Company had decided that applicants who could not hear well or who were facially disfigured were not suitable for working with other people's children or for visiting people in their homes. The seminary notes and Sisters' individual records include many marginal references to those sent home because one or other of these impediments had become apparent. The Company tested whether an aspirant was 'lacking the strength for a Daughter of Charity' by requiring hours of scrubbing on hands and knees during postulancy and seminary. Women, like Marie Lomax of Liverpool, who had many desirable qualities and came from very good Catholic families, were reluctantly sent home on health grounds during one or other of these two stages.[97] The limestone flags of the wide corridors in the Paris seminary were a dual test of obedience and stamina, as were assignments in the wash-houses and the kitchens.

Education, qualifications and personal qualities

A solid education in the three 'R's was regarded as desirable for all entrants and most possessed the minimal level, although a few were noted as having very little education at all. The directions Sister Servants received on this matter were clear: 'at this present time...it is highly important for a Daughter of Charity to be able to read, write and cipher'.[98] Beyond these basics, a 'good education' was highly regarded by the community. Yet it is clear that superiors did not equate a nursing or teaching certificate with being 'well educated': entrants who already possessed certificates were regularly noted as having a 'basic education' or 'little education'.[99] It seems rather to have referred to the education that higher-class

---

95 Letters of instruction from Paris to Sister Chatelain 1876, 1877, MS Letter Book Carlisle Place. Box X DCParis.

96 Records relating to aspirants have not survived as they have for the period after 1885, but the rigour seen in these later records is the application of existing Company practice.

97 Marie Lomax, daughter of an eminent English Catholic family living in Liverpool, went to the seminary in 1869 at the age of 25 where she spent 'nearly all her time in the Infirmary' and was sent home to her family. As a promising Young Sister they gave her a second chance. With her health seemingly restored she was readmitted in 1871 and sent to work in Dublin. Even though she was described by the Sister Servant as 'good hearted, with a great love of the poor, and very kind to her companions' her poor health 'took all her energy' and, it being judged that 'she would always be weak', she was finally sent home in May 1872 and was told kindly but firmly not to ask again because her health was not strong enough for a Daughter of Charity. Seminary Notes p. 39 and Letters to Externs in Letter Book, p. 254, Box X. DCParis.

98 *Directions to the Sister Servants*, p. 30. 3-1-10 DCMH.

99 Postulants' Book 1884–1893; Postulants' Book 1919–1933; Aspirants' Book 1924–1934. 13-2-1 DCMH.

women received at home or in convent schools and which included a knowledge of European history and culture, languages, music, religion and the finer types of sewing as well as deportment and manners as practised in that social class.

Society was moving towards the need for qualifications in teaching and in nursing but this question created tensions within the community during the 1870s. Opposition to qualifications derived in part from class-based antipathies to certification on the part of the upper-class Sisters and in part from a belief that too much concern to achieve them might lead Sisters away from their real vocation of service to the poor. One incident in Scotland illustrates the issues at stake. In 1874 the Company withdrew the four Sisters from Coatbridge, a mining and manufacturing town near Glasgow. Sisters Costello, Halligan, Duffy and Prendergast had arrived in 1867 following the request of Father Michael O'Keeffe for Sisters to teach and visit among the predominantly Irish members of St Patrick's parish where sectarianism was rife and the indigenous community was 'not in the least disposed to appreciate the Sisters of Charity'.[100] The Sisters soon established themselves with three day schools, two night schools and three Sunday schools and Michael O'Keeffe worked hard to raise the money to extend the schools. But in 1874 he notified Archbishop Eyre that the Sisters did not meet the Board of Education's criteria for teachers in its schools. O'Keeffe was 'most anxious that the Sisters should not be removed from Coatbridge' but Eyre was concerned that the school might lose its Privy Council grant. What the Sisters themselves thought is not known, but the difficulties raised by the question of competence measured by certification played a part in causing superiors to withdraw the Sisters at the end of the year.

So critical was the situation over teaching qualifications in Britain that in September 1875 the general council had almost decided the Sisters should be trained for certification. Étienne asked Sister Chatelain in London to consult with two other Sister Servants about a proposal to send capable Sisters to take the examination. When he discovered they found the idea of Sisters having to pass exams 'repugnant' the scheme was dropped, a significant concession to the feelings of the Sisters given the importance of the incident that had prompted concern.[101] Father Michael Burke writing from Sheffield commented that the Sisters' objections were based on their fear that those 'holding diplomas would become conceited and lose their vocation'.[102] No such anxiety existed among sisters in the many religious congregations that had been founded for teaching and so it seems likely that aspirants with a strong attraction to teaching would have entered one of these dedicated and professionalising communities. The Company did not give priority to formal training and certification in their recruitment or admissions of Sisters at this time and it is likely that the social class of the Sister Servants played a part in

100 *Notices of Deceased Sisters* (1916), Sister Teresa Angland, p. 25. 10-3-1 DCMH.

101 MS Letter Book, Carlisle Place, 1875. DCParis.

102 Typescript 'The Sisters of Charity in Sheffield'. 11-29-1 #2 DCMH.

developing an implicit policy which shaped the profile of the community in this generation and even into the next.

No single personality type seems to have been favoured in the selection but a number of personal qualities consistently used as admission criteria by the Company's superiors in Britain were of greater importance than certificates or training courses completed. The Company's records on individual Sisters make clear which qualities were favoured: good judgement, solid piety, even temper, humility, discretion, uprightness, a 'good spirit' (often meaning generous-spirited in community life) and willingness to work hard at improving herself as she was advised by superiors, in a spirit of obedience. Superiors repeatedly used terms such as 'simplicity', 'frankness' and 'openness' to signify constructs that were rather more nuanced than might first appear. 'Simplicity' described an absence of self-consciousness or ego, yet without foregoing individual personality. 'Cheerfulness', a much prized quality, had nothing to do with a ready smile but indicated the capacity to be positive and to see God's grace in all circumstances. A sense of humour was appreciated. Contrarily, undesirable qualities included being 'guarded and closed', particularly with superiors, which indicated pride. Singularity, 'sulkiness', defensiveness against advice and being easily influenced by others were seen as significant negative qualities. As one Sister put it, 'gloom is far removed from sanctity'.[103] Clearly, subjective opinion was involved and Sisters might find themselves misjudged, but as it was customary to move Sisters who did not fit in well or who asked for a change, being misunderstood was counter-balanced by the opportunity of a second or even third opinion. Some Sisters never fitted in anywhere but nonetheless were accommodated by the community, moving frequently from one house to another every few years, as often as every two years in a few instances. They were the bane of superiors' lives. The criteria did not produce clones and a wide range of personalities can be glimpsed among the first generation: from 'wild Agnes' Robinson 'independente et exubérante' (1860), and 'lively' Sarah Cullen who arrived on horseback for her first interview with Sister Middleton in Liverpool, to Caroline Norton (1864) who 'shunned the world almost to excess'.[104]

Leaders of the founding generation

By 1884 there were 21 Sister Servants in England and Scotland, each responsible for a house, its sisters and its work projects. Vincent de Paul had consulted Sisters on adopting the name 'Sister Servant' for the house superior, recommending the term 'servant' because it had been 'assumed by the Blessed Virgin when she consented that the will of God should be fulfilled in her'.[105] Sister Servants were to

103 'Remarks on Sister Petre' (1950), p. 5. 10-3-1 DCMH.

104 For Robinson see *Sister Chatelain*, p. 36 and *Notices of Deceased Sisters* (1898), p. 28; for Norton, *Notices of Deceased Sisters* (1916) p. 1. 10-3-1 DCMH.

105 11 June 1642, Leonard, *Conferences of St Vincent de Paul*, p. 63.

be those best suited to directing but, in their thinking and attitudes, 'there should be such perfect equality that…it might be possible for the Sisters to replace one another as Sister Servant on an annual basis'.

However, by the nineteenth century Sister Servants, who were appointed and had no fixed term of office, often remained in place for long periods. During his term as Superior General in the mid-nineteenth century, Étienne paid very particular attention to the Sister Servants, 'aware of the unique role played by [them] in the transmission of the spirit of evangelical Charity' and in the maintenance of unity and uniformity.[106] He brought Sister Servants together for special retreats, wrote *Advices* to help Sisters make the transition to Sister Servant and provided clear handbooks about the duties of the role which emphasised its importance.[107]

A Sister Servant's responsibilities were many and varied. She would interview aspirants who applied through her house and make the initial judgement about whether her companions would be permitted to renovate their vows or be held back for remedial action. She organised the work of the house, negotiating as necessary with any authorities, and she had sole charge of money management, each house being required to balance its own books. If the house had an oratory with the Blessed Sacrament reserved she must uphold proper respect for this sacred place and it was her role to maintain the prayer schedule and give the Friday conference to her companions. She was to report all serious concerns to superiors and implement recommendations that came from the regular visitation of the house. Regardless of these many duties and opportunities, records show that the greatest preoccupation and worry for a Sister Servant came from concerns about the individuals in her care and their relationships.[108] A Sister Servant might have scope for more or less initiative depending on the situation of the house and her own personality, but in the first generation before provincial government was established the role offered real opportunities for someone of energy and vision.

The requirement that Sister Servants should be able to read, write and converse in French with the secretariat at the mother house and with superiors in Paris determined that these women came from the upper-and upper-middle classes. Table 4.7 shows that families of the first-generation Sister Servants in Britain were predominantly (70 per cent) from the landowning and upper professional classes with the minority (30 per cent) being from intermediate professional and farming entrepreneurial families.

---

106 *Genesis of the Company*, p. 77. 1-7-2 DCMH.

107 'Directions to the Sister Servants of the Daughters of Charity given by Our Most Honoured Father, J.B. Étienne 1854', a typescript in English dated 1927, 13-7-1-1 DCMH.

108 Conclusion drawn from a reading of the 'Letter Book' for Great Britain, Box 10 DCParis.

SOCIAL CLASS (father's occupation)	% Sister Servants	% of total membership
I Owners of capital and land and upper professionals: landowner, proprietor, senior military, barrister, architect.	50%	26.0%
I/II Professional and intermediate: medics, clergy, bankers, professors, publishers.	20%	7.5%
I/II Combined	70%	34.0%
II Farmer, wholesaler, tradesman, teacher, civil servant, shop-keeper.	30%	56.0%
COUNTRY OF BIRTH	% Sister Servants	% total membership
France	16.6%	3.0%
England	29.2%	31.0%
Ireland	54.2%	60.0%
Elsewhere	0%	6.0%

4.7: SISTER SERVANTS IN BRITAIN BY CLASS AND NATIVITY 1884

Number = 21   not known = 1

Social class, 'respectability' and education combined with a flair for good management, and of course solid piety, was what the French superiors looked for in a Sister Servant. The only national presence that was carefully planned was French. Once they had placed two French Sister Servants in England and two in Ireland, entrusting Sister Chatelain in London and Sister de Virieu in Dublin with oversight in each island respectively, evidence suggests that Superiors General were less concerned about whether other Sister Servants were Irish, English or Scottish. What mattered was her ability to direct others, her education and general demeanour. Research has concluded that several significant congregations in Scotland excluded Irish women from leadership positions on the strong encouragement of the hierarchy there (and there has been a similar suggestion about one of the largest congregations working across Britain).[109] But the Company's French superiors appointed Irish Sister Servants to several of the community's flagship houses in England and Scotland in this period, including Anne Farrell in Smyllum and Mary Ann Costello, Sister Servant of the house in the parish of St James's Spanish Place in London's West End.

In Britain and Ireland, from 1855 to the end of the twentieth century there was slightly more than a one in five chance that a Sister would be appointed as Sister Servant at some point during her life, suggesting that there has generally been a regular rotation of Sister Servants.[110] But first-generation experience was distinctive and exceptional in this respect as in others. Satisfactory Sister Servants of this generation once appointed to a particular house were left in position for a long time, into old age and even to the moment of death. A number became something of a legend in their own lifetime. Anne Farrell was Sister Servant for 38 years at Smyllum; Ann Gunning had charge of the Manchester house in Ancoats for 40 years; Henriette Chatelain remained at Carlisle Place in Westminster for 42; Mary Ann Costello at Marylebone for 46; and Eleanor Maxwell reached a 'golden' 50 years at the Blind Institute in Liverpool. It seems these 'foundation stones' of the mission were left in place partly for pragmatic reasons, including their capacity to communicate in French with superiors in Paris, and partly because they symbolised stability. The fact that this was not always in the best interests of developing the work or the Sisters, or that the Sister concerned might have benefited from a change, seems to have been a lesser consideration.

Governance of the mission in Britain before 1884 was conducted through correspondence and by regular formal visitations by superiors. The organisation model was fairly 'flat', deploying an authority pattern of 'hub and spokes' with the mother house at the centre making the strategic decisions. Carlisle Place in Westminster, where Henriette Chatelain was Sister Servant, acted as an informal headquarters, reinforcing the French identity of the institution. Sister Servants communicated with officers in Paris whenever they wanted advice and received information and instructions by letter. Between 1870 and 1884 approximately 3300 letters were exchanged between the various houses in the United Kingdom and the mother house, almost all of them to and from Sister Servants.[111] All manner

---

109 Kehoe, *Creating a Scottish Church*, pp. 92-101 has found that the appointment of Irish women into leadership of women's congregations was avoided in Scotland because of ethnic antagonisms. The presence of Anne Farrell as the dynamic Irish Sister Servant at Smyllum Park Lanark, may be an exception to the norm described by Kehoe whereby religious communities in Scotland avoided the appointment of Irish sisters to leadership. But Farrell was not the only Irish Daughter to take a prominent role in Scotland. Kehoe cites Barbara Walsh's conclusion in relation to the Sisters of Notre Dame de Namur, that very few Irish sisters held leadership posts. Walsh, *Roman Catholics*, p. 143. See also Karly Kehoe, 'Border crossings: being Irish in nineteenth-century Scotland', in D.A.J. MacPherson, Mary J. Hickman eds., *Women and Irish Diaspora Identities: Theories, Concepts and new perspectives* (Manchester: Manchester University Press, 2014), pp. 152–167.

110 Of the 2810 sisters on the Provincial data base (which includes those who left after making vows), 611 had been Sister Servant at some point. The 1:5 ratio is calculated from these figures.

111 Number totalled from the entries in the Letter Book 1871–1929. Box 10 DCParis.

of topics were discussed, from the movement of Sisters between houses to arrangements for annual retreats; from new applications to condolences on the deaths of Sisters' close relatives and arrangements for the care of a Sister who was ill.[112] Disciplinary matters and tensions between Sisters and between a Sister Servant and local priests were also handled in this way.[113]

A system of annual house statistical reporting was used by the superiors to obtain key management information about the Sisters and about the financial state of each house. Meticulous record-keeping was given a very high priority: copies of contracts with bishops, priests and boards of management were made and stored in Paris. The Company's general council met weekly and its minutes recorded all decisions about strategic developments in different countries. The letter books maintained by Sisters in the secretariat noted operational details and decisions between Paris and Sister Servants in Britain and Ireland. The centrally held confidential record on each Sister gave instant access to the opinion of superiors about her spiritual and professional journey in the Company from postulancy to death, including her potential to be appointed as a Sister Servant. Visitations of the houses in Britain were made by appointed Sisters and Vincentian priests, including one made by Superior General Étienne in 1863 and another by his successor in 1875 when comments on each Sister and the general well-being of the community and its work were recorded.

Although their origins lay in pre-industrial society, these governance and administrative practices appeared essentially modern to a nineteenth-century progressive like Florence Nightingale. Writing in 1860 to Dr Balfour, the Secretary of the Royal Commission on Nursing, Nightingale conveyed something of her astonishment and admiration as one professionally minded woman observing the management practices of others:

> If anyone has ever been behind the scenes of the Maison Mère of the Sisters of Charity...and seen their Counting House and Office, all worked by women, an office which has twelve thousand officials (all women) scattered over the known world...an office to compare with which in business habits, I have never seen any, either Government or private, in England...they will think like me that it is this...power... which keeps these enormous orders going. [114]

The similarity with modern industrial production was what struck Etheldreda Howard who, wanting to capture the essence of the Paris seminary, described it in

---

112 Letter Book 1871–1929. Box X DC Paris.

113 Sister Elizabeth Crawford was exasperated by the interference of one of the Vincentian priests who had claimed that she opened the Sisters' letters to priests, which she strongly denied. Letter Book 1871–1929. Box X DC Paris.

114 Florence Nightingale letter to Dr Balfour, the Secretary of the Royal Commission on Nursing 12 July 1860 quoted in Richard Weallens, *The Passage: A History Part 1 1863–1913* (London: The Passage, 2005), p. 14

a letter home to her mother as 'a great manufactory of Sisters' in which 'characters are formed and reformed…through the same mould, just as a piece of clay is made into a china cup'.[115] Nightingale's and Howard's observations capture vital aspects of the management of the mission to the British Isles by the Paris superiors, indicating the particular characteristics of their approach to administrative systems and management. Through these means the mother house worked hard to convey its cultural norms and practices to the first generation. It was an intention it sought to preserve when the decision was made to create a Province of Great Britain in 1885, setting in motion a new era in the history of the Company's work in Britain and Ireland.

---

115 *Memoir of a Sister of Charity*, pp. 55–6.

A mission for Britain 1847-1884

Sisters from France

After the failure of the Company's first house in England (Salford 1847-1849) and the successful establishment of three houses in Ireland (1855-1857), the Paris superiors made a second attempt in England. They sent a small number of French Sisters to assist in the establishment and development of the mission to the United Kingdom in the nineteenth century.

Marie Henriette Chatelain 1823-1897 Born in Paris to a bourgeois family, orphaned as a girl and entered the Company in 1845, serving in France and then in the Crimean War before being sent to Sheffield in 1858 where she learned English. Her younger sister Gabrielle, another Daughter of Charity, was also sent to Britain where she was Sister Servant (Superior) in Salisbury.

Sister Chatelain was sent to Westminster in London in 1860 as Sister Servant, moving the small community twice before it settled in Carlisle Place, Westminster on land and property bought by Sister Catherine Eyston.

She worked closely with Dr (later Cardinal) Henry Manning who was a neighbour. When the Paris superiors recalled Sister Chatelain to France in 1880 Manning sent two priests to Paris with a letter pleading for a reversal of their decision: unusually they complied.

At Carlisle Place Henriette Chatelain oversaw a *misericorde* (a house of mercy) with a crèche for children of working mothers, a day school, girls' orphanage and training workshop for fine sewing, a soup kitchen and night schools for men. This house also acted as the proto-provincial house in the years before the Province of Britain and Ireland was erected (1885). It was busy with senior Sisters passing to and from France on their way to conduct visitations and with packages arriving from Paris containing items for the work of the Sisters.

A senior French Sister, Charlotte de Virieu, was appointed to the house in North William Street, Dublin, to play a similar role for the work in Ireland. Nine of the French Sisters who came to Britain and Ireland before 1885 lived and died on the mission.

Sisters from Ireland

In the period 1857-1924 Irish-born Sisters comprised just under sixty percent of the total number of those taking vows. A majority came from families who owned moderate sized farms.

Mary Anne Costello 1835-1917 was born in Dublin to a 'comfortable family' but orphaned at a young age. In 1856 all her brothers and sisters emigrated to the United States while she entered the Company, travelling to Paris for her formation.

Her first fifteen years were spent in a series of newly opened foundations as the mission took off: Dublin 1857-1864; St Mary's Lanark and Smyllum Park Orphanage, Lanark 1864-1867. Aged 32 she was made Sister Servant of another new foundation in Scotland in the mining district of Coatbridge. This foundation struggled with extreme poverty and was closed by the community in 1870. Sister Costello was sent to a new foundation in Marylebone in the West End of London. By her death in 1917 she was Sister Servant to 20 Sisters managing a crèche, a workroom to train young women, an orphanage, day schools, night schools and home visiting.

There are few photographs of the early Sisters and none of Sister Costello. This image is from a later prayer card produced by the Company.

Sarah, Honorah and Ann Byrne

Three Byrne sisters of Rathdrum Co. Wicklow – Sarah (b. 1835), Honorah (b. 1839) and Ann (b. 1844), the Sister Vincent whose gravestone is pictured) – became Sister-companions during the 1860s. Kinship ties between members of the Company were fairly extensive, particularly among Irish-born sisters. The Byrne sisters were representative of Irish members in coming from a family of modest independent farmers.

Between them they served in Sheffield, Dublin, Liverpool, Salisbury, and Darlington – Honorah as Sister Servant in Liverpool and Darlington. In the 1860s they were together in the same House.

Sisters from Britain

A striking number of British women who entered the Company in this mission period were from 'old' Catholic English families, including aristocratic and landed families. Only a very small number of women from Scotland and Wales entered in these decades.

BURNS & OATES, Limited
28 ORCHARD STREET, LONDON, W.

Mary Cecily Arundell 1845-1925 was born at Wardour Castle in Wiltshire and entered the Company in 1864. She was the daughter of William, 11th Baron Arundell of Wardour and his third wife Theresa Stourton, herself the daughter of a Catholic Baronet. Sister Arundell was placed first in St Mary's Lanark, Scotland. In 1887 she was placed in St Elizabeth's orphanage and small boarding-school in Bullingham, Hereford where she served as a teacher and parish visitor until her death in 1925.

Garden at Dover drawn by Sister Josephine Bullen (DC 1878-1924)

Mary Burns 1843-1912 was born in London to Scottish Presbyterian parents who were received into the Catholic Church with their five daughters in 1847. James Burns was a publisher. The firm he established later became a designated publisher to the Holy See. Mary was educated by Ursuline nuns in France. Her father strongly opposed her becoming a 'Sister of Charity' and made her wait until she was 20. After seminary in Paris she served in St John's Institute for deaf children in Boston Spa. In 1880 she was named Sister Servant of St Agnes' Poor Law School and Orphanage for boys at Leyton, an initiative of Cardinal Manning's. In 1887 she was transferred to Mill Hill where she became Bursar to the new Province and Sister Servant of St Vincent's Poor Law School and home for boys.

Frances Dunk 1835-1922 came from the village of Sellindge in Kent where her parents, William and Eliza, were publicans of the Duke's Head coaching inn on the road between Ashford and Folkestone. By 1861 her parents had sold their inn and become the owners of a 200-acre farm in Norton Priory in Kent. Frances entered the Company in 1856 and served in the House at Dover from 1857 to 1904 when she was moved to Boulogne where she remained until her death in 1922.

Administering the mission from France

Individual Sisters' records were kept at Paris. Her 'fiche' recorded a series of dates and places: birth; entry into the Company; the date of receiving the habit (*prise d'habit*); vows taken for the first time; Houses where she was placed. Also recorded are the judgements of superiors about her personal maturity, spiritual progress and aptitude for work. This particular record is for a Scottish Sister, Honora McGarry, who entered in 1867 and was described as a serious, hard-working and generous Sister. However, as time went on her sufferings with her chest are noted. With regret, her Sister Servant at Coatbridge, Lanark notes that the time has come for her to leave the community and in March 1878 she went back to her family.

Traité A contract was drawn up by the Company and had to be signed by any third parties involved (benefactor, priest, bishop, administrators) before Sisters could be sent to serve in a parish or institution. The terms of the contract were negotiable, but the template was one developed by the Company in the seventeenth century. It was specific: how many Sisters, what accommodation, who would pay the rates and utilities, the annual stipend for each Sister, arrangements for Mass and the Blessed Sacrament in the House and the procedures for terminating the contract.

The 'Traité' shown on the right is for the Sisters to take charge of the Liverpool Blind Asylum in 1871 and is made between the superiors in Paris and the Board of Administration.

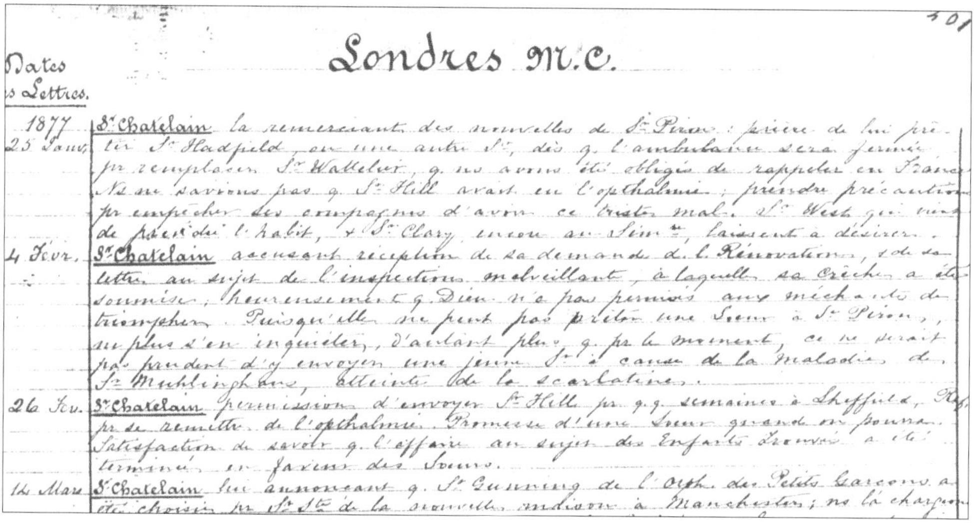

[Handwritten letter book page with entries dated 1877, including columns for "Dates des Lettres." and entries beginning "25 Janv.", "4 Fevr.", "26 Fev.", "12 Mar." referencing "S.r Chatelain" — text largely in cursive French script]

Communication

Before the Province of Great Britain and Ireland was erected the oversight and discipline of each House lay between superiors in Paris and the local Sister Servant.

Above is a page from the United Kingdom letter book maintained by the Paris secretariat. It contains a summary of the approximately 3,300 letters sent by Sister Servants in Britain and Ireland in the period 1870 to 1884.

Illustrated is a part of one page for Carlisle Place in 1877 (M.C. = Maison de Charité)

Training and formation

Seminary Sisters doing the laundry in the courtyard of the Maison Mère rue du Bac, Paris.

Seminary formation for Sisters from the British Isles took place in Paris until 1885. In the seminary, Sisters had lectures; studied the Rule and St Vincent's conferences; practised the Company's prayer life; undertook hard physical labour; developed sewing and laundering skills and 'recreated' – which was also a formation in behaviour. Some French lessons were provided, but many of the Sisters had to rely on translation provided by British and Irish Sisters

who could already speak French. The Sister would receive the habit before being sent to one of the foundations of the British mission. Her nine months in Paris meant that she brought back an experience of 'how things were done in the Maison Mère'.

Early houses and works: visiting and welfare

Solly Street, Sheffield
The Sisters' first permanent house in Britain (1857). The community lived in the top two floors of this terraced house in the White Croft district, working alongside Vincentian confrères who served St Vincent's chapel. Their initial work was poor relief and visiting among the local predominantly Irish community. Sodalities and evening classes were established.

Carlisle Place, London The earliest part of the building, to the right of the tower, was built in 1863, the tower in 1877, and the extension to the left in 1909. The House is adjacent to the site where Westminster Cathedral was later built in the 1890s.

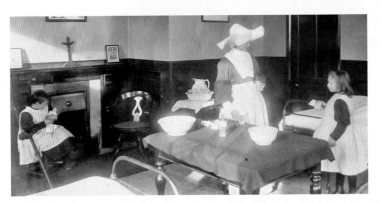

St Joseph's Howard Hill, Sheffield: a Reformatory for girls (opened 1861) which in 1887 became an Industrial School for girls who came through the courts and were regarded as vulnerable.

Disability care: a specialism emerges

Liverpool Blind Asylum founded by Reverend Dr Youens in 1841, was funded initially by subscription and run by a diocesan Board of Administration. In 1871 the Administrators asked the Daughters to take over running the home. This photograph from the 1880s is the earliest extant and shows the child and adult female residents. Several older girls are wearing their Children of Mary Immaculate ribbon and medal.

St John's Catholic Institute for the Deaf later known as 'Boston Spa' in the deaf community because of its location in Boston Spa, West Yorkshire. Founded in 1870 by Belgian priest and deaf educationalist, Monsignor de Haerne who noticed there was no Catholic provision in Britain. In 1871 the Daughters agreed to run the Institute and did so until they withdrew in 1989. The tradition continues at St John's Catholic School for the Deaf, a specialist day and boarding school funded by the state for hearing impaired pupils aged 3-19.

Healthcare and nursing

St Mary's Hospital, Lanark, Scotland

The poverty of the Catholic community in Britain combined with other factors made it difficult for the Sisters to develop hospital work. In Lanark, however, local circumstances enabled them to open their first hospital and pharmacy in Britain.

Wealthy benefactors (Messrs Bowie and Monteith) built the new church of St Mary's and in 1859 they succeeded in bringing the Vincentians to take charge of the parish. These benefactors invited the Sisters to Lanark in 1860 for parish visiting and teaching. In 1872 Sister Alice Blundell, appointed Sister Servant, received permission to use her private wealth to build a new hospital (glimpsed left of photograph).

Italian Hospital, Queen's Square, London was founded in 1884 by an Italian businessman, Commendatore Giovanni Battista (John) Ortelli, in response to the language difficulties faced by his compatriots in London hospitals. He donated two houses in Queen's Square, later demolished to make way for this modern hospital building. The Daughters were invited by Ortelli and the lay Board of Administration to take on the nursing and domestic provision of the hospital, with a particular request that they provide Italian-speaking Sisters. By 1901 there were 52 beds and an operating theatre managed by 9 Sisters, including 3 from Italy.

At the end of 1884, just before the Province was founded, there were 21 foundations in Britain and 4 in Ireland managed by 290 Sisters.

5

Founding a province of the islands

> About this time [1884] the Superiors were contemplating establishing
> the British Province, although there were only about thirty [sic] Houses
> in Great Britain; they hoped this measure would increase the number of
> Vocations and develop the works.'[1]
>
> (Sister Marcellus)

The creation of a British and Irish Province in 1885 was a watershed event in the development of the Company's mission to the two islands. It achieved the general council's aim of encouraging more women from Britain and Ireland to enter, mainly because the provincial seminary replaced the Paris seminary as the location for the greater part of a Sister's formation. As a result, expansion was the most obvious feature of the community's history in the ten years after the erection of the Province. But the administrative changes that accompanied this new status were also of great importance for the new bonds of community and identity they created between the Sisters of Britain and Ireland. In the provincial seminary, Sisters forged bonds with their own seminary directress and officers as well as with one another. The houses of Britain and Ireland were now overseen by provincial officers rather than by officers from Paris and it was the former who conducted house visitations. Sister Servants became responsible to the visitatrice as their provincial officer. Retreats were held at the *maison central* (as the provincial headquarters were known) or in another large house of the Province, with companions from Britain and Ireland, rather than in Paris with Sisters from all over France. Taking all these measures into account, it is easy to see how the provincial officers became a shared focal point and why ties between Sisters of the Province strengthened. At the same time, the bond of unity between the Province and the mother house remained vital to all members. New members were still to be formed as 'true' Daughters of Charity, always conscious of the rue du Bac as their mother house. It was the role of Sister Servants working closely with the visitatrice and provincial officers to transmit the spirit and traditions of the Company, inculcate the disciplines of the mother house and develop in every Sister an appreciation that she was part of the larger transnational Company community.

---

1 *Memoir of Ma Soeur Marcellus* (privately printed, Mill Hill, 1928), p. 24. 2-1-7 DCMH

In one of the few studies of women's religious institutes as transnational communities, Gertrud Hüwelmeier has noted that 'we still know little about the transformations and discourses within religious communities and the maintenance of their social and political ties with branches, houses and sub-groups in other parts of the world'. She advocated further research into the 'strategies of religious women as female actors in transnational activities'.[2] This chapter and the next are concerned with the strategies that the Company's senior officers deployed to maintain ties and to support a shared identity across the community's global operations. In the terms developed by historians of transnational movements and organisations, the Company's structures were designed to enhance 'ways of belonging' and its practices framed to encourage particular 'ways of being'.[3] It was intended that individual women who entered the Company would experience a transformation of identity through a wide range of practices from daily rituals and common symbols to the exchange of goods, news and prayer.[4] It was further intended that a Daughter in Newcastle and another in Ningbo in China would not only look the same and undertake similar ministries within an identically structured day, but also that each would be aware of the other and conscious that their endeavours were part of one divinely inspired mission under God's Providence.[5] Membership in real communities at local and regional level and participation in the 'imagined community' of the global Company became part of every Daughter's identity.[6] Because of this her outlook and experience was broadened in some aspects even as it was circumscribed in other ways.

Provincial governance

The nature of provincial authority and the way it was exercised in the Company are good starting points for exploring the issues identified by Hüwelmeier. Over time, was provinces have become normative in those Catholic religious orders and institutes, male and female, whose work crosses boundaries of diocese, region and nation. In general they have proved effective as a way to divide members into manageable territorial units while uniting them to one another through a

---

2 Gertrud Hüwelmeier, 'Women's Congregations as Transnational Communities.' Paper presented at the 6th EASA conference in Kracow, July, 2000. See also Carmen M. Mangion, 'Filles de la charité et sourds-muets: une histoire transnationale (1869-1901)', in Brejon de Lavergnée (ed.), *Quatre siécles de cornettes, pp. 291–307.*.

3 Transnational scholars whose work has influenced the approach taken here include Thomas Faist, Peter Haas and Peggy Levitt.

4 See Peggy Levitt, 'Redefining the Boundaries of Belonging: The Institutional Character of Transnational Religious Life', *Sociology of Religion*, Vol. 65, No.1 (2004).

5 See, for example, Marcellus Circular Letter with 'an extract from a letter of one of our English sisters in China, written in Ning-po' encouraging them to set up the Association of the Holy Childhood where they work. 9-2 DCMH. Also M. L. H., *Sister Xavier Berkeley.*

6 Benedict Anderson, *Imagined Communities: Reflections on the Origin and Spread of Nationalism* (London, Verso, 1991).

chain of authority between provincial and superiors general.[7] Dominican and Franciscan friars devised the model in the thirteenth century as they spread from one district and country to another. From the sixteenth century onwards the model was adopted by new apostolic men's religious orders and congregations such as the Society of Jesus or the Congregation of the Mission and adapted to their more hierarchical and centralised exercise of authority.[8] Neither the structure nor its impact was uniform. For example, the degree of autonomy and responsibility delegated to provinces varied between institutes, as did the extent of the participation from provinces in governance through general chapters.[9] What was consistent and shared, however, was the concern for the operation of authority across borders and for unity between all members.

The Company was one of the first female Catholic communities to develop such structures, inaugurated under Superior General Bonnet in 1712. With few exceptions, institutes of women religious did not develop provincial structures until the nineteenth century. When religious sisters in the new active congregations initially attempted to follow the lead of male orders and move in this direction, they often encountered episcopal opposition. Their difficulties have been explained by reference to the 'power struggle between the Curia and the dioceses', which 'to a large extent took place on the backs of the religious institutes'.[10] In her study of authority in women's religious congregations, Elizabeth Cotter observes that not only were 'all women's congregations subject to the local bishop except in matters for which they had exemption' but also this was to a much greater degree than male institutes.[11] Papal exemption had to be granted and the process was often contested by bishops. Disputes over authority between two sets of clergy – diocesan and Roman curial – necessarily involved women religious in gender politics and gender power relations, the histories of which have been told only recently.[12] By the later nineteenth century, however, the generalate-provincialate model had won the day over local arrangements, not least because curial officials found that it reduced their administrative burdens at a time of exponential

---

7 There were exceptions, and because authority was over personnel rather than territory, this was not anomalous.

8 Elizabeth Cotter, *The General Chapter in a Religious Institute* (Oxford and Bern, Peter Lang, 2008), p. 22 and p. 52. See more generally Cotter's thorough examination of canonical and theological concepts of power and authority in institutes of consecrated life.

9 John Rybolt, *The Vincentians, Vol. 3*, p. 361.

10 The Dominican order with its representative general chapter was more collegial than Vincent de Paul's Congregation of the Mission, which invested more in the dominative authority (by virtue of office) of its superiors. See Jan de Maeyer *et al., Religious Institutes in Western Europe*, p. 24.

11 Cotter, *General Chapter,* p. 51.

12 See Mangion, *Contested Identities*, ch. 8; Mary Wright, *Mary Ward's Institute: The Struggle for Identity* (Sydney, Crossing Press, 1997). See also the struggle over the role of the mother house in the history of the Congregation of Our Lady of Charity of the Good Shepherd of Angers in which the foundress lost to bishops who wished the Good Shepherd nuns to have novitiates outside of France. A. M. Clarke, *Life of Reverend Mother Mary of St Euphrasie Pelletier* (London, Burns and Oates, 1895), p.185.

expansion in women's apostolic religious life.[13] The establishment of a separate Sacred Congregation of Religious in the Curia, in 1908, increased pressures in favour of the erection of general-provincial structures and the amalgamation of smaller autonomous institutes in the interests of higher standards of formation, rationalisation and uniformity.[14]

What took place in the nineteenth-century Company of the Daughters was a fusion of these general Church trends with its own earlier and distinctive history. From the late seventeenth century, in a proto-provincial development, Sister Servants had been appointed to oversee a cluster of houses in a particular district. At the same time senior priests of the Congregation of the Mission had been given canonical and clerical responsibilities as directors for Daughters' houses at a distance, for example in Poland.[15] A more formal provincial structure developed out of these two practices. In 1712 the Company's activities and members were divided into 14 provinces, each co-led by a director and a Sister who was given the title 'visitatrix' (known as 'visitatrice' in Britain and Ireland and hereafter).[16] This title reflected the fact that the visitatrice discharged her responsibilities for maintaining the Company's spirit in her area primarily through the conduct of regular visitations of each foundation. Appointed rather than elected, she derived her authority by delegation from superiors general and exercised it according to statutes.[17] Every six years the visitatrices of the different provinces met in general assembly with the general councillors to discuss the needs of the whole Company and to draw up any new regulations and directions.

For his part, the director of the Province, who was always a priest of the Congregation of the Mission, was appointed by the Superior General of the Congregation of the Mission, (the Superior General of the Company) to conduct canonical visitations of the Daughters' foundations. Because of this delegated responsibility, as we have seen, the Company had 'exempted status' in canon law; that is, each house was exempted from the normal requirement for visitation by the local bishop. The director reported his findings directly to the superior general who, in turn, was responsible to the pope of the day for canonical oversight of the Company. It became established practice for the superior general to appoint senior and capable Vincentians as directors.[18] Guidance was drawn up about the

---

13 Jan de Maeyer, *Religious Institutes*, p. 22. See also R. MacGinley, *Dynamic of Hope*, p. 277 and Cotter, *The General Chapter*, p. 32.

14 R. MacGinley, *Dynamic of Hope*, pp. 276-277 for a good summary of the legislative changes. See Anselm Nye for a detailed discussion of the application of the process to the English Dominican Sisters, *A Peculiar Kind of Mission*, ch. 5.

15 B. Martinez, 'Specific Contribution of St. Vincent and St. Louise to the Identity and Spirituality of the Daughters of Charity', *Vincentiana*, July–October 2001, 45, pp. 292-3.

16 The term 'visitatrix' was used in France but in Britain 'visitatrice' was preferred. Visitatrice was replaced by the term 'Provincial' in 1970.

17 Brejon de Lavergnée, *Histoire des Filles*, pp. 254.

18 ibid., pp. 248-9.

manner of conducting their visitations[19] and during the eighteenth century the overall structure of provinces, offices and delegated procedures had become well established before it was totally disrupted by the French Revolution.

After the Company was restored in 1801 it did not reinstate provincial governance. Experience of disunity and division in both parts of the double family encouraged a concentration of authority at the level of the general council in Paris. Such trends were taken to a new level by the centralising preferences of Superior General Jean-Baptiste Étienne (1843-1876).[20] As a consequence there was no formal provincial administration at all in the Company of the Daughters between 1801 and 1876. Instead, with a few exceptions, such as in the United States, the increasingly global operation of the double family was managed from the centre.[21] As Étienne saw it:

> The multiplicity of houses springing up on all points of the globe imperiously demands incessant vigilance ... in order to preserve the unity of the spirit, to assure the success of the works, to perpetuate the graces of vocation, and to realise the marvellous destiny of the Company.[22]

It was only after his death in 1876 that the Company re-established European provinces, beginning with France, Belgium and Switzerland. Their council memberships mirrored the general council: visitatrice, director, assistant to the visitatrice and provincial bursar (*économe*). Sister-officers lived together in a Central House where the seminary was also located. The seminary directress, although not a member of the council, was an influential office holder regularly consulted on matters concerning the Sisters.

The distinctive role of the director

Although provincial councils were to be found across many nineteenth-century female congregations, the Vincentian director's role, with its blend of canonical visitation, spiritual animation and internal decision-making responsibilities put 'the Company in a unique situation' among religious communities of women.[23] The origins of the office of director, as we saw in Chapter 2, lay with Louise de Marillac. Benito Martinez has argued that Louise worked persistently to achieve a form of governance closest to her unrealised vision for a single mixed institution of

---

19 *Genesis of the Company*, p. 52. 1-7-2 DCMH.

20 Rybolt, *History of the Vincentians*, Vol 3, p. 387.

21 John E. Rybolt, *The Vincentians: Expansion and Reactions*, Vol 4, pp. 47-52.

22 *Genesis of the Company*, p. 80. 1-7-2 DCMH.

23 F. Quintano, [Director General of the Daughters of Charity] 'Mission and Charity,' in *Vincentiana*, 45 (July–October 2001), p. 236 and B. Martinez, 'Specific Contributions of St. Vincent and St. Louise to the Identity and Spirituality of the Daughters of Charity,' pp. 292–7 in the same volume.

confrères and *filles*.[24] She persuaded Vincent de Paul to institute the role of director and ensured that holders of the office had to be Vincentian priests so as to protect the Company's spiritual integrity and safeguard it from episcopal control. In Louise's view, it 'would be better that the Company disappear completely rather than be under another direction'.[25]

Just how the role of provincial director was put into practice between the 1870s and the 1970s is a little-explored subject in Vincentian histories. It has recently been described by Daniel Hannefin DC, in her history of the American Daughters of Charity, as being 'advisory' and confined to principles, canon law and spiritual guidance.[26] Hannefin makes the point that when the Elizabeth Ann Seton Sisters of Charity of Emmitsburg affiliated to the Company in 1850, the appointment of a Vincentian provincial director gave them a 'greater voice in their own destiny' because for some time they had had priest-superiors whose ill-defined role boundaries and tendency to intrude made for difficulties.[27] The experience of the American Sisters of Charity at this time (for example in New York),[28] suggests that the appointment of a Vincentian director brought them relief from overbearing priestly interference. In addition to sharing a history and spiritual tradition with their new directors, they appreciated the checks and balances built into Vincentian structures. Even so, there is reason to believe that the approach of directors could be more instrumental and less consultative in the management of a province than this one example implies.[29] That was certainly the case with one or two of the directors in the British Province in the period before the renewal of the second Vatican council. At the very least, we need to be attentive to what it might mean for the Sister-officers always to conduct provincial business in the presence of a priest-director. There was no exact definition of the role and no training for it: the way it was carried out inevitably varied according to the personalities of the visitatrice and director. Equally inevitably, conduct was influenced by contemporary thinking about the roles of men and women and by the hierarchy that was deeply embedded in clerical-lay relationships. It was the director, for example, who signed off the minutes of each council meeting. His annual report on the health of the Province was sent to the superior general unseen by the visitatrice. Whereas before the establishment of the Province Sister Servants had negotiated directly with diocesan

---

24 B. Martinez, 'Specific Contribution', p. 296.

25 Quintano, 'Mission and Charity', p. 229.

26 Hannefin, *Daughters of the Church,*, p. 93.

27 ibid. See also Betty A. McNeil, 'The Sulpicians and the Sisters of Charity: Concentric Circles of Mission', *VHJ*, (1999), Vol. 20, issue 1, article 2.

28 See Maureen Fitzgerald, *Habits of Compassion*, pp. 44ff on the activities of Archbishop John Hughes of New York to manage the Sisters of Charity of New York.

29 Florence Nightingale, for one, judged the role of the Vincentians in the management of the Sisters' affairs to be intolerably interfering by her own benchmark of female autonomy. See Lynn McDonald (ed.), *Florence Nightingale – European Travels v.7, The Collected Works of Florence Nightingale* (Waterloo, Ontario, Wilfrid Laurier University Press, 2004), p. 755.

and religious clergy, after 1885 the director became the intermediary.[30] This change seems to have increased the Province's negotiating power even as it reduced that of individual Sister-officers. The evidence suggests that the Daughters experienced fewer direct conflicts with clergy than many other women's congregations and that any difficulties, for example, over money, buildings or authority, were resolved more quickly by the director.[31] Even allowing for the possible tensions between diocesan clergy and the Vincentian directors as regular clergy, priests seem to have been more comfortable doing business with another cleric than with women.[32] When the Company's practice was exempted from the new canonical legislation of 1901, which prohibited clergy from membership of the councils of women's congregations, the singular nature of clerical involvement in the Company and its particular pattern of co-working with the Congregation of the Mission was confirmed.[33]

Questions of unity and diversity

The introduction of general and provincial councils in Catholic women's religious orders and congregations in the nineteenth century has usually been seen as bringing about increased self-governance.[34] While this was the case, it was also true that in a number of congregations an increasingly hierarchical approach developed alongside the new structures. In her history of the Society of the Religious of the Sacred Heart, Margaret Williams noted how the Society developed a 'rigidity of government along vertical lines' in the second half of the nineteenth century.[35] She identifies the origins of rigidity in concerns for unity that were 'solved' by an insistence on uniformity, a conclusion that could equally be applied to the Company of the Daughters of Charity. In the Society of the Sacred Heart, this meant that 'a centrifugal force ... from the life of the mother house was felt to the fringes of the Society.'[36] According to Jan de Maeyer these tendencies were fairly widespread even before the promulgation of the 1917 Code of Canon Law, but were strengthened by it.[37]

---

30 Letters from Byrne to Mgr Ritchie of Glasgow, January 1922, 11-44 -2 1-1 #28a DCMH.

31 Some examples are explored in later chapters. This judgement about conflicts is made in the light of my archival research in a dozen religious institutes.

32 In a number of places (e.g. Darlington), a strong working bond already existed between the Sister Servant and a local priest, and this continued.

33 Cotter, *General Chapter*, p. 61.

34 This is the position adopted, for example, by Wright, *Mary Ward's Institute* and O'Brien, 'The New Orders', in S. Gilley and B. Stanley (eds.), *World Christianities*, Vol. 8. *Cambridge History of Christianity* (Cambridge, Cambridge University Press, 2006), and is implicit in many studies.

35 Margaret Williams, *The Society of the Sacred Heart: History of a Spirit 1800-1975* (London, Catholic Book Club, 1978), pp.117–18.

36 Williams, *Society of the Sacred Heart*, p.118.

37 Jan de Maeyer, *Religious Institutes*, p. 22.

The Company's own extensive efforts to sustain uniformity were a response to concern at the centre about the potential for divergence once a province evolved. The example of the Spanish Province, where leaders were thought to have led the Sisters astray from 'obedience and uniformity' (including the wearing of a different style of cornette), was a sensitive point in the Company and often cited to stress the importance of conformity.[38] Anxiety of this kind underlay Sister Charlotte de Virieu's response to the very news that a province was to be established for Britain and Ireland. Known for rigorous control of her emotions, de Virieu, the Company's most senior Sister in Ireland, is said to have experienced 'an extreme repugnance' because of her fear that 'it would tend to separate them from the mother house and major Superiors'.[39] She, like many Sisters, and the Company's leaders themselves at this time and for long after, tended to conflate the essential spirit of the Daughters of Charity with its 'Frenchness'. French civil legislation reinforced this way of thinking. By 1880 the Company had more houses outside than inside France.[40] However, the state defined the Company as a French institution and successive French governments 'would never allow a non-French citizen to govern the Congregation of the Mission and the Daughters of Charity'.[41].

Deciding on a British Province

In response to two pressing concerns – how to manage its globalised mission and how to safeguard its survival from the growing threat coming from political secularisation in France after 1880 – the Company established a significant number of provinces towards the end of the nineteenth century. By the eve of the First World War, 41 provinces had been created.[42] Even so, there was nothing inevitable about adding the United Kingdom of Britain and Ireland to the list in 1885.[43] Nor was there any uniform pattern for provinces followed by other Francophone institutes working in Britain and Ireland. The Sisters of Notre Dame de Namur continued to send novices to Belgium until the outbreak of World War I. After the war, because of the requirement of the 1917 Code of Canon Law, they opened a

---

38 Rybolt, *History of the Vincentians, Vol. 4*, p. 286. It should be noted that the variation in religious habit among the Spanish Sisters was a source of continual concern to the general superiors. It was not resolved until the new habit was introduced in 1964 and was, indeed, an important motivation for its introduction.

39 *Pioneer Sisters*, p. 9.

40 *Genesis of the Company*, p.105. 1-7-2 DCMH.

41 Rybolt, *History of the Vincentians, Vol 3*, p. 317. When the American, Father William Slattery, was elected as general superior in 1947, the first not to be a French citizen by birth, the Congregation's procurator general pleaded with him to renounce his US citizenship and take out French citizenship 'to save the Congregation', and he did so. Zimmerman, 'Recollections of Father Slattery', p. 53. Legal changes were then made to bring this stipulation to an end. The current (2016) Superioress General of the Company, Kathleen Appler, is American.

42 *ibid.*, p. 92 and p. 98.

43 For example, as soon as Ann Seton's Sisters of Charity affiliated with the Company in 1850 they were formed into the province of the United States. Distance, size and history ruled out any other practical form of governance.

British novitiate in Sussex in 1920 but continued without provincial governance.[44] The Religious of the Sacred Heart created a vicariate of England and Ireland as early as 1858 when there were only five houses across both islands, but this was an administrative device. Sacred Heart novices from Britain and Ireland continued to travel to Conflans for formation and the vicariate did not have its own leadership. In 1918 when there was a reform and provinces with leaders were created, the Society 'put the Celts together' in a Province of Ireland and Scotland.[45]

The Company's superiors regarded the number of foundations and Sisters in Britain and Ireland as small enough to be managed from Paris. This protective position contrasted starkly with the position adopted in relation to the much smaller and more fragile community of priests and brothers in Ireland, which affiliated to the Congregation of the Mission in 1839 and was given provincial status in 1848.[46] Senior French Sisters regularly visited Britain and Ireland on behalf of the superiors. Marie Rouy, for example, visited seventeen houses between September and December 1880 and a further seven in 1881, spending up to three days with each community and interviewing all the Sisters privately. She left every community with a set of tailored notes listing the disciplines that would improve fidelity to the Company's spirit. Her reports to the mother house detailed the physical health, personal disposition and spiritual state of every Sister.[47] Ease of travel and regular communication between the United Kingdom and northern France, combined with a concern about the corrupting influences abroad in Protestant Britain, predisposed the Company's superiors towards maintaining direct oversight. It was the level of difficulty experienced in recruiting and retaining members in the United Kingdom that brought about a change of thinking.

In the early 1850s the Company's superiors had made some optimistic assumptions about the ease with which British and Irish women would adapt to French culture and become an extension of the French mission. 'Young ladies because they are entering a French community', stated their first prospectus for Ireland, 'have to learn the French language':

> It is part of the plan that once their vocation has been approved, they will spend a certain time in France living in one of the communities of the Daughters of Charity. In this way, they will be admirably prepared for their high vocation, speaking the two languages most widespread throughout the world.[48]

In reality, transnational institution building proved to be rather more difficult.

44 *Jubilee: Sisters of Notre Dame de Namur Celebrate 150 Years in Britain, 1845-1995* (privately printed), p. 63.

45 Williams, *History of a Spirit*, p. 208.

46 Rybolt, *History of the Vincentians, Vol 4*, pp. 465-489.

47 Boston Spa. Hardback notebook of visitations 1880-1992. 11-78-2 DCMH and Box 03 529/1 DCParis.

48 Prospectus for a missionary convent in Ireland 1852, 529, Letters, Great Britain, DCParis.

Either because the teaching was inadequate or because they found it difficult to learn in the time available, the French language was a stumbling block for many British and Irish Sisters in the seminary, a situation that gave rise to poor communication between them and the seminary directresses. Sister Alix Merceret, assistant to the superioress general, was unusually frank about the poor formation that resulted. Of French parentage but brought up in America, Merceret was a regular visitor to England. She got to know some of the Sister Servants in Britain and to sympathise with their problems. Writing to Sister Rose Austen in Liverpool about a problem of 'discontent' with a particular Sister, Merceret exasperatedly commented that vocational difficulties were happening too often among the British Sisters. In her view the problems began in the seminary because of how 'little the Directresses seem to know them'.[49]

The language barrier reduced opportunities for the serious process of personal transformation that was required to make a solid beginning in a vocation, particularly in a situation where there were so many Sisters in training at once. Etheldreda Howard, who was fluent in French and an experienced traveller, commented on the disorientation experienced by many Sisters from the United Kingdom who, like herself, felt themselves to be 'a mere unit in a crowd'. The seminary, with its new routines and its food that was 'strange and unpalatable to English tastes' was like 'a bed of nettles, where everything seemed to prick'.[50] Howard appreciated that the seminary was not intended to be a bed of roses, and she always loved to return to the mother house,[51] but it proved too demanding for some. Others felt its often ill-explained disciplines were an inadequate preparation for the tough realities of the mission in Britain.[52] Florence Nightingale, who visited the mother house in the 1850s, was highly critical of the seminary 'where they learn nothing but how to peel carrots and blind, not intelligent, obedience, which is worth nothing'.[53] Half of those accepted for the seminary between 1866 and 1885 – that is, after the initial sifting and the three-month postulancy – did not persist and 'too many'Young Sisters (in their first three or four years) were dismissed or left.[54] Historians have found similar rates of withdrawal in other communities in England at this time (which occurred in part because of the lack of cultural familiarity with religious life), but such a rate of loss fell outside the Company's own experience and was seen as too high.[55]

---

49 Letter dated 9 March 1875, Series 2 V D/17 LAA.

50 *Memoir of a Sister of Charity*, p. 35. 2-1-8 DCMH.

51 See, for example, Mary Ann Costello who entered in 1858 who 'on returning from Paris after a retreat shared with us the happiness which had been hers...' *Notices of Deceased Sisters* (1919), p. 64. 10-3-1 DCMH.

52 See Letter Book, British Province Box 10 DCParis.

53 McDonald (ed.), *Florence Nightingale – European Travels v.7*, p. 750.

54 Discussed in Chapter 4. 'Information about Sisters 1866-1889'. Box X DCParis.

55 See, for example, Nye, *A Peculiar Mission*, pp. 86 and 98.

By the early 1880s unease about the number leaving had grown. Vincentian priests working in Scotland and England argued that more suitable formation and better support for Young Sisters in their early placements could be given locally through a provincial seminary and provincial administration.[56] They stressed, moreover, that recruitment would increase because aspirants would not have to be assessed and trained in Paris – or in French.[57] Subsequent events bore out these claims. In the four years before the Mill Hill seminary opened a total of 66 women from Britain and Ireland entered the Paris seminary. In the four years after 1885 the number doubled exactly to 132.[58] Tellingly, the proportion who entered and stayed for life in the two decades after the establishment of the Province was more than double that of the two decades before.[59] But this is to get ahead of the story of what was involved in establishing the Province.

Locating Central House

The search for a suitable property and location for a Central House began in the autumn of 1883.[60] Several individuals acted on behalf of the general council: Sister Stephanie Crawford of Sheffield, Sister Henriette Chatelain of London and Father Battembourg, procurator general of the Congregation of the Mission, 'whose duties on behalf of the Community often brought him to England'.[61] The Company agreed to advance a loan for the purchase and the Sheffield solicitor W. Hadfield, uncle of Sisters Mary and Frances Hadfield, was commissioned to act for the Sisters. The ideal property had to be large enough to accommodate the seminary as well as the administration, with land for expansion and the potential to create a garden and walkways for the benefit of Sisters on retreat or recuperating from illness. There would need to be a chapel capable of accommodating a large gathering and space for a community cemetery in which some of the Sisters would be buried.[62] Ideally the provincial director would live nearby with a small community of *confrères* in a house that was clearly separate from the Central House environs.

Provincial houses had purposes and carried meanings that went beyond the functional. According to Carmen Mangion, this was a 'geographic space ... symbolic of the beginning and end of religious life', which held a 'special resonance' for

---

56 'Fr Michael Gleeson CM 1826-1889,' *Colloque* No. 3 (Autumn, 1980), p. 73.

57 'About this time the Superiors were contemplating establishing the British Province, although there were only about thirty Houses in Great Britain; they hoped this measure would increase the number of Vocations and develop the works.' *Memoir of Ma Soeur Marcellus* (privately printed, Mill Hill, 1928), p. 24. 2-1-7 DCMH.

58 Calculated from the Province database.

59 In 1870-1879 there were 97 Sisters who did so; in 1890-1899 there were 217.

60 General Council Minutes, Book 32, p. 979. See Minute for 26 September 1883 and note inserted. DCParis.

61 Typescript history 1940, Provincial House, 11-100, 12A DCMH. Battembourg is referred to in the General Council Minutes for 1884 and 1885, DCParis.

62 It was usual for Sisters to be buried in the parish church of the place where they were serving when they died.

women religious as 'their alma mater'.[63] Even though the Company steadfastly resisted the culture of stability associated with monastic life, and although it always promoted the rue du Bac as the heart of the community, it was anticipated that Central House would become hallowed for the Sisters of the Province. Its location was a matter for careful consideration. Two possibilities were considered and rejected. A house offered for sale at Victoria Park in Manchester by the Good Shepherd nuns came to their notice via the bishop of Salford but was judged by Elizabeth Crawford to be too small and the area too unhealthy for Sisters in formation.[64] Fallow Lodge at Fallow Corner in Finchley, Middlesex was given serious consideration, but at £15,000 it was more than they could afford and was not thought to be good value for money.[65] In June 1884 Henriette Chatelain suggested a house and estate known as 'Littleberries', located at the Ridgeway in Mill Hill, Middlesex, about ten miles north-west of central London, which was on the market.[66]

The Ridgeway was an ancient route that had become increasingly important for those travelling north out of London. A number of large houses and estates had been laid out there during the second half of the seventeenth century by wealthy London merchants who wanted a country house not too far from their London businesses. In the early nineteenth century two of these estate houses were turned into institutions: Mill Hill School for the sons of dissenting clergy and merchants was founded at Ridgeway House, and St Joseph's Missionary College, the first Catholic missionary training centre in Britain, was opened in 1866 at Holcombe House by Father Herbert Vaughan. By 1885 St Joseph's had moved into new purpose-built buildings nearby. Holcombe House had been transferred to a congregation of Franciscan nuns brought there by Vaughan and re-named St Mary's Abbey. Adding further to the Catholic character of the district, the college's new church had been dedicated as the national shrine of St Joseph. A 14-foot copper-gilt statue of the patron saint surmounting the 100-foot tower in the grounds could be seen from some distance, rising above the woods in an apparent gesture of blessing. It seemed a good sign.

Superioress General Marie Dérieux, assistant Alix Merceret and the Company's bursar, Eugénie Marcellus, visited Littleberries towards the end of 1884.[67] They agreed that 263,189 francs (approximately £10,000) was a good price for the size of the property and its good location.[68] Littleberries had thirty-nine acres of farmland and was situated at the crest of a hill with fine views over the countryside to

---

63 Mangion, *Contested Identities*, p.157.

64 Letter book, Great Britain, p. 239, Box X, DCParis and General Council Minutes, 13 February 1884, 979 Book 32 DCParis. This property was later bought by the Province for an industrial school.

65 General Council Minutes, Book 32, 20 March 1884, 979 DCParis.

66 ibid., 25 June 1884, 979 and Book 33, 26 November 1884, DCParis.

67 *Memoir of Ma Soeur Marcellus*, p. 24 and General Council Minutes, Book 32, 979, 22 June and 25 DCParis.

68 Cost in pounds sterling given in *The Tablet*, 4 July 1885, p. 26.

Totteridge.[69] It was a wholesome location for seminary Sisters. The original house, modest in size, had been extended and modernised by previous owners with the addition of Gothic lodges, two wings and an upper storey. Pleasure gardens behind the house included ornamental fish ponds, walks, gardens, monkey-puzzle trees, and three descending grass terraces that provided a commanding vista to a summer house in the form of a small Ionic temple, and then to rolling hills beyond. There was a distinction to the gardens and main house, with its projecting rear pavilion, that the Company's superiors were not afraid to embrace.[70]

But it was strategic rather than aesthetic considerations that had influenced the decision to locate the new Central House in this particular part of the British Isles. In principle the Company's superiors had a choice between Ireland, birthplace of more than half the Province's Sisters to date, and England, location of the majority of their United Kingdom foundations. There are no indications that Ireland was ever considered but clear reasons were articulated for the choice of England. Senior members of the Company believed England to be 'clearly destined' to resume its 'place ... in the bosom of the Church of Christ' if vigorous Catholics such as themselves played their part.[71] A more Catholic England was a worthy goal in its own right, but would be even more of a prize given metropolitan Britain's large influence in the world.[72] If there was something to be said in evangelical terms for a location in England there was much to be said for it in ecclesial terms because of the positive welcome of the English bishops.[73] There was a particularly strong case for locating in the Archdiocese of Westminster. The community already had four foundations there, including two of its largest *misericordes*, with their multiple welfare works and outreach (see map Chapter 3). More importantly the Sisters had won the trust of the cardinal archbishop, Henry Manning, whose seniority and campaigning on behalf of the Catholic gave him national influence. The Sisters had developed a sturdy working relationship with Manning over a 30-year period, from the time when he was provost of the Westminster Chapter and a close neighbour.[74] Henriette Chatelain had collaborated on his project to find homes for London's destitute Catholic children who were being transferred from Poor Law institutions.[75] He was said to be 'in almost daily touch' with Sister Joanna

---

69 Ralph Calder, *Mill Hill: A Thousand Years of History* (London, 1993), p. 42 and *Notes and Queries*, 21 January 1882, pp. 41-43; Provincial House 11- 00, Box 1 DCMH.

70 Notes made on St Vincent's Provincial House by the Greater London Council Department of Architecture and Civic Design in 1970. 7-1-1-3 DCMH.

71 *Notices of Deceased Sisters*, Juliette Minart (1891), p. 44. 10-3-1 DCMH.

72 ibid. Rybolt, *History of the Vincentians, Vol 4*, p. 479. More generally on this perspective being held by French congregations, see Susan O'Brien, 'French Nuns'.

73 Discussed and compared to the Irish bishops' response in Chapter 3.

74 Manning was confessor to the Sisters in York Street. Later he lived at 22 Carlisle Place.

75 See, for example, *Memoir of a Sister of Charity*, pp. 40-41.

Donor, who was 'frequently summoned by him to settle matters for the poor'.[76] It was known that Manning wanted the Sisters to have their headquarters in his diocese. As a final point in its favour, Littleberries was on a good route to central London where government business could be done, major benefactors contacted, and trains to all destinations, including the Channel ferry, could be caught.

Despite these positive factors in play, Irish history and the growing political movement for home rule, as well as the sheer number of Irish first and second-generation Sisters in the Province, meant that the decision for a single Province for Britain and Ireland (with its headquarters near London) carried tensions and ambiguities. Some of these ambiguities were reflected in the unstable naming of the Province in records. Formally the Province was 'Grande Bretagne'. But in both informal notes and forms exchanged between Sisters in the Paris secretariat, it was sometimes 'Province des Isles Britanniques' and sometimes simply 'La Province d'Angleterre'.[77]

Transforming 'Littleberries' into 'St Vincent's'

Littleberries had considerable potential for development but some aspects of the property were out of keeping with the simplicity and poverty of Daughters of Charity. And it was not yet a Catholic environment, let alone a Vincentian one. A process of transformation was managed by Sister Howard who was transferred from Plymouth for the purpose. Ornate gilding on the elaborate original plasterwork in the main reception rooms, such as the 'naked figure of Venus standing in a shell, with a cupid crouching at her feet', was removed.[78] The wooden carved panelling with its fruits, birds and flowers, identified by Etheldreda Howard as a fine example of the work of the seventeenth-century Dutch-British artist Grinling Gibbons, was judged unfitting for a Sisters' house and more usefully converted into cash. Panels were sold to a private American buyer and the resulting bare brick walls were covered with stretched canvas and later painted over in dark pitch by the Sisters. Some secular artwork was covered over with drapery and the plasterwork of 'two naked sea-nymphs seated back to back on a rock', was removed and replaced with devotional art and artefacts sent over from France.[79] A life-sized bronze statue of St Vincent, donated by Superioress General Derieux and blessed by Superior General Fiat, was placed on the front lawn in a prominent position.[80] A statue of Virgo Potens (linked to the 1830 apparition at the rue du Bac) was sent from Paris for the seminary. Engravings of Our Lady of Perpetual

---

76 *Pioneer Sisters*, p. 33 and Sister Josephine O'Driscoll typescript, 'Sidelights from the Seminary', p.1. 13-4-3 DCMH [hereafter O'Driscoll 'Sidelights'].

77 For example, in the statistical records in the mother house archives.

78 *Notes and Queries*, 21 January 1882, p. 42.

79 ibid., p. 43.

80 'Supplies made out to Central House of Mill Hill', Provincial House Box 11-100 1-4, #2 DCMH.

Succour and framed paintings of St Vincent and Louise de Marillac were among the other larger items purchased from the mother house in 1885. Crucifixes, holy water stoups and small images of subjects favoured by the Company were placed in every room. Together they sanctified the new environment and transformed it into a Daughters' domain and a sacred space.[81]

Living rooms, drawing rooms, bedrooms and servants' quarters were reconfigured as work rooms, lecture rooms and dormitories before the Sisters took up residence. A temporary chapel was created out of the former dining room, with the pantry used as the sacristy. The hall, previously a billiard room, was partitioned off to create the chapel entrance. In total the Province spent almost £1,000 on modifications and repairs to the property. The effort made to transform Littleberries into St Vincent's illustrates Carmen Mangion's conclusion that a 'provincial house provided a space that allowed for the development of ... collective identities'.[82]

The small community moved in on St George's Day (23 April) 1885. The newly appointed visitatrice, Juliette Minart, arrived from Alexandria in Egypt via Paris and Dover.[83] The appointment of French Sisters to the office of visitatrice was intended to secure the Company's spirit and traditions and would be maintained until the new Province was thought ready. Anne Farrell travelled down from Lanark to join Etheldreda Howard as the second provincial officer. Sisters Warren and Duffy took up sacristy and domestic offices.[84] To mark the occasion they were joined by Henriette Chatelain and Mary Ann Costello, the two senior London Sister Servants. The next day, anniversary of the birthday of St Vincent, Mass was celebrated by a priest from St Joseph's College and the seminary was opened with the reception of four seminary Sisters. William Gavin CM, appointed as director of the Province, joined the group on 25 April.[85] On 8 May the community was ready to welcome the Superioress General for a two-day visit, accompanied once again by Sisters Marcellus and Merceret.

At an extraordinary provincial council meeting, Superioress Marie Dérieux formally witnessed William Gavin hand the visitatrice's patent to Juliette Minart and thus inaugurate the new Province.[86] Dérieux's presence was more than ceremonial. She met with architects and builders and, presiding over the first council meeting, set the provincial wheels in motion. Several significant decisions were taken at this meeting: the council was to build an orphanage for younger boys on the Littleberries' estate as Cardinal Manning wished; it was to construct a chapel for the Sisters and build a presbytery for a small community of *confrères*.

81 ibid.

82 Mangion, *Contested Identities*, p. 157.

83 General Council Minutes, Book 32, 22 April 1885 DCParis.

84 ibid., 7 April 1885 DCParis.

85 *Pioneer Sisters*, p. 29.

86 General Council Minutes, Book 32, 10 May 1885. DCParis.

Financial arrangements for all of these projects were recorded, as was the £10,000 loan from the mother house and interest payments at three and a half per cent to be paid quarterly by the Province until the debt was paid off.[87]

Dérieux also laid out her plans for seminary formation. Seminary Sisters were to spend about six months in Mill Hill and then travel to Paris for between one and three months' formation that would culminate in their *prise d'habit* in the mother house chapel. Care was to be taken to prepare seminary Sisters for their time in Paris. There was greater sensitivity to the cultural challenges than previously, but the same insistence on the irreplaceable role of the mother house in building corporate identity. French was to be studied for five or six months at Mill Hill so that when the Sisters arrived in the rue du Bac, 'they could take advantage of the powerful and serious instructions made there'.[88] When at the mother house, the seminary Sisters would study in French and English alternately, but they would learn all the community prayers in French so they could be united in prayer with all other Daughters throughout the world. The practice of placing some Sisters in France for a period was to continue. Eventually, 97 Sisters out of 596 second-generation Sisters (those entering between 1885 and 1919) were to serve in France for a time: a much lower, though still significant, proportion than the 128 of 280 first-generation Sisters who did so. With these measures in place, the French officers left and the visitatrice with her provincial councillors began the task of administering the new Province.

Administrative processes were to play an important part in building corporate identity. The provincial council met fortnightly on a Monday, a day chosen by the visitatrice so as to expedite business with the general council meetings in Paris, which were held on alternate Wednesdays.[89] Attention to detail of this kind lay at the heart of the Company's transnational operation. It meant that responses to questions and recommendations made at one provincial council meeting were received from the mother house in time for the next.[90] Just as there had previously been a constant flow of letters between individual Sister Servants and the mother house, now there was a considerable volume of transactions between the *maison central* and the *maison mère*, occurring on at least a weekly basis and sometimes more frequently. They were being dealt with in Paris by a secretary appointed for the Province. Communication was made even easier for the Sisters once the Duke of Norfolk, in his ministerial capacity as Paymaster General (1895-1900), arranged for a post box to be set into the perimeter wall of the Central House grounds.[91] All formal business and communication was in French. Even the notes of the provincial council meetings were recorded in French and, as far as it is possible

87 ibid.

88 Provincial Council Minute Book, 1 December 1885. 9-0-2-1 DCMH.

89 Ibid., 10 May 1885, DCMH.

90 Conclusion drawn from analysis of Provincial Council Minutes, Book 1. 9-0-2-1 DCMH.

91 O'Driscoll, 'Sidelights', p. 8. 13-4-3 DCMH.

to know with any certainty, the council meetings themselves were conducted in French out of respect for the succession of French visitatrices appointed by superiors to lead the Province between 1885 and 1926.

6

Leadership and identity in a transnational community 1885–1926

> God chose France to be the place where the Company was born.
> He had his reasons for this. This circumstance entered the designs
> of Providence. This design inspired Saint Vincent not only to form
> our constitutions and our rules but also our maxims, usages, and
> customs. From France, the Company has spread to other parts of
> the earth with the same spirit and in the same conditions that
> characterize it here. The community is not to appropriate to itself
> the spirit and the habits of other peoples, but it is to implant its
> own particular customs and institutions in their midst. We do not
> accept their forms, but on the contrary we try to persuade them to
> accept ours so that we may do good among them.[1]
>
> (Superior General Étienne 1861)

> The good spirit of the Central House, the example given here, is so
> important, for it affects the whole Province.[2]
>
> (Visitatrice of Great Britain and Ireland
> Louise Hannezo 1919)

The appointment of a French visitatrice was a major component in the Company's strategy to ensure a transfer of its charism and institutional culture. For a number of reasons, the era of French visitatrices in the Province of the United Kingdom lasted for forty years, involving the appointment of not just the first, but the first three visitatrices: Juliette Minart from 1885 to 1890; Eugénie de Martin de Marcellus from 1890 to 1919 and Louise de Hannezo from 1919 to 1926. Minart's period of office was cut short by her death at the age of sixty-eight, Marcellus was allowed to retire from office at the age of seventy-nine, and Hannezo was recalled to France in 1926 because by this time the Superiors General were ready to appoint a Sister native to the Province. It was a lengthy period for an apprenticeship. The fact that no native Sister held this position during the first sixty years of the community's

---

1 Quoted in Udovic, *Jean-Baptiste Étienne*, p. 265.

2 Typescript about Sister Louise Hannezo, third visitatrice. 9-3 DCMH.

history in Britain was not without consequences for the evolution of Provincial identity and for 'being' and 'belonging' as Anglo-Saxon and Celtic Daughters in the Company.

However, despite the stress on uniformity and unity and the lack of an indigenous visitatrice, the Province evolved a sense of its own identity through these four decades from 1885 to 1926. Just as there was always the possibility of individual Sisters inflecting the corporate identity according to social background, nationality, personality or even location, there was also inflection at Provincial level. Questions of being and belonging were both fluid and multi-dimensional. By exploring the nature of the leadership offered by the second and third visitatrices and their officers, it is possible suggest the significance of the interactions between national identity (British, French and Irish) and Company identity formation in the Province's founding decades.

Juliette Minart, First Visitatrice 1885–1890

While the business of purchasing Littleberries was under way, the process of selecting a visitatrice was set in motion. Early in 1885 Juliette Minart, Sister Servant in Alexandria, Egypt, was summoned by telegraph to 'come immediately' to the mother house.[3] French-born Sister Minart had lived for thirty-five years, her entire life as a Daughter of Charity, in Eastern Europe and the Eastern Mediterranean, holding the offices of Sister Servant in Galati north of Bucharest and as assistant to the visitatrice of the newly founded Constantinople Province. Taking the first boat from Alexandria to Marseilles, she travelled to Paris with no knowledge of why her superiors had recalled her. Aged sixty-three and in weakened health, she was asked to undertake 'a testing and delicate work' and to 'realise the desires of the superiors in putting together the new Province of Great Britain'.[4] Hers was an intriguing appointment: she had no contacts in the United Kingdom and her English was far from fluent.[5] What she had, however, was a great deal of experience of working out of France and in environments where Catholicism was a minority faith.

Never at ease in the English language, Minart relied to a considerable degree for translation on the French secretary she brought with her. She turned to the Sister-councillors and the director to understand the different contexts of Britain and Ireland. In the five years before her death in 1890, Juliette Minart faithfully followed out the plan left by Superioress General Deriéux. She oversaw the creation of a provincial 'campus' at Mill Hill and at the same time expanded the Province's work in other parts of Britain.

---

3 General Council Minutes, 11 February 1885, 979 Book 33 DCParis.

4 Ibid.

5 Obituary, *The Tablet*, 14 June 1890, p.37.

In meetings of the council, Minart and the other officers discussed matters related to individual Sisters, the works of the Province and the use of financial resources. They considered all applications for entry and made recommendations to the general council about whether Sisters were ready to move from one stage of admission to the next. It was their responsibility to make recommendations about moving Sisters between houses and the appointment of Sister Servants but the final decisions was reserved to the general council. When a Sister did not settle, was ill or was unsatisfactory in her role, or when relationships between Sisters in a community were not good, the matter was referred to the general council if it could not be resolved. Requests for new foundations came to the Provincial council, which had to take a position and, again, make recommendations. A similar process applied to requests from Sister Servants for major internal expenditure.

By 1890, the complex of buildings at Mill Hill comprised a sizeable late Gothic provincial chapel that doubled as a parish church for the Catholics of Mill Hill, a solid presbytery housing a small group of Vincentian priests and brothers, a retreat block for the Sisters and a community cemetery, and St Vincent's residential Poor Law School for 200 Catholic boys under the age of nine referred by London Boards of Guardians. Ministries had been taken on for the first time in Glasgow, York, Hull and Torquay. In total ten new foundations were made in Britain in five years, a sound bequest to leave for the Province's second visitatrice. The record of these years can be reconstructed from the sources but, despite an obituary in the Catholic weekly *The Tablet*, there is little to reveal the manner of Juliette Minart's leadership and personality.[6] No biography was ever written of her by the Province other than the expected obituary in the Company's internal publication.[7]

Eugénie de Martin de Marcellus 1890–1918: adaptation and fidelity

Juliette Minart's death had been a shock to the Sisters of the Province and to the Superiors General. Only five years into the life of the Province it was predictable that another French Sister would be chosen to replace her. But in other ways the appointment of Eugénie de Martin de Marcellus was out of the ordinary.[8] Only 18 months previously she had been appointed visitatrice in Portugal. Her transfer to Britain indicated a perception among the Company's leaders that the British Province needed particular care. Marcellus was fifty years old in 1890 and described by an English companion as 'young, alert and active'[9]. Despite her relative youth she had already held the senior office of Company bursar for five years and had conducted Company business on visitations to Turkey,

6 Obituary, *The Tablet*, 14 June 1890, p.37.

7 Juliette Henrietta Minart, 9-1 DCMH.

8 Sources for Eugénie Marcellus are *Memoir of Ma Soeur Marcellus* (Mill Hill, 1928 privately printed), written by Sister Mary Langdale, and O'Driscoll,' Sidelights' 13-4-3 DCMH. Very few of her own records have survived in the Mill Hill archive, although the entire record of the Council during her period of office is available. 9-2 DCMH.

9 *Memoir of Ma Soeur Marcellus*, p.30.

Constantinople, Jerusalem and Beirut. She brought to her leadership of the British Province considerable experience of central and provincial governance and an understanding of the Company's operation in different contexts. Marcellus had already visited Mill Hill twice as Company bursar and had shown her support through the gifts of Stations of the Cross and a true relic of the cross, which she had given the new Province.

Marcellus had been born into the Bordeaux nobility and her forebears included the canonised eighteenth-century Jesuit, John Francis Regis, and grandparents who had been guillotined for their faith. Although, like Juliette Minart, Sister Marcellus was not fluent in English, she refused to have the support of a bi-lingual French secretary offered her by superiors. Instead she did her best to work in English, laughing at her own mistakes.[10] Pedigree and personality, combined with transnational and financial experience, gave the Province's second visitatrice a confident approach to leadership. Straightaway she 'adopted the Province as her own' and actively sought to know it for herself.[11] Within her first few months Sister Marcellus visited Ireland twice, travelling alone on the second occasion. Declaring the people to be 'so polite' that she did not need a companion, and that accompanying her was a waste of another Sister's time, Marcellus insisted on travelling everywhere by herself unless she was away for any length of time, allowing herself to be exposed to others and to the way things were done locally, rather than being shielded.[12]

Over time she introduced changes that made the Province more 'British' and less 'French'. The use of French was gradually replaced by English on significant community occasions. In 1893, the 1 January Act of Consecration was made in English for the first time and in 1901, French language retreats were phased out altogether. From 1905, community prayers were said in English and Latin rather than in French.[13] In a marked shift from the earlier position already discussed, the desired skills in entrants changed from knowledge of French (decreasing from one third to one quarter having any French between 1900 and 1919) towards the qualifications in teaching and nursing (increased from a quarter to almost 40 percent in the same period).[14] Far fewer Sisters were sent to serve in France after 1900, not least because France became a very difficult place for religious institutes after the 1905 legislation separating Church and state. But it was the personal efforts that Marcellus made to support rather than suppress the emotional culture she found in her adopted land that endeared her to the Sisters of the Province.

---

10 ibid. p. 29 and pp. 46–7.

11 ibid. p. 29

12 ibid. p. 30 and p. 29.

13 'In fact, until 1905, when the first English catechism appeared, our morning and night prayers, our conferences and accusations were all in French and one can imagine the labour of Seminary Sisters in trying to master them, especially the commandments of God as they are said in French – it called for heroic effort.' O'Driscoll, 'Sidelights', p.5 13-4-3 DCMH

14 Calculated from the *Catalogue of Sisters of the British Province* 13-1-1 DCMH.

She was willing to accept the local humour and banter among the community's 'clients' and to enter into it. No one thought of her as an easy-going person (the term 'strict' is used by several Sisters), but none the less she adapted to the less formal approach to relationships that prevailed in her adopted Province and grasped the cultural importance of low-key practical kindness. Recognising that Irish Sisters placed in Britain missed their home country, she allowed them to make their retreats there from time to time. Sister Servants were given scope to lead if they were capable, but the challenges facing them through the poverty of the time meant she went through their annual accounts herself and 'almost always gave back at least half, it not all, of the amount of money' they had sent her as their surplus.[15]

We know something of these elusive matters because Eugénie Marcellus comes to posterity framed by a biography published on behalf of the Province in 1928, the year after her death. Its author, Sister Mary Langdale, had been her close companion and collaborator from 1890 to 1918, first as seminary directress and then as provincial bursar. Langdale was also the Province's first unofficial historian; her accounts of the early houses indicate a natural historian's mind at work.[16] Her portrait of Sister Marcellus is strongly drawn and it goes beyond a merely edifying narrative. Four themes permeate *Memoir of Ma Soeur Marcellus*: (1) the visitatrice's personal kindness; (2) her generous and intelligent adaptability to the British context; (3) the harmony of relationships between Sister-officers at Central House; and (4) the visitatrice's rigorous fidelity to the Company and its Rule. The memoir's underlying insistence on the compatibility between 'adopting' the two islands and being faithful to the Company leaves the impression that Langdale is defending Marcellus from criticism, perhaps that she went 'native' to the detriment of the principle of unity through uniformity. Either intentionally or subconsciously, Mary Langdale engaged with the question of how fidelity was interpreted and her text reveals the way that being a 'true Daughter of Charity' was defined by the visitatrice and her companions in Britain.

When Langdale proclaimed Marcellus a 'true Daughter of Charity', one aspect she highlighted was her 'affability' towards the poor and to her companions: it was the quality of her relationships that were singled out. On visitations, for example, she asked each Sister about her own personal interests and enquired after her family to good purpose. Financial help was discreetly given to Sisters' families in need.[17] Callers looking for a meal or alms were treated with dignity. Concepts of kindness, amiability, tenderness and encouragement are used repeatedly by Langdale to describe Marcellus.[18] Yet, at the same time, it is made clear to the reader that 'when there was any question of enforcing any rule, or guarding

15 *Memoir of Ma Soeur Marcellus*, p. 89.

16 See, for example, her account of the events that led to Canon Donlevy evicting them from Edinburgh in 1898.

17 ibid. p. 38

18 'Kindness' was used 27 times in this short text. For example, see *Memoir of Ma Soeur Marcellus*, p. 33..

against what might tend to abuse, Sister Marcellus was inflexible, and perhaps even strict'.[19] Fidelity to Company practices is shown to have been as much part of her identity and leadership as sensitivity to local customs. At the end of her life, we are told 'three things remained...her duty to her Superiors, the habit of observing her Holy Rules, and fidelity to her exercises of piety'.[20]

The most significant instance of Marcellus defending the Company's Rule from serious challenge from outside the community concerned early rising. Vincent de Paul had taught that; 'The grace of vocation depends on fidelity to meditation, and the grace of meditation depends on fidelity to rising at 4 o'clock'.[21] Given the northerly latitude of Britain, adherence to this precept meant a daily sacrifice by the Sisters. In the depth of winter, Sisters in Scotland and northern England were up and at work and prayer four or five hours before daylight, a routine that was unknown for other sisters in active ministry. The Irish Vincentian Province had long ceased to practise this aspect of their rule despite a serious effort by no less an enforcer of uniformity than Étienne.[22] While no Sister was expected to rise at this hour if she was infirm or unwell - and all Sisters could take an extra hour's rest or 'repose' once a week – the discipline of early rising was regarded as the mark of a generous and honed spirit. In Britain, the Province's officers set the example and were known for their early rising. Sister Marcellus' alertness 'even in the early morning', we are told, 'was like an alarm clock for those who shared her dormitory'.[23]

This Company custom was sustained in the face of sharp criticism from bishops and priests in Britain who were concerned both for the Daughters' health and for the effectiveness of their mission. 'The social customs of the English people are such,' observed the bishops of England and Wales, 'that in order to yield more from the charitable work of the Daughters of Charity, it is necessary to make a prudent modification to the present hours of the community'.[24] The Sisters were up before the later-rising British and went to bed earlier than they did. According to some priests this made it more difficult for them to provide evening classes, religious instruction, confraternities and clubs for workers after the end of the working day. A third problem was identified by the bishops. For the Company horarium to work effectively, Mass should be at six in the morning. But it was rare in Britain for a priest to say Mass before seven o'clock in the parish churches attended by the Sisters, or to agree to come to their house to do so. Since the whole pattern

---

19 ibid. p. 98.

20 Ibid. p. 119.

21 Quoted in Circular Letter to Sister Servants from Superior General Verdier, 27 November 1921. 4-26-2 1-1 DCMH

22 Rybolt, *History of the Vincentians, vol 4.*, p.482.

23 *Memoir of Sister Marcellus*, p.39: 'Always up at four o'clock, her example encouraged us to be permitted to do likewise' was how one Sister remembered Mary Langdale, provincial bursar.

24 Letter from the Sacred Congregation of Propaganda Fide Cardinal Ledochwski to Mgr Notre Très Honoré Père Verdier, Rome, 1 January 1901. 42-6-2 1-2 DCMH. See also *Memoir of Sister Marcellus*, p. 91.

of the day, including times of breaking fast, followed from the morning routine (shown in Figure 6.1), there were many difficulties attendant on such early rising.

Horarium	
as specified in the Book of Customs	
16.00 a.m.	Rise at the sound of the bell and go to chapel or oratory
16.30 a.m.	Community prayer and meditation
5.10 a.m.	The Angelus
Mass	Mass to be said as close to the end of prayers as possible, as at the mother house, but adapted to local custom*
	15 minutes' meditation, at least, after Mass
Breakfast	According to the hour of Mass.
11.30	Particular examen (if possible according to office)
12.00	Dinner and recreation
14.00	Spiritual reading for 15 minutes
17.30	Meditation, examen and prayers
18.15	Supper
19.00	Recreation
20.00	Evening reflection followed by night prayers retire

* If Mass could not be said until 7.00am Sisters worked before Mass.

6.1: HORARIUM BEFORE THE SECOND WORLD WAR

Cardinal Herbert Vaughan had worked with the Daughters in Salford when he was bishop there and did so again as Archbishop of Westminster, but he also knew about their life from his sister, Teresa, a Daughter who had died young in 1861. He advocated that the Sisters be allowed to rise at 5.30 a.m. or even 6 a.m. and retire at 9.30 p.m. or 10 p.m..[25] When he found Sister Marcellus immovable about 'the idea of changing what had been in the rule of the Community from its very origin',[26] Vaughan took the matter to the annual meeting of the bishops of England and Wales in 1895. (In this context it is worth noting that the horarium in first Rule of

---

25 Letter from the Sacred Congregation of Propaganda Fide Cardinal Ledochwski to Mgr Notre Très Honore Père Verdier, Rome, 1 January 1901. 42-6-2 1-2 DCMH.

26 *Memoir of Ma Soeur Marcellus* ,p. 91.

the Company had begun with 5.30 a.m. rising and 10 p.m. retiring)[27]. He gained their agreement to approach the Company's Superior General, Father Fiat, via Cardinal Ledochwski of the Sacred Congregation for Religious in Rome, to ask that an exception to the rule be made for Daughters in Britain.

Fiat 'was much distressed' at the thought that 'some Sisters in the British Province had perhaps raised difficulties' about their horarium with priests or bishops.[28] Marcellus had to reassure him that the request came from the clergy. To satisfy the bishops the Sisters were asked for their views on 'the question of altering this rule'. Perhaps we should not be surprised that 'the very great majority of Sisters unhesitatingly expressed their support' for the existing horarium, given the circumstances of the consultation and what was at stake.[29] Because many of them struggled to rise so early and sometimes failed,[30] their support for the status quo showed they had favoured unity and identification with the Company's custom rather than the possibility of a practical and not unreasonable adaptation of their rule to the context. The issue of rising times provides an insight into the Sisters' desire to identify with the Company culture and with other Daughters throughout the world, even at some cost to themselves. Sister Marcellus herself continued to rise at 4 a.m. when nearing the age of eighty. The many adaptations and adjustments to British culture she made as visitatrice need to be set alongside persistent affirmation of Company identity as in the difficult case of the horarium. Taken together, they demonstrated the potential for a fidelity with flexibility (or plurality in unity) that the Superiors General were not yet ready to accept and apply across the Company. It was only after the Second Vatican Council that the Company began to debate how decentralisation and adaptation to local culture could operate without threatening unity.

Provincial officers and the question of identity 1885–1920

Sister Marcellus did not, of course, lead and manage the Province alone. Between 1885 and 1919 the three Sisters already identified, Mary Burns, Etheldreda Howard and Mary Langdale, held all the major provincial offices between them, sometimes being appointed by the general council to hold more than one office simultaneously for a number of years, as shown in Table 6.2.

---

27 John Rybolt, 'From Life to the Rules', *VHJ*, vol. 12, iss. 2, article 6, p. 184.

28 ibid. p. 92.

29 ibid.

30 Their actual time of rising in general was noted by the Sister Servant and recorded at visitations.

Visitatrice	Assistant	Bursar	Seminary Directress	Secretary	Assistant Officer	Director
Minart 1885-1890	Burns 1885-1913	Howard 1885-1913	Howard 1885-1888	Howard 1885-1920	Blundell 1913-1920	Gavin 1885-1898
Marcellus 1890-1919	Howard 1913-1920	Langdale 1913-1920	Langdale 1888-1925			Walshe 1898-1909
						Byrne 1909-1922

6.2: PROVINCIAL OFFICE-HOLDERS 1885–1919

From a practical perspective this situation was only possible because of their youthfulness at the time of appointment. In 1890, Marcellus was the oldest at the age of fifty and Langdale the youngest at thirty-four. Similarities in social background as well as a shared generational identity gave the group a strong coherence. All were well educated in languages, culture and literature and the English Sisters had all lived in France for varying periods before entry.[31] They were women from aristocratic and upper middle-class or professional backgrounds, whose families were actively engaged in religious, political and civic matters. Etheldreda Howard's brother was not only England's premier duke and earl but also a Conservative Unionist and a member of the Privy Council from 1895 to 1900. Her Scottish nephew, Philip Kerr, Marquis of Lothian, was Secretary to the Prime Minister between 1916 and 1921.[32] Langdale's forebears included Henry Grattan, of Celbridge Abbey in County Kildare (described as 'the principal architect of the Irish Parliament of 1782-1800')[33] and Charles Langdale, England's leading Catholic MP (for Beverley in Yorkshire) in the mid nineteenth century. Mary Burns' Scottish father, James, founded the internationally known Catholic publishing house of Burns & Oates, and Louisa Blundell was descended from the Blundells of Little Crosby, the staunchest of recusant English Catholic gentry families. It would be difficult to overstate the degree to which these Sister-councillors were connected to elite Catholics in England and Scotland. Their appointment to office certainly enabled them to make strategic use of their networks and private funds for the benefit of the Company's mission, but it also meant that their social perspective dominated the culture of the Province's decision-making and leadership.

---

31 On noting the time Louisa Blundell spent at school in Boulogne, her biographer writes: 'there was a somewhat large contingent of Catholic families at Boulogne at that time, besides the Blundells, there were the Cliffords, the Langdales, the Neves and the Eystons, all of whom had either members or relatives among St Vincent's daughters'. *Memoir of Sister Louisa Blundell* (Sisters of Charity: Mill Hill, n.d.), p.11. See Typescript 'Remarks on the life of Sister Mary Langdale', Personal File 10-2 DCMH.

32 Etheldreda Howard's sister, Anne, married Major-General Lord Ralph Drury Kerr, son of the 7th Marquess of Lothian.

33 Anne M. Brady and Brian Cleave, *A Biographical Dictionary of Irish Writers* (Dublin, The Lilliput Press, 1985), p. 92.

These Sisters were also particularly well equipped and motivated to transfer the Company's French institutional culture and spirituality. They had spent, and continued to spend, longer periods in the rue du Bac than most Sisters and they loved the mother house, although not uncritically so.[34] At the same time they had sufficient unity of purpose and outlook to leave their own imprint on the Province and, working with Sister Marcellus, they introduced the cultural shifts already observed. In publishing Mary Langdale's biography of Sister Marcellus, these senior members of the community wanted posterity to appreciate the lightness of touch that had prevailed in Central House under her leadership; not for its own sake but for its influence towards 'cordiality and charity' throughout the Province.[35] 'How we loved the family feasts at Mill Hill', one Sister reflected after Marcellus' death in 1928:

> There was a magnet which attracted us; indeed, one might say, the magnet was not a unity but a trinity. So closely were Ma Soeur Marcellus, Sister Howard and Sister Langdale united that they seemed to form but one, and the Sisters visiting had a three-fold welcome.[36]

The striking image of 'a blessed trinity' was used not only about the three officers listed here but about Sisters Marcellus, Howard and Mary Burns.[37] These overlapping trios were linked by the bond between Marcellus and Howard, referred to elsewhere by Langdale as 'kindred spirits'.[38] The Province's leaders were, indeed, kindred spirits and their extraordinarily long incumbency shaped the experience of 'being' and 'belonging' in the second generation (those entering between 1885 and 1919). The memory of it was to last even longer.

The benefits of stability and coherence in the Province's leadership can be seen in the steady growth of the community from 290 Sisters to more than 800 over this thirty-five year period (Figure 6.3).

---

34 Etheldreda Howard, for example, had been prepared for office as seminary directress by a further period in Paris in 1884 where, as she wrote, 'I have nothing to do but to look and listen and write, copying out rules etc.'. *Memoir of a Sister of Charity*, p. 55.

35 *Memoir of Sister Marcellus*, p. 100.

36 ibid.

37 *Memoir of Sister Marcellus*, p. 37.

38 *Memoir of a Sister of Charity*, p. 75.

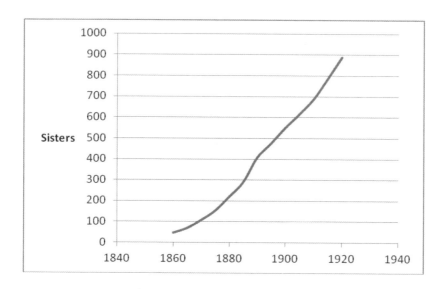

6.3: NUMBER OF SISTERS IN THE PROVINCE 1860–1920

However, that very same stability meant a lack of new perspective and fresh energy as the years went on. And whatever characteristics had been missing at the outset – in social class, nationality or personal experience – continued to be absent. In 1888, when an opportunity for change occurred with the creation of a separate seminary directress role, superiors decided to reallocate offices between the existing office-holders, seemingly satisfied that Sister Langdale would represent the Irish voice. When the next opportunity for change occurred in 1913 at the death of Mary Burns, it seems clear from the intricate way in which they steered round the question that the inclusion of an Irish Sister on the council greatly exercised the provincial officers, but again they acted to maintain the status quo.

On this occasion, Marcellus, Langdale and Howard recommended to Superiors General that offices be reassigned to the latter two Sisters, who would be helped with the added work by the creation of a new role of assistant officer with a seat on the council. Sister Louisa Blundell was recommended for this role. Superiors General accepted their recommendations. Louisa Blundell, who had worked for nine years in the Sisters' North William Street House in Dublin and ten years as Sister Servant in Dumfries in Scotland, winning affection in both places, was clearly intended to be a unifying choice. Her aunt, Alice Blundell, was also well known in both Scotland and Ireland, having been Sister Servant firstly in Lanark and then in Dunmanway in County Cork, where she had made a great impression in the local community. Louisa Blundell was a very carefully considered choice but her appointment still served to reinforce the English upper-class family and establishment character of the council. By way of a counter-balance, therefore, the more senior role of second directress of the seminary was given to an Irish Sister, Catherine O'Driscoll, who had been an officer in the seminary since 1895 and had proved to be of crucial importance in the welcoming and settling of young women from Ireland. In time she was to play a central role in the Province and to be a bond between the generations and the nationalities.[39]

The new appointments did not satisfy everyone. In November 1927 (the year after Etheldreda Howard's death), at the specific request of Superior General Verdier, Mary Langdale wrote an account of tensions that had arisen between the members of the provincial council between 1913 and 1921. She noted that in 1915–1916 the provincial director, William Byrne, had pushed to 'introduce a stronger Irish element into the Council'. Byrne had consulted one of the senior French missioners, Père Plancon, then in England at Isleworth with a group of confrères because of the 1905 anti-clerical legislation, about his concerns over the imbalance. According to Langdale (who wrote the account in the third person), 'The latter told Sister Marcellus and Sister Langdale that he was not of the same opinion as Father Byrne for he considered the Irish interests well-safeguarded in the Council, since the Director himself was Irish, and Sister Langdale half Irish, and her sympathies known to be favourable to Ireland'.[40] It seems unlikely that Plancon appreciated either the degree to which Ireland had changed since Mary Langdale last knew it or the pace of continuing change in political thinking about Home Rule. William Byrne could not take the matter any further at the time but he was to do so in 1919, when Sister Marcellus retired.

After a long period of great activity followed by years of frailty, it was a relief for Sister Marcellus to learn that she was to be replaced. Under her leadership the Province had expanded from 38 foundations to 87, of which 69 were in Britain and 18 in Ireland. The Sisters had developed a range of new ministries (discussed in detail in Chapter 7). It had been Marcellus' intention that the Daughters should be more active in Scotland and she had opened new houses in Dumfries, Edinburgh, Glasgow and Dunfermline. In England she was keen for the Sisters to have a strong presence in the East End of London, accepting invitations that established them at Bow Common, Limehouse, Wapping and Millwall. At Central House she had overseen the building of the Mary Immaculate Elementary School (1896), a retreat block for the Sisters (1899) and new accommodation for them, as well as carrying out further work to enhance the beauty of the chapel. In retirement she was to be allowed to stay on at her beloved Mill Hill, where Sisters on visits and retreats would be able to spend time with her.

---

39 Catherine O'Driscol was appointed first directress (1920–26) and later assistant to the province (1931), after which she remained at Central House until her death in 1958. See 'Remarks on Sister Josephine O'Driscoll', Personal File 10-2 DCMH.

40 Confidential account written at the request of Father General Verdier , Sr Langdale concerning the incident of Sister Mary Howard's change from the Provincial House to St David's Ealing', Nov/Dec 1927. 4-26-5 1-1 DCMH.

Sister Marcellus had, in fact, been asking permission to retire since 1909. Describing the deterioration in her health around that time, Mary Langdale discreetly noted that she 'had asked several times the favour of being relieved from her office [but] circumstances were not favourable to the change'.[41] The 'circumstances' were more likely to have been the growing political and military crises over Home Rule for Ireland than, say, the situation in France caused by the anti-clerical and laicisation legislation. By this date, more than twenty years after the establishment of the Province, it would have been reasonable for Marcellus to be replaced by a Sister native to it. But a native Sister would be a sensitive decision, because it would mean making a choice between the appointment of an Irish or an English visitatrice (there being no senior Scottish Sisters at this time).

The steady hibernicisation of both the membership and leadership of the houses in Ireland between 1901 and 1911 is an indication of the change in sentiments taking place at this time.[42] The general council decided to leave the situation as it was and, as we have seen, a further holding arrangement was put in place in 1913. Superiors did visit the Province in 1914 to assess its needs, but the outbreak of the First World War later that year brought a halt to any changes they may have been planning. Given the war in Europe, Sister Marcellus was asked to stay in office. The increased tensions between the English and Irish caused by the Easter Rising of 1916 in Ireland must have made Sister Marcellus' continuation in office imperative. The author Brendan MacThormaid recorded that James Connolly, founder of the Irish Citizens Army and Republican and socialist leader, on the occasion of his execution paid tribute to the work of priests, and he singled out also the 'big bonnets', as he called the Daughters. 'I have seen and heard of the brave conduct of priests and nuns during the week', he said, 'and I believe they are the best friends of the workers.' MacThormaid continued Connolly's tribute with specific reference to the Daughters:

> Evidently Commandant Daly in a dispatch to Connolly told him of the wonderful help and co-operation he had got from these dedicated nuns of the Big Bonnets at North Brunswick Street...But then those of us who know the Big Bonnets know their big hearted dedication...In the Roll of Honour of Easter Week must go Sisters Louise, Brigid, Patrick, Monica and Ma Soeur O'Grady.[43]

---

41 *Memoir of Sister Marcellus*, p. 110.

42 In 1901, some 84 *Ma Soeur* out of 117 were Irish-born; in 1911 , a total of 134 out of 160 were Irish-born. As non-Irish Sister Servants retired or were transferred they were steadily replaced by Irish Sisters and Irish Sisters were appointed to lead the four new foundations made between 1911 and 1919. O'Sullivan and Prunty, *Daughters of Charity in Ireland*, Appendix III, pp.257–79. With thanks to Rosalie Ní Mhaoldomhnaigh for drawing my attention to this shift.

43 I am grateful to the work of O'Sullivan and Prunty, the authors of *The Daughters of Charity of St Vincent de Paul in Ireland*, (p.150) for the references in this section..

A photojournalist image of the Daughters distributing bread to the hungry on O'Connell Street in Dublin has become a well-known image of the Easter Rising.[44] One Sister, Mary Cullen, was hit by a stray bullet while going about her charitable business and lost an eye.[45] Sisters of the Province were involved in nursing both the wounded in this internal United Kingdom struggle and the one being waged on the Continent, where several served on the front and were decorated for their services.

At the end of the First World War, Sister Marcellus' retirement could be delayed no longer, but Britain and Ireland were themselves now at war and the possibility of a negotiated Home Rule settlement was receding. The declaration of Irish Independence and the declaration of war by the Irish Assembly in January 1919 meant that a native appointment as visitatrice was now an even more sensitive matter than it had been ten years earlier. The strength of intra-nationalist identities within the community are not visible in any of the official records and were, in any case, contained or submerged by the normal discipline of community life. But they can be glimpsed occasionally. Ernest Cleveland, a fiercely patriotic English lad at the Sisters' Poor Law home in Hull between 1917 and 1926, reacted against the compulsory celebration of St Patrick's Day by the Irish Sisters who ran St Vincent's and objected to the lack of attention paid to St George. His rebellion took the form of wearing a piece of red ribbon instead of the green on 17 March which, he later recalled, was 'considered to be a sacrilege'. Nonetheless he felt happy that he had 'made a stand against overwhelming odds'.[46] A number of the Sisters' houses in England and Scotland were, like St Vincent's in Hull, served entirely by Irish Sisters and most of the houses had a majority of Irish-born Sisters (leaving aside second- generation Irish), with a substantial minority of English Sisters and a very small number of Scottish Sisters. At Central House and at Carlisle Place in Westminster, however, the reverse was true. Although there is so little concrete evidence about the dynamics in the community regarding Irish independence, incidental evidence indicates that Sisters had a national – as well as a community – identity. In the event, the Superiors General thought it wisest for a third French visitatrice to be appointed, even if for a short period.

Louise Hannezo 1919–1926: reform and renewal

In 1919, based on the insights of their 1914 visitation of the Province and William Byrne's reports,[47] the General Council appointed as visitatrice a Sister whose outstanding mental qualities were forensic analysis, clarity, energy and attention

44 A painting of this photograph was made by artist Muriel Brandt and hangs in Cork's Crawford Art Gallery.

45 O'Sullivan and Prunty (eds.), *Daughters of Charity in Ireland*, p. 81.

46 Ernest Cleveland, *St Vincent's Home Boys* (Hartlepool, Cormorant Publishing, 2008), p. 72.

47 William Byrne visited Paris to make clear his point of view. Confidential account written at the request of Father General Verdier by Sister Langdale concerning the incident of Sister Mary Howard's change from the Provincial House to St David's Ealing'. 4-26-5 1-1 DCMH.

to detail; someone whose personality enabled her to carry out ideas that were not immediately popular. Louise Hannezo, the daughter of an Assistant Public Prosecutor in Nancy, had entered the Company in 1878, aged twenty-seven. Thereafter all her appointments were to the Paris seminary. She progressed through the offices of assistant, third directress and second directress to the senior and influential office of seminary directress, responsible for the formation of thousands of seminary Sisters from various parts of the world. Her reputation in the Company was as a restorer of tradition, researching original documents and 'revising the old traditions' in order, as she said, to preserve 'in its primitive purity, the spirit of our Holy Vocation, and the source from which it flows to be diffused throughout the whole Community'.[48] Aged sixty-eight, Hannezo crossed the Channel as one steeped in the culture of the mother house and the history of the Company.

At the same time she was a supporter of innovations that would modernise the Sisters' work, declaring that 'Saint Vincent would have done it. We must keep up with the times.' [49] It was many years since she had worked in direct service of the poor or lived away from the atmosphere and regime of the mother house, but she worked with determination to find new ministries for the Sisters that would be fitting for post-war Britain. Hannezo's briskness as visitatrice can be measured in the opening of eighteen houses in six or seven years and in the closure of another four.[50] She was described as 'rarely at home for any length of time'.[51] Even more significant was the fresh direction she encouraged through the development of three new hospitals either managed or owned by the Province (St David's Ealing for disabled servicemen; The Marillac sanatorium in Warley in Essex and St Vincent's Hospice in Liverpool), plus a hospital and residential home in Rosewell outside Edinburgh for children with neurological damage or learning disability, and another in Edmonton in London for children with physical impairments from conditions such as polio. Three clinics in urban centres and a dispensary were also opened, and district nursing provided, in Glasgow. Not all of her initiatives proved viable but these health works were a major legacy for the Province in the inte-rwar years and beyond.

Sister Hannezo's decisiveness can be seen, too, in her vigorous approach to the reform of the Province. Her first priority was to refresh the council with new members. In considering its composition, she supported William Byrne's view about the need to strengthen Irish representation. Hannezo had also concluded that 'the great influence that Sister Howard exercised in the Province' and 'the high

---

48 Typescript notes concerning *Ma Soeur Hannezo* p.29. 9-3-1 DCMH.

49 ibid. p. 130.

50 Marcellus closed only two houses: North Hyde, a small nursing House for schools run by Brothers; and Edinburgh Albany Street where the decision had been taken by Canon Donlevy.

51 O'Driscoll, 'Sidelights', p. 68.13-4-3 DCMH.

esteem' in which she was held 'might easily be an obstacle' to her own influence.[52] Given the sensitivity of the situation, she asked Superior General François Verdier to come to Mill Hill to make the change personally. He arrived to do this in July 1920. In fact, Sister Howard, who was unwell and 'felt she had lost Father Byrne's confidence', had already confidentially asked the new visitatrice not to renew her in office. When he arrived, Verdier appointed Sister Howard as Sister Servant of the newly opened St David's Hospital in Ealing. Regardless of her unquestioned personal probity and loyalty to her superiors, the Superioress General later confirmed that it had been 'necessary for her to leave Mill Hill, as there could not be two visitatrices in the same house'.[53] The changes made to the council in 1920, brought in Johanna Hurley, Sister Servant of Fairview in Dublin, to the office of provincial bursar and Catherine O'Driscoll was appointed as seminary directress. By the end of 1920 the provincial leadership comprised a French visitatrice, a French secretary, an Irish director, an Anglo-Irish assistant (Langdale) and two Irish Sisters holding the offices of bursar and seminary directress respectively.

With a new council in place, Sister Hannezo felt better able to implement the reforms she had been asked to make by the Superiors General. Working through Sister Marie Gouin, the French secretary who accompanied her to Mill Hill, Hannezo immediately created a French style of secretariat 'in the way that it existed in other provinces', with an increase of staff and 'more exact record keeping'.[54] She was not impressed with what she had inherited by way of information and she set about improving the records. Sister Lucy Pilley was appointed as First Secretary and trained by Gouin, serving in this role until after the Second World War and thus ensuring that the Paris administrative method became a matter of routine at Mill Hill.[55] In 1921, every Sister Servant was required to fill out a comprehensive form giving information about the origins of her house, the terms of the original contract, income, debt, benefactions and the Sisters' current stipends.

A series of wider reforms were instigated by the third visitatrice in the spirit of the new Code of Canon Law. Chief among them were requirements that Sisters seek permission for travel, for overnight stays out of the house, for the use of personal and community money, and for the location of their retreats. This latter applied especially to Irish Sisters making retreats in Ireland, the one opportunity for those placed in Britain to visit their homeland and possibly see relatives. Sister Hannezo's primary concern was with discipline, but the impact of post-war inflation on the community's finances created the need for economies and tight fiscal control.[56] Further instructions were issued to Sister Servants on a wide

---

52 Confidential account written at the request of Father General Verdier by Sister Langdale concerning the incident of Sister Mary Howard's move from the Provincial House to St David's Ealing. 4-26-5 1-1 DCMH.

53 ibid.

54 Typescript notes concerning *Ma Soeur Hannezo* p. 29 9-3-1 DCMH

55 'Secretariat Mill Hill: account written for its golden jubilee 1919–1969'. 11-100 unnumbered file. DCMH.

56 See, for example, Plymouth. 11-13-1 DCMH.

range of matters from notepaper and envelopes ('too much fancy tinted paper that is not correct is being used') to reminders that nothing should be added to morning and night prayers without permission from Superiors General. The practice of retaining local house income rather than pooling resources into the Central House fund met with stern criticism: 'The salaries of Teaching Sisters are palpably Community Property and should be treated as such. No doubt a certain sum for the support of each Teaching Sister should be paid into the funds of the House, but the remainder of her salary should go to the Provincial Fund.' [57]

It was only to be expected that the admission of applicants received Sister Hannezo's close attention. Reform to the selection of new Sisters was the most dramatic intervention she made, by reversing the cultural adaptations of the previous regime. She had three aims: first, the seminary was 'to be an exact copy of that in the Mother House'; [58] secondly, the number of aspirants and seminary Sisters was to be increased in number; and third, it was to become more socially diverse. Figure 6.4 and Table 6.5 show very clearly that she succeeded in the second of these aims.

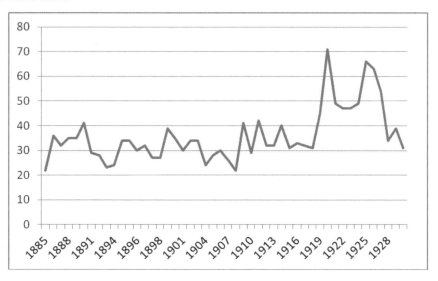

6.4: YEARLY ENTRANT NUMBERS 1885–1930[59]

Growth was achieved by admitting an increased number of younger (and older) entrants. The view prevailing among the Province's previous leaders, that it was prudent to be cautious about the admission of younger women, was set aside,

---

57 Sister Hannezo, Letter to Sister Servants, January 1924. 9-3 DCMH.

58 ibid., p. 30.

59 'Statistical Survey since 1847' 9-5-0-1-5 and 'Statistiques de la Province' Book 1 10-1 DCMH.

as Table 6.5 illustrates. Between 1920 and 1926 the proportion of members who entered under twenty years of age went up from the 2–3 per cent level at which they had been held by the Province since 1885 to 14 per cent.

	Total known	Aged 20 or under	20–24	25–29	30–34	35 +
1880–89	198	12 (6%)	95 (48%)	63 (33%)	21 (11%)	3 (2%)
1890–99	217	7 (3%)	108 (50%)	85 (39%)	16 (7%)	1(1%)
1900–09	218	4 (2%)	86 (39%)	100 (46%)	23 (10%)	6 (3%)
1910–19	246	5 (2%)	89 (36%)	87 (35%)	54 (22%)	12 (5%)
1920–25	246	33 (14%)	95 (38%)	66 (27%)	27 (11%)	25 (10%)
1926–29	127	6 (5%)	54 (42.5%)	35 (27.5)	16 (12.5)	16 (12.5)

(Sisters who made first vows only)

6.5 TOTAL NUMBER AND AGE PROFILES 1880–1929

Similarly, Sister Hannezo concluded that officers had been overscrupulous when it came to applicants who had worked in factories and domestic service. She told Sister Servants that their attitude was not 'in the spirit of St Vincent' and instructed them to widen their social criteria.[60]

Hannezo's more egalitarian policy on age and on social background was laudable in principle, but in practice it had a cost for individuals and the Province. Sixty years later, in 1985, Sister Jean Miller was given the task of copying 'a list of all the women who have ever been in the British Province'. She described how the excitement and inspiration she had initially derived from the task when recording the earliest years gave way to a 'certain sense of unease and trouble'. This was because she 'was writing about a difficult period' in the 1920s that she called 'the exodus' and 'the purge', when 'row upon row of sisters were sent home'.[61] It led her to remember her own days as a young Sister, when 'the older sisters were

---

60 Sister Hannezo, [cf f/n 57] Letter to Sister Matthews, 9 February 1923. 9-3-4 DCMH.

61 'Writing the Centenary Roll-book of the British Province, 1985: Letters from Sister Jean Miller DC to Sister Esther McDermott DC', *Colloquy Journal of the Irish Province of the Congregation of the Mission* Spring 2008, no.55, p.519. Jean Miller misdates it to the early 1920s but makes it clear that the visitatrice who undertook the 'purges' was Sister Boyle, who was visitatrice from 1926, and her successor Sister Thomson from 1928.

still talking about it', that is, 'the exodus'. According to them, 'there had been a visitatrice who was a little too concerned with numbers' and the next visitatrice 'had the distasteful task of weeding out the unsuitable people...'.[62] Her memories find an echo in the anecdotal history of Central House written by Sister Catherine O'Driscoll in 1948 from her own notebooks as seminary directress and later as bursar. She noted of the mid 1920s, without commenting, that 'many subjects came to the seminary who were most unsuitable and had to be sent away later'.[63] The statistics confirm these impressions: of those who entered the seminary between 1920 and 1926, some 23 per cent were later dismissed compared to the rate of around 10 per cent for the comparable groups between 1900 and 1909 or between 1909 and 1919.[64] By the time the problems surfaced, Sister Hannezo had left the Province.

The problems may have been created by Sister Hannezo being 'too concerned with numbers', as was later thought in the community. But perhaps it was her desire to implement practices that had worked well in France which led her unwittingly to transgress the subtle boundaries of class and national relationships that had enabled the Province to function effectively until this time. There had been a practical wisdom garnered from experience that, in the British context and at this time, it was better for applicants to wait until they were aged twenty. But the veto on admitting women from the industrial working classes reflected the culture of social class in Britain from the perspective of its most privileged members. It was they who were in a position to decide, and their decision needs to be considered in the light of the Daughters' very particular way of life. Unlike in many religious communities, only a thin curtain – not distinct grades of membership or cell walls - separated Daughters of Charity from one another: they (including provincial officers) shared dormitories, meal tables, prayer and recreation. Sisters were not separated by social class as in most religious orders and congregations, where even prayer was different for choir or teaching and lay sisters. Daughters of Charity had aprons, collars and even underclothing in common. Sister Hannezo thought the question of 'suitability' could be solved quite simply: in France, Sister Servants checked on each candidate by visiting her home and family 'to look carefully at their manners, reputation'.[65] This had never been the practice in Britain and Ireland. Since there was no one who felt able to tell the visitatrice that such behaviour crossed an invisible line of cultural sensibility about privacy and intrusion in both islands, her plan for the expansion of entrants went ahead without the accompanying checks she had requested. What had been unspoken remained so, with consequences that have left their mark in the ebb and flow of admissions and dismissals.

---

62 ibid. 'Writing the Centenary Roll-book', p. 519.

63 O'Driscoll, 'Sidelights',p. 78. 13-4-3 DCMH.

64 Calculated from the registers of entrants and departures. 13-2-1 DCMH.

65 Sister Hannezo, [cf f/n 57] Letter to Sister Matthews, 9 February 1923,.9-3-4 DCMH.

But in their decision to move Sister Howard from Mill Hill to Ealing, the French Superiors were met with a direct and outspoken response from British and Irish Sisters that confounded their expectations about the practice of obedience and acceptance of decisions. When 'the Province heard about the appointment, regret and astonishment prevailed'.[66] The Sisters felt it unjust and unkind that Sister Howard would not be allowed to end her days at Mill Hill, and they said so. 'Many letters expressing these views were addressed to our Venerable Superiors.' Nor was this only the view of English Sisters. When he travelled over to Ireland, Father Byrne was 'visited by many Sisters who gave expression to the same opinion'.[67] Irish, English and Scottish Sisters were united in feeling with their companions. Nor did these feelings give way with the passage of time. In 1923, whenSuperioress General Inchelin visited the Province 'she was surprised at...the universality of the request made her by the Sisters that Sister Howard...should be allowed to return to Mill Hill.' The Sisters prevailed. Later that year' the ailing Sister Howard returned to Central House.[68]

The overall impact of Hannezo's period of office was to tighten controls at the centre over matters large and small and to attempt the transposition of practices from the mother house. In an exhortation to the Province which can be read as a critique of her predecessors, and which was in tune with her own spirit and the stoical spirit of the inter-war years, Hannezo wrote that:

> The good spirit of the Central House, the example given here, is so important, for it affects the whole Province. It is not learning or extraordinary gifts which sustain the works, but the practice of the virtues of our vocation – humility, simplicity, charity, work done for Our Loving Lord in silence, recollection, union of hearts, and respect for Superiors, seeing in them Christ Himself, which allows of no criticism.[69]

Tellingly, at her departure from the Province in 1926 she was thanked for having 'spread the true spirit of St Vincent throughout the Province'.[70] Uncritical obedience was once again being asserted as the 'true spirit of St Vincent'.

Louise Hannezo had undoubtedly pinpointed important limitations in the class and national perspectives of the provincial leadership group, and she brought about much-needed retirements of officers and Sister Servants who had been in post too long. At the same time she underestimated the effectiveness of the more adaptive approach taken by Sister Marcellus on such matters as permitting

---

66 ibid.

67 ibid.

68 According to Sister Langdale's confidential account before Sister Howard died in 1926. both William Byrne and Sister Hannezo expressed appreciation for her 'great strength of soul' and her devotedness.

69 Typescript notes concerning Ma Soeur Hannezo 9-3-1 DCMH.

70 Provincial Council Minutes, 9 October 1926 vol. XIII. 9-0-2-1 DCMH.

Irish Sisters to make retreats in Ireland or allowing Sister Servants more room for individual initiative. Hannezo was, perhaps, inclined to interpret harmony in relationships between the Sisters as a lack of proper distance in relationships between them, and to see it in a less positive light than did her predecessor.

What matters is not so much who was 'right' about the nature of 'the good spirit of the Central House', but that there were differing benchmarks and perspectives on this important matter. The Sisters of the Province themselves had always believed that they followed the norms of the mother house to the last letter and often re-counted stories about their own fidelity. 'On returning from Paris after a retreat', it was said of Mary Ann Costello, 'she shared with us the happiness which had been hers':

> We hung on every word which fell from her lips while she spoke to us of the dear Company and our venerated Superiors...She loved to quote the Mother House as our model' on poverty and order. 'One day a lady asked her if our costume had not undergone some modifications for our English climate' 'Certainly not' she replied almost with indignation' and if there was even a pin differently placed, I would remove it at once.[71]

Hannezo's criticisms of the Province show not only that she did not agree with the Sisters' own assessment of their fidelity to detail, but also that she assumed French ways to be best and that they should prevail. Her views about a number of practices in the Province illuminate the tension between adaptive and centralising tendencies common in transnational institutions.

The conduct of leadership in the British Province offers a window on the realities of membership in a transnational community at a time when provincial identity, with all its internal nuances, was being forged. On the inside of the community, bonds of unity were strong, yet the identity of a Daughter of Charity in the United Kingdom of Great Britain and Ireland was experienced with different inflections from those in France. Daughters in Britain acted together to defend aspects of their Company identity, such as their habit or their daily schedule, when it was under threat from external sources. Yet, in other ways, such as permitting the exercise of local initiative or loosening administrative exactness, provincial leaders in this era inculturated what was familiar, rather than advancing the model preferred in the mother house. Finally, when their own sense of natural justice was offended, as in the case of Sister Howard, British and Irish Sisters united to speak out to Superiors. In practice, if not in theory, there were multiple ways of being and belonging. The fact that a united community was sustained through the severe tests of a troubled quasi-colonial relationship, a failed negotiation for Home Rule, and finally the rupture of the United Kingdom in the Irish War of Independence

---

71 *Notices of Deceased Sisters* (1919), writing about Mary Ann Costello, p. 64. 10-3-1 DCMH.

and Anglo-Irish Treaty of 1922, is testimony to the strength of the Sisters' identity as Daughters of Charity. But it also speaks volumes about the benefits for British and Irish companions of membership in a transnational institution where, at this time, responsibility lay in the hands of its French leadership.

The period from the creation of the Province to 1920 was a time in the community's history when the elite of the first generation held posts of responsibility and the (large) second generation entered with all the confidence and energy that came from being born into a firmly post-Emancipation Church. Whatever their shortcomings when measured against more recent expectations about acculturation, subsidiarity and consultation, the various strategies used to construct a Daughter's being and belonging across borders in the period 1885–1925 were remarkable for their mission effectiveness. There was an energising sense of important tasks needing to be done for the Church's mission among the poorest in society, to which we now turn.

7

The practice of charity in the first and second generations

> An Administrator one day said to her: 'Sister, before putting
> butter on the bread for your children, you should pay the
> interest on your debt.' Our sister calmly replied: 'Well then,
> you must ask my Superiors to change me from this office,
> for as a Sister of Charity I will never deprive the children
> of the butter on their bread: the poor will be served first,
> I will then occupy myself with your interest.' [1]

The main business of the Province's leaders lay in their oversight of its works and initiatives to minister to people in poverty. From the day of its establishment the new provincial council could not keep up with requests to make foundations and even with the increase in the number of Sisters the pressure continued. Between 1909 and 1912, for example, the council turned down 18 invitations from places as far apart as Camborne in Cornwall and Troon in Ayrshire, each for a specific project. [2] Some invitations were refused because their supporters were unrealistic about financial viability or had in mind a project unsuited to the Daughters' mission and purpose, others were taken up at a later date. But more often than not there were simply not enough Sisters to send. When it came to the practice of charity, demand outstripped supply.

In recent years historians have begun to reframe the charitable and educational activities of nineteenth- and early-twentieth-century Catholic sisters. They are no longer confined within a denominational narrative as they once were. [3] Scholars of women religious have shown that their activities are to be understood within the history of wider Christian and secular social movements,

---

1 *Notices of Deceased Sisters* (1933), p.8–18 10-3-1 DCMH.

2 Provincial Council Minutes for those years, vol. IV, 9-5-0-2-1 DCMH. Sisters did go to Troon in 1915.

3 See Mangion, *Contested Identities*, pp.8–18.

such as philanthropic poverty relief, the education revolution,[4] the development of healthcare[5] and social work,[6] and the emergence of professions for women, as well as within the history of Catholicism.[7]

Although these studies have revealed that the thrust of the sisters' work was the same almost everywhere, a comparison across countries highlights the extent to which its meaning and consequences have differed according to the religious, political and social context of the country concerned. In Ireland, for example, the education and social work of women's congregations was pivotal to the project of constructing Irish national identity as Catholic and to the provision of education as a means for social mobility,[8] but it also increasingly promoted religious conformity and sexual discipline within an emerging nationalist culture.[9] In France Napoleon reinstated institutes of active sisters for the benefit of the state and society while attempting to control the influence of the Church, but Catholic sisters – often financed by state authorities – promoted Catholicism vigorously, renewing the post-Revolutionary French Church through services that were popular with the people and thus helped the Church to resist *laïcité*.[10] If the part played by Catholic sisters in nineteenth-century nation building differed according to context, so too did their relationship to the emergence of professions for women. Some scholars have argued that the services provided by sisters contributed to 'processes of professionalisation and the rise of social and human rights'.[11] Others have shown that where Catholicism was the majority religion, as in France, Belgium and Ireland, the labour of sisters could be used by public authorities to provide low-cost welfare and education to the detriment of employment opportunities for other women or to women's engagement in philanthropy.[12] In a further variant where Catholicism was a minority faith, such as Denmark and the American north-eastern seaboard

---

4 Bart Hellinckx, Frank Simon and Marc Depaepe, *The Forgotten Contribution of the Teaching Sisters: a historiographical essay on the educational work of Catholic women religious in the 19th and 20th centuries*, Studia Paedagogica 44 (Leuven: Leuven University Press, 2009); Sarah A. Curtis, *Educating the Faithful: Religion, Schooling and Society in Nineteenth Century France* (Dekalb, Ill.: Northern Illinois University Press, 2000).

5 Katrin Schultheiss, *Bodies and Souls: Politics and the Professionalization of Nursing in France, 1880–1922* (Cambridge, MA: Harvard University Press, 2001).

6 Schultheiss, *Bodies and Souls*; Wittberg, *From Piety to Professionalism*.

7 Margaret Regensberg, 'The Religious Sisters of the Good Shepherd and the Professionalization of Social Work' (unpublished PhD thesis, State University New York, Stony Brook, 2007).

8 Magray, *The Transforming Power of Nuns*.

9 Maria Luddy, *Prostitution and Irish Society, 1800–1940* (Cambridge: Cambridge University Press, 2007) and *Women and Philanthropy in Nineteenth Century Ireland*.

10 Ralph Gibson, *A Social History of French Catholicism* (London: Routledge, 1989); Hazel Mills, 'Women and Religious Revival in Nineteenth-Century France' in Emily Clark and Mary Laven eds., *Women and Religion in the Atlantic Age, 1550-1900* (Farnham, Surrey: Ashgate, 2013).

11 Annalies van Heijst, *Models of Charitable Care: Catholic Nuns and Children in their Care in Amsterdam, 1852– 2002* (Leiden and Boston: Brill, 2008), p. 18.

12 Maarten Van Dijck, 'From Workhouse to Convent: The Sisters of Saint Vincent de Paul and Public Charity in Eeklo, 1830–1900', and Luddy, 'Power, Authority and the Funding of Convents in Ireland, 1780–1900' both in Maarten Van Dijck et al. eds., *The Economics of Providence* ; Luddy, *Women and Philanthropy*.

states, the sisters' welfare and education initiatives were often counter-cultural, challenging restrictive ideas about charity and women's work.[13] And where there was little social homogeneity, such as in the American West or the Canadian and Australian 'frontiers', it has been argued that charitably entrepreneurial sisters played a key role in community building as they established institutions to provide for the social needs of all with support from across the community.[14] It would seem that, regardless of the similarity of their motivations and the patterns of their social works, neither the practice of charity by sisters nor their relationships with Church and State have had identical or unambiguous meanings. Newer interpretations have highlighted that even in transnational institutes with a strong centralised identity the particularity of context remains powerful.

In Britain during the second half of the nineteenth century Daughters worked in a context of radical economic transformation and destabilised social structures combined with relatively resilient political structures. The established Churches of England and Scotland were politically powerful; evangelical Protestantism as represented by the broad church movement of the period was culturally normative and Catholicism, despite its growth, remained both marginal and marginalised.[15] Yet it was also the case that the principle of a pluralist religious state had been established and one of its consequences was gradually to create greater equality of treatment for Catholics by the state. Moreover, a space in civil society was open to Catholics through the voluntary principle of social organisation that was such a feature of British public life.[16] Voluntary bodies had long played a part in the democratic and civic vision of the British nations and were understood as a vital 'moral space between rulers and ruled'.[17] In the nineteenth century they grew in importance, scale and diversity.[18] The Victorian state actively fostered a 'mixed economy' of welfare provision 'consisting of the state, voluntary action, and support by the family'. New Roman Catholic voluntary organisations, which included communities of Catholic sisters, were able to incorporate themselves

---

13 Yvonne Maria Werner, *Nuns and Sisters in the Nordic Countries after the Reformation: A Female Counter-Culture in Modern Society* (Uppsala: Studia Missionalia Svecana LXXXIX, 2004); Fitzgerald, *Habits of Compassion: Irish Catholic Nuns and the Origins of New York's Welfare System, 1830–1920.*

14 Butler, *Across God's Frontiers: Catholic Sisters in the American West.*

15 See Stewart J. Brown, 'The Broad Church Movement, National Culture, and the Established Churches of Great Britain, c.1850–c.1900,' in Hilary M. Carey and John Gascoigne eds., *Church and State in Old and New Worlds* (Leiden and Boston: Brill, 2011), pp.99–128.

16 Matthew Hilton and James McKay eds., *The Ages of Voluntaryism: How we got to the Big Society* (Oxford: Oxford University Press, 2011) and Bernard Harris, 'The historiography of voluntary action: where have we come from, and where are we going?', paper given on the occasion of the 20th anniversary of the Voluntary Action History Society, www.vahs.org.uk/about/background accessed 28.April.2015).

17 F. Prochaska, *Christianity and Social Service* p.5, quoting Quentin Skinner; Paula Bartley, 'Moral Regeneration: Women and the Civic Gospel in Birmingham, 1870–1914', *Midland History*, vol. 25, (2000), pp. 145–148.

18 Only a minority of Victorian philanthropy bodies were directed towards the relief of acute poverty. See Harris above and Sarah Morris, 'The greatest philanthropic tradition on earth? Measuring the extent of voluntary activity in London, 1874–1914,' unpublished paper given to the Voluntary Action History Society seminar, 9 February 2006, www.vahs.org.uk (accessed 25 April.2015).

within this mixed economy.[19] Under persistent pressure from Catholic lobbyists state support was extended to Catholic charitable initiatives, most strikingly so in the case of schooling, but also to a range of other activities from Catholic Poor Law schools to child welfare clinics and Catholic probation work.[20] As we will see, this aspect of British national culture was of considerable importance to the charitable practice of the Daughters of Charity.

Most research into the history of Catholic sisters in Britain and Ireland has concerned their educational work: studies of their other charitable or philanthropic activities remains underdeveloped.[21] For their part, historians of Victorian and Edwardian Britain have made the assumption that British philanthropy in this era was a Protestant project.[22] Catholic outreach activities, where acknowledged, have simply been absorbed within the mainstream narrative without inflecting it.[23] We are told that 'Catholics founded innumerable charities that mirrored Protestant ones'[24] and that 'the most striking thing about Catholic philanthropy is its imitative and defensive character', having a 'narrowly denominational emphasis greater than any other denomination'.[25] Yet there are also hints of its possible difference in the intriguing and unsubstantiated view expressed in Bishop Arthur Doubleday of Brentwood's 1929 essay on philanthropy that 'Catholics have their own methods of benevolence'[26] and in the evidence provided by Sheridan Gilley for the early Victorian era that Catholics and Protestants in Victorian Britain had 'notably dissimilar notions of almsgiving and a notably dissimilar charitable ideal'.[27]

The framework used here to explore all these assumptions and conclusions further in relation to the Daughters of Charity is adapted from Dutch historian

19 Lewis, 'The Voluntary Sector in the Mixed Economy of Welfare,' in Gladstone ed., *Before Beveridge*, p. 10; Kate Bradley, *Poverty, Philanthropy and the State:Charities and the Working-Classes in London* (Manchester: Manchester University Press, 2009) available at in http://www.history.ac.uk/reviews/review/900.

20 F. Prochaska, *Voluntary Impulse* (London: Faber and Faber, 1998).

21 See Luddy, *Women and Philanthropy*, p. 45 who notes that their educational work in Ireland has been 'better treated by historians than have other aspects of their work such as the provision of facilities and care for the poor, destitute and outcast'. See also the works already cited by Kehoe for Scotland and by Mangion, Nye, White and Walsh for England.

22 Prochaska, *Christianity and Social Service in Modern Britain*, p.5.

23 For example, Frank Prochaska, *Women and Philanthropy in Nineteenth Century England* (Oxford: Clarendon, 1980), pp. 109, 147, and 189; Prochaska, *Christianity and Social Services*, p. 30 and pp. 64–65.

24 Frank Prochaska, *Schools of Citizenship : Charity and Civic Virtue* (London: Civitas, 2002), p.18. See also the seminal work on this subject David Owen, *English Philanthropy 1660-1960* (Cambridge MA and Oxford: Harvard University Press and Oxford University Press, 1965) as well as more recent monographs and overviews such as those by Prochaska and Robert Whelan based on research by Barendina Smedley, *Helping the Poor: Friendly visiting, dole charities and dole queues* (London: Civitas, 2001), p. 6.

25 Josef Althoz, 'Social Catholicism in England in the Age of the Devotional Revolution,' in Stewart J. Brown and David W Miller eds., *Piety and Power in Ireland 1760–1960: Essays in Honour of Emmet Larkin* (Notre Dame, Ind: University of Notre Dame Press, 2000), pp.217–8.

26 Bishop of Brentwood, 'Catholicism and Philanthropy,' in *Catholic Emancipation 1829 to 1929: Essays by Various Writers* with an Introduction by Cardinal Bourne (London: Longmans, Green and Co., 1929), p. 175.

27 Sheridan Gilley, 'Papists, Protestants and the Irish in London, 1835–70', in G.J. Cuming and. Baker eds., *Popular Belief and Practice* (Cambridge: Studies in Church History 8, 1972), p. 261.

and ethicist Annelies van Heijst's extensive work on Catholic charitable care. Unlike many other historical approaches she attempts to get below the surface of welfare institutions to understand the ideals that motivated Catholic sisters and to account for the everyday details of life as experienced by both care givers and care recipients. Her approach focuses on the welfare work of sisters as a *charitable care practice* that comprises three important elements: their ideas and values; their practices of charity; and the nature of the care itself. She begins by noting that since the 1960s and 1970s the concept of 'charity' has been treated with a degree of suspicion in academic and policy discourse.[28] It can indeed be a double-edged sword since paternalism and repression as well as compassion and generosity were inherent in certain Victorian and Edwardian ideas about charity.[29] Abuse of power, moreover, could hide under the blanket of care on occasions. But because the concept of *caritas* was essential to the Daughters' self-understanding, it is vital to explore what their espoused values system meant in this period.

Care is adopted here as the primary descriptor for the Daughters' activities across residential homes, training institutions, community social support, home visiting and pastoral parish work.[30] It can be an elusive term,[31] but it has the advantage of being more accurate a description of the Daughters' activities than welfare and of bringing out the gendered nature of their daily labours.[32] So much of care, often associated with women's domestic work, is easily taken for granted. For those without the fundamentals of life it means the provision of shelter, clothing and prepared meals, a clean orderly environment and sick nursing. Care requires that someone undertake these tasks directly through the taking of personal responsibility for the well-being of others and the making of a relationship with them. In the case of children it extends to include all that is meant by 'upbringing' (education, preparation for work and life, moral and spiritual development), shaped by the social, cultural and religious frameworks within which it takes place.[33]

'Practice' refers here to the implementation of care on a daily basis as distinct from general attitudes, strategies or theories.[34] Decisions made by the

---

28 van Heijst, *Models of Charitable Care*, p. 18

29 See Jones, *The Charitable Imperative*, pp. 16–17.

30 Janet Boddy, Claire Cameron and Peter Moss eds, *Care Work: Present and Future* (Abingdon: Routledge, 2006).

31 Boddy et al., *Care Work*, pp. 3–18. See also Warren Thomas Wright, Project for the History of Care, University of Georgetown, http://care.georgetown.edu/The%20Project. and various publications.

32 Ninna Eghard, 'A Gendered Perspective on Welfare and Religion in Europe,' in *Welfare and Religion in 21st Century Europe: vol. 2, Gendered, Religious and Social Change* (Farnham: Ashgate, 2011), pp. 62–106.

33 Social care has been defined as 'the activities and relations involved in meeting the physical and emotional requirements of dependent adults and children and the normative, economic and social frameworks within which they are assigned and carried out' M. Daly and J. Lewis, 'The concept of social care and the analysis of contemporary welfare states.' *British Journal of Sociology* 51 (2) 2000: 281–289 quoted in Eghard, p. 65

34 See Mark Smith, *Residential child care in practice: Making a difference* (Bristol: Policy Press, University of Bristol, 2013), p. 1.

Province about who to care for and in what ways to care for them, for example, tell us what priorities the community had. The choices made about how to allocate and use financial resources were likewise an expression of priorities. Individual Sisters had their personal views, but the Company set the tone for the practice of individual Sisters. In turn these actions and attitudes could be life-determining for the children and young people in their care, and they mattered – to a greater or lesser degree – to the adults with whom they engaged. In considering the nature of their charitable care practices, fresh questions can be asked about the Sisters' attitudes, relationships and daily routines. In what ways, if any, were they distinctively Catholic and Vincentian?

Charitable priorities, 1870–1925

> Oh what happiness, if...the Company had to serve only the completely destitute poor.
>
> (Louise de Marillac)[35]

The commitment of the Company's founders to work with those in greatest material and spiritual need set the benchmark for the Daughters' priorities. In Britain, as already described, the clerical priority was education, both as a means to prevent or reduce so-called 'leakage' from the Church and to promote social betterment.[36] All Catholic sisters were under tremendous pressure from the hierarchy to take part in this great drive which was, of course, a key means to prevent destitution in the first place. Building on their first projects in Sheffield, London, and Lanark, the challenge for the Daughters in Britain therefore was to stay close to their traditional service rather than succumb to the pressures to move into elementary teaching on a large scale.[37] We start with an analysis of the projects undertaken by the Sisters between 1885 and 1925 to show the extent to which first-and second-generation Sisters sustained Vincentian social and spiritual priorities in the British context and also to tease out the pattern of service that emerged.

Institution-based care of children and young people

Highest priority was given to children and young people up to the age of fourteen. Residential care homes were the most numerous of the institutions the Daughters either founded themselves or, more usually, managed on behalf of others. This category encompassed a much greater range of initiatives than might be inferred or imagined by the single label. It included emergency short-term accommodation for children living on the streets or at immediate risk (refuges); secure units as

---

35 Louise de Marilliac, *Spiritual Writings*, p. 833. Written in 1660.

36 Tenbus, *English Catholics and the Education of the Poor*.

37 Maureen Fitzgerald discusses how this was a challenge in the USA too: *Habits of Compassion*, p. 38.

an alternative to prison for children and young people under fourteen sentenced by the criminal justice system (reformatories); residential training homes for those committed by magistrates because they were on the streets, thought to be neglected or involved in petty crime (industrial schools);[38] homes for former residents of reformatories and prisons (probation hostels); after-care for working boys and girls who had no other home (hostels); special needs residential care for children with conditions such as deafness and blindness, and homes for children with cognitive impairments, often in combination with physical disabilities; and convalescent and holiday homes by the coast or in the countryside. Most numerous of all were the residential homes for children who might be orphans but more often had lost one parent, leaving the other unable to cope because of poverty, ill-health or both. These too were of different kinds: Poor Law schools, diocesant owned homes or those owned by the Daughters themselves. Table 7.1 shows the range of institutions managed by the Daughters and their changing relative importance to the Province between 1885 and 1925.

Type of project	1885	1905	1925
Children's homes: voluntary funded	5	8	9
Children's homes: Poor Law	2	7	13
Reformatory/approved school	1	1	-
Industrial school	5	8	4
Special needs residential schools	2	3	6
Convalescent and holiday homes for city children	1	1	4
Children's refuge (emergency care)	1	2	3
Hostels for young workers and job seekers	1	5	12
Probation hostels	-	2	3
TOTAL	18	37	54

7.1: INSTITUTION-BASED WELFARE PROVISION FOR CHILDREN AND YOUNG ADULTS IN BRITAIN 1885-1925

NB many Houses conducted more than one activity

38 For a full discussion of which groups were eligible to be admitted to reformatories and industrial schools and an analysis of registers see Gillian Carol Gear, 'Industrial Schools in England, 1857–1933: 'Moral Hospitals' or "Repressive Institutions"? (University of London, Institute of Education PhD thesis, 1999), Chapter III.

Not revealed by these overall figures is the striking way that the Sisters became significant providers of boys-only residential homes, including those for boys over the age of nine, as already suggested in Chapter 3. Their Rule, like that of other women's communities, had restricted them to work primarily with their own sex and with younger boys.[39] The strength of this restriction is illustrated by the fact that when Elizabeth Ann Seton's American Sisters of Charity affiliated to the French Company in 1850 and were informed they had to give up their boys' homes some branches chose to go it alone rather than comply when the Paris superiors would not adapt to the provision for boys.[40] Nor was it normal in the British context for women to have overall responsibility for boys' homes: they were often run by a married couple with the wife as Matron.[41] When Thomas Bowman Stephenson, founder of the Methodist National Children's Homes and Orphanages Society established and trained a Sisterhood of the Children (1878) to work in Methodist boys' homes, he erroneously regarded this as an entirely new departure; 'Ours is the only [institution]' he wrote, 'in which the training of boys in all routines and influences of domestic life is committed to women'.[42] The government's own chief inspector of reformatories and industrial schools, the Anglican Reverend Sydney Turner, could have told him otherwise. In 1869, six years after the Daughters had taken on the management of St Vincent's boys' home in Beacon Lane in Liverpool, Turner conducted his first inspection of the home. He gave St Vincent's the same kind of glowing report he had bestowed on St Joseph's girls' home in Sheffield (see Chapter 3). The home had not been an attractive or easy proposition for the Daughters; there was insufficient funding to pay for even quite basic levels of food and clothing and the boys, in rebellion over the austere regime, had taken control of the keys from the male lay staff who previously had charge so that they could come and go as they pleased.[43] Moreover, the chapter of Liverpool Cathedral had only been persuaded to offer the Daughters a trial period managing the home (then called St Louis Gonzaga's) after they had run out of all other options and

39 I am grateful to Dr Sarah Curtis for confirmation from her own research that in general boys over the age of seven were taught and managed by religious brothers and priests in France. See Sarah Curtis, *Educating the Faithful*.

40 See Fitzgerald, *Habits of Compassion*, pp. 46–52. With great reluctance most agreed, hiring 'extra matrons to care for boys and retaining administrative control over...orphanages' but where they did not, the issue became the cause of a separation.

41 For the staffing of reformatories and industrial schools more generally see Gear, 'Industrial Schools in England,' Chapter V.

42 http://www.theirhistory.co.uk/70001/info.php?p=13 (accessed 8 December 2014).

43 Susan O'Brien, 'The Daughters of Charity and the revival of Religious life for women in nineteenth-century Britain' in Brejon de Lavergnée ed., *Quatre siècles de cornettes*, pp. 274–90.

on the assurance of Monsignor James Nugent that, although women, they were capable. Known in the diocese as 'Nugent's folly' the renamed home was turned round by the Daughters.

In 1870 Cardinal Manning asked the community to manage a second boys' home at Leyton in the Westminster Archdiocese. It was proving difficult for bishops to find a sufficient number of men's religious communities to undertake this work, not only in Liverpool but in other parts of Britain too.[44] Several factors were at work. Girls were well-catered for by the increasing numbers of women's communities. There were fewer male communities with experience compared with France, Italy or Ireland, and in any case several well-publicised instances of sexual abuse and ill judgement about discipline in Catholic boys' reformatories and industrial homes run by male religious gave them a poor reputation with the authorities. At the same time, partly because society was preoccupied with safeguarding girls and young women from sexual predators, those in the field considered that the vulnerability of boys was being overlooked.[45] Boys cost more to clothe and feed, were more often left to fend for themselves and were less likely to remain with their mothers if the family broke up.[46] Manning expressed his own concern that boys 'had nowhere to live and often no parents or friends' and after 1888 re-focused the Westminster Diocesan Fund on provision of 'Homes for Destitute Boys'.[47] What started as something of an experiment in Liverpool became a more systematic response to social need in Britain until it developed into a distinctive feature of the Daughters' charitable care practice there, as Table 7.2 illustrates.

Type of project	Boys	Girls
Industrial schools (state aided)	4	5
Orphanages (state-aided Poor Law schools)	8	6
Orphanages (voluntary funded)	6	11

44 See David Lannon, 'Bishop Turner, the Salford Diocese and Reformatory Provision, 1854–1872,' *Recusant History*, Vol. 23, 3 (May 1997), p. 396 and Report of the Commissioner appointed by the Secretary of State on 24 September 1894 to inquire into the allegations made regarding the treatment of children in the St. John's Industrial School for RC Boys at Walthamstow. *Parliamentary Papers 1895* (107) LXXX. The authorities had a strongly held view that the absence of matrons and other women staff in institutions run by male religious orders was detrimental for children and led to a harsher environment.

45 Reports of Inspectors of Prisons, Reformatory and Industrial Schools. 6th Report 1863, p. 34.' 18th Report 1875, pp.17–18 House of Commons Library; and Lannon, 'Bishop Turner and Reformatory Provision'.

46 House of Commons, 'Physical Infirmities, Institutes, 1891 Census' *Sessional Papers, 1891, Population* vol. 8, pp. 366–8, quoted by Jessica Sheetz' p. 569.

47 V.A. McLelland, *Cardinal Manning: His Public Life and Influence, 1865–92* (Oxford, 1962), p..47.

Type of project	Boys	Girls
Residential schools for deaf and dumb (mixed funded)	2	2
Residential schools for blind (mixed funded)	2	2
Hospital and school for disabled children (state aided)	1	-
Sub-total	23	26
Hostels for young workers (aged over 15) (voluntary and self-funding)	4	16
Total	27	42

7.2: RESIDENTIAL CARE BY SEX 1915

In total the Province opened or took on the management of more than 40 children's homes of various kinds in Britain between 1885 and 1925. These included instances of all categories of institutional care funded by the state for the welfare of children and by already established charities such as the Liverpool Catholic Blind Institute and St John's Institute for the Deaf and Dumb, the only Catholic provisions for these special needs in the Victorian period.[48] Writing in 2006 to persuade a sceptical readership of social workers that there was a continuing place for residential care, Ian Milligan and Irene Stevens felt it vital to overcome the prevailing 'stereotypical images about "typical" residential child care...' The reality, they argued, is of a great diversity that ranges 'from "mainstream" children's homes, to residential schools, to specialist disability services, to secure units'.[49] The standards of accommodation, the degree of accountability and the professional practices associated with early twenty-first-century residential care, including the understanding of childhood trauma and psychology, differ markedly from one 100 years earlier, but it was the earlier generations who initiated the now familiar range. The Daughters in Britain participated in the diversification and specialisation of social care, sometimes going beyond the remit set by either the State or the Church as they drew on their own practical experience and sought to fulfil the Company's charitable mission.

48 Carmen M. Mangion, 'Filles de la charité et sourds-muets: Une histoire transnationale (1869–1901)', in Brejon de Lavergnée ed., *Quatre siècles de cornettes*, pp. 291–307.

49 Ian Milligan and Irene Stevens, *Residential Child Care: Collaborative Practice* (London: Sage Publications, 2006), p. 9.

Parish-and community-based ministries

If the Sisters' institution-based work can be said to belong in the category of welfare support known in Britain as 'indoor relief', their practice of home visiting fitted into the category of 'outdoor relief'. Both were a blend of material and spiritual ministries. Priests asked for visiting Sisters not only because of their discreet and self-directed distribution of welfare, but because, as we will see, their visits extended the Church's sacramental provision and evangelical mission into places of multiple deprivation and into the homes of Catholics at the margins of observance. When a small group of parish Sisters combined visiting, parish and sacristy work with teaching in the elementary school they could be a powerful addition to the life of the parish and community. Table 7.3 indicates that community-based parish work, which might be initiated by a priest, a lay benefactor, or by the Province itself, developed most strongly after 1905.

	1885	1905	1925
Parishes visited	8	c35	131
Prisons visited	-	3	7
Houses running evening classes, parish sodalities and clubs.	12	28	40
Crèches for infants of working mothers	2	2	3
Dispensaries		3	2
Child welfare clinics	-	-	2
Parish elementary schools	7	·15	36
Continuation schools (state aided)	-	-	2

7.3: PARISH- AND COMMUNITY-BASED MINISTRIES 1885-1925

Hospital and other institutional work

In France, the United States and elsewhere, hospitals, nursing and dispensaries were significant in the mission of Daughters of Charity. Like home visiting they continued a practice which had begun in seventeenth-century France.[50] In Ireland healthcare of various types accounted for ten out of the eighteen foundations

---

50 Kristine Gunnell, *Daughters of Charity: Women, Religious Mission and Hospital Care in Los Angeles 1856–1972* (Chicago: De Paul, 2013); Mann Wall, *Unlikely Entrepreneurs*; Katrin Schultheiss, *Bodies and Souls*.

made by the Province between 1885 and 1925.[51] Although the Sisters founded their first small hospital at Lanark in 1860 and added other healthcare activities from 1870 onwards, this category made up a relatively small strand of their work in Britain. It proved difficult to secure funding and, despite the significance of Anglican sisterhoods in nursing in the years from 1850 to 1880, a secular and local non-sectarian approach to voluntary hospital provision had become firmly established in Britain by the final decades of the century, as Florence Nightingale had intended.[52] Perhaps for these reasons the Daughters' activity in this field, like that of all Catholic providers, was small-scale and intermittent before 1920, as demonstrated in Table 7.4.[53]

WORKS	1885	1905	1925
Private schools[1]	2	2	3
Hospitals, sanatoria, hospices	2	3	7
Infirmary for seminarians (priests)	-	-	1

7.4: OTHER SMALL-SCALE PROJECTS 1885–1925

The First World War and its tragic legacy of injury and poor physical and mental health became the spur to found four further hospitals, hospices and nursing homes between 1920 and 1925. It was after the War too that the Sisters were persuaded to take on the domestic and infirmarian support services for seminarians in the Archdiocese of Liverpool (1920). They did so very reluctantly on the grounds that it was 'morally impossible' to refuse the Archbishop's request, but remained for as short a time as was decent on the grounds that 'this is not our work'.[54] This was also the case with the private school work which made up a very minor strand of their activity with special cases being made for their Catholic provision in rural Herefordshire and in Darlington where they began the first Catholic post-elementary school for girls in an environment that was particularly hostile to Catholics.[55]

The number of Sisters engaged in each broad category of work is perhaps the best indication of its relative importance in the community at any particular time.

---

51 Prunty and Sullivan, eds., *Daughters of Charity in Ireland,* Appendix IV.

52 Nightingale believed passionately in health and welfare provision being under civil authority even if she admired the discipline that religious orders imposed on nursing and nursing sisters. Carmen Mangion, 'Developing Alliances: Faith, Philanthropy and Fundraising in Late-nineteenth-century St Helens,' in Maarten Van Dijck, ed., *The Economics of Providence*, pp. 205–26.

53 Peter Coman, *Catholics and the Welfare State* (London: Longman, 1977), p. 60.

54 Provincial Council Minutes 2 December 1919, Vol VI, p. 96. 9-5-0-2-1 DCMH.

55 The Darlington school accepted many girls from families unable to pay the fees and found various ways to subsidise their education.

From the figures it seems clear that residential welfare work consistently occupied most Sisters of the first and second generations, although because houses often had multiple activities it is difficult to be absolutely sure of an exact calculation. In 1900, the year for which the most accurate figures are available, of the 364 Sisters working in Britain, 207 were in houses undertaking institution-based welfare work, 124 in houses of charity for parish and community welfare and teaching, and 33 in other work not directly connected to people in poverty, including 15 at Central House for administration and the training of seminary Sisters and a small number of elderly or sick Sisters.[56]

Living alongside poverty, 1885–1925

> This Company must never depart from nor change its poor manner of life. Thus, should Divine Providence provide them with more than is necessary, let them go to serve the corporally and spiritually poor at their own expense.
>
> (Louise de Marillac)[57]

The places where Catholic sisters lived can be a good indicator of mission priorities according to Barbara Walsh, who has mapped convents across England and Wales between 1857 and 1937.[58] A marked change in convent geography took place at the end of the nineteenth century, signifying the move of many religious sisters away from the urban poor in central London, the poor industrialised urban areas of the North-West and the West Midlands, towards the South-East, particularly around London. There, Walsh argues, they benefited from 'the emergence of a prosperous service sector in which Roman Catholics played an increasingly prominent role', many of them providing convent schooling for the better off, including those who were not Catholic.[59] Older convents remained in the original areas, but after 1880 the choice of location and the work of nuns 'reflected the broader changes in the social structure of the country' towards greater prosperity.[60] In this context the continued location of the Daughters' houses in or close to the urban and working classes in northern cities is an expression of their charitable practice.

Not only did the Province sustain the nineteenth-century foundations made in the poorest inner city areas such as Ancoats in Manchester, the Crofts district of Sheffield, Everton in Liverpool, Clerkenwell in London and in Glasgow's East End, but in the first two decades of the twentieth century it opened additional foundations in similar districts elsewhere. After 1900 the Sisters went to the

---

56 1900 Statistical Return to Paris. 9-5-0-2-5 DCMH.

57 Louise de Marillac, *Spiritual Writings*, p. 833. Written in 1660.

58 Walsh, *Roman Catholic Nuns in England and Wales*, pp. 87–88.

59 Ibid.

60 Ibid.

dockside in Dundee, the manufacturing districts of Middlesbrough, and to Bristol's immigrant district of Easton. The number of houses in London increased when several new foundations were made in Bow Common, Limehouse and Wapping in the East End and at Walworth in south-east London. Real progress was also made in expanding the Province's work in Scotland, with houses opening in poor districts of Glasgow, Edinburgh and Dundee as well as in Dumfries, Dunfermline, and Troon. The focus on London and in the East End is striking (Figure 7.7), but equally so is the proportion of the community's activity across the north of England and in the west of Scotland (Figures 7.5 and 7.6).[61]

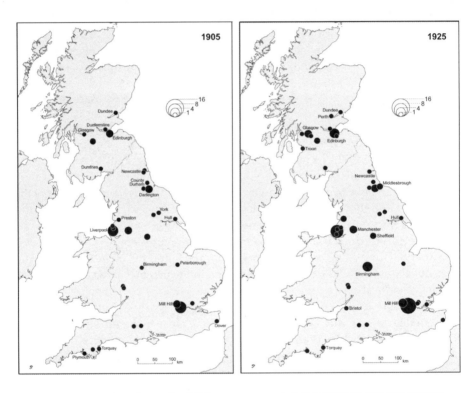

7.5: LOCATION OF HOUSES IN 1905

7.6: LOCATION OF HOUSES IN 1925

61 Carmen Mangion's analysis of the regional distribution of ten congregations by English dioceses led her to conclude that by the end of the nineteenth century only 'the Sisters of Mercy and Daughters of Charity of St Vincent de Paul were spread throughout England', Mangion, *Contested Identities*, p. 41. Barbara Walsh's mapping of the presence of all convents in England in 1917 confirms that at this later date only the Sisters of Mercy (whose convents were autonomous rather than governed by a province) were more widespread than the houses of the Daughters of Charity.

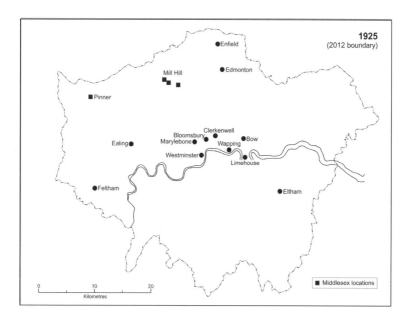

7.7: FOUNDATIONS LONDON IN 1925

Despite the decision to locate Central House in the leafy South-East bordering London, and the fact that management committees preferred to locate children's homes in healthier and morally less 'polluting' rural locations, the proportion of the Province's houses in the industrial North and in central and east London gave it a distinctive geographical profile congruent with to its espoused values (see Table 7.8). By the start of 1925 of the Province's 80 houses in Britain just over half (43) were in inner city areas, seven had more prestigious urban locations, while the remainder were children's homes outside cities or houses of various categories in smaller rural and seaside towns.[62]

Region	1917 All convents (N = 800)	1917 Daughters of Charity (N = 53)
London	19%	21%
Midlands	11%	11%

---

62 These were the teaching sisters' house for the girls' secondary school in Darlington, a donated house near Moor Park in Preston for visiting sisters and the Sisters' parish house in Morningside, Edinburgh. Central House in Mill Hill has been excluded for this purpose since it was not a house of charity but for training and administration.

Region	1917 All convents (N = 800)	1917 Daughters of Charity (N = 53)
North-East and Yorkshire	12%	25%
North-West	17%	23%
South-East excluding London	22%	9%
South-West	9%	9%

7.8: COMPARISON OF DC LOCATIONS WITH ALL CATHOLIC CONVENTS IN ENGLAND, 1917[63]

With the exception of those living at Central House, all Sisters lived alongside the people they served. Unlike most other women involved in visiting and welfare work at this time, the Sisters did not go back to a comfortable home, more often than not kept clean from dirt by women born into the very environment they had visited.[64] Daughters not only lived close to poverty but shared with poor women the reality of cleaning and cooking for others as well as doing their own housework. When domestic servants were employed to help with the large amounts of cooking, cleaning and laundry in children's homes, it was *alongside* and not in place of the Sisters.[65] Sister Servants - even duke's daughters –cleaned pans and floors.[66] Scions of Catholic elite families such as Mary Langdale and Louisa Blundell were remembered respectively as 'our leader in all the most laborious work....securing to herself the most repulsive washing'[67]and as 'living in the wash house'.[68] Such behaviour conformed to ideas about gender roles but was firmly counter-cultural

---

63 This table owes much to the work of Barbara Walsh. Walsh, *Roman Catholic Nuns in England and Wales*, p. 178. The dates have been selected to enable an exact comparison with Walsh's data.

64 The tension between Virginia Woolf as a progressive and feminist, her total reliance on her domestic servants and the ambiguity of her feelings about this situation is discussed in Alison Light, *Mrs Woolf and the Servants: The Hidden Heart of Domestic Service* (London: Penguin, 2007). Light recognises that Leonard Woolf was in the same position but did not feel it as an anomaly. The gap between moralising about domestic skills by middle-class reformers and their own lack of personal experience is mocked in Seth Koven's *Slumming: Sexual and Social Purity in Victorian London* (Princeton and Oxford: Princeton University Press, 2004), pp. 184–204. Van Heijst also discusses the 'presence of a private domain where tasks are unjustly divided' in the lives of upper and middle-class reformers, *Models of Charitable Care*, p. 159.

65 There was no domestic help at Central House, for example, until 1937 because the seminary Sisters undertook this labour.

66 *Memoir of a Sister of Charity*, pp. 34–6 and 38.

67 'Remarks on the Life of Sister Mary Langdale', typescript in personal file, 10-2 DCMH

68 Anon. *The Life of Sister Louisa Blundell* (London: Sisters of Charity, Mill Hill, c1930), p. 47. 2-1-12 DCMH. It is worth noting the emphasis on cleaning and washing in the British Province's records in the light of Florence Nightingale's scathing observation about the lack of hygiene in the Paris mother house and other French houses of Daughters. See McDonald ed., *Florence Nightingale's European Travels vol 7 Collected Works*, pp. 748–758.

when viewed from a social class perspective, making sense only through the prism of the Company's practice of Christian discipleship and its theology of vocation.[69]

Although after 1900 the extreme poverty of the earliest communities with their lack of chairs, pots, pans and even beds became honoured memory, living conditions for the Sisters continued to involve much self-sacrifice.[70] Only the sick or dying, for example, had the luxury of an individual sleeping room: even the visitatrice shared sleeping quarters. Sisters slept in shared rooms or larger dormitories separated from one another by a curtain around bed, chair and washstand. In children's homes a Sister on night duty slept in a partitioned cubicle in a corner of the dormitory, always aware of the sneezes, coughs and the other movements inevitable with a room full of children. There was no privacy for the children but little either for the Sisters. For clothing they were given two habits, one for work and one for best, the former usually a carefully patched hand-me-down and the latter given to her new at the *prise d'habit* or vows and intended to last. Clogs were worn indoors and outdoor shoes were often mentioned in memoirs as being ill-fitting. Work aprons, pockets, cornettes and chemises were communal property, Sisters taking from the week's clean laundry the size that best fitted them. Food was sufficient in quantity, something the Company had insisted upon from the days of the founders,[71] but it was unvaried and plain.[72] Sisters who worked in homes and orphanages ate separately from the children but had the same diet. There was the occasional treat for feast days but the regular house income and the stipends for Sisters' individual expenses created little opportunity for regular treats, even if their understanding of their vow of poverty had permitted it.[73]

Money and the practice of charity

Writing in 1921, Hilda Plater, former Sister Servant at St Vincent's boys' home in Torquay, informed her successor that she had left 'a detailed account of all the money received and spent', reflecting cheerfully that 'it was often a mystery to me where the money came from' but 'we had many good friends'.[74] Finances have certainly been something of a mystery in convent histories, but money is

---

69 See, for example, Lucy Lethbridge, *Servants: A Downstairs View of Twentieth-Century Britain* (London: Bloomsbury, 2013).

70 Ibid., p. 31 and *Pioneer Sisters*, p. 16. The first Edinburgh house opened in 1893/4 was as poor as the first houses in England, *Memoir of Ma Soeur Marcellus*, pp. 86–87.

71 See Jones, *Charitable Imperative*, p.176.

72 See Etheldreda Howard's comments about the diet given to the seminary Sisters in Mill Hill, recorded in *Memoir of a Sister of Charity*, pp. 72–73.

73 Ibid, in many places.

74 Sister Teresa Plater DC to the Sister Servant at Torquay, August 1921, Box 11-13-1.1 DCMH.

an opaque subject in the study of modern Christianity more generally.[75] Susan Mumm's point that 'we learn as much – if not more – about an organisation's real priorities from its budget allocations than we do from the proclamations of its leadership' is well-made.[76] In addition to the vital question of how the bills were paid, a study of income and expenditure can suggest much about the practice of charity. Scrutiny of income reveals something about the nature of the 'charitable gesture': who gave what and for what reasons.[77] Since money was critical to the level of support available to those in need and the degree of comfort that could be afforded in residential care, such a study can also shed light on how the Province's spirit of charity operated within the resources at its disposal.

Between 1870 and the early 1920s the Daughters had four main sources of income: donations from private benefactors, including from a number of Sisters; public funding in exchange for specific services undertaken for the state (residential child care, teaching); fees charged for a range of charitable services (hospital treatment or hostel board) and for their own labour and that of others in their care (commercial laundry work, sewing, shoe repairs, basketry); and, fourthly, fundraising appeals and events which drew in members of the local community as well as regular Catholic supporters. A small number of houses had income from stocks and bonds and, as noted, those who had land stretched their money by keeping chickens and growing fruit and vegetables.[78] All Sisters darned, mended and recycled in the manner of thrifty housekeepers with insufficient means.

Until 1920 the Company's traditional 'business' framework of contracts and stipends was still largely in place. However, much more of the burden for discharging financial responsibilities now fell to the Sisters themselves than had been the case in the Company's early years.[79] No work for third parties, such as bishops or trustees, was begun without a contract setting out the Sisters' stipends and their other undertakings but this did not mean the Sisters were simply employees without financial management cares. Like priests they received a stipend. Stipends were for the Sisters' personal and community expenses: clothing, travel to retreats, medical needs, postage and stationery, payment to priests for saying Mass and, if it was not provided as part of their work, food. But

75 Sarah Flew, 'Money Matters: The Neglect of Finance in the Historiography of Modern Christian History,' in Peter D. Clarke and Charlotte Methuen eds., *The Church on Its Past: Studies in Church History 49* (Ecclesiastical History Society with Boydell Press, 2013), pp. 430–46. See the important work by Maarten Van Dijck, et al. eds., *The Economics of Providence.* The introduction notes how little the topic has been researched. For a subtle re-reading of women's giving see Jill Rappaport, *Giving Women: Alliance and Exchange in Victorian Culture* (Oxford: Oxford University Press, 2012).

76 Susan Mumm, 'Women and philanthropic cultures,' in Morgan and deVries eds., *Women, Gender and Religious Cultures in Britain*, p. 56.

77 Davies and Taithe, 'From the Purse and the Heart', *French Historical Studies*, vol. 34, No. 3 (Summer 2011), pp. 413–432.

78 For example in 1921 Carlisle Place received income from investments of more than £8,000 variously from railway stocks and a War Loan. 1921 Survey of Houses, 9-5-0-1-2 DCMH.

79 See Jones, *Charitable Imperative*, pp. 176–84.

it was the Sister Servant's responsibility to balance the house books and to make an annual donation towards provincial running costs. In reality she often found herself generating income to cover the costs of care itself since what was given, particularly in diocesan homes, was inadequate. Both the general council and the provincial council could be asked to loan money for major capital expenses, but this had to be repaid.

Most Sisters' stipends were modest; some were minimal. Work took place in what Jill Rappaport has described in another context as an 'economy of redemption' that 'separated professionalism from pay'.[80] In the early twentieth century, Sisters working in residential care where board was covered, even in 1920 when wartime and immediate post-war inflation had been rampant, received an annual stipend of £10-£20. This sum was considerably less than the £30–£40 paid to an experienced live-in cook in a large household before the war.[81] The 19 Sisters serving at Smyllum children's home in 1916, for example, spent just over £7 a head on personal and community expenses, about one 1 cent of the home's total expenditure.[82] Parish Sisters and teaching Sisters, who had to cover their food and heating, normally had a stipend of £30 at this time.

Most foundations had one main source of funding but had to use a mix of two, three and even four income streams to make ends meet. In Dundee, for example, where the Sisters opened a house of charity in 1905 to work among the many migrant Irish women working in the city's jute factories, the main financial support came from the local conference of the St Vincent de Paul Society (SVP). Its members collected a contribution of £100 a year for the four Sisters as well as partly funding the emergency women's refuge managed by them. Local priests paid something extra for visiting work and the Sisters earned a small amount from the crèche they opened in 1908 to help working mothers. Around 1920 when they took on prison visiting and probation work they were paid £35 a year by the city authorities. In Birmingham six Sisters visited in four parishes linked to St Chad's cathedral and ran a hostel for young women 'many [of whom] have been turned adrift by useless parents, because they were out of work, or not earning sufficient to support themselves'.[83] In 1901 when they were living with 24 residents aged between 13 and 27 and two domestic servants, the total income was just over £790. Outgoings were almost £850. The Sisters' visiting stipends (£88) went into the common pot as did the £66 grant towards the rent from the Catholic Women's League. A further £69 came from donations and £36 was raised through a jumble sale and a 'Pound Day', but the hostel could not have paid its way without the

---

80 Rappaport, *Women Giving*, p. 95.

81 http://www.womenshistorykent.org/themes/workingwomen/domesticservice.html (accessed 3 January 2016).

82 Box 11-67-1 8-11 #14 DCMH.

83 Appeal Letter from the Sister Servant of St Joseph's House Princip Street, 1922. Centenary House History Birmingham, DCMH.

£432 earned by the public laundry where most of the girls and young women of St Anthony's worked at least part-time.[84] By 1922 the Sisters had opened a new hostel, St Joseph's. Now they aspired to make a 'Home in the true sense of the word' for the young women – by which they meant a family atmosphere and no laundry work. This entailed relying on weekly payments for board and lodgings. But of the 72 residents only 21 paid the full cost, others contributing what they could, and some nothing at all.[85] The Sisters and the Archdiocese had to set themselves to raise the shortfall in funding in other ways.

Benefactions and donations took many forms. It was common for small change to be pressed into the hands of the readily-identifiable Sisters by anyone who wanted prayers and a share in their acts of charity.[86] Although research has eroded stereotypes of 'puritanical' Protestants and 'indulgent' Catholics when it came to attitudes to assisting the destitute,[87] a recent reassessment of the emergence of national policies towards poverty relief has argued that different dominant theological traditions did indeed shape the varied approaches developed by European states and their citizens.[88] Direct almsgiving was less likely to be promoted in Protestant states where charity was socialised (paid for by rates or taxation) earlier.[89] Research into fundraising for the Church of England's home mission in Victorian London has identified a model that used church collections, collecting districts with secretaries, and public donations underpinned by a theology of stewardship that operated effectively before the 1880s, particularly with men, in a culture of public accountability.[90] But almsgiving without formal accountability continued to be valued by Catholics as a personal exchange between giver and recipient in which both parties were giver and recipient. All gifts were

---

84 1900 Report for the Birmingham Catholic Girls' Aid Society, 14th annual report relating to St Anthony's Home, D204 Birmingham Archdiocesan Archive (BAA).

85 Appeal Letter from the Sister Servant of St Joseph's House Princip Street, 1922. Centenary House History Book Birmingham, DCMH.

86 This was so commonplace an occurrence as to be almost unrecorded by the Sisters. Oral interviews confirmed that the practice took place frequently and, when the Daughters changed their habit and lost the cornette in 1964 one of their main concerns was that people would not recognise them to ask for prayers, for help, or to make donations.

87 Jones, *Charitable Imperative*, p. 2 and Colin Jones, 'Some recent trends in the history of charity,' in M. Daunton, ed., *Charity, self-interest and welfare in the English past* (London: UCL Press, 1996), pp. 51–63.

88 See, Sigrun Kahl, 'The religious roots of modern poverty policy: catholic, lutheran and reformed protestant traditions compared,' *European Journal of Sociology*, vol. 46, Issue 01 (April 2005), pp. 91–126.

89 Catholic teaching on grace and merit is often misunderstood. '[G]race is preceded by no merits. A reward is due to good works, if they are performed, but grace, which is not due, precedes [good works], that they may be done' (Canons on grace 19 [AD. 529] Council of Orange). Richard Finn has shown how, in the early Church redescribing the poor as fellow Christians in need rather than as lower social status individuals meant that they had an honourable relationship with the donor and meant too that the donor's gesture could be characterised as virtuous. Richard Finn, *Almsgiving in the Later Roman Empire: Christian Promotion and Practice 313–450* (Oxford: Oxford University Press, 2006)

90 See Sarah Flew, *Philanthropy and the Funding of the Church of England 1856–1914* (London: Routeldge, 2015) and the discussion in Lynda R. Pearce, 'Catholic Philanthropy in Mid-Nineteenth Century Britain: The Reformatory Work of the Female Congregations' (University of Kent PhD thesis, 2003).

given and received as acts of mercy that, if performed through God's grace, would confer merit on benefactors. The Daughters were seen as an ideal channel for such gifts, close to the poor and trustworthy through their vows. An understanding that they would offer their own prayers for the donor became part of a complex spiritual exchange in which it was assumed that all the parties offered prayers for one another.

The largest benefactions were used for capital projects. We have already noted the considerable Scottish benefactions made by converts Robert Monteith and Thomas Bowie to projects in Lanark. Lady Georgiana Fullerton, Lady Fitzgerald and Mary Stanley underwrote the Daughters' first work in London.[91]Author and philanthropist Lady Herbert of Lea, another convert, paid more than £5,000 in the early 1870s towards the industrial school in her home town of Salisbury, a property she then bequeathed to the Province.[92] Lady Mary Petre of Thorndon Hall in Essex, who in time had a daughter and two nieces in the Company, gathered subscriptions and donations from others totalling more than £16,000 to buy two house in Marylebone's Seymour Street, both of which were kept in trust with the Westminster Archdiocese for the Daughters' works.[93] Gender bonds between women and bonds between family members explain why some benefactors gave to the Daughters rather than to another worthy Catholic charity. It is difficult to calculate the amount given by the 14th Duke and Duchess of Norfolk, Sister Howard's parents, or her brother the 15th Duke between the 1860s and the First World War.[94] At a later date Lord and Lady Lovat of Beauly sponsored the construction and equipment of an operating theatre for St Vincent's orthopaedic hospital school at Pinner where their daughter, Sister Muriel (Joseph) Fraser, served as an orthopaedic nurse and manager from 1918 to 1942.[95] Other major benefactions were given as memorials. Mrs Lucy Moore paid for a large house at Leigh-on-Sea in memory of her daughter, Edith, who had been accepted as an aspirant in 1915 but had died before she could enter. Named St Edith's, the house was endowed with funds to pay for respite care for mothers and children from London's East End because Edith had volunteered there.[96] Many other individuals, some of them members of the Association of Ladies of Charity, donated money,

---

91 Augustus Craven (trans. Henry James Coleridge), *The Life of Lady Georgiana Fullerton* 2nd ed. (London: Richard Bentley & Son, 1888), p. 310.

92 11-68-1 DCMH.

93 11-75-3-1 DCMH.

94 They paid the rent at Sheffield and gave for the poor. The Duke donated £1,000 for a chapel at Howard Hill, the Duchess £3,600 to building extensions at Carlisle Place in Westminster and about £2,000 to develop Central House, and £2,000 in her will to complete the chapel and seminary. The family bought a house for the boys' home in Plymouth and paid for new outfits for all the children.

95 11-115 DCMH.

96 Lady Anne Kerr, sister of Etheldreda Howard, bought a property in Ealing and established St David's Nursing Home for Disabled Soldiers in memory of her son, David, who had been killed the First World War. 11-91 DCMH.

shares, food, clothing, fabric, equipment, chapel furnishings and property to the Daughters' projects across the nation and were remembered in Masses and prayers offered for benefactors.[97]

Individual Daughters were among the Province's most generous benefactors in this era. Since they were not canonical religious, Daughters who had private wealth before entering continued to manage their own money.[98] They were at liberty, with permission from superiors, to donate it to the Province as and when they chose, and to suggest, but not dictate, how it might be used.[99] Purchase of the land and the cost of the first building at Carlisle Place in Westminster (£30,000)[100] was financed by Sister Catherine Eyston who also left a legacy of just over £10,000;[101] Wealthy widow Sister Margaret Brown Younger paid off the £10,000 loan owed to the mother house on Central House at Mill Hill;[102] Alice Blundell built the hospital at Lanark from her own resources (1872) and Monica Weld paid for a new elementary school to be constructed at Walkley in Sheffield (1889); Blanche Lamb bought Steinway Hall in Seymour Street to provide rental income for the Province in the 1880s; Edith Noel gave 'her fortune' of £8,000 to build St Vincent's boys' home at Mill Hill (1886);[103] Sister Mary Anne Burke paid the annual stipend of £100 for three Sisters at Torquay and left a £2,000 legacy, while over the years Sister Norton gave about £2,500 to St John's Institute for the Deaf, where she was Sister Servant.[104] Hilda Plater (sister of the Jesuit Charles Plater) and her family developed St Philip's hostel at Torquay, where she was Sister Servant, to give working boys a sense of family and further education, as well as board and lodging. In 1921 Sister Ethel Pickwood bought Warley House in Essex for £4,000 and gave it to the Province for the sanatorium which the provincial council wanted to open at that time. At her death in 1926, Sister Etheldreda Howard, whose considerable benefactions to various works over her lifetime are as difficult to calculate as are those of her parents and other relatives, left more than £4,000 for the use of the Province.[105] Given the number and scale of donations made by women to enable the Sisters'

---

97 'Foundation Masses to be said in the Chapel at Mill Hill. 11-100-1 #9a DCMH. The Association of Ladies of Charity, founded by Vincent de Paul before the Daughters were established. Branches were established in London (based at Carlisle Place), Birmingham, Dover, Edinburgh, Glasgow, Manchester and Preston in the late 19th and early 20th centuries. 20-1 DCMH.

98 *Manual of the Daughters of Charity, containing the Words of Our Lord; the Words of St Vincent to the Daughters of Charity; and an Instruction of the Vows made in the Community.* Translated from the French (1883), p. 354 14-1-2 DCMH.

99 Although they could proceed to make the decision, as Sister Lamb did in purchasing Steinway Hall. The Council had already turned down her offer to donate her money to Mill Hill which the Superior General regretted. O'Driscoll, 'Sidelights', p. 54 13-4-3 DCMH.

100 11-83-1, 1-1 #19 DCMH where the sum for land and building is given as 700,000 francs.

101 National Archives, Probate Records.

102 O'Driscoll, 'Sidelights', p. 18 13-4-3 DCMH.

103 1921 House Survey, 9-5-0-1-2 DCMH.

104 Ibid.

105 Etheldreda Howard, 10-2 DCMH.

social works, particularly to construct the buildings that housed them or to initiate new projects, their gifts underscore Kathleen McCarthy's claim that women were 'shapers of civil society through their donations of time and money',[106] a point echoed in Jill Rappaport's conclusion that 'Victorian women's gifting...established civic authority that otherwise remained beyond their reach'.[107]

If private donors paid a significant proportion of capital costs in this period, public funds from local authorities and national departments of state provided the main running costs for many projects. Catholic dioceses and religious communities were among the small percentage of voluntary bodies that received public funding for poverty relief and works of moral reform under the 'mixed welfare economy' already alluded to.[108] As voluntary bodies they could apply to manage industrial schools and reformatories in buildings they owned, using staff they employed. If approved they received a weekly per capita allowance for a specified number of children from the Home Office. Local Boards of Guardians allocated funding on the same basis as Poor Law homes, as did the Ministry of Pensions after 1916.[109] Most straightforward administratively and best supported were elementary schools, given grants by school boards and later by local education authorities to pay teachers' salaries and other costs in England (in Scotland the Catholic Church did not accept this payment until 1918). Because the stipends taken from school managers by the Province for its teaching Sisters were lower than provided for in the school grant (the average salary for a woman teacher in 1900 in England was £86 and for a Catholic teacher in Scotland about £60), some of the surplus funding was available to support visiting sisters in an internal cross-subsidy.[110] The grant for two or three teachers' salaries was spread across small teams of four to six parish Sisters in Dunfermline, Little Crosby, Wardour and York among other places.[111]

The three-way partnership between the Church, state and the British Province, each playing a different role in the relationship, enlarged the capacity of all the partners to fulfil their overlapping but different goals.[112] The Diocesan Church's capacity for outreach was transformed by income from the state which was given for the services provided by the Sisters. As the state's concept of welfare expanded

---

106 Kathleen D. McCarthy, *Women, Philanthropy and Civil Society* (Bloomington, Ind: Indiana University Press, 2001), p. 1.

107 Rappaport, *Giving Women*, p.6.

108 Jose Harris, 'Society and the State in Twentieth Century Britain,' in Thompson ed., *Cambridge Social History of Britain* vol. 3. p.67. See Finlayson, *Citizens, State and Social Welfare*.

109 Between seven and twelve shillings in 1921.

110 Library of House of Commons Standard Note SN04252 (1) where the teaching Sisters' stipend was £30. W.W. Knox, *A History of the Scottish People* http://www.scran.ac.uk/scotland/pdf/SP2_1Education.pdf accessed 4 January 2016).

111 Number of Sisters and range of work in these houses is given in the Annual Statistical Return to Paris 1900, 'Statistics'. 9-5-0-2-5 DCMH. See, for example, York St George's School and St Vincent's nursery school or crèche, 1921 Survey of Houses, p. 869 9-5-0-2-5.DCMH.

112 The best study of residential care provision from a diocesan perspective is Jim Hyland, *Changing Times, Changing Needs: A History of the Catholic Children's Society (Westminster)* (Catholic Children's Society, 2010).

and new legislation was enacted, fresh community-based welfare interventions such as probation work, child welfare clinics, and school meals were supported financially from taxes and rates. The Daughters responded by adding these activities to their portfolio of projects in particular places or, in the case of school meals, claimed funding for a project they had long undertaken charitably.[113]

By the end of 1920, when there were 74 foundations in Britain (excluding the Central House), 64 of them are known to be in receipt of some state funding. For 45 of them it was the main source of income, a situation illustrated in Table 7.9.[114] Caution is needed in interpreting the data in this table since the proportions refer to proportion of houses and not of income, but the evidence is nonetheless suggestive of the range of income and the relative importance of different funding sources.

Funding Source
* Includes Society of St Vincent de Paul
  and religious orders
+ Includes lodging charges, fees,
  fundraising, rents, farms
	No. of
	houses
		% of
		houses
			%
			houses
			where this
			was
			main income

Public funding received	64	91.4	67.1
Church funding received*	14	20.0	11.0
Benefactors and charitable trust received	24	34.3	7.1
Sisters' social enterprises excluding laundries+	16	23.0	} 14.3
Laundry work (Sisters and girls)	5	7.1	}
Houses with 3 or more sources of income	17	24.3	-
No main overall source of funding	9	13.0	-

7.9: HOUSE SOURCES OF FUNDING, 1921

Total number. of houses = 75
Total known and used for calculation = 70

This brief survey of the priorities, locations and economics of charity among the Daughters of the British Province allows us to draw a number of conclusions about their practice of charity. Their firm commitment to a Vincentian construct of charitable care practice is mapped out in the places they lived and benchmarked

---

113 At St George's School in York for example and at Carlisle Place in Westminster.

114 Analysis of the 1921 House Survey forms. 9-5-0-2-5 DCMH.

A Province and expansion 1885-1925

The Province of Great Britain and Ireland was founded in 1885. Provinces were administrative units supervising the work of the Company in specific geo-political areas. They enabled the Company to work on a large scale across different parts of the world while continuing to be one body united in a single identity under the authority of the Motherhouse in Paris. Each Province was governed by its own officers who lived in the Central House. The founding of the Province inaugurated a 40-year period of growth. In 1925 there were 82 foundations in Britain and a further 18 in Ireland, managed by more than 1,000 Sisters.

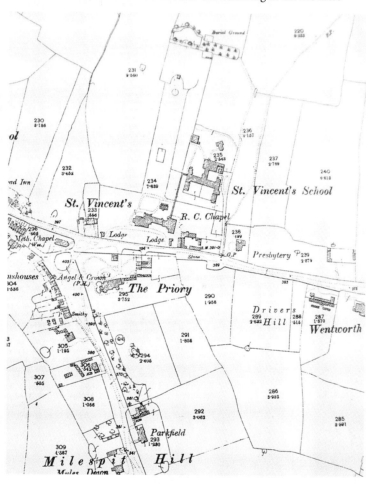

Provincial House

Littleberries estate on the Ridgeway, Mill Hill, Middlesex, ten miles from central London, was bought by the Company to be made into the Central House of the new Province. Littleberries (renamed St Vincent's) comprised a seventeenth-century country house and 46 acres of land. Here a seminary was opened, a large chapel built, and a cemetery consecrated. The Sisters built a presbytery for the Vincentian Director, a large Poor Law School for boys sent by London Boards and Immaculate Conception elementary school. Other buildings on the Ridgeway (The Priory and Wentworth Hall) were later acquired for the Province.

Front aspect of St Vincent's Mill Hill, Provincial House
'Poor man's gate' extreme left where food was given to tramping men, chapel at extreme right, seminary centre right.

Provincial leaders

The Province was led by a Council comprising the Visitatrice, the Assistant, the Bursar and the Father Director. The seminary Directress was the other important officer but she was not a member of the Council. Between 1885 and 1926 there were three Visitatrices, all of whom were French. A very small group of Sisters held all the offices until 1920.

Eugénie du Tyrac de Martin de Marcellus 1840-1927 2nd Visitatrice of the province, 1890-1919, was born into the French nobility in La Gironde. She had served as a visiting Sister and as Sister Servant in two Houses in Paris before being made Bursar to the whole Company until 1889. At the unexpected death of Sister Minart (1st Visitatrice, 1885-1890) she was recalled from her new office as Visitatrice of Portugal to take up office as 2nd Visitatrice of Britain and Ireland. She was described as 'small, alert and selfless' with a gift for understanding people's characters and capabilities. She travelled by herself when conducting visitations, saying that it was a waste of another Sister's time to accompany her.

Etheldreda Fitzalan Howard 1849-1926 daughter of the 14th Duke of Norfolk, the premier duke in the British realm and its premier earl. Etheldreda Howard entered the Company in 1868 at the age of 18. She was Directress of the Seminary from 1885 to 1888, Bursar from 1885 to 1913 and Secretary to the Provincial Council from 1885 to 1920, remaining on the Provincial Council until 1922. Sister Howard was a very influential Sister in the Province for more than three decades, being regarded as virtuous as well as highly capable. Her family connections in state and society were extensive and her relatives gave of their personal wealth to support the Daughters in Britain.

Provincial Directors

The office and role of the Director was initiated in the time of St Vincent and St Louise to support the Vincentian spirituality of the Daughters. Directors were always senior Vincentian priests and were the formal clerical Visitors for the Sisters' Houses in place of the local bishop. They were appointed by the Superior General in Paris from among the Irish Vincentian Province.

Very Revd William Gavin CM, Director 1885-1898

William Gavin was made novice master of the Irish Vincentian Province in 1873, a post he held for twelve years before being appointed first Director to the Daughters in Britain and Ireland. He was described by them as being sympathetic and gentle. Sister Marcellus 'found him a wise and prudent guide, ever ready to second her efforts for good'. His health was delicate. He served as Director until 1898 when his health broke down altogether and he left Mill Hill.

(*Left*) Miraculous Medal stole made by a Sister for the Province.

Very Revd Joseph Walshe CM, Director 1898-1909
Also Provincial of the Vincentians of Britain and Ireland. The Sisters' account of him tells us that 'he guided and seconded Sister Marcellus in her various projects for the development of the Province and was 'much beloved by the Sisters' for his kindness and devotion.

Very Revd William Byrne CM, Director 1909-1922
Also Principal of St Mary's Training College Twickenham from 1899-1909. He was regarded by the Sisters as a capable, intelligent and learned man and a valued spiritual guide. He was Principal of St Mary's Teacher Training College at Twickenham 1899-1909.

Very Revd John O'Connell CM, Director 1923-1938
John O'Connell was 58 when he was appointed as Director, having held senior posts in his own Province. He was known for his goodness and remained a friend and confessor to Daughters after he ceased to be their Director.

The Seminary at Provincial House

Seminary Sisters photographed in 1924 round the lake on the lawn at the back of Provincial House and in front of the 18c. ornamental summer house, known as The Temple. The peak year for entrants to the Seminary was 1920 when there were 71. Two other peak years were 1925 (66) and 1926 (63).

The Seminary period was 7-9 months and was followed by a month or two in Paris that included a retreat and *prise d'habit* (taking the habit).

The Seminary Heart

The Heart, with its flame of love echoing the seal of the Company. The names (above) of every woman to enter the seminary of the British Province was placed in the cavity of the Heart.

On Feast Days the Heart was placed close to the statue of the Blessed Virgin.

Kitchen and housework
The Province employed very little domestic help in any of its houses and none at Central House (shown left) before 1937.

Sisters' tableware was numbered. The Sister Servant was Number 1 and all other Sisters were numbered according to their years of Vocation. These two drinking cups (imported from France) are also marked for Sister of Office and Sister Économe (Bursar).

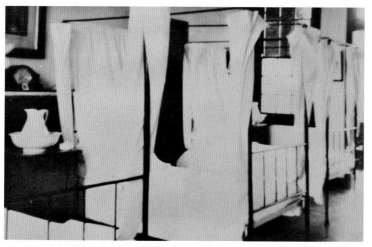

Sisters' dormitory (photo from the 1950s just after it had been refurbished)

Thin tin sheet known as 'the plaque' for starching the cornettes
The white linen of the cornette was starched and stretched over the plaque to dry in the sun before being folded. The damp climate in Britain meant that cornettes often drooped.

Development of the Sisters' works

St Vincent's Boys Orphanage, Torquay Opened in 1889. St Vincent's Torquay provided residential care until 1982 when it closed. It had an active Old Boys' Association. (Photograph 1921)

The Daughters in Britain were unusual for the number of boys' orphanages they ran. They concluded that there was a particular need for provision for boys who were more neglected by society and less well provided for by the Church than girls were. Homes were often overcrowded because the Sisters did not turn anyone in real need away. They accepted children whose parents could not cope, even though they might not be orphans or be eligible for any form of state funding. As a consequence of this policy and of the limited funding there was little privacy for children or Sisters.

St Vincent's Home Preston built by the Diocese of Liverpool in 1895 with public donations. This photograph shows staff and youngest residents the year after opening.

This home closed in 1956 when a family group house was opened at Ashton-on-Ribble.

Crèches for the children of poor working mothers were first opened by the Sisters in the 1860s. **York Fishergate Street** (opened 1903) is illustrated here.

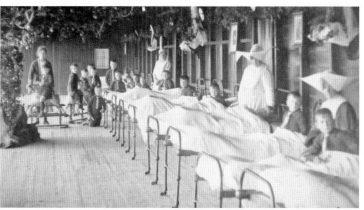

Healthcare

St Vincent's Orthopaedic Hospital Pinner founded in 1907 in Clapham and moved to Pinner in 1912. It was only the second orthopaedic hospital in Britain. By World War I it had beds for 114 boys and an operating theatre.

Tollcross Institute near Glasgow 1911

The opening of Tollcross with specialist teaching and facilities for blind and deaf children represented the end of a fund-raising campaign to improve provision for Scottish Catholic deaf children. Uniquely in Britain it used Irish sign language at one time.

Changing representations

In 1847 when the first group of Daughters to arrive in England took up residence in the north-west manufacturing city of Salford they were subject to intense physical and verbal harassment. Their Paris superiors withdrew them in 1849.

The representations shown here, both from the north-west of England, indicate the gradual shift in attitude.

1885 Beecham's Pills based in St Helen's Merseyside adopted the Daughters' image for brand endorsement. The image of the Daughters as trustworthy and steadfast nurses lay behind the use of the cornette to sell health products. French proprietory products such as tisanes and tonics used the same kind of imagery.

Reproduced with permission of the Advertising Archive

Salford street scene from *Manchester Old and New* (1890).

St John's Cathedral is in the background – Daughter of Charity centre. This is the very area of the Daughters' initial failure in Britain. Here the Sister is shown as part of the ordinary scene in this book about Manchester – walking the city streets.

against the groups which had priority in the allocation of their labour. It was literally cashed out too in the use individual Daughters made of their personal financial resources and the resources devoted to their own needs. The way that all Sisters, regardless of personal wealth, lived their vow of poverty, particularly in the balance between what they spent on themselves and what they directed towards the care of others, contributed greatly to the support they could give. It appears that they were able to draw on a wider range of funding than was available to other women engaged in philanthropy and fundraising.[115] Their own trusted position within the Catholic community and a Catholic spiritual economy of gift exchange attracted private donations while their Vincentian commitment to providing direct services to those in need meant they were eligible to receive public funding. Looking at the range of the Sisters' charitable projects in Britain before 1925 it seems reasonable to conclude that the Province's choices were influenced to by the availability of public funding for some activities (Poor Law schools and probationary work) rather than others (nursing and hospital work). But even when they followed where the funding led, the Sisters did not have to distort or dilute their Vincentian mission to the poor. No requirements came with the grants beyond regular inspection against specific criteria and public reports about these works, to which they no longer objected. Rather, as a voluntary body, the Daughters found ways to use some public finance to support innovative projects that were not as yet the business of the state. If there was a price to be paid in Britain for taking the Queen's or King's shilling in support of their Vincentian mission, other than the risk of sudden policy changes, it lay in having to set aside the Company's historically inclusive policy and confine themselves to Catholic admissions to their state-funded institutions, or at least when it came to state-funded admissions to these institutions. No authorities in England or Scotland were willing to pay for Protestant or potentially Protestant children to be accommodated within Catholic institutes. It was sufficient to fund Catholics to take care of their own members – and there were plenty of them in need of such care.

Care practices

Sources that allow us to get close to the Daughters' daily care interventions and relationships, either from their own perspective or that of recipients, are scarce.[116] One readily available viewpoint is that of government inspectors and visitors

---

115 For a comparison with the funding of other women's philanthropic work see Frank Prochaska, *Women and Philanthropy* and the recent work of Sarah Flew on Anglican fundraising.

116 See the comment made to the same effect by Gillian Gear, 'Industrial Schools in England,' p. 140

from the Boards of Guardians.[117] Their nineteenth-century reports were almost uniformly full of praise about the good health, cheerfulness and independence of the children in the Daughters' care. But because inspectors and visitors only ever saw a snapshot of daily life, their comments have been used simply to test the portrayal that follows rather than as sources in their own right.[118] Several categories of documentation, some concerned with ideal practices and behaviour and others indicative of actual practices from the point of view of care givers and receivers, do, however, exist. Together they help to establish something of the texture of care, provided their limitations are recognised.[119]

The Company's espoused values were expressed in many different ways and across all the community's core texts. It hardly needs saying that all Catholic sisters believed the most important task for parents and for themselves as guardians was to bring up a child with knowledge and love of God and of redemption from human sin through Christ's sacrifice of himself. In addition each Catholic institute had a unique spirituality and set of precepts that shaped its care giving. Every Daughter of Charity in the late nineteenth century would have been thoroughly familiar with the Company's Rule, Customs, Vow Catechism and many of the conferences of St Vincent.[120] These texts were taught in the seminary and were read aloud in the daily lecture, a 30-minute period of communal spiritual reading that usually took place at 2.00 p.m. They were preached at the annual retreat, permeated the annual circulars from superiors and were available to each Sister in her personal copy of *The Manual of the Daughters of Charity*.[121] We can be certain what values Daughters of Charity in Britain espoused (discussed in Chapter 2). Because she was serving Christ in the poor the relationship between a Daughter and anyone she served had to be a direct and personal one. Her attitude was to be one of compassion based on verse 25 of St Paul's first letter to the Corinthians, in Vincent de Paul's words: 'When we go to visit the poor we should so identify with them that we share their sufferings'.[122] At the same time the founders were realistic about how personally challenging it was to live up to the Company's precept that

---

117 Reports of the Inspector of Prisons – Reformatory and Industrial Schools, 7th Report PP 1864 (3378) XXVI to 59th Report PP 1916 (8367) XV House of Commons Library. Children were sent to the homes by many different local boards, depending where they lived. Each board sent a group of visitors regularly. In 1894, for example, more than 50 different inspecting visitors went to Smyllum on 22 different occasions. Smyllum Log Book, 1882–1934. 11-67-1 #5-1 DCMH.

118 Gear, Industrial Schools in England' uses these sources extensively in her own work but warns that 'these inspectors spent very little time in each school and rarely, if ever, saw more than they were meant to see' p. 141. She quotes from the inspectors' reports of St Joseph's Sheffield managed by the Daughters as an example of the best practice at the time. Ibid., pp. 170–172.

119 van Heijst, *Models of Charitable Care* is the basis for this approach. See also, Smith, *Rethinking Residential Child Care*, p. xi.

120 The first printed edition of the core texts was published in 1804 and the first English edition in 1880.

121 *Manual of the Daughters of Charity*, 14-1 Box 1 DCMH.

122 Louis Abelly, *The life of the venerable servant of God Vincent de Paul: founder and first superior general of the Congregation of the Mission* 3 (New Rochelle, N.Y.: New City Press, 1993), vol.3. p. 118.

'the poor are our Masters' and acknowledged the inevitable ambiguity inherent in the relationship between giver and recipient in which only love redeemed the situation:

> It is not enough to give soup and bread. This the rich can do. You are the servant of the poor, always smiling and good-humoured. They are your masters, terribly sensitive and exacting masters you will see. And the uglier and the dirtier they will be, the more unjust and insulting, the more love you must give them. It is only for your love alone that the poor will forgive you the bread you give to them.[123]

By contrast with the large body of formational literature from which to identify espoused values, texts that reveal the Sisters' actual practices and feelings are rare. As one biographer noted 'a Sister of Charity has little time for correspondence' – or for written reflection.[124] A remorseless emphasis on work, moreover, and on the virtue of simplicity and the importance of community identity combined to make the very idea of reflecting critically about practice unthinkable at this time, despite its importance at the time of the founders. Where they can be heard, therefore, the Sisters' voices are usually mediated. The richest and most consistent source, Sisters' obituary notices, falls into this mediated category.[125] The Company had its own tradition of publishing obituaries in the form of 'Notices of Deceased Sisters'.[126] Each is a miniature biography containing stories to honour the Sister and to illustrate the particular way she exemplified the Company's Vincentian spirit of charity. Obituaries straddle teaching text and personal life story. Written by a provincial officer who knew the Sister and sought out the views of her companions, many were lively and detailed accounts. Importantly, they seem to have been the one occasion that a Sisters' individual personality was formally celebrated, making use of the memories and attestations of companions, priests and, even on some occasions, care recipients. To set alongside these internal records we have at least one significant external source that unintentionally gives witness to the Sisters' practices. The court materials generated by an investigation in 1876 of the foundling home for babies in one of the Daughters' London houses of charity provide a rare insight into the Sisters' care practices, making clear that a clash of values existed between the Sisters and representatives of the civil authorities about what constitutes 'true charity'.

---

123 This quotation is one of the most often cited. Scholars are not sure if Vincent de Paul used these actual words but agree that its spirit reflects the many teachings and maxims he gave. famvin.org/en/2015/08/02/the-giver-in-the-gift-from-what-to-who-fr-tom-mckenna/ (accessed 11 November 2015).

124 Kerr, *Edith Feilding*, p. 25.

125 Caroline Bowden, 'Collecting the Lives of Early Modern Women Religious: Obituary Writing and the Development of Collective Memory and Corporate Identity', *Women's History Review,* vol. 19, Issue 1, 2010.

126 A very small number of sisters had a longer memoir published about them, but far more were memorialised by a 'Notice'.

The views of care recipients, particularly those that are unmediated, are also scarce.[127] But one substantial memoir was left by Ernest Cleveland, who, with his three brothers, was sent by relatives to St Vincent's Home in Hull in 1917 when his mother died and his father was away serving on a minesweeper. Ernest lived in St Vincent's from the age of seven to fourteen. In the late 1970s, after he had retired from a lifetime's work as a trawler man and seafarer, he wrote an account of his time at St Vincent's which does not seem to have been seen by anyone until after his death in 1985. His son and daughter found 'a suitcase in the loft' and edited and published the papers it contained.[128] Apart from its sustained length, this memoir about life in a Catholic children's home is unusual among others published in the early twenty-first century because it was not written with knowledge of the public discourse about experiences in children's homes, particularly those run by nuns, which has developed since the 1990s. The memoirs of a second man, also brought up by the Daughters from the age of seven to fourteen during the 1920s after the death of his parents, this time in Smyllum in Lanark, form a second shorter but still extensive narrative recently donated as a manuscript to the Daughters' archive by his daughter.[129] Since the donor wished it to remain anonymous, I have used the pseudonym 'John'. A William Harding, resident at St Vincent's in Preston at almost the same time (1918-1927) as Ernest and 'John', donated his recollections to the archives of the Catholic Children's Society which has published them on its website.[130] A fourth much shorter source, a tribute to Sister Mary Ann 'Augustine' Leonard who died in 1921, published by the Old Boys' Association of St Vincent's Beacon Lane in Liverpool, gives the voice of a further care recipient.[131] These four reflections from the same period, none of which is by a woman about her girlhood, may be difficult to use as the basis for generalisations, but the rare personal insights they give into the daily experiences in the homes and the feelings of those who received care are invaluable to any attempt to describe and assess the sisters' care practices and pastoral work.

---

127 A.Van Heijst, *Models of Charitable Care*, Chapter 6.

128 Ernest Cleveland, edited by Margaret Monk and Barrie Cleveland, *St Vincent's Home Boy* (Hartlepool: Cormorant Publishing Ltd., 2008), p. 124. See also Ernest Cleveland, *Trawlers and Trawler Folk* edited by Barrie Cleveland, Jonathan Monk, Margaret Monk (Kent: Pneuma Springs Books, 2009).
For a profile of Ernest Cleveland see http://www.pneumasprings.co.uk/Featuredauthors.htm#Ernest Cleveland (accessed 10 January 2016). Every effort has been made to trace the editors for permission to quote from the memoirs, a copy of which they had sent to the Province.

129 Anonymous resident, 1918–1927 11-67-1, 1-2, #1 DCMH.

130 William James Harding, 'Memoirs of my schooldays at St Vincent's Orphanage from 1918–1927,' published on www.catholiccaringservices.org.uk from their archives.

131 'Sister Augustine, An Appreciation' by the Rev.D.J. Quigley designed and printed by the editor of 'The Old Boys' Journal' and issued by The Members of the Old Boys' Association as a Small Tribute To The Memory of One Who Was Their Friend' Beacon Lane. 11-48-1 1-2 #1 DCMH.

Institutional care of children

In 1924 at the age of fourteen Ernest Cleveland, like other children in care, not only had to leave St Vincent's school but also the place that had been his home. In recollecting that his relatives 'found my conduct exemplary' and that 'my shyness, cleanliness and general behaviour astonished those I came into contact with', he articulates some of the impact on him of the Sisters' upbringing.[132] Ernest was due to go to sea but at first he felt 'bewildered', often wanting 'to return to the haven the home provided'. He concluded that 'the training gained from those nuns proved well worth possessing' and recorded how, as a lad, he wanted to make his fortune so he could give back to the home.[133] At the same time Ernest was clear-eyed and regretful about the Sisters' lack of ambition for him when he had showed an aptitude for education. Some of his best memories concerned one of the secular teachers who had taken a more personal interest in him.[134] 'John' noted that 'we all had to have good manners and know how to get on with people and carry ourselves off right'.[135] According to his recollections, 'we were well able to take care of ourselves when we went out into the wider world'.[136] William Harding's summary of his years stressed the extent to which the home in Preston was a world of its own: 'you could say we were happy because we had no knowledge of the outside world and the plight of some of the families that were suffering'.[137] For him what mattered was that he made many friends for life: the other boys and the routines of life are to the fore in his memoirs, but he also appreciated being smartly clothed, warm and well fed.

Food was central to these memories of childhood. William described the diet at St Vincent's, Preston, as porridge and bread and butter or margarine with cocoa for breakfast, meat, potatoes and vegetables for midday meal, and two slices of bread with tea before bed. The same diet (plus references to rice pudding and bread and dripping) was to be found at the boy's industrial school at Beacon Lane in Liverpool, in St Vincent's home in Hull and at Smyllum.[138] In Hull, as in a number of other homes, the Sisters and children kept chickens and grew fruit and vegetables so that the diet could be enlivened from time to time. 'John' accredited their good health in Smyllum to the fresh air and the 'good food off the farm'.[139] Ernest vividly recalled the poultry run with its 30 or so hens and 'John' remembered that the boys'

132 Cleveland, *St Vincent's Home Boy*, p . 1.

133 Cleveland, *St Vincent's Home Boys*, p. 113. 'Joe' notes that the Sisters 'did everything they could for us to be all right when we left them'. 11-67-1, 1-2, #1, p. 7 DCMH.

134 Cleveland, *St Vincent's Home Boys,* , pp. 50 and 85.

135 Anonymous resident 1918–1927 11–67-1, 1-2, #1 DCMH.

136 Anonymous resident 1918–1927 11-67-1, 1-2, #1, p.4 DCMH

137 Harding, 'Memoirs of My Schooldays'.

138 Beacon Lane, Liverpool Box 11-48-1-1 2c DCMH.

139 Anonymous resident 1918–1927 11-67-1, 1–2, #1, p. 4 DCMH.

nickname for Sister Patricia, who kept the hens, was 'Turkey'. From time to time the Sisters killed poultry and the boys learned how to pluck them for the table.[140] Even so, it was only at Easter, when the Sisters saved up a supply and decorated them, that there were sufficient eggs for every boy to have a whole one to himself.

Routine, discipline and a sense of personal responsibility were among the hallmarks of the life described by all three men. To some degree these characteristics of daily life were a matter of practical necessity. At St Vincent's Hull, for example, there were only seven Sisters to 120 boys aged from about four to fourteen, with no more than two teenage girls as additional support in the laundry and kitchen, a situation Ernest regarded with hindsight as 'remarkable'.[141] In retrospect and with experience of his own family life 'John' felt the same, asking 'how on earth did they get any sleep with all those children to look after'.[142] It was imperative, because of the amount of work to be done, that the boys made their own beds and took part in the cleaning of the home. Because no men were employed and it was against the Sisters' rule for them to touch the boys' naked bodies, the older boys, observing extreme modesty rules about keeping covered, helped out by bathing the younger ones.[143] These were adaptations forced by necessity. But it was also part of the Sisters' approach that every child (girl or boy) should learn self-discipline and useful skills. Cleveland notes how from a young age all the boys had their chores. He was happy with kitchen duty because it meant extra bits of food and chatting to the kitchen maid.[144] 'Polishing the long corridors...was fun, with cloths tied round our feet we skated all over the floors'.[145] John's memory is that 'what seemed like work to adults was a chance for fun to us'.[146] All the children, boys as well as girls, were taught by the Sisters to knit and

---

140 Cleveland, *St Vincent's Home Boys*, p. 28.

141 Ibid., p. 42.

142 Anonymous resident 1918-1927 11-67-1, 1-2, #1 DCMH

143 Cleveland describes the modesty practice of wearing towels in the bath, insisted on by the Sisters. There is no suggestion this was not adhered to. Ibid., p. 42 I found only one reference to sexual abuse in these accounts. 'John' notes that a boy told the priest in confession that the new music master 'had done something to him. The priest asked if the nuns knew and the boys said No (he was too upset) so the priest said would the boy let him tell the nuns and the boys said 'Yes' ...The next thing the Music Master was thrown out and told he would never again work with children because they would make sure every school in the area knew about him.' 'Smyllum 'John' p. 15. Sister Monica Cowman, one of the Province's most experienced child care Sisters, answered my questions about her experience at St Vincent's Torquay during the 1930s to 1960s very openly. She recalled a sexual abuse incident with a house master which the Sisters reported to the police and he was prosecuted. Sister Monica Cowman, 'Childcare: A Synopsis of Personal Experiences 1931–1965', typescript in author's possession. See the important contribution to the discussion about the lack of evidence about sexual abuse in the Victorian and Edwardian history of residential child care made by Lesley Hulonce, https://lesleyhulonce.wordpress.com/2014/08/31/sexual-abuse-silences-and-sources-did-the-victorians-better-protect-their-vulnerable-children/ and https://www.academia.edu/4991787/Journal_of_Victorian_Culture_online_The_elephant_in_the_room_Questioning_the_absence_of_paedophilia_in_children_s_histories (accessed November 2014).

144 Cleveland, *St Vincent's Home Boys*, p. 85.

145 Ibid., p. 99.

146 Anonymous resident 1918–1927, 11-67-1, 1-2, #1, p .2 DCMH.

mend their own stockings and to repair their clothes, all regarded as useful life skills.[147] Another memory, from the Sisters' perspective, tells how

> Sister always knitted with [the boys], as all the needles clicked busily... she would propose riddles and funny experiences, and the happy laughter of Sister and her boys would echo and re-echo through the whole place.

To these regular tasks were added even more serious responsibilities. In his last year at school William Harding was made Head Captain which meant he had to 'take the boys to the classrooms, line them up for mealtimes and bed times, see them washed at different times...'[148] When he was a senior, Ernest looked after the coke-fired boiler at St Vincent's and maintained the radiators. He learned his trade from one of the Sisters 'who could use a spanner and a rake, stoke a fire and swing a hefty shovel of coke'.[149]

Children who failed to exercise self-control or fell short of expected behaviour were disciplined.[150] The Sisters used the cane or strap or even bare hands for physical punishments. But there were deprivations such as bed without supper, or 'fringe chopping' and other humiliations that Ernest felt were much worse than physical pains.[151] Those who crossed a line and seemed too difficult to control were sent to the Catholic reformatory, a threat he remembers as hanging over the boys. The Sisters' determination to ensure discipline can be felt throughout Ernest's and 'John's' memoir but, despite the reality of punishment, neither boy lost his curiosity and sense of adventure. Not infrequently Ernest calculated the balance between the pleasure of a forbidden activity (such as leaving the house for fish and chips or stealing an entire supper of rice pudding waiting on the kitchen table for seven Sisters) against the risk of anticipated punishment. He made his choices – refusing the fish and chip escapade but indulging himself with the rice pudding and taking the punishment.[152]

It was axiomatic that religious practice was woven into the everyday routine, and was as much a part of the discipline of life as making beds and

---

147 Cleveland, *St Vincent's Home Boys, pp. 43 and 99* Anne Duffy *Notices of Deceased Sisters,* 1956, p. 41.

148 Harding, *Memoirs,* Chapter 15.

149 Cleveland, *St Vincent's Home Boys,* p. 90.

150 For a full discussion of the discipline regimen permitted in industrial schools and the actual practice see Gear, 'Industrial Schools in England'.

151 Cleveland, *St Vincent's Home* Boys, pp. 50 and 98. Cleveland notes that children who wet the bed had to have a cold bath before dressing: 'Every morning there followed the screams of the poor unfortunates who had wet their beds and were given cold baths, summer or winter', (p. 42). He makes no reference to the practice of children having to wear their wet bedding on their heads or round their shoulders. 'John' gives a very detailed account of how bed wetters at Smyllum were put together in St Joseph's dormitory, about 20 of them when he was there. They had a waterproof ground cloth over the mattress 'and the bed had no sheets, just blankets'. Anonymous resident 1918–1927, 11-67-1, 1-2, #1, p. 2 DCMH

152 Cleveland, *St Vincent's Home Boys,* p. 80.

attending school. The children's prayer life was as regular as the Sisters' and so it was abnormal measured against typical family behaviour. Ernest described the chapel in St Vincent's Hull as 'an impressive place' but also 'intimate, informal and different from church'.[153] Boys began and ended the day with prayers, the Angelus was said three times a day, grace was said before and after all meals and there was weekly Mass and regular confessions. Sundays were observed as quiet days with three church attendances. Occasions for treats were often (but not always) religious, such as the Feast of St Vincent and St Patrick in addition to Christmas and Easter. Children participated in exposition of the Blessed Sacrament for the Forty Hours, some were altar servers, all learned the catechism by heart and there was an annual retreat which was another occasion for instruction.[154] Even on the annual two-week holiday from St Vincent's Hull, one of the ex-army huts they used was converted into a chapel.

Expressions of tenderness were not part of the Sisters' regular care practice, but this did not mean they were entirely absent either. When Ernest's mother died and he was sent to let the Sisters know, he recalls how, 'deeply concerned, two of them cradled my head in their arms whilst the third hurried away to my home'.[155] His situation was a tragic one, permitting this rare physical consolation. A similar sense of the extra-ordinary obtained with disabled children whose need for physical affection in place of words also allowed the transgression of normal barriers, including that of 'having of favourites'. One of Sister Theresa Caraher's favourites was 'a poor idiot [sic] child whom she cared for from the cradle until in her sixteenth year it pleased God to call this child to Himself'. This Sister 'washed her, dressed her and fed her like a baby, and this every day until the end'. For her part, the girl 'unable to restrain herself at the sight of Sr Josephine [Theresa Caraher] would begin to dance'.[156] A few, like Mary Burns, when she was Sister Servant at St Vincent's Mill Hill, felt able to express her enjoyment in all the children openly. At her death in 1913 one of them recalled how 'She always took delight in her boys, each and all, and in their feast-days, the parties and entertainments which she provided with a lavish hand ... Her kindly smile showed that our happiness was hers.' [157] Others, who were less emotionally open, expressed pride and pleasure in the children in different ways. Thomas Whiteside, Archbishop of Liverpool, 'was often very amused because she [Helena Jinks] never had any unsatisfactory boys in the house: 'My boys are not angels, My Lord,' she would reply to him, 'but they are real boys''. Her obituarist felt confident that 'Her

153 Ibid., p. 33.

154 Cleveland, *St Vincent's Home Boys*, pp. 32-35.

155 Ibid., p. 25.

156 *Notices of Deceased Sisters* (1908), p. 82. 10-3-1 DCMH.

157 *Notices of Deceased Sisters* (1914), p. 89. 10-3-1 DCMH.

boys knew she loved them', although we do not know that directly from the boys themselves.[158]

From the recollections of those who were brought up by the Sisters, however, we can see that care was not always carried out according to the espoused Vincentian values of gentleness and patience. That Sisters varied in their patience and even in their fairness is well reflected in memoirs that show clearly that children could tell the difference between the occasional loss of temper under duress and a mean temperament. 'Some [Sisters] could be hard hearted, or so we thought,' was Ernest's comment, 'others were gentleness itself'.[159] 'John' notes that Sister Gertrude 'had the heart of corn. I can't talk about her', while Sister Patrick was 'as soft as anybody would want for a granny ... useless at keeping order', and Sister Teresa who 'carried a cane' and 'was sharp and quick to act' would also play football with them and 'we loved it'.[160]

But other Vincentian care practices *were* consistently practised. Mary Anne Costello, Sister Servant at Marylebone for many years, simply 'could not understand that a Daughter of Charity would willingly relinquish to others the care of our Lord and masters...if you had only a piece of bread to give some poor unfortunate, give it with your own hand,' she exhorted.[161] The Sisters gave care directly and exercised a personal presence alongside the children day by day. 'It is not by watching your children doing their work, with your arms folded that you will teach them', reminded Sister Teresa Angland, 'but by setting to work with them, and not being afraid to soil your hands.' [162] Because it was essential to the Company's vision of Christian compassion, the daily tasks of care were performed personally by Sisters, regardless of social class or background. It was in the everyday and the ordinary that God was to be found.

If routine and discipline were the scaffolding of the homes, emphasising their institutional character and the limited scope for deeper personal relationships, the beneficial mirror images of these characteristics were security and continuity of care. Provided they were able to cope, it was the Province's policy to leave residential home Sisters in place for many years for the sake of stability. Ernest was aware that 'the sisters were seldom transferred to other similar establishments'.[163] Sister Christie was at the Enfield boys' home for 33 years and Helena Jinks was Sister Servant for many years at Preston. The effect of this steadfastness was a high degree of continuity of care for children and young people. Of course, if the Sister was liked this longevity of service was a good thing; but it could be otherwise. Hence Ernest's recollection that 'when Sister Louise, mainly in charge of us was

158 *Notices of Deceased Sisters*, (1932), p. 33 10-3-1 DCMH.

159 Cleveland, *St Vincent's Home Boys*.

160 Anonymous resident 1918–1927, 11-67-1, 1-2, #1, p. 13 DCMH

161 *Notices of Deceased Sisters* (1919), p. 64 10-3-1 DCMH.

162 *Pioneer Sisters*, p. 63.

163 Ibid., p. 88.

moved, so were we – to loud cheers of relief.'[164] The Sisters knew that continuity of service provided points of familiarity and recognition when former children came back to visit what was often their only home. They continued to be available for former residents after they had left, making this a matter of entitlement for those who had been their charges. It was their practice to give moral and spiritual support to individuals for as long as they looked for it in adult life. Sister Mary Ann (Augustine) Leonard, who was at St Vincent's Liverpool from 1865 until she died in 1921, was remembered by her former charges as a 'cheerful giver' and a 'hidden hero'. She would 'hour by hour sit, reading, talking, praying by the bedside of sick boys' but 'it was not only while the boys were in her care...that she served and mothered and uplifted them: but when they had gone forth to all parts of the world [her] prayers and interest followed them'.[165] Helena Jinks was held up at her death as one who 'always found time to receive the boys after they left and returned to present their fiancées or when married brought their wife and children to see her'. They often came back if they were unemployed or fell on hard times when 'she gave them new clothes, kept them for several days so as to give them the chance of making a good confession, and thus put them on their feet again, both spiritually and socially'.[166] Taking an interest in how their lives unfolded was the Sisters' way of care and of honouring and respecting each one as a unique individual.

The same was true of all the small gestures to provide some of the pleasures of normal childhood treats, many of which loom large in the memories of former residents. Every home had a small sweet shop run by a Sister, even if it was only out of a suitcase.[167] Presents given to individual children were accepted only on the understanding that they would be shared out, which may have seemed hard on the recipient. At Christmas in Hull every child received a small present, a treat that did not take place at Smyllum in the 1920s, perhaps because of its size and lack of sufficient benefactors by this time. Outings, days out at the fair and annual holidays were as much a part of the rhythm of the year as church seasons and feasts and it seems that they were regular and could be anticipated with certainty. For Christmas at the home in Liverpool, a former resident recalled how 'No boy who was ever at St Vincent's needs a fairy wand or magician's cave to aid his imagination as long as he can recall Sister Augustine and her Christmas tree.'[168] Few working-class city children in the first two decades of the twentieth century would have had a holiday, but St Vincent's in Hull closed for two weeks when the entire household moved to an ex-army camp at Cowden on the coast 'where we had a really good time', bathing, walking, cliff climbing and sports and games

164 Ibid.

165 *Sister Augustine: An Appreciation.* Beacon Lane, 11-48-1 1-2 #1 DCMH.

166 *Notices of Deceased Sisters,* 1933, p. 33 10-3-1 DCMH.

167 Cleveland, *St Vincent's Home Boys,* p. 46.

168 *Sister Augustine: An Appreciation.* Beacon Lane, 11-48-1 DCMH.

on the sand.[169] By the time of the First World War seaside holidays were taken by many of the homes.

At the same time living conditions were usually spartan and often overcrowded. Both Ernest and William commented on the large dormitories with their many beds close together. The Sisters' own care ethic was to admit a child who had nowhere else to go, even if this meant accepting more than were provided for by public capitation or private sponsor. According to their own values it was better to share the goods more thinly than to turn away children in need or expose Catholic children to a Protestant upbringing, a judgement not shared by everyone. While crowded dormitories, visible from publicity photographs proudly taken in this era to show the clean white bed linen, ample blankets and central heating, were a consequence of a Vincentian care practice that did not always accord with the norms and standards set by others in the interests of children, it was also the case that the material provision and hygiene standards far exceeded those of poor working-class households.[170]

The most vivid illustration of the clash of care values between the Sisters and more mainstream opinion was the public censuring of Sister Henriette Chatelain, investigated in 1876 by the Board of Guardians of St George's Hanover Square (the responsible authority) for accepting too many babies into the 'foundling' home at Carlisle Place in Westminster. The *maison de charité* at Carlisle Place became a cause célèbre in the press and public eye and drew in John Henry Newman (not at that time a cardinal) in support of the Sisters. Although local and national papers adopted different tones ranging from 'Massacre of Innocents' to 'Orphanage Mortality', 'the problem was portrayed as a case of scandalous neglect'. Prejudice and a propensity for exaggeration in the interest of sales led one paper to describe Carlisle Place as 'the Black Hole of Calcutta'. According to one guardian 'The children would have had a much better chance of living if they had been thrown over an area railing.' [171] Jessica Sheetz has painstakingly unpicked the evidence.[172] Infant mortality at Carlisle Place was unquestionably high. Ballard, the Hanover Square guardian, had found that in 17 years of operation 503 of the children, one-third of the total, had died, of whom 402 were less than one year old. He felt 'bound to add' that 'the infants are kindly and tenderly nursed. Each has a nice cot, everything about the infants is very clean and an experienced nurse is engaged

---

169 Cleveland, *St Vincent's Home Boys*, p. 48.

170 Ernest Cleveland recalled that he slept in one of two dormitories 'each with forty single metal beds', a memory shared with William Harding who described 'very large dormitories with a complement of 36 boys in each...', *St Vincent's Home Boys*.

171 A St George Guardian quoted in *The Globe*' 17 January 1877.

172 Jessica Ann Sheetz 'Just Deserts': Public and Private Institutional Responses to Poverty in Victorian London: Space, Gender, and Agency' (University of Milwaukee at Wisconsin PhD thesis, 1999).

to attend to them'. [173] The fundamental cause of the high death rates, according to the medical report, was the lack of a restrictive admissions policy combined with insufficient resources for wet nursing. In other words, the Sisters did not refuse dying infants but accepted them as an act of charity in order to look after them in their last days. In 1872 Sister Chatelain had spelled out their approach to the Superintendent: we 'have no stated Regulations for admission of children... The urgency of the case of the applicant is generally the only and best test for admission...these cases of Infants are generally speaking the most distressing cases'.[174] At the 1876 hearing she repeated this: 'Really, many of these little ones came only to die', adding that 'we should not have received them if it had not been for the baptisms', in other words to ensure salvation for them according to Catholic teaching.[175] The Company's approach to admissions was only one, if the most important, of the ways that its approach to 'foundlings' differed from the model the Guardians had in mind.

At the Board of Guardians' hearing the Daughters work was compared very unfavourably with that of the famous London Foundling Hospital run along English philanthropic lines. By this time the Foundling Hospital interviewed and screened all mothers with questions about their background, work, family, health, good character and sexual history, including the place and number of occasions of sexual intercourse with the child's father, all of which was regarded as responsible action by the Board. The Sisters, on the other hand, had a very different charitable ethic, the integrity of which was difficult for the Guardians to understand. The Sisters kept only a note of the mother's and father's names (if available) and the date of the infant's birth. They did not enquire into the circumstances of the birth or cross-examine the mother for her moral rectitude. By the nineteenth century the Foundling Hospital Board was 'far more likely to reject reclamation applications' than it had been in the eighteenth century because it set clearer conditions about the financial capacity of a parent to support a reclaimed child,[176] whereas the Sisters allowed the mother free access to her child and freedom to reclaim it. Many of the mothers who came to Carlisle Place, Chatelain said, 'had been sent out of the workhouse with infants in their arms at two weeks old... and they come and beg of us to let their babies in'. 'What', she said, 'can the poor Mothers do without an

---

173 Report upon the Mortality which has occurred among Infants under the care of the Convent Carlisle Place, 'Westminster.' Enclosure in a letter from A.F.O. Liddell to Clerk to the Guardians of St George's Union, 20 December 1876, Folio 13, Westminster Diocesan Archives, quoted by Sheetz, 'Just Deserts', p. 632.

174 Correspondence between Sister Chatelain and Superintending Architect of Metropolitan Board of Works, November 1872, Box 11-83-3 1-5 #1a, 1b, 1c. DCMH.

175 Marie Chatelain to Rev Thomas Seddon, 11 January 1877, Folio 13, 43-4 Westminster Diocesan Archive, quoted by Sheetz, 'Just Desserts', p. 641.

176 Amy Gillimore, "Restored to its mother': Reclaiming Children at the London Foundling Hospital in the Nineteenth Century', p. 13 http://www.bristol.ac.uk/media-library/sites/history/migrated/documents/2013gallimore.pdf (accessed 11 July 2016).

abode, without a penny, and without a character to be able to get a livelihood?'[177] In reply the Guardians told her that 'it is better to let the children die in the streets than receive them here'. 'That is one way of looking at it', Chatelain responded, 'but it is hardly the charitable way'.[178] Her 'charitable way' was to give what she had, which included baptism, even if this could not prevent physical death, rather than to close the door.[179]

The Carlisle Place case was a highly publicised example of practices that pertained at a less dramatic level across the homes and refuges run by the Daughters throughout this period. When she died in 1898 Sister Chatelain's life was the first in the Province to be memorialised in a published biography, held up to all the Sisters as an exemplary model of the practice of charity expected from a Daughter of Charity.[180]

Care in the community

The Company's precepts for home visiting were put into practice as soon as the Daughters arrived in Sheffield and they remained largely unchanged for the next hundred years. By 1925 Sisters were visiting in 133 parish communities in England and Scotland at the invitation of the parish priest and with the permission of the local bishop.[181] A number of inner-city houses in Birmingham, Dundee, Edinburgh, Liverpool, London, Manchester and Preston were dedicated entirely to visiting work, housing up to eight full-time visiting sisters who between them might cover five or six city parishes and go beyond the parish into the wider community.

Visiting Sisters are remembered vividly in the written and oral traditions of the Province yet their activities are not easily quantified or amenable to systematic description. Every Sister was required to record the number of visits she made each week and to give these figures to her Sister Servant, but very little even of this data has survived. Yet the lack of recording and of case notes is itself revealing of the Daughters' practices. Sisters did not write during their visits, there were no forms to be completed either by the Sister herself or by those she visited: any notes she made later were simply aides-memoire for her private use and were destroyed. Her practice in this regard contrasted fundamentally with the

177 Marie Chatelain to Edward Ballard, 13 December 1876, Folio 13, Westminster Diocesan Archives, quoted Sheetz, 'Just Desserts', p. 644.

178 'Awful Mortality in a Convent', *The Catholic Times and Catholic Opinion*, 2 February 1877.

179 [805]Others seem to have understood this: 'Agnes Wickes was charged at the Westminster Police Court with exposing two children, of the age of three and four years respectively, at the Convent of the 'Sisters of Charity of St. Vincent de Paul,' at Carlisle-place, Victoria-street, Westminster, adjoining the London and County Bank.—It appeared from the evidence for the prosecution that the prisoner had been deserted by her husband for eight months, and left with four children in a state of destitution. The children had been left at the Convent, as it was generally supposed that should they be placed on the doorstep of that Institution they would be taken in and well cared for.' *The Tablet*, 30 May 1885.

180 Lady Amabel Kerr ed., *Sister Chatelain: or Forty Years' Work in Westminster* (London: Catholic Truth Society, 1900). The episode here is referred to in Chapter V.

181 Statistics for 1925 for Paris Report, 9-5-0-2-5 DCMH.

large number of district visiting associations working in Victorian and Edwardian Britain. Records were essential, in their view, to being effective agents of poverty relief. Case notes were highly desirable in the cause of both fund-raising and professionalism.[182] After 1869 when many district visiting associations were brought under the umbrella of the Charitable Organisation Society, each assisted family was centrally registered and case-note records kept. Church of England and other organisations involved in district visiting, religious and secular, held case meetings; district visitors reported to co-ordinators who in turn reported to committees where cases were discussed and decisions recorded.[183] Because of its casework approach commentators agree that modern social work has its origins in church-based district visiting.[184] The Daughters' approach to visiting was different. Visits might be very regular but remained informal. A high level of confidentiality was expected and respected, somewhat in the tradition of the confessional. Support might be material or it might be practical. 'One day I did not expect her because it was late,' one mother in Willesden, London, wrote about Sister Barbara Burke (Augustine), 'when a knock came and it was our Sister Augustine':

> She saw I was getting worried over something as I was trying to get the eldest girl's dress ironed, but the little one was crying... Sister said, 'Give me the iron' and up went her sleeves and she ironed the dress for Mary and washed and dressed her...Another time I had to go to hospital and good Sister Augustine, not being able to find a temporary home for my little ones, kept them at Our Lady's House [where Burke lived in Willesden]...when she came into your house she brought the good news and the sunshine with her, and she always had a kind word for everyone.[185]

Sisters like Barbara Burke, or Bridget Kelly who visited in St Columba's parish in Edinburgh between 1903 and 1931, became part of a locality long enough to build strong networks, being known across family generations and by all parts of the community. The same was true for Sisters who visited part-time as an addition to their main office. Eleanor Maxwell, the cook at Beacon Lane boys' home in Liverpool in the 1860s, visited in the large Everton parish of St Francis Xavier at the request of the Jesuits who had charge of it. After she had cooked the boys' midday dinner she 'walked one and a half miles each way' to Everton, 'taking a sandwich in her pocket to eat when an opportunity arose' and only returning home at six in the evening in time to make her meditation in the parish church. She continued

---

182 J. Lewis, *Women and Social Action in Victorian and Edwardian England* (Stanford, CA: Stanford University Press, 1991).

183 Whelan, *Helping the Poor.*

184 F. Prochaska, *Christianity and Social Service*, Chapter 3 'Visiting'.

185 'Remarks on Sister Barbara Burke, Sixth Visitatrice who died 1947', p. 13 Personal File, 10-2 DCMH.

with this daily routine for ten years. Long days and a good deal of walking were typical for visiting Sisters. Margaret Brohan was sent to the Sisters' Commercial Road house in London's East-End in 1914 and 'was indefatigable' in her work 'among London's poorest slum dwellers'. Her feet 'became quite deformed, through tramping the streets of London in ill-fitting shoes'. At another time she 'visited in a London district so far from her home at Carlisle Place in Westminster that she was given a room in the City, where people could 'find her'.[186] According to her obituary notice 'only those who lived with her in London have some idea of the prodigious work she did amongst the poor'.[187] Like other visiting Sisters she walked and worked alone. At Sister Margaret Duff's funeral the presiding priest told a large Glasgow congregation that 'Our Lord had walked side by side with her through the slums of just about every city and town in Scotland',[188] a tribute that referenced the Company's famous seventeenth-century 'charter' that the streets of the city were a Daughter's cloister.[189]

Visiting Sisters could be alerted to a family in crisis through one of their teaching Sister companions or through a priest or a neighbour. They were able to pass on small gifts of food and clothing and sometimes money in discreet ways, using their own judgement and without reference to anybody else.[190] The same was true of their prison visiting. Sisters began visiting in Holloway Prison in 1909 and were also present in prisons in Manchester, Birmingham, Liverpool, Plymouth, Edinburgh and Dundee before or just after the First World War, usually in partnership with the Catholic Prisoners' Aid Society, supporting women at the point of discharge, regularly giving out clothes and small amounts of money. The visiting Sister at Holloway, for example, gave out items to just over 100 women in January of 1912 and again in January 1914 (two sample dates chosen randomly), dispensing winter coats, shoes, underwear, warm skirts and also tools and goods to help the women restart in a trade, such as baskets and flowers for selling, supplies for laundresses and book folding tools.[191]

If their visiting did not conform to emerging new practices, neither can it be said simply to continue the more traditional practice of visiting rounds that had been practised by elite women on family estates or in local villages. It was too systematic, and in its own way, 'professional', for that. What little sporadic quantitative evidence there is about the Daughters' visiting indicates that full-time

186 Personal File, *Notice of Deceased Sisters*, p. 1 10-2 DCMH.

187 Ibid., p.5.

188 Joseph Sheedy CM 'Writings' typed and bound, vol II, p. 3. 8-5 DCMH.

189 'Your monasteries are the houses of the sick; your cell, the hired room; your cell, the parish church; your cloister the streets; your enclosure, holy obedience; your grill, the fear of God; your veil, holy modesty'. *CDC* #111, 24 August 1659, *CDC*, p. 1213. This now famous set of precepts is currently known in the Company as 'the charter' .

190 See the description of visiting undertaken by Sister Edith Feilding in York c.1890 in Kerr, *Edith Feilding*, p. 21.

191 Carlisle Place, Box 14, Books 25 and 26. 11-83-3 DCMH.

visiting Sisters typically made between eight and ten visits a day, six days a week for fifty weeks in the year. The visiting Sister in Walworth parish in south-east London, for example, undertook more than 2,500 family visits in 1921, an annual total consistent with the figures given thirty years earlier in a report from the Birmingham Catholic Girls' Aid Society (Table 7.10) that had employed two visiting Sisters, and not very different from the situation as late as 1960.[192]

Parish	Visits to families		Visits to sick		Weekly over 50 weeks	
	1890	1891	1890	1891	1890	1891
St Chad's	1121	1730	243	196		
St Joseph's	937	1422	152	76		
Total for Sister A	2058	3152	395	272	41	63
Oratory District	1124	1857	132	138		
St Patrick's	1061	1470	169	91		
Total for Sister B	2185	3327	301	229	44	67
Total	4243	6479	696	501		

7.10: BIRMINGHAM PARISH VISITING, 1890 and 1891[193]

As for the overall scale of the Province's visiting work, some idea of it can be gained from the figure of 320,303 visits for the year 1936/37 submitted by the Province to the mother house by special request for the Paris Exposition that year.[194] It seems reasonable to deduce a fairly consistent figure of around 300,000 annual visits throughout the previous 15 years because the total number of Sisters and works remained fairly constant throughout this period.

Anyone who requested a visit would have expected it to be a religious or spiritual occasion. The salvation of souls was part of this ministry. Edith Feilding, visiting in Sheffield in the late 1890s, was typical in regularising marriages, getting mothers to have their babies baptised and reserving church benches for female factory workers so they would be more likely to attend Mass.[195] Many Sisters were regarded by priests as very fine evangelists. A 'dignitary with long experience

---

192 11-34-2 DCMH.

193 'Annual Report of the Catholic Girls' Aid Society for 1900', Birmingham Archdiocesan Archives (BDA) D204. 1891 'Annual Report of the Catholic Girls' Aid Society for 1901' BDA D443.

194 Statistical Information for Paris, March 1937, 9-5-0-2-5 DCMH. This was to be used by the Company at the International Paris Exposition of 1937.

195 Kerr, *Edith Feilding*, p. 23.

gave it as his opinion,' recalled Father Joseph Sheedy (director of the Province, 1938–1961) in his funeral oration, 'that Sister Joseph of Tollcross [Margaret Duff] had been a means of saving more souls in Scotland than any prelate, priest or religious within living memory'.[196] The parish priest of St Mary Magdalen's parish in Willesden, north London, described Sister Augusta Magdalen Walsh, who visited in the parish from 1923, as 'a remarkable woman who completely revolutionised the place, doing the work of at least two priests'.[197] Canon Hayes, later parish priest of Troon in Ayrshire, reminisced about meeting the Daughters of Charity when he was a new assistant priest at Dumfries and 'resolving that I would seek that co-operation in the work of the sacred ministry in whatever mission or parish the Bishop may assign me', which he duly did.[198] Of Margaret Brohan it was said that 'only God knows' how many she brought to Him: her twice-yearly confirmation classes 'revealed her harvest: lawyers, professors of music, clerks, businessmen, labourers, young ladies, grandfathers and grandmothers'.[199] Indeed, some of the evangelised, like an old woman instructed by Barbara Burke, would rather the Sisters had actually done the work of the priest. On being informed which priest would hear her general confession, the 'old woman listened very attentively and when Sister had finished said: "Och! Now look here Sister, could I not make my confession to you? I would rather do so than go to Father N".[200] It was part of the daily round for a visiting Sister to persuade a non-Catholic husband to allow a priest to visit his sick wife for anointing or to help a mother make arrangements for the baptism for her baby.[201] Unlike the other aspects of the visit each of these sacramental events was meticulously recorded for the provincial statistical returns to Paris, with few details surviving in Britain. In 1936 we do know that the Sisters arranged for 1520 infant baptisms; regularised almost 500 marriages; instructed more than 500 converts; encouraged 1219 baptised Catholics to receive their First Holy Communion; and facilitated more than 600 occasions of anointing of the sick by a priest.[202] Evangelisation and sacramental intervention sat comfortably with the provision of practical care and assistance.

Thus in many of their community care practices the Daughters differed from the general exercise of philanthropy as it evolved into social work in Britain after the 1870s. In particular, their methods were at odds with emergent practice in casework as articulated and implemented by the Charity Organisation Society (COS), or with social work underpinned by new approaches to social investigation

---

196 Reverend Joseph Sheedy, *Conferences and Sermons* ,Typescript vol. II, p. 2. 8-5 DCMH.

197 11-109-1 DCMH.

198 *Life of Sister Louisa Blundell*, p. 33.

199 *Notice of Deceased Sisters* Margaret Brohan, p. 5, Personal File, 10-2 DCMH

200 Typescript 'Remarks on Sister Barbara Mary Bernard Burke, Sixth Visitatrice of the Province, p. 14. Sisters' Personal File, 10-2 DCMH.

201 *Notice of Deceased Sisters,* Margaret Brohan p. 5 Personal File 10-2 DCMH.

202 Statistical Information for Paris, March 1937 9-5-0-2-5 DCMH.

as developed by, among others, Beatrice Webb (1858–1943) or Helen Bosanquet (1860–1925).[203] The COS, guided by Octavia Hill, firmly believed in the unpaid and part-time volunteer who 'was a member of a family with other duties...better still a wife and mother' who could bring 'a gleam of sunlight' from her own home 'into many a monotonous life among the poor': the visiting Sister not only had no family of her own but lived in the same 'monotonous' neighbourhood as those she visited; was a full-time visitor or at least a full-time 'worker', and she received a modest stipend for her visiting work.[204] Jesuit priest and writer, Peter Gallwey, represented a Catholic perspective when he stated that, for work with people in need, 'We want the Nun...those who have chosen poverty for their portion'.[205] The COS was hostile to giving irregular alms on the grounds that this kind of support kept 'a whole class on the very brink of pauperism who might be taught self-control and foresight if we let them learn it'.[206] The model presented to young Sisters, through the stories told about honoured deceased companions and the example of more experienced ones, was to show mercy, to practise judgement and not to discriminate if someone who appeared desperate came to the door. When Helena Jinks, was described as someone who 'would never refuse any', this was clearly presented as a virtue.[207] The Sisters' approach was customary rather than professionalised, informal and continuous rather than investigatory. It was modelled not only by Sister Henriette Chatelain but by second visitatrice Eugénie Marcellus who, even though 'she quickly discerned the true from the false, she ever acted on our Lord's exhortation "the merciful shall obtain mercy"'.[208]

The First World War and the global economic changes that came in its aftermath changed the environment for the practice of charity and had a major impact on the Daughters' ministries. The war 'brought the liberal economic order of the late 19th century to an abrupt halt'.[209] The impact of this collapse, combined with new ideas about child care, led to a decision by the government to rationalise and close its provision for children within the criminal justice system. Five of the Daughters' industrial schools closed. Difficult economic conditions also affected the Province's own income. With increased pressure to raise the standards of buildings and training and new developments in social security and welfare, there was some rethinking about the range of charitable work it was practical for the Sisters to undertake. Although there was much continuity of work and of location thereafter,

---

203 Lewis, *Women and Social Action*.

204 Octavia Hill, 'District Visiting' in *Our Common Land and Other Essays* (London: Macmillan, 1877), p. 24.

205 Father P. Gallwey, *Convent Life and England in the 19ᵗʰ Century: Two Sermons preached in the Church of the Immaculate Conception Farm Street, Mid-Lent Sunday March 7ᵗʰ 1869 On Occasion of An Appeal on behalf of the Little Sisters of the Poor* (London: Burns, Oates, 1869).

206 Lewis, *Women and Social Action*, p. 43.

207 *Notices of Deceased Sisters*, Helena Jinks (1934), p . 33 10-3-1 DCMH.

208 *Memoir of Ma* Soeur *Marcellus* (Mill Hill, 1928), p .49.

209 R. Findlay and K. O'Rourke, *Power and Plenty* (Princeton: Princeton University Press, 2007), p. 249.

by 1925 a particular era in the practice of charitable care by the Sisters was drawing to a close. As it did so, a new chapter in the Province's devotional history opened. Chapter 8, which takes the long view of Marian devotional transmission in the British Province, also argues for a connection between charitable practice and the exceptional increase in Marian devotion in the inter- and post-war decades.

1 These were: a small girls' school at Carlisle Place, Westminster; a larger mixed boarding and day school at Bullingham in Hereford; and a large girls' high school at Darlington which became voluntary aided. For short periods there were other small-scale private girls' schools opened and closed by the province according to the capacity of a particular Sister Servant (Lanark) or the fact that the province took over a property and larger project from other sisters that included a girls' school (Kilburn in 1932 and in West Hounslow in the 1920s). See Appendix II.

Part III
1925–1959 Enduring and Evangelising

8

Marian devotional mission 1880–1950

The chapel at the rue du Bac is one of the most wonderful places
in this world. Here Our Blessed Lady appeared to her who is now
St Catherine Labouré. The chair on which Our Lady sat is there
for all to touch...the tabernacle from which Our Lord manifested
himself to St Catherine is there; the statue Our Lady commissioned
St Catherine to have made is there; and the heart of St Vincent de
Paul rests there, as do the bones of the Holy Foundress of the Sisters
who made our Pilgrimage possible, St Louise de Marillac. Finally ...
there rests the incorrupt body of St Catherine Labouré.[1]

(Kay Trainer, Child of Mary Immaculate, Troon, 1948)

On 25 August 1948, Kay Trainer, a clerical worker from Troon on the west coast
of Scotland, set out for Paris and Lourdes on a centenary pilgrimage of the
Association of the Children of Mary Immaculate. She joined a group boarding
the night train from Dumfries where the pilgrims were given a 'stirring send-off
by many Dumfries parishioners led by several of their priests and the Sisters of
Charity who had made all the arrangements'. There were prayers and blessings
before the train pulled out of the station 'leaving the [Lourdes] "Aves" floating away
with us from those on the platform, and back from us to them'.[2] Kay Trainer had
never travelled to London before, let alone to France. She appreciated seeing the
Houses of Parliament and the Tower of London, but it was the grotto at Lourdes and
the chapel of Apparition of Our Lady of the Miraculous Medal in the rue du Bac
that made the greatest impression on her. 'I think that one of the most marvellous
moments of my life,' she confided to her pilgrim journal, 'was that moment when
I realised that I was actually looking at a Canonised Saint who had beheld Our
Blessed Lady in that very chapel. Such moments come but seldom in a lifetime so
it is small wonder that we guard the memory of such occasions very preciously.'[3]
    This Marian pilgrimage was the project of Sister Barbara Burke, sixth visitatrice
of the British and Irish Province who proposed it as a fitting way to mark both the

---

1 Journal kept by Miss Kay Trainer 'Sisters of Charity Centenary Pilgrimage to Lourdes and Rue du Bac, Paris
26 August 1948 to 6 September 1948', p. 53. Dumfries 11-88 DCMH.

2 ibid, p. 2

3 ibid, p. 54.

1947 canonisation of Sister Catherine Labouré, visionary of the Blessed Virgin, and the forthcoming centenary of the Company's sodality, the Children of Mary Immaculate. 'I wanted to terminate this great year 1947 by something special', she wrote to the Sisters, 'and thought of two things – the re-awakening of the "Louise de Marillac Association" and...a pilgrimage for the Children of Mary to Paris next year, perhaps including Lourdes'.[4] Barbara Burke died unexpectedly before the end of that 'great year', but her shocked and bereaved companions honoured the pilgrimage project. More than 500 Children of Mary Immaculate from Britain and Ireland, with a contingent of Daughters of Charity, undertook the centenary pilgrimage to Paris and Lourdes. Once in France they joined forces with 10,000 others from all over the world who converged on Paris to participate in public rosaries and masses, to process while singing Marian hymns, and to watch tableaux re-enacting the story of the apparitions.[5] This post-war Marian occasion was both a transnational event and a high point in the reinvigorated Marian mission initiated by the Daughters of Britain and Ireland after the First World War.[6] Its progress mirrored the intensification of Marian devotion in the Church that started in the nineteenth century, took on a new anti-communist and apocalyptic dimension with the apparition at Fátima in Portugal in 1917,[7] and culminated in the promulgation of the doctrine of the Assumption in 1950 and the declaration of 1954, the centenary of the definition of the dogma of the Immaculate Conception, as the first ever Marian Year by Pope Pius XII.[8]

Pilgrimages of the kind undertaken in 1948 were once-in-a-lifetime occasions but they grew out of daily devotional practices, those aspects of Catholic spirituality expressed in extra-liturgical prayer and embodied piety. To apply historian Robert Orsi's insight, Kay Trainer's pilgrim experience gave her access to the 'radical presence' of the divine.[9] As she expressed it; 'The chair on which Our Lady sat is there for all to touch'. After a lifetime's study Orsi has concluded that relationships – human and divine – are key to the power that devotional practices have in the

---

4 Remarks about Sister Barbara Burke 1896–1947. p. 30. Personal File, 10-2 DCMH.

5 The 10,000 figure comes from http://vincentians.com/saint-catherine-laboure-of-the-miraculous-medal-xiv-the-medal-and-ratisbonne/ (accessed 3 March 2016).

6 See the many references to the centenary events in *The Echo of the Mother House* for 1953 and 1954, e.g. 'An Account of the Marian Year Celebrations at the Central House, Mill Hill', August/September 1954, pp.245–249. 1-5 DCMH.

7 See Sandra Zimdars-Swartz, *Encountering Mary: From La Salette to Medjugorie* (Princeton, Princeton University Press, 1991).

8 'Centenary Congress of the Children of Mary Immaculate from England, Ireland and Scotland. Paris Sept 2nd to 5th 1948', Pilgrims' Handbook produced by the Central House Mill Hill. Dumfries. 11-88 DCMH.

9 Robert A. Orsi, 'Abundant History: Marian Apparitions as Alternative Modernity.' in Anna-Karina Hermkens, Willy Jansen and Catrien Notermans eds., *Moved by Mary: The Power of Pilgrimage in the Modern World* (Farnham, Ashgate, 2009), p. 218.

lives of individuals.[10] These relationships challenge the frameworks within which modern scholars interpret human experience, where 'the social somehow exists prior to the transcendent'.[11] For Orsi, devotions are best understood as 'lived religion', that is, as a way for people to bring 'the structures of their everyday lives into "dynamic relationship" with their religion'.[12] As he reminds us, although they connect to the transcendent, 'relationships with Mary are never lived apart from the circumstances of particular times and places'.[13] In exploring the Daughters' mission to live and teach a path of holy living through devotion to the Blessed Virgin, this chapter attempts to hold together the spiritual realities of devotions for practitioners with their changing social meanings over one hundred years from 1860 to 1960, with a particular focus on the period from 1920 to 1950. At the same time, it also seeks to maintain the connections between devotions and the Daughters' care ministries as they evolved through this period.

Mary Immaculate, Catherine Labouré and the Miraculous Medal

Pilgrimage to the chapel in the Daughters' mother house connected Kay Trainer to the occasion in July 1830 that had begun a fresh Marian mission in the Company.[14] The Company's Marian dimension, however, had deep roots in the personal devotion to Mary common to both Vincent de Paul and Louise de Marillac.[15] Louise de Marillac's intense personal devotion meant that the prayer practices of the Company were strongly Marian.[16] 'Let us celebrate, in a special way', she wrote, 'the Church feasts honouring Mary.'[17] The Sisters were to 'say part of their rosary at different times, such as one after morning prayer...'[18] Most significantly for the long-term devotional life of the Company, Louise de Marillac added a sixth decade to the Company's recitation of the rosary and established the practice that every

10 Ibid., p.220 and p.221. Robert A. Orsi, *Thank you St Jude: Women's Devotion to the Patron Saint of Hopeless Causes* (New Haven, Yale University Press, 1998) and *Between Heaven and Earth: The Religious Worlds People Make and the Scholars Who Study Them* (Princeton and Oxford, Princeton University Press, 2005). See also Chris Maunder, 'Apparitions of Mary', in Sarah Jane Boss ed., *Mary: the complete resource* (Oxford, Oxford University Press, 2007), p.426.

11 Orsi, 'Abundant History', p.217 quoting Dipesh Chakrabarty, *Provincializing Europe: Postcolonial Thought and Historical Difference* (Princeton, Princeton University Press, 2000).

12 Robert A. Orsi, *The Madonna of 115th Street: Faith and Community in Italian Harlem, 1880-90* 2nd edition London, (Yale University Press; 2002), pp. xiii-xiv. See, for example, Meredith B. McGuire, *Lived Religion: Faith and Practice in Everyday Life* (Oxford, Oxford University Press, 2008) and Jeff Astley and Leslie J. Francis eds., *Exploring Ordinary Theology: Everyday Christian Believing and the Church* (Farnham: Ashgate Press, 2013).

13 Orsi, *Madonna,* p. 217 and Orsi, *Between Heaven and Earth*, p. 60.

14 Orsi, 'Abundant History', p. 215.

15 See, for example, Superior General Slattery, 'The Devotion of Saint Vincent and Saint Louise de Marillac to the Most Holy Virgin', in *Echo from the Mother House* June 1954, pp.151-54. 1-5 DCMH

16 See various editions of the 'Formulary of Prayers and Pious Practices for the use of the Daughters of Charity, with appropriate instruction'. Prayer Books. 14-1 DCMD.

17 Sullivan, *Spiritual Writings of Louise de Marillac*, pp.785-786.

18 *CCD*, 13b, p.147.

decade would conclude with a prayer she had composed. It is this prayer that gives greatest insight into her theology and her specific devotion to Mary's Immaculate Conception.

> Most holy Virgin, I believe and confess thy holy and immaculate Conception, pure and without stain; O most chaste Virgin, through thy virginal purity, thy Immaculate Conception, thy glorious prerogative of Mother of God, obtain for me from thy Divine Son, humility, charity, great purity of heart, mind and body, holy perseverance in my dear vocation, the gift of prayer, a good life and a happy death. Behold the handmaid of the Lord. Be it done to me according to Thy word. O Jesus be to me a Jesus. Now and at the hour of my death. Amen.

As early as 1644, on a pilgrimage to Chartres, the foundress had dedicated the Company to the Virgin[19] and on her deathbed she instructed the Sisters that they were to regard Mary as their *only* Mother.[20] In his discussion of Vincentian spirituality, Corpus Delgado notes that 'Mary's presence in St. Louise's correspondence and writings is rich, abundant and sometimes even written in a systematic way'.[21] The rosary prayer, along with her paintings of the Blessed Virgin, formed part of her spiritual bequest to the Sisters.[22] Moreover, because Louise de Marillac had made her own vows on the Feast of the Annunciation (25 March), as already noted, this date was eventually chosen for all Sisters to renew their annual vows. The feast aligned the Sisters' dedication to Mary with their personal vocational commitment. It is not difficult to see how the rich Marian tradition of the Company was the fertile seedbed for the Marian events of 1830 beginning on 19 July in the rue du Bac. What those events changed, however, was the Company's Marian public identity and identification with the Blessed Virgin.

On that July day a young Daughter of Charity, Sister Zoe (Catherine) Labouré, a seminary Sister at the rue du Bac, experienced an apparition of the Blessed Virgin. She later spoke of two further supernatural encounters in the same chapel in November and December 1830 when the Blessed Virgin instructed Catherine to have a medallion made and told her what should be inscribed on it.[23] It was to be widely distributed so that 'abundant graces' could be poured out on those who wore it. Labouré described the medal to her spiritual director, Vincentian Father Jean-Marie Aladel, and in 1832 he, in turn, gave the details to Parisian goldsmith Adrien Vachette. The first batch of medals struck by Vachette had as its obverse

---

19 ibid. p.122.

20 ibid. p.835.

21 http://famvin.org/wiki/Marian_Spirituality_and_the_Vincentian_Charism (accessed 20 February 2016).

22 Anne Neylon, 'Historical Marian Devotional Practices Among the Daughters of Charity', in Prunty and Sullivan eds., *The Daughters in Ireland*. p. 88.

23 This account is largely taken from Laurentin, *The Life of Catherine Labouré*.

the image of a womanly Mary, erect of posture, one knee slightly flexed, arms extended as though reaching out to petitioners. It was immediately recognisable as a representation of the Immaculate Conception: the serpent beneath her feet, crushed by the sinless one, confirmed this.[24] But in a departure from the familiar, this Mary Immaculate wore jewelled rings and from them emanated striking rays of grace 'as if in bundles', widening as they spread from Mary's hands towards the ground.[25] Arranged round the outside of the image was the prayer, 'O Mary conceived without sin, pray for us who have recourse to thee.' The medal's reverse was a new arrangement of well-known Christian and Catholic icons: a plain cross standing on and above a strong bar that was intertwined with the letter 'M'. Beneath were two hearts – one encircled with a crown of thorns (the Sacred Heart of Jesus), the other pierced with a sword (the Immaculate Heart of Mary), and the whole was encircled by 12 stars.

Sister Catherine later insisted that Mary's arms had not been outstretched: the rays of grace came from rings on hands that had held a small golden ball. This, the Virgin had told her, '...represents the whole world, especially France, and every individual'.[26] The confusion over the Virgin's representation has never been satisfactorily explained: although the evidence has been scrutinised minutely, the dramatic popular reception of the medal overtook all other considerations and left the question behind.[27] Stories circulated almost immediately about cures, conversions and consolations linked to the medal, leading to its popular sobriquet as the 'Miraculous'.[28] In 1836, the Medal was circulating in the United States and soon made its way to China and Russia via Vincentian missionaries.[29] By 1842, 12 years before Pope Pius IX defined the dogma of the Immaculate Conception, an estimated 100 million Miraculous Medals had been made and distributed. It is

24 For a discussion of the artistic representations of Mary Immaculate, see Joyce Polestina, 'The Image of Mary of the Miraculous Medal: A Valiant Woman', *Nineteenth-Century Art Worldwide* (Summer, 2012), Vol. 11. no.2. (accessed 26 January 2016) and Eli Heldaas Seland, 'The visual rhetoric of medals representing nineteenth-century Marian apparitions', in Laugerud and Ryan, *Devotional Cultures of European Christianity*, pp.75-95.

See also Laurentin's comparison with earlier representations of the Immaculate Conception and of the representation in Catherine Labouré's parish church, *Life of Catherine Labouré*, p.88, and Maurice Vloberg, 'Iconographic Types of the Virgin in Western Art', in Sarah Jane Boss ed., *Mary the Complete Resource* (Oxford, Oxford University Press, 2007), pp. 569-72.

25 Laurentin, *Catherine Labouré*, p.79. Art historian Joyce Polistena claims that the rays 'marked a feminine personification of spiritual agency new in Catholic art' which she links to the iconography of the Valiant Woman of scripture: Polestina, 'Image of Mary of the Miraculous Medal', referring to the Book of Proverbs 31:10-31.

26 Laurentin, *Catherine Labouré*, p.153.

27 The usual explanations given are either that Aladel and other authorities believed that the globe was too much of a deviation from the accepted representations of Mary Immaculate and would confuse the faithful or that there was more than one apparition and that Catherine was unclear in her narrative about the globe. For discussion of these points, see the discussion in Laurentin (pp.219 and 262-5) which is critiqued in the dispassionate non-apologetic review of evidence in Stafford Poole CM, 'Pierre Coste and Catherine Labouré: The Conflict of Historical Criticism and Popular Devotion', *VHJ* (1999), Vol. 20, iss. 2, pp.253-302.

28 It was originally called 'The Medal of the Virgin of the Rays' or the 'Medal of the Immaculate Conception', 'Seland, Visual rhetoric', p.76.

29 See Jeremy Clarke, *The Virgin Mary and Catholic Identities in Chinese History* (Hong Kong, Hong Kong University Press, 2013), pp.74-78.

highly likely, and often claimed, that they played a part in laying the immediate ground for the promulgation of the dogma *Ineffabilis Deus* of 1854.[30] Daughters and Vincentians took a share in distributing the Medal in hospitals and schools and on home visits, but there were many other channels for circulation, among which the Marian devotional centre, Notre-Dames-des-Victoires in Paris, was the most important.[31]

In accounting for its immediate success during the 1830s, which was not the result of any organised papal or episcopal campaign, historians have emphasised the political and social atmosphere in France[32] and the general concept of 'ultramontane' devotions (those approved and promoted by Rome). Given the Medal's popularity among Catholics living in very different environments, and given its French rather than Roman origins, other and additional explanations must be sought. For curator and historian Eli Seland, the visual appearance of the Medal has always been vital to its popularity and effectiveness. Atypical of the genre of apparition medals, it does not include an image of either the location of the vision or the visionary herself. All attention is therefore 'directed at the object of the vision'. The 'presence of the Holy Virgin on earth' becomes the focus, and devotees find evidence of its truth in the 'working' of the Medal.[33] In summary, the Medal is a portable sacramental, a symbolically rich aid to the user's own religious imagination that is felt by believers to 'work' because of the abundance of grace promised and subsequently verified by countless individuals.[34]

The apparition and its message led to the foundation of the Association of the Children of the Blessed Virgin Mary Immaculate (Children of Mary Immaculate), a pious association whose emblem and medal was the Miraculous Medal.[35] Pope Pius IX approved the fledgling organisation in 1847 as an association for young women operating exclusively under the guidance of the Vincentian family and affiliated for privileges and protocols to the Sodality of Our Lady, Prima Primaria, founded by the Society of Jesus in the sixteenth century. Its manual was written by Jean-Marie Aladel, and in 1850 the Vincentians' request for permission to establish branches of boys and young men under their guidance was granted. Throughout the nineteenth century the Association's headquarters was in the mother house of

---

30 See Trent Pomplum, 'Mary' in James J. Buckley, Frederick Christian and Trent Pomplum eds., *The Blackwell Companion to Catholicism* (Malden MA and Oxford: John Wiley, 2011), p. 317.

31 The parish church of Our Lady of Victories in Paris, rededicated in 1836 to the Immaculate Heart of Mary by its priest Abbé Desgnettes, became a major distribution network for the medal, not least through the confraternity Our Lady, Refuge of Sinners, established by Desgnettes which took the Miraculous Medal as its badge and had 640,000 members by 1845.

32 See, for example, Richard D.E. Burton, *Holy Tears, Holy Blood: Women, Catholicism and the Culture of Suffering, 1840-1970* (Ithaca, NY, Cornell University Press, 2004).

33 Seland, 'The visual rhetoric of medals', p. 83.

34 This phenomenon has been discussed in relation to, for example, the relics of St Thérèse of Lisieux: Sophie Deboick, 'Image, Authenticity and the Cult of Thérèse of Lisieux' (unpublished PhD thesis, University of Liverpool, 2011).

35 Laurentin, *Catherine Labouré*, p. 146.

the Congregation of the Mission, in the street neighbouring the mother house of the Company of Daughters. By 1870, more than 300 branches were in operation in different parts of the world and by the end of the century across all the branches, male and female, more than 600,000 members had been registered.[36] It achieved canonical recognition as a distinct lay society in the Church in 1904 and became one of the largest lay Catholic organisations in the world.[37]

Catherine Labouré herself remained for her entire community life in the same house, a home for impoverished elderly men at Reuilly in the environs of Paris. Living not far from the mother house, and therefore under the discreet surveillance of Superiors General, she lived a straightforward life of service, caring for the residents and tending the extensive kitchen garden and livestock. Despite the persistent myth that the Sisters did not know which among them was the visionary, Stafford Poole describes it as an 'open secret' among the Sisters that it was Zoe Labouré.[38] But her identity as the visionary was not made known publically to the Sisters or externally until after her death in 1876. An 'official' history of the apparition and the Medal with an account of Sister Catherine's life was published under Aladel's name in 1877 (although not written by him).[39] In the light of the role played by Marian shrines in French Catholic revivalism, above all at La Salette (1846) and at Lourdes (1858), Catherine died believing that the Blessed Mother had ensured there were other places of pilgrimage and sites of grace accessible to the people since the chapel at rue du Bac remained closed to them.[40]

Superior General Jean-Baptiste Étienne (1843-74), a close friend of Aladel, made no attempt to push or promote a devotion that had not been verified by the Church.[41] But after 20 years, he began to give credit to the Blessed Virgin of the apparition for the unity, vigour and the global missionary outreach of the double family through the graces she had bestowed on it. 'Can we find another reason,' Étienne wrote of the Congregation and the Company, 'for such *incomprehensible numbers* of vocations that are showing themselves everywhere?'[42] The Company did take tentative steps towards making the chapel more accessible in 1880, the golden jubilee of the apparitions, when it was enlarged and opened to the public for the first time. Respecting Catherine's persistent wish for a statue of the Blessed Virgin holding a globe, one was sculpted in 1880. After an initial ruling by the Holy See that it be removed as confusing to the faithful, the statue, known as Virgo Potens

36 John Rybolt, *History of the Vincentians: Vol 4*, p. 77.

37 *Catholic Encyclopedia* 1911 http://www.newadvent.org/cathen/03659d.htm (accessed 10 February 2016).

38 Poole, 'Pierre Coste and Catherine Labouré, p. 253.

39 The work was entitled *La Médaille Miraculeuse: origine, histoire, diffusions, resultants* by J. M. Aladel, (Paris, Pillet et Dumoulin,1878).

40 Laurentin, *Catherine Labouré*, p.162. For a study of other Marian pilgrimage sites, see Sandra Zimdar-Swartz, *Encountering Mary: From La Salette to Mdjugorie* (Princeton NJ, Princeton University Press, 1991).

41 John Rybolt, *The Vincentians: Vol. 4*, p. 70.

42 Laurentin, *Catherine Labouré*, p.1 31.

(Virgin Most Powerful), was approved and placed at a side altar as Catherine had specified.[43] At this stage external pilgrims were still from the local area and few in number. The chapel had very short public opening hours because it was in use by the Sisters: there is little sign that the Company was promoting it as a pilgrim site, and the Company's own identity remained firmly focused on serving the poor at home and abroad.[44]

At the request of Superior General Antoine Fiat, Pope Leo XIII instituted a Feast of the Virgin Mary of the Miraculous Medal (27 November) in 1894, with a proper (specific texts) for the Mass and indulgences. By this time the Medal's popularity had led to the creation of a large number of unregulated local 'Miraculous Medal associations' in several countries. Concerned that many 'were influenced by some spiritual trends that were completely foreign to the message of the rue du Bac', the Vincentians moved to gain control of the devotional practices associated with the Medal.[45] With the Company's Superiors, they convinced Pope Pius X to approve the establishment of a new and highly unusual 'association of the faithful', the Association of the Miraculous Medal, open to clergy, Religious and laity as equals (canon 298). Its only membership criterion was that members 'receive the blessed medal [blessed by a priest] and carry it with them repeating frequently the words inscribed on it'.[46] Since only Vincentians could approve other priests to give the blessing, the Association was particularly strong where the Vincentian fathers had a presence.

The Medal, the Children of Mary Immaculate and the Association of the Miraculous Medal spread throughout many parts of the Catholic world. For many commentators they are prime examples of the 'ultramontane' (Roman) devotions that characterised the nineteenth-century Catholic revival. However, to use this term to describe a wide range of popular devotions whose initial dissemination and reception owed nothing to papal or Vatican intervention is 'to force the issue beyond an acceptable point'.[47] It seems more helpful, as we turn to look at what happened to the Medal in Britain, to see it and the Children of Mary Immaculate as transnational devotions whose reception in each nation or territory was inflected according to history and context.

---

43 On the grounds that it was a novel representation based on a private revelation, Poole, 'Coste and Catherine Labouré', pp.288-9.

44 J.M. Planchot, 'The Chapel of the rue du Bac,' trans J. Ryan 2003 http://famvin.org/wiki/Rue_du_Bac (accessed 1 February 2016). Planchot gives an estimated 2.5 million visitors to the chapel in 2003. Poole notes that the Superior Generals were 'quite reluctant' to start the process for the beatification of Catherine Labouré, 'Coste and Catherine Labouré', pp.292-94

45 Enrique Rivas Villas, 'The Association of the Miraculous Medal: A Uniquely Vincentian Association', *Vincentiana*, Vol. 53, No 6, (2009), p.467.

46 ibid., p.456.

47 Heimann, *Catholic Devotion*, p.36.

The devotional history of nineteenth-century Britain

If we are to understand the Medal's reception in Britain, we must begin by asking what kind of devotional landscape existed at the time when the Sisters began their work and how it changed in the later decades of the nineteenth century. We know more about Catholic devotional life in England than in Scotland but, despite the development of the history of 'lived religion' and the history of religious material culture in recent years (statues, medals, pictures and cards, for example), there has been little systematic research carried out for either nation in the modern era, particularly in relation to devotion to the Blessed Virgin.[48] This is surprising because Catholics in Britain, whether Scottish, English or Irish, were acutely aware that the honour they afforded Mary was the most salient signifier of their religious identity.[49] Indeed, changes in Protestant thinking after 1840 about the mother of Jesus increased her potency as a religious identity marker.[50] Anti-Catholics used devotion to the Virgin Mary to distinguish between what they believed to be 'a stalwart, rational, British Protestantism and a weak, effeminate, continental Catholicism' with its tendency to idolatry.[51] It was not an obviously encouraging climate into which to introduce a Marian devotion originating in a miraculous event that had taken place in France.

The classic study of devotional life in nineteenth-century England is Mary Heimann's *Catholic Devotion in Victorian England*.[52] In turn, Heimann's work was the spur for Bernard Aspinwall's essay 'Catholic Devotion in Victorian Scotland'.[53] Heimann put forward several new arguments about devotional practice in Victorian England that are relevant to the history of the Daughters of Charity. Firstly, she was able to show the continuing vigour of Catholic piety in the early nineteenth century. It drew its strength from Richard Challoner's eighteenth-century *Garden of the Soul* and other prayer books based on this text and from its constancy in the practices of Benediction and the rosary. Catholic devotional life in England had developed its own 'English' tone and tenor, quiet and serious, undemonstrative but intense.[54] Secondly, there was no sudden change in the nineteenth century wherein these traditional forms of piety were replaced by new 'Roman' devotions

---

48 For other countries, the literature in these fields is substantial and growing, particularly using the methods of 'lived religion' and the history of material culture. Some of it is referenced in this chapter. Sheridan Gilley sets out the challenge to historians of writing a history of the entire 'Devotional Revolution' in Britain in his essay 'Devotions and the old rite' in Henning Laugerad & Salvador Ryan eds., *Devotional Cultures of European Christianity 1790-1960* (Dublin, Four Courts Press, 2012), pp.34-47.

49 Herringer, *Victorians and the Virgin Mary*.

50 ibid., p.22

51 ibid., p.4.

52 Heimann, *Catholic Devotion*.

53 Bernard Aspinwall, 'Catholic Devotion in Victorian Scotland', in Martin J. Mitchell, ed., *New Perspectives on the Irish in Scotland* (Edinburgh, John Donald, 2008), pp.31-43.

54 Heimann, *Catholic Devotion*, p.172. See also her quotation from J. D. Crichton, at p.10 'somewhat reticent, solidly instructed and devout with a deep interior piety.'

through an effort by the papacy and certain bishops to centralise Catholic life: the older forms persisted as new ones were gradually introduced.[55] In a third argument, Heimann made the case for these 'English' devotions as the unifying force that brought together English recusants, Irish migrants and converts from the Church of England to form an English Catholic community.[56] The same levels of usage and popularity for Benediction and the reprinting of Challoner's prayers were found in Scotland.[57] We will return to Aspinwall's other conclusions shortly.

At the same time, devotion to Our Lady of Lourdes was 'conspicuous by its absence' before the First World War, Heimann concluded.[58] She confirmed what had been noted in 1920 by the well-known Jesuit historian, Herbert Thurston.[59] Reflecting on the reception given in the British Catholic press to the apparitions at Lourdes and La Salette, he notes how muted it was. The scathing response of *The Times* and *The Daily Telegraph* at the time of the apparitions, Thurston considered, may 'have tended to make English Catholic editors cautious' about encouraging the devotions, a caution that was shared by most of the bishops, particularly in relation to the visions at La Salette.[60] Paris and the Miraculous Medal do not even merit mention in Thurston's thorough survey of devotions, despite the Medal being worn by John Henry Newman.[61] But the existence of a culture of caution towards modern French Mariology is confirmed, Heimann suggests, by the decision taken at the 1908 meeting of the bishops of England and Wales to oppose a request for 'the extension in England of the Feast of the Miraculous Medal'.[62]

In Scotland, Aspinwall has argued, the situation was different. A range of European devotions were well received there, not least because of the shortage

---

55 Denis Gwynn, *The Second Spring 1818-1852: A Study of the Catholic Revival in England* (London, Burns Oates, 1942); Derek Holmes, *More Roman than Rome: English Catholicism in the Nineteenth Century* (London, Burns and Oates, 1978). This process was described as long ago as 1972 in relation to Ireland in Emmet Larkin, 'The Devotional Revolution in Ireland 1850-1875'. See also A. Taves, *The Household of Faith: Roman Catholic Devotions in Mid-Nineteenth Century America* (Notre Dame, IND, University of Notre Dame Press, 1986).

56 Ibid., p.172-173.

57 Aspinwall,'Catholic Devotions in Victorian Scotland', p. 36.

58 Heimann, *Catholic Devotion*, p. 92.

59 It is worth noting that a chapel and altar dedicated to Our Lady of Lourdes was erected in the prestigious Jesuit Farm Street church in 1887 where Thurston was living. There were at least six other new churches in England dedicated to Our Lady of Lourdes before the First World War.

60 H. Thurston, 'The Début of Lourdes before English Opinion', *The Month*, Vol. 143. no. 719, May 1920, p.408. On the difficulties in Rome caused by aspects of La Salette, see Poole, 'Coste and Catherine Labouré', p. 289.

61 Newman wrote to Pusey on 22 August 1865: 'It is twenty years to the day since I saw my way clear to put a Miraculous Medal round my neck.' Francis J. McGrath and Charles Stephen Dessain, *The Letters and Diaries of John Henry Newman: The Final Steps* Vol. 11, 1 November 1843-6, October 1845 (Oxford, Oxford University Press, 2006). On Newman's gratitude for the prayers offered for him at Notre-Dames-des-Victories in the weeks before his abjuration, see Marina Warner, *Stranger Magic: Charmed States and the Arabian Nights* (Cambridge MA, Harvard University Press, 2012), p. 232.

62 Heimann, *Catholic Devotion*, p.167. Decision taken at the Annual Meeting of the Bishops of England and Wales Low Week 1908, 'Bishops' Meetings 1858-1909', p. 387. Westminster Archdiocesan Archives. No further comment was made other than that they had received a petition for this extension, with no petitioner named. See also Heimann, 'Mysticism in Bootle: Victorian Supernaturalism as an Historical Problem', *Journal of Ecclesiastical History*, Vol. 64. iss.2 (April, 2013), pp. {335-356}.

A Marian era: enduring and evangelising 1925-1960

In this period the life of the Province was significantly shaped by political and economic events on the world stage. Financial constraints in the years after the First World War were serious and created increased pressures. Even so, between the two World Wars the Sisters began new healthcare works and opened city hostels for young working women. With the advent of the welfare state and new childcare legislation came requirements for greater professionalisation and different approaches.

In the 1920s the Province began a more overt mission to promote the Company's Marian spirituality, stimulated in part by the process to canonise Louise de Marillac and Catherine Labouré but also by threats to religion from Communism. The promotion of sodalities and Marian devotional practices became one of the outstanding features of the Province's activity across schools, institutions, hostels and parishes, reflecting and intensifying a strong Marian orientation in the Church at this time.

The Chapel of the Apparition of the Miraculous Medal in the rue du Bac as it looks today. The chapel was extended and renovated in 1930 in readiness for the centenary of the apparitions. After 1930 the chapel grew in importance as a Marian apparition pilgrimage site that also contained the remains of St Louise and a major relic of St Vincent. After her canonisation in 1947, the body of St Catherine Labouré was placed in the chapel, to the right of the sanctuary.

Virgo Potens (Powerful Virgin) Catherine had seen the Virgin holding a globe, representing the whole world.

Canonisations of Saint Louise and Saint Catherine

Celebration of the Canonisation of St Louise de Marillac, Mill Hill 1934

Seminary Sisters and Sister Directress and her assistants surround the new statue of St Louise depicted giving the Rules and Customs to a Sister. This statue, paid for by donations from Sisters across the Province, was placed in a prominent position behind the Provincial House. Starting in the late nineteenth century, the Company undertook a project to collect Louise de Marillac's correspondence and writing and to promote knowledge of her as co-founder. The cause for her canonisation was opened in the 1880s leading to her beatification in 1920.

Celebration for the Canonisation of Catherine Labouré, Mill Hill 1947

Superiors from Paris and Mill Hill with Cardinal Griffin of Westminster at Mill Hill for the occasion of the Triduum (3 days of prayer and liturgy) to mark the canonisation of Catherine Labouré.

Back from left: Fr Sheedy CM (Provincial Director); Sisters Rafferty, Whalen, Brennan and Rainford.
Front: Sister Burke (Visitatrice); Fr Slattery CM (General Superior); Cardinal Griffin; General Superioress Blancot; Sister O'Driscoll (Directress of the seminary)

Formation for spiritual mission

Feast of the Miraculous Medal, the Mill Hill Seminary

This temporary altar (shown here in 1955) was erected and decorated each year by the seminary Sisters. The Virgo Potens statue is now in the Sisters' seminary in Kenya.

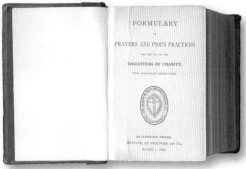

The Formulary of the Daughters of Charity containing 'Prayers and Pious Practices for the use of Daughters of Charity'.

Chaplet (rosary) of a Daughter of Charity. The beads are dried berries. In addition to the crucifix, the chaplet had a 'crown of thorns' head of the Lord, a Miraculous Medal and a medal of St Benedict. The rosary was threaded on green tape, green representing the virtue of Hope. The chaplet has six decades.

A Marian mission in Britain

Cards and medals distributed by the Daughters In 1923 the Province opened the Virgo Potens office in Dublin to promote the Medal and a new magazine dedicated to Mary of the Immaculate Conception, also called *Virgo Potens*. Additional centres were opened in Britain to promote the Medal and the Red and Green Scapulars, two other Company devotions.

May procession and outdoor altar to Mary Immaculate in the parish of the Immaculate Conception Church, Commercial Road, East London, early 1950s.

Fr Frederick Higley invited the Daughters to the parish in 1911. He built the new church of the Immaculate Conception. In his will he left an endowment to support the work of four Sisters in the parish.

1952 Corpus Christi Procession, Immaculate Conception School, Darlington

Immaculate Conception School was founded by the Province in 1905.

Children of Mary in York c. 1925 (above) and in Lanark 1949 (below)

The Children of Mary Immaculate – a Vincentian confraternity – began in France and received Pontifical Approbation from Pope Pius IX in 1847. It had male and female groups by 1850 and was described in the Approbation as 'a pious Society under the title of Immaculate Virgin Mary'.

Members met weekly for prayer. They wore a Miraculous Medal on a blue ribbon. The Association experienced an increase in fervour at the time of the canonisation of St Catherine Labouré in 1947, which coincided with the immediate post-war years and the onset of the Cold War.

Hostels

The Sisters had provided and managed hostel accommodation for young working women in several cities since the turn of the century with an initial emphasis on ports such as Liverpool, Plymouth, Dundee and Hull. This service became a more significant activity during the 1920s, 1930s and 1940s when they opened hostels in half a dozen central and north London locations and in Glasgow, Edinburgh, Cardiff and Birmingham.

ST. LOUISE'S GIRLS HOSTEL, MEDWAY ST., LONDON, S.W.1.
RUN BY SISTERS OF CHARITY OF ST. VINCENT DE PAUL.

St Louise's Hostel London Medway Street SW1. The hostel began as a series of houses around Medway Street which were replaced by a purpose-built hostel owned by the Province shown in this contemporary postcard.

In 1938 St Louise's housed 166 single working women and 25 homeless women.

St Joseph's Hostel, Birmingham staff and residents, 1947

In 1924 the Province bought and converted a former button factory in the city centre into a hostel for working women and those looking for work, undertaking much of the manual labour of conversion themselves.

From left to right: Sisters Agnes Tobin, Adrian Foyle, Gertrude Furlong and Rosalie Hughes.

Healthcare

The Sisters greatly developed their nursing and healthcare services between 1920 and 1950. In Britain a new hospital for men with severe war injuries was opened in Ealing in 1920; buildings for two sanatoria were bought and staffed as were locations for two general hospitals, one in Liverpool and one in London. In addition the Province expanded its children's orthopaedic work at St Vincent's in Pinner and opened three hospitals for children with disabilities needing long-term nursing, educational and social care.

Marillac House (The Marillac), Warley in Essex was bought by a Sister in 1921 for a sanatorium, primarily for religious sisters in the early stages of TB. Margaret Sinclair, a Scottish Poor Clare nun in the Nottingham Hill Carmel, later revered for sanctity in Catholic circles, came here to be nursed in her final months of life. As the need for specialist TB treatment declined Marillac House changed its focus. It became a hospital for the chronically sick and is now a nursing home for young adults with acquired brain injury.

St Joseph's Hospital and Home, Rosewell near Edinburgh 1924 This large Jacobean revival style country house had been used as a Red Cross hospital during WWI and was bought by the Province in 1924 to develop a hospital and home for children with cognitive disabilities. The Hospital was licensed by the Board of Control and run by a Management Board. In 1942 the Province established St Joseph's Training School for Nurses for the Mental Handicapped Register here.

St Vincent's Sanatorium and Hospital Kingussie 1934 This was the most northerly of the Sisters' Houses. The sanatorium had been built in 1901 and run privately by its doctor-proprietors until 1934 when the Sisters bought it for the same purpose. During the 1950s the hospital was adapted for geriatric nursing with a new wing and chapel being added.

Holidays and lighter moments

St Mary's Grangetown parish outing 1924
The ladies of the parish on an outing, possibly to York. Two of the parish Sisters are with them. Daughters arrived in the parish of St Mary's, Grangetown in 1921 and taught generations of the same families in the infant and primary schools.

Photo credit John O'Neill
Around Grangetown, reproduced with kind permission of the publishers

Sisters Vincent Carroll (l) and Mary King (r) with their scout troop on Barry Island, 1933. The Sisters had provided holidays for London children since the late 1880s when they were given a house in Dover.

In the 1920s it became much more common for the Sisters to take children from the homes to a nearby sea resort for one or two weeks.

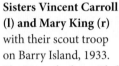

London Marillac Association summer outing to Mill Hill 1937. Mrs O'Toole of Poplar and Sister Mary Petre, Sister Servant of Carlisle Place, Westminster.

Sister Mary Thompson and boy at St Vincent's Orthopaedic Hospital Pinner make the most of the severe winter of 1947.

Community customs

4.00	Rising bell*
4.30	Morning prayer and Meditation
5.10	Angelus and concluding prayers
5.15	Work in the house
7.00	Mass and thanksgiving**
7.30	Breakfast
	Works and offices
11.30	Examen and prayer
	(or later for teaching Sisters)
12.00	Dinner with reading aloud
13.30	Recreation or return to work
14.00	Reading from Rules or Conferences
	(or later)
	Works and offices
17.30	Evening Meditation and Examen
18.00	Supper
19.00	Recreation together
20.00	Night Prayers
	Great Silence

* Sisters were given permission to remain in bed for an hour once a week

** In France it was customary for Mass to be earlier than this but in Britain and Ireland it was rare for Mass to be available before 7.00 a.m.

Daily Order

From the time of the founders there was a daily order with prescribed times for rising and retiring, for prayer and particular examination of conscience (examen), spiritual reading, Mass and general silence.

Priests and bishops in Britain expressed concern for the Sisters about the hardship of such an early start to the day in northerly parts, especially Scotland. In 1895 Cardinal Vaughan asked the Company's superiors if they could rise later, only to find that the Sisters objected strongly to what they saw as a cause for disunity between themselves and the rest of the Company.

The structure of the day was still being observed in the 1930s, with variations according to the day of the week and liturgical season.

Apart from during World War II the first major change came in 1947 when Sisters in Britain had special permission to rise at 5.00 a.m.

Marking a special occasion

Composing a song and decorating a card was the way Sisters of the Province marked a special occasion such as making Vows or completing seminary.

Sister Joan Tindall's card reflects her previous career as a WAAF driver and her love of all fast vehicles, hence the Guardian Angel hovering protectively behind her.

Sister Morwenna Fogden's card marked her start of seminary in 1950. It shows a spirit of self-mockery about 'virtue and piety' and at the same time leaves no doubt about the sheer physical labour of the Seminary Sister.

World War II

At the outbreak of war in 1939 the seminary was moved to Torquay, returning to London in 1942. Children and Sisters were evacuated from many other Houses; seven were closed altogether including one in Bow, London that was bombed. The Province operated on a wartime footing with little communication from general superiors. Daughters in the Province were given permission by general superiors to rise at 5.00 a.m. rather than 4.00 a.m.

Evacuation of toddlers from St Anthony's home in Hounslow in 1939.

This photograph was printed in the Westminster Rescue Society publication 'The Net' in 1939.

(Reproduced by kind permission of the Catholic Children's Service, Westminster)

French children with their French Sisters being evacuated to the Daughters' home in Lanark.

Basque refugee children fleeing the Spanish Civil War in 1937 were given shelter in the Daughters' homes in Gainford and Tudhoe Co. Durham. Later the refugees presented the Gainford home with an inscribed statue of Our Lady of Begona.

Inspecting the bomb damage at St Vincent's Pinner, October 1940.

The chapel at St Vincent's Pinner was almost destroyed by an enemy bomb and the chapel at St Vincent's Mill Hill was also hit. No one was killed or seriously hurt.

Professionalisation

After 1910 more entrants arrived with nursing, teaching, domestic science or secretarial qualifications. After WWII there was further pressure for the Province to meet rising expectations in relation to qualifications in social and welfare work as well for teaching and nursing. Releasing Sisters to be trained added to the work for other Sisters and was therefore a difficult decision. In 1960 the Province supported 38 Sisters in studies and another 110 on short courses.

St Vincent's Orthopaedic Hospital Pinner In 1947 a nurse training college was opened at St Vincent's. Sisters were among its first graduates, shown above.

St Vincent's Institute for the Deaf and Blind, Tollcross, Scotland 1963

Sisters Esther Cavanagh and Margaret Wigley testing the hearing of a 3-year-old. Sister Cavanagh graduated from Edinburgh University and gained qualifications as a teacher of deaf students and of blind students. In Holland she studied new techniques in deaf education, becoming Headmistress of Tollcross in 1970.

The Braille Book Project, 1964-1966. Sisters of Liverpool Blind Institute at HMP Liverpool

Sister Kathleen Fothergill initiated this scheme to teach prisoners to produce Braille texts for 'A' level students at the Institute, visiting the prison fortnightly to give lessons. She undertook a study tour in the USA and was awarded the Arthur Pearson Prize for excellence in blind education and welfare.

Appeal to the new generation

By the late 1940s a decline in vocations to both the priesthood and religious life was being recognised across Catholic Europe. It led to the adoption of new approaches to 'vocations work', as the effort to encourage vocations became known.

In Britain the first vocations exhibition was held in 1949 in Blackburn, Lancashire. In 1952 Cardinal Griffin, Archbishop of Westminster, and 6 diocesan bishops backed a large-scale exhibition in Olympia, London. The Daughters had a stall at this and other exhibitions in Manchester, Liverpool and Glasgow.

1953 Olympia Vocations Exhibition – the opening Mass.

Two Daughters can be seen in the bottom left quarter.

Vocations brochure designed for the Province circa 1962. The brochure had sections on formation and on all aspects of the vocation of a Daughter of Charity. It ended with the page shown right and a challenge in verse:

Rise for the day is passing
And you lie dreaming on.
The others have buckled their armour
And forth to the fight have gone,
A place in the ranks awaits you.

of diocesan priests and the consequent importance of missionaries such as the Redemptorists. Scotland's nineteenth-century devotional history comprised both 'continuity *and* a devotional watershed'.[63] Familiar devotions were blended with those freshly brought into Scotland and a significant role is claimed for the 'Irish, French and English nuns' who 'inculcated their devotions in the classroom, sick room, boarding and Sunday school' in a process of devotional blending. The popularity of the Miraculous Medal is cited as an example of this blending.[64]

Aspinwall's claim highlights significant gaps in British devotional history in relation to the Blessed Virgin and regarding the work and influence of Catholic sisters in devotional life. It seems self-evident that women religious would have played some part but, again, there is little written on the subject.[65] Religious sisters fully supported and reinforced church-based devotions; this much is clear from biographies of nuns and from congregational histories. Yet, just as this was not the sum total of their devotional activity, so also the parish was not the sole source of an individual Catholic's devotional practice. A focus on the devotional work of Catholic sisters directs attention to piety as it was practised outside of church; in the home, in schools, Catholic institutions and on the streets.

There is much to be gained for the history of devotional life in Britain from exploring the influence of Catholic sisters.[66] It was they who directed many local branches of confraternities and sodalities to deepen personal piety; they provided suitable spaces and increased opportunities for collective devotional practices in their schools, chapels and convents; sisters made or provided many of the materials that supported and enhanced devotional events (banners, altar dressings, sashes and cloaks, the adornment of statues as well as medals and holy cards); they attended to the dying and laid out the dead. In some places, their own chapels, usually well endowed with statues and pictures connected to specific devotions, were where people attended Mass until a parish church was built.[67] In schools and in night-classes they talked and taught about Mary as model, as

63 Aspinwall, 'Catholic Devotions in Scotland,' p.31.

64 Ibid.,p.33.

65 For an attempt to outline the possibilities, see Susan O'Brien, 'Making Catholic Spaces: Women, Décor and Devotion in the English Catholic Church, 1840-1900', in Diana Wood ed., *The Church and the Arts*, Studies in Church History, Ecclesiastical History Society, 28 (London, Blackwell, 1992), pp. 449-464; 'French Nuns in Nineteenth Century England', *Past and Present* 154 (February 1997), pp. 142-180; Susan O'Brien, 'Religious Sisters and Revival in the English Catholic Church', in Emily Clark and Mary Laven eds., *Women and Religion in the Atlantic Age, 1550-1900* (Farnham, Surrey, Ashgate, 2013), pp.165-193.

66 Heimann, *Catholic Devotions*, p.138. Heimann's later essay 'Catholic revivalism in worship and devotion' makes clearer the importance of a wide range of Marian devotions and about the significance of 'the feminine' in devotional life than *Catholic Devotions*, pp. 71 and 82. See also Turnham, *Catholic Faith and Practice*, p.9 and Nancy Jiwon Cho, 'Martyrs of England! Standing on High!: Roman Catholic Women's Hymn-writing for the Re-invigoration of the Faith in England', in Laurence Lux-Sterrit and Carmen M. Mangion eds., *Gender, Catholicism and Spirituality: Women and the Roman Catholic Church in Britain and Europe, 1200-1900* (Basingstoke, Palgrave Macmillan, 2011), pp. 131-48.

67 For example, the Daughters' chapel at the Central House served as parish church until the church of the Sacred Heart and Mary Immaculate was opened in Mill Hill in 1923. Similarly the industrial school chapel at Walkley in Sheffield was used by the local people for many years.

path to Jesus and as the compassionate maternal one who 'prays for us' to God the Father. As Catholic schooling developed and the number of convents grew (more than 500 in Britain by 1891),[68] so did the influence of Catholic sisters active in parish and school life. Because many of these religious communities were French and continued to form their British members in France, devotional practices that originated in Francophone Europe became part of a diversifying British devotional landscape.[69] The Daughters' history of devotional transmission and transnational exchange belongs in this tradition.

The Daughters and Marian devotion in Britain, 1860–1914

The definition of the dogma of the Immaculate Conception (1854) gave new status to an already traditional belief about Mary and was easily absorbed into Catholic teaching and texts in Britain.[70] By 1880, thirty-eight new churches in England and six in Scotland had been dedicated to the Immaculate Conception or to Mary Immaculate, with more to follow.[71] One of the effects of the definition was to give a new impetus in Britain to devotional practices focused on Mary's Immaculate Conception and on the virtues of chastity and purity. Sodalities and confraternities for children and adults dedicated to Mary Immaculate were the most significant of these practices because of their formative influence on young Catholics.[72] They helped to shape the piety of many individual observant Catholics in the period between 1850 and 1940 and their members provided the backbone of parish-based Marian devotions. Peter Doyle counted 47 branches of the Children of Mary linked to various religious communities in the diocese of Liverpool in 1886, making it the most widespread sodality after the Living Rosary Society. Between them, these two Marian devotional groups far outstripped all others in membership.[73] Evidence from the diocese of Middlesbrough and from many parish histories suggests that this pattern was repeated elsewhere in England and Scotland.[74]

---

68 Nye, *A Peculiar Kind of Mission*, p .17.

69 O'Brien, 'French Nuns in Nineteenth Century England', pp. 142-180.

70 Heimann, *Catholic Devotion*, p .112.

71 *Catholic Directory* and information confirmed by website search.

72 Colm Lennon and Robin Kavanagh, 'The flowering of the confraternities and sodalities in Ireland, c1860-c1960', in Lennon ed., *Confraternities and Sodalities in Ireland*, distinguish between sodalities and confraternities: the former being more likely to be private and the latter public with a more formal code and uniform, although the lines could be blurred, p. 78.

73 Peter Doyle, *Missions and Mitres, Mitres and Missions in Lancashire: The Roman Catholic Diocese of Liverpool 1850-2000* (Liverpool, The Bluecoat Press, 2005), p.125.

74 Although she gives no figures, Margaret Turnham states that the Children of Mary was 'one of the most popular sodalities for children between the ages of eight and fourteen' in the Middlesbrough diocese by the 1880s. *Catholic Faith and Practice in England*, p. 88.

The Children of Mary Immaculate

The Daughters of Charity made a distinctive contribution to the growth of confraternities and sodalities in Britain through their Association of the Children of Mary of the Immaculate Conception. Like many such sodalities, its main aim at this time was personal salvation, in the words of the manual 'to lead its members to love God above all things...thus securing their own salvation'. The means to achieve this came 'through honouring the beautiful privilege of [Mary's] Immaculate Conception', who was the 'ark ordained by God for this epoch'.[75] More unusually, the Association's earliest members were young people from the working classes, many of them in the Daughters' orphanages or workrooms.[76]

The structures and rubrics of the Children of Mary Immaculate were modelled on the consecrated life and they played a part in creating a sacred and solemn organisational environment for members. New members went through a period of Aspirancy. If accepted, they were vested with the Miraculous Medal with the words 'Receive, my child, this Ribbon and Medal as the livery of Immaculate Mary, and the marks of your consecration to this tender Mother'.[77] Associates met weekly on a Sunday under the guidance of a Directress. Meetings opened with the *Veni Sancte*, followed by a reading 'always preferring those which treat of the devotion to the Blessed Virgin, her virtues, her life, its mysteries'. Each member was invited by the Directress to speak about how he or she had spent the week, to which 'they should reply simply and humbly'. Meetings closed with a canticle in honour of the Virgin, a Marian anthem, prayers and verses. Each month there was a Mass and a more elaborate 'solemn' meeting which included the Act of Consecration to Mary Immaculate.[78] Between meetings, Associates were expected to live up to 'the duties of a Child of Mary'. These included prayers at rising and retiring, daily attendance at Mass, examination of conscience and a daily 'visit to the Blessed Virgin' to say the rosary or another Marian prayer. Indulgences were available for many of the above practices, properly undertaken. Guidelines were given about leisure and recreation, how long for sleep, and what to read. Members' daily work was spoken of as ennobling and emphasis was laid on the many opportunities to exercise the virtues of charity and mercy at work.[79] Children of Mary were public witnesses on behalf of their parish, taking a leading part in parish, diocesan or town-wide processions, most usually during May, when the female members, dressed in blue cloaks, gloves and white veils, walked beside a banner dedicated to Mary Immaculate. Membership created spiritual kinship between associates but

---

75 *Manual of the Children of Mary for the use of the orphan asylums and the schools of the Daughters of Charity* translated from the French (Dublin, James Duffy, *c.* 1890), p.13.

76 *Manual of the Children of Mary,* frontispiece.

77 ibid., p. 99.

78 ibid., pp. 46-48.

79 ibid., p. 206.

there was social bonding too, through the annual outings to the seaside or parks, and other social activities. It is hardly surprising that it proved to be a pathway into the Company for a significant number of the women.

By 1900, the Province had branches in Darlington, Dover, Dumfries, Dunfermline, Hereford, Hull, Lanark, Liverpool, Clerkenwell, Marylebone and Westminster in London, Plymouth, Salisbury, Sheffield, Torquay, and York. There are few records providing numbers of members, but in Sheffield in 1877 between 42 and 50 attended weekly.[80] New branches of the Children of Mary were established in Birmingham, Edinburgh, Middlesbrough and Peterborough between 1900 and 1914 and by the First World War branches were to be found in the widely different settings of the Catholic Blind Institute in Liverpool, St Joseph's industrial school in Sheffield, the boarding school in Herefordshire and Smyllum orphanage in Lanark, as well as one for the factory workers of Dundee.

Priests and people came to expect that Sisters in their parish would establish the Children of Mary. Sodality work was not discussed by the provincial council as a major dimension of its work nor was it given the resources that went into other activities, but wherever they had opportunity to develop the Association particular Sisters did so. In this period it seems that its spread was dependent on the enthusiasm and gifts of individual Sisters rather than on a provincial strategy, although the work was never lost sight of or neglected. It was understood that an Association directress's influence on the devotional sensibility of individuals could be powerful. Vera Harfitt, born in Salisbury in 1907, treasured all her life a booklet and note from the Daughter of Charity who was her Association directress. Addressed 'To my very dear daughter on the day of her Reception as a Child of Mary', the note expressed the Sister's hope that she would 'be faithful to your promises of today' and that 'Our Blessed Lady will love you as her special child'.[81] In her nineties, Vera Harfitt recalled that her 'most vivid memories' of being a young Catholic were about her time as a Child of Mary.[82]

The Miraculous Medal

Associates of the Children of Mary Immaculate were among those in Britain who learned directly about the apparitions at the rue du Bac from Sisters who knew the story and the chapel well, but there was very little literature available in English about the events of 1830. To coincide with the fiftieth anniversary of the apparitions in 1880 author Lady Georgiana Fullerton, friend and benefactor to the Sisters, translated and abbreviated the full history of the Medal from the 1877 French

---

80 St Vincent's Schools Sheffield, 1877, Box X DC Paris.

81 June Rockett, *Held in Trust: Catholic Parishes in England and Wales 1900-1950* (London: The Saint Austin Press, 2001), p. 29. I have deduced that the sister was a Daughter of Charity from other internal evidence quoted from Rockett's interview with Vera Harfitt and from the fact that the Daughters had been in Salisbury since 1868.

82 See Mary Eaton, 'What Became of the Children of Mary?' in Hornsby-Smith ed., *Catholics in England 1950-2000*, pp. 219-241.

original.[83] This fully illustrated text gave prominence to Catherine Labouré's life, told the story of the apparitions, detailed the early graces granted through the Medal, and provided a history of the establishment of the Association. In a new conclusion written for this edition, Fullerton listed more recent Marian apparitions; at Marpingen in Prussia (1876), Gietrzwald in Poland (1877), and Knock in County Mayo Ireland (1879).[84] In commending a second edition of the book in 1894, *The Tablet's* reviewer remarked that Pope Leo's recent permission for the Feast of the Miraculous Medal would 'give a fresh impulse to [its] already widespread use'.[85] This edition sold well enough for Burns and Oates to follow it with a third in 1895, giving some indication that the Feast, the indulgences and the Little Office had a following in Britain and Ireland by this date. In fact, the book's publishing history is one of the few firm pieces of external evidence of reception of the Paris apparitions and the Miraculous Medal in Britain during the nineteenth century.[86]

The Daughters themselves took the opportunity provided by the golden jubilee of the apparitions on 27 November 1880 to disseminate the devotion in their foundations. The Sisters of St Vincent's Carlisle Place in Westminster, a very deprived area at that time, 'decorated our chapel as much as our poverty would allow us' and reported that:

> The invocation 'O Mary conceived without sin', in large gold letters, made a halo whose effect was charming, especially when the gas was on. Placed in front of the front door, this statue attracted attention and hearts at once; Our Lord was exposed on the altar, and the whole day was spent in adoration before Him.

The chapel was visited by 'a large number of people from outside...for Mass' and for the service of Benediction that ended the day. There was singing, silent prayer, and a great sense of devotion. The Sisters felt the occasion had 'essentially revived devotion to the Blessed Virgin in raising awareness of the precious Miraculous Medal'.[87] In Lanark, there was a 'grand celebration' in St Mary's parish supported by its Vincentian priests, and likewise at their parish of St Vincent's Sheffield, where 'the altar of the Holy Virgin was decorated tastefully and the whole church decorated like at the biggest feasts':

---

83 Lady Georgiana Fullerton, *The Miraculous Medal: The Life and Visions of Catherine Labouré, Sister of Charity* (London, Burns & Oates, 1880).

84 Fullerton, *Miraculous Medal*, p.227.

85 *The Tablet*, 24 November 1894, p.11.

86 Another of the community's benefactors, Lady Herbert of Lea, translated the life of visionary Apolline Andriveau (of the Red Scapular) for publication in 1897: *Sister Apolline Andriveau and the Scapular of the Passion* trans from the French by Lady Herbert (London and New York, Art and Book Company, 1897).

87 *Annales de la Congrégation de la Mission*, Vol 46: 1881,p. 257. http://via.library.depaul.edu/annales/ (accessed 23 February 2016) and Kerr, *Sister Chatelain*, p. 96 2-1-9 DCMH.

> There was not an empty seat in church when it came the solemn day...
> there were at least a thousand communions over the different masses.
> Benediction of the Most Blessed Sacrament crowned this beautiful feast
> day which was a real triumph for Mother Immaculate.[88]

Care was always taken by the Sisters to link the Miraculous Medal to the Eucharist
and the Blessed Sacrament through Mary Immaculate. At Walkley in Sheffield,
where St Joseph's industrial school chapel served as a Mass centre, the Sisters
'were amazed at the influx of people who came, from the early morning until
evening, to enjoy the indulgence and to satisfy their piety'. The priest distributed
Miraculous Medals and at the end of the day 'not one remained in the house'.[89]
Sisters in London found that after the celebrations they could hardly keep up
with the requests because Westminster diocesan priests were now telling their
parishioners about the Medal.[90]

All these Medals came from the mother house and, indeed, this continued to
be the case in the twentieth century and to the present day. Once the Province
was established in 1885, it became easier and more efficient to organise the flow
of packages from Paris. Medals arrived with a wide range of other supplies that
Sisters in Britain were required to obtain from the mother house: herbs and
medicines; material for habits; statues; and holy picture cards. In March 1888, for
example, the Sisters at Mill Hill received two gross (288) of ordinary Medals, and
dozens of silver ones; about the same number were sent each month during that
single year and the next, the only ones for which a record has survived.[91] Sisters
returning from the Paris seminary or from retreats would arrive home loaded with
rosaries, Miraculous Medals and blue ribbon for the Children of Mary, as well as
the artificial flowers bought from the Maison Jeanne d'Arc.[92] And although people
could obtain the Medals through other channels, those supplied from the rue du
Bac bestowed the special privilege of having been blessed in the chapel and placed
on the very chair where the Blessed Virgin had sat.[93]

There is no evidence of Medals being made in Britain at this time. Most of those
owned in Britain by working-class men and women in the nineteenth century are
likely to have been distributed by Sisters as part of their pastoral practice, whether
that was in family homes, hospitals and prisons, in their own children's homes or
within the parish schools where they taught. The Sisters' use of the Medal suggests
that giving it to someone could be an expression of maternal care in which, as a

---

88 *Annales de la Congregation* Vol. 46, p. 259.

89 ibid. p. 260.

90 ibid. p. 258.

91 The Central House Mill Hill Accounts 11-100 #10 DCMH.

92 O'Driscoll, 'Sidelights', p. 5: 'no sister returned from her retreat [in Paris] without some exquisite artificial flowers'. 13-4-3 DCMH.

93 This was the normal practice. Helen Chadwick, *Remarks on Deceased Sisters* (1962), p. 21.10-3-1 DCMH.

spiritual mother, she entrusted the recipient to the Blessed Mother for protection and blessing.[94] Mary Burns, Sister Servant at St Vincent's boys' home at Mill Hill (1849–1913), 'made sure every child in the orphanage' wore a Miraculous Medal. She 'attributed to this many escapes from accidents'.[95] Louisa Blundell (1859–1929), who 'had a great devotion to the Miraculous Medal', on one occasion gave one to a five-year-old girl, Chuckey, whose mother 'was much addicted to drink and had left the child to run wild', only to watch her 'tear it off' amidst a 'volley of foul language'. Later, she had the satisfaction of seeing Chuckey 'quite reformed [in] her morals and her language'.[96] Helen Chadwick, whose decision to enter the Company in 1880 had been encouraged by being shown a picture of Our Lady of the Miraculous Medal', later became Sister Servant of the girls' orphanage at Tudhoe where she established the Children of Mary and worked assiduously to spread devotion to the Miraculous Medal throughout County Durham.[97] Margaret Brohan (1880–1949), who after being a visiting Sister in London for many years was missioned to Australia where she continued to supply people with a wide range of material support, 'a spiritual word to console them...and, of course, a Miraculous Medal'.[98] Of Catherine O'Driscoll (1864–1958), who occupied several offices in turn at the Mill Hill seminary and in the Central House, it was said that 'she never lost an opportunity of distributing our dear Medal',[99] including the occasion when she returned a lost umbrella to its owner and put medals inside it.[100] A far more serious occasion arose in 1914 when troops billeted in the school of the Immaculate Conception at the Central House asked for 'rosaries and medals' before departing for the Front. Both were 'freely distributed by the Sisters' as the best expression of care and pastoral support they could offer the young men being sent to the slaughter fields.[101]

Despite these indications that the Miraculous Medal was disseminated and well received, the historian searching for evidence that it was known and used in Britain before 1914 is, however, likely to be disappointed. John Henry Newman is a rare example of an individual known to have worn the Medal, cited by Marina Warner to show that it was not simply the 'unlettered' who had a devotion to it.[102]

---

94 Seland, 'Visual rhetoric', p.90. Seland's insight that medals were experienced as carrying a blessing and that the blessing was specified by its motifs (protection and grace freely given in the case of the Miraculous Medal) resonates with the fact that people asked for a Miraculous Medal when they were under pressure or in distress.

95 *Remarks on Deceased Sisters* Mary Burns (1914), p. 91. 10-3-1 DCMH.

96 *Sister Louisa Blundell*, p. 21. 2-1-12 DCMH.

97 *Remarks on Deceased Sisters* Helen Chadwick(1962) p. 21. 10-3-1 DCMH.

98 *Remarks on Deceased Sisters* Margaret Brohan (1949), p. 4. 10-3-1 DCMH.

99 *Remarks on Deceased Sisters* Catherine O'Driscol (1958), p. 28. 10-3-1 DCMH.

100 O'Driscoll, 'Sidelights', p.70. 13-4-3 DCMH.

101 Ibid., p.36.

102 Warner, *Stranger Magic* ,p. 232.

Peter Doyle described it as 'extremely popular' in the Liverpool diocese[103] and Bernard Aspinwall, as we have seen, mentioned the Medal as one of the devotions that 'infiltrated' Scotland through the activities of the Sisters.[104] But even these references may be a projection backwards of impressions from the inter-war period when the Medal's presence is more visible.[105] What might its absence from sources mean? Without overstating the case, it seems likely that it 'was hidden in plain sight' precisely because its field of action was *outside* churches and chapels: it was to be found in the home, on the body, in bags and pockets, tucked into prayer books and letters (and even lost umbrellas). Like many other material and embodied devotional practices, the use of the Medal largely fell outside of church-based events. Like other devotional objects that became familiar through prayer and touch, the Medal activated meaning and brought its owner into close relationship with the divine in ordinary and everyday places.[106]

The rubric in Pope Pius X's brief of 1905 establishing the Association of the Miraculous Medal was designed to 'reorder' its use by bringing it under the control of the Vincentians: anyone who wished 'to share in this rich treasury of Indulgences' attached to the Medal had to 'be invested in the MEDAL by a priest having the faculties to do so and wear the medal on the breast suspended from the neck'.[107] But the fact that such a rubric was judged necessary is an acknowledgement that Medals (the millions that had been distributed or bought) were used by individuals in ways that were not controlled in this way: placed in children's clothing for protection, hidden close to someone whose conversion was prayed for, buried in gardens and fields to aid or prevent purchases.[108] In these acts of faith we can see how people wove their living relationship with Jesus and his Blessed Mother into their daily activities.[109] They are also just the kind of religious behaviour likely to make some bishops cautious in an environment such as that in Britain, where such activities could be 'misunderstood'.

The last years of the nineteenth century and the early twentieth were a transitional time when Marian devotional practice in Britain was becoming more overt and visible yet was still not fully out in the open. In 1889, the Guild of Our Lady of Ransom under the patronage of the hierarchy was established to pray for the conversion of England, and in 1893 Pope Leo XIII requested Cardinal Vaughan to reconsecrate England and Wales to the Blessed Virgin. Just as new churches

---

103 Doyle, *Mitres and Missions*, p. 130.

104 Aspinwall, 'Catholic Devotion in Victorian Scotland', p. 33.

105 A search through more than 30 diocesan and parish histories yielded no concrete evidence.

106 See Orsi, *Between Heaven and Earth*, p. 164, and Morgan, 'Materiality of Cultural Construction', p. 228.

107 http://www.stcathek.org/Our_lady_of_the_miraculous_medal.htm (accessed 14 March 2016).

108 These are all widely attested uses made of the Medal and have been consistent since the 1830s. In 1922, the Sister officers at the Central House 'threw' Miraculous Medals into the fields adjacent to their property when they came up for sale . O'Driscoll, 'Sidelights', p. 62. 13-4-3 DCMH.

109 Orsi, *The Madonna of 115th Street*, pp. xiii-xiv.

were dedicated to Welsh, Scottish, Anglo-Saxon and Celtic saints to express local identities and a significant number were named for Mary Immaculate, a small but increasing number were dedicated to Our Lady of Lourdes, publicly aligning a parish to a French and transnational Catholic identity.[110] There was even one church with its own shrine dedicated to Our Lady of Salette in Bermondsey, south-east London as early as 1861. Catholics in Britain, England as well as Scotland, seemed at ease in holding together familiar devotions with an array of new devotions, often Marian and most usually from France.[111]

The Daughters' devotional practice was part of this diversification. St Vincent's Central House, for example, was well endowed with Marian iconography from the outset. The statue of Our Lady of Lourdes donated by Sister Anne Farrell in 1885 was joined in the same year by a statue of the Virgo Potens, a gift of the Superiors General. A replica of the statue of Mary Immaculate in the rue du Bac chapel followed in 1891. But Sisters also supported a wide range of Marian devotional life beyond their own, including the annual Madonna *festas* instituted by Britain's two largest Italian communities, one in Ancoats in Manchester and the other around St Peter's 'Italian Church' in Clerkenwell, London run by the Pallottine Fathers. Daughters ministering in these two parishes at the request of their priests became actively involved in the Marian *festas*. The *festa Madonna del Carmine* in Clerkenwell was born in 1883, the year the Daughters arrived. The *Madonna del Rosario festa* in Manchester was part of the Whit Walks by 1890 and on each occasion the large procession assembled and started out from the Daughters' house in St Vincent's Street.[112]

Although there is still much to be learned about the devotional activities of Catholic sisters, the influence of the Daughters of Charity in the nineteenth century is instructive. It was typical in being French in origin and Marian in orientation yet unique in its association with the Paris apparitions and the Miraculous Medal. Typical too was the fact that the Sisters' Marian mission was integral to their educational and pastoral ministries. More distinctive, however, was the freedom Daughters had to take their portable devotional emblem into homes, prisons and hospitals as they went about their work.[113] From the perspective of the Province's history, given its primary focus on establishing and expanding its work in this period and the wider anti-Marian cultural context, it is perhaps not surprising that there was nothing large-scale or dramatic about their devotional mission in

---

110 Acton (1877), Harrow (1882) [a co-dedication with St Vincent de Paul], Liverpool (1884) and Uxbridge (1891).

111 Alana Harris calls this an 'integrating strategy'. See her 'Astonishing scenes at the Scottish Lourdes: masculinity, the miraculous and sectarian strife at Carfin, 1922-1945', *The Innes Review*, 66.1 (2015), p. 107.

112 http://www.ancoatslittleitaly.com/author.html (accessed 23 June 2014). See also Terri Copli, 'The Scottish Italian Community: *senza in campanile?*', *The Innes Review*, Vol. XLIV, no. 2 (autumn, 1993), pp. 153-167 which has a photograph of the Manchester procession in 1905.

113 See. Supple-Green, *The Catholic Revival in Yorkshire, 1850-1900* (Leeds, Leeds Philosophical and Literary Society Ltd, 1990), p. 68.

the period before the First World War, but it was nonetheless real and constant and it constituted a field of independent devotional action.

Devotional life 1920–1960: Mary, Louise and Catherine

> We must not forget that we are the messengers of Mary, her chosen ones...Since the year 1830, our special mission has been to spread the Medal, to teach all the faithful the special road to the blessed Chapel, to the Altar where they will receive many graces, and to take charge of the Association of the Children of Mary. We must not keep our treasure to ourselves alone, we must spread the Medal far and wide.[114]
>
> (Marie Inchelin, Superioress General 1925)

In her annual circular letter of 1 January 1925, Superioress General Marie Inchelin, (1922–1928), urged Daughters throughout the world to renew their special Marian mission. Her lengthy exposition expressed the high Mariology of the Company's spirituality at this time, quoting St Augustine's conceptualisation of the Blessed Virgin as 'the Mould of God': in Mary alone 'a Man-God was formed' and so in Mary alone can man be formed in God. As inheritors of the Blessed Mother's message to Sister Catherine Labouré, their particular responsibility was to 'throw into this divine mould...the souls of the numerous children' confided to their care.[115] During the 1920s, this message was repeatedly reinforced in Inchelin's letters and conferences and through the printed conferences given by Superior General François Verdier (1918–1933), all of which were sent to each house and read aloud at the Sisters' Friday conferences, or at meals, and reprinted in the Company's new monthly newsletter, *The Echo of the Mother House,* founded in 1926.[116]

This Marian renewal message was of critical importance to the Company itself as it sought to re-establish its own identity in the wake of the French anti-clerical legislation of 1904–1905, the catastrophic First World War, and the social and economic dislocation of the post-war years. These were very challenging times. In France, the Company and the Congregation experienced a reduced number of new members which, in a call to renewal, Verdier attributed to a reduction in their direct work with the poor.[117] The Company's decision to focus on Louise de Marillac, whose public reputation had been overshadowed by Vincent de Paul for so long,

---

114 Marie Inchelin, General Superioress of the Daughters of Charity, Circular Letter to all the Sisters, 1 January 1925. 6-44-21 1-1 DCMH.

115 Ibid. pp.1-2.

116 A comparison of Verdier's conferences and those of a predecessor, Antoine Fiat (1878-1914), shows that the latter contained close readings of scripture and a strong sense of the history of the Company, both being used to ensure universal discipline. Those of Verdier by contrast were almost exclusively Marian in focus. He took the Magnificat and used it, line by line, as the basis of his circulars over many years. General Superiors Circulars 4-23-4 and 4-26-4 DCMH. *The Echo of the Mother House* began in 1926 and was translated from the French by the American Daughters of Charity. 1-5 DCMH.

117 *Genesis of the Company 1633-1968*, p.125. 1-7-2 DCMH.

and to point out the link between its female founder and its Marian mission, proved to be essential to the process of restating and updating the Company's identity in the spirit of the nineteenth century 'feminisation' of Catholicism, as Brejon de Lavergnée has argued.[118] The cause for her canonisation, begun in the 1880s, was pursued steadfastly after 1900.[119] The 'recovery' of Louise, whose letters and writings were gradually collected and ordered, gave the Company a more publicised heroic female Catholic past which it increasingly connected to the apparitions and to Catherine Labouré.[120] The causes of both women linked the foundational work of the Company's service to the poor with its more recent Marian devotional mission, and to divine intervention: Louise and Catherine, servants of the poor, and women directly touched by God.

Between 1900 and 1934, a great deal of Company effort and many prayers went into the canonisation processes for Louise de Marillac and Catherine Labouré. The two proceeded simultaneously in some years and at other times one made more progress than the other, but Louise's cause was the superiors' first priority. Even with the cause in progress, the details of her life were very little known or publicised. One of the reasons she and the Company remained obscured from historical view, even after her beatification and canonisation, was because of the superiors' 'overdeveloped sense of discretion about the origins of cofounder St. Louise' as the illegitimate daughter of nobleman Louis de Marillac.[121] Because of their caution there was little sense of the 'real' Louise in the pious hagiographies produced in the period before 1950. 'Only in 1958 was it publicly acknowledged that she was illegitimate' (and then only because a biography of her had been written outside the community), and it was not until after 1970 that her personality began to be explored in the Company's own research efforts.[122] Inside and outside the community it was so often Catherine Labouré, not Louise de Marillac, who attracted the more committed following.

Still, the earlier efforts for her cause were the start of this long process of recovery. Louise de Marillac was beatified in 1920 (20 May) and on the same day this honour was granted also to the four Daughters of Charity martyred at Arras during the French Revolution. Since this was the week chosen by Pope Benedict XV for the canonisation of Joan of Arc (16 May), the way these honours were brought together reflects the desire of the French Church and the Holy See to re-Catholicise

---

118 Matthieu Brejon de Lavergnée, 'Du mythe des origines. Les Filles de la Charité et leurs fondateurs, XVIIᵉ-XXᵉ siècle', in Brejon de Lavergnée ed., *Quatre siècles de cornettes*, pp. 27-35.

119 See the account of the process given by McNeill, 'Spes-Unica Path to Glory', pp. 113-26.

120 The remarkable process by which the letters were gathered is told by Carmen Urrizburu DC http://famvin.org/wiki/Letters_of_Louise_de_Marillac_to_the_Daughters_of_Charity_(I) (accessed 29 January 2016)

121 Colin Jones, review of Mattheiu de Brejon Lavergnée, *Les Filles de la Charité, The Catholic Historical Review*, Vol.98, no. 4 (October, 2012), pp.816-7. The significance of 1958 was the publication of a life of St Louise which revealed this fact, something that only the most senior Daughters knew.

122 ibid.

the French nation through holy women and the Blessed Virgin, to whom they were so close.[123] It was Pope Benedict who wrote of Louise de Marillac that 'Honour due to the Daughter mounts also to the Mother'.[124] This was not the first time such an approach had been taken: Pope Pius X's declaration in 1907 of a feast day for the whole Church to honour the appearance of the Blessed Virgin at Lourdes was one response to the legislation separating Church and State, and his description of Louise de Marillac as 'the valiant woman of France' when declaring her Venerable in 1911 was another.[125] In the Company itself, the beatifications of 1920 acted as a spur for more prayers and devotional activism to press for the canonisations of Louise and Catherine, conferred in 1934 and 1947 respectively.

Sisters in Britain and Ireland were drawn fully into the fervour that surrounded these events. A more vigorous devotional mission was given impetus by Louise Hannezo's appointment in 1919. As we have seen, visitatrice Hannezo was both energetic and committed to renewal. A stronger devotional focus on the part of the Sisters at this time corresponded to an extension of the public devotional life of an increasingly confident Catholic community in Britain. Manifested most clearly in the increased circulation of devotional magazines, the building of parish shrines, membership of sodalities and participation in retreats and pilgrimages, the material aspects of devotional life in Britain underwent serious development between the wars.[126] Across Britain, parishes, schools and Catholic institutions everywhere built replica Lourdes grottoes in their grounds and erected statues representing the many aspects and apparitions of Mary. Such borrowing coexisted with campaigns to restore or create national Marian shrines and with popular participation in large-scale pilgrimages. Mass pilgrimages, attracting upwards of 15,000 pilgrims, had started in the 1890s with the historic holy sites of Holy Isle, Iona and Canterbury, but these had been connected to Catholic history on the island rather than to the miraculous or the Marian.[127] The medieval devotion to Our Lady of Willesden, the Black Madonna, had been revived at the Catholic mission in Willesden where a new statue was dedicated by Cardinal Vaughan in 1892, and the first post-Reformation pilgrimage took place in 1897 to a recently

---

123 See   http://vhrn-depaul.ning.com/profiles/blogs/vincentiana-purchase-of-the-week-beatification-of-louise-de-marillac for photographs of the medals struck for these beatifications. (accessed 16 February 2016).

124 *The Echo of the Mother House,* May 1954, p. 114. 1-5 DCMH.

125 McNeill, 'Spes-Unica Path to Glory'.

126 Works for this period in other English-speaking contexts include James M. O'Toole ed., *Habits of Devotion. Catholic Religious Practice in Twentieth-Century America* [Cushwa Center Studies of Catholicism in Twentieth-Century America] (Ithaca, New York, Cornell University Press, 2004); Colm Lennon ed., *Confraternities and Sodalities in Ireland: Charity, Devotion and Sociability* (Dublin, The Columba Press, 2012).

127 Katherine Haldane Grenier, '"Public Acts of Faith and Devotion": pilgrimages in late nineteenth-century England and Scotland', in Alisa Clapp-Itnyre and Julie Melnyk eds., *'Perplext in Faith': Essays on Victorian Beliefs and Doubts* (Newcastle:Cambridge Scholars Press, 2015), pp.149-67, and Anne C. Parkinson, *A History of Catholicism in the Furness Peninsula 1127-1997* (Centre for North-West Regional Studies, University of Lancaster, 1998), pp.82-4. For an early example of the restoration of a medieval Marian site, see Jean Treacy's account of the revival of devotion to Our Lady of the Dales in 1889, *'Poor but willing Folk': a brief history of the Catholic Church in Ilkeston 1858-1990* (Ilkeston: Our Lady and St Thomas of Hereford Parish, 1990), p. 9.

restored shrine site at Walsingham in Norfolk, but at this time modestly attended with a symbolic pilgrim group of about 50 people.

What was different about the pilgrimages after the large-scale massacres of the First World War and the Bolshevik revolution in Russia was their focus on Mary and on Marian apparitions, whether medieval and pre-Reformation or nineteenth century and modern (including the apparition at Fátima in 1917), and their scale. At Willesden, a new Romanesque church was opened as a national shrine in 1931. In 1934, church authorities obtained papal permission to dedicate the Slipper Chapel at Walsingham as the Catholic National Shrine to Our Lady, opening up an entirely new phase in the shrine's history as a popular place of pilgrimage for Catholics. The shrine to Our Lady at Penrhys in Wales was restored at this time and the first modern pilgrimage took place in 1936.[128] In Ireland, where the first mass pilgrimage in 50 years made its way to Knock in 1929, a new movement developed in the 1930s to rescue the shrine from neglect.[129] Yet the first large-scale Marian pilgrim site in Britain, preceding these latter restorations, had been an entirely fresh creation that had reproduced a full-size re-creation of the grotto at Lourdes in the Scottish countryside. The remarkable new shrine site built by unemployed working men at Carfin in Lanarkshire in the early 1920s began with a full-scale replica of Lourdes. The site progressively incorporated shrines to many other saints, becoming a site of mass pilgrimages: more than 50,000 pilgrims on one day alone in June 1926. In a rare scholarly incursion into the history of devotional life in Britain in the first half of the twentieth century, Alana Harris has argued persuasively that, at a time of political and economic insecurity between the wars and in a period of acute sectarian tensions in religious life in Scotland, Carfin represented a 'self-confident articulation of Scottish Catholic identity which was, at the same time transnational'.[130] Her approach can be fruitfully applied to that of the Daughters' devotional mission in the inter-war years.[131]

Devotional promotion

> Everywhere, thank God, we notice at present a wonderful devotion to the Miraculous Medal. Priests from all over the country are writing for faculties to bless the medal and enrol people in it. The Novena devotion

---

128 Nigel Yates, 'Walsingham and Interwar Anglo-Catholicism', in Dominic Janes and Gary Waller eds., *Walsingham in Literature and Culture from the Middle Ages to Modernity* (Farnham: Ashgate, 2010), pp. 131-46, and H. M. Gillet, *Walsingham: The History of a Famous Shrine* (London, Burns, Oates and Washbourne, 1950); Madeleine Gray, 'Sacred space and the natural world: the holy well and shrine of Our Lady at Penrhys', *European Review of History*, vol. 8, no. 2 (2011), pp. 243-260.

129 William Allen, 'A nation preferring visions: moving statues, apparitions and vernacular religion in contemporary Ireland' (PhD thesis, University of Cork, 2014), Ch. 2.

130 Harris, 'Astonishing Scenes at the Scottish Lourdes', pp. 104-5.

131 I have been influenced by Harris's insight of a process of re-inscription at work.

has made rapid strides in recent years and the power of the medal is becoming universally recognised.

(Joseph Sheedy CM, Director of the British Province, 1953)[132]

If there was a single action taken by the Province which explained the developments later described by Joseph Sheedy, it was the decision to open an office in Dublin to promote the Company's devotions in the two islands. In 1923, Sister Hannezo asked Sister Mary Cullen to take charge of a new office whose work was to make the Company's devotions better known, first and foremost through publication of a new monthly devotional magazine. Mary Cullen (1866–1940) was a highly capable Sister, the daughter of Hugh Cullen, director of the Liverpool Bank, and his wife, Elizabeth Leonard. As Sister Servant of the foundation in North William Street in Dublin, one of the Company's senior houses in Ireland, she had long experience as directress of a branch of the Children of Mary. The first edition of *Virgo Potens: the Crusade of the Miraculous Medal*, as the magazine was called, was published on 8 December 1923, selling at twopence. Its content was designed to teach Vincentian spirituality as well as Marian devotion and it included stories, poems, songs, prayers and reflections which could be used by readers in their own private devotions, or by groups under guidance.[133] With her January circular to the Sister Servants, Hannezo sent samples of the first edition and informed them it was their duty to support the project because this was 'not a private affair but fulfils the intention of Superiors'.[134] Its circulation was around 15,000 in the 1930s with magazines being sent over to Britain from Dublin either direct to subscribers or for dissemination by Daughters.[135]

The decision to open this office in Dublin was noteworthy on a number of levels. It was the first important work any Irish house had ever carried out explicitly on behalf of the whole Province and, significantly, this took place one year after the establishment of the independent Irish Free State. Moreover, the initiative was led by the Sister who had sustained an injury in the week of the Easter Rising. Marian devotional life was far better developed and more confidently lived in Ireland than in Britain, giving the magazine a stronger base from which to draw its content and a ready-made readership.[136] Finally, visitatrice Hannezo hoped that this initiative would be a recruitment vehicle for postulants. The Irish vocations environment

---

132 Revd. William Sheedy, Director of the British Province, 1938-1961, 1 January 1953, Permissions letter. 8-4. DCMH.

133 I am indebted to the description given by Anne Neylon in her essay 'Historical Marian Devotional Practices among the Daughters of Charity', in Prunty and Sullivan eds., *Daughters of Charity in Ireland*, p. 91.

134 Hannezo, 1 January 1924, circular to Sister Servants. 9-3-1 #20a. DCMH.

135 Staff salaries, Folder Virgo Potens, Box North William Street, Daughters of Charity Archives, Dublin, [DCD]

136 James S. Donnelly, 'The Peak of Marianism in Ireland, 1930-1960', in Stewart J. Brown and David W. Miller eds., *Piety and Power in Ireland 760-1960: Essays in Honour of Emmet Larkin* (Belfast and Notre Dame IND, University of Notre Dame Press, 2000), pp. 252-283 ,and Lennon, ed., *Confraternities and Sodalities in Ireland*.

had become increasingly competitive, particularly from the newer missionary congregations that were being founded in the post-Independence years.[137] *Virgo Potens* magazine promoted the full range of associations and sodalities connected to the Miraculous Medal, and the *Virgo Potens* office also promoted and distributed the Company's Red Scapular of Our Lord and the Sacred Hearts of Jesus and Mary (known as the Scapular of the Passion) and the Green Scapular (known as the Badge of the Immaculate Heart of Mary).[138] The demand had grown enough by 1950 to justify the employment of three paid staff who kept the accounts, conducted the correspondence on behalf of the Province and cut and made scapulars.[139]

Publication and writing was a new form of ministry for Daughters in Britain. *Virgo Potens* proved to be such an effective form of evangelisation and devotional encouragement that other Sisters were allowed to take up their pens. Sister Edith Burd, the author of *Virtue and Christian Refinement*, also wrote *The Spirit of Margaret Sinclair* (1932) to communicate the inspiring life of the young working-class Scottish Carmelite nun who spent the last months of her life in the Daughters' sanatorium at Warley. In 1933, Burd published *Blessed Catherine Labouré*.[140] Sister Muriel Fraser, daughter of Lord and Lady Lovat of Beauly,[141] who spent most of her active life as a Daughter managing and nursing in St Vincent's orthopaedic residential hospital for children in Pinner (1914–1942) before being moved to the sanatorium at Kingussie, published a meditational guide – *Rosary Mysteries and Prayers* – under her religious name 'Sister Joseph Fraser'.[142] Sisters' relatives were also enlisted to write. Sister Fraser's mother, the Catholic author Alice Lovat, wrote the first ever English biography of Louise de Marillac (published 1916) as 'a labour of love', dedicating it to 'the English-speaking members of the Company'. And it was to Etheldreda Howard's niece, the Catholic writer Lady Anne Cecil Kerr, that the Province turned when it wanted a popular short history of Catherine Labouré and the Miraculous Medal for the centenary in 1930. Cecil Kerr's work went into many reprintings and still forms the basis of the Catholic Truth Society pamphlet *The Miraculous Medal* (2015).[143]

---

137 For example, the Missionary Sisters of the Holy Rosary formally established in 1923 and the Missionary Sisters of St Columban formally instituted in 1924.

138 These two devotions were initiated by visions experienced by two French Daughters and approved by Pope Pius IX in 1857 and 1870 respectively.

139 Staff salaries, Folder Virgo Potens, Box North William Street, DCD.

140 Edith Mary Burd, Individual File. 10-2 DCMH.

141 *Scottish Catholic Observer* 14 July 1989, obituary. See also *The Oban Times* 13 July 1989 which describes her farming skills, exercised at St Vincent's Home Kingussie where she retired and where she also 'pursued her hobby of making rosaries' for distribution at her death. Muriel Fraser Personal File. DCMH.

142 Muriel Fraser Personal File. 10-2 DCMH.

143 (Anne) Cecil Kerr had already written the lives of Etheldreda Howard (1928) and went on to write that of Edith Feilding (1933).

Associational life

After 1920, under Hannezo's leadership, the work of supporting the Children of Mary was given greater priority in the Province. Retreats, intended to form an integral part of the sodality's devotional life, had never featured in Britain. This now changed. The first weekend retreat for Children of Mary from the London area was held at the Central House in 1920 under the charge of Sister Lucy Pilley who was given responsibility to develop the programme. It started modestly with 23 retreatants. Their numbers had grown to 174 by 1937, some travelling considerable distances.[144] Members arrived at Mill Hill on Saturday 'coming straight from business' and started the retreat after tea. It closed on Monday morning with 5.00 a.m. Mass and breakfast before work. The hours between were spent in conferences and scripture study led by Daughters and Vincentians. There was Mass and private prayer in the chapel and walks in the grounds. Waited on by the seminary Sisters, the young women 'simply loved that retreat'.[145] At other times of the year, social events, such as a day trip by charabanc to Southend in 1923, were also part of the calendar.[146] Similar, if simpler, retreat programmes were held in other cities in England and Scotland and continued until they were brought to an end by the outbreak of war.

Newer Company associations, founded to diversify and extend the connection between the Sisters and young people, were trialled by some Sisters in Britain. As part of its effort to increase awareness of Louise de Marillac, the Company had established the Marillac Association in 1901. It was aimed at young women who wanted to be involved in pastoral activities rather than in a prayer-based sodality and it occupied a place somewhat akin to the Vincent de Paul Society (which was restricted to men until 1963), with a feminine gendering to its work. The first branch in England was started in 1919 by Dorothy Bowlby, (Sister Apolline). As visiting Sister in the Stonehouse district of Plymouth, which was 'very poor, mostly wives of soldiers and sailors with large families', Bowlby asked permission to establish a Marillac Association so that young women could be formed to work with her. Twelve attended the first meeting, a group made up of girls in their last year at school and young working women.[147] Their volunteering was wide-ranging; as one of them said, 'We Marillacs never knew what we would be asked to do next, but we were ready for anything.[148] Regular ministries included catechesis of the Catholic children of the neighbourhood, helping to run clubs in the parish such as Mothers' Meetings and clubs for children, including drama and music, and the

---

144 O'Driscoll, 'Sidelights', p.76. 13-4-3 DCMH.

145 Ibid., p. 77.

146 Ibid., p. 68.

147 *A Sister of Charity in China during the Wars, 1926-1942* (London, Sisters of Charity, 1946), pp.23-4. 2-1-14 DCMH.

148 Ibid., p. 25.

important visiting work, particularly to the elderly. Their method followed that of the Vincent de Paul Society.

> We each kept a little book in which we entered the number of hours spent in catechism classes, clubs etc., the number of visits to the Poor, and any relief we had given in food or clothing...[149]

Sister Bowlby rented a house in Stonehouse. Its largest room was a club room, open for long hours in the week. But on a Sunday it was transformed into a chapel with the reservation of the Blessed Sacrament so as to reach out to local, mostly unchurched, Catholics. In the words of one of the first Marillacs, 'Sister thought that if [the women] had a little chapel of their own, they would soon return, and before many months, had the joy of seeing this hope realised'.[150] Soon they rented a larger house in which a room was given over as a dedicated chapel with the Sacrament present at all times, and always open for people to drop in. By the time Bowlby left for the missions in China in 1926, there were 32 Marillacs in Plymouth, of whom seven became Daughters of Charity.[151] The first Marillac branch in central London was started in 1926 and others followed, including in the East End, but unfortunately there are no surviving records. It is possible that the Association was overtaken by the attraction of the Legion of Mary, the lay apostolic association founded by Frank Duff in Dublin in 1921 which was Vincentian in its spirituality but gave women an equal role in a mixed Catholic action organisation.[152] Duff had been President of a St Vincent de Paul Society conference in Dublin and had a strong personal Vincentian identity. When he found difficulties in extending the Legion to Britain, Duff made contact with Daughters of Charity in Glasgow and London 1928 and they were instrumental in opening doors to the hierarchy in both Scotland and England, after which the Legion of Mary grew steadily.[153] Clifford Williamson has recently argued that the interweaving of the Legion's Catholic social action and its Marian devotion was well-suited for the Church's challenge to communism in Scotland.[154] The Daughters continued to support the Legion in various ways, seeing it as a work of God rather than a rival to their own activities.

The Company's new association for younger children was the Guild of Our Lady's Crusade. On a visit to Britain in 1924, Superioress General Inchelin had requested that the Guild be established in all the schools managed by the Sisters

---

149 ibid., p. 25.

150 ibid.

151 ibid. p. 27.

152 Finola Kennedy, *Frank Duff: A Life Story* (London, Continuum, 2011), Ch.6.

153 ibid., pp.125-127.

154 Clifford Williamson, *The History of Catholic Intellectual Life in Scotland, 1918-1965* (London, Palgrave Macmillan, 2016), Ch. 6 'Inter-War Marianism and the Legion of Mary', pp.125-143.

(35 at this time).[155] The first British branch opened at the Immaculate Conception school in Mill Hill in 1924 to set an example for the whole Province. Children enrolled were given a medal and a blue ribbon and were gathered together each dinner time (midday) to say the rosary. With its establishment, a ladder of associational life had been created from the early years of elementary school through to adulthood.

Pilgrimage

The 1948 Paris-Lourdes pilgrimage for the Children of Mary centenary with which this chapter began had been preceded in 1930 by the first large-scale pilgrimage to France organised by the Sisters of the Province. The year 1930 was the apparition centenary and it was marked by the opening of the newly extended and decorated chapel at the rue du Bac. At their meeting on 12 January 1930, provincial officers decided to advertise the centennial celebrations in the *Catholic Times*, *The Universe*, *The Standard* and *The Glasgow Observer* and to invite participants for a British pilgrim party. A group of 700 lay people with Sisters and Vincentians left St Pancras by night train for Paris on the 10 August. The organisation had been considerable; 'the arrangements with Cook's [travel agents] and Sister Reeves about the pilgrimage never ceased' was how Catherine O'Driscoll remembered it.[156] She herself arranged for the Sisters to thread 700 Miraculous Medals on blue ribbon to be sent out to participants with the tickets via Cook's because it had been decided that all their pilgrims would wear one.[157] The arrangements were a mammoth undertaking but all efforts were repaid when they saw 'the special train coming from under the tunnel with the words MIRACULOUS MEDAL TRAIN in great letters on the front of it'. As the pilgrims took their places 'they all sang Bl. Catherine's Hymn...and then, as they set off...the Hail Holy Queen'.[158]

This centennial pilgrimage 'inaugurated the new era of large pilgrimages' to the chapel and launched the Company's shrine work which after the war was increasingly internationalised.[159] When Kay Trainer went to Paris in 1948, an important part of her pilgrimage experience was its internationalism. Among the 10,000 present, she met Children of Mary from Germany, Belgium, Italy and Spain. 'Here', she wrote of the rue du Bac, 'as we had experienced at Lourdes...the "one-ness" of our Association prevailed over race ...I was much struck on several occasions with the request to pray for France and the promise of prayers for

155 *Echo from the Motherhouse: Supplement for British Province* April 1926. 1-5 DCMH

156 O'Driscoll, 'Sidelights', p. 89. 13-4-3 DCMH.

157 ibid., p. 89.

158 ibid., p. 90.

159 Jean Daniel Planchot, translated by John Rybolt, 'The Chapel of the Rue du Bac' famvin. website (accessed 10 November 2015). Since 1980, when the chapel was extended once again and re-opened by Pope John Paul II, it has seen a further internationalisation and increase in visitors.

Scotland. Truly it was an International Congress.'[160] It is not difficult to understand why, in the immediate aftermath of the Second World War, this would have been such a powerful experience of healing and hope.

The Daughters' close association with the rue du Bac is likely to explain the requests received by the Province for Sisters to undertake hospitality and spiritual work at the shrines in Carfin in Scotland and Knock in Ireland. In August 1925 the founder of the Carfin shrine, Monsignor Thomas Nimmo Taylor, visited Mill Hill to ask for Sisters on site. The provincial council took up the invitation without hesitation, immediately getting down to practicalities; 'for a start', they agreed, 'we could offer a Sister who could travel from Tollcross by tram (20 minutes) every morning to Carfin after Mass and return at 5 in the evening'.[161] Four years later in 1929, when the council received a request from 'the ecclesiastical authorities in Knock for a foundation for the pilgrims', there was again no hesitation in deciding to accept the management of a pilgrim hostel or hospice (whichever was needed) on site.[162] As part of its commitment, the council decided to give £2,000 to build the hostel. In 1930, when the restored shrine opened, Anne Thomson, fifth visitatrice, attended the opening. Daughters of Charity have served the shrine at Knock ever since.

Devotional events

From the account already given, it is apparent how extensive was the redirection of attention and energy in the community in the inter-war years towards supporting a wide range of devotional activities and relationships. Almost inevitably, the Sisters' own devotional life and their activities were influenced by this new orientation. The Central House was not only the administrative headquarters of the Province and its seminary but increasingly important as a retreat centre for the Sisters. The already powerful Marian imagery of the site was augmented in 1926 when a statue of Our Lady Immaculate was erected over the high altar in the provincial chapel, to which the 'rays' of the apparition were added in 1930. A side shrine to Catherine Labouré was built in 1933 to mark the beatification, featuring a statue of the beatified bought in Paris and gifted by Sister Mary Cullen in Dublin.[163] And in 1935, to mark the founder's canonisation, a large-scale statue of St Louise was erected on the terrace behind the Central House, entirely paid for by donations from Sisters.[164] In a representation of Louise that highlighted her maternal relationship to all the Sisters, she is depicted handing a copy of the Rule to the kneeling figure of a newly habited Sister. The detail of dress, rosary

160 Kay Trainer, 'Sisters of Charity Centenary Pilgrimage', p. 51. Dumfries 11-88 DCMH.

161 Provincial Council Minutes vol. VIII, 28 August 1925, 9-5-0-2-1 DCMH.

162 Provincial Council Minutes vol. IX 13 March 1929, 9-5-0-2-1 DCMH.

163 O'Driscoll, 'Sidelights', p. 106. 13-4-3 DCMH

164 ibid. p. 122.

and other accoutrements are minutely observed and the statue quickly established itself as an iconographic identity statement for the Sisters.

Because the Central House was the location for a number of significant liturgical events in the inter-war years, it welcomed many more visitors than before the 1914–18 war. A good deal of community time was invested in preparations for these events. No fewer than three celebratory Triduums (three-day liturgical events) were organised and held between 1930 and 1934. The apparition centennial between 25 and 27 November 1930 brought 500 Children of Mary, Ladies of Charity and benefactors of the Province to Mill Hill on different days. On entering the chapel, they saw 'the statue of Our Lady surrounded by the invocation "O Mary conceived without sin etc" in brilliants, gauze clouds surround[ing] her'. The final Mass on the Feast of the Miraculous Medal was attended by Cardinal Bourne himself, with Bishop Arthur Doubleday of Brentwood as preacher. The Sisters had invited all the priests with whom they worked in and around London and after Mass gave them a grand dinner, cooked by the Sisters but served by hired waiters from Harrods. At the end of the final Mass, the Sisters presented Cardinal Bourne with a solid gold Miraculous Medal, which he duly received with thanks, an exchange which indicates the devotional distance travelled between 1908 and 1930.[165] A second Triduum was held in 1933 over 26–29 November in honour of the beatification of Catherine Labouré. A relic of the Blessed was available for veneration. The third occasion was to celebrate the canonisation of St Louise and was held 17-19 June 1934, again with a relic of the saint for veneration. Masses and devotional events were organised in Ireland and Scotland throughout the year, a small group of Sisters attended events in Rome and Paris and, in addition, all Sisters could read lavishly detailed reports of the actual events in Rome published in *The Echo of the Mother House.*

It would appear that the inter-war years were ones of confidence and even some public élan for the British Province. There were many celebrations and a good deal of public engagement. But, as we will see in the next chapter, beneath the surface there were real anxieties about money, the selection of ministries and, in the later 1930s and 1940s, about vocations. By contrast with the long nineteenth century when Daughters had joined forces with other Catholics to combat poverty and Protestantism, this was a time when bold and straightforward goals at home proved elusive and some degree of confusion over purpose can be detected beneath the impression given by peak numbers, large buildings, extended liturgies and canonisations. Although it might seem to have been something of a distraction to spend so much community time and energy (and even money) on Marian activities, at a time of unease and readjustment these very enterprises served as a community focus, gave scope for expression outside the new canonical strictures, and carried a sense of optimism for the future. It also placed the Province in harmony with the wider Church and with Pope Pius XII. Through their involvement with Marian and

---

165 ibid. p .91.

Marillac Associations, their promotion of devotion to the Miraculous Medal and their involvement in local and transnational pilgrimages, this chapter has charted how Daughters in Britain reinscribed their identity in the inter-war years so that it had two strong dimensions, one practical and the other devotional; both of which were integral to their pastoral ministries.

9

Mission in empire and beyond

> A Sister of Charity may be for years engaged in hospital
> duty in England, in France, in Germany, or in Italy. On a
> particular morning she may receive an order to start for China,
> the following day. No leave-taking of friends – no packing-up
> of luggage – no elaborate arrangements for this long journey of
> sixteen thousand miles...With her little bundle containing a
> change of clothes, her few books of devotion and her rosary,
> she departs at the appointed hour. (John Murphy, *Terra Incognita* 1873)[1]

Missions at home and overseas had more in common than might first appear to be the case, including dissemination of the Company's devotion to Mary Immaculate and distribution of the Miraculous Medal.[2] John Murphy's 1873 pen portrait is romanticised but nonetheless captures some essential features of the reality for a Sister of Charity called to work on overseas missions; the three day's notice prior to moving, the lack of fuss and the departure from a familiar role in a safe environment for a destination only previously imagined. The same routines for changing *placement* applied also to every domestic change made by a Daughter, but the practices of obedience and detachment were dramatically heightened in the case of a move to the overseas missions. In the eyes of observers like Murphy the sense of difference was intensified by the Sister's association with 'exotic' continents and their peoples. The departing Daughter is depicted as going into exile; 'fearlessly and cheerfully go[ing] forth to pass the remainder of her days in the land of the barbarian'. Like most nineteenth-century missionary literature Murphy emphasised the 'otherness' of the recipients of the gospel message. Where his writing differed from most contemporary texts about either sisters or about missionaries was in its straightforward acknowledgement that the Daughters were missionaries.

---

1 J. N. Murphy, *Terra Incognita*, p. 136.

2 See for example, Jeremy Clarke, *The Virgin Mary and Catholic Identities in Chinese History* (Hong Kong, Hong Kong University Press, 2013), pp.74-78.

The Company's missionary history

Vincent de Paul intended the Daughters to be missionaries. In conference with them in 1655 he counselled that to be 'be good Daughters of Charity' they should be willing to go 'wherever God may wish to send you', whether 'into Africa, to the army, to the Indies, to whichever places ask for you, it does not matter; you are Daughters of Charity and so you must go'.[3] His vision that the Daughters would work outside France in collaboration with the priests and brothers of the Congregation of the Mission was counter-cultural in his own day and was not put into practice outside Europe for another two hundred years.

In Vincent de Paul's lifetime the confrères of the Congregation of the Mission worked in Italy (1642), North Africa (1645), Ireland (1647), Madagascar (1648), Poland (1651) and briefly in Scotland (1650).[4] By the end of the seventeenth century they were also in China.[5] Before the French Revolution they increased the number of their foundations in the Ottoman Empire and began working in parts of Latin America as well as in Spain, Portugal, Italy and Russia. Daughters of Charity arrived in Poland before the Vincentians (1652), but there were to be no further developments in their work outside France until some Sisters were missioned to Italy in 1788 via Piedmont and to Spain from Paris in 1790.[6] At the time of the Revolutionary regime, when it was almost impossible for them to work in France, a few Sisters went to work in Lithuania (1795) and Russia (1796). By the start of the nineteenth century the Company was already more decidedly transnational than it had been before the Revolution but, even though it went on to make a new foundation in Switzerland in 1810, there were no further advances abroad in the next quarter of a century. It was not until the late 1830s that Sisters crossed a fresh European boundary to work in Portugal (1838). Then in 1839, in step with France's new expansionism, the Company pushed beyond the boundaries of Europe for the first time to Turkey and then to Algeria (1842).

These latter two developments were significant, but it was during Superior General Étienne's period of office (1843–1874) that the Daughters fully realised Vincent de Paul's missionary vision. Étienne travelled to the Levant in 1840 on behalf of the French government[7] and recognised that in Middle Eastern societies the Sisters could gain access 'where the Missionary [Vincentian confrère] could

---

3 Leonard, *The Conferences of St Vincent de Paul*, p.743. Conference 18 October 1655, 'On the End of the Company'.

4 José María Román, trans. Joyce Howard, *St Vincent de Paul: A Biography* (London: Melisande, 1999), pp. 432-442, (Madagascar), 394-398 (Ireland and Scotland), 416-26 (North Africa), 404-410 (Poland).

5 See, Antonino Orcajo, 'Reflections on Missions "Ad Gentes" in the light of St Vincent', *Vincentiana*, Vol 40, No.3. (1996), pp.1-7 for the missionary spirit of the Congregation; Robert P. Maloney, 'Our Vincentian Mission in China, Yesterday, Today and Tomorrow', *Vincentia*, Vol. 45, No.1 (2001).

6 Maria Ángeles Infante, http://famvin.org/wiki/The_Daughters_of_Charity_in_the_History_of_Military_Health_Care_and_in_the_History_of_Nursing (accessed 12 May 2016).

7 Rybolt, *The Vincentians, Vol. 4*, pp, 28-31.

never hope to enter'.[8] They, not the confrères, could meet women and families in Muslim and traditional rural cultures. He realised that the Sisters could 'exercise a powerful influence over hearts', bringing individuals closer to 'the true faith', especially through their health-care involvement with women and the education of girls. As superior general he expanded their activity in the Levant and North Africa.[9] The Company's decision to pursue missionary practice with vigour during the 1840s marked a significant turning towards globalisation.

With the addition of a mission to Egypt in 1844 an extensive field of activity opened up for the double family across much of the Ottoman Empire. A group sent to Mexico in the same year did the same for the Company's work in Latin American nations. Following the Treaty of Nanking (Nanjing) in 1842 between Great Britain and China, which ended the First Opium War and opened up China to British and French economic imperialism, the first Sisters went to China in 1848. By the 1880s the Company was firmly established across Latin America, the Middle East, North Africa and Eastern China. At a practical level the scale of this activity was made possible by two factors: the considerable increase in entrants to the Company in France after 1830 and the Company's policy of accepting indigenous women into membership unless proscribed from doing so by diplomatic protocol.[10] As a consequence, although the French government continued to reserve the designation of 'missionary' for priests and brothers when registering Europeans operating in its protectorates in the Middle East and China,[11] the most numerous group of missionaries working under its aegis by 1870 were actually Catholic sisters, among whom the Daughters of Charity formed the largest group.[12]

Catholic women in missionary historiography

Missionary history has come out of the cold during the past twenty years, moving beyond the clichés of the reductionist historical writing that had portrayed it as merely a prop for western imperialism and capitalism.[13] Christopher Bayley's magisterial study of the modern world has shown that missionary activities were common to Christianity, Islam and other major religions of the world in this era. Mission developed out of the religious revivalism they all experienced and stimulated the rise of 'empires of religion' that were not identical to territorial

---

8 Curtis, 'Charity Begins Abroad', in White and Daughton (eds.), *In God's Empire*, p.92.

9 ibid. p.93.

10 The number of Daughters increased from just under 2,000 in 1823-24 to 7,000 in 1861. Curtis, 'Charity Begins Abroad', p.90, quoting from Langlois, *Le Catholicisme au feminine*, pp. 334-335.

11 Curtis, *Civilizing Habits*, p.15.

12 Elisabeth Dufourcq, *Les Congrégations religieuses féminines hors d'Europe de Richelieu à nos jours: Histoire naturelle d'une diaspora*, 4 vol, doctoral thesis (Paris: Librairie de l'Inde, 1993), Vol. 4, pp.857-864.

13 Norman Etherington, 'Afterword' in White and Daughton, *In God's Empire*, p.280-282. See also J.P. Daughton, *An Empire Divided: Religion, Republicanism and the Making of the French Empire, 1880-1914* (New York: Oxford University Press, 2006) and Andrew Porter, *Religion versus Empire?:British Protestant Missionaries and Overseas Expansion, 1700-1914* (Manchester: Manchester University Press, 2004).

empires.[14] Although there were many convergences of interest between Christian missions and the French and British empires, scholars have now shown that Christian missionary activity was neither wholly defined nor controlled by forces of trade and territorial expansion.[15] In Sarah Curtis's words 'the fact that the church and state were often partners in colonization does not mean that their objects, methods, or impact always coincided...[missionaries] saw themselves first and foremost as agents of God rather than agents of the French state'.[16] The French state was, in any case, always ambiguous about Christian missionary activity and often hostile. For their part, no missionary societies were ever wholly a 'French' enterprise.[17] These wider considerations apply to the Company. It operated everywhere out of its French culture and mores but on the missions it worked through a transnational network of Sisters drawn from many nations and cultures, including the local culture of the mission place. On the missions the primary identity of its members as Daughters of Charity, rather than as nationals of their homeland, was vital to their charitable effectiveness.

Yet the concept of who does or does not qualify for missionary status has been neither straightforward nor self-evident. The French administrative system for colonies and protectorates that named clergy and brothers as missionaries, classified the sisters primarily as teachers and nurses, a label that served to obscure their missionary work from the view of historians. As Tara Manning observed with reference to the work of the Loreto sisters in India and Canada, 'despite the plentiful wealth of material in congregational archives very little historical space has been awarded to the thousands of sisters who served as missionaries overseas'.[18] This field of research has opened up only relatively recently among French historians. Elisabeth Dufourcq's study (1993) has laid a firm and comprehensive foundation by tracking the thousands of French sisters across continents in time, place and numerical strength.[19] Sarah Curtis has gone on to make the case that their participation was transformative for the Church's missionary work. Sisters increased the Catholic Church's approach and effectiveness on the mission field because they brought Christ to people through the practice of charity and this was often more attractive and powerful than the preaching of doctrine to pre-literate peoples. In Muslim countries it avoided the problem of direct proselytism.[20] Missionary work, moreover, gave women themselves a new kind of Christian

14 Bayley, *Birth of the Modern World*, Ch. 9.

15 Etherington, 'Afterword' in White and Daughton, *In God's Empire*, p. 280

16 Curtis, *Civilising Habits*, p. 13.

17 White and Daughton, *In God's Empire* p. 20.

18 Tara Manning, 'Sisters in the Field: The Courageous Stories of the Pioneering Loreto Sisters to India and Canada', in Máirtín Ó Catháin and Mícheál Ó Haodha (eds.), *Irish Migrants in New Communities: Seeking the Fair Land* (Plymouth: Lexington Books, 2014), p. 60.

19 Dufourcq, *Les Congrégations religieuses féminines hors d'Europe*. See also Elisabeth Dufourcq, *Les Aventurières de Dieu: Trois siècles d'histoire missionnaire française* (Jean-Claude Lattès, 1993).

20 Curtis, 'Charity Begins Abroad', p.1 03.

subjectivity in which they had direct experience and knowledge of working directly with people from other cultures and in a wide range of new circumstances.

Managing mission in the Company

As it extended its reach the Company developed procedures for administering and managing its missionary initiatives. Some systems already developed in the Congregation of the Mission were applied in the Company.[21] Influential, too, were the methods of the Paris Foreign Mission Society (MEP), the French Church's specialist missionary seminary, established 1658-63. Since 1666 the MEP's headquarters had been at 128 rue du Bac, almost next door to the Daughters' post-Revolutionary *maison mère*. The MEP's approach to mission was theoretically based on three principles: supporting the development of an indigenous priesthood, adaptation to local culture, and close collaboration with the Congregation for the Propagation of the Faith in Rome rather than with any particular national territorial or ecclesial authority (although this was often more honoured in the breach than the observance).[22] Like the MEP and the Congregation of the Mission, the Company encouraged its members to learn the local language, to support local women who wished to enter and to encourage progress towards provincial status.

Over time the Company developed two routes for its missionary work. The first, which was by far the most important in the nineteenth and early twentieth century, was the *mission ad gentes*, a centralised mission department operated by and from the mother house. The second route involved an individual Province assuming responsibility for a particular mission field on behalf of the Company. This decentralised approach became increasingly important in the twentieth century and often made use of the sphere of influence between a colonial or former colonial power and its colonies or post-colonial territories. Sisters from Britain and Ireland became missionaries through both of these routes at different times.

Any Sister in the Company who had made vows was at liberty to volunteer for the *mission ad gentes*. This self-offering signalled her willingness to be placed where the superiors decided (although she could express a particular vocational attraction), with an understanding that they might not accept her offer at all. It was an advantage if a Sister already spoke French, the *lingua franca* of the Company's missions, and that she was known to be self-reliant and with a definite skill to practise, such as nursing or teaching, or else an aptitude for what would now be called project management. Before departure (certainly in the years before the First World War) she would travel to her mission placement via Paris to receive her foreign mission cross and a blessing from superiors and then be sent out to the

21 See Rybolt, *The Vincentians, Vol. 4*, p. 13 for a summary.

22 See Ji Li, 'Measuring Catholic Faith in Nineteenth- and Twentieth-Century Northeast China', in White and Daughton, *In God's Empire*, pp.173-194.

sound of the seminary Sisters singing the Company's mission song 'Embarquons pour la terre etrangère'.[23]

Mission communities were of mixed nationalities, predominantly French but including other Europeans as well as a growing number of indigenous Sisters (except in Muslim countries). Sisters owed obedience to the local Sister Servant who, in turn, was responsible to the vice-visitatrice or regional superior of the mission appointed by Paris. Missionary Sisters, however, continued to be counted as members of their own Province and would return there if they ceased to be on mission. Contact with provincial superiors was the primary external source of moral, spiritual and practical support for a missionary Sister. Conversely her letters home, copied and circulated, were a source of edification and inspiration for her own community. These letters were also used to inspire lay friends to give support and to create networks capable of leveraging funding. Far from being the concern simply of the individual missionary Sister and of the Company's leaders, a missionary Sister's work and experience was of interest to the whole community, helping to inspire all members and to underline the fact that their real and ultimate work was the salvation of souls.

British and Irish Sisters in the mission field

More than 500 Sisters of the British and Irish Province served outside the two islands between 1870 and 1970 (about one quarter of the membership in total).[24] The majority of this number (289) worked on the Continent. As we saw in Chapter 4, many of this group (148) were first-generation Sisters who served in France for a period either for their own training or because their knowledge of English was needed. The latter applied, for example, in the case of Sisters sent to the hospital at Chantilly between 1903 and 1923 to nurse English and Irish jockeys injured at France's largest racecourse and likewise in the very different circumstance of those who were sent to nurse British and Irish soldiers on the French front in the First World War.

Once we have deducted the number of such Sisters from the total there remain 191 members of the British and Irish Province who served outside Europe, mainly in the Middle East, the Far East, Africa or Australia but occasionally in Latin America. Analysing this number by generation reveals significant patterns and shifts in the missionary participation of the Province. Before 1930 Sisters went primarily to the Middle East and Far East. But from the late 1920s Australia became a significant new destination, followed by Ethiopia and Nigeria after 1950, as Table 9.1 illustrates.

---

23 *A Sister of Charity in China (Sister Apolline Bowlby) during the Wars 1926-1942* (London: St Vincent's, 1946), pp.32-33. 2-1-14 DCMH.

24 Numbers in all places in this chapter are derived from an analysis of the provincial Sister Database, DCMH.

Destination	1st	2nd	3rd	4th	Total
Middle East (Turkey, Lebanon, Egypt, Palestine-Israel)	15	23	7	2	47
Far East (China, Japan)	11	26	6	1	44
Australia		22	12	3	37
Africa (Algeria, Ethiopia, Eritrea, Nigeria)	-	5	16	38	59
Totals	**26**	**76**	**41**	**44**	**187**
Other extra-European locations	2	2			**191**

Note: 1st generation born before 1865; 2nd 1866–1900; 3rd 1901–1925; 4th 1926–1950

9:1 DESTINATIONS OF MISSIONARY SISTERS BY GENERATION, 1860–1970

In some places their work might involve Sisters in little exposure to local people and culture, being confined instead to émigrés, colonisers and traders.[25] But many Sisters 'on the missions' moved between different groups of people: local and incoming; powerful and poor; the baptised and the un-baptised. Some undertook a spell of overseas missionary work and returned home. Others passed their entire community life outside Britain and Ireland, moving from one missionary field to another and never returning permanently; yet others stayed and died in the place where they had first been sent. In total fifty-eight Sisters of the Province died outside Europe.[26]

Because this is not a history of the Company's missionary work, our focus in this chapter is on the Sister-missionaries themselves and on the impact of their missionary work on the Province, its members and the wider Catholic community at home rather than on the impact they had on those among whom they worked. A different and considerable history on that subject is still to be written. Within this more modest framework four themes emerge as significant: (1) missionary work as exemplification of the Company's transnational nature and the transnational mobility of some Sisters; (2) the 'missionary option' as a path for those attracted to a bolder and less conventional form of dedication; (3) missions as a focus for collaboration between Sisters and lay networks; (4) the impact that the missions

25 Julia Clancy-Smith, 'Muslim Princes, Female Missionaries, and Trans-Mediterranean Migrations: The Soeurs de Saint-Joseph de l'Apparition in Tunisia c.1840-1881', in White and Daunton (eds.), *In God's Empire*, p.114 describes this growing group in the Levant as an ethnically mixed population of 'thousands of non-Muslim or non-subject residents, job-seekers, the down-and-out, vagabonds, and labor migrants passing through'.

26 See headstone in provincial cemetery in Mill Hill which gives the numbers of Sisters dying overseas in each location.

had on the Province. The changes that took place in the Sisters' approach to missionary activity and formation after 1960 will be introduced but considered in more detail later. Because of important shifts that occurred between the first and third generations in terms of mission location from the Middle and Far East to Australia and Africa and from the *mission ad gentes* to provincial responsibility, a broadly generational approach is helpful in exploring these four themes.

First-and-second generation missionary Sisters: Ottoman Empire and China

> How privileged we Sisters of the Foreign Missions are. We live and work so near to souls. In the Foreign Missions, it is much easier; every day we should thank God for the great grace and privilege we have to be so near souls in all that we do.[27]
>
> (Sister Agnes (Xavier) Berkeley, missionary in China 1890–1944)

The Ottoman Empire

In the 1840s and 1850s the lack of opportunity to minister in their homeland increased the likelihood that British and Irish Daughters would be placed (rather than volunteering) in the Middle East, particularly in Turkey and Egypt. Some became missionaries by virtue of becoming Daughters at a particular historical moment. Although the number of British and Irish Sisters serving in this part of the world may not have been large the experience they gained, particularly in health care, proved to be an important asset to the Company's expanding work in the English-speaking world, including in the British Isles itself. The Company established a number of hospitals, dispensaries and clinics in the region before the Crimean War and afterwards increased its work as French interests in the region grew. Sarah Curtis has described the Ottoman Empire as 'a central focus of [the Daughters'] evangelizing efforts' and one that absorbed 'increasing numbers of personnel and resources'.[28]

Because of its strategic value the port city of Alexandria was afforded priority in the allocation of Company resources. A cosmopolitan city with a large European population at this time, its military and trade base shifted from France to England during the second half of the century. This transfer was even more marked following the British bombardment of Alexandria in 1882 after which Egypt was occupied by British troops in the era of the so-called 'veiled protectorate' (1882-1914). A need for English-speaking Sisters helps to explain the increased presence of second-generation Sisters from the British Province (Table 9.2).

---

27 *M.L.H.* (Margaret Lucy Hughes), *Sister Xavier Berkeley: Fifty-Four Years in China as Missionary Sister of Charity* (London: Burns Oates, 1949), p.127. 2-1-10 DCMH.

28 Curtis,'Charity Begins Abroad', p.89.

Generation	Egypt	Lebanon Syria	Palestine– Israel	Turkey
First	4	1		10
Second	10	5	2	6
Third	4	3	2	-
Fourth	1			1

9.2: UK SISTERS SERVING IN THE MIDDLE EAST BY GENERATION

The predominance of English-born rather than Irish-born Sisters in the region contrasts with their relative ratios in the British Province itself and is likely to reflect the importance accorded to specifically English networks and influence by the Company's superiors (Table 9.3).

	English	Irish	Scottish	French	Other
Egypt	10	4	-	2	2
Palestine–Israel	2	2	-		
Lebanon	7	1	1		
Turkey	7	5	-	2	2
	26	12	1	4	4

9.3: NATIONAL ORIGINS OF UK PROVINCE SISTERS IN THE MIDDLE EAST

From Alexandria the Company spread slowly outwards, to Ismailia on the west bank of the Suez Canal where it opened another hospital in 1888, then to Port Taufiq (now Suez Port) in 1889 and Cairo and Port Said in 1905 and 1906 respectively.

This activity began with the arrival in Alexandria in January 1844 of a group comprising three Vincentian priests, two brothers and seven Daughters.[29] Their presence was supported by the European consuls and the apostolic vicar of Egypt and was conducted under the patronage of Muhammed Ali, the modernising wāli and khedive (governor) of Egypt and Sudan. The Vincentians were to run a secondary school and an Arabic-language printing press, the Daughters a school, hospital and clinic. By the late 1840s two communities of Sisters were dedicated

---

29 Rybolt, *The Vincentians, Vol. 4*, p. 408.

to school and hospital work respectively, but had also opened a house of mercy (1845) and were undertaking home visiting, going out into the villages close to Alexandria. Among these Sisters in the late 1840s and early 1850s were Dorothy Beahan from Drogheda, who entered in 1844 at the age of thirty-one and was sent to serve in Alexandria after formation in France, and London-born Eliza MacDonough, who entered the community in 1847 and arrived in Alexandria in 1853 after service in France.[30]

Nothing is recorded about these two Sisters while they lived in the newly-named Street of the Seven Sisters, but the letters and diaries of Florence Nightingale dating from the winter of 1849 and spring of 1850 shed considerable light on their community and its activities. Nightingale was travelling with close friends Charles and Selina Bracebridge. Aged twenty-nine at the time, she had not been able to follow her strong attraction to nursing because of steady family opposition. On the journey by train from Paris to Marseilles their party fell into conversation with two Daughters of Charity making their way to Auxerre.[31] The previous year Nightingale had visited the Daughters' hospital in Rome with another friend, Elizabeth Herbert. The seriousness of her interest being obvious, the two Sisters offered to provide an introduction to St Vincent's Institute, the Daughters' clinic in Alexandria. Nightingale spent so much time at the clinic during three weeks in the city that she described herself as like 'a tame cat there'.[32] One morning she arrived at 8.30 and watched all day as three Sisters, with no other assistance, saw 300 patients; 'discipline', she noted of their conduct, 'quickness and kindness; beautiful'.[33] Selina Bracebridge observed them 'bleed and dress wounds; dispense medicines and compound them'. Both women were impressed by the impact of such a modest operation: 'The poor flock by hundreds to them for advice and medicine and with no fixed revenue, it is wonderful how much they do', Bracebridge concluded.[34] Nightingale counted nineteen Sisters in Alexandria who 'seemed to do the work of 90'.[35] Their accounts confirm Curtis's conclusions that the Daughters 'served far more than a displaced European community', their 'ultimate goal' being 'Christian conversion through charity'.[36] At the Sisters' Mass for the Feast of the Presentation Nightingale witnessed '...the Levantine, the Smyrniot, the

30 Provincial Sister Database. DCMH.

31 Anthony Sattin, (ed.), *Letters from Egypt: A Journey on the Nile 1849-1850* (London: Parkway Publishing, 1998), p.24.

32 Ibid., p.205.

33 Anthony Sattin, *A Winter on the Nile: Florence Nightingale, Gustave Flaubert and the Temptations of the Nile* (London: Hutchinson, 2010), p.14.

34 Ibid., p.12

35 Ibid., p.14.

36 Curtis, 'Charity Begins Abroad', pp.96-97.

Overseas Mission and Development

This headstone in the Daughters' cemetery Mill Hill was erected in 2012 in tribute to Sisters of the Province who died on mission overseas between 1870 and 2003.

There were two routes a Daughter could take to become a missionary: through the Company's 'Mission Ad Gentes' department or through a mission that was being managed by her own Province.

Mission Ad Gentes was the central department for mission based at the rue du Bac. Any Sister could volunteer for the missions, making herself available to be sent anywhere that the Company chose. When on mission Ad Gentes she was on loan from her own Province to the department. The mission in China was managed in this way.

Provincial Mission. A Province might be given or might initiate responsibility for a mission to a particular country or region. Such missions and 'sub-provinces' usually developed into independent Provinces over time.

SPES UNICA

IN LOVING

MEMORY OF

OUR 74 SISTERS

WHO DIED

ON MISSION

OVERSEAS.

1870 - 2003

R. I. P.

ALGERIA - 1
AUSTRALIA - 27
CHINA - 16
EGYPT - 3
ETHIOPIA - 1
FRANCE - 12
GREECE - 2
ISRAEL - 4
ITALY - 1
LEBANON - 3
NIGERIA - 1
SPAIN - 1
TURKEY - 2

British Daughters in China

Daughters of Charity arrived in China in 1848.

Agnes Berkeley 1861-1944 (Sister Xavier) of Spetchley Park Worcestershire had a strong call from childhood to serve as a Sister of Charity in China. She entered in 1882 aged 22 (left) and went to China in 1890, serving there until her death. She became influential in the Chinese Catholic missionary world, partly because of her innovative work on the ground and partly through her wide correspondence with American and Irish bishops and superiors of missionary orders. American Maryknoll missionary and bishop in China, James A. Walsh, referred to her as Maryknoll's co-founder because of her insistence on the need for Maryknoll sisters in China. Her House of Mercy at Chou-shan (Zhoushan) was a model and she was known locally as 'Mandarin of the Poor'. Shown (right) at the age of 71.

Dorothy Bowlby 1877-1942 (Sister Appoline) was the daughter of an army colonel. Her sister was received into the Catholic Church and became a Daughter of Charity (Sister Philippa Clerk), her family then severing all links. Dorothy married and was also received into the Church in 1903. Widowed in 1911, having had no children, Dorothy herself entered the Company in 1913 aged 36, with dispensation for her age. After ten years in London and Plymouth Sister Bowlby put her name forward for the China mission not because she wished to go – she actually had an aversion to the idea – but because she believed God wanted her to make a sacrifice. She was twice refused but was accepted in 1926 aged 50. She extended the workshop in Ningbo, built a primary and secondary school and reformed the hospital in Hangchow. She died in Shanghai where she had been sent by the Japanese occupying force prior to expulsion.

Photograph taken prior to departure for China in 1926.

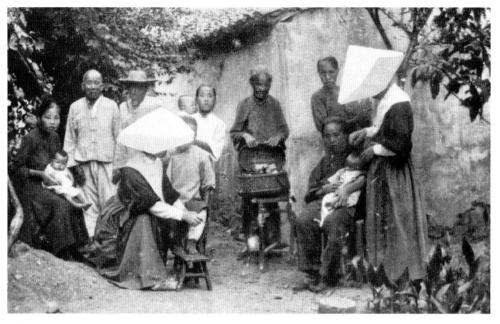

Mobile health clinic in the countryside near Shanghai.

The Sisters would also baptise any infants brought to them who were unlikely to live. (Photo mid-1920s)

Ningpo (Ningbo) Technical High School Embroidery Workshop established by the Sisters to provide skilled employment making silk garments and cotton towels. Sister Berkeley established 'fair trade' retail outlets in Britain and America, for example, with Fortnum and Mason in London.

Sister Louise Liou with men from the hostel in Chou-shan (Zhoushan), 1920s. Local women entered the Company soon after it started work in China.

Australia 1926

The Australian foundation was a mission from Britain and Ireland at the request of Vincentian Bishop Michael O'Farrell, Bishop of Bathurst, New South Wales, developing into a Vice-Province in 1936 and a Province in its own right in 1963.

in 1926 the four pioneer sisters were Sisters Hannah (Catherine) McGuire, Margaret (Vincent) Valentine, Elizabeth (Mary) Fagan and Elizabeth (Joseph) Leonard. In total 37 English, Irish, Scots and Welsh Sisters were sent to Australia from the Province of Great Britain and Ireland. Hannah McGuire was the first Vice-Visitatrice.

Croagh Patrick Home for Boys, Orange, New South Wales (1929) which cared for 35-40 boys aged from three to twelve. The first to arrive were Tom (10), Keith (8), Kevin (6) and Danny (4) Byrne whose mother had recently died. In the early 1950s there was a community of seven

Sisters here, five of whom also taught in the local school attended by the boys. There were no lay staff and the Sisters also visited families after school and instructed converts.

Sister Judith Greville and children in Sydney in the late 1960s. Sister Judith was born in England, emigrated to Australia in 1952 and entered the community in 1954. After training as a teacher she specialised in the education of perceptually impaired children, working in Australia until 1976 when she returned to England. She later trained as an archivist at London University and as the Province's first professional archivist organised its archive and Heritage Room.

Nigeria 1963

Bishop Moynagh of Ikot, Ekpene asked for Daughters from the British and Irish Province. 80 Sisters volunteered from whom three were missioned. The Sisters who went on this mission were joined from 1973 onwards by many Nigerian entrants. In 1970, when an Irish Province was created separately from that of Britain, the Nigerian mission was linked to the Province of Ireland.

1963 Send-off. Sisters Daly, Gaynor and Hughes leave Mill Hill for a retreat in Paris en route to Adiaha Obong.

'We send you forth to Nigeria
Our Sisterly Pioneers – three
With best wishes from the Mother-land
To all across the sea.'

1965 Alice Daly and Margaret Hughes (Sisters Xavier and Gabriel) giving lectures and practical demonstrations of food preparation using the bulgar wheat and rolled oats donated by the American Wheat and Grain Programme.

The Sisters are wearing the missionary version of the new habit, introduced in 1964.

Alice Daly returned to Africa in 2002 as a member of the new community in Kenya.

Nigerian Seminary Sisters 2001.

In 2001, when the Province of Nigeria was inaugurated and Sister Francesca Edet installed as first provincial, there were almost 150 Nigerian Sisters.

Ethiopia

Theodora Cubitt 1897-1989 (Sister Gabriel) was the first Sister of the British Province to be missioned to Ethiopia. She entered the Company at the relatively late age of 32. At almost 6' tall and older than the other seminary Sisters she was always distinctive – and because of her capabilities (which included fluent Italian and French) was soon identified as a Sister for the missions.

In 1937 she was sent to China and remained there until she was expelled by the Communist government in 1951. After a short period in Egypt she was missioned to Ethiopia, a region that the Company had administered from Italy and then France.

In Ethiopia Theodora Cubitt found her life's ministry, over the years passionately making the case to the British Province that it become more involved.

She assisted people with leprosy, helped to set up a clinic in Mekele (the Poly Clinic), and begged food and funds from everywhere, daily visiting the most marginalised people who lived in the cemeteries because they had nowhere else.

In 1968 Emperor Haile Selassie awarded her his personal Gold Medal for Humanitarian Achievement. She was the first woman to be recognised in this way.

In 1966 the General Council asked the British Province to take responsibility for the mission that had been opened in Ethiopia and in 1967 Sister Angela Murray was appointed as Councillor for Ethiopia.

Bridget Lally in Ethiopia Bridget Lally (Sister Helen), 1919-2012, was one of 11 children born near Knock in Co. Mayo to a farming family. Aged 18 she moved to Sheffield to train at Sheffield Royal Hospital with a view to offering herself to the DCs as a qualified and experienced nurse (pictured, right, in 1945 on qualification). After Seminary she was placed in St Vincent's Hospital, Liverpool and North Infirmary, Cork becoming Matron and Sister Servant. In preparation for Ethiopia she trained in midwifery. From 1970 Sister Helen worked at St Mary's Clinic in Addis Ababa, ran vaccination schemes and ante-natal programmes supported by Oxfam and Caritas International. She served as Ethiopian Regional Superior from 1979-1983 and remained through the Communist era 1974-91, the famines of the 1980s and Revolutionary war of 1987-1991, returning to England in 1997.

Sisters in Mekele mid-1980s with Sister Zoe O'Neill (12th Provincial 3rd from left): Sisters Genevieve, Gabriel, Zoe, Frevienie, Aster, Mary Dixon and seminary Sisters.

Many British and Irish Daughters served here and many Ethiopian Sisters have spent time in formation and on retreat in Britain.

Seminary Sister c.2000

Ethiopia became a Vice-Province in 1995 and a Province in 2001

Today the Daughters run five primary health care clinics and outreach stations and a specialized eye clinic. They provide education facilities ranging from crèches and kinder-gartens through primary and secondary schools to a third level Montessori Teacher Training Institute. Social work in all areas includes such activities as women's empowerment, safe houses for abused women, working with street children, prisoners, the elderly, young people, people with disabilities, and leprosy patients.

The new 'missionary momentum' of the 21st century

The Company has adopted the concept 'The Boldness of Charity for a new missionary momentum' as part of a strategy to re-galvanise its mission and international development activities for the 21st century. New practices include trans-provincial collaboration.

Trans-Provincial mission collaboration: Kenya

In a collaborative venture under the leadership of the Irish Province the Kenyan mission draws on a network of support from two USA Provinces and the Provinces of Nigeria and Australia as well as Ethiopia-Eritrea and Britain.

In 2002 'Sisters in Kenya' was formed of 3 Sisters from the Irish Province, 2 from Britain and 3 from the Ethiopian-Eritrean Province. Lay volunteers share their skills for short periods. A seminary was opened in Nairobi in 2008 and the Kenyan mission is thriving.

Sisters Marie Raw and Anne Redmond from the British Provincial Council visit Thigio, Kenya. A decision was made to focus on special needs education in Thigio Kenya because there were no facilities in any of the schools. Daughters work with Kenyan teachers trained in special educational needs who had no resources or classrooms. There are now seven such class-rooms in primary schools and two centres for special needs adults.

International Strategic Projects: HIV/AIDS

The DREAM Center in Kubwa Abuja was opened in 2007, the first of its kind in Nigeria to offer free services for people living with HIV/AIDS. DREAM stands for drug resource enhancement against AIDS and malnutrition and is a proven, scalable model designed for sub-Saharan Africa deployed by Daughters of Charity in Nigeria, Kenya, Cameroon, DRC, Mozambique and Tanzania. This strategic approach is another aspect of the new movement.

Maltese, the Egyptian, people of all nations and tongues uniting in the worship of the one God'.[37]

Nightingale's visit to Egypt marked a significant turning point in her own life and played a small part in the history of nursing in Britain.[38] The long apprenticeship served by British and Irish Sisters in the Ottoman Empire was to underpin their subsequent service in more significant ways. After five years in Alexandria, Dorothy Beahan, for example, was among the pioneer group sent to Santiago in 1853 to start the Company's work in Chile, remaining in leadership there until her death in 1875.[39] Eliza MacDonough's three years with the Alexandria community was followed in 1856 by her appointment to the important office of directress of the seminary in the United States of America. Her mother tongue and an Anglo-Saxon cultural outlook combined with French and global community experience convinced the Company's superiors that she could transfer the Company's disciplines to the American seminary. During the American Civil War Sister MacDonough's Alexandrian nursing experience led her to the battlefields and hospitals of Gettysburg, furthering her own integration into the American Province.[40]

Experience gained in the Ottoman Empire was equally important to the emerging mission in the British Isles. Dublin-born Teresa O'Callaghan had been with Eliza MacDonough in the Paris seminary in 1847 but was sent to the Company's hospital in Constantinople rather than Alexandria. From there she was placed in Smyrna and then successively in military hospitals in Algiers, Lyons and Sedan. In 1867 she returned to her native land as first Sister Servant of North Infirmary Hospital in Cork when the Daughters assumed responsibility for its management.[41] As the Company's first hospital in the United Kingdom, North Infirmary was where Sisters from Britain and Ireland could gain nurse training in the Company's own tradition. In 1903 Sister O'Callaghan was given permission by the Cork authorities to open a nurse training school attached to North Infirmary. Fifty years after the Crimean War her extensive nursing experience abroad not only proved itself in the effectiveness of the Daughters' work in Cork but left a wider legacy in the nurse training given to Sisters of the Province.

---

37 Sattin, *Letters from Egypt*, p.24.

38 See, for example, Lynn McDonald (ed.), *Florence Nightingale: An Introduction to Her Life and Family*: Vol. 1*Collected Works of Florence Nightingale* (Waterloo, ON: Wilfrid Laurier University Press, 2002), p.18 and Gérard Vallée ed., *Florence Nightingale on Mysticism and Eastern Religions*.: Vol 4: *Collected Works of Florence Nightingale* (Waterloo, ON: Wilfrid Laurier University Press, 2003).

39 Provincial Sister Database, DCMH.

40 Hannefin, *Daughters of the Church*, p.123.

41 Prunty and Sullivan (eds.), *Daughters of Charity in Ireland*, pp. 121ff.

China

If first-generation British Sisters were placed by superiors in the Ottoman Empire to gain experience and meet the Company's needs, only those who volunteered for China and demonstrated a strong commitment were accepted for this mission, regarded as a special and arduous calling. Such a precondition did not, however, create a problem of supply. Of the many missionary openings available to second -generation British and Irish Daughters, it was China that most fired imaginations and dreams of sacrifice.

The possibility of service in China attracted some young women to enter the community in the first instance. Agnes Berkeley (1861-1944), born into a landed recusant Worcestershire Catholic family, declared an intention to become a Daughter of Charity in China at the age of six. Her inspiration was the Association of the Holy Childhood, the transnational lay organisation founded in France in 1843 in aid of Catholic missions, to which she and her siblings belonged and whose membership card depicted Daughters in China.[42] Her cousin and exact contemporary Edith Feilding (1862-1918), daughter of the Earl of Denbigh, also entered the Company with a 'life-long wish and heart's desire' to work in China. As a fourteen-year-old she had contemplated missionary martyrdom in China on hearing about the deaths of ten Sisters of Charity in the Tsien (Tianjin) uprising of 1870. Hers was not the only vocation aroused by thoughts of martyrdom in China.[43] Bridget Coleman, whose background was on a family farm in County Wexford, had a long-standing desire for the China Mission. When Sister Berkeley visited Mill Hill from China in 1923 wearing Chinese cloth shoes that fell apart in the rain Sister Coleman, at that time in charge of the Mill Hill kitchen, retrieved them and wore them at recreation until she received the awaited call to go to Peking (Beijing) in 1925.[44]

The commitment of these Sisters belongs within the Western and orientalist fascination with China that developed from the 1840s onwards. A wide readership developed for all types of writing about China – scientific, geographical, historical and religious. Among a range of subjects, interest was particularly piqued by aspects of the treatment of girls and women, the subject of moral outrage in Europe. The writing of missionaries such as Gabriel Palatre (1830–1878), a French Jesuit missionary, aroused Christians to action,[45] as did the literature of the Association of the Holy Childhood. Hugely popular with laity and clergy the Association had

---

42 M.L.H., *Xavier Berkeley*, p.xii. 2-1-10 DCMH.

43 Kerr, *Edith Feilding*, 'When 14 years of age (1874) Edith heard a sermon on the Chinese martyrs which was destined to have a lasting effect upon her.' 'Wouldn't it be lovely', she asked her sister Clare, 'to go to China and be martyred.' The idea 'never left her mind'. pp.13-14. See also *Lives of Deceased Sisters* Margeurite Dargouges (1916), p. 73. 10-3-1 DCMH.

44 *Sister Xavier Berkeley*, p.123-124.

45 Michelle T. King, *Between Birth and Death: Female Infanticide in Nineteenth-Century China* (Stanford, CA: Stanford University Press, 2014), pp.98-110.

built up its annual income to nearly two million francs by 1869.[46] Although the Holy Childhood supported missions in many countries, its promotional materials concentrated on China, appealing directly to Catholic children in Europe and America to give up their pennies to save the lives and souls of Chinese babies in peril through infanticide and the high incidence of infant death. Like much of the contemporary literature it exoticised and stereotyped Chinese life and culture.[47]

The overlapping interests of Western academic studies, a project to 'civilise' foreigners that included greater protection of girls and women, and a cross-denominational missionary effort for the salvation of souls in China, form the context for the publication of biographies of Chinese missionary Sisters by the British Province. Only nine full-length biographies were ever published by the Province; seven before and two after 1940. Sisters who served on the Chinese mission were the subject of four, and theirs were the only missionary lives selected for such memorialisation.[48] All four biographies were published between 1928 and 1949, starting with an English translation of *The Heroine of Pe Tang*, the life of French Sister Helene de Jauria who lost her life during the Boxer Rebellion in 1900. This was followed by biographies of three English Sisters who between them saw service in China between the 1880s and 1940s. A substantive and well -illustrated biography of Agnes Berkeley (Sister Xavier) was written by Margaret (Sister Anne) Hughes, herself a missionary who had known Sister Berkeley in China. Published with a forward by John Wu, Chinese Minister to the Holy See, it found a wide readership, and was to be found in many convent and convent school libraries.[49] The life of Edith Feilding, who was in China from 1903 to her death in 1918, was commercially published in 1933.[50] The story of Dorothy (Sister Apolline) Bowlby, published by the Province in 1946 with illustrations, was largely told through her own letters.[51] This slim volume went into four reprints in 1946 and 1947, the profits going to the China mission. The genre of missionary lives to which these biographies belong was not only highly popular between the 1850s and 1950s but has 'long [been] considered an integral part of missiology'.[52] As religious communities were well aware, it was also an excellent form of publicity

---

46 See Henrietta Harrison, '"A Penny for the Little Chinese": The French Holy Childhood Association in China, 1843-1951', *American Historical Review* (February, 2008), pp. 72-92.

47 For a new reading of Catholicism in China and of the missionary push see D.E. Mungello, *The Catholic Invasion of China: Remaking Chinese Christianity* (Lanham, MD: Rowan and Littlefield, 2015).

48 Notable leaders inevitably formed one group of biographies; the Company's foundress Louise de Marillac, and three prominent Sisters of the province - Henriette Chatelain, the 'mother' of the province, its second Visitatrice, Eugenie Marcellus, and Etheldreda Howard. The Visionary Sisters Catherine Labouré of the Miraculous Medal and Apolline Andriveau of the Red Scapular made up a second category.

49 M.L.H. [Margaret Hughes], *Sister Xavier Berkeley*. Author's own observation of the holdings in convent libraries during the 1980s and 1990s , before many were dismantled.

50 Kerr, *Edith Feilding*.

51 *A Sister of Charity in China during the Wars, 1926-1942: Sister Apolline Bowlby*. 2-1-14 DCMH.

52 Stanley Skreslet, *Comprehending Mission: The Questions, Methods, Themes and Problems and Prospects of Missiology* (Maryknoll, NY: Orbis Books, 2012), p.188.

for vocations. Care was taken to set each Sister's life, extra-ordinary though it was, in the context of everyday Vincentian practical charity and spirituality..

The existence of these detailed biographies means that we know about the China Mission largely through the lives of the upper-class cousins Sisters Berkeley and Feilding, and of Dorothea Bowlby, a widowed convert to Catholicism from a middle-class army family background. Their presence and that of a number of other upper-and middle-class Sisters on mission from the Britain Province in the Levant and China confounds the conclusion drawn by Norman Etherington that 'few European or American missionaries of any denomination were recruited from the upper-or upper-middle classes' and undermines Julia Clancy-Smith's conjecture that Daughters of Charity were 'more compliant and socially more modest' than the Sisters of the Apparition of St Joseph with whom she compares them.[53]

With 17 British Sisters and 19 Irish, the former were disproportionately represented on the China Mission in relation to the overall composition of the Province, but the latter's presence was also strong. Offsetting the misleading impression given by the biographies that the Province's Chinese missionaries were exclusively English, is the special place accorded to Drogheda-born Alice (Sister Louise) O'Sullivan in the Company's collective memory. Alice O'Sullivan was the first Sister to go to China from either Britain or Ireland, arriving in 1867. As one of the group of ten Daughters murdered and violently mutilated in the 1870 Tsien (Tianjin) uprising against Westerners she is honoured as a martyr in the Company's history.[54] When the Sisters returned to Tianjin in 1877 the new group included another Irish Sister, Catherine McCarthy (Sister Vincent), from Co. Cork. This community rebuilt the Sisters' work there after the calamitous events of 1870, working quietly to regain the trust of local people.

Despite Sister McCarthy's presence in the 1880s, the active involvement of the British and Irish Province in China dates from 1890, reaching its peak between the wars and then ceasing to be replenished after 1939 because of the outbreak of war (Table 9.4).

---

53 Norman Etherington, 'Afterword: The Missionary Experience in British and French Empires', in White and Daughton (eds.), *In God's Empire,* p.290 and Julia Clancy-Smith, 'Muslim Princes, Female Missionaries and Trans-Mediterranean Migrations', in White and Daughton, p.113.

54 See Louise O'Connell, 'Irish Daughters of Charity on International Mission', in Prunty and Sullivan (eds.), *Daughters of Charity in Ireland,* pp.221-244. For a contemporary account see *The First Martyrs of the Holy Childhood* by a French priest trans. by Lady Herbert (London and Leamington: Art and Book Co. 1900) and for a recent analysis see King, *Between Birth and Death,* pp.155-158.

Generation	Number
First	11
Second	24
Third	3
Fourth	1

9.4: UK SISTERS SERVING IN CHINA BY GENERATION

In 1930, when several first-generation Sisters in China overlapped for a period with a number of the second generation, there were thirteen members of the Province on the mission, more than in any other part of the world at that time.[55] The commitment required, coupled with the need to learn at least enough of the language to get by, and the demands of living in a very different culture, meant that almost all the Sisters of the Province who went to China remained there until death or until they were expelled by the Communists in the early 1950s.

Unlike Sisters from France and Poland, or the American Sisters who arrived in 1923, members of the British Province were not clustered as a community to manage a particular work but were spread across a large number of houses singly or in twos. Some were appointed Sister Servant to a house of mainly French and Chinese Sisters, others served under a French Sister. (I have found no evidence at this time of Chinese Sister Servants in houses where there were Europeans). When Sister Berkeley was moved from her first placement in Jiujiang where Catherine McCarthy was Sister Servant she remarked that 'we hardly expected two English Sisters to be left long together, we are precious from rarity out here'.[56] In saying so she was simply recognising the value of their native language to the Company. As the only native English-speakers on the Vincentian mission before 1923, Sisters from the British Province were able to conduct negotiations in the treaty ports where English was an official administrative language and to communicate, with more or less sophistication, between French, English and the local Chinese dialect.

The English language was a valuable tool, too, when it came to building networks of support for the funds that were vital to sustain and develop the Daughters' China Mission. Although the Holy Childhood Association paid some of the basic costs of the mission, these were inadequate. Sister Xavier Berkeley was a prolific correspondent, making skilful use of private letters and public annual 'report letters' to large numbers of adult and child donors. Her efforts yielded considerable results. At the most straightforward level she was able to interest her wealthy family and close friends in Britain sufficiently for them to

---

55 At this date there were also 3 Sisters in Palestine, 3 in Egypt, 1 in Turkey, 1 in Chile and 2 in Spain. Annual statistical return to Paris for 1930. 9-0-2-5 DCMH.

56 *Sister Xavier Berkeley*, p.38.

send out regular medical supplies and hospital equipment,[57] bales of cloth to make children's clothing, seeds and agricultural implements,[58] and to donate capital that was invested to provide a cash flow to improve the diet of the children in their care.[59] But she also developed a number of new fundraising models. The first of these was the establishment of 'fair trading'. At the turn of the century Sister Berkeley created workshops in Ningpo (Ningbo) that provided training and employment for young men and women in the manufacture of silk, satin and cotton raw materials and 'high-end' embroidered panels and goods. This initiative was successful only because she secured investment for equipment at one end of production and outlets for commercial retail distribution at the other. Initially this was done through her own efforts in contacting individuals and large department stores in London and New York, such as Liberty's, Harrods and Macey's. But when supporters formed the London Committee for the Technical Schools in China (chaired by the Duke of Norfolk), a structure was put in place that enabled the endeavour to be backed more securely and replicated in other locations.[60] The workshops received additional publicity in an article written by the English Consul-General in China, J.M.H. Playfair, for the British press. 'There are two specially noteworthy points about this School of Embroidery', Playfair wrote:

> It is almost Utopian in its co-operative constitution. Here Capital is associated with Labour in unique terms. The convent supplies the Capital, the workers constitute the Labour and ALL THE PROFITS GO TO THE WORKERS. Secondly....it is strictly undenominational. Pagans and Christians are welcomed alike, which is the apotheosis of tolerance.[61]

When Sister Berkeley left Ningbo the work suffered for a period but was revived by Sister Bowlby whose initiatives included publication of an eight page bookle printed by the Jesuit press in Shanghai and illustrated with photographs about the work to distribute to backers and adaptation to lace-making as European tastes changed.[62]

American dollars became increasingly important to the whole range of Daughters' projects in China, and it was the British and Irish Sisters in China who created an American support network. This was the second of Sister Berkeley's funding projects. From the later 1890s her contact with the American Foreign Aid Society in Boston found funds for many new building and farming projects in

57 Sister Xavier Berkeley, p. 50.

58 ibid., p. 115.

59 ibid., p. 75.

60 ibid., p. 56-57.

61 ibid.p. 65.

62 *A Sister of Charity in China*, pp. 38-41.

Ningbo and on Zhoushan Island: a children's home, a men's hospital, a women's and children's hospital, the purchase of an island for growing food and timber. Boston was followed by contact with other American Foreign Aid Societies. In another large-scale American collaboration, Berkeley created a system of 'god-mothers' for abandoned children through which American donors sent money for care of an individual child and received regular information about his or her progress. Margaret Hughes' claim that 'Sister Xavier opened up American alms to all the Sisters' Houses in China' was not exaggerated.[63] Sister Berkeley in turn was full of praise for American generosity. 'America fed Chusan' she wrote about the difficult First World War years when European money for China missions dried up.[64]

The Province's Irish Sisters in China joined forces with her to extend the reach of these appeals directly into their own Irish-American networks. Sister Gertrude Hanley, for example, 'had many good friends and relatives in America and she appealed to them' for funds to build a hospital for poor men on Zhoushan after the War. Again, Sister Berkeley noted that 'the hospital was built by Boston friends'. These were networks that the French superiors and Sisters could not have forged. It was little wonder that 'Priests, European and Chinese, looked on her [Berkeley] as a fairy godmother to supply their many wants.'[65]

In 1923, at the age of sixty-three, Agnes Berkeley returned to England for the first time since her departure in 1890. The superiors general had ostensibly recalled her to represent the Holy Childhood Association at the Missionary Exhibition being held in Birmingham, although their real motivation was to enable her to meet her elderly mother one final time. Superior General Verdier asked her to travel back to China via the United States so that she could meet leading American missionary support organisers, give lectures on the China Mission and speak to the Sisters of the American Provinces 'in their own tongue...and to smooth away some of the initial difficulties' of their own mission to China.[66] Here was the transnational Company operating to maximise its effectiveness for the sake of the mission.

The heart of this American support network was in Boston where Father James Walsh was Director of the Boston Propagation of the Faith office. In 1911 he, Father Thomas Price and Mary Joseph Rogers co-founded the Catholic Foreign Missionary Society of America, better known as the Maryknoll Missionaries, male and female, who were very active in China during the 1920s and 1930s. By his own statement, Walsh's extensive correspondence with Sister Berkeley over the years had influenced him to make such a foundation; she had continuously stressed the need for American missionaries, men and women for China, at a time

63 *A Sister of Charity in China*, p.53.

64 Ibid., p.113.

65 Ibid., p.97.

66 Ibid., pp.116-124.

when American priests and religious were not engaged in overseas mission.[67] Although Price was not alive to hear it, the lecture Agnes Berkeley gave to the Maryknoll seminarians in 1923 was a tribute to a friendship built on a common passion for mission. It was also an illustration of the many ways that normal gender boundaries could be dissolved on the mission field and in the name of mission.

Given her own doughty approach it is unlikely that Sister Berkeley emphasised physical suffering in her Maryknoll lecture, but it was an almost inevitable dimension of the China Mission given the prevalence of cholera and the tendency of Europeans to contract tropical sprue. The experience of loneliness often had to be faced too. Dorothy Bowlby was forewarned of the latter just before her departure in 1926. 'Sister Visitatrice spoke to me so very sympathetically', she recalled, 'of the loneliness I should feel owing to my extremely unintellectual companions'.[68] The entry in her spiritual notebook for January 1929 recorded her own reflections on this experience:

> Next month we shall have another European Sister, and after 16 years of Community life one is used to a certain isolation of heart and mind, which one cannot, and ought not to try, to avoid. It is this that makes the supernatural part of our life, for the body soon gets used to exterior mortifications, but the mortification of the intellect and heart will always remain, and will, I hope, help us to gain Heaven.[69]

Yet Sisters from Britain and Ireland also found considerable scope for action and fulfilment for their zeal on the Mission. As this brief account has indicated the Sisters' charitable activities were wide-ranging. They included medical care in hospitals and dispensaries, travelling dispensary work, shelter and education for children, care of elderly men and women, and the organisation of fair-trade enterprises to provide employment for young people, as well as many other personal and individual acts. They involved building projects and land negotiation, the need to learn a new language and to live among people whose customary practices were so different. But the challenge of the missions lay as much in the demand it made on the personal responsibility and responsiveness of Sisters as in the range of the works. Like other 'frontiers', the China Mission was less supervised, less formal and less constrained by familiar social expectations than service at home and there was freedom to work for God in less conventional ways.

This brief account has consciously left to one side the controversial history of the Sisters' ministry of saving the souls of abandoned and dying babies through baptism in order to give the subject separate consideration. Baptism of dying

---

67 This is repeated in histories of Maryknoll. See, for example, the entry for James Walsh in *The Biographical Dictionary of Chinese Catholicism* http://www.bdcconline.net/en/stories/w/walsh-james-edward.php (accessed 12 May 2016) and also *Xavier Berkeley*, pp. 113-115.

68 *A Sister of Charity in China*, p. 40.

69 ibid., p. 49.

infants was the aspect of missionary work emphasised above all others in official Holy Childhood Association publicity. The Association's literature and its sensationalised campaign, 'A Penny for the Little Chinese', was, without doubt, its most effective fundraising campaign and message, popular with adults and children alike.[70] However, neither benign nor harmless, this campaign and the activity of infant baptism served to deepen misunderstandings about attitudes to infants in China that were widespread in Western culture, simplifying a more complex moral and existential aspect of society in some regions of China. In China itself the ill-informed actions undertaken by some early missionaries in their concern for babies unwittingly exacerbated existing East-West tensions. In 1870 these tensions spiralled into the horrific violence in the city of Tianjin, already mentioned, when the French consul and twenty other Westerners, most of them French, including ten Daughters of Charity and two priests, were killed and mutilated by an enraged mob. The events of 21 June almost triggered an international incident as the new transnational telegraph sent the news across Europe and North America.

There was no single cause for the Tianjin uprising and for the others that preceded and came after it. But the cultural misunderstandings surrounding the inter-related issues of Chinese infanticide on the one hand and the Catholic missionary practice of baptising dying infants on the other, played its part in arousing xenophobia. Where Westerners came to believe that infanticide, particularly female infanticide, was 'a totemic cultural marker', of Chinese-ness (and therefore in need of reform),[71] many of the local Chinese who saw or heard about the practice of baptism believed that their children were being bewitched and prepared for death so that their organs could be removed and used by the missionaries in their orphanages.

The subject of infanticide in China has been the subject of recent scholarly research, although that of infant baptism still awaits a more nuanced interpretation. From a close reading of Chinese as well as Western texts historian Michelle King has arrived at a number of revisionist conclusions. She confirms that infanticide was practised in particular areas of China in the later nineteenth and early twentieth centuries and was more likely to be practised on female infants, but shows that it was not as widespread as the scientific and religious literature, including the Holy Childhood Association's literature, promoted. The practice was, moreover, debated and criticised in moral debates among Chinese social and intellectual leaders: it was not simply accepted. King draws attention to the very significant parallels between the culturally different infant abandonment practices that existed across Western Europe, Russia and China at different times. They

---

70 See Henrietta Harrison, "A Penny for the Little Chinese" *passim*.

71 King, *Between Birth and Death*, p. 8.

varied in the form they took (the Chinese in relation to gender, for example),[72] but all had their common root in the poverty of people who had more children than they could support, something she suggests which would have been an unpalatable truth for the donors to the Holy Childhood Association.[73] Her interpretation brings us back to the work of the Daughters. To read their own accounts of child rescue in China is to be reminded that their infant 'rescue' work began as a result of the child neglect and the high rate of infant deaths in seventeenth- and eighteenth-century France and continued into the nineteenth-century in many places, including Britain and Ireland.[74] There are even parallels between the accusations the Sisters faced of being baby murderers in England and the same charges made in China, not least because of the high rates of death among the very poorly nourished and often sick infants brought to them.[75]

But what did the Sisters of the British Province themselves make of this *Médecin Baptiseur* aspect of their mission? In her life of Agnes Berkeley, Sister Margaret Hughes' clearly wished to correct misunderstandings that had arisen from pressures to fund-raise. 'Some people', she wrote, 'have the idea that the Sisters roam about the countryside merely looking for dying babies to baptise and doing nothing in effect to cure sick babies. This is not true. They go to nurse the sick poor in their houses....the Sisters baptise only when they feel sure that the baby will not recover...' Their real work was to 'nurse and restore to health a sick mother or father with a big family'.[76] She wanted to emphasise the restorative and ameliorative activities of the Sisters in nursing, teaching, providing food and a livelihood.

Yet we must recognise that the ministry of baptism was an important dimension of the work of the Sisters in China and that it fired up support at home. In Catholic doctrine the administration of the sacrament of baptism was the ultimate salvific work that could be performed for anyone who was dying unbaptised: for a baby it was believed to guarantee a certain passage to paradise that would otherwise be denied.[77] In life and death situations baptism became the one sacrament that missionary women (or laymen) could perform equally with the ordained. The exercise of this responsibility marked an important difference between the ministry

---

72 D.E. Mungello, *Drowning Girls in China: Female Infanticide since 1650* (Lanham, MD: Rowan and Littlehead, 2008) is an excellent study of the subject.

73 King, *Between Birth and Death*, p.8, who cites extensively from the literature on infant abandonment in Europe. See the important study Cliona Rattigan, *Single Mohers and Infanticide in Ireland 1900-1950* (Dublin: Irish Academic Press, 2012).

74 See, for example, Rachel Ginnis Fuchs, *Abandoned Children: Foundlings and Child Welfare in Nineteenth-Century France* (Albany: State University of New York Press, 1984); A. Kiday, *A History of Infanticide in Britain, c.1600 to the Present* (London: Palgrave Macmillan, 2013); Catherine Panter-Brick and Malcolm T. Smith (eds.), *Abandoned Children* (Cambridge: Cambridge University Press, 2000).

75 See Ch. 7.

76 *Sister Xavier Berkeley,* pp.76-77.

77 This was the theology of the 'Limbo of Infants', never an official teaching but not denied either.

of Catholic and Protestant women missionaries. Although so much emphasis was placed on this practice in the literature and narrative about China, it was practised on occasion by the Sisters in all places. The emphasis on baptising infants to save their souls and to care for them in their dying days held the same imperative for Sister Henriette Chatelain in London during the 1870s as it did for Dorothea Bowlby in 1920s China. It was the way the practice was fetishised in scientific, historical and religious literature about China, along with the gender specificity of Chinese infanticide and child abandonment practices and the counting of souls saved which made it appear altogether specific.

Sister Berkeley, who had strong views about the priority of health reform and the education of girls, was more likely to have talked about these activities than about hordes of 'angel baptisms' when she 'entertained the Mill Hill seminary Sisters at recreation with the wonders of her mission' during her visit to England in 1923.[78] We cannot know the content of those conversations, but we do know that they had an immediate impact. No fewer than 70 Sisters of the British Province offered themselves for China in 1923. The first group of four travelled back with Sister Berkeley but others followed during the 1920s and early 1930s, sustaining the Province's strong commitment to the China Mission. Interest was kept high when only two years after Berkeley's visit home the provincial house played host to two Chinese Sisters. Their recital and singing of the community prayers in their own language made a deep an impression on the seminary Sisters, helping them to grasp the global nature of the Company to which they belonged.[79] The work of the Chinese Sisters, only glimpsed in the English biographies, had been a vital part of the Company's Mission since the first Chinese Sister entered in 1864. Most of the British and Irish missionary Sisters worked alongside them and the work depended on them in many ways, as Xavier Berkeley's long community relationship with Sister Pauline Souen or the work of Sister Louise Liou, for example, makes clear.[80] When the last 75 Western Sisters had to leave China in 1953 there were 287 Chinese Daughters of Charity left to live out their vows as best they could under the hostile Communist regime. More than 70 of these Sisters were still alive and self-identifying as Daughters of Charity in the mid-1990s when the Company's superiors visited discreetly for the first time since the expulsions.[81] Together with a number of recent entrants at various stages of formation they had already been quietly supported for some time by the vice-Province of Taiwan, recently established with this responsibility.[82] As the remarkable faith stories

---

78 O'Driscoll, 'Sidelights' p.67. 13-4-3 DCMH.

79 ibid, p. 82.

80 *Sister Xavier Berkeley*, p.74 and pp.174-185.

81 'Evolution of the Company in the Last Six Years', address of Superioress General Elizondo to the General Assembly of the Company, 1997, p.3 and p.16. There were 2 Sisters under vows, 6 seminary Sisters and 5 postulants in 1996. 15-3 DCMH.

82 ibid., p. 16.

of these women were told it became clear that, despite the efforts of the regime, the chain linking the youngest entrants in the late twentieth century back to the missionary Sisters of 1848 had never been broken.[83]

Third and fourth generations: Australia, Ethiopia and Nigeria

During the 1930s the Province's main contribution to the Company's missionary work came from its agreement to sponsor and take responsibility for mission in a specific country. In 1926 the Province made a new foundation in Australia, sponsoring it until the community there was granted provincial status in 1963. Just as this process reached its end in 1963, a new mission began in Nigeria. Between these two initiatives there was one other: Ethiopia. Although it was only in 1966 that the Province accepted responsibility for the work of the Company in Ethiopia, it had played an increasing role there since the later 1950s, taking on a mission originally founded from Italy but partly managed from France after 1936. Both Ethiopia and Nigeria became Provinces in 2001.

Australia

Around the time in 1926 that the Central House community hosted the two Chinese Sisters, it also welcomed a visitor from Australia; Michael O'Farrell, Bishop of Bathurst in New South Wales. O'Farrell was a confrère of the Congregation of the Mission and made the journey to Mill Hill to ask the Province to begin a mission of the Company in Australia in his diocese. A favourable decision was made by the provincial council in May and approved by the general council. Once the contract with Bishop O'Farrell had been signed it was only a matter of months before the first group of Sisters departed. The foundation was begun in Orange County, New South Wales on 6 December. Over the next ten years a further 28 Sisters transferred from the British Province to Australia. The Daughters in Australia opened 11 additional houses in New South Wales in a twenty-year period, later extending their work to Perth and Roebourne, Brisbane, Melbourne and Adelaide. Australia became a vice-Province of Britain in 1936 and its seminary and central house were founded in Sydney in 1939. Full provincial status was granted to Australia in 1963.

In her personal history of the Australian Province Emily Rowe (Sister Teresa) begins by confronting two difficult questions about the work of the Company on the Antipodean continent. Why come to Australia at all, since this would be a mission primarily to the already baptised? And why come when there were so

---

83 Prunty and Sullivan, *Daughters of Charity in Ireland*, p.231. Personal conversations held by the author in England and in China during a two-week study visit to China in 2006 with Cultural Exchange with China, an organisation of the Catholic Church in Britain. At least one Sister of the British province went to teach English in China in the 1990s.

many other sisters and congregations already ploughing the Australian furrow?[84] As Rosa MacGinley's listing of women religious in Australia shows there were 32 different congregations of sisters in this British dependency when the Daughters arrived. The first – the Irish Sisters of Charity – had left Ireland for the colony in 1838. Indigenous (settler) religious communities were founded in the nineteenth century and flourished.[85] In MacGinley's survey the pioneer Daughters of 1926 are sufficiently late in the day to be located in a chapter entitled 'Consolidation and New Initiatives'.[86] Reflecting further on the questions raised by Sister Rowe helps us to understand aspects of the Company's missionary priorities and the history of mission more broadly conceived, as well as the Daughters' position within the mission of the Australian Catholic Church.

Bishop O'Farrell's request for Daughters of Charity in Australia was not the first. Forty years earlier, in 1886, the Company had been approached by Cardinal Moran, Archbishop of Sydney, for the same reason. The superiors general had declined his invitation. In the community it is understood that their refusal stemmed from the belief that 'there were no poor in Australia'.[87] This may be the belief, but there were other factors at play. Given the status of Australia as a British colony, the obvious course of action in 1886 would have been for the British and Irish Province to take responsibility for the mission on behalf of the Company. Not only was the majority of its migrant and settler population British or Irish at this time but, as a consequence of Cardinal Cullen's militantly missionary approach to Australia, Irish bishops, priests and religious dominated the Australian Catholic Church.[88] The appointment in 1884 of Patrick Moran, who was Cullen's nephew and private secretary, as third Archbishop of Sydney and first Australian cardinal, represented the zenith of Cullen's policy for the Australian Church. Moran was 'to lead what he termed the "Irish spiritual empire"'.[89] A year after his installation Moran invited two of his old Vincentian priest friends from Castleknock to join him in Australia. They conducted retreats and helped Moran to establish a new school – 'the Castleknock of Australia' - which became the base from which the Congregation of the Mission grew in Australia.[90] It was this connection, a powerful

---

84 Typescript History of the Australian Province (1989) originally compiled by Sister Teresa Rowe and prepared for publication in serial form in the provincial newsletter by Sister Louise Dilly. 7-3 DCMH.

85 MacGinley, *A Dynamic of Hope*, p.349, Table 1.

86 Ibid., p. 298.

87 Typescript History of the Australian Province, p.2. 7-3 DCMH.

88 James Jupp (ed.), *The Australian People: An Encyclopedia of the Nation, Its People and Their Origins* (Cambridge: Cambridge University Press, 2001), p. 461.

89 Lindsay J. Proudfoot and Dianne P. Hall, *Imperial Spaces: Placing the Irish and Scots in Colonial Australia* (Manchester: Manchester University Press, 2011), p.209. See also A.E. Cahill's entry on Patrick Francis Moran (1830-1911) in the *Australian Dictionary of Biography* db.anu.edu.au/biography/moran-patrick-francis-7648, (accessed 17 May 2016). MacGinley, *A Dynamic of Hope*, discusses Moran's impact on religious congregations, pp. 223ff.

90 Mary Purcell, *The Story of the Vincentians* (Dublin: All Hallows College, 1973), p. 174.

and promising one for the work of the Company, that had lain behind Moran's 1886 invitation to the Daughters.

An Australian mission would no doubt have been considered overly ambitious at a time when the Province of Great Britain itself had been established for only a year; but a holding answer could have been given, as so often happened if the Company had a strategic interest in a project. Not only did this not happen but in 1908 when Michael Gallagher, Bishop of Golburne Diocese, asked for Sisters for a hospital, he too received a negative response. The Company's superiors showed little enthusiasm for a mission to Australia or, indeed, for any of the extensive parts of the globe where the imperial or colonial language spoken was English rather than French or Spanish. Their lack of interest in serving those parts of the world where the dominant Western power was Britain (India, Canada, Australia, South Africa, West Africa) might seem a predictable position for a French religious community, but it was not inevitable. Many modern Francophone congregations were among the earliest missionaries to these regions. Some, like Sophie Barat, founder of the Religious of the Sacred Heart, were motivated to come to Britain and Ireland as much for their missionary potential in the British Empire as for their own sakes. 'I was interrupted in this letter', Barat told one correspondent in 1842, 'by a call to see the bishop of New Holland who is asking me for a colony in Sydney at once...Everywhere so many souls to be brought to the Sacred Heart! As the language there is English, if in fact we had a house in Ireland or England, as we would have plenty of subjects [entrants], they would be able to supply the various missions. So for two reasons the most pressing foundation is that in the British Isles and we must make one at whatever cost.'[91] One of the main reasons for the arrival of the Daughters of the Cross from Liège in Britain in 1858 was for the advantage it would bring to the community's new mission in India.[92] In Australia itself two French congregations, the Sisters of St Joseph of the Apparition and the Good Shepherd nuns, were among the pioneers.[93]

The Company not only declined the first Australian opportunity but did the same when invited to begin a mission in India in 1910. Lady Anne Kerr, one of the Province's steadfast benefactors, offered to finance a hospital for poor women in India. The provincial council turned down the invitation, regretting that 'it is necessary to refuse this good work'.[94] Vincentians did not arrive in India until 1922 and there were no Daughters of Charity there until 1940, and none in Canada until

---

91 Barbara Hogg, 'Society of the Sacred Heart in England, 1842-1870' (undated typescript), p. 3. Religious of the Sacred Heart Archives, Roehampton, London.

92 The Faithful Companions of Jesus responded to a call from Vital Grandin, the (French) Bishop of the diocese of St Albert in Canada in 1882, who knew that they 'had some English-speaking sisters'. Their Superior General replied that they would 'do it for God' and sent 18 predominantly British and Irish sisters between 1883 and 1885. *Journeying through a Century: Sister Pioneers, 1883-1983* (Edmonton, AL: FCJ, 1983), p. 11.

93 MacGinley, *A Dynamic of Hope*.

94 Provincial Council Minutes, Vol V. 28 July 1910. 9-5-0-2-1 DCMH

1948.[95] In the nineteenth century the Company's missionary work avoided those places where Anglo-French colonial rivalry had ended in British victory in order to concentrate on those where French colonial power or the influence of Spain and Portugal extended. Far from learning English, Sisters on the missions were expected to know French in addition to the language of the mission country. It seems reasonable to conclude that under Étienne and extending later, the Company's Gallicanism was reinforced and tinged with a form of French nationalism that was not necessarily shared by other Francophone women's religious communities.[96]

However, by the later 1920s the world of empires was changing: the creation of the Irish Free State in 1922, with its semi-autonomous 'Dominion' status, had presaged that change. The Balfour Declaration of 1926 recognised Ireland, Australia and New Zealand, Canada, India, Ceylon (Sri Lanka), Pakistan and South Africa among others as 'autonomous Communities among the British Empire'. Moreover, the number of Sisters in the British Province was experiencing its most rapid increase at this time and the Province felt it could send Sisters. The first four Sisters who went on the Australian mission in 1926 - Chicago-born and Irish-raised Hannah MacGuire, Elizabeth Fagan from County Antrim, Margaret Valentine from Liverpool, whose blood sister, Alice, had recently died on mission in Egypt, and Mary Leonard from Drogheda – expected and received a warm welcome from the Vincentian community. They were overwhelmed, however, by the unexpected support extended by other communities of religious sisters: the Sisters of Mercy,[97] the Dominicans,[98] and the Sisters of St Joseph: it was a lesson learned early about the openness and hospitality of a new frontier society.[99] Unsurprisingly they also found plenty of people in poverty to serve, even more than was usual because of the global economic depression. Nor was there any lack of 'unchurched' Catholics for them to bring back to the faith, or seekers to instruct and encourage. The work of evangelisation and conversion, as the number of 'unchurched' Catholics in Victorian Britain had shown, was never confined to so-called barbarian lands; much of the Daughters' daily activity was missionary at heart, whether it was in Britain, Australia, China or Ethiopia.

The Sisters' initial visiting and school work in William Street, Orange was soon augmented by a boys' orphanage, Croagh Patrick, in Orange. A second group of four Sisters travelled out in 1927 and a third in 1929. In 1930 a fourth group took on the management of a large hostel for working girls and women in Victoria, a crèche

95 An earlier attempt to make a foundation in Canada had not succeeded but there were a number of congregations in Canada, for example the Sisters of Charity of Providence (1843) who followed the Company Rule.

96 See the discussion of Etienne's Gallicanism and the constitutional Gallicanism of the Company in Edward Udivoc, *Jean-Baptiste Étienne and the Vincentian Revival* (1996). *Vincentian eBooks.* Book 3.
http://via.library.depaul.edu/vincentian_ebooks/3.

97 'Typescript History of the Australian Province', p.5. 7-3 DCMH.

98 ibid., Ch. 4.

99 ibid., Ch. 5.

and parish visiting in Woolloomooloo, one of the most deprived parts of Sydney. Another group arrived in 1933 to manage a second boys' orphanage in Mayfield, New South Wales and the last pre-war group (1936) comprised Sisters destined to be office holders for an Australian seminary and to staff Central House, which opened in its own new building in 1939. From 1936, when the seminary opened, it was no longer necessary for entrants to travel to Britain or Ireland.

'The Australian seminary was modelled closely on the one in Mill Hill', as Sister Judith Greville remembered from the early 1950s era. 'Because of the great distance between us the 't's were crossed and the 'i's dotted earnestly.' They ate 'fried bread or porridge for breakfast on alternate mornings' and had 'cocoa for supper', even in sub-tropical summers.[100] In 1926 it was the culture of the British Province that was transferred to Australia, a culture that had seemed semi-French to the British and Irish Sisters and all too British to the French visitatrice Hannezo. Its 'Frenchness' was now further challenged in the translation to what by this time was a genuinely Australian society with its 'own distinctive social context'.[101] By 1911 as a result in the fall-off in migration 85% of the population was already Australian-born. Australia was both familiar and different for the migrant Daughters. From the outset, for example, the Sisters in Australia were able to operate within a Vincentian (and largely Irish-Australian) world: their first retreat, in December 1926, was given by the Vincentian Father Rossiter, whose own family were their neighbours in Orange. Fund-raising for their projects was led by Dr Maurice O'Reilly, Vincentian provincial in Australia, and they had the support of several Vincentian bishops.[102] But the level of support given by Church and by the people was of a kind that was simply never experienced in Britain. For example, when the women's hostel, St Anne's Hall, was opened the Solemn Blessing was attended by the Apostolic Delegate, three archbishops and three bishops and 'a huge crowd' who 'flocked to inspect the house'.[103] Whenever the Sisters began a new project, their house, no matter how simple or austere, was handed over to them spotlessly cleaned by the women of the parish or mission. Differences of another kind reminded them they were not at home. Distances between places were on another scale while, in the words of Sister Judith Greville, 'Nature was never very far away.' She wrote memorably of the everyday presence of the natural world in which

> A colony of fruit bats circled round the stair well on the top landing and were sometimes seen hanging upside-down on the brass rails around the Sisters' beds...The children brought turtles to school...if left over-night...they would rummage in forgotten wastepaper baskets and upend anything in sight. Frogs were extremely vocal night and day,

---

100 Judith Greville, 'The Australian Connection: A Daughter of Charity remembers, 1954-1976', p. 368.

101 MacGinley, *A Dynamic of Hope*, p. 279.

102 'History of the Australian Province', p.7. 7-3 DCMH.

103 ibid., p.13.

especially in the cisterns where they held family parties, or sat in pairs on the toilet seat, waiting for other guests.[104]

Despite the welcome and support, there was still loneliness for early British and Irish Sisters on the Australian mission, as there had been in China. Hannah (Sister Catherine) McGuire, previously Sister Servant at Drogheda, who had been named to lead the Australian mission and was later its first vice-visitatrice, experienced an acute sense of isolation. Just over a year into the mission she lost her 'best friend' when Bishop O'Farrell collapsed and died on a visit to the community. Only a few months later she learned that Sister Mary Boyle, the Province's visitatrice whom she had known well, had died in the second year of her office. This loss had to be borne at a distance, separate from the rest of the community family. Moreover, as a consequence of this news the provincial director, John O'Connell, at the time on his way to visit Sister McGuire and the Australian Sisters for the first time, turned back for London.

One of the Province's concerns had been that such a late arrival might adversely affect recruitment because other communities were well established. Entrants were indeed slow to apply: it was almost ten years before the first appeared. New groups from Britain were regularly sent, therefore, to take up the work being offered to the Sisters: 31 in total between 1926 and 1954. Their ethnic composition more closely reflected the overall balance in the Province: 7 English-born Sisters, 19 Irish, 3 Scottish, 1 Welsh and 1 American citizen. In time there were more vocations to the Australian community but perhaps they were never as many as might have been if the Sisters had been established earlier: in 1951, twenty-five years after its foundation, there were 70 Sisters in the vice-Province.

Ethiopia

The Province's connection to Australia is more readily explained than that to Ethiopia. Ethiopia was not on the Sisters' horizon in any way in 1950 but the place, its people, its tragedies and development in the second half of the century became part of the lives of all the Province's Sisters from the late 1950s, whether or not they were on the mission itself. There were several reasons why this level of provincial commitment and involvement took place. Timing was important. The Sisters had recently 'lost' China, a mission that had long occupied a central place in the Province's imagined community beyond its own islands. But more compelling than this from the early 1950s, and most notably through Pope Pius XII's address to an international assembly of teaching sisters gathered in Rome, the papacy increasingly emphasised the need for Catholic sisters to be more outwardly turned and to be more evangelical.[105]

---

104 Greville, 'The Australian Connection', pp. 371-373.

105 See commentaries in Skinner, Keller and Reuter, *Encyclopaedia of Women and Religion in Modern America*, (Indiana University Press, 2006).

At a time when the new Communist regime was persecuting Christians in China and when the spread of Marxism-Leninism was finding a ready following in parts of Africa and Latin America, Pius XII issued his encyclical *Evangelii Praecones* (EP 1951), translated as 'On the promotion of Catholic missions'. He used it to emphasise the need for the tenets of Catholic social teaching and the traditional forms of Catholic Action to be combined with the work of evangelisation and of charity. On the one hand the Pope urged the importance of training and, in particular, of more trained medical missionary work on the ground, and on the other, pressed the case for local churches and their people to have control over their own affairs, supported but not dominated by outside missionaries.

Writing of charity in places of extreme poverty around the world, the encyclical noted 'Charity indeed can remedy to a certain extent many unjust social conditions. But that is not enough. For in the first place there must be justice which should prevail and be put into practice.' [106] It went on to teach how the role of Catholic missionaries was to put into practice the Church's ideals of the 'dignity of the human person and the right of all people to share the goods of the earth'.[107] Other aspects of the encyclical's tone and content were also fresh: its commitment to qualifications and preparation as well as zeal, and its straightforward recognition that sisters were missionaries, integral to the Church's endeavours.[108] Pius XII followed this encyclical with another in 1957, *Fidei Donum*, dedicated to the subject of Catholic missions in Africa and to addressing mission in the context of Africa's experience of 'such speedy changes in social, economic, and political life that the entire future of that continent appears to depend upon their outcome'.[109] These teachings were not remote and unread: they were immediately summarised and commented upon in magazines and periodicals read by Church personnel and lay people.[110] The orientation of papal teachings during the 1950s was a forerunner of later Vatican II and post-Vatican II teaching, such as Pope Paul VI's *Evangelii Nutiandi* (1975), which 'introduced the word "evangelisation" as a rich, complex and dynamic term' according to Frans Wijsen. Together these teachings transformed the Church from being defensive and separatist to being willing to form relationships and enter into dialogue for the sake of converting the world.[111]

---

106 *Evangelii Praecones* 1951, paragraph 51.

107 Arij Roest Crollius et. al., *Creative Inculturation and the Unity of Faith* (Rome: Editrice Pontificia Universitá Gregoriana), p. 15.

108 *Evangelii Praecones* Paragraph 47.

109 *Fidei Donum*, Paragrah 13.

110 *Fidei Donum* was referred to in the Company's monthy newsletter, *The Echo of the Mother House* for March 1957, DCMH. See also Timothy Connolly, 'Pope Pius XII and Foreign Missions', *The Furrow*, Vol. 8, No.3 (March 1957), pp. 150-155.

111 Frans Josef Wijsen, *Mission is a Must': Intercultural Theology and the Mission of the Church* (Amsterdam and New York: Rodopi, 2002), p. 109.

Such teachings inspired many communities of women to engage in missionary activity for the first time or to increase their existing commitment. In the Company's case it was more a matter of renewing and refashioning an existing dimension of the community's vocation. The new Vatican vision was seized with energy at the Company's General Assembly of 1968. Papers on 'The Missionary Vocation of the Daughters of Charity' were written and their content summarised for circulation throughout the Company, bringing the present and past into relationship.[112] Even so, it was a bold step for the British Province to commit itself so fully in the matter of human and material resources at the very time when its own underlying demographic trend was towards ageing and reduction in numbers, and then to sustain and develop its commitment after the creation of the Irish Province in 1970 further reduced its capacity.[113] To understand this level of boldness we must look to the part played by individual personalities: the eighth and ninth visitatrices of the Province, Sisters Anne Whalen (1952–1966) and Gertrude Andrew (1966-1978), and the remarkable missionary Sisters; Theodore Cubitt, Margaret Cunnane, Angela Murray, Helen Lally, Mary Dixon, Zoe O'Neill, Jane Heery and Barbara Quilty among them. More than 40 Sisters of the British Province served in Ethiopia-Eritrea between 1954 and 2001, many for long periods. National composition is shown in Table 9.5.

	English	Irish	Scottish	French	Other
Eritrea	1	1			
Ethiopia	19	18	3		4
Nigeria	1	7	2		
	23	26	5		5

9.5: UK SISTERS IN ETHIOPIA, ERITREA AND NIGERIA
BY NATIONAL ORIGINS

The mission field has always been a place (physical and metaphysical) where particular individual Christians both found and fully expressed their personalities and gifts. In the nineteenth century and even up to the 1970s it could also be a place unlike any other for less conventional women to feel at home, perhaps in a way that was not possible when they were more literally 'at home'. Her

---

112 For example, Joseph Jamet CM 'The Missionary Vocation of the Daughters of Charity', *The Echo of the Mother House* (February, 1967), pp.107-115. 1-5 DCMH.

113 This is discussed more fully in Ch. 11.

biographer hints that this was so for Agnes Berkeley who 'could not sew' and was so uninterested in her own appearance that her ancient patched habit was stripped from her back when she visited the mother house on her way to England and a new one made (which she did not wear). There was a physical reason she was described by local Chinese people as 'Big Momma' and the 'Big English Sister'.[114] Sister Hughes observed that 'difference in nationality sometimes brought opposition' from French Sisters to Sister Berkeley's way of working.[115] She could 'be misunderstood' because she thought nothing of what was extreme behaviour for others (such as fasting until 2.00 p.m. if there was a chance of receiving Communion) and unwittingly made demands on them that they found very hard.[116] Yet, such was her ardour and vigour that she was their first nurse when they fell ill.[117]

The Province's mission in Ethiopia began with another such individual, Theodore (Sister Gabriel) Cubitt. It was her presence in Ethiopia which gave reality to the Church's teachings on mission in the modern world for the Province, thus pushing open a door through which it stepped into missionary partnership in Africa. Sister Cubitt was among the group of Daughters who had stayed in China during World War II. She had arrived there in 1939 at the age of forty to serve in a new leper colony after a preparatory orientation period in Cochin China (Vietnam). As the leper colony location became too risky she had to be content with working in a Shanghai hospital. Interred for two years in a Japanese prisoner-of-war camp between 1943 and 1945 she lost one lung to TB but remained totally committed to a missionary life and never returned again to England. When she was expelled from China along with other foreign missionaries in 1951 the Company placed her first in Egypt, and then in 1954 asked her to go to Ethiopia as the first English-speaking Daughter to serve there.

Roman Catholics comprised a small minority of the Ethiopian population in the 1950s. Arguably the first nation in the world to accept Christianity, Ethiopia's majority church has always been in the Coptic Orthodox tradition. Vincentian missioners had been active in the country from 1837. One of them, an Italian Lazarist, St Justin de Jacobis, played a significant role in revitalising Catholicism there in the mid nineteenth century and was canonised for his heroic sanctity.[118] In terms of European influence, Ethiopia has the distinction of being the only African nation never to have been colonised, its annexation to the Italian colony of Eritrea as the largest component of Mussolini's Africa Orientale Italiana (AOI)

---

114 *Sister Xavier Berkeley,*p.68, pp. 73-74, p. 124.

115 Ibid., p.67.

116 Ibid., p.68, p.112, p.122 and p. 206.

117 Ibid.,p.144 and p.205 quoting one of the Chinese Sisters: 'When you were ill she would nurse you as your own mother would.'

118 His biography was translated into English by Lady Herbert of Lea: A. Devin, *Abysinnia and its Apostle* (London: Burns and Oates, 1867).

being short-lived and superficial. Even so, given the Italian colonial presence to the north in Eritrea and to the south in Somalia, it was Italian Catholicism that formed the most significant European Catholic presence in the region in 1950.

Daughters of Charity from France had first gone to the capital Addis Ababa in 1927 where they opened a girls' school. The school was allowed to continue when Haile Selassie was crowned Emperor in 1930, but in 1936 during the Italian occupation of Ethiopia, when the Emperor was forced into exile, these French Sisters were also forced to leave. Their primary and secondary schools were handed over to one of the Italian Provinces of the Company to manage. Italian occupation ended in 1941 when the Allies led by Commonwealth and British forces were victorious in their East African campaign. Emperor Haile Selassie, recognised as the legitimate ruler by the Allies and always predisposed to favour the growth of British influence in his country as a counter-balance to Italian and Russian influence in neighbouring Eritrea, returned to govern Ethiopia in 1941. His ambitions in the region, which included the annexation of Italian Eritrea, were acceded to by the United States and Britain in 1950 on the grounds of 'the strategic interests of the United States...and...world peace'.[119] In reality they created the conditions for continuous warfare and enmity in the region, conditions that affected everyone including transnational organisations working there.

It was not until the end of World War II that the Italian Daughters returned the property to their French companions who then resumed the mission but asked for more assistance from the Company's *mission ad gentes.* Theodore Cubitt's availability for this mission seemed providential to the Company's superiors and to Sister Gabriel herself. She was from an establishment English family but also a member of the Italian aristocracy, her father being a member of the Cubitt building family and her mother an Italian contessa. Already fluent in French and Italian with a facility for languages, she had proved herself on the mission field as a dedicated nurse and natural communicator across nations and social classes. At the age of fifty-seven Sister Gabriel took to this new mission immediately, serving in the dispensary just opened by the Company. Her immediate contribution was to recognise that she must go out to the people in the countryside who were too sick to travel. She became a one-woman peripatetic clinic. The figure of the tall sister (she was just under six feet in height) with the butterfly hat, mounted on an elderly white horse, soon became well known in the district. It was not long before she began to meet people with leprosy and to dress their wounds. In 1956 she was joined by Sister Margaret Cunnane. Together they pioneered a new medical-based work for the Daughters in Ethiopia, treating adults and babies and

---

119 John Foster Dulles, 'From the point of view of justice, the opinions of the Eritrean people must receive consideration. *Nevertheless* the strategic interest of the United States in the Red Sea basin and the considerations of security and world peace make it necessary that the country has to be linked with our *ally* Ethiopia.' quoted Bereket H. Selassie (ed.), *Eritrea and the United Nations and Other Essays* (Trenton, NJ: The Red Sea Press, 1989), note 5, p. 155, citing Linda Heiden (June 1978)'. 'The Eritrean Struggle for Independence', *Monthly Review Press*, 30 (2), p. 15.

later developing their treatment and support for victims of leprosy, still working as part of a vice-Province under Paris.

Sisters Cubitt and Cunnane began to make a case to their own provincial leaders that the British Province become should more involved in the Ethiopia mission:

> there are ordinary day-to-day problems in a country where there is absolutely no state-aid for widows, orphans, the old, the blind, the mentally ill...There are many cases where these poor people would die of starvation and exposure if the Sisters didn't help them, and often this help has to continue over a long period.[120]

Even though the British Province was beginning to feel the impact of reduced numbers of young Sisters, its superiors asked for volunteers for Ethiopia. Two more Sisters were sent in 1958 along with donations of money and goods, marking the beginning of regular material support. Gradually the Ethiopian international mission community, managed from Paris, transmuted into a British and Irish community while that in Eritrea continued to be managed by the Naples Province. In 1962 an aspirant from Ethiopia, Sister Zoudé, travelled to join the provincial seminary in Mill Hill and Dublin, the first in a line of Ethiopian and Eritrean women to make the journey and experience the profound cultural challenge involved. Over the next three decades, two dozen others followed, often for shorter periods but sometimes to complete two-and three-year-long courses in nursing and midwifery.

In March 1966 the mother house formally asked the British Province to consider taking direct responsibility for the Company's houses in Ethiopia. Initially the council declined, not least because it had opened a mission in Nigeria in 1963. But in February 1967 it agreed to a pressing second request, laying down firm conditions for doing so. They would not include the Italian-Eritrean house in their responsibilities and would manage the Ethiopian houses as part of the British Province and not as a vice-Province. Sister Angela Murray, provincial councillor, was appointed to a new role as Councillor for Ethiopia for twelve months during which time she made a number of critical decisions about the appointment and placement of Sisters.[121] This temporary role was formalised as Regional Superior thereafter. The tensions between Eritrea and Ethiopia made the Province cautious. Added to this challenge the formation programme needed particular attention, since what was suitable in Britain was not transferrable to Ethiopia: the Sisters responsible had to make adjustments just as the new entrants did.

---

120 Letter February 1957 from Sisters Cubitt and Cunnane to Central House. Sister Cubitt's letters from 1954 onwards were regularly been reproduced in the monthly newsletter, *The Echo of the Mother House*. 1-5 DCMH.

121 Provincial Council Minutes, Vol. XX. 18 March 1967 and 16 September 16, 1967. 9-5-0-1-2 DCMH

On the other hand, for a short period, the handover benefited from the background support it received from Haile Selassie's government. Only the previous year the Emperor had bestowed his highest personal award, the Haile Selassie Humanitarian Award, on Theodore Cubitt, who became the first foreign woman to receive it. The formal citation noted that 'Sister Gabriel and her colleagues have sacrificed all personal gain for the good of the less fortunate and given invaluable service. The Poly Clinic operated by her has treated 324,080 people over the last thirteen years, treated 19,000 babies over the same period and has brought much needed relief and loving care to thousands of Ethiopians...200 leprosy victims are regularly visited and treated.' [122]

What was not in the formal citation but was recalled by Sister Maeve O'Brien was the fact that the people with leprosy whose sores she dressed – and whom she always called 'my special friends' – lived in the large cemetery of Medhane Alem because they were not permitted to mix with other people. Nor was there any special provision until Sister Cubitt was able to get sufficient funds to establish it. 'I was so shocked and taken aback' Sister Maeve remembered with honesty,'I couldn't believe they were human beings and that they were living on top of the dead...I felt so nauseated and repulsed.' But, she continued, 'everything changed when Sister Gabriel came amongst them. These disfigured faces were transformed by smiles.' [123] Some years later, when Cardinal Basil Hume visited Ethiopia as part of the global humanitarian response to the great famine of 1983–1985, Sister Gabriel took him to see her'special friends', those with leprosy.'When I watched her going among those people the remarkable happened,' he recalled when the news came of her death, 'I saw etched into her face the face of Christ.' [124]

By 1979, following the civil war that ended in victory for the Ethiopian Communist side, the Daughters' Ethiopian Regional community was operating across Eritrea and Ethiopia. It had houses in Addis Ababa, Alitena and Mekele in Tigray Province, Bonga in Kaffa Province and Dembidollo close to the Sudanese border. A total of 31 Sisters (15 Ethiopian, 12 from Britain and Ireland, and 1 each contributed by France, Australia, the Philippines and the Netherlands) had developed a wide range of medical, social development and educational works, according to the local needs. In the remote mountain region of Alitena this was a boarding-school for girls who came from miles around, medical work out in the field and a clinic funded by the Catholic international organisation, Caritas. In Bonga the Sisters 'had the upgrading of the women as a priority', which meant training in agriculture and domestic science, social welfare and home economics. Their clinic concentrated on mothers and babies but there was also a clinic hospital

122 Citation. Sister Cubitt Personal File. 10-2 DCMH.

123 Maeve O'Brien, 'The Tall Woman: the life of Sister Gabriel Cubitt D.C. O.B.E. 1897-1989' Typescript, 2010, pp. 5-6. 7-5 10-2 DCMH.

124 *The Universe*, 11 September 1994. Reports of her work were also carried in *The Guardian*, 26 November 1976; *Daily Mail* 'At 87, the Angel with so much still to do', 15 November 1984; *Today* newspaper, 'The heiress who grew to be a saint', 15 June 1986.

with out-stations in the countryside. The community in Mekele ran one clinic in town and another outside attended by large numbers of people, a primary school, and a workroom to provide employment for women. It also had a ministry to the refugee camp first established during the 1973 famine.

An important aspect of the work of the Mekele Sisters was the formation programme for young Ethiopian women who were usually in need of primary and then secondary education as a preparatory stage to postulancy. Some of the first Eritrean-Ethiopian women to enter the community played crucial roles in this preparation and in sustaining the community's outreach in rural or politically sensitive districts. Sister Tsion Weldegiorgis (entered 1955), for example, served in this way in Bonga, making use of the six or seven local languages that she spoke,[125] as did Sisters Marie Tesfae and Dashe Beyesse. Taken together, the Sisters' service blended development, aid, medical, educational and catechetical activities. 'All in all, we are face to face with reality,' the community reported to the Provincial Assembly held in London in 1979, 'and in spite of some heavy strains from within and without, we have a healthy community and spiritual life.'

These strains, particularly in the northern communities, were considerable. There had been twenty years of fighting and food shortages. Conflict over the kind of nation Ethiopians wanted had led to a devastating civil war ending in the establishment of a Communist regime in 1974 and the imprisonment of the Emperor. There had been the famine of 1973, and even when that was over levels of poverty had increased. Unknown to the Sisters who wrote in 1979 to share the joys and needs of their mission with the Sisters gathered in the Provincial Assembly in England, the devastating and globally infamous famine of 1983–1985 was round the corner. But in 1979 the concerns were political and economic. The Communist regime removed some of their equipment, forbade or restricted movement between houses and threatened expatriates (as they called themselves) with expulsion. One of the main points put forward by the newly established domestic assemblies (local consultative meetings of the Sisters) in the Report from Ethiopia, concerned the need for a new form of governance that would suit the different situations of Eritrea and Ethiopia and help them to overcome the obstructions put in their way by the regime. The story of the way the Province responded to this request, and how it prepared the Ethiopian Sisters 'to assume full responsibility',[126] belongs in the post-Vatican II decades and deserves its own history. Even so, we can note how the comprehensive and analytical 1979 Report from Ethiopia and its full consideration by the new decision-making Provincial Assembly not only indicates the way the community had changed in the years following the Second Vatican Council, but underlines the closeness of the relationship between the Province and its mission in Ethiopia.

---

125 *Dictionary of African Christian Biography* at www.dacb.org (accessed August 2014).

126 'House Reports from Ethiopia' for the Provincial Assembly 1979, p.56. 15-4-3-1979 1-7 #10 DCMH.

Nigeria

In September 1963 three Sisters from the British Province, Margaret Hughes (Sister Gabriel), Alice Daly (Sister Xavier) and Mary Gaynor (Sister Catherine), arrived in Paris for the customary mission retreat and blessing. They were on their way to Nigeria. At the mother house they found themselves immersed in the Company's missionary world. 'Our missionary spirit was kept alive', Sister Hughes wrote,

> by little items such as Lebanese Sisters singing 'O Mary conceived without sin' in Arabic; Sister Kelly's arrival from Japan; Sister Hargreaves on her way to her mission in Ethiopia. We also had wonderful news of Notre Mère [superioress general] going to Madagascar to give the cornette to 47 Malagasy Sisters and to install the first Malagasy Sister Servant. Could we be blamed for dreaming into the future and wondering when there might be a similar ceremony in Nigeria.[127]

Her dream, looking ahead to a time when Nigerian Daughters would manage their ministries under the guidance of their own provincial, is emblematic of the changes that had taken place in Catholic missiology and in the Company by this time: the orientation was towards the inculturation of the community and the withdrawal of European missionaries.

As in Australia the invitation to found a mission in Nigeria came via an Irish bishop, Bishop James Moynagh, a priest of St Patrick Missionary Society, and followed almost immediately on from the arrival of Vincentian priests from Ireland. The first Vincentians arrived in 1960. It was a time of great change, the year in which Nigeria was granted independence from British rule, and when the Church began to name Nigerian priests for senior posts.[128] When the invitation to the Daughters arrived in August 1961, it was immediately given favourable consideration by the provincial council. 'The Bishop of Calabar is anxious to have Sisters in his diocese', the minutes recorded, 'for a Domestic Economy School, the Technical training of native Sisters and parochial visiting. The sisters for the first of these works will need to satisfy Government requirements. As the Vincentians from the Province are already in this mission, the matter was considered favourably. When further details have been received, the matter will be put before the General Council of the Community.'[129] Permission from Paris was received within weeks and the Province set about applying to the Nigerian government for approval to establish

---

127 Quoted in *Nuachtán Chúize na hÉireann* (Journal of the Irish Province), Autumn/Winter Issue, 2001, p. 5. 12-1 DCMH.

128 For example, in Calabar, Dominic Ignatius Ekandem was appointed auxiliary bishop in 1953 and Brian David Usanga as auxiliary bishop in 1963 and bishop in 1970.

129 Provincial Council Minutes Vol. XIX. 28 August 1961. 9-5-0-2-1 DCMH.

the technical school, above all having to demonstrate that the teaching Sisters had appropriate qualifications.[130]

This time the Province was able to draw on its experience in Australia and Ethiopia and on the informed discussions about modern missionary work taking place in Catholic journals and between religious congregations. One development was the provision of preparatory programmes for new missionaries. The group for Nigeria was sent on one such programme in All Hallows College in Ireland. But the inexperienced Sisters who went to Nigeria did not have to work alone. By the early 1960s the inter-community co-operation that had so surprised the first Sisters in Australia in 1926 was widely practised by the English-speaking missionaries working in Nigeria. At the airport the Sisters were welcomed by the Our Lady of the Apostles nuns[131] and their first temporary home in Nigeria was Cornelia Connelly College belonging to the Holy Child sisters who had gone from England to Nigeria in 1930.[132] Through their schools and teacher training colleges the Holy Child nuns were heavily orientated towards the advancement of women through education, which was also to be the purpose of the Daughters' initial project.[133] At other times the Sisters visited the Holy Rosary Sisters and the Medical Missionaries of Mary, regularly meeting up with other sisters for training sessions, worship and important events in the life of the Church in Nigeria.

Adiaha Obong Girls' Secondary Commercial School in Uyo was established within months of the Sisters' arrival in Nigeria and, although the Sisters began with nothing and had to have the building constructed from nothing, it soon flourished. This project did however strain resources and meant that the provincial council had to turn down a request for support for new works in Ethiopia at the time.[134] On the other hand when Bishop Ekandem of Ikot Ekpane, a suffrage diocese of Calabar, requested a second group of Sisters 'to begin a small clinic with parish visiting and welfare work which, it is hoped will develop into a Maternity and General Hospital eventually', they accepted the project because of 'the desirability of having a second house within easy distance of Uyo which is also another type of work'.[135]

The first Nigerian postulants were accepted in 1973, and in 1975 the British Province ceased to have a formal role in the development of the Company's work in Nigeria, because the newly established Province of Ireland was given that responsibility, while Britain retained responsibility for Ethiopia. The vice-Province

---

130 Provincial Council Minutes Vol. XIX. 31 October and 2 November 1961. 9-5-0-2-1 DCMH.

131 Nigerian Journal Vol. I. 7-4 DCMH.

132 Nigerian Journal Vol II, No.3. January 1964, p. 40. 7-4 DCMH.

133 Rose Uche Nwosu, 'Nigeria Calling' and Teresa Okure, 'The Beginning of an SCHJ Vocation: A Personal Story' in *History: Society of the Holy Child Jesus,* Issue I, 'Beginnings' (published by Society of Holy Child Jesus, 1996), pp.74-81 and 90-100.

134 Provincial Council Minutes Vol. XIX. 30 May 1963. 9-5-0-2-1 DCMH.

135 ibid., 19 February 1964. 9-5-0-2-1 DCMH.

of Nigeria developed quickly and confidently. By 1995 there were 85 Sisters, of whom 66 were Nigerian, including 4 in the office of Sister Servant. A report for that year expressed the contemporary missiological approach: 'The Irish Sisters have done a magnificent job,' it noted. 'They have become less and less as the Nigerian Sisters have become more and more.' [136]

Missionary work outside Britain and Ireland was a primary vocation for a minority of women who entered the community of the Daughters of Charity. For some the missionary context gave scope for exercising personal initiative directly in service of people in poverty that was less readily available in Britain and Ireland, particularly after the First World War, when the pioneering phase gave way to consolidation, as we will see in the next chapter. But the Province's participation in missionary activity, first through individuals and then through a more institutional commitment, went far beyond the personal. Its importance to the Province, reflected in news, in financial sacrifices and in collective activities involved all the Sisters. It was through the missions that the Province participated most fully in the Company's transnational nature and that its members became more aware of political and economic situations across the globe. Moreover, the Province's missionary work drew lay networks in Britain and Ireland (and America) into engagement with questions of global poverty and development. The Sisters' approach to mission continued to be based in Vincentian praxis and service to all, and the Company had a consistent orientation towards building indigenous communities. The age of heroic individual endeavour, awesome in itself and inspiring though it had been to the Daughters back in Britain and Ireland, had also been the age of colonial paternalism. Gradually the lessons of engagement with the modern world, of subsidiarity and of collaboration as proclaimed by the Second Vatican Council began to take root in the Province. Two changes in particular stand out, and both came to fruition after the Council. Firstly, equality between Sisters from the global North and global South became a reality rather than simply an espoused value. Secondly, alongside the works of mercy and charity which had always characterised the Sisters' activities, those of social justice and human development took on increasing importance. What also emerges from this overview is the way that the overseas work of the Province developed its eventual character from its unique place at the juncture of British colonial and post-colonial networks, the Irish ecclesial diaspora and the Company's missionary spirit.

---

136 'Daughters of Charity in Nigeria', typed note summarising the situation in 1995.. 7-4 DCMH.

10

1925–1959: a golden era?

> The Catholic Church had grown almost continuously
> since the late 1920s, and now, in the post-war period,
> it had never had it so good...There was no sudden change;
> it had been a steady process continuing all through the
> 1920s, the 1930s, 1940s and 1950s.[1]

The Daughters who were missioned to China and Australia in the inter-war era and to Ethiopia after the Second World War were a tiny minority. Almost all the Sisters' ministry took place at home. The period from 1925 to 1959, the subject of this chapter, is a relatively short one. Even so, in the history of Britain generally it has been customary to divide it into two or even three parts and to emphasise the distinctive character of each: the inter-war years, the Second World War, and the post-war era of austerity and the new welfare state.[2] In the history of the Catholic Church in Britain on the other hand it is almost always understood as a single coherent narrative, starting around 1920 and going through to the late 1950s or the mid-1960s.[3] These decades even have their own Catholic label; the pre-conciliar era – that is, before the Second Vatican Council (1962–1965). The name signals the many characteristics that have been attributed to the period, both real and re-imagined, and at the same time denotes the Second Vatican Council as the point of change into a new, post-conciliar, age.[4]

Here, then, was an island of time, often described in terms of a golden era for the Catholic Church in Britain.[5] The steady growth in the number of the faithful, priests and churches was its most obvious feature, often contrasted by historians

---

1 Adrian Hastings, *A History of English Christianity 1920-1990* (London, SCM Press, 1986), p. 473 and p. 475.

2 More recently this approach has been challenged in favour of taking a longer view that sees the connections between the inter-war era and the 1950s and 1960s. See for example Heiko Feldner, Clare Gorrara and Kevin Passmore (eds.), *The Lost Decade? The 1950s in European History, Politics, Society and Culture* (Newcastle: Cambridge Scholars Press, 2011) and the discussion in Harris, *Faith in the Family*, Ch. 2.

3 Sheridan Gilley, 'The Years of Equipoise, 1892-1943', in V. Alan McClelland and Michael Hodgetts (eds.), *From Without the Flaminian Gate: 150 Years of Roman Catholicism in England and Wales 1850-2000* (London: Darton, Longman and Todd, 1999), 'this world was at its height in the 1940s and lasted until the 1960s', p.55.

4 Harris, *Faith in the Family*, p. 38 for a discussion of the historical use of these terms.

5 Gilley,. 'Years of Equipoise', p. 23.

and sociologists with the position of other Christian denominations over the same period.[6] Expansion and gradual upward mobility, moreover, did not diminish individual and community religious identity.[7] If anything Catholic identity became more distinctive in Britain between the wars and during the 1950s. Its hallmarks were the Latin Mass, a separate Catholic schooling system, Marian devotions, a prohibition on marrying 'out' without permission, and an ideal of family life that after 1930 diverged increasingly from the mainstream concept of a 'responsibly-sized' family as comprising two children.[8] Its strong Irish component, now reaching back through three or four generations of migration and settlement, was also part of its identity. The Church of this period enjoyed an internal stability that came from 'settled beliefs', a universal catechism and universal jurisdiction codified in canon law since 1917. Even the unimaginative leadership given by many senior clergy in Britain in the period contributed to the sense of solidity.[9] Growth, internal peace and a coherent identity created the environment – often dubbed a 'ghetto' or 'fortress Church'[10] – for the development of a rich associational life and an increasing social and cultural confidence. Identity was expressed through a degree of engagement in the public sphere via the Catholic Social Guild, Sword of the Spirit and other Catholic Action organisations,[11] and in the creative and intellectual sphere in the nationally acclaimed works of overtly Catholic artists, novelists and essayists.[12] According to one historian of the English Church in this period, 'there was a swagger about the Church in the 1950s.'[13] Large numbers of highly visible Catholic sisters and nuns were an essential, almost taken-for-granted, part of the overall story of growth, distinctiveness and flourishing.[14]

6 Ross McKibben, *Classes and Cultures: England 1918-1951* (Oxford: Oxford University Press, 1998), p.273. However, recent debate has challenged the established notion of a 'secular' Britain before 1960 and even later. See Jane Garnett *et al.*(eds.), *Redefining Christian Britain: Post-1945 Perspectives* (London: SCM, 2006). On the other hand the Catholic Church was the only church to experience growth.

7 Coman, *Catholics and the Welfare State*, pp. 15-30.

8 There is no clear statistical evidence about the difference between Catholic family size and that of other groupings because the data is not identified by religion. Siân Pooley notes that 'it is time to move beyond "average" national narratives, both qualitatively and quantitatively', in 'Parenthood, Childrearing and Fertility in England, 1850-1914', *History of the Family* 18, (1) (March 2013), pp.83-106. But see Ru-Chi Chou and Susannah Brown, 'A Comparison of the size of families of Roman Catholics and non-Catholics in Great Britain', *Population Studies*, Vol.22, No.1. (March 1968), pp.51-60; McKibbin, *Classes and Cultures*, p.310 and Michael Hornsby-Smith, 'Catholic Family Life', in Hornsby-Smith (ed.), *Catholics in England*, pp.10-11 and p.69.

9 Hastings, *English* Christianity, p.287 and p.478.

10 See, for example, Hornsby-Smith, *Catholics in England*, p.12 and Kester Aspden, *Fortress Church: The English Roman Catholic Bishops and Politics 1903-63* (Leominster: Gracewing, 2002).

11 See Michael Walsh, 'Catholics, Society and Popular Culture', in McLelland and Hodgetts, *Flaminian Gate*, pp. 360-366.

12 See Adam Schwartz, *The Third Spring: G.K. Chesterton, Graham Greene, Christopher Dawson and David Jones* (Washington DC: Catholic University of America, 2002).

13 Aspden, *Fortress Church*, p.274.

14 Sandra Schneiders writes that 'many people have suggested that the 1940s–1960s were the most developed and distinguished period in the history of ministerial Religious Life'. *Finding the Treasure: Locating Catholic Religious Life in a New Ecclesial and Cultural Context*, p.165.

The Daughters' history in this period appears to fit comfortably within such a golden age narrative. The three peak years for entrants took place during the 1920s and the Province's peak total membership size occurred in the early 1950s. Centenaries of foundations, a sure sign of stability, began to come round; the first, celebrated in Sheffield in 1957, was soon followed by those of Little Crosby, Carlisle Place in Westminster and Lanark. With the passage of time many of these establishments had become features in the charitable landscape of neighbourhoods and dioceses as well as forming part of the Province's own identity. As we have seen, between 1920 and 1950 the Company had enjoyed the privilege of two canonisations and the Province had experienced increased participation in its devotional societies. With their traditional habits and cornettes in place, it would have seemed to outside observers that the Sisters were impervious to the seismic changes that had occurred in British society between the end of the First World War and the late 1950s.

Research into women's history in Britain during this period has developed strongly over the past twenty years but the study of Catholic women and Catholic sisters in these decades has barely begun.[15] Although there has been little archival research it is not uncommon for assumptions to be made that the second quarter of the twentieth century was when Catholic women's congregations were at their zenith.[16] This was certainly the case on grounds of size. Two recent studies of individual congregations suggest, however, that the story was more complex.[17] Given the paucity of research on the one hand and the strength of impressions on the other, retrieval of this largely unwritten chapter in the history of religious sisters in Britain is overdue. How did the Sisters and their practice of charity evolve in the changing economic, political and social context between 1920 and 1960? With greater understanding of this question we will be in a better position to reassess the pre-conciliar era in the Church in Britain as a whole, through the lens of the history of its institutes of consecrated women. The subjects of vocations, leaders, ministry and finance, modernity and way of life have been selected because of what they can add to what we have already learned about Marian devotions and overseas missions in the evolution of the Province in this period.

---

15 See Sheridan Gilley's historiographical comments in 'A Tradition and Culture Lost', in Hornsby-Smith (ed.), *Catholics in England 1950-2000*, pp.32-33, on the lack of study about the religious experience of the Catholic community post WWI. Earlier histories, such as George A. Beck (ed.), *The English Catholics 1850-1950* (London: Burns Oates, 1950), concentrated on the long nineteenth century, while more recent ones, such as Hornsby-Smith (ed.), *Catholics in England 1950-2000*, are concerned with the second half of the twentieth century. For more recent work that is breaking new ground see essays in D.A.J. MacPherson and Mary J. Hickman (eds.), *Women and Irish Diaspora Entities: Theories, Concepts and New Perspectives* (Manchester: Manchester University Press, 2014) and Alana Harris, *Faith in the Family*.

16 Hastings, *English Christianity*, p. 475.

17 Two recently published congregational histories are invaluable for their pioneering work on this period: Anselm Nye, *A Peculiar Kind of Mission* and Teresa White, *A Vista of Years: History of the Society of the Sisters of the Faithful Companions of Jesus 1820-1993* (privately printed, 2013).

Vocations

Changes in vocational numbers have proved an absorbing subject for historians and Church commentators, and have often been used as a benchmark for the health of an institute. At first sight the trajectory of the Province's growth seems to mirror that of the Catholic community in Britain. Closer analysis, however, shows that the total number of Sisters between 1930 and 1960 did not increase but rather remained remarkably steady, as Figure 10.1 shows.

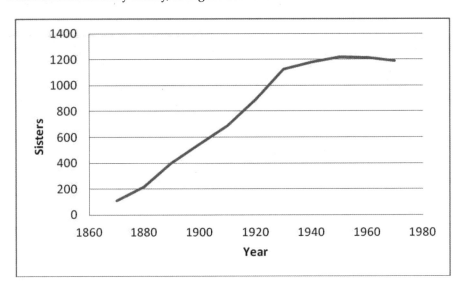

10.1: TOTAL NUMBER OF SISTERS 1870–1960

In fact, once the numbers of Sisters on the Australian mission (increasingly Australian-born) are excluded from the total, a slowdown in growth can be seen to have taken place in the 1940s and the first signs of numerical decline can be dated to the early 1950s.[18] What is even more striking is the exceptional growth of the 1920s.[19] The lower numbers either side of this decade, which themselves comprised the next two largest decadal intakes, underline this phenomenon.[20] Between 1920 and 1929 the Province admitted 465 to the seminary, compared with 297 for the decade before and 331 for the decade after: the (smaller) numbers completing seminary and receiving the habit are shown in 10.2 below. These 1920s entrants were the equivalent of the 'baby boomers' after the Second World War

---

18 There were 1124 Sisters in 1930, 1217 in 1950 (62 in Australia) and 1215 (118 in Australia) in 1960.

19 See Chapter 6 for a discussion of this large-scale recruitment in the 1920s also led to a larger than usual withdrawal and dismissal rate.

20 See Nye, *A Peculiar Kind of Mission*, p.138 for a similar pattern of high recruitment (and high defection) in the English Dominican Sisters during the 1920s.

(see Table 10.2): a demographic wave whose size was to influence the Province at every stage of these Sisters, community life from arrival to death.

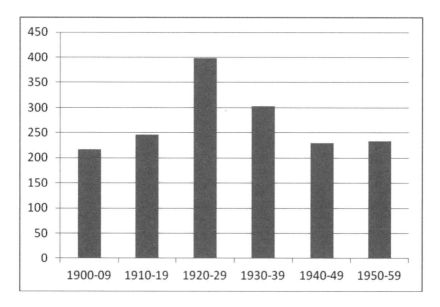

10:2 SISTERS RECEIVING THE HABIT BY DECADE 1900–1960

As was later to become clear, the large intake of the 1920s was not simply part of a continuous upward movement but was brought about by a number of convergent factors never likely to be repeated.[21] The deaths of more than 700,000 men from the British Isles in the First World War (9% of all those under the age of 45) meant that the gender balance for the generation of women born between 1894 and 1902 could not be restored.[22] At a time when there was a gap between the numbers of men and women of marriageable age, the possibilities for single women to support themselves with dignity and to live purposeful lives continued to be limited.[23] Catholic young women coming to adulthood during and after the war had been more fully exposed to the ideals of a life consecrated to God than any

---

21 See, for another context, Sonja Bezjak, 'Catholic Women's Vocations in the Twentieth Century: The Slovenian Case', *Review of Religious Research,* Vol. 54, Issue. 2 (June, 2012), pp. 157-174.

22 Jay Winter, *The Great War and the British People 2nd edn.* (Basingstoke: Palgrave Macmillan, 2003) makes this point but also notes out that there was nothing new in a high percentage of 'never marrieds'. Virginia Nicholson, *Singled Out:How Two Million Women Survived Without Men after the First World War* (London: Penguin, 2008); Katherine Holden, *The Shadow of Marriage: Singleness in England 1914-60* (Manchester: Manchester University Press, 2007); '"Surplus Women': a legacy of World War One?' (http://ww1centenary.oucs.ox.ac.uk/?p=2345) by Rosemary Wall (accessed 1 July 2016).

23 Elizabeth Roberts, *Women's Work: 1840-1940* (Basingstoke: Macmillan, 1988) notes that a higher percentage of women were in the workforce in 1911 than in 1921 because so many women had to give up their jobs after the war. On the changing work opportunities for young women, see Selina Todd, *Young Women, Work and Family in England 1918-1950* (Oxford: Oxford University Press, 2005).

earlier generation in Britain while in Ireland the well-established culture of the convent was clearly present as a life choice. The war itself left some with an urgent personal need to live out Christian ideals of peace, solidarity and service.[24] It is hardly surprising that more individual Catholic women looked for meaning and fulfilment in consecrated community life or that collectively their search had an impact on the Province's recruitment.

Despite this large intake of the 1920s the Province's demographic profile was already ageing by 1940, as Table 10.3 indicates.

age	1920	1940	1960
% under 40	40	30	29
% 40–64	50	51	47
% over 65	10	18	24

10.3: PERCENTAGE AGE DISTRIBUTION 1920, 1940 AND 1960

In the early 1950s, for the first time in its history, the number of deaths and departures exceeded the number of those taking first vows in the Province. It was a phenomenon that occurred in many women's congregations in Britain at varying points between 1930 and 1960, for example, in the Faithful Companions of Jesus and the Religious of the Sacred Heart.[25] During the 1950s the latter appeared to have steady overall numbers, but their historian warns that these figures were 'deceptive'. 'Vocations were waning while the age level was rising; the pyramid was becoming inverted,' she notes.[26] Qualitative evidence confirms the statistical data. When the Vincentian Bishop Vicar Apostolic of Bulawayo in South Africa requested in 1949 that the Daughters of Britain and Ireland make a foundation in his diocese he was refused because 'Our vocations are few, and we have a very small number in our Seminary – not anything sufficient to meet the needs of our Province.'[27] There were in fact 30 seminary Sisters in 1949 of whom, given normal average departure rates, 20 would continue onto first vows. But the strain of supporting existing commitments was already being felt. It was to be felt even more in the 1950s when the annual average number of entrants reduced further to 23.[28]

---

24 D. Nash, *Christian Ideals in British Culture: Stories of Belief in the Twentieth Century* (Basingstoke: Palgrave Macmillan, 2013).

25 White, *A Vista of Years*, p. 178.

26 Williams, *The Society of the Sacred Heart*, p. 230

27 Provincial Council Minutes Vol XV, 30 August 1949. 9-5-0-2-1- DCMH.

28 A more firmly downward trend in recruitment caused the English Dominican Sisters to begin closing smaller houses as early as 1929. Nye, *A Peculiar Kind of Mission*, p.173. Nye notes that this was unusual and cites the expansion of the Sisters of Charity of St Paul. However it is possible that this expansion also belied an underlying ageing demographic.

In 1928 the Province had sensibly decided to use The Priory, a large Edwardian house and grounds purchased on the opposite side of the road from the Central House to serve as an extension for the seminary, as a house for the care of its most elderly and infirm Sisters.[29] The Priory was convenient for visitors, close to the Vincentian presbytery and to the provincial chapel. Its location meant these frail Sisters could continue to be at the heart of the Province. The wisdom of this practical decision not to extend the seminary was underlined in 1931 when the superioress general asked the provincial council to discuss a proposal to open a seminary in Dublin as a 'as a means of drawing vocations'.[30] Visitatrice Thomson recorded her doubts, anticipating the negative impact she believed this would have on the seminary in Mill Hill. Irish-born women had made up at least two-thirds of the seminary intake throughout the 1920s. Sister Rainford, provincial secretary, was also cautious. Sisters O'Driscoll (assistant) and Shannagher (bursar) were enthusiastic and Provincial director, Father O'Connell, was 'absolutely and unreservedly in favour of it', considering 'the project providential... and calculated to increase vocations'.[31] There was a detectable division of opinion along national lines, but all agreed this development would encourage Irish vocations. Superioress General Lebrun opened the Irish seminary at Blackrock outside Dublin on 8 September 1932 and installed Catherine Rickard, previously seminary directress in Mill Hill, as its first directress. The predicted impact was immediate: numbers at Mill Hill declined sharply. Irish vocations on the other hand were sustained (although they did not increase) despite the strong competition from the new Irish missionary institutes which were proving particularly attractive to women in Ireland at this time.[32] As the number of British-born entrants decreased, the proportion and contribution of Irish Sisters to the Province rose even higher during and after the Second World War, reaching three-quarters of new members in the 1940s and 1950s.[33]

From the late 1930s there were also significant changes in the age profile of women accepted for entry. The age range had always been a very wide one but, as we have noted, for fifty years the average and modal age of entrants had fluctuated between 24 and 26 years. In the 1940s and 1950s, however, these figures, shown in Table 10.4, moved sharply downwards.

29 Provincial Council Minutes Vol. VIII, 21 December 1928 .9-5-0-2-1 DCMH.

30 Provincial Council Minutes Vol IX, 19 March 1931, 9-5-0-2-1 DCMH.

31 Ibid.

32 For example Missionary Sisters of the Holy Rosary (1924) or the Marie Martin's Medical Missionaries of Mary (1937). On the importance of the Irish missionary movement of the 1920s and 1930s see Deidre M. Bryan, 'A "Peculiarly Fitting" Institute: The Origins of Marie Martin's Medical Missionaries of Mary', PhD thesis, Boston College, 2007, p.6.

33 The exact percentages were: 1930s: 64%; 1940s: 76%; 1950s: 75%.

	No.	under 20	20–24	25–29	30–34	35 +	Mode	Ave
1920–1929	398	46 (11%)	154 (39%)	118 (30%)	40(10%)	40(10%)	21/28	26.0
1930–1939	303	48 (16%)	107 (35%)	84 (28%)	39(13%)	26 (8%)	24.5	25.0
1940–1949	228	64 (28%)	97 (42.5%)	40 (17.5%)	18 (8%)	9 (4%)	19.0	22.5
1950–1959	233	100 (43%)	88 (38%)	32 (14%)	5 (2%)	6 (2.5%)	18.0	21.0

10.4: AGE AT ENTRY 1920–1960
(Sisters who made first vows only)

The much higher percentage of entrants who were under the age of 20 contributed to the Province's vitality, but they also constituted a new phenomenon in its history that is worthy of note. The change may simply have mirrored the increased willingness of the community to accept younger entrants at a time of greater competition for vocations or it may reflect what was happening to the average age of marriage for women in Britain and elsewhere.[34] Table 10.4 also shows that the presence of older entrants (over the age of 30), which had been a constant feature of the life of the community in Britain since the later nineteenth century, diminished significantly at this time. For the first time the seminary reality moved very close to the popular image of novitiates as full of very young women.

The fact that aspirants associated the Daughters with a wide range of ministries and missionary work seems to have helped recruitment, but even so vocations continued to be a concern for the Province. In this context the persistent rejection of factory or mill workers is striking and puzzling, particularly since it had been made clear to the Province's leaders that automatic refusal was not a Company precept.[35] Even as late as the 1930s the provincial council regularly turned down factory workers recommended by Sister Servants in Preston, Manchester and Dundee. It was a restriction that seriously affected recruitment from England and Scotland.[36] Just before the outbreak of the Second World War, perhaps inspired by the establishment of 'aspirancy' schools by a number of American religious communities,[37] or by the existence of junior seminaries for the priesthood, provincial officers proposed the idea of a 'Vocation School' for those either too

---

34 This shift almost exactly mirrored what was happening to the average age of marriage for women in Britain and other parts of the Western world, which by the end of the 1950s had moved from its long-term historic average of 26 to an unprecedented new average of 21. Tomkin, *Social History of the Twentieth Century*, p.52. But the same did not take place in Ireland until the late 1950s. See Cormac Ó Gráda, *A Rocky Road: The Irish Economy since the 1920s* (Manchester: Manchester University Press, 1997), p.192.

35 Discussed in Chapter 6.

36 Provincial Council Minutes Vol X, 24 November 1933 and 3 March 1935, 9-5-0-2-1 DCMH.

37 For these aspirancy schools in the USA, see Helen Rose Fuchs Ebaugh, *Out of the Cloister: A Study of Organizational Dilemmas* (Austin, TX University of Texas Press, 1977), p.70.

young to enter or in need of more training.[38] This proposal did not gain the approval of superiors and, in any case, the war changed all such plans. From 1939 to 1942 the British seminary was evacuated to Torquay and during the war there were, understandably, few entrants. Only 32 Sisters received the habit at Mill Hill or Torquay between 1940 and 1945.

By this time the decline in vocations to religious life and the priesthood across Europe had become a matter for open discussion in the Church. Writing in the *Clergy Review* in 1950, Rev. G. W Shelton noted the marked fall in numbers in England and also that 'the present devotees appeared tired, worn out and overworked.' [39]Addressing a Congress of Mothers-General in Rome in 1952, Pope Pius XII spoke of the 'crisis of vocations'.[40] Reviews of 'vocations work' now took place within a new discourse about 'the modern girl'; a discourse the Pope played a key part in initiating on a Church-wide scale.[41] In his 1951 address to the International Congress of teaching sisters meeting in Rome he posed the question

> The modern girl! ....Was there ever such a time as the present when a girl had to be won and trained interiorly, according to her convictions and will, for Christ's cause and a virtuous life? [42]

Pope Pius invited congregations to respond by looking at themselves and their adaptation to modernity. This was now a matter of concern for the whole Church because since 1917 the concept of consecrated active religious as 'living parts of the institutional Church, rather than private entities' had gained force, a situation that women themselves had struggled to attain in previous centuries.[43]

In Britain religious communities and dioceses reached out to modern youth through public vocations exhibitions after the war, making use of this popular format for the Church's purpose. The first exhibition, held in Blackburn in Lancashire in 1949, was the initiative of the recently founded Vocation Sisters. Thereafter a committee of religious and priests took responsibility for organising exhibitions held in Manchester, Liverpool, Glasgow and elsewhere. The Daughters participated in many of these regional events and they had a significant presence

38 Provincial Council Minutes Vol X, 7 January, 1939, 9-5-0-2-1 DCMH

39 G. W. Shelton, 'Religious Vocations for Women', *Clergy Review* 33(1950), pp.73-81.

40 Pope Pius XII *Report of the First Congress of Superior Generals of Pontifical Right*, Rome, 11-13 September 1952. Original at http://www.vatican.va/archive/aas/documents/AAS-44-1952-ocr.pdf.

41 See for example the publications of the Dominican Sister Mary Laurence, such as *Nuns are Real People* (London: Blackfriars Publications, 1955); Edward Murphy, 'The Teaching Sister and the Modern Girl', *The Furrow,* Vol. 9, No. 10 (October, 1958), pp.633-645. For a broader context see The Modern Girl Around the World Research Group and its publication *The Modern Girl Around the World: Consumption, Modernity and Globalization* (Durham, NC and London: Duke University Press, 2008).

42 Pius XII, 'Counsel to Teaching Sisters', an address given to the first International Congress of Teaching Sisters' 15 September 1951. http://www.papalencyclicals.net/Pius12/P12TCHRS.HTM (accessed 21 August 2016).

43 Council of Major Superiors of Women Religious (ed.), *The Foundations of Religious Life*, Introduction.

at the largest, held at Olympia in Kensington in London from the 5 to 12 July 1953.[44] More than 150 religious communities were represented at Olympia and each used great ingenuity to attract and inspire the tens of thousands of visitors. The event culminated in the ordination to the priesthood of 30 students of St Joseph's Missionary College in Mill Hill by Cardinal Griffin, attended by 11,000 people.[45] At the Daughters' stand 'our Virgo Potens presided [and] a statue of Saint Catherine Labouré with a bunch of medals in her hand.' There were maps showing the global work of the Company and a large display of tiny model Sisters undertaking every aspect of the Province's work.[46] In writing a report on the Olympia exhibition for *The Echo*, an unnamed British Daughter captured the great excitement and genuine delight of religious communities at the public interest shown in them and their work. The exhibition was an 'out of the catacombs' milestone for the Church in Britain[47]she concluded, and 'more exciting than the pictures'.[48] Such enthusiasm not withstanding, in 1958 the Province decided not to participate on the grounds of cost and, more importantly, because the exhibitions had not been effective in increasing vocations.[49]

This historical evidence calls into question the often categorically held view that the decline in vocations in North America and Europe came in the wake of the Second Vatican Council, as in this opening sentence of Gerald Arbuckle's influential text *Strategies for Growth in Religious Life* (1987):

> In 1966 the recruitment and the retention rates of many religious congregations were at an all time high. Within two years, the situation had dramatically reversed itself. Why?[50]

More recently, and with a wider evidence base, Rodney Stark and Roger Finke (2008) stated that 'cross-national data show that the declines began in Europe and North America immediately following actions taken at Vatican II.' But a strong element in their argument was the data they presented from the United

---

44 *The Tablet*, 28 February 1953, p. 16.

45 ibid., p. 180 and p. 186 says 105 women's congregations and orders and 54 for men. *The Tablet* gives slightly different figures.

46 'The Vocations Exhibition', p. 182.

47 ibid., p. 184.

48 ibid., p. 182.

49 Council Minutes, 1 July 1958. 9-5-0-2-1 DCMH. It should be noted that they did take a stall again in 1965.

50 Gerald Arbuckle, *Strategies for Growth in Religious Life* (New York: Alba House, 1987), p.1. The evidence behind Gerald Arbuckle' statement, for example, was drawn from his own Marist congregation and from other male orders and congregations of whom he was aware. I am grateful to Father Arbuckle for this information and for his interest in the evidence from women's congregations. (Private correspondence, September 2016). See also James Sweeney, 'Religious Life after Vatican II', in Hornsby-Smith (ed.), *Catholics in England*, p.279, writing about Britain: 'vocations crashed immediately on the close of the Council'.

States.[51] We will explore the Company's and Province's engagement with Vatican II in the next chapter, but at this point it seems right to question these globalised generalisations and the interpretation of the impact of Vatican II on the basis of evidence from women's congregations in Britain and several countries in mainland Europe, including that presented here about the Daughters of Charity

Leaders

Third-and fourth-generation leaders of the Daughters in Britain experienced first the expansion and then the beginning of the serial decline in recruitment. Between 1925 and 1960 six Sisters held the office of visitatrice. The frequency of these changes, greater than in the previous 35 years, was mainly brought about by illness and premature deaths rather than by deliberate policy. As a consequence there were times when the provincial council struggled because of its lack of experience and there were periods when the Province was unsettled by such change. It is all the more significant, therefore, that superiors general appear to have given considerable weight to the question of nationality in making new appointments to senior offices.

In 1926 after seven years as visitatrice and having set in motion the process of transition from the 'old order' of council officers as described in Chapter 6, Louise Hannezo was recalled to France. With her departure no member of the council, officer or director, remained from 1918. Appointed in 1919 Hannezo had held the Province through the Irish War of Independence, the Civil War which followed and the establishment of the Irish Free State, with the partition of Ireland into North and South. All members of the community lived through experiences that were momentous in Ireland and for Irish Sisters and Vincentian confrères, even if no word of them appears in the records of the Province. By 1926, when the political settlement seemed more secure, superiors general made the decision to pass the leadership of the British and Irish Province from French hands to one of its own. Sensitivities about national origins and loyalties were still sufficiently important, however, for them to be taken into account in making new appointments.

Mary Boyle was named as fourth visitatrice. At the age of 64 she was old enough to have undergone the full seminary formation at the mother house and she was proficient in French. Her personality – 'alert, full of "go" and vivacity, active and energetic' – had made her well suited to her first placement in St Vincent's boys' industrial school in Liverpool.[52] This was where she had remained for forty years, many of them as a Sister Servant, trusted to help open new foundations in

---

51 Rodney Stark and Richard Finke, 'Catholic Religious Vocations: Decline and Revival', *Review for Religious* (2000), Vol.42. Iss. 2, p.131. 'Most discussions of the decline in female religious vocations in the United States', they noted, 'have ignored a vital fact that following World War Two there were nearly two decades of consistent and substantial growth in the number of nuns...only then (1965) did the numbers begin to decline', which they related to the changes that took place following the Council.

52 *Remarks on Deceased Sisters*, Sister Mary Boyle (1930), p.2. Personal file 10-2 DCM.

Bebington and Upholland in 1920. In 1920 she was chosen to accompany Sisters Langdale and Blundell to Rome for the beatification of Louise de Marillac and the martyred Sisters of Arras.[53] When in 1923 she was moved to London as Sister Servant of the house of mercy in Marylebone (Wigmore Street), she was greatly surprised at being changed, but with hindsight it seems clear she was being prepared to replace Louise Hannezo when the moment came.

The daughter of an independent farming family, Mary Boyle was the Company's historic ideal type of Sister and well placed, therefore, to help the Province make the necessary transition from the elite English and French women who had previously dominated its leadership. But just as important was her origin as a native of Termonery Co. Derry in Northern Ireland. Sister Boyle embodied both the Province's Irish and United Kingdom components. The fact that her brother was a Vincentian priest who was superior of the Irish College in Paris only enhanced this providential bridge-building aspect of her appointment. Her death only two years later at the age of 66 was not only a great loss to the Province but it meant that superiors general had to face again in 1928 the issues of unity and cohesion they had confronted in 1926.

On this occasion they selected Anne Thomson. In appointing one of the relatively few Scottish-born members of the Province at this time they neatly side-stepped any Anglo-Irish sensitivities. Anne Thomson had been brought up in the Catholic enclave of the 'holy vale' in Fochabers in Morayshire, where her family had upheld the faith for generations and her father found work in the large estates of Gordon Castle. Thomson entered in 1903 with a strong commitment to nursing and she remained in her first placement in St Mary's Hospital in Lanark for twelve years, becoming Sister Servant in 1922. Always described as having a spirit of 'interiority' and as an excellent listener, she would not have been widely known in the Province when she was appointed to the office of provincial assistant in 1926. But within two years she found herself unexpectedly installed as fifth visitatrice. A series of changes in council membership involving eight Sisters between 1928 and 1932 indicates the level of difficulty in establishing a new leadership group at this time.

The new council configuration which emerged surely reveals the concern of the superiors general to ensure a balance and a parity between the Province's national communities at a time of tension. It was inevitable that the two islands would now develop ever more separately and that their governments would have different and sometimes conflicting interests.[54] The latter manifested itself during the 1930s in the Anglo-Irish economic war. More concretely for the Province the new state's legislative programme for education and social welfare created a new working context in Ireland. After 1929 governments and Church in the Irish Free State worked together to forge a post-colonial national identity and a moral culture

---

53 Remarks on Deceased Sisters, Sister Mary Boyle (1930), p. 4. Personal file 10-2 DCMH.

54 Moulton, *Ireland and the Irish in Interwar England* , Introduction.

that would clearly differentiate the new nation from Britain.[55] Although the rhetoric overstated the reality of a rupture in Irish history at this time, the idealisation of 'small' agriculture and of traditional Catholic ideas about gender roles and the family had a real impact on economic and agricultural policies, as they did for policies related to family life and welfare.[56]

In this context it seems more than a coincidence that the provincial council between 1928 and 1947 comprised one officer from each of England, Ireland, Northern Ireland and Scotland. To support Anne Thomson, the council appointed as her assistant, Catherine (Sister Josephine) O'Driscoll, who had left Mill Hill in 1925 after forty years as an office holder in Central House but was now restored, first as bursar and then as provincial assistant. It was a reversal that 'astonished' O'Driscoll, then in Herefordshire, but it made sense in the circumstances.[57] Almost every Sister, whether in Ireland, England or Scotland had been known to her in the seminary where she was a popular and respected figure. She made it her business, furthermore, to maintain a personal link with all the Sisters in Australia.[58] Catherine O'Driscoll, born on the Island of Valencia in Co. Kerry, one of Ireland's most westerly points, became the 'glue' and the memory of the Province in its transitional time, linking the community of the inter-war and wartime era to its own past and across its national boundaries.[59] She and Sister Thomson remained in office throughout the Second World War giving consistency of direction and a comforting sense of continuity and familiarity at a time when, in addition to the dangers and austerities of war, the Province could no longer make direct contact with its superiors in Paris. The Province was, moreover, divided in terms of wartime experience by Éire's position of neutrality on the one hand and the British dedication to the Allied cause on the other. One year after the end of war and at the age of 67 Anne Thomson was allowed to step down and return to Scotland. Sister Josephine O'Driscoll retired from office the following year and superiors looked to create a new leadership era.

Barbara Burke was appointed sixth visitatrice in 1946, the first English woman to hold the office. Her father had qualified as a doctor in County Cork and migrated to practise in Plymouth where he married an Exeter woman from a merchant family. Barbara Burke was a well-educated middle-class woman with no particular professional orientation. A Voluntary Aid Detachment volunteer during the First

---

55 See the discussion in Diarmaid Ferriter, *The Transformation of Ireland 1900-2000* (London: Profile Books, 2005), pp. 319-335, 344-355, 376-379 and Louise Ryan, *Gender, Identity and the Irish Press, 1922-37: Embodying the Nation* (New York: E. Mellen Press, 2002).

56 See, for example, Lorraine Grimes, '"They go to England to preserve their Secret": The emigration and assistance of the Irish unmarried mother in Britain 1926-1952', *Retrospectives* Vol 5 (1) (Spring, 2016), pp. 51-65.

57 *Remarks on Sister Josephine O'Driscoll* (1958), p.19. Personal file 10-2 DCMH.

58 ibid., p.26. She made it her business to write personally at Christmas to each of the Sisters in Australia, including those she had never met.

59 Her legacy, 'Sidelights of the Seminary', a personal history of Central House based on diary entries and notes helped to pass on the history to seminary Sisters for years to come. 13-4-3 DCMH.

World War, she had been sent to Boulogne where her fluent French made her useful. In 1922 she entered the Company via St Teresa's orphanage in Plymouth and became the visiting Sister Augustine we have already met ironing Mary's dress in Willesden, north London (Chapter 7). After a period as Sister Servant in Willesden she was appointed Secretary at Central House in 1938 and thereafter often accompanied Sister Thomson on visitations. Liked across the Province for her warm, spontaneous and straightforward personality her death from heart failure within eleven months of appointment was, in the words of Sister Thomson, 'a frightful blow to us all'.[60] It knocked the Province's equilibrium and its capacity to respond to the post-war welfare state legislation, which not quickly restored over the next few years.

On the last day of 1947 Mary McGee, was installed as seventh visitatrice. In her journal of events at Mill Hill, Josephine O'Driscoll noted that 'we can all understand what a surprise it was to dear Sister McGee in Dublin.' By way of explanation she continued sympathetically 'one can only guess the cost of that sacrifice which must have been an especially heavy burden as Sister had spent all her community life from the time she left the Seminary, in Ireland.'[61] Just as Barbara Burke had been the first English visitatrice, Mary McGee was the first appointed from Éire. Since receiving the habit in 1921, she had been nurse, matron and Sister Servant in hospital settings in Abbeyleix and Dublin. She was not familiar with the British context, where most of the Sisters' works took place.

By this date, however, it would be true to say that almost any Sister appointed from either island would have felt the 'heavy burden' of having much to learn about 'the other'. Provincial officers from Mill Hill undertook regular visitations to Ireland and Irish Sisters continued to move between the islands to take up placements and to make their annual retreats. But, even as early as 1920, Sisters serving in Ireland were almost entirely Irish-born, which had not been the case in the later nineteenth century.[62] This change was almost inevitable, given the imbalance of entrants. Moreover, the establishment of the Blackrock seminary had meant that cohorts of new Sisters no longer bonded across national boundaries as they had done previously, sharing memories of formation and of seminary officers. During the Second World War the regular movement of Irish Sisters into the Province's houses in Britain had been much reduced and travel between the islands undertaken only infrequently by officers.[63] When the war ended normal

---

60 *Remarks on Sister Burke* (1940), p. 34, Personal file 10-2 DCMH.

61 O'Driscoll, 'Sidelights', p. 181. 13-4-3 DCMH.

62 See Breege Keenan, Appendix III 'Daughters of Charity recorded in the Censuses of Population of 1901 and 1911', in Prunty and Sullivan, *Daughters of Charity in Ireland*, pp. 255-279. British-born Sisters were no longer appointed to Ireland on any regular basis after 1914. In 1960 there were 3 British-born women out of a total 398 serving in Ireland. Annual Statistics 1960. 9-5-0-2-5 DCMH.

63 Provincial director Joseph Sheedy was detained by the authorities under emergency restrictions and not allowed to return to England when he made a visitation to the Sisters in 1943. Provincial Council Minutes, May 1943, 9-5-0-2-5 DCMH.

communications were resumed, but with the passage of the Republic of Ireland Act of 1948 they did so in the context of a new relationship between the Republic and the United Kingdom. The advent of radical new education and welfare state legislation in England and Scotland after 1944 increased the complexities of management for Sister councillors. An emerging theme in the council minutes at this time was the pressure placed on those in authority because of the size of the Province and the strain caused by working across three legal and education systems, the latter requiring their own certification and qualifications. In recognition of this factor Sister Rickard, directress of the Irish seminary, was appointed in 1948 to a new role of provincial vice-visitatrice with particular responsibility for the Irish houses and the Sisters in Ireland, North and South.[64] A further step was taken to ensure that the provincial council received sound advice by the appointment of a consultative council for the Irish houses in 1952 in addition to the vice-visitatrice role.

Superiors could reasonably have hoped that Mary McGee would serve to the age of 70. But in 1952, after just four years, she asked to be released from office on grounds of ill health. It would appear that the role, and possibly the unfamiliar context, had overwhelmed this normally capable and energetic woman. It was noted that her assistant, Anne (Sister Margaret) Whalen had steadily taken on more of the tasks of office because of Sister McGee's state of health.[65] The notification of Mary McGee's departure for Ireland in *The Echo* stated her belief she could no longer do justice to the requirements of her office 'because of a loss of strength'.[66] Restored to health, she later served as Sister Servant in Crumlin and died in 1970. It was her assistant, Anne Whalen, who became eighth visitatrice and took on this increasingly difficult role at the relatively young age of forty-nine.

The daughter of a coal miner from Co. Wexford who had migrated to Bishop Auckland for work and there married a local woman, Anne Whalen was one of ten children, seven of whom survived childhood. Growing up in a two-up two-down terraced house with her siblings and an Irish grandmother as well as her parents she knew working-class life at first-hand.[67] At 14 she had left school, giving up the prospect of a scholarship to the Daughters' school in Darlington to look after her sick mother and younger brothers and sisters. At the age of 21 she was free to enter the community. After a short period at Tollcross specialist school for deaf and blind children near Glasgow, she spent the next twenty years in Central House as an officer in the seminary before being appointed as directress in 1946, and then as provincial assistant in 1947 on the death of Barbara Burke. It was Sister Whalen who held office during the pivotal period from 1952 to 1966 which saw the Company and the Province begin to modernise and adapt many aspects of their work and way of life.

---

64 Council Minutes, 19 April 1949, 9-5-0-2-5 DCMH.

65 'Life of Sister Anne [Margaret] Whalen' p. 4, Personal File 10-2 DCMH.

66 *The Echo of the Mother House* Supplement for Britain and Ireland, p.139 1952, 1-5 DCMH.

67 1911 Census.

The Company's appointments in this period not only demonstrate a sensitive concern on the part of superiors general for a balance of national origins among the leadership of the British Province but show a determination to shift it in the direction of greater social inclusivity. Before 1925 authority had lain entirely with women from aristocratic, gentry and upper middle-class professional families. From 1926, even though there was the opportunity to select from Sisters from similar backgrounds, office holders, including at the highest level, were drawn from professional, farming, trade and labouring families. Of the six Sisters who held the office of visitatrice, however, only Anne Thomson and Anne Whalen, daughters of a gardener and coal miner respectively, held the office of visitatrice long enough to influence the direction taken by the community in response to the changing British and Irish contexts in the inter-war and post-war eras.

Ministries and funding

At the end of 1925 the community was managing 82 foundations in Britain (64 in England and 18 in Scotland), each with its own works. A quarter of a century of strong growth between 1900 and 1925 had seen 60 foundations made and 12 brought to an end. In 1959 the number of foundations was still 82. Yet this was not a static or stable period. During these years the Province made 26 new foundations and closed or withdrew from another 26, almost all of this activity being concentrated in the second quarter of the century. The Second World War was responsible for the permanent closure of six houses, including three in London and one near Glasgow which suffered bomb damage, and two that once requisitioned never resumed their works. But the many other decisions made during the 1920s and 1930s amounted to a re-configuration of the community's work that was quite distinct from the emergency circumstances and decisions of wartime. The nature of this re-configuration is not immediately obvious, partly because there was so much continuity of activity and partly because the changes comprised a number of modest trends rather than any single new development. The map of the Sisters' foundations in 1945, for example, shows a good deal of continuity with the map of twenty years earlier (Figure 10.5).

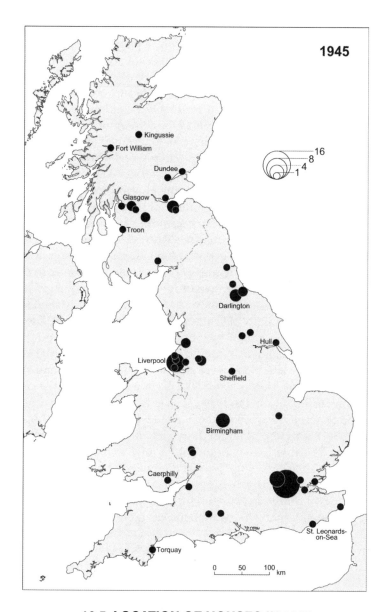

10:5 LOCATION OF HOUSES IN 1945

No overall strategy or policy was ever articulated at this time and it seems unlikely that one existed, but a clear sense of direction can nonetheless be read into the provincial council's responses to the invitations and requests received during these years and in the initiatives taken by the Province.

The most important growth trends lay in health-care services and in hostel provision. A third strand was the strengthening of parish work – the combination of visiting, teaching and sacramental activities. A further development, one that reflected the need for increased professionalism and training, was the establishment by the Province of a small number of nurse and nursery nurse training institutions. Concomitantly, a gradual but continuous downward trend was taking place in the number and scale of the community's homes for children. It began with the Home Office rationalisation and reduction of industrial school provision in the early 1920s which led to the closure of the Province's Home Office homes in Salisbury, Liverpool (2) and Manchester. In a second round of review in the early 1930s the Home Office closed the Howard Hill industrial school in Sheffield as part of the abolition of all industrial school provision in Britain. The girls were transferred to St Helens which became one of the new approved schools which the Daughters were invited to manage. The real reductions of the early 1930s came about when the Province was asked by individual local bishops to relinquish the management of four diocesan homes or orphanages, two homes in Edinburgh and one each in Plymouth and Brentwood, largely as a consequence of financial pressures but in the latter instance because Cardinal Hinsley wished to transfer its management to a community of brothers. Several other children's homes, such as St Vincent's Beacon Lane, judged by the authorities not to be 'keeping pace with the general trend of development in similar establishments',[68] that might otherwise have been closed in the late 1930s, were sustained during the Second World War out of necessity when the children and Sisters were evacuated.[69] The closure of a number of large institutions in the 1950s, such as St Vincent's Preston, St Vincent's Newcastle and St Mary's Gravesend, came about when these homes implemented the reforms of the Curtis Report on childcare and its Scottish equivalent, the Clyde Report, discussed further below. In total 18 homes managed by the Sisters on behalf of others (11 for girls, 6 for boys and 1 mixed), and a handful of smaller homes of their own were closed between 1921 and 1959.

The economics of charity help to explain the expansion of some ministries and the decline of others. A short post-war boom was rapidly followed in 1921 by 'the most severe recession the British economy had ever experienced'[70] and then by the depression of the late 1920s, which created pockets of very high unemployment, all of which had serious implications for the Daughters' practice of charity.[71] One

---

68 Letter from Home Office, 21 October 1929 Mr Crapper to Sister Provincial, 11-481-1 #10, and Father Sheedy to Canon O'Connel,l concerning the sale of Beacon Lane, 21 March 1939, 11-48 1-1 #21. St Vincent's was evacuated to Capel Curig during the war and them to Market Harborough before closing in 1965.

69 A large number of children and Sisters were evacuated, for example from St Mary's in Gravesend in Kent to Ugbrook Park, Chudleigh in Dorset and from St Vincent's Hull to Scarborough. See Gazetteer.

70 Ed Butchart, 'Unemployed and Non-employed in Interwar Britain', Oxford University Discussion Papers in Economic and Social History No.16 (May 1997), p .16 https://www.nuffield.ox.ac.uk/economics/history/paper16/16www.pdf (accessed 28 August 2016).

71 ibid for discussion of the relationship between increased wages and high unemployment.

consequence was a drop in the post-war purchasing value of the government's per capita allocation for children in care. Another was the impact on benefactions. The landed families and individuals who had been the mainstay of the Province's private benefactions were those who lost most from the war and the Province never recovered the pre-war levels of financial support it had enjoyed.[72] The same applied to Daughters who had entered with their own funds. In the context of these changing circumstances the failure to respect the Province's stipendiary system by those who had the benefit of the Sisters' labour was all the more serious.

By 1925 the council noted that 'in many cases our Sisters engaged in works managed by Committees, who have sufficient funds at their disposal, receive a mere pittance as a stipend.'[73] Yet it was often difficult for the Province's officers to persuade the clergy who chaired the management committees that the Sisters' needs were real. In the most intransigent situations their only recourse was to withdraw, so leaving children to whom they were committed and a place in which they had invested time and money over a sustained period, as well as creating difficulties in their relationship with the bishop concerned. Since collaboration with bishops and clergy was an essential part of the Company's historic culture, this was avoided wherever possible. By the late 1920s, however, it had become clear to officers that the Province's financial situation was worsening and that they could not allow matters to continue. Early in 1927, for example, when there was a change of bishop in the diocese of Hexham and Newcastle, they asked the new incumbent for an increase in the 'very inadequate' stipend for the Sisters at St Vincent's Industrial School.[74] Shortly after this the committee of the Catholic Blind Asylum in Liverpool was asked to review stipends because 'the Committee has great resources at its command and the money allowed to our Sisters engaged in the various offices is merely nominal. The Council feels bound in justice to the Community, at present heavily in debt, to ask for an adjustment.'[75] The adjusted rate they proposed for a teaching Sister, for example, was £100[76] at a time when the average teaching salary for a certificated woman teacher was £244. The Asylum's Committee counter-proposed £800 for all the Sisters serving there, a sum lower than the proposed revised individual stipends. In reluctantly accepting an arrangement that was not in keeping with its own way of working, the council gave notice that 'should any of the teaching Sisters fall out, we shall not be able to replace them unless the standard salary is given'.[77]

---

72 See Pamela Horn, *Country House Society: The Private Lives of England's Upper Cass after the First World War* (Stroud: Amberley Publications, 2013).

73 Council Minutes, 8 September 1929, 9-5-0-2-5 DCMH.

74 Ibid., 3 February 1927, 9-5-0-2-5 DCMH.

75 Ibid., 29 March 1927, 9-5-0-2-5 DCMH.

76 Ibid., 24 June 1927, 9-5-0-2-5 DCMH.

77 Ibid., 12 September 1927, 9-5-0-2-5 DCMH.

In 1929 officers summarised the Province's financial position as 'deeply in debt'. That year a serious effort was made to influence the committees of St John's Boston Spa residential home for Catholic deaf children, the committee of St Charles Institute at Carstairs for children with multiple special needs managed by the Archdiocese of Glasgow, and the Westminster Diocesan Catholic Rescue Society, for whom the Sisters ran St Charles' in Brentwood, St Joseph's in Enfield and St Anthony's in Feltham, to raise the Sisters' stipends. Between them these institutions had the services of more than 50 Sisters. The revised rate offered by the Westminster Rescue Society was £25 a year for each Sister with a donation of £100 'for Noviciate purposes', regarded as an 'impossible' offer by the council.[78] Provincial officers noted the much higher rates paid by Southwark Diocese from the identical publically funded rates they received to cover costs. Although it attempted to reach the same arrangement with the Westminster Rescue Society, the council eventually had to settle for significantly less 'in deference to the wishes of His Eminence Cardinal Bourne'.[79]

The matter of inadequate stipends at St John's Boston Spa rumbled on for several years without settlement and was, therefore, referred to Father John McHale, assistant to Superior General Verdier, when he made a visitation of the Province in January 1931. McHale raised the matter with Father Wilson, the administrator at St John's, and reported to the council that Father Wilson 'quite agrees that the sisters are not receiving enough and seems willing to raise the sum, though his last letter to [Sister] Visitatrice appeared to imply the contrary'.[80] Agreement was finally reached in March 1932 when the council accepted the offer of £50 for each Sister, including those with specialist qualifications for teaching blind or deaf children.[81] As for the situation at St Charles at Carstairs, the Sisters withdrew in 1936 when they had been unable to reach agreement with the archdiocese of Glasgow about stipends or management practices.

These were matters of economics for the Province, but also of social justice and of an expectation that the Sisters' work be respected. While these awkward and unrewarding tussles were taking place, the Province regularly responded in the affirmative to requests for financial support from its own retired employees, former Sisters who had left the community, impoverished family members of the Sisters, and priests who asked for stipends for their own services.[82] In the later 1920s and 1930s, for example, it paid priests in the Westminster diocese at the rate of £100 a year for part-time chaplaincy services in hospitals or nursing homes and

78 Council Minutes, June 1929, 9-5-0-2-5 DCMH.

79 ibid., 22 April 1930, 9-5-0-2-5 DCMH.

80 ibid., An Extraordinary Meeting, 27 January, 193,1 9-5-0-2-5 DCMH.

81 ibid., 29 March 1932, 9-5-0-2-5 DCMH.

82 See for example, Council Minutes for 26 September 1929 Decide to give Mrs Oliver who has worked for them in the Central House Laundry for over 30 years and now: 'has poor health, a pension of 7/5 a week until she is eligible for the OAP.' 26 April 1932, DCMH.

did not pay less than £40 for daily Mass to be said in the house by local parish priests.[83] From its decisions and comments it is clear that the provincial council knew when a parish priest or a diocesan or Catholic charity committee genuinely could not afford to pay the full stipend and when, on the other hand, the Sisters and their charity were being taken for granted. When the parish priest of Poplar, for example, wrote in 1927 to ask them to help him 'in his difficult and charitable work of providing schools for Catholic children drawn from the Board Schools, by forgoing the visiting Sister's stipend of £40 per annum', they agreed because the two teaching Sisters' salaries had made the house self-supporting.[84] The rector of Mile End, on the other hand, who wrote in 1939 to ask to have the visiting Sister's stipend reduced because he was struggling, was informed that £50 a year was not too much to ask for a Sister's labours but on this one occasion they would return him £20 for the poor of his parish.[85]

Despite these kinds of difficulties visiting work was sustained at a significant level throughout this period, continuing in the vein described in more detail in Chapter 7. By the 1920s Catholics in Britain associated the Sisters so closely with visiting that when they arrived in a locality for the first time, even if it was to do other ministry, parishioners expected them to visit. Sister Matthews, who was in Holly Road, Liverpool to open a nursery nurses' training school in 1927 and had no diocesan permission for visiting, wrote to the visitatrice asking permission because 'Three or four people came and asked me to go and visit their sick friends; they were people that knew the Sisters and cannot understand Sisters being in a parish and not visiting the sick.'[86] The Sisters were making in the order of 320,000 to 330,000 visits annually during the 1930s and continued the practice throughout the war wherever possible.[87] Many, like Patricia O'Sullivan who lived at Montague Place in Poplar and visited in the parish of SS Mary and Joseph for more than sixty years (1935-1995), became well-known in a neighbourhood. For Tony Galcius, whose family lived in Stepney and stayed during the blitz and bombing, the sight of a Sister 'struggling' in her cornette 'to get through the doorway and narrow hall to reach the kitchen...to ensure my mother and father and six children had enough to eat' was an early childhood recollection.[88] The Province's continued commitment

---

83 See for example Council Minutes, 28-29 October 1939, 9-5-0-2-5 DCMH. The average wage for a full-time male worker at this time was £1126. See Stephen Broadberry and Carsten Burhop, 'Real Wages and Labour Productivity in Britain and Germany, 1871-1938 (2009) http://www2.warwick.ac.uk/fac/soc/economics/staff/sbroadberry/wp/solgeruk7a.pdf (accessed 27 August 2016).

84 Provincial Council Minutes, 19 January, 1927 9-5-0-2-5 DCMH.

85 ibid., 14 July 1939, 9-5-0-2-5 DCMH.

86 Sister Matthews of Guardian Angels Home, Holly Road, Liverpool to the Visitatrice, 1927, 11-17 1-1 DCMH. Because visiting had not been agreed with the diocese for this house, she was advised to do so privately and only where there was an over-riding need.

87 Statistical Information for Paris, March 1937, 9-5-0-2-5 DCMH.

88 Tony Galcius, 'Olympic Nuns: Daughters of Charity of St Vincent de Paul', *Catholic Life*, (October, 2012), p.29.

to visiting is in stark contrast to what happened to the district visiting societies in the Church of England and other churches which never resumed after the war: 'visiting society after visiting society collapsed', states Frank Prochaska,'for want of money, volunteers and purpose'.[89]

Nonetheless, the reduced public funding, the Church's lack of funds for its childcare work and the near collapse of the Province's own private charitable funding sources had serious implications. In many places there was an institutional drabness in the quality of the environments provided for children that had not been there earlier.[90] It became difficult to modernise and to meet the improved standards of the late 1920s and 1930s, as several inspection reports show. St Teresa's home in Plymouth for example, a diocesan home for girls, was in a very poor state of repair by 1929. Although the building belonged to the diocese, the Sisters had contributed between £15,000 and £17,000 since going there in 1875 in order to extend it and keep up the standard of decoration. Often they had paid from their private purses. Now they could no longer afford to do so. The new bishop declared that he had no funds and that it was for the Sisters to solve the problem by buying a new house or upgrading the current one. In 1930 the home's medical officer felt that something needed to be done, observing in his report to the management committee 'Whether this house is worth renovating is for an expert to decide...I don't wish to say more only I feel there is a very great responsibility placed on the Sisters and also on myself and I do not feel justified in continuing as Medical Attendant if representations are pushed aside.' [91] A resolution of kinds was reached early in 1932 when Bishop John Barrett decided to transfer the work to the Poor Sisters of Nazareth who, in the words of the diocesan treasurer to visitatrice Thomson,'do not expect or demand any help from Diocesan Funds nor do they expect payment from the Rescue Society for any child they take into the Orphanage', although, he added,'I am confident they will lose nothing by this attitude, as one is naturally anxious to help a community, which so courageously takes over a tremendous burden and confidently carries it on'.[92] The new community provided its own building and the sisters' main source of funds and food was begging.[93] When St Teresa's was eventually sold the Province received nothing and, uncharacteristically, decided to ask for a share of the sale price as promised by the previous bishop. In 1937 they were offered the interest on £500 for as long as they continued to manage St Vincent's in Torquay, regarded as 'paltry recompense' by the council whose members had felt hurt by the entire

---

89 Prochaska, *Christianity and Social Services*, p. 97.

90 See for example St Joseph's Rosewell in this period, St Vincent's Beacon Lane Liverpool and St Joseph's Darlington.

91 Dr Keily's Report 31 December 1930 11-13-1 1-1 #37 9-5-0-2-5 DCMH

92 Plymouth File Rev. John Berger to Visitatrice Thomson, 13 January, 1932 11-13-1 #177 DCMH

93 Alice Maynell, *The Poor Sisters of Nazareth* (London:Burns Oates, 1889), p.17 and Francesca Steele, *The Convents of Great Britain* (London: Sands and Co, 1902), p. 262.

handling of the matter and what they experienced as a disregard of their years of service.[94]

A similar set of events took place in Edinburgh in 1930, when the new Archbishop, Andrew McDonald, adopted the same solution at a time of great economic pressure.[95] He replaced the Sisters at two homes, one for boys and one for girls, writing that he had been 'fortunate in securing an offer which will relieve the diocese of all responsibility in regard to the property and the buildings' and had therefore 'felt compelled in justice to the diocese to accept the advantageous terms offered'.[96] The Sister Servant described the children's removal by the nuns who took over their work as 'a terrible day. I hope never to see or hear of one like it again.'[97]

Financial pressures and the almost continuous need to negotiate with church authorities about money framed the Province's decisions to develop works which gave them greater independence. The financing for hospitals and health services, challenging though it was, was not as dependent on dioceses as were children's homes. In this period the Province itself bought several properties for the new hospital and health care works it established, using its capital to invest for the longer term and to give it control over some of its works. While not an entirely new approach, as Table 10.6 suggests, it was an increasing trend.

Ownership	1925	1965
Private benefactors	2%	4%
Church (dioceses, parish and diocesan trustee boards)	61%	42%
Province	37%	54%

10.6: OWNERSHIP OF FOUNDATIONS IN BRITAIN
1925 AND 1965

Hospitals had lay boards of management whose members worked hard to raise funds, fees were charged for patients who could afford them to off-set charges to poorer patients, and many patients were sponsored by employers, the SVP, religious orders, or the Ladies of Charity. War pensions covered some of the nursing cost for the disabled soldiers in St David's and, in the case of residential children's nursing care, for example at St Vincent's orthopaedic hospital in Pinner, or the two St Joseph's homes for children with multiple and complex needs

---

94 Plymouth File, Sister Rainford to Visitatrice Thomson, 3 June 1936, 11-13-1 # 4 DCMH.

95 W.W. Knox, *A History of the Scottish People 1840-1940* Ch. 10 an on-line publication of SCRAN http://www.scran.ac.uk/scotland/pdf/SP2_10Economy.pdf (accessed 28 August 2016).

96 Blacket Avenue, 22 November 1930, Archbishop McDonald to Visitatrice Thomson, 11-21-2 1-1 and Restalrig 11-24 DCMH.

97 Restalrig 16 and 18 July, 1933, Sister Brannelly to Visitatrice Thomson 11-24, DCMH.

in Rosewell, near Edinburgh, and in Sheffield, local authorities paid a weekly allowance for each child.

Other factors, however, played an important part in the emergence of these trends in the Sisters' works. It is surely relevant that the foundations for involvement in health-care laid by visitatrice Hannezo between 1920 and 1924 were strengthened and extended by visitatrice Thomson, a trained and experienced nurse. Another important influence was the increased attraction of nursing to women as an alternative profession to teaching, both as a consequence of the war and of the establishment of the College of Nursing in 1915 and the Nurses Registration Act of 1919. In Ireland the number of nurses grew steadily during the twentieth century, overtaking the number of teachers by 1946 and becoming an important source of nurses for Britain.[98] Just as a significant number of women applying to enter were interested in missionary service so an increasing number hoped to nurse. To the six hospitals she inherited in 1928, Anne Thomson added a further six by the time of her departure from office in 1947: a private maternity home in Salford which took married and unmarried women (1932); an open-air residential school for sick and delicate girls in St Leonards-on-Sea that expanded when it moved from Dover (1934); a sanatorium in the Scottish Highlands (1934); a certified home for girls and young women with serious cognitive impairment and physical disabilities in Sheffield at Howard Hill (1935); Virgo Potens General Hospital with facilities to nurse the chronically sick in Liverpool (1939); and their own clinic with operating theatres in Notting Hill in London (1941).

A small number of new hostels made up the second strand of development. In common with many other organisations (most notably the Young Women's Christian Association and the Girls' Friendly Society) the Province had been running small-scale hostels for young women in major cities since the 1890s.[99] Unlike the YWCA and GFS, however, the Daughters' early hostels had straddled categories by sheltering women at risk. The same hostel might offer a bed for temporarily homeless women, a hostel place for young women on probation, board and lodging for unemployed women in exchange for work, and lodgings for working women who could pay their own costs. The Sisters saw hostels as both a work of charity and an opportunity for the catechesis and spiritual formation of young women. Many of these hostels, like the ones in Dundee, Manchester, Hull and Liverpool, and the large London houses in Westminster and Marylebone, carried on into the inter-war years, offering a specifically Catholic environment for residents. A few, like the Birmingham hostel that had first opened in 1895

---

98 See Nicola Yeates, 'Migration and Nursing in Ireland: An Internationalist history', *Translocations: Migration and Social Change* 5, (1) (2009) Open Access E-Journal and Jennifer Redmond, 'The Thermometer and the Travel Permit: Irish Women in the Medical Profession in Britain during WW2', in MacPherson and Hickman, *Women and Irish Diaspora Identities*, pp. 92-111.

99 Emily Gee, '"Where Shall She Live?"' Housing the New Working Woman in Late Victorian and Edwardian London', in Geoff Brandwood (ed.), *Living,Leisure and Law: Eight Building Types in England, 1800-1941* (Reading: Spire Books, 2010), pp.89-109.

and had moved locations, were greatly expanded and updated at this time. What changed in the latter period, however, was the scale of several new hostels and the intention to provide for young women arriving from Ireland in search of work. St Louise's hostel in Medway Street close to Victoria Station was opened in 1933, when Cardinal Bourne asked the Daughters to work with the Westminster Ladies of Charity to provide accommodation for women who came to London, mostly from Ireland, a work which also had the enthusiastic support of the provincial director, John O'Connell. Within a couple of years St Louise's offered accommodation for 166 working women with 25 additional night shelter places. It eventually expanded to provide 300 places.[100]

Inspired by the success of St Louise's, Bishop Butt, Vicar Capitular of Westminster Archdiocese, asked the Sisters to do the same near Euston Station for 'the great number of Catholic girls who come from Ireland and Scotland to find work and have no friends or family in the city'.[101] St Teresa's Hostel in Gower Street was opened in 1936 with 80 places. Still very new at the time of the outbreak of war, these hostels were used by the government between 1940 and 1945 for women engaged in war work.[102] With the existing hostels and two other new smaller hostels, one in Willesden and one in Kilburn, the Sisters' provision reached its height in London during the 1950s and early 1960s, corresponding to the peak in Irish migration during that decade (500,000) and responding to the concern in Ireland about the moral and spiritual safeguarding of young Irish women in Britain.[103] A pocket-sized booklet given out free to migrants as they boarded the boats to Britain is representative of this anxiety and of what Yvonne McKenna has called an Irish 'reverse othering' of the British that was sometimes a component of post-colonial Irish nationalism.[104] The first section of *A Catholic Handbook for Irish Men and Women Going to England*, entitled 'Know Your England', alerted Irish youth to aspects of English life that were perilous and degrading to their moral well-being and eternal salvation.[105] Although England was the main focus for this concern, because migrants also went to Wales and Scotland, the Province opened a new hostel centre in Cardiff in 1949 and expanded its hostel in George Square

---

100 Typescript Account of Medway Street, 11-97 DCMH.

101 11-52 DCMH.

102 Mary Muldowney, 'New Opportunities for Irish Women? Employment in Britain during the Second World War', *University of Sussex Journal of Contemporary History*, 10 (2006), pp. 1-18.

103 Grimes, 'They go to England', p. 53, notes the frequency of sermons in Ireland on the subject of innocent Irish girls falling prey to 'the smooth-tongued, well-dressed stranger' in British cities. See Jennifer Redmond, '"Sinful Singleness"? Exploring the Discourses on Irish Single Women's Emigration to England, 1922-1948', *Women's History Review*, Vol. 17, Iss.3 (2008), pp. 455-476.

104 McKenna, *Made Holy*, p. 100. McKenna found evidence of this reverse othering in women's religious congregations with Irish and British sisters, where the othering concerned the inferiority of Catholicism in Britain compared with Ireland.

105 *A Catholic Handbook for Irish Men & Women Going to England* (Dublin: Catholic Truth Society, 1953). Cited in Clair Wills, *The Best Are Leaving: Emigration and Post-War Irish Culture* (Cambridge: Cambridge University Press, 2015), p. 88.

in Edinburgh. The Cardiff house, bought by the Province, included a night shelter that was part-financed by a donation from the Mothers' Union and by annual income from a Trust established by a local businessman.[106] The presence of the Sisters in all these hostels provided the young women with instant companionship, warmth, hearty meals, the constant promise of a prayer in times of need and a way to reassure their own families. Hostel ministry was seen by the Province as requiring pastoral experience and dedication on the part of the Sisters but no specific training, a position that came to be questioned by the Sisters themselves during the 1960s.

Ministries and professionalism

> The Archbishop being in London called on me in Mill Hill. He wanted to know if when vacancies of Sisters' positions occur in future in schools in Edinburgh, we could guarantee to offer Sister candidates as well qualified for the posts as the lay teacher applicants – having a BA, MA and BSc degrees. He believed that the Religious teachers in schools should be as qualified as the lay ones. Of course I knew we could not touch this standard.
>
> (Visitatrice Thomson to Superioress General Lebrun 1930)[107]

In his approach to the question of the professional qualifications of Catholic sisters, Archbishop McDonald was in advance of many other prelates and leaders of women's communities. At one level the Archbishop's expectation was unreasonable. Few women had degrees in 1930 and the number of Catholic sisters in Britain who had graduated, although increasing, was still small. Only three Daughters in the Province had degrees in 1930, and the Province had no policy to send Sisters to university on any scale. Yet McDonald was under strong pressures from the local authorities (most of which were dominated by Presbyterians) for Catholic sisters to match the qualifications expected from lay Protestant teachers. Several Catholic women's communities working in Scotland, such as the Sisters of Notre Dame de Namur and the Religious of the Sacred Heart, had shown that a high standard of educational attainment was possible, but Catholic schools in general lagged far behind in the quality of their buildings and the proportion of trained teachers.[108] The 1918 Education (Scotland) Act had brought Catholic schools into the state sector with full state funding in order to close the gap in attainment

---

106 This was John Curran who wanted to give £2,000 to buy the house but agreed instead to create a trust to fund running costs. 11-82-1 1-1 #10 DCMH.

107 August 1930, Thomson to Lebrun, 11-21-2 1-1 #2 DCMH.

108 For example, Lucy Carter, as Sister Bernadine of Jesus, Sister of Notre Dame de Namur was the first woman (and the second person) to gain a PhD in science at Glasgow University when she graduated in 1921. http://www.universitystory.gla.ac.uk/biography/?id=WH1308&type=P (accessed 30 August 2016). Other sisters graduated at MA level from the early 1900s.

that had opened up between them and state schools. The Church was expected to approve all teachers in Catholic schools as to their religious beliefs and character but the local education authority had the right of appointment and was emphatic about qualifications and experience.[109]

Five years after this visit to Mill Hill McDonald pressed the subject of qualifications and standards again, this time in relation to the Sisters' residential nursing care for children with multiple disabilities including cognitive impairment at St Joseph's in Rosewell. In the wake of a critical report from the Diocesan Visiting Committee (March 1935), he remarked pointedly that 'The time is long past since inefficiency can be condoned merely because an institution is under Catholic control, and the time is further past since an Institution must necessarily be considered well run because it is under the control of Sisters.' [110] Archbishop McDonald was determined that the Church should not be found wanting, even more so given the increase in sectarianism taking place in Scotland at this time. There is, however, no record that he (or any other bishop) ever offered to fund even part of the training of Catholic sisters. A contemporary Sister at St Joseph's noted that 'Finance was a big problem as the only income was 23 shillings a week paid for the children. Quite a number of ladies came with great suggestions, but there were no funds to support their ideas, so Lady Poverty reigned supreme.' [111]

Although no rebuttal was made to the Archbishop, the Province was making a real effort to release Sisters for training. In August 1926, for example, the council noted that Sister Sloan had recently completed two years in the Edinburgh teacher training college and could be sent on the specialist deaf education course at Manchester University with a view to a placement in the Tollcross Institute near Glasgow.[112] The importance of qualifications was well understood by the Sisters, being initially most urgent in the fields of nursing and teaching and after 1945 increasingly so for special needs, children's social care and social work. It was a serious challenge; although a significant number of entrants had had British Red Cross experience during the First World War, the third generation was not more professionally qualified than the second.[113] The need to maintain current works while releasing suitable Sisters to study for qualifications made it difficult to upgrade training; the community did not employ 'externs' to cover for study leave on grounds of cost and of ethos. Moreover, because the Sisters in care and nursing homes worked very long hours it would have taken two employees to cover for each one. A subsidiary problem was the question of where Sisters should train at a time when it was not acceptable for them to spend protracted periods

---

109 On the increase in sectarianism at this time of high unemployment in Scotland, see W.W. Knox, *History of the Scottish People*, Ch.10.

110 McDonald to Director O'Connell, 25 March 1935, 11-117 1-2 #12a DCMH.

111 Sister Louise Hannigan, *St Joseph's: the First Years*, (booklet n.d. *c.* 1984) p.4 11-117 1-1 #18 DCMH

112 Provincial Council Minutes, 22 August 1926, 9-5-0-2-5 DCMH.

113 Seminary Records, 13-4-1 DCMH.

living outside the community. From around 1910, teaching Sisters had been sent as day students to Mount Pleasant College in Liverpool run by the Sisters of Notre Dame, to St Charles' Training College in Kensington Square in London belonging to the Religious of the Sacred Heart, or to one of the two Scottish colleges run by these same orders.[114] They were able to live in one of the Province's own houses in any of these cities, although the travel was often time-consuming.[115] It was only in 1950 that Sisters were allowed to reside at Mount Pleasant College in Liverpool for the first time.[116] The question of training was linked to the question of community identity and to the practice of deliberately reducing outside influences that was normal within religious institutes and the training for the priesthood at this time.

The Province made some progress in establishing its own nursery nurses training colleges before the Second World War, one at St Vincent's Mill Hill and the other at Yelverton in Devon (the one in Liverpool having run into difficulties), both approved by the Home Office and the Royal Society of Nursery Nurses. When the Yelverton college was requisitioned during the war, a facility was opened at Feltham in Middlesex where the Sisters were already managing children's homes and another operated in Salford between 1941 and 1945. From the mid-1920s nursing Sisters regularly participated in professional bodies' meetings, such as the central Council for District Nursing in London, on which the Province was represented and in the international congresses of Catholic nurses and Religious nurses.[117] These bodies and congresses were increasing in number and range. When the third International Congress of Catholic Nurses was held in London in 1937, it was attended by Superior General Verdier and Superioress General Inchelin (who led several of the sessions) and senior nursing representatives from Germany, France and Peru as well as from Britain.[118]

It is possible to gauge how far these efforts had gone by the time of the Second World War. In the spring of 1941, when the Province had to register all Sisters in Britain under the age of 60 for war purposes and to state their qualifications, a quarter were certificated teachers. A further ten per cent were qualified nurses, and a small but growing number had qualifications as nursery nurses, or in clerical skills or domestic science.[119] Even so, at least half of the Sisters under the age of 60 had no professional qualification. During the war itself significant progress was made in the field of nurse training when the Province founded St Joseph's Training School for Nurses for the Mental Handicapped Register at Rosewell

---

114 Blandford Street Centenary History 1985, DCMH.

115 More than one Sister had to withdraw from her course because of the fatigue of travel combined with study and work.

116 Provincial Council Minutes ,13 March 1950 and 4 August 1950, 9-5-0-2-5 DCMH.

117 ibid., 14 November 1926, 9-5-0-2-5 DCMH.

118 *The Echo of the Mother House,* September, 1937, pp 177-180, 1-5 DCMH, and *The Tablet,* 24 July 1937, p. 27.

119 'Memorandum of the Sisters and their Works in England, Scotland, Wales and Northern Ireland ', April 1941 and List of School Sisters 1941, 9-0-2-5 DCMH.

in 1942, initially for Sisters only. Fifteen Sisters achieved their State Diploma as specialist mental handicap nurses in the first seven years. After 1949 St Joseph's became a Catholic training provider in Scotland by accepting other trainees. A second specialist nursing school, this time in orthopaedic nursing, was established at St Vincent's Pinner in 1947. The fruits of this investment were clear by 1960 when there were 25 Sisters in Britain with a mental handicap nursing diploma and 20 qualified in orthopaedic nursing in addition to the 57 State Registered Nurses.[120]

Training for childcare, however, was not well developed anywhere in Britain at this time (or even much later).[121] The many Catholic sisters involved in childcare in orphanages and Poor Law schools were given a new opportunity for professional training from a Catholic perspective for the first time in 1948. Prompted by the Report of the Care of Children Committee (Curtis Report, 1946) the first Home Office approved and inspected full-time Catholic childcare course of training was offered by the nuns of the Society of the Holy Child Jesus at their college in Cavendish Square in London. The course required six months of classroom study and the same length of practical work under supervision. Nineteen sisters were selected for admission in 1948,[122] two Daughters of Charity among them.[123] The Province also accepted an invitation from the Holy Child nuns to have a seat on the steering committee for the course. Despite this commitment, the two Daughters put forward by the Province to attend the course in 1950 were withdrawn before it began 'because of pressure of the works'.[124] It was a problem the Cavendish Square nuns experienced with many congregations despite the excellent reputation their course enjoyed among religious sisters.[125]

During the 1930s and 1940s professional development for sisters was fully endorsed by the papacy. Pope Pius XI, for example, used the occasion of the second International Congress of Catholic Nurses (1935), to state that it was the duty of every Catholic nurse to belong to a Catholic association of nurses. His address, quoted in *The Echo*, the Company's monthly internal journal, on his death in 1939, discussed the 'double field of action; a professional field and a moral field' and urged sisters to add to their qualities as Christians, 'this honour of being excellent in your professions'.[126] After the war Pope Pius XII gave further impetus to the drive to improve the professional competence of women religious. In a number of key addresses to the leaders of women's communities he connected the fall in vocations to the poor standards of professional training expected and practised by nuns. His forthright and unmistakable views on qualifications for

---

120 Statistical return to Paris for 1960, 9-0-2-5 DCMH.

121 See Mark Smith, *Rethinking Residential Child Care: Positive Perspectives* (Bristol: Policy Press, 2009), p.157.

122 Annals of Cavendish Square D51, p. 51, Archives of the Society of the Holy Child Jesus, Oxford.

123 Provincial Council Minutes, February 1948, 9-5-0-2-5 DCMH.

124 Ibid., 8 February 8 1950, 9-5-0-2-5 DCMH.

125 Annals of Cavendish Square D51 p. 58, Archives of the Society of the Holy Child Jesus, Oxford.

126 *The Echo of the Mother House*, October 1939, DCMH.

sisters were difficult for community leaders to ignore, even if they had wished to do so. Excellence, he told the First International Congress of Teaching Sisters held in Rome in September 1951, 'presupposes that your teaching sisters are masters of the subjects they expound'.[127] A year later the major superiors from around the world gathered in Rome for their own Congress were told to be 'broadminded and liberal' in the training of their sisters and to 'admit of no stinginess'.[128] There seemed to be an assumption that religious sisters could pay for this training, so that questions of cost did not enter into the discourse.

Professionalisation brought with it communication and engagement with other bodies – state, Church and specialist. It was a direction pursued energetically in the Company in France during the 1950s, building to some extent on work begun before the war. Superioress General Lebrun had created a new bureau in 1932, the Secretariat for the Works, which was to give modern direction to the Sisters' activities across professional fields. In 1954, under Superioress General Lepicard, this Secretariat enlarged the physical space it occupied and its role. Under the dynamic leadership of Sister Suzanne Guillemin, the Centrale, as it was known, began to guide the whole Company by means of symposia and through the articles it published in *The Echo*.[129] Although the administrative and state structures with which it was most concerned were French, the general thrust towards expertise and external engagement was applicable to all Provinces as were many of the new theories.

As a consequence *The Echo*'s content during the 1950s underwent a dramatic shift in emphasis away from the devotional orientation it had had in the 1930s. Sisters could read articles on such topics as 'Pedagogy for Training Schools for Hospital Nurses',[130] 'Bowlby and maternal deprivation',[131] 'Social Work in the Service of the Poor' and professional qualifications for the 'Sister of Charity Visiting the Poor'.[132] In November 1956 *The Echo* informed them of new 'Pontifical Directives for religious in nursing, teaching and the adaptation of Institutes to Modern times'.[133] The British Province was able to contribute to this exchange of good practice from its experience of implementing a new model of residential childcare.[134] The 'family group' approach, recommended in the Curtis and Clyde Reports, was described by a Sister of the Province at some length in a 1956 *Echo*

---

127 Pope Pius XII, Address to the First International Congress of Teaching Sisters, Rome, 8 September 1951.

128 Pope Pius XII *Report of the First Congress of Superior Generals of Pontifical Right*, Rome, 11-13 September 1952. Original at http://www.vatican.va/archive/aas/documents/AAS-44-1952-ocr.pdf.

129 Anon. *Mother Suzanne Guillemin* (no place but thought to be Paris; no date but known to be 1970), pp. 55-70. DCMH.

130 *The Echo of the Mother House* April 1954, p. 95 DCMH.

131 ibid., November 1954, DCMH

132 ibid., July 1955, p. 168, DCMH.

133 ibid., November 1956, p. 243, DCMH.

134 ibid.

article. It was a significant step away from institutional care, often formerly conducted on a large scale, and one that the British Province had taken for the first time in 1956. In the process of change expert working parties visited the homes run by the Sisters and their reports, such as the one on the Children's Refuge in Bellevue in Glasgow in 1956, could be painful to receive in their forensic analysis of shortcomings.[135] The author of 'Social Work for Religious in the Light of the Curtis Report' noted that 'Voluntary Homes and organizations were, up to the time of the Curtis Report, endeavouring with very slender resources and inadequate facilities to fulfil works which have since been acknowledged to be State responsibilities and are now State-aided.'[136]

Although there were concerns about the higher rates of loss of faith that might come from a policy favouring adoption and worries about a likely decrease in stability of care through increased use of fostering, the new developments in childcare were welcomed by childcare Sisters as enabling them to work more effectively.[137] Sister Monica Cowman, for instance, who was in front-line care at St Vincent's home in Torquay from 1931 to 1963, singled out the new availability of information about children's backgrounds (it had previously been withheld by the children's placement societies) and the encouragement to join professional networks as particularly important.[138] At the same time Sister Cowman continued to practise distinctively Vincentian care priorities that were not cultivated within the new professional culture. Through her involvement with the very active Torquay St Vincent's Old Boys Association, for example, 53 years after she had accompanied twelve boys on evacuation from Feltham to Torquay in 1943, and long after they had all left Devon, she and five of the former evacuees were still in regular contact. It was an illustration of the sustained human relationships that could be formed in residential childcare with Vincentian values.[139]

As the Province's involvement in general residential childcare reduced from the early 1950s it began to engage in a radical overhaul in special needs residential provision for blind children in Liverpool, deaf children in Boston Spa and children with both special needs in Tollcross. This was undertaken in collaboration with the Ministry of Education and the management boards of institutions. Sisters were sent on specialist university courses, a few visited the United States to study methods there and all began to work with new pedagogical methods and technologies. In

135 Copy of a Report made after a visit of Working Party on Family Grouping to the Children's Refuge, Bellevue, Glasgow 19 June 1956 and Report of the Committee Appointed by the Archbishop and Bishops of Glasgow to investigate the position of the Children's Refuge Rutherglen following Report by the Working Party. 11-44 DCMH.

136 *The Echo of the Mother House,* January 1956, p. 24, DCMH.

137 ibid., pp. 21-32.

138 Monica Cowman, 'Childcare: A Synopsis of Personal Experiences 1931-1963'. (Response to questions put by the author, 2005 private typescript), pp. 9-10. The same point is singled out in Nye, *A Peculiar Kind of Mission,* p. 193.

139 Monica Cowman, *Footsteps: Journeying Together through All Seasons of Life* (Dublin: privately printed, 1996), pp. 67-68. 2-1-16 DCMH.

1954, in a name change that heralded a complete programme of modernisation, the Liverpool Blind Asylum (a diocesan-owned provision) became the Liverpool Blind Institute. The following year the Institute hosted the Association of Teachers of the Partially Sighted and began a major fundraising drive to expand and upgrade its facilities.[140] The purpose was 'to ensure comparable education and life opportunities for visually impaired children so that they could integrate into the workplace and community'.[141] Two Sisters working at the Liverpool Institute won the Sir Arthur Pearson Prize for outstanding contributions to blind education and welfare during the 1950s. A very similar pattern of development took place at St John's Institute for the Deaf in Boston Spa during the late 1950s and early 1960s, particularly under the leadership of Sister Barbara Walsh who, with others, 'moved the school from a vocational institute to an international centre of intellectual achievement where an extraordinary numbers of deaf students moved on to higher education and university'.[142]

To summarise, by 1960 home visiting, the care of children and mainstream teaching were still core activities but a significant number of Sisters now ministered in health-care, hostel work and special needs residential schools, as Table 10.7 shows.

Works	Sisters deployed
Children's Homes and Special Needs Residential Care	120 86
Visiting Sisters: home and prison	106
Nursing of all types and Nurse Training	97 4
Hostels	50
Maternity and nurseries	14
Convalescence and holiday homes	14
Teachers mainstream Approved School Special Needs	86 4 26

10.7: DEPLOYMENT OF SISTERS BY MINISTRY IN BRITAIN 1960

140 11-84-1 DCMH.

141 Sister Kathleen G. Fothergill, 'The Development of a School for Visually-Handicapped Children in the Light of Educational Thought and Practice with special reference to the period 1944-74', MEd dissertation, University of Manchester, 1977), p. 17. 11-84-2 1-1 #6 DCMH.

142 St John's History from the school's current website http://www.stjohns.org.uk/history-of-st-johns/ (accessed 20 October 2017). In 1979 Barbara Walsh was awarded the OBE for her services to deaf education.

The Province now exercised greater control over its own work because of its ownership of newer foundations. Collaboration with the state increased as works for dioceses decreased. This was true of several of the hospitals, even though all Catholic hospitals had been exempted from transfer under the 1947 (Scotland) and 1948 (England and Wales) National Health Service Act as a consequence of the position unilaterally negotiated by the Catholic bishops for all Catholic provision in Britain.[143] The Sisters continued to work under contract for the NHS and to value this connection.[144]

Looking at the Sisters' work as a whole it seems fair to conclude that the focus on the most marginalised in society, so clear in the long nineteenth century, was not sustained as completely in this period. In part this was for the persistent financial reasons already explored, and in part because of the distributive benefits of rationing during the Second World War and the introduction of the welfare state and the National Health Service afterwards. But it was also the case that the culture of religious life in this period was more conformist and less bold in seeking out new forms of poverty and discrimination. From the mid-1950s onwards there are many signs of new approaches and methods in the Sisters' works but there were also more tensions when it came to reviewing and renewing their way of life.

Modernity and way of life

> Religious Sisters have for long been the most
> devoted and yet the most neglected members of the
> Body of Christ. That is to say, their great and
> wholehearted work in so many fields, both active
> and contemplative, has been taken for granted; everyone
> else calls on them as soon as there is a need...and expects
> them to be there. Yet the same people can be heard
> criticizing the Sisters as scrupulous, narrow-minded or
> out of touch with reality. (*Life of the Spirit* 1954)[145]

Dominican Sister Mary Laurence quoted this extract from a recent Catholic publication in her 1954 book for young women discerning a vocation to the religious life. Her intention was to counter a discourse critical of the way of life of Catholic sisters that had developed in recent years, largely among the clergy, that sisters were out of touch with modern post-war life. As we have seen, from 1950 Pope Pius XII regularly addressed the superiors general of women's congregations living in Rome on this subject. He spoke openly about 'updating'

---

143 Coman, *Catholics and the Welfare State*, p. 40. See also pp. 60-61.

144 As evidenced by the individual House assessments of the Particular Works, 1968, which asked every foundation to comment on its relationship to civil authorities. 15-4-1-1968, 1-7.

145 Quoted in Mary Laurence, *Nuns are Real People*, p. 15. *Life of the Spirit* was a periodical founded by the Dominicans in Britain in 1920 for Catholic reflection on current events.

and 'adapting' their 'outmoded' forms of penance, devotional life, unhygienic dress and impeding headwear.[146] At one of these meetings the superiors were addressed in a frank manner by the secretary of the Congregation for Religious, Claretian Father Arcadio Larraona, on the subject of congregational custom books. 'Notwithstanding all their good qualities'

> it is undeniable that custom books, because of their
> detailed regulating of many aspects of daily life,
> can and do become oppressive or at least embarrassing.
> There are superiors of all types and temperaments, and
> some of them are unduly attached to the letter of the
> prescription, without considering the 'spirit'.[147]

What Larraona and Pius XII had in mind was the climate that sister-historian Teresa White describes as a 'narrow and rigid' interpretation of the constitutions that took place in her own congregation between 1920 and 1950, leading it to become 'more monastic...more private...more remote from the 'outside world'.[148] Sisters were not to read newspapers but to have suitable articles clipped for them by superiors. They should never speak to strangers, keeping silence when out. An uncannily similar picture is painted in Anselm Nye's history of the English Dominican Sisters: 'many aspects of everyday conventual life became further removed from the lived experience of the women who entered religion after 1918, and less comprehensible to them'.[149] Nye aptly names the problem as the sacralising of customs and traditions.

Most modern readers are likely to sympathise with the spirit of the clerical reformers, represented above all by Cardinal Josef Suenens, whose widely-read book, *The Nun in the World* (1962), gave cogent voice to many of the issues.[150] Although he spoke for women rather than giving them their own voice, Suenens'analysis of the 'problem' was most unusual for its historical and sociological approach and for its orientation towards freeing women religious to flourish.[151] But not even Suenens placed responsibility for the prevailing malaise squarely where it belonged with the anti-Modernist actions of the Church in the early decades of the twentieth century. Alongside many sensible prescriptions derived from experience and tradition, a spirit of centralisation and of hostility to modernity had pervaded the General Norms accompanying the Apostolic

---

146 Pius XII *Report of the First Congress of Superior Generals of Pontifical Right*, Rome, 11-13 September 1952.

147 September 1952. Quoted in Ann Casey, *Sisters in Crisis* (Huntingdon, IN, Our Sunday Visitor, 1997), p. 20.

148 White, *A Vista of Years*, p. 202.

149 Nye, *A Peculiar Mission'*, p. 137.

150 See Cardinal Joseph Suenens, *The Nun in the World* (1962), p.vi, and prefaced by a letter from the Vatican Secretary of State A. Dell'Acqua who thanked the Cardinal on behalf of the Holy Father for 'devoting his time and talents to a problem which today forms the main concern of many pastors'.

151 Suenens, *Nun in the World*, pp. 38-51.

Constitution *Conditae A Christo* (1900) and the 1917 Code of Canon Law.[152] In 1922 this spirit was carried into the detailed precepts for episcopal visitation and for the quinquennial reports required by the Sacred Congregation of Religious for congregations professing simple vows.[153] Every five years 105 questions had to be answered. These included 'Do the Sisters practise any works of charity (such as the taking care of infants, of confinements or surgical cases) which appear improper to virgins consecrated to God and wearing the religious habit?' (No. 98) and 'Have the Superiors allowed Sisters to dwell in the houses of seculars and for how long?' (No. 100); or 'practised any art or industry that brings them in too frequent contact with outsiders?'(No.99).[154] All congregations had been required to rewrite their constitutions to conform to a template inspired by this more monastic attitude which allowed no place to incorporate their own spirit or charism into the drafting.[155] It is not surprising that the underlying thrust of the General Norms and revised constitutions were internalised by many sisters and taken as the source of authority by any mother general who lacked confidence or felt threatened by more adventurous spirits than her own.[156] As Kester Aspden observed 'it was not just in the realm of thought that the atmosphere became oppressive.' [157] There was a hard irony in women religious being preached to once again, this time to release themselves from the prescribed path they had followed after 1917, now seen as outmoded.[158]

We might not expect to find the same degree of restriction, monastic culture and separation from everyday life among the Daughters of Charity. Indeed, the perception of the Sisters as freer, less restricted than nuns and more 'ordinary' at this time was a strong theme to emerge from a survey completed by 80 Sisters of the Province in 2005 on motivations for choosing to enter the Company, discussed in the next chapter. One noted that 'the Sisters seemed to be on the streets in the many cities I visited' and another that 'they were more like ordinary people chatting and always in contact with people' or they had 'the freedom to go to the poor'. 'I felt that they were human, warm, individual not nunnish or odd', one commented when she met them in the nursery nurse training school at Mill Hill,

---

152 See Aspen, *Fortress Church*, p. 3.

153 D.I. Lanslots, OSB (ed.), *Handbook of Canon Law for Congregations of Women under Simple Vows* (New York: Frederick Pustet Co., 1922), Appendix C, pp.260-274d.

154 ibid., p. 274b.

155 Sandra Schneiders, *Finding the Treasure: Locating Catholic Religious Life in a New Ecclesial and Cultural Context* (Mahway, NJ: Paulist Press, 2000), p. 283.

156 This was the conclusion that Teresa White drew in her study of the Faithful Companions of Jesus, *Vista of Years*, pp. 185-88.

157 Aspen, 'Fortress Church', p. 4.

158 Mary Anne Confoy, 'Religious Life in the Vatican II Era: 'State of Perfection' or Living Charism?', *Theological Studies*, 74, 2, pp. 321–46. Reprinted in David Schultenover (ed.), *50 Years On: Probing the Riches of Vatican II* (Collegeville, MN: Liturgical Press, 2015).

while for another the deciding factor was 'seeing a Sister carrying her bag visiting the poor. Still a very vivid picture even though I did not know her.' [159]

At the same time Daughters of Charity had always practised many quasi-monastic disciplines. The founders had required that they live 'with holy modesty' and be 'more zealous of observance [of the rules] than of life itself' to safeguard their reputation, to ensure a spirit of poverty, for the sake of the common life and as 'a path of salvation'.[160] They wore common dress, practised the great silence after 9.00pm, asked permissions of superiors for many actions and accepted that their correspondence would be read by superiors. During the second half of the nineteenth-century Superior General Étienne promulgated norms for every office and for many aspects of life, as we have seen.[161] Some of the original Company customs, such as not accepting the offer of food or drink from the poor families they visited on the grounds that this would mean showing preference for some and taking from those in need, metamorphosed into a complete ban, including even members of the Sister's own family, that served to cement a clear status separation (and caused much heartache). The ecclesiology of the early twentieth century, reflected in the new canonical provisions, saw the Company accrue a further rigidity of community life and customs more associated with religious sisters, such as the wearing of a special postulancy outfit rather the simple black secular dress as previously.[162] One commentator noted 'a certain imitation of the 'religious life' as having taken place 'to bring us into accord with the Code'.[163]

The achievement of uniformity (and control) was always a challenge of course and we should not mistake prescription for implementation. The development of means for communication, brought about in the Company in 1926 through the monthly publication of *The Echo of the Mother House* was, therefore, an important new dimension for the insistence on certain behaviours. In the 1930s, for example, the pages of *The Echo* paid great attention to the details of dress and behaviour. A regular Question and Answer column dealt with 'customs' through means of questions purportedly coming from Sisters who was answered by the Vincentian director of the Company. A Sister who asked, for example, whether she might use her spare time arranging flowers for the chapel were told in no uncertain terms that a Daughter of Charity had no spare time and that flower arranging was only possible if it was an office she had been given by superiors.[164] In August 1934 this column was augmented with a serialised essay by the superioress general on 'The

159 'Survey of the Sisters' held at the 2005 Provincial Gathering held at Ushaw College. Author's own data.

160 Leonard, *Conferences*, p. 1005 (91) 30 December 1657.

161 See Miguel Flores, 'Father Richardson and the Daughters of Charity', *VHJ*, (1996), Vol.17, Issue 2, Article 7, p.95.

162 See the article by Father Joseph Jamet, Director General of the Company in *The Echo of the Mother House*, April 1968, which makes precisely this point. DCMH.

163 Ibid., p.3. 15-4-1-1968, 1-3 DCMH.

164 *The Echo of the Mother House*, March 1937, DCMH.

Importance of Our Pious Customs' which covered such matters as not wearing 'a
Vow Chapelet with medals differing from those of the Community' or 'an apron not
made according to custom, or a chemisette fitted to the figure' or a watch on a chain
rather than on a piece of black or green string.[165]   Chaplain's reflections continued
in November 1934 with directions about 'uniformity and simplicity in furnishings
and apartments'.[166]   Such articles sat side-by-side with detailed descriptions of
the elaborate ornamental displays created in the Company for Marian feasts, the
canonisation of Louise de Marillac and the beatification of Catherine Labouré.

The inter-war period seems to have been a time of contradictions, a time
when boundaries were tested by some Sisters and insisted on by authorities.
The apostolic life of the Sisters was experienced as 'freeing' and the Sisters were
seen as being 'ordinary' in their work in comparison with nuns, but their lives
otherwise were restricted and controlled by norms that correspond to a high view
of consecrated life. The installation of telephones for example, even when justified
on grounds of the apostolate, was not permitted. Sisters were instructed to decline
invitations to outside events such as the one from the Catholic Women's League
in 1929 for a women's Congress at the Albert Hall. Permissions to accompany
parishioners, like the request made in 1935 by the Sisters at Dundee to accompany
the women of their Mother's Guild to London, were refused.[167]   As late as 1938
Sisters asking to accompany the children in their care to a matinee were instructed
to reread the advice given in *The Echo* in 1926 forbidding such outings to public
entertainment, which were indeed forbidden to clergy and religious.[168]

Although Sisters were wholly obedient to these rulings they did not give up on
making a case for a telephone or requesting permission to accompany the children.
In 1932 they successfully proposed abolishing the use of the title 'Ma Soeur' for
Sister Servants because 'it creates a distinction amongst the Sisters.'[169]   Above all
they did not desist from asking for a change to the early rising rule of 4.00 in the
morning. The council regularly received requests from individual house for an
exemption on particular grounds. Only very exceptionally was permission given.
When in November 1939 the houses in Scotland were instructed to rise at 6.00 and
retire at 10.00 it was the exigency of war that had led to the change, then extended
across the Province. Wartime experience had re-opened this vexed question and
in January 1948 the provincial council 'considered [it] advisable to represent to the
Council in Paris that it would be more suitable for the works in these Countries if
the Sisters could rise at 5.00 a.m'.[170] This time, in an historic decision, change was
approved. When in 1956 it was decided that the Sisters should not rise until 5.30

165 Ibid., August 1934, p. 215, DCMH.

166 Ibid, November 1934, p. 273, DCMH.

167 Provincial Council Minutes, 26 August 1929, 31 October 1929, 1–5 February 1935. 9-5-0-2-5 DCMH.

168 Ibid., 1–3 February 1938, 9-5-0-2-5 DCMH.

169 Provincial Council Minutes, 29 March 1932 9-5-0-2-5 DCMH

170 Ibid, Vol. XV, 10 January 1948. 9-5-0-2-5 DCMH.

so that they could have seven and a half hours sleep it was clear that a spirit of adaptation was already in train.

The Sisters' prayer life, like the horarium a core foundation of daily living, was also updated. A new edition of the community prayer formulary was published in 1953 but only three years later the British Province went further than this to experiment with a monthly 'mutual catechism', a new form of spiritual life derived from the methods of St Vincent. The new rite for Holy Week promulgated by Pius XII in November 1955 was put into practice in Central House at Easter 1956, and in 1957 the Province introduced yet a further new form of community prayers. For anyone outside the Company the first visible sign of reform was the demise of the cornette in 1964. For Daughters themselves the adjustments to the horarium along with an updating of community prayers had already signalled that more fundamental changes in their way of life were possible in the interests of health and in keeping with the Company's lay status.

After 1964 it was understandable that in some memories and narratives of the pre-conciliar Catholic community an assumption was made that an 'ideal' had existed that could have been sustained. But as Eamon Duffy has remarked 'it was a way of life which, which though it seemed immemorial, was actually a cultural construct, the product of a network of specific circumstances.'[171] It is at least open to question whether the Province responded to Superior General Verdier's 1928 call to the Company to 'do the work for which we were established',[172] or whether under the economic and cultural pressures of the inter-war and post-war years there was a move into 'safer', albeit still physically very demanding, ministries. The Second World War and the new expectations of working-class people and of women marked a turning point that was rapidly followed by a new climate of debate in the Church about the work of active Sisters. A great impetus for change in the 1950s co-existed with a wish to reassert the norms of a peaceful and more domestic era. Recent reassessments of post-war history that have identified the 1950s as a 'period when old and new co-existed' find ready parallels in the experience of the Sisters.[173] The changes that came during the 1960s and 1970s were already underway in the 1950s for pragmatic or sociological reasons. It was the Second Vatican Council and the movement for renewal that anchored future

---

171 Eamon Duffy, 'Tradition and Reaction: Historical Resources for a Contemporary Renewal', in Austen Ivereigh (ed.), *Unfinished Journey: The Church 40 Years after Vatican II* (London and New York: Continuum, 2003), p.52.

172 Superior General Verdier writing in *The Echo of the Mother House* April 1928, quoted in *Genesis of the Company* Vol. 1 (privately printed, 1968), pp.125-127. 1-7-2 DCMH.

173 On Catholicism in the 1950s and 1960s see the literature survey in Harris, *Faith in the Family*, Ch.2. For revisionist history of the 1950s more generally see Heiko Feldner, Clare Gorrara and Kevin Passmore (eds.), *The Lost Decade? The 1950s in European History, Politics, Society and Culture* (Newcastle: Cambridge Scholars Press, 2011), p. 2. See also N. Thomas, 'Will the Real 1950s Please Stand Up? Views of a Contradictory Decade', *Cultural and Social History* Vol. 5, Issue.2 (2008), pp.227-236.

changes in the Company's historic spirituality and, at the same time, placed them in a new theological and ecclesial understanding.

Part IV
1960–2017 Renewal and Revisioning

11

Responding to the Second Vatican Council 1960–1983

> Entering actively into the movement of the church
> and adapting ourselves to the world of today are a
> matter of life or death for a community... Our
> manner of going to God, our mode of union with God,
> and the place of our contemplation, are located within
> our action, in the meeting of the people we encounter
> side by side at this moment...This calls for a renewal of
> spirit and structures.
> (Suzanne Guillemin, Superioress General 1962–1968)[1]

The tercentenary of the deaths of Vincent de Paul and Louise de Marillac opened the new decade in 1960 for Daughters of Charity everywhere. Solemn ceremonies in the rue du Bac during March of that year marked this significant occasion in the life of the Company. In Britain large numbers of Daughters, Vincentian confrères, representatives of the St Vincent de Paul Society, Ladies of Charity, Children of Mary Immaculate and invited guests packed into Westminster Cathedral to participate in a Solemn High Mass presided over by Cardinal Heenan. Similar events took place in Scotland, and in all the countries where Daughters were present, apart from those under Communist rule. The occasion was also marked in the British and Irish Province by the publication of two booklets intended to reach out to a wide audience. The Catholic author and broadcaster on theological and spiritual matters, Rosemary Haughton, was commissioned to write a popular study of the history and interior spirit of the Daughters entitled *'You did it to me'*, and the province published an English translation of French pictorial lives of St Vincent and St Louise. Occurring one year after Pope John XXIII had given notice of his intention to convene an Ecumenical Council of the Church and less than two years before the opening of that Council in October 1962, these tercentenary events, with their display and solemnity and their regard for the past, could appear

---

1 Carmel McEnroy, *Guests in Their Own House: The Women of Vatican II* (Eugene, OR, WIPF & Stock, 1996), p. 178, quoting Guillemin, 'Renewal of Spirit and Structures', presentation to a colloquium of French bishops on 10 September 1966, held at Louvain.

with hindsight as the end of an era. The Council, however, with its purpose of *aggiornamento* (updating) and renewal through the principle of a return to original sources (*ressourcement*), showed a new interest in the 'authentic intention of founders'.[2] In a very real sense, therefore, the tercentenary marked the opening of a new chapter in which the needs of the present day and the presentation of the Gospel in a globalised world were explored through the lens of the founding spirit.

The Council's decree on 'The Adaptation and Renewal of Religious Life', *Perfectae Caritatis* (*PC*), was promulgated in October 1965.[3] In it 'the sacred synod confirms these religious in their vocation and urges them to adjust their way of life to modern needs' (*PC* 10). *Perfectae Caritatis* gave orders and institutes not only the specific task of renewal but also the sources and method to undertake it, and a timescale by which to do so. They were to redraft their own constitutions and at the same time to edit all customs books, prayer books and directories.'Renewal of spirit' was to have priority over 'renewal of ministry'(*PC* 2). The sources for this task were to be the life of Christ revealed in the gospels, each order's own particular charism or grace as manifested through founders and in history, the Church's mission as set out in the Council documents as a whole, and a sound and scientific knowledge of the contemporary society in which they were inserted. *Ressourcement* for *aggiornamento* was stated explicitly, as was the Council's respect for the diversity of charisms and callings of the Church's religious life. The distinctive nature of each was not only acknowledged but was to be the source of renewal.

With chapter 6 of *Lumen Gentium* (1964), the Dogmatic Constitution of the Church, the Norms for renewal, *Ecclesiae Sanctae* (*ES* 1966), and the Instruction on formation for the religious life, *Renovationis Causam* (*RC* 1969), these documents constitute the core conciliar texts for the renewal of religious and consecrated life. They were, however, always to be read in conjuction with the other Council texts, above all the whole of *Lumen Gentium* and *Gaudium et Spes*, the 'Pastoral Constitution of the Church in the Modern World' (1965). The former confirmed the ecclesiology that had been developing in the twentieth century – that vowed religious are constitutive of the Church: they are ecclesial and the holiness of the Church would not be complete without them. The latter articulated the theology of the Council, in particular its vision of the Church as the whole Pilgrim People of God *within* the world rather than in flight from the world, and the call to holiness - originally drafted in reference to religious life – but in the final draft transformed into a universal call to all God's people.

Perfectae Caritatis provided two further instructions, one permissive and the second a requirement, in which the means of renewal and its ends were intertwined. Permission was given for religious institutes to begin a period of

---

2 *Genesis of the Company,* Vol. 1. Introductory Letter from Superior General William Slattery, 15 March 1968. 1-7-2 DCMH

3 *Perfectae Caritatis,* in A. Flannery, (ed.), *Vatican Council II: The Conciliar and Post Conciliar Documents* (Dublin: Dominican Publications, 1992), pp. 611-623. *Ecclesiae Sanctae* (1966) available on-line in English.

experimentation so that they could test out the value of interim constitutions and customs before committing to a final text. All institutes were required to convene a special renewal chapter before the end of 1969 to draft such interim constitutions. A general commission of each institute was to be established to prepare for this extraordinary chapter by 'full and free consultation of the members...for example by consulting conventual and provincial chapters, by establishing commissions, by proposing a series of questions etc' (*ES* 1.4). It was stated as an expectation that each institute would proceed with the 'cooperation of all the members'. The Congregation for Secular and Religious Institutes (CSRI) envisaged that new constitutions and other texts would be submitted for approval in the early 1980s when the commission that had been established to renew and rewrite the 1917 Code of Canon Law in the light of the Council was also due to complete its work. At this point the experimental period would be over. The men and women who led these organisations were required, as organisational management theory would describe it, to embark on a whole-institution management-of-change process. It was a top-down initiative which was at the same intended to be a Spirit-inspired renewal for individuals and their institutes 'so that their witness may be seen by all and our Father in heaven may be glorified' (*PC* 25). There was to be sufficient renewal for this to happen without discontinuity taking place. From an organisation perspective the Council Fathers had set out a daunting prospectus for religious orders and institutes, particularly given the confusing nature of the categories 'updating', 'renewal' and 'reform' in the original documents and subsequent magisterial teaching.[4]

The writing of constitutions in the light of authentic historical sources, the return *ad fontes*, was of particular importance to the Company and to the Congregation of the Mission. Even during the war-worn 1940s the Holy See had pressed again for the Company to have constitutions approved in the light of the 1917 Code of Canon Law.[5] Negotiations about constitutions that respected the Company's privileged vows (neither private nor public) and exempted status (from visitation by the local bishop) began in 1944 and were completed only in 1954 with the pontifical approval for the first time of constitutions and rules.[6] In the year before the opening of Vatican II, Rome approved, again for the first time in the Company's history, a set of regulations for the provincial directors in relation to canonical visitation and for the relationship between the Congregation of the Mission priests and the Daughters.[7] These approved constitutions had certainly not 'bedded down' in the practice of the Company by 1962, and were regarded negatively by some

---

4 See Nicholas Lash, 'Vatican II: Of Happy Memory – and Hope?" in Austen Ivereigh, (ed.), *Unfinished Journey: The Church 40 Years after Vatican II* (London & New York: Continuum, 2003), p. 19.

5 Letter from Cardinal Lavitrano, Prefect of the Congregation of the Affairs of Religious to general superior Slattery, 17 October 1946. Printed in *Genesis of the Company*, Vol 1, pp. 131-133. 1-7-2 DCMH.

6 Described at length in *The Echo of the Mother House*, June 1954, pp. 154-158, and May 1955, pp.117-119. 1-5 DCMH.

7 Ibid, May 1955, pp. 134-135.

in it, as 'drawing it closer to the religious state'.[8] The requirement to write new constitutions in the light of authentic sources was, therefore, entirely welcomed as the opportunity to adjust canon law to the Company's own charism.

Despite the importance of recognising the implementation of the Council's work as an 'unfinished journey',[9] there was nonetheless a defined conciliar phase for religious institutes which came to an end in the early 1980s with the presentation and approval of revised constitutions and the approval of the new Code of Canon Law in 1983. It is with this period between 1962 and 1983 that we are concerned here, and specifically with the reception of the Council by Daughters in Britain, their participation in the Company-wide processes for renewal during the 1960s and 1970s, and with the first outcomes.

If the history of Catholic sisters in the inter-war decades is characterised by a paucity of historical and research literature, the opposite has been the case with the post-Vatican II years. Questions of change in organisation, in ministries and in the outward appearance of Catholic sisters have attracted a significant amount of analysis and comment. There might have been little new in the willingness of outsiders to comment on the lives of nuns and sisters, but the readiness of sisters themselves to engage in public discussions of their life and to participate in public debate on the nature of the Church and her mission in the modern era was novel. The insights of theology, spirituality, sociology, anthropology, history, life-writing and psychology have been deployed in differing combinations in doctoral theses, autobiographies, specialist journals for religious, symposia proceedings and books on the 'question' of apostolic women religious and Vatican II. This literature constitutes what may well be the largest discourse on the nature of religious and consecrated life in the history of the Catholic Church; it is certainly the largest contributed by women concerning their own vocation and way of life.[10] Oral histories, moreover, along with interviews and surveys, have given access to the memories, reflections and responses of a wide spectrum of sisters.[11]

At the same time it is important to remind ourselves that most of these narratives in the English language, whether they come through sociological surveys and analysis or through personal stories, speak about the experience of sisters in

---

8 Joseph Jamet, CM director general of the Company, 'What Are We?', *The Echo of the Mother House*, April 1968. 1-5 DCMH.

9 See, for example, Ivereigh, (ed.), *Unfinished Journey*.

10 This section taken from Susan O'Brien, 'Religious Life for Women', in McClelland and Hodgetts, *From Without the Flaminian Gate*, pp. 129-130.

11 For example, Carole Garibaldi Rogers, *Habits of Change: An Oral History of American Nuns* (Oxford & New York: Oxford University Press, 1996). See the extensive oral history project run by the KADOC (Interfaculty Centre for Research and Documentation on Religious, Culture and Society), Leuven University, Leuven.

the United States of America.[12] This context, out of which so much outstanding intellectual work on the religious life for women has come, is also the most sharply polarised anywhere about the impact of *aggiornamento*.[13] Against Sister Sandra Schneiders's three-volume analysis and study of an artificially constrained past and hopeful future for women's consecrated life[14] Ann Carey's *Sisters in Crisis: The Tragic Unraveling of Women's Religious Communities*, with its self-explanatory title, stands as representative of the alternative perspectives.[15] The meaning of Vatican II has been a matter for debate since the 1970s, even, for some at least, a 'battle' for the historical memory of the Council.[16] Consecrated women and their way of life have been at the heart of that debate since the later 1960s.

For all the points of similarity between the American and British contexts and between the sociology and history of consecrated women in United States and Britain, it can be misleading simply to read meaning from the former to the latter, as tends to happen by default.[17] Because the Council itself spoke about unity in diversity and taught the principle of subsidiarity as essential to healthy hierarchical governance, it intentionally promoted decentralisation and encouraged inculturation. This direction of development was deepened by the strong encouragement given to religious institutes to read the 'signs of the times' in their own particular part of the world. A good deal remains unexplored concerning the influences and cross-currents which passed between different provinces in transnational institutes during the process of renewal, and how these were managed by generalate authorities, but further study also requires an

12 The leading sociologist of women's religious life, Patricia Wittberg, takes a global perspective but has an American lens. Patricia Wittberg, *From Piety to Professionalism and Back? Transformations of Organized Religious Virtuosity* (Lanham, MD: Lexington Books, 2006); *Pathways to Recreating Religious Communities* (New York: Paulist Press,1996); *Creating a Future for Religious Life: A Sociological Perspective* (New York: Paulist Press, 1991) and with Mary Johnson and Mary Gautier, *New Generations of Catholic Sisters* (New York: Oxford University Press, 2014).

13 Two separate organisations speak officially on behalf of two sets of religious orders and institutes of women in the United States, representing the two positions: the progressive Leadership Conference of Women Religious (LCWR) and the more traditional Conference of Major Superiors of Women Religious (CMSWR). A Vatican Apostolic Visitation of U.S. Women Religious, carried out between 2009 and 2012 in which it was the LWCR affiliated institutions that were under scrutiny, exacerbated the tensions.

14 Sandra Schneiders, *Religious Life in a New Millennium*, 3 vols (New York: Paulist Press). Vol I *Finding the Treasure: Locating Catholic Religious Life in a New Ecclesial and Cultural Context* (2000): Vol II *Selling All: Commitment, Consecrated Celibacy and Community in Catholic Religious Life* (2001) and Vol III *Buying the Field: Catholic Religious Life in Mission to the World* (2013).

15 Ann Carey, *Sisters in Crisis: The Tragic Unraveling of Women's Religious Communities* (Huntingdon, IN, Our Sunday Visitor Publications, 1997).

16 Massimo Faggioli, *Vatican II: The Battle for Meaning* (New York/ Mauwah, NJL Paulist Press, 2012) and *A Council for the Global Church: Receiving Vatican II in History* (MNL Fortress Press, 2015). Faggioli's *The Battle for Meaning* gives an even-handed account of the two viewpoints as they developed at and since the Council. See also his bibliographical essay "'Council Vatican II: Bibliographical Overview 2007-10', *Cristianesimo nella Storia*, 32 (2011-2012) pp. 755-791. http://www7.uc.cl/facteo/centromanuellarrain/download/faggioli.pdf (accessed 21 September 2016). For another perspective see M.L. Lamb and M. Levering (eds.), *Vatican II: Renewal with Tradition* (Oxford & New York: Oxford University Press, 2008) and Nigel Zimmermann (ed.), *The Great Grace: Reassessing Vatican II Today* (London & New York: Bloomsbury, 2015).

17 See Gemma Simmonds (ed.), *A Future Full of Hope?* (Dublin: Columba Press, 2012), p.18.

understanding of the particular historical experiences in specific locations.[18] This chapter has three aims. The first is to explore how the processes and mechanisms for renewal established by the transnational Company of the Daughters were implemented in the British Province and influenced by the British context. The second is to present an argument that the Daughters' history in Britain supports an interpretation of 'change within continuity'.[19] This argument is made partly by drawing attention again to the changes that had already occurred before 1965 and partly by highlighting the stability of life that continued into the 1970s and beyond in ways that do not conform to many characterisations in the literature about the implementation of Vatican II.[20] Connected to this second aim, a third intention is to enable the Sisters in Britain to speak about their own experience of Vatican II and to reflect on its impact from lived experience.

Vatican II Voices of Daughters in Britain

In 2005 Sisters of the British Province, who had come together for a provincial meeting, were invited by me to complete a short survey comprising a series of open questions (see Appendix III) two of which concerned Vatican II. More than 80 Sisters answered these two questions of whom 31 had entered before 1955 and 29 had entered between 1956 and 1964, the date at which the Company changed from the cornette and traditional habit to a new habit. When asked 'What was your first reaction to the changes brought about in the Company after the Second Vatican Council?' the oldest group remembered the following:

> Huge relief! Many of the practices both of the Church and Community had become meaningless for me, but I'd never dared express this. It was affirming when these practices were dropped or changed. The joy my parents experienced when we were allowed to spend time at home was worth its weight in gold. The freedom experienced in the teaching of R.E. and the creativity that was allowed.

> I compared it to Christ impressing his followers that he 'did not come to change the Law and the Prophets – but to fulfil it'.

18 Carmen Mangion, 'A New Internationalism: Endeavouring to "build from this diversity, unity" ', paper given at conference 'Nun in the Modern World', Cushwa Centre May 2015.

19 See Christopher M. Bellito and David Z. Flanagin (eds.), *Reassessing Reform: A Historical Investigation into Church Renewal* (Washington DC: Catholic University of American Press, 2012) Intro. p.9. This is the position taken by Alana Harris in *Faith in the Family* (Manchester, Manchester University Press, 2016).

20 Roger Finke and Rodney Stark, 'Catholic Religious Vocations: Decline and Revival', *Review of Religious Research*, Vol.42:2 (2000), pp. 125-145.

> I have always thanked God I lived before Vatican II. I
> appreciated so much what change came about. The discipline
> in our lifestyle stood by me. I am grateful for the openness in
> many aspects of our lives.

> It was very exciting. Then we began having Local Assemblies
> and Provincial Assemblies where we all felt at last we have a
> 'Voice'. Just to answer the questionnaires, we felt now we can
> tell PARIS our feelings and views.

> A great sense of excitement and each one eager for renewal in
> community life.

> Delighted, relief, progress at last! Less control from Paris and
> Mill Hill! But fear of adapting and of neglecting renewal, which
> (the latter) is the work of the Holy Spirit.

> Joy at the wonderful changes that came about allowing for
> freedom of speech, discussion, dialogue etc.[21]

Only three in this group recalled any kind of anxiety as their most significant memory, represented by a Sister who found it 'Difficult to take on board. Well-known structures collapsed; my path was no longer mapped for me. Pain because so many sisters left. Insecurity.'

Among those who had entered between 1956 and 1964 one Sister identified her main memory as anxiety: 'I was wary of too many changes too quickly', she wrote, 'Aware of moving too soon without enough reflection.' Three others recalled being both delighted and fearful, challenged and yet relieved. One expressed her initial dislike at the loss of the cornette (1964) but most were glad not to wear the heavy habit (it weighed twelve pounds) and the change to a more hygienic habit. The great majority of the Sisters in this group expressed strong memories of their own joy at what took place in the mid- to later 1960s:

> My first reaction was one of joyful liberation. It was high time
> for a change in the Church and in the Community. I was very
> privileged to share in that change.

> I revelled in being turned upside down and inside out. Besides
> becoming a voice for the voiceless – we became aware of our
> own voice, a woman's voice.

> I saw each change as for the better as it came along. We lost a lot

---

21 Quoting from returns to the survey which are in the author's possession.

of 'nunnish ways' which had crept in and returned more to our
original foundation state and spirit.

The openness, the way we could speak up and tell our story,
be part of decision-making, have our say.

I was young but I was also aware of moving forward with the
tradition of the Company and a sort of 'keeping faith' with the
past but being and becoming more inserted into the changing world.

I found it exciting – especially the attitude which helped to
deepen my spirituality and ways to reach out to others.

It was wonderful! I was only young in the Community –
still at College – a new vision of hope and openness was there.
Hans Kung's book 'The Council and Reunion' [1960] I can
still remember. Liturgy became a joy.

The words used by the Sisters to recall their own reception of the Council bear
out historian John O'Malley's proposition that the 'horizon of interpretation' of
the Council is embedded in its language and its style.[22] O'Malley argued that the
Vatican II decrees, constitutions and declarations contrasted with earlier council
texts not only in their overall pastoral orientation but in their consistent use of new
language categories. A coherent discourse was created by the use of horizontal
language such as the Church as the 'People of God'; the reciprocal language of
dialogue and collaboration; words of friendship (human family) and humility
(servant); and words of interiority (joy and hope; anxiety and grief). Even if the
language of hierarchy remained, the form of the documents and their language
comprised a model-shift for 'what the Church should look like' and a 'profile of
the holy Christian'.[23]

If O'Malley is right then ecclesial bodies which obeyed the call to renewal
closely, as did the Daughters of Charity, would be expected to experience that
model-shift for themselves. One of the most striking aspects of the expectation
placed on religious orders and institutes by Vatican II was that of consultation and
of giving a voice to all members. When asked in 2005 to select what each one now
believed to have been 'most important to the province' from the process of conciliar
renewal, Daughters in Britain were in agreement that it was, to employ O'Malley's

---

22 John O'Malley, 'Vatican II: Did Anything Happen?' *Theological Studies* Vol. 67 (2000), p.27 ff.

23 O'Malley, Ibid., p.30 quoting *Acta synodalia* 1, Part 1, pp. 166–175, at 172–73. See O'Malley's extended
argument in *Vatican II: Did Anything Happen?* (New York: Continuum, 2008) and *What Happened at Vatican II*
(Boston, MD Harvard University Press, 2010). For his penetrating thinking about the historical significance of
form as content and style as substance, see other works, for example, John O'Malley, *Catholic History for Today's
Church: How Our Past Illuminates our present* (Lanham, MD: Rowman & Littlefield: 2015), p. 219.

terms, the shift from the vertical to the horizontal and from instruction to dialogue. The 67 responses to this question from Sisters of all ages were analysed for themes and coded by frequently recurring terms. There was strong agreement across the generations in what was identified and even in the order of importance given to each. As Table 11.1 shows clearly, four dimensions of community life stand out ahead of all others, the first pair concerning questions of governance, responsibility and decision-making and the second pair describing 'the Vincentian spiritual path' and spiritual renewal through scripture, prayer and liturgy:

.

TOP 8 RESPONSES Respondents' own language and terms The number in bold is the rank and that in brackets refers to the number of references	50 + years of vocation Number = 29	21–50 years of vocation Number = 38	Total Number=67
Inclusive governance, consultation	**2** (15)	**1** (26)	**1** (41)
Personal responsibility, co-responsibility	**1** (18)	**2** (17)	**2** (35)
Deeper understanding of Vincentian way of love and service of people in poverty	**3** (9)	**3** (13)	**3** (22)
Spiritual renewal through access to Scripture, Office of the Church, Charismatic Renewal	**3** (9)	**3** (13)	**3** (22)
Normalisation of life. Discarding 'nunnish' customs, French dominance,	**7** (4)	**5** (12)	**5** (16)
Deeper personal and community relationships	**5** (7)	**7** (8)	**6** (15)
Appreciation of individuals for who they are; anti-uniformity	**6** (5)	**6** (10)	**6** (15)
Collaboration with others	**8** (2)	**8** (7)	**8** (9)

11.1: QUESTIONNAIRE RESPONSES VATICAN II 'THE CHANGES MOST IMPORTANT TO THE PROVINCE'

Additional responses included: appreciation of the Company's place in the Church, the importance of justice alongside charity, and the development of the Sisters' talents. We will return in the final chapter to the significance that such a high degree of agreement has had for the Province as time has passed, but at this point our interest is on how, by what means and processes, these changes came about.

Dialogue and decision-making

> Before Vatican II our Sisters did not express opinions
> unless specially invited by superiors. That was rare.
> We were to follow the authority of superiors. This was
> how it was and we accepted it in obedience.[24]

On 8 October 1967 the eight Daughters living in the St Augustine's community in Darlington convened themselves as a Local Assembly of the British Province. This was the first of five weekly meetings which would enable them to formulate proposals to the first ever Provincial Assembly, scheduled to meet at Mount Pleasant College in Liverpool in late December that year. Like the Provincial Assembly, Local Assemblies were an entirely new development for the Company. Each meeting was formally chaired and minuted, delegation papers and voting papers were circulated and scrutineers appointed. Specific topics were scheduled for each occasion: the spiritual life; the Vows in general; service of the poor; community life; vocations; government of the community; apostolic activities and particular works, the Blessed Virgin and the Company. The Sisters at St Augustine's put forward a total of 18 proposals. These included the subdivision of the Province into regions to speed up decision-making; the renaming of the Miraculous Medal as the 'Medal of Our Lady'; the reading of Scripture to be integrated into the Rule; more emphasis on ministry with the elderly and lonely; a minimum community size of six Sisters; and each Sister to be entitled to one free recreation time a week.[25]

In a letter circulated to all the Sisters in February 1968, Sister Gertrude Andrew, visitatrice of the Province, informed them that it had been a major work 'to classify the two or three thousand proposals which had resulted from the Local Assemblies', but she would shortly circulate them.[26] As events transpired, the Provincial Assembly had to be postponed two weeks before it was due to take place because an outbreak of foot-and-mouth disease in England posed the risk

---

24 Interview (unstructured), Sister C, 12.10.10.

25 St Augustine Darlington Domestic Assembly Log Book, 1967-73. 11-55-1, 1-12 #5 DCMH.

26 Letter sent to Sister Servants by Sister Gertrude Andrew, 17 February 1968, to be read to all the Sisters. 15-4-1-1968 , 1-3, #9a. DCMH.

of Sisters travelling to and from Ireland transferring the infection there.[27] It was no mean feat to reschedule a ten-day programme for more than 200 delegates and officers at such short notice, but a new time was found in April.

Local (or Domestic) Assembly consultation was one of several strands in the preparations made for the Provincial Assembly, which itself fed into the Extraordinary General Assembly of the Company in June 1968, the first to have legislative powers in the Company's long history.[28] A second form of consultation had preceded Local Assemblies and had formed part of the preparation for them. In June 1967 Sister Gertrude informed Sisters that they would soon receive the first part of a two-part questionnaire compiled in Paris on behalf of Superioress General, Mother Suzanne Guilleman. Reminding them of the Vatican Council Fathers' expectation that 'every member of the Community must have a voice in the General Assembly', Sister Gertrude impressed on the Sisters the importance of conscientious and responsible completion of the questionnaire. 'Each one of us has something to say,' she wrote, 'because each one of us, if we are living our religious life, is in contact with God.'[29] At a time when there were more than 45,000 Sisters in the Company the process had been designed 'to allow each Sister, even those who are diffident, to express their ideas...to help the Sisters deepen and clarify their opinions concerning the problems the Community now has to face... and to begin the remote preparation for the work of the Domestic Assemblies'. Undertaken between June and September 1967 the questionnaire comprised more than 200 questions divided into sections covering all aspects of the life and work in the Company. It required answers to such fundamental questions as 'What, in your opinion, is the religious value of community life?' as well as to enquiries specific to the British and Irish Province such as, 'Should the Province be divided? If, so in what way?' and 'Should the charitable name of the Province be changed from Sisters of Charity to Daughters of Charity?'[30] The anonymised responses were collated and analysed by a team of 50 Sisters from the Province. Sisters working in Special Commissions for each of the thematic headings of the questionnaire then turned the results into a series of reports. Behind each report lay the statistical evidence which showed not only how opinions ranged in relation to each question, but also how the responses compared between Sisters of different years of vocation.[31] If the authors of *Perfectae Caritatis* had intended to effect organisational transformation through process they were supremely effective in the case of the Daughters of Charity in Britain.

---

27 Letter from Sister Joan Tindall to Sister St John, Sister of Notre Dame de Namur, 14 December 1967. 15-4-11968, 1-1 #5 DCMH.

28 This General Assembly combined the business of the regular General Assembly that had been scheduled for 1968 to elect general officers with that of the Extraordinary Assembly mandated by *Ecclesiae Sanctae*.

29 Letter sent to Sister Servants by Sister Gertrude Andrew, 2 June 1967. 15-4-1-1968, 1-2, #1. DCMH.

30 Raw data on the Questionnaire Returns 1968. 15-4-1-1968, 1-6 DCMH.

31 Provincial Assembly 1968 Commission Reports. 15-4-1-1968, 1-12, #1 DCMH.

A third preparatory strand investigated the individual ministries or works of the Province. Questions were designed to tease out the position of each activity in every location in relation to the civil authorities, to the mission of the Church and to the specific vocation of the Company. Was it a work of the Church and did it meet the test of being a true work for people in poverty? Which social class were they primarily working with and were they qualified for the work? Sisters met in working communities to assess how well their particular apostolate measured up to these criteria. The resulting reports provided both a set of factual answers about the civic and ecclesial status of the work and a subjective assessment by those carrying it out, summarised in Commission Reports for the Assembly.

Responses to this enquiry demonstrated how the Sisters on the ground were living out their Vincentian vocation in ways not necessarily apparent from a simple categorisation. For example, it was noted about one hostel which provided accommodation for young women of 15-23 years old, that the residents included 'many coloured girls who find great difficulty in getting suitable accommodation, girls in the care of Children's Department and from broken homes, quite a number from our own homes find happiness and security in a homely and friendly atmosphere'. It was essential, the Sisters reported 'that the sisters be suited to this work for youth and find it congenial otherwise they are unhappy and so are the girls' but they also noted that they should be trained in youth leadership and social welfare for better 'apostolic results'.[32]

Data from these three processes formed the investigative and consultative basis for the Provincial Assembly's deliberations. Summaries were circulated to delegates along with a Directory of the norms for the conduct of business. The electing of delegates was itself new. All those participating, who had been advised months earlier to obtain and read the documents of the Council, were recommended to re-read Supplements to *The Way* (published by the Society of Jesus) on *Perfectae Caritatis* and on Religious Renewal.[33] To these sources were added a Meditation on Renewal composed by Father James Jamet, director general of the Company, and a copy of his trenchant summary of the history of the Company's Rules and juridical status from 1633 to the present day, starkly entitled 'What Are We?'[34]

As is apparent from this brief account of the detailed processes that fed into the 1968 Extraordinary General Assembly, every Sister in the Province who was capable of involvement had not only been consulted but had participated in modern social science and organisational research. It is hard to overstate the transformations that were effected or set in motion by the processes described above, although it is right to be cautious in estimating the speed with which their

---

32 'Particular Works' Code No..205. 15-4-1-1968, 1-7, DCMH.

33 Letter Sister Gertrude Andrew to Sister Servants to be read to all Sisters, 17 February 1968. 15-4-1-1968 1-3, #9a DCMH.

34 Father Jamet's piece was also printed in *The Echo of the Mother House* in April 1968. 1-5 DCMH.

meaning was absorbed into the lifeblood of the community and by each individual. In 1972, in preparing for the second Provincial Assembly of 1973, the team of Sisters who wrote a 'Report on the Assessment of the Works' commented that 'there was a realisation on the part of many Sisters that the past few years of renewal and self-criticism had awakened them to their personal responsibilities...many also feel that they have a greater understanding of people in poverty and their needs.'[35]

As the 2005 survey shows, in the view of the Sisters, it was the changes in governance, consultation and shared responsibility which were the most significant outcomes of the Council's call for renewal. All other aspects of renewal – in prayer life, spirituality, the common life, and the apostolate – flowed out from an application of the conciliar precepts of subsidiarity, dialogue, the role of conscience and respect for human dignity. Daughters experienced a 'model-shift' that transformed relationships at every level when they began to put into practice both what the Council had required by legislation and the language and style in which it had spoken. But another conclusion is also indicated: such an undertaking could only have been set in motion and managed by leaders at Company and provincial levels who were committed to renewal and had the personal gifts to see the process through.

Leading renewal in the Company and Province

The election in 1962 of Suzanne Guillemin as superioress general of the Company carried the same potential of renewal for the Daughters that Pope John XXIII intended for the whole Church through the work of the Council.[36] Mother Guillemin was a towering figure among the leaders of Catholic women religious during the 1960s. Only ten Catholic women superior generals were invited to attend the third and fourth sessions of the Second Vatican Council as auditors and as one of them Suzanne Guillemin embraced the messages of the Council.[37] Since her appointment in 1954 to head the Company's Social Services Department, based in Paris, Guillemin had developed a reputation as someone able to move with ease between care of her own community and engagement in the wider Church, between the individual Sister and consideration of issues on an international scale with secular and Church agencies.[38] She had proved to be an inspiring teacher and communicator, initiating a series of seminars for Sisters to learn about new

---

35 'Report on the Assessment of the Works' (March 1972), p.6. 15-4-1-68 1-5 DCMH.

36 Suzanne Guillemin, *Circular Letters Vol 1 1963-65* and *Circular Letters Vol 2 1966-68* (Paris: Privately printed for the Company, 1968). 6-50 DCMH.

37 McEnroy, *Guests in Their Own House*. McEnroy's is the only study of the women auditors, who also included lay women. McEnroy gives invaluable information about all the women auditors that was gleaned through interviews and correspondence. Women were not invited to the first and second sessions and Cardinal Suenens played a significant role in changing this situation.

38 *Mother Suzanne Guillemin*, p.52 ff. This biography was put together by several Sisters after her death, one of whom paid for its private publication. There are few copies in circulation. 6-50 DCMH See also Betty A. McNeil 'Unfolding the Legacy: Key Figures in the Tradition', *VHJ* (1998), Vol.,19, Issue 1, Article 5.

developments in social services and to discuss them freely. Moreover, she had a way of integrating work and prayer, spiritual and social service that meant the supernatural horizon was never set aside.[39]

During the Council it was Suzanne Guillemin who was invited to advise the French bishops on the problems facing women religious before they voted on *Perfectae Caritatis*. She did the same for the African bishops in October 1965.[40] Already known to many of the superiors general of women's congregations for the role she played in the cross-congregational sister formation movement of the 1950s, she was also asked to address them too. In 1967 Pope Paul VI appointed Guillemin as consultor on the Commission for Justice and Peace charged with applying the social teaching principles promulgated in the encyclical *Populorum Progressio* (the development of peoples).[41] The following year she was appointed as consultor of the Congregation of Religious. It is indicative of Guilleman's capacity and her reputation, but also of her priorities, that she turned down an invitation to serve as the first President of the International Union of Superiors General, the post-conciliar collaborative body of women religious, which she had helped to establish.[42] Despite the Church's historical difficulty in finding the 'right' canonical status for the Company, it was recognised that Suzanne Guillemin's contribution to discussions about *aggiornamento* from the particular perspective of a Daughter of Charity was of value to the renewal of all active women's congregations.

Well before the close of the Council, Mother Guillemin was already laying the groundwork for the renewal of the spirit of the Company. Dissemination of the Council's messages to all the Sisters was a priority and she employed all the existing means of the Company to accomplish this end. In the *Echo of the Mother House* in October 1962, for example, she contributed a piece entitled 'With the Church in the Council' and continued with essays on 'Rome in Council' (1963), 'Tensions of the Religious Life: Apostolic Values' (1964), 'Formalism and Truth' (1965), and 'Social Justice' (1966). The *Echo* was a place where a Sister could read extensively in the theology of the Council through the many essays contributed by Vincentian scholars. It seems, however, that few had the time for such reading: publication and circulation did not mean that reception had taken place.[43] A monthly *Echo* could run to 300 pages in the conciliar and immediate post-conciliar years and it bore little relation to its 1930s counterpart. More definitely received by the Sisters at large were the superioress general's annual circular letter for the start of the calendar year and her conference for the Feast of the Presentation, which were read aloud to the Sisters.

---

39 See *Circular Letters*. 6-50 DCMH.

40 *Mother Suzanne Guillemin*, pp. 161-64. 6-50 DCMH

41 Promulgated 26 March 1967.

42 McEnroy, *Guests in Their Own House*, p. 197.

43 Interview (unstructured) Sister D. 13.9.2104.

Mother Guillemin's letters linked the promulgation of council documents to the Sisters' own lives and ministries, for example relating *Pacem in Terris,* about which she wrote in 1963, to harmonious and peace-building ways of working and to the bedrock of prayer.[44] After the close of the Council she took passages from individual documents as the source for her annual meditations,[45] and likewise statements made by Pope Paul VI.[46] In this way she consistently created a connection between the Council, the historical spirit of the Company, and the Sisters' continuing formation as Daughters of Charity. An even more direct form of dissemination was the extensive programme of visitations she made to different countries with their opportunity for oral presentations to the Sisters. In 1963 she travelled to Japan, Vietnam, Belgium, Portugal, Madagascar and the United States of America, and called in on the Sisters in the Philippines, Greece and Turkey.[47] Mother Guillemin did not visit Britain or Ireland but her influence was felt, for example in the letter she wrote to Young Sisters about to make their retreat at Mill Hill in 1966 rather than travel to Paris, as had always been the case previously. Characteristically, the focus in this letter of encouragement for the Sisters at such a key moment for them was a quotation from chapter 6 of *Lumen Gentium* about Christ as the wellspring of all holiness.[48] For others in the Province her influence was felt indirectly through circular letters and conferences and through a thorough implementation of the methods she had devised for bringing Sisters together in day-long seminars for updating, sharing information and for community building.

It was a hallmark of Mother Guillemin's approach to *aggiornamento* that she did not depart from the Company's normal rhythms and channels but rather sought to model application of the principle of *ressourcement.* 'It is not a case of making a clean sweep of the past, of rebuilding everything into something new', she wrote:

> It is a question, on the contrary, of imitating the father of the family in the Gospel who brought out of his treasures new things and old. What, then, is this treasury if not the Gospel [,] our Holy Rules [,] the teaching of our Holy Founders [,] the directives of the Church.[49]

Research into the Company's history and the sources of the founders was extended by Guillemin and Superior General Slattery and the fruits made available to the Sisters. In September 1967 Mother Guillemin circulated a new Company Calendar to be used from 1 January 1968. Significant historical events in the life of the

---

44 *Circular Letters* Vol I, 2 January, 1964, p. 26. 6-50 DCMH.

45 *Circular Letters* Vol. II, 2 February 1966, p.21 on *Lumen Gentium.* 6-50 DCMH.

46 *Ibid.,* 2 February 1967, p. 60.

47 *Mother Suzanne Guillemin,* p.136. 6-50 DCMH.

48 In 1966 she wrote to the Sisters making their Seminary retreat in Mill Hill, the first year that Sisters did not travel to Paris for the prise d'habit. 1 August 1966. Letter in personal possession of Sister Maria Parcher.

49 Ibid., p. 184

Company, from the seventeenth to the twentieth centuries were listed in a pithy form 'to help us to know better and to appreciate more this great Community of which we are members, this Community of whose past we are the heirs and of whose future we are the builders'.[50] Other historical material was designed in part to assist discussion about the constitutions. A concise and cheaply produced history of the Company entitled *Genesis of the Company 1633–1968* was published by the mother house in 1968, much of which would have been new and highly informative for the Sisters, particularly concerning the vicissitudes of their exempted status.[51] 'Treasures' from the storehouse served other purposes too. In the early 1970s the Company's superiors 'rediscovered' Marguerite Naseau, the countrywoman and shepherdess who Vincent de Paul had described as the founding Daughter of Charity. Matthieu Brejon de Lavergnée has argued that the Company was able to propose and promote her as a role model for the Sisters in a less hierarchical era in which the 'option for the poor' was being articulated.[52]

The historical perspective was vital, but renewal was necessary in Mother Guillemin's view because religious communities, like all organisations, experienced a life cycle. Each began 'with an enthusiasm and fervour that endowed fluidity'. Out of these attitudes came success, then 'as experience has shown, nearly always methods of procedure become concretized...[and] the activity in question begins to be threatened by sclerosis on the one hand, and on the other by a partial isolation from the world'.[53] It was a soundly based sociological analysis, as was Guillemin's observation that because women's position in society had changed and social needs were different, it was time for women religious to be 'inserted' into the Church and the world.[54] Real insertion would mean a renunciation of certain privileges that went with their status, so as to 'enter into the life of those who were formerly called the poor, but whom, in reality, we must know as our brothers [sic]'.[55]

Under Mother Guillemin the Company conducted a General Assembly in 1965 between the final two sessions of the Council, holding it in Rome for the first time. This too had been preceded by a questionnaire to all the Sisters on their vocation as a Daughter of Charity, the results of which were studied at the Assembly. It was the last General Assembly to be restricted to the visitatrices and presented

---

50 *The Echo of the Mother House*, Supplement October 1967. 1-5 DCMH.

51 A second volume, printed in English in Emmitsburg, Maryland, in 1973 presented themes in the development of the Company's life from 1935 to 1971, including a summary of the Extraordinary General Assembly of 1968-1969 and its decisions.

52 Matthieu Brejon de Lavergnée, 'Du mythe des origines: Les Filles de la Charité et leurs fondateurs, XVIIᵉ-XXᵉ siècle', in Brejon de Lavergnée (ed,), *Quatre siècles de cornettes*, pp. 27-35.

53 *Mother Suzanne Guillemin*, p. 170. 6-50 DCMH

54 ibid.,p.65 'We are at the moment when women are preparing to play a very different role in the world. Up to the present a woman was shut up, as it were, in her role of wife and mother...Things are not complete nor balanced, and are good only when both [men and women] have been given their opinions, when both have agreed, as it were, in judging things.'

55 ibid., p. 170. The French sense of 'fraternalism' loses its sense of inclusivity when translated into English.

an opportunity to prepare the 75 provincial leaders for the work ahead as well as to agree modifications to customs.

The visitatrices who met in Rome in 1965 not only discussed a new range of topics in a fresh language, their appearance was also entirely different. They were wearing the new habit that had replaced the cornette and traditional habit on 20 September 1964. The timing of its introduction meant that when Mother Guillemin walked to her first Vatican Council meeting and took her place in the Visitors' Gallery she was, in effect, modelling the new habit for the waiting press. It was a newsworthy event, prompting a comment from President de Gaulle of France and in Britain featuring on the BBC news and in the *Daily Telegraph*, the *Guardian,* the *Daily Mail* and the *London Evening Standard.* A change of habit and headdress had been announced to the Sisters on 10 January 1964 by Superior General Slattery. Planned to happen on the same Sunday worldwide, like so much about the management of change by Suzanne Guillemin and her councillors, this event had required meticulous coordination and communication, and a great deal of practical work. From the Sisters it required obedience and trust. As one of the two older Sisters from the British Province noted, 'Changing from the Habit and Cornette was such a surprise – one felt reluctant to appear, but presently it was OK.' For the other 'the change of the Habit was a big emotional thing to all at the time. But I think the most important thing was we now began to realise that we are "The Church".'

The Company had been discussing the updating of the habit for some time.[56] Its advantages as a 'trademark' and for identifying Sisters as they went about the streets was offset for them by their increasingly anachronistic and conspicuous appearance (certainly not part of their founding charism), the impediment to mobility, especially car driving and cycling, and, as one Sister expressed it, the challenges of the traditional wool habit at a time when expectations about personal hygiene had been revolutionised.[57] Several younger Sisters who were at that time in college or in the seminary noted 'relief and delight' at never having to wear the cornette. Moreover, by making this change, Superiors General Guillemin and Slattery achieved a global uniformity that had defeated even Étienne's efforts to move the Spanish Daughters (who were numerous) from the black habit and veil they had adopted when they had gone under episcopal protection at the time of the French Revolution. Guillemin herself wrote little about the habit change. The speed and efficiency with which she brought this about, compared with the consultative care that pertained in so many other areas of renewal, suggests that she knew this was one matter for decisive leadership.

Between 1963 and 1968 Suzanne Guillemin laid deep foundations for the Company's response to Vatican II. She was not, however, given the time to develop or embed this work herself. Her death from a post-operative embolism in

---

56 Joan Tindall, 'A Sprinkling of Memories: Before I forget', p. 14. Personal File 10-2 DCMH.

57 Comments in the 2005 Survey of the Sisters of the British Province.

March 1968, shortly before the opening of the Company's Extraordinary General Assembly, was described by her biographer as 'sudden and unexpected'. Guillemin herself had considered it a possibility and reminded the Sisters gathered round her hospital bed that 'les evenements, c'est Le Dieu.'[58] It was her successors, Christine Chiron (1968-1974) and Lucie Rogé (1974-1985) who took on the task of leading the Company's renewal, including the rewriting of its Constitutions.

In Britain it had been visitatrice Margaret Whalen who had attended the 1965 Assembly in Rome. In 1966, when her term of office expired, Mother Guillemin appointed Gertrude Andrew, one of the provincial councillors at the time and Sister Servant of the large house of mercy in Blandford Street in London. Installing Sister Andrew as visitatrice, Sister Mary Basil, English-speaking Councillor from Paris, spoke of the grave responsibility that superiors faced to bring about 'organic development' within the Company's historical tradition.[59] The evidence strongly suggests that Gertrude Andrew was well-equipped to lead the renewal of the Province within the spirit and template already developed in the Company.

A Lancashire woman from Oldham and the daughter of an iron works foreman, Gertrude Andrew had been educated in Manchester by the Faithful Companions of Jesus and had a higher level of formal education than most of her companions in the inter-war era. She graduated from Manchester College of Technology in 1934 with a Masters in Technical Optics.[60] Working as an assistant optician in Manchester she joined the Ladies of Charity and became known to several Sisters in the city before enquiring about her own entry to the community. 'I like her', wrote Sister O'Halloran in recommending her, 'and think she is very much in earnest'.[61] This earnest young Sister was soon identified as having the potential to lead. Most of her life in community was lived at Provincial House or The Priory. In 1947 she was appointed directress of the seminary and in 1952 became provincial secretary to Sister Whalen. Later reflections about her tend to see her as a personality as holding juxtapositions in harmony. One who knew her well described her as someone who could appear rather nervous but was actually very capable of being decisive. She was a private person and yet was also attentive to other Sisters and trusting of their capabilities. Sister Joan Tindall, who was Andrew's driver for many years, described her as rarely talking on long journeys, using the time to make notes. Tindall saw her as both 'trapped in herself' and yet, as provincial, showing 'her true breadth of vision by her courage in steering the Province smoothly and gently through the momentous change that took place

58 *Mother Suzanne Guillemin,* p. 217. 6-50 DCMH.

59 *The Echo of the Mother House Supplement for the British Province* March 1966. 1-5 DCMH.

60 Later University of Manchester Institute of Science and Technology.

61 Letter dated 28 January 1936, from Sister O'Halloran in Ancoats. Personal File, Gertrude Andrew, 10-2 DCMH.

in our way of life after Vatican II'.[62] An historian has the advantage of seeing the risks that she took on occasion and the overall re-education programme that she embarked on with the Sisters.

It was Sister Andrew who not only managed the provincial consultative programme already described but who instituted gatherings of Sisters for less formal conversations. She adopted Guillemin's model of bringing Sisters together in groups according to vocational age or ministries for 'Renewal Days', and this personal dialogue proved to be the most effective form of transmitting the meaning of Vatican II. On these occasions there was always an extended opportunity, sometimes lasting from 1.45 until 6.00 p.m., for Sisters to ask any questions they might have and to explore questions together. The Sisters' appreciation of these events both to consider the implications of *aggiornamento* and as effective ways to build community, was considerable. Meetings held in Scotland and England in 1971 for Sisters between 3 and 12 years of vocation, for example, concentrated on what it meant to live in community. 'All our thoughts were discussed openly,' a Sister reported, 'We laughed and talked with many of our friends as well as discussed seriously. We are grateful to our Superiors for their thoughtfulness, consideration and openness to our thoughts and ideas'.[63] Another session in the same year for Sisters of 13 to 23 years of vocation took as its topic 'The Community and Service of the Poor'. Of this it was said 'we all felt immediately a bond deepening between ourselves, as common problems were presented and answers were sought.[64] The reporter on the Manchester session for this age group praised the way that the provincial, director and Sister Catherine Barrett had 'given themselves to be completely at our disposal during the day, as well as the example they gave of open-mindedness and respect for each individual's opinion had perhaps taught us more about"Community Living"than talks or discussions'.[65] Reports of these sessions convey a sense of the authenticity that was experienced. When the Sisters in training had their session, for example, the topic of shared spontaneous prayer was raised by them. Because some had no experience of it 'in the evening Sister Gertrude and Sister Margaret led voluntary groups. For myself I found this a very helpful way of prayer, and was very much aware of the Holy Spirit with each member of the group individually and in the group as a whole...I think this was the general feeling.'[66] Reading such comments sheds light on Joan Tindall's conclusion that Gertrude Andrew, for all her quiet manner 'shared the vision of St Vincent in holding the service of the poor paramount, and letting go of peripherals. She was a woman for her time – far-seeing, broad-thinking, and

62 Sister Joan Tindall on the occasion of Sister Gertrude Andrew's funeral, 2005. Gertrude Andrew, Personal file 10-2 DCMH.

63 'News Around the Province', No. 7, p. 7 May 1971. 1-7-3 DCMH.

64 ibid., No. 8. July 1971, 1-7-3 DCMH.

65 ibid.

66 ibid., No.14. February 1973 1-7-3 DCMH.

encouraging.'[67] There was a clear respect for office but the boundaries that existed in the days when Sisters knelt as soon as the visitatrice entered the room were entirely gone.

Part of the effectiveness of these events lay in the relationship between the provincial and the provincial director. In 1961 Father James Cahalan had been appointed to replace Father Joseph Sheedy who had held the position since 1938. At one time provincial of the Irish Vincentians, Sheedy was greatly respected in the Vincentian community and his internally published sermons were much appreciated by many Sisters. But he was something of a traditional patriarch in his dealings with the Sisters, and he could dominate.[68] Cahalan was an entirely different proposition. A visionary priest with a gift for teaching and an instinctive inclusiveness, he would only say what was essential. Sister Joan Tindall observed that one of the first things James Cahalan did on appointment was to buy a car. Then 'he drove for miles round the Province – England, Ireland, Scotland, Wales – visiting the Houses and the Sisters, listening to them and encouraging them. Informality was his trademark.'[69] One Sister, who had entered in the early 1960s, remembered that 'Father Cahalan's eighteen months with Gertrude Andrew was powerfully changing.' Many Sisters spoke of how he had 'guided change by using the opportunities presented by the different attitudes of the young Sisters', such as handling responses that arose when, to the shock of some of the older Sisters, they went to see a Beckett play and spoke about its content.[70] In this he worked with the seminary directress, Madeleine Ryan, also described as a quiet 'change agent', who introduced unstructured free time for seminary sisters and oversaw the new process of postulancy and juniorate introduced after the 1965 General Assembly.[71] For a number of Sisters of the fifth generation he, and his successor Father McAtarsney, were remembered as instrumental in keeping them from leaving. In talking matters through with the director they were able to bridge the gap that existed between their experience before entering and their life in community.[72] Sisters of all ages found James Cahalan's spiritual challenges enriching. 'Have we in fact sold all?' he asked in a 1965 conference on vocations that challenged each member to think about herself rather than vocation exhibitions as the source of vocations, to *be* rather than to *do*:

---

67 Sister Joan Tindall on the occasion of Sister Gertrude Andrew's funeral, 2005. Personal file 10-2 DCMH

68 This comes across in his many conferences, of which there are two typed and bound volumes in the Mill Hill Archive, and it is the view of Sisters who knew him.

69 Joan Tindall, 'A Sprinking of Memories', p. 17. 10-2 DCMH.

70 Group interview with 5 Sisters held on 10.10.2005 at Christopher Grange, Liverpool.

71 ibid and unstructured interviews of individual Sisters in 2016. On the postulancy and juniorate, see reports in 'News Around the Province' and *The Echo of the Mother House.*

72 Group interview with 5 Sisters held on 10.10.2005 at Christopher Grange, Liverpool.

Have we burned our boats or do we cling tenaciously to any purely natural plank, fearful of the complete darkness which sometimes surrounds complete commitment to God. It cannot be repeated too often that our greatest missionary instrument is our transformed personalities, the evidence to the world that we are indeed new.[73]

When he was appointed provincial of the Irish Vincentians and had to relinquish the office of director, James Cahalan continued to be in demand in the Province as a retreat leader. But it was his successor Felix McAtarsney who worked with Sister Gertrude over a number of key transitional years. Quiet, scholarly, thoughtful and particularly gifted with the seminary Sisters, he and Sister Andrew established a working relationship that allowed the changes to happen seamlessly and in harmony. In circumstances where the structural relationship between the two parts of the double family did not yet function as a partnership of equals, it was important for the process and progress of renewal in the Province that the directors were far in advance of their day in their interpretation of the role as one of 'brother' and accompanier.[74]

Division of the Province

It was almost inevitable that in each Province some questions of real importance not directly connected to the question of *aggiornamento* became caught up in renewal processes. In the British and Irish Province it was the question of whether to divide the Province to achieve a more effective and personal governance across Ireland, Northern Ireland, Scotland, England and Wales. From 1966 to 1970, when the decision was made to create one Province for Ireland and one for Britain, this was a recurring issue. In January 1966 when the vice-visitatrice for Ireland became ill, councillors believed her heavy burden of responsibility to be the root cause. It was agreed to recommend that her replacement be freed from responsibility as Sister Servant of Dunardagh and to change her office to that of Councillor for Ireland.[75] Sister Louise Hughes was installed in this role two days after Gertrude Andrew was installed as visitatrice and this was the situation at the time of consultation in preparation for the Provincial and General Assemblies of 1967 and 1968.

Consultation on the matter of governance produced seven different proposals that were considered by the Provincial Assembly. They ranged from the creation of a separate Province for Ireland to no change, and included a number of alternative

---

73 James Cahalan CM 15February 1965 Conference on Vocations, 8-7 DCMH.

74 In 1964-1965 the Company had drawn up the first Directory for the provincial directors starting with a draft created by Felix Contassot, one of the assistants general of the Congregation of the Mission, who consulted all the provincials of the Congregation and all the provincial directors of the Daughters, but not the Daughters themselves. The most recent Directory for Directors identifies three aspects to the role: animation, formation and accompaniment.

75 Provincial Council Minutes, 27 January and 8 March, 1966, 9-5-0-2-1 DCMH.

compromise arrangements involving the establishments of Regions or an enlarged provincial council.[76] A proposal to transfer the Provincial House to Ireland was voted on and rejected.[77] In the 'Record of the Assembly Proceedings' it was noted that the 'question as to whether or not the Province should be divided in some way, and if so, how, had been occupying everyone's mind and prayers since the opening of the Assembly.' It was decided to deal with it first 'as everything would depend on the outcome of that'. As provincial director, Felix McAtarsney advised them to set aside all other considerations than 'the context of the Church and Her mission', what was best for the mission in both countries.[78] The outcome was a proposal to the General Assembly for powers to extend the membership of the provincial council 'in view of the special circumstances existing in the Province of Great Britain and Ireland'.[79] Writing to the whole community the week after the Assembly, Gertrude Andrew conveyed openly 'the atmosphere of frank discussion, perhaps particularly felt when we were discussing the proposals regarding the organisation of the Province'. Of all the issues voted upon, this was the one about which she chose to provide advance information ahead of the circulation of the report. Informing Sisters of the outcome she noted that 'the proposal to divide the Province was rejected by a large majority and yet each member of the Assembly was keenly aware that there are big problems and that there must be some reorganisation.'[80] This decision, approved by the General Assembly, was refined further during August and September 1968, to ensure that the Assistant Provincial and a Councillor were resident in Ireland and were supported by specialist advisory groups for each of the fields of work.[81] Yet, within eighteen months, in January 1970, the provincial council decided that time was now 'opportune that the approval of the General Council be sought for the erection of Ireland as an autonomous Province'. The new Province was to encompass the whole island and not to follow national contours. Four points were articulated as the basis for this recommendation, of which the difficulty superiors had 'to maintain the contacts with the Sisters that are necessary to really do justice to the work of renewal' was primary. It was recognised that the works in England and Scotland would face difficulties because of the loss of Irish vocations but it was nonetheless decided to proceed as quickly as possible. All the Sisters in Ireland over eight years' vocation were to be consulted about the new Provincial and her officers. The provincial council proposed the apportionment of continuing responsibility for the mission in Ethiopia to Britain and Nigeria to Ireland on the basis of the strength of past relationships. Irish Sisters currently placed in Britain would be free to choose

76 Proposals to the Provincial Assembly, April 1968, p. 44 Division of the Province. 15-5-1-1967 1-2 #2 DCMH.

77 Proposals Rejected, Provincial Assembly, April 1968, p.6 15-4-1-1968 1-15 #3a DCMH.

78 Record of the Proceedings of the PA, 1968, p. 9. 15-4-1-1968 1-11 #1 DCMH.

79 Proposals from the Provincial Assembly to the General Assembly, No. 30. 15-4-1-1968 1-11 #3c DCMH.

80 Letter of Gertrude Andrew to all the Sisters, 1 May 1968. 15-4-1-1968 1-3 #16 DCMH.

81 Provincial Council Minutes, 10 August and 3 September 1968. 9-5-0-2-1 DCMH.

whether to remain or to move to the Irish Province, a highly risky proposal that respected individual choice.

Between January and September 1970 the council worked with Paris on financial arrangements; the General Council appointed Catherine Barrett as first Irish provincial and she proceeded to consult the Sisters in Ireland about officers. At the beginning of September Sister Hilda Gleason travelled from Paris to install Catherine Barrett as first provincial of Ireland. Also present was Sister Gertrude who 'thanked the Sisters of Ireland for their loyal co-operation at all times'. She wanted them to know that they would 'never forget the deep debt of gratitude which the British Province owes to the Irish Sisters. Almost fifty per cent of the Sisters in Great Britain are Irish and without them the works could not carry on.' She hoped that there would always be co-operation between the two Provinces and repeated what Sister Hilda had already said – that 'where there is love there can be no real separation.'[82]

What seems to have made a decision for division critical at precisely this time was the urgent need to carry out a review of the works in the light of two imperative forces: *aggiornamento* and the reduction in the number of Sisters in active service. Although the significance of the start of 'The Troubles' – the sectarian and political conflict over the constitutional status of Northern Ireland – in October 1968, cannot be ruled out as an influence, no mention was ever made of it in notes and minutes or in any record. On the other hand the repeated governance reforms since the end of the Second World War indicate increasing concerns that the Sisters and works in Ireland were not receiving the attention needed. The call to renewal served to bring matters to a head. The division was painful and even traumatic for Sisters who had not understood the degree to which the council had wrestled with the issue over years. For Irish Sisters placed in Britain it meant that the question of whether or not to request reassignment to Ireland would always be a live one since no time limit was set on the permission. For British-born Sisters there was a grave sense of loss, both of historical identity and personal relationships. At the same time there was the opportunity for both Provinces to develop a more specific approach to the cultures in which they worked and to collaborate.

Reassessment of the works and the question of vocations

The newly configured Province of Britain comprised more than 700 Sisters in 1970. During the 1970s 26 Irish-born Sisters placed in Britain made the decision to join the Irish Province and a small number followed in the 1980s and 1990s, as some Sisters chose to live closer to family once they were no longer in full-time active ministry. Although the numbers transferring in the 1970s were not large and did not cause a sense of crisis, they further depleted an already insufficient number of Sisters for the Province's existing commitments. A more serious loss, given

82 'Provincial Newsletter', Issue 5, 5 September 1970, p. 4. 1-7-3 DCMH.

that it was absolute, was the departure from the community altogether of vowed Sisters, a phenomenon that happened with increasing frequency in the post-war years. Whereas only 25 vow Sisters made the decision to leave the Company in the whole period from 1925 to 1950, almost the same number made this decision during the 1950s, a number that was replicated in the 1960s.[83] At the same time, as already discussed, the number of aspirants was continuing to decrease. Between 1955 and 1965 an average of ten women entered the Mill Hill seminary each year of whom six, on average, would continue on to make vows.

This was already a considerable reduction on the pre-war flow of new companions coming from England, Scotland and Wales, yet it seems that many in the Province were unaware of the gravity of the situation.[84] The lack of communication and consequent lack of a shared understanding became apparent at an early stage of the first Provincial Assembly in 1968. When Sisters studied the works of the community through commission reports, presentations and discussions, such as the hostel example given above, 'this exchange of experiences, of information on what each one is doing came as a revelation';

> Works that had come in for criticism as not being the service of the poor took on a new meaning as we heard of what was being done...The main cry was for more personnel, more Sisters...It came as a surprise generally that nowhere is the supply meeting the demand.[85]

Analysis of the entry figures would have shown the degree to which the gap between supply and demand in Britain would be greatly exacerbated by a division of the Province on either side of the Irish Sea.

While the Vatican Council was in session and during the post-conciliar consultations and meetings, provincial officers were already making decisions about which foundations to close. During the 1950s, although two houses in England and one in Scotland were closed, the issue had been avoided. Instead the number of Sisters across the houses had been reduced and no new foundations had been made. The status quo was maintained as energy was devoted to restoring normality after the war and then to adjusting to the changes brought about by the welfare state and post-war education reforms. The nettle was only grasped during the 1960s as it became clearer that the number of new entrants would not replace the number of older Sisters retiring from full-time ministries.

Between 1960 and 1969 a total of 18 foundations in Britain were closed. Although three new ones were made, this still meant that an 18 per cent decrease in the number of houses occurred in this single decade. These closures were

---

83 Calculated from the provincial data base and registers. DCMH.

84 Some of the entrants to Mill Hill were always Irish-born and aspirants were never limited as to the place of entry.

85 Record of the Proceedings of the Provincial Assembly 1968 15-4-1-1968. 1-11 #1 DCMH.

entirely unrelated to the impact of Vatican II, having multiple causes in the social environment and in the longer-term cultural shifts that had themselves prompted Pope John XXIII to call a Council. When, in 1971, the question was considered of how to renew the work of the British Province in the light of Vatican II, each assessment of ministries had necessarily to take account of the rapidly changing downward demographic. The psychological and spiritual challenge to update and renew in a context of diminishment has been the reality the Province has faced and met since the 1960s. Over time provincial leaders have drawn on and developed the methods of consultation and research initiated by the renewal process to make their decisions and in this sense Vatican II has become a resource for change.

The decisions about closures during the 1960s signalled a continuation of the trend to reduce residential childcare in the light of national policy changes and reduced need (Darlington, Liverpool, Preston and Rutherglen near Glasgow). But, at a time when the number of Catholic school places was at a high, they also reflect the fact that teaching Sisters could not, and would not, be replaced when they retired (Birmingham, Edinburgh, London Clerkenwell, Troon and Wardour). A more strategic approach, however, can be seen in the cases of the closure and redevelopment of the houses in central Manchester (Rumford Street) and around the East End of London. The Province had a longstanding and strong commitment in both locations. Its properties were old and were in areas marked for slum clearance. The decision was taken in the early 1960s to stay in these localities but in updated properties which would help the Sisters to reinvigorate their community-based social ministries and integrate them into state social services where possible.

After five years of planning, De Paul House in Commercial Road in East London opened in 1967 as a centre for around 20 Sisters who had previously lived in five or six small houses in Poplar, Mile End and Limehouse. At De Paul House the Sisters ran a nursery school, a small hostel for homeless individuals, a drop-in centre which also provided hot dinners, and a Family Centre, while other Sisters resident in the house went into the community as social workers, district nurses, teachers and catechists. The central Manchester project which had opened in 1965 was broadly similar but had its own blend of ministries and projects. Some of these were long-standing services such as the Seton Night Shelter that had relocated and some, such as the Ephesus Youth Centre, represented a typical emerging strand at this time.

Neither of these developments arose from post-conciliar renewal, although they do show the influence of the evidence-based and integrative approach advocated by Suzanne Guillemin as head of the Company's Social Services. The decision on De Paul House was taken by the provincial council in 1962 and the Hathersage Road complex was opened in 1965. Both centres fit squarely into the Company's long tradition of city centre 'misericordes', with Sisters living in an area of deprivation to offer a range of services flexibly in the community and local parishes. Even so, the impact of renewal processes, particularly the 1967 Local

Assembly and 1968 Provincial Assembly, can be seen by examining three aspects of the work in these two centres.

First, the requirement for qualifications, for example in social work and district nursing or youth work, was taken seriously by the Province, and from 1960 a steady stream of Sisters was sent for training. Just as important, however, was the attention given to the skills and knowledge evolved by experienced visiting Sisters, and the perceived importance of transmitting and developing it. Visiting was maintained as a core ministry, and ways were sought to update it without making it bureaucratic or technocratic. Gabriel Taylor, visiting Sister in Cardiff, who gave talks on visiting to other communities, published a paper entitled 'The Usefulness of Visiting' in the recently launched provincial newsletter, 'News Around the Province', during 1970. This discussed in separate sections the aims and principles involved, the need, the techniques, and the qualities necessary.[86] Several Daughters went on to play an active role in the new organisation established by various religious sisters in pastoral ministry as more congregations, previously focused on education, moved into this field.[87]

Secondly, the need for collaboration with other charitable agencies, local authorities, and the National Health Service was now a goal and not something to be avoided in the interests of Catholic separatism. One of the proposals to the 1968 Provincial Assembly, for example, was a request that the Bishops of England and Wales reverse the policy that had led to exemption for Catholic healthcare institutions so that 'Clinics could become annexes to bigger hospitals and thus come into more direct contact with the poor.' [88] The nursery at De Paul House, likewise, was the result of a conscious plan to collaborate with the officers of Tower Hamlets Local Authority. Sister Margaret Campbell chaired a series of meetings in 1969 attended by other Sisters from the house with council officers to promote liaison with the Health Department, the Local Authority Welfare Department and the Children's Committee. The Committee warmly welcomed the Sisters' offer to provide day care 'for children who, might otherwise have to be received into care by the Council'.[89] De Paul House and the way it worked had a wide influence in the Province, not least because a large number of Sisters were placed there at one time, including those in formation.

The question of relationships with co-workers from outside the community and with other partners was the third dimension of *aggiornamento* that can be identified as taking place at De Paul House and in the Manchester centre. The topic was much discussed during renewal sessions in the later 1960s and early 1970s and in

---

86 'Provincial Newsletter', pp. 4-11 No. 4, July 1970. 1-7-1 DCMH.

87 Association of Sisters in Pastoral Ministry, founded in 1974 after course at Spode Hall, a Dominican Priory, in 1972 and 1973.

88 'Proposals to be presented to the Provincial Assembly, 1968', 15-5-1-1967, 1-2, #2 DCMH.

89 Letter from J. Wolkind to Sister Margaret Campbell 3 July 1969. DCMH.

The era of Vatican II, 1960-2000

On 25 January 1959 Pope John XXIII announced the Church's twenty-first Ecumenical Council – the Second Vatican Council – for the spiritual renewal of the Church in the modern world. The Council met between 1962 and 1965 and promulgated a series of documents about the Constitution of the Church. The document *Perfectae Caritatis* addressed the renewal of religious and consecrated life by calling on all religious orders and institutes to recover the spirit of their founders (*ressourcement*) and to update it for the modern world (*aggiornamento*).

The renewal movement took place in a context of decline in vocations to consecrated life. The year before the Council opened the number of Sisters in the Province fell for the third year in succession – a trend that was to continue and that was experienced by other communities.

Honouring the past

1960 Tercentenary of the deaths of St Vincent and St Louise. The occasion was marked with solemnity by the Company of Daughters and the Congregation of the Mission. Cardinal Griffin, Archbishop of Westminster, presided over a High Mass in the Cathedral attended by the Vincentian family of Daughters, Vincentians, their sodalities and associations and the SVP.

Sisters assembled in Westminster Cathedral for the Tercentenary Mass.

Facing present and future

Suzanne Guillemin, Superioress General of the Company of the Daughters of Charity (1962-67) at the Third Session of the Second Vatican Council in 1964 (extreme left; note she is wearing the new habit).

Ten women, leaders of international orders and institutes, were invited by Pope John XXIII to audit the 3rd and 4th sessions of the Council. Guillemin was appointed to the Justice and Peace Commission by Pope Paul VI. She proved to be a courageous and forward looking leader.

Under her guidance the Company worldwide was prepared for an Extraordinary General Assembly in 1968 to review its life and work in the light of the Vatican Council. Suzanne Guillemin died of a post-operational embolism two months before this Assembly.

Visible change: the habit

Pope Pius XII had spoken of the need for more practical habits in 1951. The Company's Superiors tried out several versions of a new habit before selecting one. The changeover day for all Daughters throughout the world (more than 44,000) was Sunday 20 September 1964.

The new and the old being modelled for the local press by (l to r) Sisters Sheila Hurley, Brigid Costello and Ita Healey of Cathedral Road, Cardiff. (photograph credit: John O'Sullivan)

Because people had always been able to identify the Sisters easily by their cornette, they could approach them in the street with requests and concerns. Its imminent replacement spurred the British Province to embark on a media campaign to alert the public to their new appearance. The Sisters co-operated with the BBC to make a feature film that was shown on its news broadcast ahead of the change.

And though our cornette is no more,
We know great blessings are in store
For us all, of every nation,
If we accept this adaptation

As was their custom, Sisters of the British Province marked the occasion with a spot of doggerel – but the seriousness of the change was experienced by all.

And though our cornette is no more
We know great blessings are in store
For us all, of every nation
If we accept this adaptation
Cheerfully, without a grouse
Out of doors, or in the house,
For it is by the Church decreed
Out-dated dress should not impede.

Postulants and seminary Sisters also had a new look. Experiments took place in formation too: from 1966 they no longer went to the Paris seminary but received the habit at Mill Hill.

1969 entrants: postulants (l) and seminary Sisters (r).

Visible change: liturgy

Chapel of the Sacred Heart, Mill Hill 1947 as it was decorated for the High Mass to mark the canonisation of St Catherine Labouré.

The first Mass was celebrated here in 1887 although the transepts were not finished until 1890, the left side being used by the boys of St Vincent's and the right side as the official parish church for Mill Hill (until December 1923). The window and the altar were the gifts of two individual Sisters.

The first Easter Vigil (a key aspect of the liturgical reforms of Pope Pius XII) was held in 1956. Mass was televised live on Low Sunday 1966.

In 1967 the sisters began to use the Breviary or Office of the Church for community prayer, replacing their own traditional book of prayers.

1974 The chapel was reordered in line with the liturgical recommendations that followed the Second Vatican Council and after consultation with the Sisters. The stained glass window remained, the tabernacle is off-centre so that the eye is drawn first to the large sculpture of the risen Christ commissioned from the artist Seán Crampton (1919-99). Crampton also made the sanctuary furnishings.

Internal change: leadership

Gertrude Andrew 9th Provincial 1966-1978 (left) entered in 1936 after taking a degree in Technical Optics in Manchester. She was identified for leadership and held the offices of Seminary Directress, Provincial Secretary and Councillor.

At her funeral in 2011 she was described as 'a woman for her time – far-seeing, broad-thinking and encouraging. From narrow, constricting customs she took us to a more reasonable and human way of living.' Illustrative of this thinking was her invitation in 1974 to American Daughter, Sister Zoe Glenski, photographed here (right), to give retreats to the Province. This was the first time a Sister had done so.

James Cahalan Director of the Province 1961-1967 and Provincial of the Irish Vincentians 1966-75, remembered fondly by many sisters as an encouraging and visionary priest with a gift for teaching. This extract from his Conference to the Sisters, Feast of St Vincent 1965, is characteristic:

'It would be the greatest travesty of Vincentian doctrine to imagine that we meet the challenge by doing things the way Vincent did them, for that way belongs to the period. But to be real Vincentians we must THINK the way St Vincent thought and then without any doubt we repeat Christ in the world of today…The second recipe of Vincent is ADAPTATION 'because "it is the Will of God that we should adapt ourselves… to the times and to places".'

Margaret Barrett 11th Provincial 1987-1996 (left) with Superior General Robert Maloney, Sister Julia Denton, General Councillor for Australia and Fr Frank Mullen, Provincial of the Irish Vincentians at Damascus House.

Joan Dwyer 10th Provincial 1978-1987 had been brought up in Mill Hill and entered in 1942 after completing teacher training. Intellectually and musically gifted she studied on her own for an external London degree in 1956 while teaching in Salisbury. She was made headmistress at Immaculate Conception secondary school in Darlington at the age of 30. Sister Joan was a natural administrator but above all was seen as a quiet enabler and a spiritual person who, at a time of change and upheaval, encouraged Sisters to stay focused on what mattered by deepening their prayer life.

Sister Margaret Barrett later became Assistant to the Mother General of the Company, the first Sister of the Province to have been a member of the General Council.

Internal change: consultation

Sisters went from no systematic individual or group consultation to experience extensive consultation processes in preparation for an Extraordinary General Assembly of the Company in 1968. These involved individual questionnaires, Local Assemblies at house level, and Provincial commissions.

Provincial Assemblies The text and visual style of this programme coversheet, designed for the first Provincial Assembly in 1968, express both the *ressourcement* (return to sources) and *aggiornamento* (updating) principles of the Second Vatican Council. 207 Sisters attended the Assembly in Liverpool of whom 110 were elected delegates – an entirely new approach.

Consultation for the second Provincial Assembly followed the same process as for the first, set out in the diagram received by Sisters in February 1973.

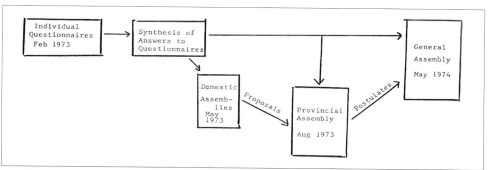

Division of the Province, 1 September 1970. At the 1968 Provincial Assembly the best form of governance for the size and diversity of the Province was discussed frankly. The historic decision in favour of division was made by the provincial council in January 1970. The Irish Province comprised the island of Ireland and the

British Province comprised England, Scotland and Wales. Sisters placed in Britain whose family home was Ireland were free to choose between Provinces. In August 1969 the province of Britain and Ireland had comprised 1187 Sisters. On 1 September the British Province comprised 734 Sisters.

External change: work

In the early 1970s there was a root and branch review of all the Province's works in the light of changes in social need, government policies, the reduction in the number of Sisters and the urging of the Second Vatican Council for religious communities to 'return to roots'. The box (right) shows the overall impact of the Province's reviews between 1972 and 1982.

Report on the Assessment of the Works 1972

A formal review that drew on questionnaire responses completed by Sisters and was divided into three fields: Social Works, Hospitals and Schools. Each field had a Provincial Commission of Sisters to co-ordinate its work.

Outcomes 1972-1982

Houses closed: 18 (out of 67)
Change of focus: 8 Houses
Houses opened: 5
Major investment: 3 Houses

THIS IS A SIGN OF THINGS TO COME....

From St. Vincent's Home to Damascus House

New focus: Damascus House Retreat and Conference Centre This brochure expresses the sense of excitement about change; in this case from a residential school to a conference centre for the diocese whose aim was 'to bring meaning, relevance and a sense of purpose to modern living'. It was a collaboration between the Daughters and the Vincentians to assist in spiritual renewal and in equipping lay people along the lines of the Council's Decree on the Laity.

Closure: Smyllum Park, Lanark Smyllum (right) had always been the largest home managed by the Daughters in Britain, accommodating around 700 children from across Scotland at its peak in the early twentieth century. It adjusted to 'family group' care in the late 1960s (groups of around 12 children and carers in their own 'house' within the building), was managed downwards in size and closed altogether in 1981.

Opening: Houghton Regis This was an area of population growth as people moved out of the East End of London to work in the motor industry. The Vincentians had charge of the two Catholic parishes here and the Daughters collaborated with them as parish Sisters, living among the people they served. There was no church building until the late 1970s and the Sisters' house (left) was a community base for the many groups they launched or supported.

Visiting Sisters and pastoral work: renewing a tradition

Visiting was a constant thread in the Daughters' service in Britain but from the later 1960s there was a renewed interest in the practice and how it could best serve a changing society and Church. Sister Gabriel Taylor, who was based in Cardiff, gave talks to the Sisters and wrote about the role, describing it in 1970 as 'a highly skilled undertaking requiring knowledge, especially of human behaviour, training if possible, and much experience'. After 1970 a growing proportion of the Sisters were missioned to visiting and to pastoral work in parishes, hospitals and prisons and in 1986 the province published a 'Policy Statement for Sisters in Parish and Pastoral Ministry'.

Glasgow visiting Sisters Wilton Crescent c1975

From l to r: Sisters Patrick Hegarty, Genevieve Gaffney, Finbar Kelleher and Brendan Cousins

Sheffield visiting and teaching Sisters 1984

Back: Sisters Joseph Kirrane and Catherine McErlean
Front l to r: Sisters Rosaleen McMahon, Mary Browne, Pauline Cruise, Cecilia Coyle, Anna McDonagh

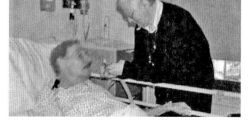

Visiting at home, in sickness, in prison and in all weathers

Clockwise from top left: Sisters Cecilia Coyle, Winifred McGovern, Lucy Regan and Frances Martin

Special occasions

Visit of John Paul II to Britain, 1982

In the summer of 1982 Pope John Paul II arrived in Britain for a six day tour. It was the first time a Pope had visited Britain for 400 years. The Pope greeted and blessed thousands of people at 16 different locations. One of these was St Joseph's Hospital in Rosewell, Scotland, owned and run by the Daughters of Charity (1924-1999) for the care of children and adults with physical and cognitive disabilities.

Pope John Paul II with a patient and Sister Joanna Danson at St Joseph's, Rosewell near Edinburgh.

1985 Centenary of the British Province

One of the ways that the Province marked its centenary was through an historical project to collect materials, to create a timeline and a family tree and to compile house histories. Professionally trained Sister-archivists have organised a provincial archive and created a Heritage Room. An important part of their work is responding to requests for information from former residents of the Province's children's homes.

One corner of the present Heritage Room in Provincial House

House Centenaries The Sisters' vocation is one of 'coming and going' according to needs, but a number of Houses celebrated centenaries in the second half of the twentieth century including: Sheffield, London Carlisle Place, Little Crosby, Dover, Darlington, York and Dunfermline.

Dunfermline centenary cake with Scottish thistles, made by parishioners to celebrate 100 years of DC presence in the town.

New Directions: The Passage and Cornerstones

The Passage at Carlisle Place in Westminster was a new work for homeless people in one of the Province's oldest houses. Started in 1980 as a collaboration between the Sisters and Westminster Cathedral it opened with the active patronage and support of Cardinal Basil Hume. The Passage took its name from the long hallway between the front door and the rooms used to welcome people.

The service began very simply with food and a place to sit and talk.

The Passage was an important initiative in its own right and has developed to become the largest day centre providing rehabilitation housing, medical, training and other practical support for homeless people in Britain. But it was also a harbinger of services started in other places by individual Daughters for adults and young people who had 'fallen through the net'.

Sisters Paula Sheehan (l) and Barbara Smith (r) Director, between 1985 and 1991, in a Passage newsletter story.

Sister Ellen Flynn, Director 2000-2008 and friend at a Passage Christmas party.

Cornerstone Ancoats, Manchester

In 1979 Sister Pauline Gaughan (left) was transferred to Manchester to work in Mary and Joseph House in Ancoats, a home for men with multiple problems. In 1990 with Canon Kevin O'Connor of St Augustine's in Hulme she began

a modest drop-in centre in a portakabin next to the church. Cornerstone (named for Acts 4:10-12) offered company, sandwiches and a safe place. It developed into a service for 120 people daily in a purpose-built cabin with 100 volunteer helpers. 'I see it as building a community. There's a lot of befriending going on.' (Sister Pauline Gaughan) Cornerstone continues as a day centre offering a range of support and training under the auspices of the Roman Catholic Diocese of Salford.

Leaving places...

From the late 1940s the ratio of older to younger sisters increased. This underlying demographic trend (masked for some time by the continuing growth in absolute numbers), accelerated after 1970. The division of the Province coincided with a sudden drop in the number of young women entering and the departure in a decade of more than 20 Sisters aged in their thirties and early forties, a trend that was also new.

Houses were steadily closed – 30 in a twelve year period from 1980-1992 – as the Province adjusted.

Closure of the York House 1992 (left) as reported in *The Yorkshire Evening News*. DCs first arrived in York in 1886.

Clockwise from top: Sisters Kathleen Fothergill, Hilda Keenan, Bride Carolan and Ann Buckridge. Sister Keenan was in York from 1957-1992.

Closure of Peterborough House 2005 Sister Anne Lambe in a story covered by the local paper. DCs went to Peterborough in 1901.

> So many years of giving
> To the hungry and
> the poor,
> So many years of
> answering
> That knock upon
> the door.

Closure of Dumfries House 2007 The Sisters were given a framed copy of a poem written by parishioner Charlotte Souter to mark 115 years service in the community.

(One verse extracted with kind permission of the author)

Sisters of The Priory, the Province's residency for sick and elderly sisters was in Mill Hill between 1926 and 2006, photographed here on the occasion of a Visitation by the Superioress General Sister Evelyne Franc (seated middle). In 2007 The Priory was closed for refitting as the new Provincial House.

…starting new projects and partnerships

St Wilfrid's Centre Sheffield DCs were invited into partnership by Mgr William Kilgannon of St Wilfrid's to manage a new drop-in centre for vulnerable and socially excluded people. The centre opened in 1991and expanded rapidly to include a recreation hall, interview rooms, kitchens, cafe, showers, and workrooms for skills development. St Wilfrid's has always been able to reach individuals, most of whom are men, who will not or cannot engage with other providers, helping more than 300,000 people since it opened. In 2005 Mr Kevin Bradley, who had worked with Sister-Directors Evelyn Warnock (picture right) and Kathleen Page, became Director. The Centre continues to thrive with paid-workers and many volunteers.

 **The Depaul Trust** was founded in 1989 to support young homeless people (aged 16-25) who were sleeping rough on the streets of London. Sister Barbara Smith, Director of The Passage, identified the need. The project, again under the patronage of Cardinal Basil Hume, brought together the DCs, the SVP and the Passage Day Centre. Sister Sarah King Turner, 13th Provincial (2002-2008), played a major role in its development as first Director of Trustees. Depaul grew quickly to become a national UK charity and in 2002 began an international expansion, starting in Ireland. In 2014 DePaul UK had 38 projects working with young people to tackle homelessness and a large number of Depaul Nightstop schemes offering emergency short term accommodation in the homes of local volunteers.

NOAH Luton (New Opportunities and Horizons) was awarded Day Centre of the Year Award in 2008. It had its origins in a collaboration between the Irish Government, the Luton Irish Advice Bureau and Sr Eileen O'Mahony who developed work with young Irish migrants in the area in 1987. What began as a day centre for migrants who had 'lost their footing' is now a wide-ranging service for those who are excluded and can benefit from its intensive personal support programmes. Sr Eileen retired in 2000 but NOAH continues to be a Vincentian-inspired enterprise.

(Image reproduced with kind permission of NOAH)

Inspiring young people the Vincentian way

In 1989 the Province piloted 'Vincentian Volunteers', a one-year experimental volunteering programme for young people which was formally launched in 1992.

Vincentian Volunteers are young people aged 18-35 from all over the world who commit a year of their lives to the service of vulnerable people in Britain in a programme of placements and spiritual formation co-ordinated by the Daughters. During their year they live in a community of three or four people and engage in voluntary work in partnership with other, well-known charity organisations in order to help people who are marginalised through poverty, homelessness or disabilities, refugees and those suffering with addictions within the local community.

VINCEN†IAN VOLUNTEERS

Early Vincentian Volunteers: Sister Joan Moriaty at the microphone

Sisters Ann Buckeridge (front) and Susan Molloy (back right – VV Director) with Volunteers

'News Around the Province'.[90] Vatican II's incarnational and Trinitarian theology pointed to the centrality of relationships in the path to Christian holiness and in evangelisation (broadly understood). But, given the strict boundaries that had been maintained by the Sisters in the past, the new emphases implied behavioural changes at both personal and organisational levels. Writing in the July 1971 one Sister noted that:

> So many workers know little or nothing of the Sisters' way of life, indeed some have weird ideas about nuns in general and I think it is a good idea they should see that we are human beings after all. When I first went into the Children's Department many of the workers came to me and said it was a revelation for them to see a Sister laughing – they honestly thought we were not supposed to laugh. (They had only seen Sisters walk along with their eyes modestly cast down).[91]

Daughters, in common with women religious, had always used the term 'externs' for their co-workers and for visitors and, of course, had not been permitted to take a cup of tea or share a meal with them. It was only in 1970 that Sisters 'over vows' (having made their vows for the first time) were permitted to stay with a member of their family for an authorised visit. Inevitably, the question of 'how far to go' in changing behaviour was a recurring one, often linked to the questions about the practice of religious poverty.[92]

Despite the many real and obvious modifications that occurred in the period of experimentation between 1966 and the approval of the Constitutions in 1983, the degree of continuity in the life and mission of the Sisters is just as striking. A sense of the relative nature of change and continuity can be glimpsed through the eyes of one Sister who reported in 'News Around the Province' on her educational visit to the United States of America in the summer of 1968. She was completing a degree in social science and undertook her block placement in practical work in the Child Guidance Clinic of the Boston Daughters of Charity. 'Many orders and more especially individual nuns have taken *aggiornamento* very literally', she wrote, 'and they want to change radically.'

> Some of the orders are wearing secular dress, with a mantilla...in some sisters have the option of leaving their convents and living in selective groups in 'living units', which is simply housing similar to the people in the neighbourhood. They choose their own means of government... While I was dumbfounded at many of the radical changes, I could not help admiring the sincerity and dedication of many of the Religious. It

---

90 This newsletter was begun in 1969 by Gertrude Andrew as an outcome of the Provincial Assembly's desire for more exchange and information.

91 'Provincial Newsletter', No. 8, July 1971, p. 13. 1-7-3 DCMH.

92 ibid., 1973 and 1974. 1-7-3 DCMH.

> was in the ghettoes I witnessed the heroism of many nuns...to try and
> help to improve the sub-human conditions prevalent there.

She went on to reassure her readers that 'As for our own community, in the House
which I visited there was no evidence of the radical changes taking place in other
Orders. I was edified at the observance of Rule and how our American Sisters
treasured the tradition of the Community....[and] it was heartening to see that
"the poor were first served."[93]

Daughters of Charity 'treasured the tradition of the Community' during
aggiornamento and increasingly had a better knowledge of it. In Britain in the
post-conciliar 1970s and 1980s they continued to live the common life with a Sister
Servant appointed for each community; there was no question of Sisters living
alone or living without the appointment of a local superior for the twin reasons
of obedience to the directions of the founders and the Church. Sisters continued
to rise at 5.30 and to come together daily for morning and evening prayer using
the breviary of the Church supplemented by Company prayers for Company feast
days. Devotion to the Blessed Virgin remained central to personal and communal
prayer. Sisters had individual free time and more holiday but they continued to
undertake community recreation and corporate retreats and to follow the same
annual rhythm for vow renovation. Their habit changed, but they continued to
wear one; indeed they were now wearing a veil contrary to the original conception
for the Company.

Some developments in the works of the community took place during the 1970s,
but they were variations on familiar Company commitments. Three foundations
were made on new housing estates at Houghton Regis, Dunstable, Bedfordshire
(1973), Deptford (1977) and Warrington (1979) which had been built with few
community or social amenities. The Sisters were not specifically parish Sisters
but, following out the concept of 'insertion', provided a resource base for the whole
community and took whatever initiatives, such as opening a crèche or running
youth ministries, seemed most needed.[94] Major strategic investments made in
the 1970s to upgrade selected institutional works such as the hospital in Lanark
were the result of strategic decisions that underline continuity. Updating can be
seen in the new partnership with Vincentian confrères, not only in Dunstable and
Warrington, but in the jointly established Damascus House Retreat Centre (1972)
that replaced the former children's residential home at Mill Hill. This too was a
creative development within the tradition of Marguerite Naseau, supporting lay
people to deepen their faith and to develop knowledge of scripture, liturgy and
the wide range of Catholic prayer practices. Retreat and formation work with
schools and parishes can also be seen as an updating of the purpose of sodalities

---

93 'Provincial Newsletter', p.4 March 1969, p. 4 1-7-3 DCMH.

94 See James Sweeney, 'Religious Life after Vatican II', in Hornsby-Smith (ed.), *Catholics in England*, p. 276-279
for a discussion of the limited application of this approach in England.

and confraternities, both of which had waned dramatically in popularity. As these examples show, the Sisters' ministries continued to be corporate and, if anything, were now measured more consciously against the community's collective sense of the vocation of a Daughter of Charity. Although they were now better trained than at any previous time there is no doubt Sisters continued to identify primarily as Daughters of Charity rather than as professionals.

Even so, the community continued to experience the same serious decline in vocations as occurred in communities which had changed in more obvious ways. The reduction in recruitment from Britain that began at the time of the Second World War did recover to some extent during the 1950s but the underlying trend was of continuous decline. Vocations remained fairly constant from 1966 to 1970 with between six and nine young women entering the seminary at Mill Hill and between two and seven of these continuing on to make vows. Between 1973 and 1979 the number who entered and remained was one or two a year while the departure of experienced vow Sisters peaked with 17 leaving during the 1970s. Many of those who left had made their vows during the 1950s, more than fifteen years previously. In the 1980s women continued to enter in small numbers but only eight of those who tried their vocation remained. It is difficult to link this decline to any loss of internal or external identity, of community or prayer life, or of loss of focus on the traditional work of the Sisters with people in poverty. Neither would it be right to imagine that re-creating the custom of wearing the cornette, never visiting family members, or rising at 4.00 a.m. would have increased the appeal of the vocation, although that is the implication of some recent writing on the subject.[95] It seems more likely, as James Sweeney as argued, that 'the lack of recruits has as much, if not more, to do with societal factors as the features exhibited by religious orders'. Among these he names increased cultural bias against tradition and the 'contemporary cultural transformations that do not favour attachment to organizations'[96] and, as the key to late modern culture, individualisation.[97] Other salient factors such as the reduction in Catholic family size, the drift from regular practice of the faith, and the new possibilities for women to live an integrated life of faith, work and family life as active lay Catholics are widely taken into account in explanations of the decline.

For the Sisters themselves the greatest sense of challenge to their identity came, not from abandonment of old disciplines or the value given to the laity (among whom they named themselves), but from what they perceived to be an increasing drift towards 'middle-class' living standards and away from detachment from material goods. Different Sisters identified this drift with watching television, an increase in community and personal possessions, the advent of a personal

---

95 Rodney Stark and Richard Finke, 'Catholic Religious Vocations: Decline and Revival', *Review for Religious* (2000), Vol.42, Issue 2.

96 Sweeney, 'Religious Life after Vatican II', pp.279-280.

97 James Sweeney, 'Religious Life Looks to its Future', in Simmonds (ed.), *Future Full of Hope*, pp.129-142.

allowance, the removal of the need to ask for permissions, for example to take a new item of toiletry, and the sub-division of dormitories into individual cubicles. Interpreting the meaning of poverty for Sisters vowed to live as 'the poor' was a recurring point of discussion in the group meetings, Local Assemblies and 'News Around the Province' and became a serious point of tension in the identity of all religious in the 1970s and 1980s, and perhaps beyond that date.

'What are We?'[98]

> Given to God for the service of the poor, the Daughters of Charity find their unity of life in that end. Service is for them the expression of their consecration to God in the Company and gives it its full significance. It nourishes their contemplation and gives meaning to their community life, just as their relationship with God and their fraternal life in common continually revitalise their apostolic commitment.
>
> (1983 Constitutions of the Company)[99]

Joseph Jamet, director general of the Company, asked the question 'What Are We?' to introduce the Sisters to the canonical history of their vows in a paper circulated to delegates of the 1968 Provincial Assembly. It had been usual for women to enter the Company without understanding the distinctive juridical place of the Sisters in the Church. As seminary Sisters they learned about the origins of the vows with St Vincent and St Louise and because they subsequently practised the annual renovation, its reality became a part of their spiritual lives. But few, if any, would have known about the struggles over three hundred years to preserve each aspect of the Company's character – privileged and annual vows, the canonical authority of the superior general, and lay status. And relatively few, before the processes created by Vatican II, would have understood the charismatic significance of these features in an explicit way that they could articulate to others. As part of the 2005 survey, Sisters were asked to say whether they had known at the time they entered that the Company was canonically different from other active religious congregations. Typical responses were encapsulated by one respondent who said simply, 'I felt but did not know that the Company was different', a response shared almost exactly by another:

> No, I did not know it but I felt it. I also felt that they were in contact with the people, not enclosed, there was something natural about them, which suited my free spirit.

---

98 *The Echo of the Mother House*, April 1968. 1-5 DCMH.

99 'Given to God for the Service of the Poor'. Constitutions of the Daughters of Charity of Saint Vincent de Paul. 2 February 1983. 2.1.3-1-8 DCMH.

Several noted that they learned about the distinctiveness once they had entered. 'At that time' one wrote, 'my one concern was to follow a call I could not resist and give my life to God. All the canonical bits came later.'

Only one of the 80 Sisters who answered this question had understood the canonical position at the point of entry and had consciously chosen the Daughters because they were lay. It is all the more interesting, therefore, how many respondents remarked on what might be seen as the fruit of the charism, often by making comparisons with named orders and congregations that they knew: the absence of lay sisters among the Daughters, the lack of enclosure and the sense of freedom of the Daughters, their focus on the poor, their friendliness and ordinariness. Insight gained from these personal memories sheds light on the discussion held at the General Assembly in 1968 where two proposals from Local Assemblies were considered: 'whether or not we are canonically a "Religious Congregation". And, if not, do we wish to become one?'[100] Some Sisters answering the questionnaire and some Local Assemblies had seen no reason why not. Vincentian canonists and scholars, however, believed that the practice of the annual privileged vow renewal and of exemption from canonical episcopal visitation was not simply historical and traditional, it was charismatic – of the essence of God's grace given to the founders. It was not, therefore, dispensable. The same was thought to be true of other practices, such as the reception of a Daughter dating from her entry into the seminary rather than the date of making first vows. The Record of the Proceedings of the British General Assembly made clear the part played by Father Jamet's articles and subsequent discussions in the decision that took place to support the privileged vows and special status. Sisters present came to understand their 'unique place in the Church' which preserved their mobility and gave a 'structure ready-built to bear the greater flexibility in our life and works that we are now seeking'. In summary,

> Little discussion was necessary for us to understand that our avenue of renewal lies, not in a change of status, but in a more intense consciousness of our consecration and a deeper understanding of the unshackled serving of Christ in the neighbour that St Vincent could see so clearly.

In 1970, the year after agreement at the General Assembly, the Sisters in all Provinces received a temporary text of the experimental Constitutions and Statutes. It seems likely that the injunction in *Perfectae Caritatis* to return 'ad fontes' - to the sources - and to involve all the Sisters in the outcomes of research, became an educational process. This was not necessarily true for all religious institutes but in the case of the Company there was not only a spiritual depth in the somewhat complex story about the Rule, but many new sources to be discovered and made

---

100 Record of the Proceedings of the Provincial Assembly 1968, p. 1. 15-4-1-1968 1-11 #1 DCMH.

available to members.[101] Above all, research continued towards the publication of accurate editions and translations of the complete writings of both Vincent de Paul and Louise de Marillac.

After the 1970 draft Constitution had been written it had become necessary for the general superiors, most particularly the superior general, James Richardson (1968–1980), to sustain discussion with Vatican canonists. Among this group 'there was a widespread difference of opinion' about the special charism of the double family and its implications. Richardson's aim was a change in canon law to recognise the charism of a community living under vows taken in the name of an authority delegated by the Church (the superior general of the Congregation of the Mission), yet whose members retained lay status. In the end this came about largely because Richardson, himself a canon lawyer, was appointed as the president of a special Vatican commission to 'orient the revisers of the new code [of canon law] so that the societies known then as "communities of common life without vows" would be respected'.[102] The successful outcome of the commission's work was the inclusion in the 1983 Code of Canon Law of an entirely new category, 'Societies of Apostolic Life'. The canons for such Societies accommodated the Company's founding charism and its vows, 'which are neither public nor private'.[103] The original seventeenth-century Rule of the Company, the new canonical status and the horizontal language of Vatican II theology were fused in composing the new Constitutions of the Daughters of Charity of St Vincent de Paul. They were approved in 1983 by the Congregation for Religious and Secular Institutes on 2 February, Feast of the Presentation of the Lord, three hundred and fifty years after the founding of the Company.

Some women religious, reflecting on the impact of the Vatican Council from the vantage point of the early twenty-first century, have concluded that the Holy See's efforts to accommodate the small number of Societies of Apostolic Life have added to the confusion of the meaning of religious life itself unleased by the Council's insistence that there were only two states of life in the Church, clerical and lay.[104] They believe that the question of the specific definition of religious life needs to be reviewed and developed, while for others the hierarchy's preoccupation with canonical definitions is confirmation of its continuing misunderstanding of the

---

101 The injunction to return to sources assumed that there was a charism and a charism story but this was not always the case. See, Mary Finbarr, 'The Complexities and Difficulties of a Return *ad fontes*', in Simmonds (ed.), *A Future Full of Hope?*, pp. 38-51 and in the same volume, Simmonds, 'Religious Life: A Question of Visibility', p. 117. Also Sandra Schneiders, *Finding the Treasure* and, for the United States the outstanding work of Margaret Susan Thompson available as a series of audio lectures. https://www.nowyouknowmedia.com/the-history-of-women-religious-in-the-united-states.html.

102 Miguel Flores, 'Father Richardson and the Daughters of Charity' (1996), Vol. 17, Issue 2, Article 7, p. 96.

103 Sharon L. Holland, 'Societies of Apostolic Life', in John P. Beale, James A Coriden and Thomas J. Green (eds). (New York: Paulist Press, 1985), p. 543.

104 Council of Major Superiors of Women Religious, *Foundations of Religious Life*, pp. 189-190 and 207-208.

charismatic dimension of consecrated life.[105] Linked to the latter, is the question of the theology of religious life, the lack of which has concerned many.[106] For her part, biblical scholar and Immaculate Heart of Mary sister, Sandra Schneiders, has argued that 'the time is ripe, for the first time since the earliest days of the Church, for a fully mature, genuinely lay spirituality and ministry to develop'.[107] Despite all the effort to create a classification that would satisfy juridical honour as seen from the Holy See and the realities of history as lived by the Company, Vincent de Paul's answer to the question 'Who are you?' remains the most compelling. Addressing a group of Sisters being sent on mission into the country in 1650 he advised, 'If he [the bishop] asks who you are...tell him you are poor Daughters of Charity and that you are given to God for the service of the poor.'[108] For Daughters in late twentieth-century Britain the challenge of the new era was to leave behind preoccupations with questions of canon law so as to concentrate more fully on the Company's spiritual way of life, lay and communal, in solidarity with people at the margins of society.

105 Diarmud O'Murchu, *Consecrated Religious Life: The Changing Paradigms* (Manila: Claretian Publications, Orbis: 2005) and ; Margaret Susan Thompson, ' "Charism" or "Deep Story"?: Towards a Clearer Understanding of the Growth of Women's Religious Life in Nineteenth Century America' in *Religious Life and Contemporary Culture*. Theological Education Process, Cycle 2 (Monroe Michigan: Sisters, Servants of the Immaculate Heart of Mary, 1998) and Sandra Schneiders, *Finding the Treasure*, Chs. 9 and 10.

106 Gregory Collins, 'Giving Religious Life a Theology Transfusion', in Simmonds (ed.), *A Future Full of Hope?*, pp. 23-27.

107 Schneiders, *Finding the Treasure*, p. 97.

108 *CCD*, Vol IX, p.432 Vincent de Paul to Sisters being sent to the country, 22 October 1650.

12
Poverty's many faces, 1980–2007

> The spirituality of our time is the spirituality of
> Holy Saturday: a spirituality of confusion and
> consternation, of ineffectiveness and powerlessness,
> of faith in darkness and the power of hope. It is a
> spirituality that carries on when carrying on seems
> most futile. This is not the time for quitting simply
> because the past is past and the present unclear.
> (Sister Joan Chittister osb)[1]

After the initial post-conciliar years of enthusiasm, consultation and dedicated renewal, the 1990s were seen by many communities of religious sisters as a time 'marked by darkness and suffering'.[2] The recurring experience was that of loss, a loss which took more than one form: the departure of long-standing members of the community and the giving up of works and houses that could no longer be sustained; and the experience, in the absence of more than a very small number of new members, of being unable to look ahead to handing on the community and its way of life to a future generation. The repeated cycle of welcoming aspirants and postulants who then did not remain might even be experienced as rejection. Greater expectations of fraternity after Vatican II meant community life was now more personally demanding and more capable of disappointing than when community had been based almost entirely around regimes and hierarchical relationships.[3] Daughters of Charity, accustomed to concentrating on the needs of others rather than themselves, and used to being part of a large and robust community in Britain, absorbed the sense of loss later than some other communities, but by 1990 had to accept the inescapable reality of diminishment. Yet even as they experienced this new form of poverty, the Province and its members

---

1 Joan Chittister, *The Fire in these Ashes: a spirituality of contemporary religious life* (London: Sheed and Ward, 1996), p. 41.

2 Sandra Schneiders, *Finding the Treasure*: locating Catholic religious life in a new ecclesial and cultural context (Mahwah, NJ, Paulist Press, 2000). p.173. Schneiders places this time in the late 1970s and 1980s but it seems likely to have varied between institutes and between countries and it is argued here that it was the 1990s before it was reached in the British Province of the Daughters.

3 'Proposals to be presented to the Provincial Assembly', p.25 'Fraternal Life' (1979) 15-4-3-1979 1-4, #3 DCMH.

continued to turn outwards and to start new, often bold, initiatives which were firmly focused on the poorest in society.

The new form of poverty they were experiencing has been described, in relation to Catholic sisters in general, as 'first a paradox, and second, a malaise'.[4] The paradox was that communities, who by any sociological criteria were at the 'decline stage' of the normal organisational birth-to-demise cycle, defied expectation by continuing to act with vigour, commitment and vision. Vigour and vision accompanied the 'pervasive sense of suffering', a 'malaise' which came from individual and communal loss and diminishment.[5] Sister and scholar of religious life, Sandra Schneiders has proposed that the diminishment in religious life and its effects were more than a sociological phenomenon, likening its spiritual roots and impact by analogy to St John of the Cross's 'dark night of the soul'.[6] As in St John's mystical poem, the purposes of the experience are those of purification (detachment) and greater unity with God.[7]

Schneiders explained the analogy in this way:

> Vatican II precipitated something analogous to a corporate experience of the active night of the spirit among Religious, especially women. Although the renewal seemed, at the outset, to be largely about external modifications such as modernization of the habit, adjustment of the horarium to contemporary timetables, democratization of community procedures, and other easily observable phenomena, in fact the renewal precipitated changes that profoundly touched the spiritual dimensions of Religious Life...As many left and few entered, Religious who stayed got in touch in a new way with the real meaning of their vocation, the God-quest at the center of their hearts...those who continued...had now to choose it in purified faith, unsupported hope, and generous love, because it was largely devoid of compensatory packaging.[8]

To the elements of loss and of transformation elaborated above, which stripped the life of its 'compensatory packaging', it must surely be right to add the experience of living through, and with knowledge of, the clerical sexual abuse and the widespread Church cover-ups and denials of abuse that began to enter public consciousness in the mid-1990s. In the context of Britain and Ireland, a growing understanding of the damage that had been inflicted on children and young people was very gradually absorbed as an injustice and wound by all members

---

4 Sandra Schneiders, *Finding the Treasure*, p. 154.

5 ibid., pp. 156-157.

6 ibid., Ch.5, pp. 156 ff. See also findings of the research conducted as part of the Religious Life Vitality Project in Britain. Report available at http://www.margaretbeaufort.cam.ac.uk/assets/documents/research%20 key%20findings%20report.pdf (accessed 2 October 2016).

7 Schneiders, *Finding the Treasure*, p. 164 and p. 167.

8 ibid., p. 164 and p. 166.

of the Catholic community, and more particularly by those whose whole identity was entwined with the Church. Even closer to home for Catholic sisters were the allegations of physical and psychological abuse made by those who had been in their care as children, which had happened mainly but not exclusively in the 1950s and 1960s. Once the first cases were brought forward in Ireland and Australia in the late 1990s, they were followed by many others, including some in England and Scotland. The reputation and standing of all Catholic sisters involved in care was impugned, whether or not they as individuals or their particular institute were involved, whether or not the allegations had been upheld. It was in 1997 that the Daughters in Britain were first made aware of allegations of physical and psychological child abuse, primarily in one former location in Scotland.[9] Because this case is still pending as part of the investigation into historic child abuse in Scotland, it is not possible to do more than indicate its existence.[10] But a consequence has been the need for the whole community to face the possibility that not all that was done by it met the standards of the day, let alone its own ideals of care-giving. This knowledge became part of what can been seen in Schneiders' terms as collective stripping down – of confidence, of self-image and good memory - akin to 'the actual loss of real spiritual goods to which one has become attached'.[11]

These losses could be experienced and understood by religious communities as the harbingers of institutional death or of a new kind of life that arises from the darkness of God. The latter understanding shows itself when sisters persist in living the life against the odds, when the community tenaciously sustains its commitment and priorities, and when sisters have the 'deep trust that God is somewhere, active, in the midst of it all'.[12] Findings from the Religious Life Vitality Project conducted in Britain and Ireland by Catherine Sexton and Gemma Simmonds CJ between 2013 and 2015, discussed further in Chapter 13, provide strong evidence from communities and individual Sisters both for Schneiders' claims about the 'dark night' and about new life arising from it.[13] There needs to be an acknowledgement that, alongside the demographic factors and the cultural

9 http://www.gov.scot/resource/doc/203922/0054353.pdf

10 The daughters have also engaged with a group of former residents involved in bringing the case and have responded to their request to erect a new monument to the 150 babies and children who died in the children's home between 1864 and 1964 (all from natural causes). The children had all received a proper burial but had been buried in unmarked paupers' graves with a shared monument erected to them. The memorial, which was erected in 2004 is inscribed with words agreed between the INCAS Care Survivors' group and the Province. The name of each child has been recorded in a parish memorial book in the local church (St Mary's) and is remembered on the date of their death.

11 Schneiders, *Finding the Treasure*, p. 163.

12 Ibid., p.207 also 181. See also Sister Gemma Simmonds at http://globalsistersreport.org/news/trends/religious-life-vital-ever-25306 (accessed 8 October 2016), reporting on the Religious Life Vitality Project (Britain) in May 2015.

13 Catherine Sexton and Gemma Simmonds CJ, *'Religious Life Vitality Project: Key Project Findings'* (Report for the Conrad N. Hilton Foundation). The key findings report is available at http://www.margaretbeaufort.cam.ac.uk/assets/documents/research%20key%20findings%20report.pdf and the final report at https://www.dur.ac.u.

and generational differences often cited to explain the demise of consecrated life, 'there may be more going on'.[14]

Many commentators have addressed themselves to one or more aspects of the situation, and to the idea of a loss of hope in the future of the consecrated life that became increasingly prevalent in Catholic thinking in the global North.[15] By the early 1990s Pope John Paul II was concerned about this possibility taking hold across congregations and institutes. In itself, this concern for the future of women's communities was evidence of the significant shift that had taken place in the Church's thinking about women's vocations to ministry since the time of Louise de Marillac.[16] The Pope's Apostolic Exhortation, *Vita Consecrata* (1996) came after the first post-conciliar Synod on Religious and Consecrated Life of 1994 and referred directly to a loss of heart. It spoke of the need to avoid 'at all costs the actual breakdown of consecrated life, a collapse that is not measured by a decrease in numbers but by a failure to cling steadfastly to the Lord and to personal vocation and mission', an interpretation that is difficult to match to the reality on the ground in so far as British Daughters, and perhaps many others, are concerned.[17] In the same year, Benedictine author Sister Joan Chittister published a work on spirituality for religious entitled *The Fire in these Ashes: a spirituality of contemporary religious life,* which captured the spirit of the moment for many sisters in Britain where she had spent a sabbatical year writing the book. Noting the disillusioning 'endless historical reviews of past forms of religious life and long excursions into futuristic speculation', she proposed that the 'task is to live this time now, our time, well so that a future model can rise from these ashes with confidence and with courage'.[18]

Whether the actions and response of the Daughters of Charity in Britain after 1980 are most helpfully interpreted through the 'dark night of the soul' framework or through that of a 'living well now' approach (they are not incompatible), will have to be left to historians some time hence whose perspective will be longer. For now, this chapter seeks to explore and understand the 'lived' experience of the Daughters by taking the experience of loss and diminishment that they suffered

14 Schneiders, *Finding the Treasure*, p. 181 and p. 207

15 See Gerald Arbuckle, *Out of Chaos: refounding religious congregations* (London, Geoffrey Chapman, 1988); Patricia Wittberg, *Creating a Future for Religious Life: a sociological perspective* (Mahwh NJ, Paulist Press, 1991); Desmond Murphy, *The Death and Rebirth of Religious Life* (Alexandria NSW: E.J.Dwyer, 1995) and Tony Flannery, *The Death of Religious Life?* (Dublin, Columba Press, 1997).

16 Many commentators have observed that the shift accompanied the incorporation into the institutional Church of the women's charismatic initiatives. See, for example, the works of Diarmuid O'Murchu and also Margaret Susan Thompson among others.

17 John Paul II, Post-Synodal Apostolic Exhortation *Vita Consecrata, On the Consecrated Life and Its Mission in the Church and in the World* 1996. Vocation statistics in England Wales, did however, support the notion of a collapse of this kind. See '*Religious Life in England and Wales: Executive Report* (study commissioned by the Compass Project, 2010). In 2016 when the figure for the number of women entering consecrated life to *all* orders and congregation, contemplative and active, was stated as 45, it was noted that this was the highest figure for 25 years.

18 Joan Chittister, *The Fire in these Ashes*, p. viii.

at this time together with the courageous commitments they made at the same time in solidarity with people in poverty at home and overseas.

Poverty in Britain

As the second millennium reached its final decades, despite post-war measures to address the five 'Giant Evils' of 'squalor, ignorance, want, idleness, and disease' and an unprecedented increase in the general standard of living, poverty was still present in many forms in Britain.[19] Moreover, the welfare regimes that had been established or developed across Europe to protect people from extreme hardship came under challenge in the final two decades of the century. New pressures coming from globalisation, the revolution of the modern family, the changing economic role of women and the emergence of ageing populations created both familiar and new forms of poverty. Social isolation and the hidden poverties of older age were on the increase along with the more familiar crises of homelessness and hunger.

Although many people prospered in the 1980s, it was also the case that a new geography of poverty and vulnerability emerged in Britain. During the 1970s, the number of people classified by social scientists as 'breadline poor' – that is living below the relative poverty line and thereby excluded from participating in the norms of society – had been falling steadily to a new low. But after 1979 the numbers started to rise again. Statistics for children living in poverty increased dramatically and remained high during the 1980s and 1990s.[20] The amount spent on welfare was not reduced but benefits were being spread more thinly over an increasing number of recipients.[21] Homelessness became a national issue once more and, because of legislative changes to benefits in the late 1980s (1986 Social Security Act), more teenagers were sleeping rough, most visibly so in London.[22] When the 1988 Local Government Act introduced the Community Charge (1989 in Scotland and 1990 in England and Wales), popularly known as the 'Poll Tax', it was widely seen as both a tax burden on people unable to pay and a likely source of further impoverishment.[23] Although the Poll Tax was replaced in 1993 by the Council Tax, the intervening years of outright confrontation, including riots,

---

19   The five 'Giant Evils' were identified in the Beveridge Report of 1942, which was itself highly influential in the development of the welfare state in Britain.

20   See Daniel Dorling *et al.*, *Poverty and Wealth across Britain 1968 to 2005: a look at how the geographical distribution of poor and wealthy people in Britain has changed in the last 40 years* (Joseph Rowntree Foundation Report available at https://www.jrf.org.uk/report/poverty-and-wealth-across-britain-1968-2005 and Paul Gregg, Susan Harkness and Stephen Machin, 'Poor kids: trends in child poverty in Britain, 1968-96', *Fiscal Studies* (1999), vol.20. no.2, pp. 163-187 and

21   John Hills, *'Thatcherism, New Labour and the Welfare State'*, CASE Paper 13 (London School of Economics, Centre for Analysis of Social Exclusion Unit, 1998), p. 5.

22   https://www.jrf.org.uk/report/single-homelessness-overview-research-britain (accessed 3 October 2017)

23   Paul Bagguley, 'Protest, poverty and power: a case study of the anti-poll tax movement', *Sociological Review.* (1995), Vol.43, no.4, pp. 693-719.

between the government and citizens' campaigning groups, highlighted growing social rifts. As churches and faith groups, along with other institutions and ways of collective belonging,[24] played a decreasing part in people's lives, social scientists began to discuss the decline in 'social capital' as a signifier of poverty.[25] The loss of relational and spiritual life was seen by many as a growing form of personal and communal impoverishment.

Several elements, including a new political landscape, combined to create what social policy analysts called a 'welfare state in transition' at this time. In a reversal of earlier policies of welfare expansion, the British government of the 1980s sought to reduce both its overall cost and direct state involvement in the provision of welfare.[26] This meant that some policy changes, such as 'care in the community' which aimed at making improvements in the quality of life for individuals, were also planned as opportunities for cost reduction.[27] One significant aspect of the ambition to 'slim the state' was to resume the practice of the historic British mixed welfare model, whereby national and local government engaged with the voluntary non-profitmaking welfare sector. A major difference with the past, however, was the encouragement now given to for-profit companies as well as charitable bodies in competitive bidding for welfare contracts. In turn, this new policy approach encouraged the formation of social entrepreneurial organisations, which aimed to combine the values of charities with the energy and effectiveness of successful businesses. Competition between a wider range of providers, always intended to be integral to the new model of welfare state, became a reality in the late 1990s.[28]

During the 1980s, churches responded to these complex changes in poverty and policy by themselves becoming much more overtly engaged as advocates on behalf of and in association with people in poverty, and as agents for community building. Many parish priests, vicars, ministers and members of religious communities were conscious of being among the few residents in their neighbourhood with social capital, education and networks outside of the neighbourhood. They were sometimes the only such residents. In the 1980s and 1990s, the highest authorities in all the mainstream churches in Britain used their voices to speak up for those being left behind in society, the best-known example being the Church of

---

24 Grace Davie, *Religion in Modern Britain: believing without belonging* (Oxford, Blackwell, 1994). See Rosalyn Harper, *'The Measurement of Social Capital in Britain'* (National Office for Statistics, 2002).

25 Greg Smith, 'A Very Social Capital: measuring vital signs of Community Life in Newham' in B. Knight, M. Smerdon and C. Pharoah (eds.), *Building Civil Society* (London, Charities Aid Foundation, 1998). B. Knight, B. and P. Stokes, *The Deficit in Civil Society in the United Kingdom* (Foundation for Civil Society, Working Paper No 1., 1996).

26 Eva Jeppson Grassman, 'Welfare in Western Europe: existing regimes and patterns of Change' in Anders Backstrom and Grace Davie (eds.), *Welfare and Religion in Twenty-First Century Europe, vol. x 'Configuring the Connections'* (Farham, Ashgate, 2010), p. 25.

27 *'Making a Reality of Community Care'*, Audit Commission for England and Wales, 1986. (Government Green Paper (Griffith Report) 1988, leading to the White Paper in 1989, *'caring for people: community care in the next decade and beyond'*.

28 Peter Alcock, *Social Policy in Britain* 4th edn (Basingstoke, Palgrave Macmillan, 2014), Ch.18.

England's publication of *Faith in the City* in 1985. Its purpose was to 'examine the strengths, insights, problems and needs of the Church's life and mission in Urban Priority Areas and, as a result, to reflect on the challenge which God may be making to Church and Nation'.[29] For the Catholic Church, the Bishops' Conference of England and Wales intervened in the debate with its statement *The Common Good and the Catholic Church's Social Teaching,* published in 1996. Distributed as part of the preparation of the faithful for the 1997 General Election, it was widely recognised as an important contribution to public discourse. 'The systematic denial of compassion by individuals or public authorities', Cardinal Hume wrote in his introduction, 'can never be a morally justified political option'.[30]

Many Catholic religious orders that had not previously been involved in community outreach work had already interpreted the renewal of Vatican II, with its injunction for them to 'discern the signs of the times', as a compelling call to become engaged with communities suffering deprivation. Their engagement took many forms, from providing community-based services and a ministry of community presence to activism and citizen organising.[31] James Sweeney, whose own Passionist order created the Passionist Inner City Mission in Liverpool, later wrote:

> While the option for the poor has application in all forms and styles of religious life...the flagship projects are those involving 'insertion': that is, those religious living as small groups among local communities in areas of deprivation, in ordinary housing rather than in ecclesiastical buildings, taking part formally (through specific projects) and/or informally (as neighbours) in the concerns of local people.[32]

From his own researches at the end of the century, Sweeney concluded that religious sisters had been more involved than orders of priests, but that 'among the older orders such projects often remain on the institutional margins' because religious communities 'are ambiguous and ambivalent about any radical departure in terms of the option of the poor'.[33] In other words, there had been more aspiration than realisation.

29   Archbishop of Canterbury's Commission on Urban Priority Areas, *Faith in the City. a call to action by Church and nation* (1985).

30   Catholic Bishops, Conference of England and Wales, *The Common Good and the Catholic Church's Social Teaching* (1996).

31   For a survey of some of the community engagement in the Catholic Church at this time, see Jenny Rossiter, *In the Middle of Our Street community development and the Catholic Church in England and Wales.* (A Report from the Catholic Agency for Social Concern In association with the Committee for Community Relations, Catholic Bishops' Conference of England and Wales, 2002).

32   James Sweeney, 'Religious Life after Vatican II' in Michael Hornsby-Smith (ed.), *Catholics in England* (Cambridge: Cambridge University Press, 1987), p. 277. See also: James Sweeney, *From Story to Policy,* (Cambridge, Von Hugel Institute, 2001). See also; Rossiter, *In the Middle of Our Street*, p.24.

33   Sweeney, 'Religious Life after Vatican II', p. 228.

For the Daughters of Charity there was no question about whether to be committed to people in poverty, the debate was about who, where and how. One of the challenges put before them by Provincial director Father Matthew Barry CM around the time of the Vatican Council, was whether the Province had been choosing what he called 'the safe poor', in other words those of their own faith, those who deferred, those who welcomed them, those who could not refuse and those who were less disturbing in their behaviours.[34] These were demanding questions but they were faced up to in the community during the 1980s and 1990s in conjunction with discussions about the best use of the community's reducing resources.

Provincial priorities

The social environment had begun to change in the late 1970s at around the same time that Sisters in the British Province entered a new and tougher stage of renewal and adjustment. The first 'Assessment of the Works' had taken place in 1971–72 in the wake of the separation of the two Provinces. That review had tested each work against the Vincentian criteria listed in Chapter 11, but it had not taken difficult decisions about closures nor developed a Provincial strategy in the light of future projections about the number and age of the Sisters and contemporary needs. It was followed up by the closure of several foundations identified as less fully meeting the criteria (the clinic in Notting Hill, for example, and the small parish school at Little Crosby in Lancashire). Other foundations, a dozen in total, were closed as the Province withdrew from institution-based work such as the mental handicap hospital in Sheffield, hostels in Cardiff, Edinburgh and London, the approved school in Birmingham and mainstream primary schools in a number of locations. But many of the closed foundations were replaced with smaller houses in nearby locations and Sisters were transferred there to take up parish or community work. Some entirely new foundations were also made. As a consequence, the total number of houses in Britain was only three fewer at the end of the decade than at the beginning despite an average reduction of 15 Sisters annually in the Province.

Ten years later, in 1990, in her opening address to the Provincial Assembly, Sister Margaret Barrett asked Sister-delegates to face the facts. The most significant of these, in her view, was that too many houses were being sustained by the Province in proportion to its size. Whereas the number of Sisters had decreased from 752 in 1970 to 469 in 1990 (including 50 in Ethiopia and 4 in Sierra Leone) and the average age of Sisters had risen from 57 years to 66, a figure which would have been higher without the Ethiopian Sisters, the number of foundations

---

34 Interview, 11 September 2016.

had only dropped from 70 to 64 (including 9 in Ethiopia and 1 in Sierra Leone).[35] In presenting delegates with evidence in the form of graphs and charts, she invited them to 'pretend that we are in the year 2000 and we are only 200 Sisters here plus 70 in Ethiopia'. The question was, 'what page of history must we close?' to 'free personnel to make new options to meet the many new needs' and in order to 'leave more time for the prayer and balance so desperately needed in our lives if we are not to become frenetic, overwrought, over-worked, highly-strung women'. Sister Margaret presented this 'objective look at reality' alongside stories and Scriptural passages, notably from the psalms. She emphasised the importance of trust in Providence and each other to make possible both the hard decision-making and the dreaming about 'the new road ahead...that will ensure that the poorest of the poor will continue to experience justice and love in the streets of the city'.[36]

Perhaps hardest for the Sisters present in 1990 was the fact that this was an invitation to make a second journey down the road of closing chapters and taking bold new steps. Ten years earlier in 1979, voting on 'Our Mission', Sister-delegates had proposed a fresh assessment of the works of the Province 'to adapt where possible so that present-day needs are met to the best advantage by the energies and personnel available' – and this had been undertaken.[37] They had wanted an approach to planning that would take into account what others were doing so as to avoid competition and focus on unmet needs. Greater collaboration with professionals and volunteers was favoured. These were ambitious goals and the Province set about the work using the Commissions (groups of Sisters with specialist experience) that it had already established for each of its spheres of activity and by appointing lay professionals – surveyors, accountants and architects – to an Advisory Committee for England and Wales, and a separate one for Scotland.[38] To guide the Provincial leadership in making choices, the 1979 Assembly wished it to prioritise visiting work, for younger Sisters as much as for the more mature, and to create more and better provision for older Sisters no longer in active ministry.

At the next Provincial Assembly in 1984 three individuals from outside the community had been invited to talk about their life experiences and had been invited 'to say what they expected and needed' from the community: Jane – a single parent; Tony (originally from India), who worked for the Catholic Commission for Racial Justice; and Peter, an unemployed married man with a young family. Above all, what each of these contributors asked for was the presence of the Sisters alongside them to listen, to pray, and to be in solidarity as advocates. At the end

---

35   The Conference of Major Superiors of England and Wales (CMRS) found that between 1975 and 1985 religious congregations had closed 340 houses and opened 290. See: Sweeney, 'Religious Life After Vatican II', p.276.

36   Sister Margaret Barrett, Address to the 1990 Provincial Assembly: 'Apostolates', p.1, 15-4-5-1990 1-6 #3 DCMH.

37   'Our Mission', 15-4-3-1979 1-5 #5 DCMH.

38   Joan Tindall, 'A Sprinkling of Memories', p. 23 Personal File 10-2 DCMH.

of this Assembly, delegates articulated three propositions as the framework for the Province's apostolic activity, expressed as 'desires':

> The desire for openness to the poor in our houses so that we can share with them all we have and are;

> The desire to be sensitive to the poor and live in solidarity;

> The desire to work with the laity, especially in our local parishes and the places where we serve.[39]

Many decisions had been taken during the 1980s by the provincial council in response to the recommendations of its advisory councils, commissions and assemblies. Some of these had less sense of deliberative choice about them, either because the community could no longer support the work adequately or because, like teaching and nursing, it could be undertaken by others. But accepting that this was so, there was none the less more underlying coherence to the shifts taking place than might have been apparent at the time. Such coherence might be seen as all the more surprising since many of the most prominent new initiatives were driven from below. But they were quietly overseen by the tenth Provincial, Joan Dwyer (1978–1987), who had the ability to encourage and manage with a light touch, and they were, ultimately, united by the Company's strong values and mission identity, so fully explored in the post-Vatican II era.

In her term of office as provincial, Margaret Barrett (1987–1996), the youngest Sister to be appointed to the office in Britain and the first from the fifth generation, helped the community to clarify and deepen its choice of commitments. Her vision for working with those at the margins of society ensured that the community developed more radically at this time than might otherwise have happened. Her successor, Zoe O'Neill, had returned to Britain after many years as Regional Superior in Ethiopia and brought to the office a personality and missionary experience that was comfortable with the idea of 'bottom up' initiatives, inclusiveness of consultation and some risk-taking. When the Province's activities across the 1980s and 1990s are analysed together, not only is there a clear pattern to them but the sense of purposefulness, far from tailing off between the first and second decade as the number of Sisters reduced and their average age rose, intensified and became more radical. The ministry and mission of these fourth and fifth generations of Daughters in Britain had its own foci corresponding to the needs of the day and the capacity of the Province: community ministries in deprived districts; projects for people sleeping rough; short-term overseas crisis missions and community-based services to replace institutions.

---

39 Provincial Assembly 1984, Sister Maureen Tinkler, 'First Impressions: Last Word', p.2. 15-4-4-1984 1-9, #8 DCMH

Community ministries

In total, provincial leaders closed 18 houses in the 1980s, many of them, such as
Hereford (1861–1984), Lanark Smyllum (1864–1981), Salisbury (1868–1982), Torquay
(1889–1982) and Tollcross (1911-1986), having a considerable history. In these cases,
because of the Province's commitment to focus resources on districts of acute
deprivation, closure meant the Province withdrew altogether from both the wider
area and the local community with which it had a long association. Sisters on
the Commissions used independent social research findings to provide evidence
about areas of social need and bishops were consulted to identify districts in their
dioceses where this need was unmet. As a consequence the community stayed
on in Hull, where it moved to a smaller property, and it opened new houses for
community ministries in Coatbridge in Lanarkshire (1982), Ancoats in Manchester
(1982), in Glasgow Easterhouse (1986), Barrowfield (1989) and Johnstone (1987)
and Seacroft in Leeds (1986). The overall effect of the decisions about closures
and foundations was to make the community's geography even more distinctly
urban in both England and Scotland and to reduce its overall spread (Figure 12.1).

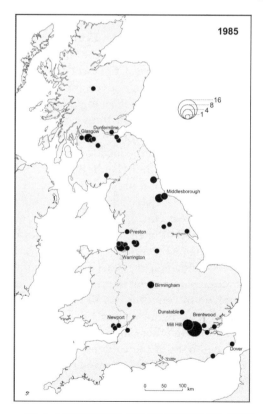

12.1: LOCATION OF HOUSES IN 1985

Even so, as Sister Margaret Barrett pointed out in 1990, its spread was still considerable, and although the houses were smaller in scale, their number had not changed dramatically. During her term of office, the community continued to move away from more 'comfortable' locations to areas of deprivation and the total number of foundations in Britain was reduced to 40 by the end of the century (it had been 70 in 1970). Her reflection to the Provincial Assembly in 1990 about the process that lay ahead of the community almost exactly anticipated Schneiders' conclusions a decade later. Noting that the effort required to renew at a time of decline only made 'sense in the context of a living faith community', she went on to say;

> This is a death/resurrection experience. There are no simple, easy answers. It could be a Calvary experience, but the seeds of the Resurrection are being sown.[40]

Increasingly the Province missioned a group of Sisters to a location for a specific (renewable) period, as was the case for the community sent to Seacroft in Leeds, to the parishes of Our Lady of Perpetual Succour and St Columba's, originally for six years. A wide range of ministries was carried out there in addition to visiting: hospital chaplaincy, confraternities and adult and Vincentian formation. After nine years, this community was transferred in 1995 to Bradford where, in consultations also involving the bishop and parish priest, the local council had made a council house available to the Province. With experience, the Province's members came to accept that short-term missions were not a sign of failure but were in keeping with Vincentian Christian discipleship. In the former mining town of Ammanford in Carmarthenshire (1991–2004), the Province bought a four-bedroomed house to work with the very poorest families in the local community and in the parish of Our Lady of the Rosary, alongside Father Haydn Blackley. This community was involved in parish visiting, sacramental preparation, visits to residential homes and hospitals, and meals on wheels. Catechetical and pastoral work with families in the valleys as well as the town was undertaken. One room in their house was registered so that they could offer respite support to local people. Another community missioned to Glasgow Easterhouse in 1986 (moved to Lockdochart in 1988 because of the levels of vandalism) was based at St Benedict's parish for more than ten years. It had a range of ministries of presence, including ministry to deaf adults, but was also involved in community building with the Salesian Fathers and Sisters, training and supporting local people to set up a credit union and co-operative shop. Collaboration with other Catholic orders, other Christian churches and organisations was a hallmark of the contemporary ministry of community insertion. A planned inter-congregational experimental project was set up in 1994 between the Daughters, the Jesuits and the Sisters of St Joseph of Peace; and for

---

40 Provincial Assembly 1990, Sister Margaret Barrett, 'Apostolates', p .2. 15-4-5-1990 1-6 #3 DCMH.

four years this community (known as Emmaus) ministered in Sunderland's East End, at that time the poorest postal district in England.[41] These examples serve to indicate the nature and importance of community insertion in the Province's work; a fuller picture of which can be gained from the Gazetteer (Appendix 1). At the same time, other Sisters resumed a renewed style of institution-building to meet the contemporary crisis of homelessness.

Poverty on the streets

The most prominent example of the Province's late twentieth-century activity in the field of homelessness is The Passage, begun in 1980 as a drop-in centre at St Vincent's Centre on the corner of Carlisle Place, next to Westminster Cathedral, one of the oldest of the Province's foundations. Over the next twenty years The Passage was to develop into a large-scale and multi-dimensional service for people living on the streets in Westminster or arriving in London via Victoria train or coach station without anywhere to live. By 2000, Daughters had also played key roles in initiating and running Cornerstone Day Centre in Manchester (1990), St Wilfrid's Centre in Sheffield (1991) and NOAH (New Opportunities and Horizons) in Luton (1993), and in co-founding a national organisation, the Depaul Trust (1989), to provide a safety net for young people at risk of homelessness.[42] The re-development of Carlisle Place was the springboard for some of these activities but it is important to note that, despite its deserved reputation, it was not the only work of this kind in the Province. A second point to note is that although each of the initiatives in the 1990s began as the work of an individual Daughter or as a collaboration with a priest who had approached the Province for support, this was because from the late 1980s the Province developed a strategy of involvement in homelessness to support the initiatives of individual Sisters who, in Margaret Barrett's words, 'had a dream'. Each of these projects became embedded in its locality, gaining vitality from local staff, volunteers and benefactors, and building the capacity that enabled all to continue after the Daughters had withdrawn from key management roles. From the perspective of the Province, these projects were the source of learning and growth. It was through them that a transition took place in praxis, moving – in the words of one Daughter, from 'counting how many sausages we served to publicly accounting for how many people we moved off the streets into a better life'.[43]

The roots of this transformation, however, lay in the familiar practice of a Daughter opening the door to a hungry stranger and inviting him or her in for a break from the streets. This is where Sisters Margaret Price, Eileen O'Mahoney and Pauline Gaughan began at Carlisle Place in the late 1970s after St Vincent's School

---

41   Pauline Farrell ssjp and Jim O'Keefe sj, '*The Emmaus Project: An evaluation review – final report*', June 1998.

42   Cornerstone 11-120-2; StWilfrid's 11-72-5; Luton 11-90-1 DCMH.

43   Private conversation,. October 2016.

had moved to new premises and a new purpose for the building had not been decided. They were women described by others as 'tough', 'feisty' or not hesitating 'to rattle a Bishop's or even an Archbishop's cage and rock a few boats'.[44] With hard graft and little funding, Carlisle Place was developed into a small centre, The Passage, opening daily for a restricted number of hours offering tea, sandwiches and a listening ear. What began as a conversation between an individual Daughter (Sister Eileen O'Mahony) and particular priests of Westminster Cathedral (Canon Kelly and Father Patrick O'Donoghue), and practical action by the Daughters in response to the growing number of homeless people in the Cathedral piazza, was given a decisive push by the personal support and patronage of Cardinal Basil Hume.[45] An important outcome was the development of additional complementary services which were established in the neighbourhood by the Cathedral, some of them with the assistance of the Daughters. Sister Eileen, for example, who dreamed beyond The Passage, inspired Cardinal Hume to initiate and put his name to a project for young people at risk on the streets. The Cardinal appealed to religious congregations for funds and the result was the Cardinal Hume Centre, which worked initially with young mothers and children living in local bed and breakfast accommodation and developed accommodation for young people.

With this project underway Eileen O'Mahoney was missioned to Dunstable in Bedfordshire and in the early 1990s developed an existing initiative into a day centre in Luton with a special focus on male Irish migrants who had slipped out of mainstream society and were struggling with addictions and loneliness. This project grew to become NOAH.[46] Pauline Gaughan, who was missioned from Carlisle Place to Manchester, volunteered full-time in Mary and Joseph House, the men's hostel in Ancoats run by the Legion of Mary. In 1990, working with Canon Kevin O'Connor and volunteers, she opened a modest new drop-in centre in a prefab hut in the grounds of St Augustine's church in Hulme to welcome vulnerable people, mainly men experiencing social exclusion – an initiative she saw as 'building a community'.[47] The starting-point at St Wilfrid's in Sheffield was an invitation to the Province from the parish priest Monsignor William Kilgannon of the Mother of God parish, to develop and lead a new drop-in centre. With the arrival of Sister Evelyn Warnock in 1989, considerable work began on preparing a suitable space in a disused church, much innovative handiwork on the premises, raising the necessary resources and support, and recruiting volunteers: the centre opened in 1991 with Sister Evelyn as its first director.[48] In time, each of these centres

---

44 Archbishop Patrick Kelly writing to inform parishioners in the Archdiocese of Liverpool of the death of Sister Pauline Gaughan DC, 7 October 2007, Pauline Gaughan Personal File 10-2 DCMH.

45 Biographies of Cardinal Hume rarely mention the Daughters' part in the initiative. See, for example, Peter Stanford, *Cardinal Hume and the Changing Face of English Catholicism* (London, Geoffrey Chapman), pp. 98-99.

46 http://www.noahenterprise.org.

47 *Manchester Evening News*, 13 May 1997, http://www.cornerstonecds.org.uk.

48 http://www.stwilfridscentre.org.

evolved award-winning services offering supported routes into a better future for clients. Their services encompassed personal assessments, substance and alcohol abuse management, medical and mental health care, skills training and mentoring support, and access to emergency and longer-term resettlement and employment – in addition to the hospitality of tea and company.

For the Sisters involved in this ministry, the journey from a space with cups of tea to the management of a sizeable enterprise, partly funded by competitively-won local authority or government contracts, was a significant one. Those who were open to it learned from professionals and agencies outside the community already experienced in supporting people with complex needs. They learned to make grant applications to charitable foundations, to network for business sponsorship and to bid for publicly funded commissioned projects. This was political work with a small 'p', since it involved knowledge about emerging policies and the ideologies behind them, about advocacy and informal lobbying. It meant a new kind of teamwork, involving more individuals from outside the community than from within, some as employees and many as volunteers.

Increasingly the Sisters involved in these initiatives came to realise that the values they themselves held implicitly, or expressed using language familiar to 'insider' Catholic virtuosi and members of the Vincentian family, needed to be articulated so that they could be understood, discussed and shared with their collaborators outside this inner circle. Much of this concerned the values and precepts of Catholic social teaching – the common good, the dignity of the person, solidarity, the primacy of the family, option for the poor and the inviolability of human life.[49] Some of it had a long Vincentian pedigree with its own emphases. These values occasionally generated organisational 'red lines' when it came to behaviours or procedures that would not be accepted, even if this meant forgoing a commissioning contract - and this too had to be understood by everyone. Just as the Sisters had to learn from professional practitioners in new fields, so they had to think about how to transfer their own value framework to others if their agencies were to be 'Vincentian' in practice as well as in name. Involvement of local conferences of the Society of Vincent de Paul and of young people on placements from the Province's own Vincentian Volunteers scheme, launched in 1992, were further ways of reinforcing the transmission of Vincentian values.[50]

During the 1980s and 1990s, The Passage in Westminster itself evolved gradually through the leadership of the four Sisters who served as directors. As first director Eileen O'Mahoney (1980–1984) worked on the many practical problems to make

---

49   See Anna Rowlands, *Catholic Social Teaching: a guide for the perplexed* (London, Continuum, forthcoming). For a report on the application of Catholic social teaching in a range of other Catholic charities and action groups, including the SVP, see Ben Ryan, *Catholic Social Thought and Catholic Charities in Britain Today: need and opportunity* (London, Theos, 2016).

50   Vincentian Volunteers is a Provincial scheme for young people from Britain and all over the world aged 18-35 to commit a year of their lives to the service of vulnerable people in Britain through a programme of placements and spiritual formation co-ordinated by the Daughters. It began with a pilot in 1989 and was formally launched in 1992. See http://www.vincentianvolunteers.org.uk/

the building more suitable for clients and to build the network of volunteers and supporters. Her successor, Barbara Smith (1985–1991), oversaw a seven-days-a-week opening, a refocus of the service, and serious fundraising to extend services. The establishment of the Depaul Trust in October 1989 as a partnership between Sister Barbara at The Passage, the Society of St Vincent de Paul and the Province, with the support of Cardinal Hume, created a new charity focused on homelessness and young people. Its first director was Sister Sarah King-Turner. After 1989 and beginning with one hostel in Willesden made available by the Province as 'seedcorn', Depaul Trust developed rapidly as a significant independent national charity in its own right working for vulnerable and disadvantaged young people.[51] By 2014, Depaul UK was assisting 4,000 young people annually and had developed into a global organisation, Depaul International. The early work of Depaul (and the Cardinal Hume Centre) allowed Sister Barbara to focus The Passage's services on those over the age of 25.[52]

By the time of Bridie Dowd's appointment as third director of The Passage (1992–2000), the day centre was well established. Her period as director coincided with the government's Rough Sleepers' Initiative in London, which was itself inspired by the unprecedented increase in the number of rough sleepers in the capital and elsewhere at a time when hostels were being closed. Sister Bridie, well known to statutory and voluntary sector agencies as well as members of the private sector and the Royal Family, worked on the development of specialist services such as employment and training and substance abuse treatment. Under her leadership. The Passage raised £2 million for the purchase and establishment of overnight accommodation for 48 clients at Passage House near Victoria Station (2000), a long anticipated provision that replaced the temporary nightshelter that had operated in Westminster Cathedral Hall since the winter of 1990.

Under the last Daughter-director, Ellen Flynn (2000–2008), The Passage became a full participant in central and local government strategies.[53] Sister Ellen's philosophy was one of engagement with the state and other agencies to bring about systemic change, an approach which on occasion produced a working relationship with senior civil servants and ministers, even to the level of Prime Minister. In 1997, the incoming Labour Government created two new units, the Social Exclusion Unit and the Rough Sleepers' Unit, the latter located in Victoria Street, a step away from The Passage, headed by Louise Casey, the former deputy director of the agency Shelter. The location of The Passage had always made it as much a magnet for politicians, policy makers and celebrities as for those at the margins of society. Diana Princess of Wales was a guest in 1990 and 1993 when

---

51 For a history of the Depaul Trust, see Nicki Arden, 'Meet the DePaul Trust', *Catholic Medical Quarterly*, (May 2003) ,available at http://www.cmq.org.uk/CMQ/2003/depaul_trust.htm (accessed 21 October 2017). See also http://uk.depaulcharity.org.

52 Sister Barbara Smith was awarded the OBE for her services to homelessness.

53 Ellen Flynn, 'The Story of the Passage' in James Keane (ed.), *Seeds of Hope: stories of systemic change* (Vincentian Family's Commission for Promoting Systemic Change,: 2008), pp. 86-98.

she opened a new wing, as were other members of the Royal Family at various times and many other figures in the public eye. Members of the new government now came to take a look. Like her predecessors, Sister Ellen sought to harness the goodwill of the privileged for the benefit of the disadvantaged, as exemplified in the annual fundraising gala concert, 'Night Under the Stars'.

By 2008, the year the Daughters withdrew from the directorship of The Passage, the charity was employing 87 full-time and 18 part-time staff to support clients, many of them specialists. Over 200 volunteers worked with these staff for the 4,000 and more individuals who used The Passage's services that year. Of an annual budget of little short of £4 million, almost half came from statutory bodies and £1.5 million was donated.[54] Three years earlier, marking the twenty-fifth anniversary of The Passage's opening, Sister Ellen wrote of the 'privilege simply of being in solidarity with people at the darkest moments of their lives' and of witnessing 'the extremes of goodness – and of evil'. 'I have watched homeless people', she said, 'caring for each other in the midst of so much fear and insecurity – in a way that many of us could learn from'.[55] In 2008, when Sister Ellen was replaced as director by Mick Clarke, The Passage, by now the UK's largest day centre for rough sleepers, became the last of its homelessness initiatives to pass out of management by Daughters, who continue to have membership on the Board of Trustees. At the present time, each of the day centres is a thriving and professionally run organisation working in the interests of socially excluded individuals and clear about its Catholic values, while The Passage itself continues to be part of an extended Vincentian family.

The collaborative approach fundamental to the Province's mission and ministry at the end of the twentieth century can be contrasted with the insurmountable but unspecified difficulties that Daughters apparently encountered during the 1920s and 1930s in their initiatives with 'externs' (for example, at St Louise's Hostel in London and the George Square hostel in Edinburgh). By 2000, collaboration had become expected by Daughters involved in projects and services. In addition, the Province co-created a new Vincentian organisation, Vincentian Volunteers, with the Vincentians and SVP. This was a partnership of the Vincentian Family to engage in the practice and formation of young adults in the Vincentian charism. Finally, we can note the conscious increase in networking and collaboration between the different members of the Vincentian family in Britain, made manifest in the formation of the Vincentian Millennium Partnership (VMP) in 1998. Its purpose was to advocate and work practically for justice, aims that were taken into VMP's twenty-first century successor, Vincentians in Partnership (VIP; from 2010). A number of Daughters have played important roles in VMP and VIP as directors and committee members.[56]

---

54 The Passage Annual Report 2009.

55 *The Passage Jubilee Report*, p. 29.

56 See http://www.vip-gb.org/ (accessed 30 October 2016).

Emergency and short-term overseas missions

Just as the Province made a short-term commitment intentionally in particular locations where it believed Sisters could make a difference, it began to respond in a similar way to emergency situations around the world. Rather than 'having a mission' to a particular country and seeing it as 'theirs' in a quasi-territorial way, Sisters were sent, often at the request of someone out on the ground, to countries where there was an immediate need for specialist support and resources, both of people and of funding. As a member of the provincial council at the time, Sister Joan Moriartywas often the first to investigate the viability and potential effectiveness of a mission. The first such was to Freetown in Sierra Leone, beginning in 1990 just before the outbreak of the Civil War (1992) and ending in 1995. Canon HerbertVeale, a former parish priest of Enfield in Middlesex who had been born in Mill Hill and gone to minister in Sierra Leone after leaving Enfield, asked for Daughters to run programmes for girls and young women who had been trafficked, raped or involved in street prostitution. The Daughters who went established a resource house called Marillac House of Light, and ran education, training and confidence-building programmes which led into employment or self-employment.[57] Just at the time of making a commitment to this project, the Province was contacted via Daughters of Charity in Romania about urgent needs in their country after the revolution of December 1989 and the death of Communist dictator Nicolae Ceauşescu. More than 50 Romanian Daughters had survived the Communist regime and were now asking for help in their orphanages, in the first instance with medical, food and clothing supplies. Sisters from Britain made two trips with loaded minibuses in 1990. When in 1992, Health Aid UK (later renamed Health Aid Romania) invited the Province to send Sisters to Bucharest to help care for and rehabilitate abandoned children who had AIDS or were HIV positive, they accepted. The Province bought a house in Bucharest and began to work in the former Colentina Hospital, judged at the time to be wholly unsuitable for the emotional and physical care of small children. With the support of Health Aid UK, the Sisters were able to plan and oversee the purchase of houses, move children into them, and put in place a programme of training for 'house parents' who were employed. A horticultural project was established to give work to the children when they finished education, because otherwise there was a bar on employment for HIV survivors in Romania. Even after it had withdrawn from the project in 1998, the Province stayed in contact with the children and the projects, sending Sisters to visit and continuing to sponsor the work. Over a span of nearly 17 years, about 20 Sisters had been missioned to Bucharest, some for short periods, others for up to three years, in a deliberate Provincial policy to share these overseas missions. It reflected the wide interest shown in them throughout the Province

---

57 Annual Report for 1995 on Marillac House of Light 7-6 DCMH.

and the policy of including as many Sisters as possible.[58] Between 1990 and 2005, the Province also missioned Sisters with specialist skills to Somalia (1992), Sudan (1993) and to Rwanda in 1994 just after the genocide. Three Sisters were sent to Cairo in 1996, staying for two years to help the local church. In 2002, Sisters went to Haiti in the aftermath of the 2002 storms and to Niger (2005) to oversee an emergency food programme. Short-term missions, along with the Province's long-term commitment to Ethiopia and Eritrea, often physically exacting and emotionally distressing, proved to be a bond between Sisters and were another source of regeneration for the whole community.

Care services in the community: St Joseph's, Rosewell

Ever since the Daughters had opened their first children's homes in the 1860s, the Province had been involved in the care of children and adults with learning disabilities. Families unable to cope left the children with them or with public bodies who sent them into care. In 1926, the community had opened its first specialist hospital in Britain for children with learning disabilities, some of whom had a motor neurone condition or other complex care needs.[59] St Joseph's, in Rosewell near Edinburgh, operated under the terms of the 1913 Mental Deficiency Act, and it became the Province's main centre for mental handicap nursing and education, establishing its own specialist nursing school, as we have seen, in 1942. The passage of the first significant reform legislation on mental capacity, the 1959 Mental Health Act, brought about a complete reversal of the state's previous policy of separation and institutionalisation of persons with a mental handicap. Integration and community care were now advocated, although almost fifty years were to elapse between the articulation of this ideal and its full national implementation. St Joseph's began to prepare some residents for rehabilitation into community living in the early 1960s but also continued to develop as a hospital.

The Province invested heavily in Sisters and money to develop St Joseph's from a drab cash-strapped and under-staffed post-war institution into a model therapeutic hospital and home and training school. New wards were built in collaboration with the statutory bodies. Departments for occupational and speech therapy and a special school were opened. A swimming pool was added in 1981 and in the same year St Joseph's pioneered music therapy. Training at St Joseph's included a unique course, 'Creativity and the Individual', to give nursing staff the opportunity to learn how to use art, music, drama and movement flexibly as education, therapy and recreation. Sister Celeste Bowe, senior tutor at St Joseph's, was an outstanding spokesperson for people with special educational needs

58   I am indebted to Sister Joan Moriarty, who visited Romania in 1992, 2001, 2004, 2006 and 2009, for notes about this mission. 7-9 DCMH.

59   The Province had developed a strong ministry in mental handicap nursing and learning disabilities in Ireland from an earlier date. See Joseph Robins, *From Rejection to Integration: a centenary of service by the Daughters of Charity to persons with a mental handicap* (Dublin, Gill and Macmillan, 1992).

and, until her early death in 1976, she promoted research with colleagues from Edinburgh University.[60] Many other Sisters excelled in the field and the reputation of St Joseph's as a centre of nursing and educational excellence in developmental disability was firmly established by the early 1980s. In 1982, when Pope John Paul II made his historic six-day visit to Britain his tour included time at St Joseph's to meet patients, residents, their families and staff. His public address from St Joseph's about the dignity of every person and the 'mission of the Church to care for all God's people' was given concrete reality by the setting.

Even as the hospital was being developed, so was provision for community care. A handful of houses acquired from Midlothian Council and Scottish Homes were made suitable for small groups of individuals who had expressed the wish to move, and support was given to them by community nurses based at St Joseph's. This was to be the model for the future services when the 1990 National Health Service and Care in the Community Act transferred funding to social services in 1993, a change of policy which made it almost financially impossible for hospitals to continue to offer care.[61] Although St Joseph's reorganised to make some savings so that it could continue to operate, closure was increasingly inevitable. To prepare for the changes, St Joseph's hosted a two-day conference entitled 'The Community Care Act 1993 and its implications for practice' for its own staff and other professionals in the field.[62] Sisters Kathleen Fox from the Centre for Adult Blind in Liverpool and Catherine McErlean, director of services at St Joseph's, shared the platform with the director of planning and a consultant psychiatrist from Lothian Health Board. Presentations and discussions included some predictable topics such as assessment, care management, care plans, quality and standards. Other topics, such as 'A Concept of Creativity – a group experience', 'Vincentian Spirituality of Caring' and 'The Feminine in Leadership and Management' (Catherine McErlean), owed their place on the programme to the particular approach of the Sisters at St Joseph's.

The hospital's long history of integration within its local community helped greatly with the projected new care model, but this did not mean that all families found it easy to accept the decision to close the hospital.[63] Further housing in Rosewell was bought or built in the neighbourhood so that friendships could be sustained and support services be offered in an effective way. After 1998, support was provided through the newly established St Joseph's Services based in Rosewell and managed by the Daughters.

When the hospital closed in 1998 the Sisters invited former staff, residents and families to a series of reunions held over several months, attended by more

---

60 Celeste Bowe was awarded the MBE for services to mental health in 1975. See *Irish Dictionary of National Biography* (Cambridge University Press online).

61 See Mike Titterton (ed.), *Caring for People in the Community: the new welfare* (London, Jessica Kingsley, 1994).

62 This took place in November 1993, 11-117 1-17 #10 DCMH.

63 'Bid to end fear over hospital closure', *Herald Scotland*, 15 April 1995.

than 400 people. An illustrated brochure was distributed to share memories and to ensure that the past, with its shortcomings as well as successes, was recorded and respected. Because of who they were as consecrated women, the fundamental human experience of 'letting go', often undertaken by companies, organisations and individuals without attention to the human needs involved, was understood by the Sisters as an eschatological moment and a missionary occasion. The endnote was to be one of rejoicing:

> Rejoice for that first journey, in the early days, when the service struggled to rise in the dawn of a new beginning. Rejoice, too, for the progression to the noontide of a service of excellence as the vision became a reality. Rejoice, now, as we prepare to leave the 'evening shell' of St Joseph's glowing in the setting sun. Rejoice for we know that a new dawn is breaking in a village called Rosewell –with St Joseph's there, resplendent with the morning sun of a new day.
>
> So let us leave this new place redolent with 'relics' of laughter, left in rooms long after weather broke in where we had been, and move to that new place of blessing.[64]

Letting go with grace: Provincial House

It was not long after this leaving and new beginning at Rosewell that the Province faced the same decisions and processes for its own Provincial House at the Ridgeway in Mill Hill. In 1985, it had celebrated the centenary of the Province and St Vincent's Provincial House with vigour and creativity. Teams of Sisters had worked on different aspects of the celebrations. A triduum was held in the Provincial House chapel in April. Every community was invited to compile a house album with history, photographs, memories and reflections. A research team led by Sister Maria Parcher worked through the records in Mill Hill and visited the archive in Paris to create a series of historically accurate materials for displays, featuring a timeline of major events in the Province's own history, a family tree of houses, representative photographs and artefacts. The resulting large-scale interpretative display was mounted and left in place throughout the year so that any Sister going to Mill Hill would have the opportunity to see it. The centenary led to the appointment of a Sister-archivist with professional training, the development of high-quality archival storage and a permanent Heritage Room at Provincial House, open for the Sisters and visitors.

Provincial House was the literal and imaginative repository for individual and community memories: seminary, retreats, respite, liturgies, meetings, celebrations, funerals and visits to the community cemetery. When in 2002 the provincial

---

64 Memorial Brochure 1998, 11-117 1-17 #12 DCMH. The quotation is from John O'Donohue.

council made the decision to explore the sale of the house it was because they had come to recognise that its size and the costs of maintenance had also become a burden and a barrier to future momentum. It was as though the old house was now a source of inertia, holding back new visions.

The possibility of selling was raised towards the end of the period of office of the twelfth provincial, Sister Zoe O'Neill (1996–2002), who gently guided the community into accepting the need for this decision and to identify the collective preference for the location of the new house. Sister Sarah King-Turner, thirteenth provincial (2002–2008), and her provincial team had the considerable task of managing this change. It was not simply a matter of finding a buyer for the large and unconventional complex of buildings, but of finding a suitable alternative provincial house. The whole community was involved in the process of consultation about alternative locations, with Manchester and Carlisle Place under consideration as well as Mill Hill itself. One of the most obvious solutions, that of moving over the road to The Priory, appeared almost as shocking to the community as the thought of closing Provincial House. It would mean moving the most vulnerable and oldest members of the community out of a house they loved, one that was at the heart of the Province. The Priory was ideal in so many ways: spacious but compact, and with manageable gardens. It gave continuity with the past, proximity to the Vincentian community in Mill Hill, access to the community cemetery - and it was financially prudent. In the event the decision was eased by the creation of nursing home places in the Province's former orthopaedic hospital, St Vincent's in Pinner, not far from Mill Hill. The management board of St Vincent's raised the funds to replace the hospital (closed as a result of NHS reorganisation) with a new 60-bed private Catholic nursing home with its own chapel and chaplain. The Province committed itself to purchasing rooms for Sisters from The Priory in need of nursing care. At the same time it expanded the accommodation in its three centres for elderly Sisters, the Daughters' own Seton House nursing home in Warley in Essex, Southport in Lancashire and St Catherine's Lanark in Scotland.

The provincial council divided the Provincial House project into its three component parts.[65] The first, and the one given the highest priority, was to ensure good-quality care for elderly Sisters, to involve each one in the change and to give her a sense of security about it. This project, named 'Rosalie Rendu' after the French Sister honoured in the Company as a post-Revolutionary model of service, was guided by Anne Redmond, one of the Province's youngest Sisters, and Aine McGuiness, Sister Servant at The Priory.[66] Each Sister in the Priory was paired with a Sister in active ministry who took care of her personally before, during and after the move, and each care location was close to a community of

---

65 New Provincial House planning and move , 11-100-2 DCMH.

66 Rosalie Rendu, 1786-1856, was a French Daughter of Charity beatified in 2003 for her extensive work of organising care among the poor of Paris. In 1833, she began mentoring the first members of the Society of St Vincent de Paul, including Frederick Ozanam.

active Sisters. Father Fergus Kelly, provincial director (2000–2012), who knew all the Sisters personally and had accompanied the provincial councillors in their decisions over the previous six years as a 'brother', made the older Sisters his priority at this time. A second component was the sale of Provincial House to raise as much money as possible while protecting access rights to the community cemetery: this task with its legal and planning complexities fell to the Provincial, Sarah King-Turner.

The third project component was the complete remodelling of The Priory to transform it from a nursing and care home into a modern Provincial House with an updated chapel, a work undertaken by Sisters Marie Raw and Eileen Glancy, provincial bursar. As part of their planning , the provincial council also identified a 'fourth dimension'. Between 1985 and 2000, as a consequence of the many closures it had undertaken, the whole community had learned the importance of carefully thought-through and inclusive farewells that resonated for individuals at a personal and spiritual level. Members of the Province had developed a collective expertise and appreciation of ritualising every aspect of closure, withdrawal and letting go through liturgy, prayer, social gatherings, laughter and memorialising. This approach, exemplified at the time of the closure of St Joseph's Hospital, Rosewell, was now fully deployed by provincial leaders when a buyer was found for Provincial House in 2007 and the time came for its closure. The Provincial Council were convinced that 'leaving well' was crucial to the community and the future of the Province. One of their number, Sister Marie Raw, was given responsibility for this part of the project.

Farewells to Provincial House started with those older Sisters unable to travel back to Mill Hill. At the start of 2007, provincial officers travelled to each of the elderly Sisters' homes for special days of liturgy, presentations and the telling of stories about Seminary days in Provincial House. Following this tour, Sister Marie and the team embarked on three months of events at Provincial House itself. On one Sunday in March the Sisters hosted over 200 Vincentian colleagues, Sisters' families and former staff for Mass, dinner, a history tour and presentation. An open house in March, for Mill Hill parishioners and local residents brought more than 70 people for the tour, a liturgy and talk. There was an invitation, too, for former Daughters to share their memories and say farewell. More than 35 gathered for an occasion of their own entitled 'Women Called to Journey'.[67]

For the Sisters of the Province themselves, there were a series of two-night 'Farewell Gatherings' before April, each involving between 35 and 55 companions. Many came over from Ireland to join a Gathering, but for those who could not do so council officers travelled to Ireland in April and led sessions there. Each Gathering at Provincial House began with an historically researched pilgrimage round the house, with presentations and time for personal memories. There was a vigil in the cemetery, Mass in the chapel and a liturgy devised for the occasion.

---

67 I owe all these details to the journal kept by Sister Marie Raw, which she generously allowed me to access.

Music, displays and art were used to heighten the occasion. During the dinner, a procession of unexpected guests made their appearance at intervals. Sisters Etheldreda Howard, Catherine O'Driscoll, Margaret McGroarty (a Scottish Sister who had been sacristan to the provincial chapel for 30 years) and Gertrude Andrew were 'enacted' by fully habited Sisters. Each spoke about her own time at Provincial House in scripts constructed from the archives. At the final Gathering, St Louise arrived and spoke to the assembled Sisters in heavily French-accented English. In this process of 'letting go', as throughout the period between 1980 and 2007, the community not only lived the 'paradox' of late twentieth-century consecrated life in their own Vincentian way, but also confronted the dangers of 'malaise' spiritually, psychologically and in the bonds of community.

After the final vow retreat during March and the final Easter Triduum, a closing Mass took place in the provincial chapel on St George's Day, 23 April 2007, the 122nd anniversary of the occasion when the first generation of provincial officers had taken up residence in 'Littleberries' and celebrated the first Mass of its life as St Vincent's *Maison Centrale*. In her journal for 2007, Sister Marie Raw wrote of the day:

> The most moving part of the Mass occurred in the silence
> after Holy Communion, when Fr. Fergus opened the tabernacle
> and, preceded, by Anne Lambe ringing a small hand bell
> and our youngest sister, Kay Trivett carrying a candle, he
> removed the Blessed Sacrament out of the chapel. Carole,
> the sacristan, blew out the red sanctuary lamp and we all
> stood in the poignant silence of the moment, realising that
> we have indeed come to the end of our time in this house.[68]

---

68 Ibid., 23 April 2007.

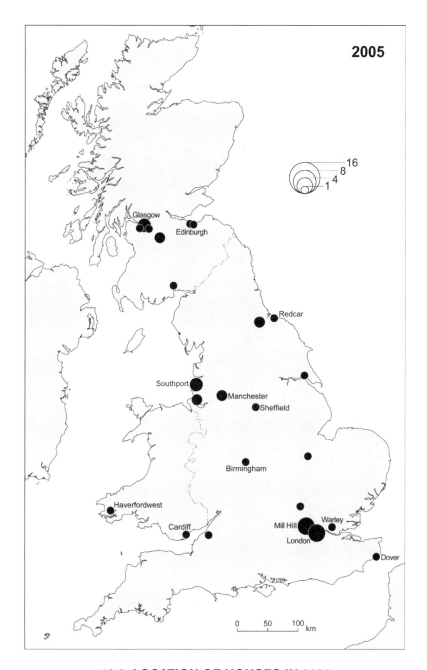

12.2: LOCATION OF HOUSES IN 2005

13

The boldness of charity[1], 2008-2017

> Sisters say they don't worry about the lack of new
> vocations because they have got the mission right;
> they are doing what they can to live their vocation and
> although it feels like dying, they believe in the Resurrection.
> (Religious Life Vitality Project, 2015)[2]

In 2015, the Religious Life Vitality Project (RLVP), conducted by academics from Heythrop College's Religious Life Institute and the Margaret Beaufort Institute of Theology, published its key findings about vitality in women's active religious life in twenty-first-century Britain and Ireland.[3] The British Province of the Daughters of Charity was one of the institutes of consecrated women (and the only Society of Apostolic Life) to participate. It did so at a time of determined activity in its own life, not only to secure continuation of its projects for people in poverty but also to sustain its own charism, the female dimension of the Vincentian double family, into the future in Britain. The findings of the RLVP and internal community sources telling the story of decisions and activities in the period between 2008 and 2016 allow this closing chapter to take stock of the Province in the second decade of the twenty-first century and to indicate the emerging directions of its still vibrant life in community and in mission.

Introducing the *Final Report* of the Religious Vitality Project, Sister Gemma Simmonds CJ noted that its findings showed how women living the consecrated life in Britain had moved 'from the socially and ecclesiastically respectable centre of church and society to the margins, both in terms of status and apostolic focus'. She called this 'part of the contemporary "turn to the subject", which 'rejects both the collective institutionalisations of the past and today's cult of individualism

---

1 'The Boldness of Charity for a New Missionary Momentum' was adopted as the theme for the whole Company at its General Assembly in 2015. Inter-Assemblies Document 2015-2021.

2 Sexton and Simmonds CJ, *Religious Life Vitality Project: Key Project Findings*, 'Reflection on the Daughters of Charity transcript', p.18. (Hereafter RLVP Key Findings). This latter part of the Key Findings report, specific to the Daughters of Charity, is not in the public domain but has been made available to the author by the Province.

3 The *Key Findings* are available at http://www.margaretbeaufort.cam.ac.uk/assets/documents/research%20key%20findings%20report.pdf and the *Fnal Report* at http://www.margaretbeaufort.cam.ac.uk/assets/documents/final%20rli%20report.pdf

in favour of union with God and others'.[4] The RLVP was intended primarily as a resource for the participating communities themselves, but it has also served to fill a gap in understanding about the contemporary experience of consecrated life for women in the particular context of Britain.[5] More than 200 sisters from 18 congregations took part in the first research phase during 2013 and 2014. Sisters from 13 of these communities, including the Daughters, went on to engage in a second phase, in which they reflected on their own data and the project's analysis.[6]

The RLVP's narrative summary for the Daughters of Charity describes the Sisters of the British Province as having 'a clear and strong sense of identity...based on a "joined-up" sense of mission, prayer and spirituality and community, and of being servants of the poor'.[7] Significantly, the summary notes that 'religious vows are explicitly mentioned as a source of vitality' by Daughters, a feature regarded as being 'done in a different and more marked way to other congregations, perhaps reflecting the fact that the Daughters of Charity renew their vows annually, in a way which is unique to them'.[8] Observing that their 'clarity of mission and purpose enables the sisters to engage in challenging ministries', the summary suggested that Sisters themselves felt that they have a 'simpler, strong focus on apostolic work' with 'ministry as 'the ground of their being', perhaps because they are not a religious order'.

These findings, and those for other participating congregations, raise questions about the interpretation of post-conciliar religious life arrived at by commentators who have concluded that what is 'troubling religious life...[is] the rather fundamental and all-embracing existential question of identity'.[9] According to many scholars, Vatican II's removal of a distinct and special status for religious, together with the decline in the salience of the very concept of 'the state of perfection', created a crisis of identity and served to deepen an existing crisis of vocations.[10] But in a clear echo of the language used by their seventeenth-century founders, the RLVP found that today's Daughters 'describe themselves as having come to do what Jesus Christ came to do and thus to model themselves on Christ's life of service and ministry'.[11] The Daughters' narrative does not support

---

4 ibid., p. 3.

5 The Project included some congregations from Ireland.

6 The Project's methodology is set out in RLVP *Final Report*, p. 4.

7 RLVP, 'Reflection on the Daughters of Charity Transcript provided by the project researchers', p. 15.

8 ibid.

9 Sweeney, 'Religious Life After Vatican II', in Hornsby-Smith (ed.), *Catholics in England*, p. 281.

10 See Schmiedl , J. 2010., 'Reception and Implementation of the Second Vatican Council' in Leo, Kenis. Billiet and Pasture eds., *The Transformation of the Christian Churches in Western Europe 1945-2000.* (Leuven: Leuve, University Press, P. .306. For a riposte and an historicisation of the concept of 'identity crisis', see Timothy Radcliffe   http://www.dominicans.ca/Documents/masters/Radcliffe/religious_identity.html   (accessed   2 November 2016).

11 RLVP *Key Findings*, p.16

the argument about an identity crisis or a crisis of meaning; rather it captures the experience of transformation. 'I often feel that' one Sister reflected,

> that we are like Christ at the foot of the cross, you know, we are stripping ourselves of houses, we are stripping ourselves of places that we have been in for a very long time, of work that we are familiar with and easy with and what are we doing we are re-clothing ourselves anew. We are re-clothing ourselves with reaching out to trafficked people, we are re-clothing ourselves by looking, looking to the refugees and asylum seekers and quite honestly that is mounting the cross and I just think that that to me is a sure sign that we are alive to the way Christ acts in our world and we are participating in that wonderful mission of Christ.[12]

At the human level it is only community belonging – and the whole community's engagement – that makes transformation possible. 'I was thinking', she went on, that 'if there wasn't the support of the Province behind it and the faith of the Province, it wouldn't be able to continue...People wouldn't be saying 'Yes'.[13] As we have seen, both the saying of 'Yes' and the high degree of continuity in identity had come about through a determined endeavour of constant renewal by the leadership and the community over more than thirty years. 'I see the constant referring to the re-visioning of our work', one Sister comments, 'as...reiterating the values of our charism.'[14] Transformation as a continuous process had become integral to the community's life and future.

In 2009, the Province had started what was arguably the most profound re-visioning it had undertaken, more so even than in 1990, although this was not realised at the outset. A number of factors combined to make it so: the rapid ageing of the community, its accumulated experience of self-assessment; the prominence of fifth-generation post-Vatican II Sisters in the leadership of the review, and their commitment to strategic outcomes that would have the support of the whole Province. Sister Marie Raw, appointed as fourteenth provincial in 2008, embarked with the new council on writing a Provincial Plan the following year. It was thought that a new approach to consultation was needed, if engagement were to be both meaningful and productive of change. A series of group conversations around the Province conducted during 2009 replaced questionnaires and top-down approaches, with regular checks to make sure that Sisters felt their views had been faithfully reflected in the summaries made. With the Plan in place, it was decided to begin implementation with the 'Mission and Ministry' section

---

12 RLVP **Final Report**, p. 15.

13 ibid. In this context it is important to note that the Province included the whole community in the research, first by presenting the findings to Sister Servants and then through a presentation from the researchers to a Province Day (October 2015), which was live-streamed to the houses of the Province for Sisters not present.

14 RLVP *Final Report*, p. 15.

because, 'it is Mission that gives meaning to our lives; everything else must flow towards and from it'.[15]

According to Seán D. Sammon, former Superior General of the Marist Brothers and a writer on consecrated life,

> 'groups that have developed a more profound understanding about their foundational spirituality and have spent time addressing important issues of community life...have reaffirmed that life together is for the purpose of mission, centred around faith and spirituality and marked by the members' genuine interest in one another'.[16]

For Daughters the life had always been for mission, a position that was only confirmed in the consultation. However, it became clear that to be effective, as Vincent de Paul himself had concluded in 1617 using different language, it was necessary to be strategic.[17] By May 2010 the council had reached a critical point.[18] They believed they faced a choice of either continuing to 'move the deckchairs around, while the ship was going down' or to undertake a radical 360-degree review of the Province.[19] Having chosen the second option, they brought in external professional help and external spiritual support for themselves.

Beginning with a meeting for all Sister Servants in autumn 2010, there was an 18 month period of Province-wide discussion, punctuated by a meeting of the whole Province in January 2011 to gain further feedback. The process culminated in another such meeting in May to present the outcomes.[20] This careful approach brought about commitment to undertake strategic change using four building blocks.

The first concerned ministry. Ministry streams encompassing the activities of all the Sisters, including the elderly and those in administration and management, were identified: local (place-based) ministries; projects and services; ministry to the Province; and ministry of prayer and presence. The second building block was to agree criteria (listed below) against which all their external activities, existing and in the future, would be measured:

---

15 Marie Raw notes for Susan O'Brien, 'Vision for the Future', p.1. All documentation for this part of the process forms part of the Province's administrative records. The process was well documented. Her statement finds support in the RLVP, see Key Findings, p. 16, where the Sisters described ministry 'as something that runs through them s through the centre of a stick of rock'

16 D Sammon, S. D. 2015.'Religious Life Reimagined', *America: The National Catholic Review,* 14 September 2015.

17 See discussion in Chapter 2.

18 Marie Raw notes for Susan O'Brien, 'Vision for the Future', p. 1.

19 'Our Vision for the Future'. Current administrative records DCMH.

20 Participant pack for Provincial Meeting at High Leigh, May 2011. Current administrative records DCMH. Documents for all aspects of the iterative process are numbered and stored as 'Marie Raw Strategic Plan'.

1. The service of those who are poor and our ability to serve them effectively

2. Sustainability of our ministries and their Vincentian Values

3. Availability of opportunities for ministry, ongoing or new, especially collaborative ministry

4. Suitability of property, its size, location, amenities etc

5. Relationship with the local church

6. Opportunities for visibility, presence and witness

A further criterion, to be applied in some cases, was consideration of the opportunity for the initial formation of new members.

Research into nationally established poverty indicators for each of the places where they were in ministry constituted the third building block. With this information and the agreed criteria it was possible to move to the fourth building block, a review of each activity to make the decision to 'maintain, develop or let go'. The difficulty of this part of the strategic planning, deciding which houses to close, was increased by the fact that the poverty indicators had shown that most of their local ministries were already taking place in the poorest areas of Britain or with people in great poverty or need. The decisions were made and the community of each house was informed confidentially of its own future before the whole picture was presented to a Province Gathering in Liverpool on 30 June 2012. 'This was a seminal meeting', Sister Marie Raw reflected, '– many tears, some relief – but a huge sense of togetherness and acceptance'.[21]

Implementation was then immediate, with one process for communities that were to be developed, and another for those that were closing. This latter group included Sheffield, the Province's first place of ministry (1857), where connections were deep; Darlington, where Daughters of Charity had ministered continuously since 1880; and Bristol, where they had first arrived in 1916. The closure of the Sheffield foundation came as a shock in the community, but it had not met the assessment criteria as comprehensively as several of the others, such as Hull and Glasgow. Again, great care was taken to handle the decision sensitively for those who would be affected, including the Sisters. Employees, collaborators, parishioners and the people served by the Sisters were informed in a particular order and in a way that was planned and co-ordinated. Where the Province was withdrawing from a place altogether, as in the three named, there were Masses and social events to mark the occasion.

The community had already decided to leave Bristol in 2011. Sheffield followed in 2012 and Darlington in 2013. In 2014, Sisters were withdrawn from Cathedral

---

21 Marie Raw notes for Susan O'Brien, 'Vision for the Future', p.3. Sister Marie Raw's address to the Gathering is part of her deposit for the archive 'Strategic Plan 2012.

House in Liverpool, leaving just one community in the city, and the Province also closed smaller communities in Glasgow, Little Hulton in Salford and Kilburn in North London, places where it continued to have a presence. One Edinburgh community that had begun at Muirhouse and moved to Inveresk was moved again to Rosewell, where a house was opened opposite the offices of St Joseph's Service. That same year, 2014, the decision was taken to strengthen the Province's commitment in Hull, by adding a second community to the one already present in St Wilfrid's presbytery, west Hull. Daughters were missioned to continue the work of a departing Congregation of Jesus community on a marginalised estate in east Hull, where the CJ sisters had set up St Stephen's Neighbourhood Centre with its own legal and financial structure and staff. Both Hull foundations work with the diocese for evangelisation and ministry in areas identified as experiencing particularly high levels of spiritual and material deprivation. Another new foundation has been established in the London area, at Abbey Wood near Woolwich, in partnership with Nigerian Vincentians serving the four parishes in the area. The environment here has some parallels with that in east Hull but has a more diverse population. With these additions, the Province's foundations now form two corridors: one on the east side of the country comprising London (Abbey Wood, Westminster, Kensal Green, Mill Hill, Pinner), Brentwood, Hull and Rosewell near Edinburgh: and one on the west side made up of Cardiff, Manchester, Liverpool, Southport, Ayr, Lanark and Glasgow.

These decisions formed the context for the Daughters' engaged with the RLVP between 2013 and 2015. But so too did the less publicly visible work of finding a new way to sustain the Vincentian charism in the life of projects that it had retained and those it would go on to found in the future. Sisters Ellen Flynn and Eileen Glancy first began to research legal structures and test out organisational models in 2009, to see which would enable projects and services started by the Province and still connected to it 'to continue and flourish with limited or no DC management'.[22] The outcome was a group structure or parent company with subsidiaries, which they called Daughters of Charity of St Vincent de Paul Services (DCSVP). This new charity sat alongside the longstanding Daughters of Charity Charitable Trust, which encompassed the Province's parish and other local ministries, its internal concerns such as Provincial House and the care homes for older Sisters, and any overseas mission activity it might undertake. As a vehicle for projects and services undertaken with others, DCSVP was set up to be simple, flexible, collaborative, sustainable and to have potential for international or transnational operation. The Province was also keen that DCSVP should have the potential to develop an affiliate membership category to draw in former Daughters of Charity projects, such as The Passage, which were already fully developed as independent charities but were interested in questions of organisational values.

---

22 'Daughters of Charity of St Vincent de Paul Services Summary Paper for Sister Evelyne Franc, Superioress General', June 2012, p.1. Current administrative records, Provincial House.

DCSVP was legally incorporated in 2012, with one subsidiary and with five other projects envisaged as becoming subsidiaries in due course. Two of these, St Joseph's Services in Edinburgh, for adults with learning disabilities, and Marillac Care in Warley, supporting adults with neurological disabilities, have roots going back into the Province's pre-Vatican II history. St Vincent's Family Project, begun in 1996 at Carlisle Place to work with fragile and vulnerable families and developing out of an earlier family project, was the first subsidiary. Two projects, joining as subsidiaries in 2014, had been established in the early years of the new century from a Province initiative led by Sister Margaret Bannerman to research potential new services that re-minted historic Company ministries to meet contemporary needs (the Naseau initiative); 'Out There' supports families of prisoners in Manchester prisons; and Vincentian Care Plus is a home-based personal care service in the Westminster area, concentrating primarily on housebound and older people. Both continue the Province's practice of working with statutory bodies.

The most recent project was founded in 2014 in Glasgow. In parallel with establishing new local ministries in Hull and Abbey Wood and as part of its revisioning, the Province wished to begin a new Naseau type of project in Scotland. Collaborating with Faith in the Community, a project of the Church of Scotland, a group of Sisters already based in Glasgow opened a place of welcome and hospitality in a former shop in Govanhill and named it simply 'The Space'. They adopted Vincent de Paul's practice of 'wait and see', to discover what might happen and how The Space and their presence might be used. Levels of poverty and multiple deprivation in the area (85% above the average for Scotland) indicated strongly that there would be a need, but the nature of the service would emerge rather than be pre-determined. Over a two-year period, Sisters, staff and volunteers at The Space found that they were working predominantly (70%) with members of the Romanian Roma community, described as 'the most vulnerable and deprived ethnic group within Europe', of whom there are around 3,500 in Govanhill.[23] The Space has found a purpose in brokering relationships for its users with GPs, schools and agencies, in accessing food and clothing, and in developing networks and relationships to empower people to transform their lives and that of their community. Describing The Space as a 'social cohesion' project, the Sisters see their own role as one of building trust and they are consciously launching and embedding a project that can continue independently without them.[24] Currently, The Space reports directly to the Daughters of Charity Charitable Trust Board but the intention is for the organisation to become an independent subsidiary of DCSVP, as has already happened with St Joseph's Services.

The new type of relationships developed between the Province and its employees, and between the professional peers and volunteers who have worked

---

23 Poole and Adamson 2007, *Report on the situation of the Roma community in Govanhill, Glasgow* (Glasgow: University of the West of Scotland), p.2. also published by Oxfam in 2008.

24 See http://dcsvpservices.org/projects-and-services#projects_the_space (accessed 25 October 2016).

on their projects since the 1980s, provide one clear and significant example of post-Vatican II 'transformation' in consecrated life where the Daughters are concerned. These relationships, however, led to a new set of questions about how the Vincentian nature of the organisations could be sustained as the number of Daughters involved in them reduced. Having created the legal structure of parent company and subsidiaries, the Province took up the vital question of how to embed Vincentian values in the subsidiaries and in organisations with a heritage from the Daughters in Britain. 'Lay people', the DCSVP *Theory of Change Business Plan* (2014) observed, 'can and have already demonstrated their commitment to continuing their service according to the charism of the Daughters of Charity. However, this does require a depth and breadth of Vincentian formation alongside their professional competence'.[25] The vehicle developed by the Province to achieve this formation is Vincentian Values Today (VIVAT).

VIVAT is intended to influence organisational behaviour, inform employees about Vincentian values and form them in values-based practices.[26] Its development has been a collaborative venture from the outset, beginning in early 2014 with a conference to bring together the Sisters and staff of the six intended DCSVP subsidiaries, for whom VIVAT is compulsory. Representatives from other organisations which would be beneficiaries (such as the Province's care homes) and those who, like The Passage and Depaul UK, had already been experimenting with their own Vincentian programmes under guidance of the Daughters, accepted an invitation to take part. The product of this first conference of fifteen organisations was the establishment of three working parties to undertake the groundwork respectively for formation programmes, a Vincentian definition of pastoral care, and the means to embed values in the policy and practices of the subsidiary organisations.

As this work was underway, a symposium of Sisters, trustees and key staff of the 15 organisations was held in November 2014, to 'distil the core characteristics that they share...rooted in the specific, inspirational 400-year-old Vincentian tradition'.[27] Five shared values were identified as being core:

> Serving people who are experiencing the effects of poverty;
> Respecting each person's dignity;
> Being compassionate and kind;
> Enabling choice and change;
> Acting in solidarity for justice.[28]

---

25 DCSVP 'Theory of Change Business Plan April 2014 to April 2017', p. 7. Current administrative record.

26 The six listed above plus Seton Care Home, St Catherine's Care Home, St Vincent's Care House, Depaul UK, The Passage, Vincentians in Partnership, and Vincentian Volunteers, and the Daughters of Charity of St Vincent de Paul, and Daughters of Charity of St Vincent de Paul Services.

27 'Vincentian Values Today: A shared statement of our Vincentian identity and purpose', p.1. Current administrative record widely available in VIVAT organisations.

28 ibid., p. 8.

Although this Vincentian values statement does not replace any statements which members might already have, it commits them to work within its framework in specific aspects of their organisational life.

The definition of Vincentian pastoral care and a Vincentian pastoral model, identified at the first conference as being essential for the subsidiaries, was underway during 2015. It was partly progressed by means of research undertaken by Sister Kathleen Page to test ideas and practices with the assistance of VIVAT's working party. This work to develop a language and praxis of pastoral care rooted in the Vincentian tradition will be taken forward by Sister Kathleen through research for a doctorate in practical theology. It is possible to see parallels between the importance placed by the Province today on a Vincentian pastoral model, capable of forming and informing front-line staff in their daily practice of care, and that placed on the formation of the early Daughters by Vincent de Paul and Louise de Marillac.

Progress on the pastoral model, the values programme and organisational policies and practices were reported for discussion to a second conference of the 15 organisations in June 2015.   Proposals were refined, the working parties were dissolved and a pilot stage was begun with the oversight of a single review group. The level of agreement reached meant that it was possible to publish a booklet, *Vincentian Values Today: a shared statement of our Vincentian identity and purpose* on behalf of the 15 organisations and a set of guidelines for the six potential subsidiaries, *Manifesting our Values*, which sets out which of their policies and practices should be influenced by the agreed value statement.

Recruitment policies and practices, induction and ongoing training were identified as the aspects of organisations that should be influenced by the statement, which is also to be used to identify and communicate 'points of difference' between the organisation and others that might appear to be the same. The aspiration is to go further than this in the longer term. As like-minded bodies, it is expected that members will explore mutual areas of interest and collaborate with one another, so as to speak out 'with a single voice on some of the major issues of poverty and inequality in Britain'.[29] Because 'a hallmark of a Vincentian approach to services for people in poverty is that it aims to be systemic', members intend to investigate and challenge the underlying causes of poverty through research, policy and advocacy, often by working together to do so.[30]

Agreement of the VIVAT statement was also followed in 2015 and 2016 by the development of training programmes for organisations at different levels, from new employees to trustees and board members. The Daughters devising these programmes are experienced adult educators and have worked in the formation of young people and adults within a variety of Vincentian organisations. The first training took place as a series of pilots in early 2016 at Marillac Care and

---

29 ibid., p. 2.

30 DCSVP 'Theory of Change Business Plan April 2014 to April 2017', p.21. Current administrative record.

at St Joseph's Services in Edinburgh.[31] The first sessions have revealed a lack of knowledge generally about Louise de Marillac and this has provided an opening in the programme to discuss women's leadership, partnership between women and men for the common good and the reasons for St Louise's 'hidden history'. In the medium term, the Daughters intend to develop different levels of courses, some of which could be accredited at undergraduate level for the benefit of employees and volunteers, and in the future will focus their own efforts on training trainers, chief executives, chairs of boards and trustees.

In the early twenty-first century, wholly at ease with their own lay status and identity, Daughters have been able to forge relationships with other lay collaborators who are following their own vocational calls. One participant at the VIVAT annual meeting in 2016 described the values of the subsidiary he worked for as 'a reason for joining and a reason for staying'.[32] Another referred to her employment as a 'vocational call, a *lay* call from the Lord to build God's kingdom'.[33] As one of the Daughters observed, some in VIVAT were travelling from a primarily professional identity to an understanding that they had a vocational call which was deepening their own lives; and others, including herself, had begun with a vocational call and only later developed a professional identity in service of that vocation.

Seán Sammon has reflected on a general movement taking place in Catholicism in which

> 'lay partners have an essential role to play in redefining consecrated life for the 21st century' because 'over time [they] along with the members of the founding congregation, become a living endowment for the institutions in which they minister, ensuring that the institutional identity is clear and the founding values respected'.[34]

But perhaps even more significant is the way that collaboration between Daughters and women and men outside their own community, undoubtedly galvanised by 'the crisis of vocations', is bringing about a transformation in keeping with Vatican II and doing so, moreover, through the ministry of women. Sister Ellen Flynn, who was designated fifteenth Provincial in 2015, believes that the Province

---

31 Marillac Care has 196 staff and 70 volunteers; St Joseph's Services has 270 full-and part-time staff.

32 Personal notes taken at VIVAT annual meeting held at the Royal Foundation at St Katharine, London, 7 July 2016.

33 ibid.

34 Seán D. Sammon, 'Religious Life Reimagined', *America: The National Catholic Review* 14, September 2015.

has 'developed a great way of serving the poor and there's no reason why it should not be lay led'.[35]

In her visit to the Province in February 2006, the year before the closure of Provincial House and in knowledge that this was imminent, the Company's superioress general, Evelyne Franc, had addressed a meeting of many Sisters at Provincial House. She looked back to the time when the new Province had borrowed 250,000 francs (£10,000) from the mother house to buy and adapt the Littleberries estate and, with the Sisters, she looked forward beyond the moment of their departure from this same house. Questioned from the floor about how the community, in leaving behind ministries and projects and not simply buildings, could also leave behind the Vincentian 'touch', Sister Evelyne responded that some juridical safeguards could be adopted and it could be done partly by veto over some decisions that might be taken in the future. But the real 'touch', she stressed, is to put the priorities of the poor first in planning. Since they were no longer professionally at the cutting edge, the question now, she suggested, is about influence. It had been easier to be a Daughter of Charity when you led a large institution. Now it had to be about culture; influence *is* cultural. These were challenges, but she expressed her confidence in the Province because, from the perspective of the mother house in Paris, the Province's reputation for being outwardly turned rather than inward looking, and for being willing to test new forms of mission, made it well placed to find its own answers to this question.[36]

Ten years later, in 2017, the Province's answers are moving from plans to practice, from ideas to embodiment. The Daughters' vision and charism ensures that efforts are concentrated on change for individuals in poverty. The major thrust in the Sisters' work has been to collaborate with others to live the Gospel together. Being outwardly turned means that the Province's members continue to play an active part in the Company's missions outside Britain too. Today, Sisters are involved in interprovincial initiatives in specific places such as Kenya and in the transnational campaign against human trafficking in response to the global exploitation of persons.

There is no doubt that the Company of the Daughters of Charity of St Vincent de Paul is globalising, collaborating within and outside itself in a movement to become a more fully transnational 'Company without Borders'. The Province of Great Britain remains committed to seeking new members and, even with its current realities, to playing its part in the wider Vincentian family in order to have greater impact on the emerging poverties of this present time.

***

---

35 *The Tablet*, 11 July 2015, p.32. Depaul UK provides an inspiring example. In 2016 it launched a new homelessness service in Sheffield, called Nightstop South Yorkshire, to provide young people sleeping rough with emergency accommodation through the involvement of volunteers. The service was awarded £200,000 from the People's Postcode Lottery.

36 Personal notes taken at the Provincial meeting with Sister Evelyne Franc, Mill Hill, February 2006.

Looking back over the 170 years of the Daughters of Charity has provided insights into the working of a transnational community of Catholic women in ministry through a British lens, allowing an exploration of how and why the relationships between the mother house and region, and between regions themselves, have changed over time. The Province itself has steadily moved in the direction of living out its own British cultural distinctiveness without losing its firm bond with the transnational Company or its identity as a part of the Company. Vincentian distinctiveness, always a strong characteristic, has become better defined and more widely understood in the community in the years since Vatican II. The practical and spiritual benefits of belonging to a wider Vincentian family have been strengthened by social media and digital networking, whether that takes the form of campaigning and advocacy or prayer and formation via websites.

The practice of charity by the Daughters of the British Province has been remarkable consistency of focus on people in poverty, but it has also widened in scope and inclusion. Over the long durée of 170 years, the Daughters' practice of personal visits to people at home, in prison and in hospital has stood the test of time as a response to a human need for companionship and support, and is currently being used as the basis for new models of care. The Daughters' history provides strong indication that Catholic practices of charity were distinctive in the landscape of British philanthropy. The argument made here would merit further exploration and updating in the light of the Province's recent commitment to what it has described as the 'radical Christian commitment to a "preferential option for the poor" that lies at the heart of the Vincentian tradition' and its work to transmit the theological values that underpin its practice.[37]

As a community of Catholic women, the Province has steadily developed autonomy in decision-making and leadership. Daughters confidently manage their own affairs with the advice of external professionals. They have a wide range of Company role models in Marguerite Naseau, Rosalie Rendu and many others, as well as Catherine Labouré. Sisters in Britain have travelled so far from Étienne's construct of the 'good Daughter' that this aspect of the Company's history, where women were instructed from on high about how to be a Daughter by someone not living the life, seems entirely alien. Equally their understanding of the part

---

37 DCSVP 'Theory of Change Business Plan', April 2014 to April 2017 p. 17 (2014).

played by Louise de Marillac in receiving and transmitting what is known as the Vincentian charism has undergone a transformation.[38]

Knowledge of Louise de Marillac's true life story, for so long hidden from the Daughters and the wider public because of her illegitimate birth, has become a source of rich reflection for the Sisters in Britain. Far from finding it shocking or shameful, as earlier generations had done, modern Daughters are able to connect Louise's own emotional deprivation to her subsequent service of others. To a contemporary, sensibility the years of depression and anxiety she suffered before finding fulfilment and a way to use her talents in the work with Vincent de Paul no longer make her 'odd', as she seemed to some twentieth mid-century interpreters, but rather believable and inspiring. The same is true for her struggle to develop an authentic relationship with God and a spiritual practice that, in time, transformed her own life and those of others. Greater knowledge about Louise de Marillac's own spirituality following the publication of her complete writings in English in 1991, has served to reinforce the Province's continuing devotion to Mary, Mother of God and Mary of the Immaculate Conception. Although the emphasis on devotion to the Blessed Virgin waned in many parishes and religious communities in the post-conciliar era, this was not the case in either the Company at large or in the British Province.[39] The fact that Daughters in Britain placed the life of Jesus at the centre of their lives and had welcomed the Liturgy of the Hours because of its scriptural basis, did not mean that the Province lost its Marian iconography or prayers.

The Daughters of Charity in Britain today believe that the key to their vitality and their future remains, as it has always done, in giving highest priority to the poorest members of society. In the words of the Religious Life Vitality Project, 'ministry is the ground of their being'.[40] For some in the community the next step is 'a true collaboration of the most challenging kind', with those who experience poverty on the peripheries of society today, 'so that they work together as equals and receive together the gifts of this ministry'.[41]

---

38 Although knowledge of Louise de Marillac had increased during the 1920s at the time of her beatification and 1930s when she was canonised, there were many suppositions about her in the double family, including the myth that she was neurotic and over-scrupulous. It was not until Joseph Dirvin's 1970 biography that her portrayal as a woman of action and spiritual insight began (Joseph Dirvin's, *Louise de Marillac of the Ladies and Daughters of Charity*, New York: Farrar, Straus, Giroux, 1970), and not until 1991, the 400th anniversary of her birth, that her complete writings were available in English; Louise Sullivan ed., *Spiritual Writings of Louise de Marillac: Correspondence and Thoughts* (New York: New City Press, 1991). That year a new interpretative selection of her writing was compiled for the Company, Elizabeth Charpy, *Louise de Marillac: A Way to Holiness*. For a short modern study see Gertrude Foley, 'Saint Louise de Marillac: Woman of Substance; Woman of God', *VHJ* (2000), vol.21, issue 2, art. 2.

39 See Charlene Spretnak, *Missing Mary: The Queen of Heaven and Her Re-Emergence in the Modern Church* (Basingstoke and New York, Palgrave Macmillan, 2004).

40 RLVP *Key Findings*, p.16.

41 ibid.

Vincent de Paul sitting among the poor as one of them, part of a triptych painted in 1990 by the Austrian artist Kurt Welther for St Vincent's Church, Graz. A copy (used here with permission) is in Sacred Heart and Mary Immaculate Church, Mill Hill, London.

Vincentian Volunteers 2015

Daughters of Charity Services

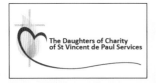

The logo of Daughters of Charity of St Vincent de Paul Services (DCSVP), the name of the legally incorporated group structure which holds the six individual charities listed on these two pages. Each charity was initiated by the Daughters but is operated in collaboration with others. The aim is for each to become a sustainable subsidiary.

Out There (supporting the families of prisoners), Manchester

St Vincent's Family Project, London

Marillac Care, Warley, Essex

Daughters of Charity Services

The Space, Glasgow

Vincentian Care Plus, London

St Joseph's Services, Rosewell near Edinburgh

Vincentian Values for Today (VIVAT)

'VIVAT' is both a formational programme for employees and volunteers and a means to influence key charity policies and practices so that they are values-based and sustain a Vincentian approach.

VIVAT sessions 2014 and 2016

Planning for change across DC Services 2015 onwards

IMPLEMENTATION

Inputs	Establishment of new legal group structure for 6 subsidiaries in three phases. Staffing New Governance structure Start up budget for two year period (ends April 2016) Finance and admin support from centralised DC Charitable Trust resources.
Activities	Support subsidiaries to improve their sustainability Legal activities to ensure subsidiaries have 'joined' DCSVP Services by 1st April 2016. 2 year VIVAT values programme rolled out. Fundraising to ensure DCSVP is self-sustaining beyond start up budget. Research processes initiated exploring emerging UK poverties requiring new DC responses.
Outputs All delivered by December 2015	Business/development plans in place in all subsidiaries. Common Vincentian Vision/Values code adopted across subsidiaries. More collaboration occurring across DCSVP Services subsidiaries. 2 VIVAT conferences held and 3 task groups established producing new Vincentian values resources/training/tools. Common Vincentian Advocacy Plan devised for 2016 implementation Monitoring of UK social policy occurring.

RESULTS

Outcomes To be measured by April 2016/17	(1) Increased understanding of Vincentian values within all layers of participating Vincentian organisations and a sustained and faithful mission focus. (2) Robust and sustainable subsidiaries in evidence delivering best quality services. (3) Growth of a range of new anti-poverty initiatives beyond initial 6 subsidiaries. (4) A more cohesive 'Vincentian voice' on UK social justice issues emerges and begins to bring its practice evidence to bear.
Impact Intended in long term. Measured in 2019	(1) Sisters' legacy is secured in UK and ethos safeguarded as a lay led group is in full operation guided by DCs at pastoral and governance levels. (2) Systemic change and advocacy occurring with and on behalf of people experiencing poverty in the UK.

Taken from the 2015 Province Business Plan

Prayer and Presence

Provincial House chapel

Threading Miraculous Medals: a long-standing occupation of older Sisters in the Province. Thousands continue to be requested and distributed each year.

Photo © Sr Bernadette Ryder DC

Station Four of the Stations of the Cross designed by Sisters in 2010 for the garden of the new Provincial House in Mill Hill.

She who has the spirit of a true Daughter of Charity is ready to go to any place, prepared to leave all to serve her neighbour. If we love Our Lord, He is to be found everywhere. And there, my dear Sisters, are the three marks of charity; to love God, to make no exception of persons and to be indifferent to all places.

Vincent de Paul 'On the Spirit of the Company' Conference of February 2, 1653

Appendix I

Gazetteer of the Daughters' Houses and Works in Great Britain since 1847

ABOUT THE CONTENT

This is a comprehensive listing of every House opened and closed by the Daughters of Charity in Britain between 1847 and 2014. The amount of information for each House varies but most entries contain: dates of opening and closing; nature of the property; a summary of the original works of the House; who invited the Daughters or collaborated with them; parish involvement; financial arrangements; whether the work was certificated by the Home Office or other government department; changes to the works of the House over time; reasons for closure; and, in some cases, a note about an individual Sister strongly associated with the work of a House. This level of detail is more than could be borne by the main text but it is hoped that such a compilation will be quarried by those interested in the history of a particular locality or in a particular theme, such as prison visiting or Catholic benefactors. Above all the list is a testimony to the scale and range of the work of the Daughters of Charity in Britain.

DEFINITION OF A HOUSE

A House (or foundation) is a group of Daughters with a Sister Servant formally instituted by the appropriate Superiors or Officers with the permission of the local Bishop. It is not the building that is being referred to but the group of Sisters and their works, which might include more than one property.

HOW THE GAZETTEER IS ARRANGED

As the name implies the Gazetteer is arranged alphabetically by geography.

- England, Scotland and Wales.

Within each country it is arranged alphabetically by region.

Within region places are organised alphabetically.

- e.g. North-East England: Darlington, Durham, Newcastle.

At the level of place the order is primarily chronological, following an individual House through time.

Some Houses were in existence for a long period during which time the Sisters and the work were relocated from one property to another within the same neighbourhood. The history of the House is followed through chronologically until closure. Some Houses were moved from one geographic area to another (e.g. within a city). Where this happened the transfer is cross-referenced.

ABBREVIATION

Society of St Vincent de Paul (SVP)

ENGLAND

- London area including Outer London Boroughs and Middlesex
- Midlands
- North-East
- North-West
- South-East
- South-West
- Yorkshire

In the East of England the Province had only one location – Peterborough.
This has been located under 'South-East'.

LONDON AREA

Central London

Arranged as follows: Central London, East London, North London, South London, West London and Outer London–Middlesex.

York Street no. 8	1859–1860 The first London House of Charity was opened at the request and with the support of four 'new' Catholics: Father Henry Manning (later Cardinal Manning) who also lived in York St in Marylebone at this time; the novelist Lady Georgiana Fullerton; Mary Stanley; and Frances Taylor (later founder of the Poor Servants of the Mother of God), both of whom had been in the Crimea with Florence Nightingale. Initially there was hostility to the presence of 'Papist Nuns'. The small rented house in York Street received destitute children for care but the Sisters soon moved because it was cold and damp with some rooms accessible only by ladder. Transferred to Park Street which was a continuation of the same House.
Park Street no. 12	1860–1863 House of Charity for visiting and running a small school. The Company missioned a highly regarded French Sister, Henriette Chatelain, as Sister Servant. This House was very close to the Jesuits of Farm Street who supported the Sisters with fund-raising activities. Of the six Sisters listed in the 1861 Census as living in Park Street with a group of children over the age of ten only three are traceable in the Province's Register, indicating the high level of 'fluidity' among the membership at this time. This House transferred to Carlisle Place in Westminster.
Westminster Carlisle Place	1863 continuing. St Vincent's House of Charity. Carlisle Place is the oldest still-active House in the British Province. The large property (extended at various times) belonged to the Province until 2004, the land having been bought and donated by Sister Catherine Eyston and the cost of building having been raised by the Sisters. Its location was in a very poor area close to Tothill Prison. In more recent decades its proximity to Victoria Station and to Westminster Cathedral has continued to keep it accessible to some of the most marginal groups in society, despite the growing affluence of the area. At the same time proximity to the Houses of Parliament and Westminster Cathedral connect it to political, social and church elites. The Sisters have made use of this location and large property to reconfigure the ministries of Carlisle Place periodically to meet new needs. In the nineteenth century Sister Chatelain developed a crèche, soup kitchen for 300/400 daily, night school for 100 men and boys, girls' orphanage and refuge, small school, day nursery, and sodalities. The finances of the House were supported by Ladies of Charity, gifts from many women of the old Catholic families and recent converts such as Lady Herbert, as well as through fund-raising events. The first *Times* newspaper appeal for the soup kitchen appeared in 1875. A new wing was added in 1877. In 1881 there were 210 residents, including 15 Sisters. Between 1898 and 1931 Sister Mary Petre was Sister Servant. Her powers of organisation and social networks played a crucial role in the educational and physical modernisation of Carlisle Place. Visiting at Holloway women's prison was started in 1909. The House continued with its wide range of night schools and poor relief. It was a centre for social activities for deaf Catholics in London. In 1914 the small private school was certified as a public elementary school (with a rooftop playground). In 1920, following the raising of the school leaving age to 14, this school became one of the first day continuation schools, developing a strong reputation for pupil achievement. In 1921 a hostel for young working women opened and continued until 1967 when it was closed to create more classroom space. By 1955 there were 720 pupils on site. In 1974 the primary

school moved to a new St Vincent de Paul school in the Cathedral precinct and the seniors joined with St Aloysius School to form Maria Fidelis Comprehensive School. By the mid 1970s the space was unoccupied and attracting the attention of property developers. For a period while its future was unclear some of the space was rented out to other Catholic organisations: the Sisters of La Sagesse for their school for children with special needs; the Servites to provide short-term housing; and the Spanish Daughters of Charity ran a nursery for the children of Spanish-speaking migrants. From St Vincent's Centre the Daughters themselves undertook support services to young Irish migrants, nursing and chiropody, Cathedral chaplaincy and emergency night shelter for young homeless women.

The main work for which Carlisle Place became known after 1980 emerged gradually once it was known that property developments would not happen. In the later 1970s the Sisters had begun to provide food for homeless people in the vicinity of Victoria Station. Cardinal Basil Hume, the then Archbishop of Westminster, had a meeting with the Sisters at which they decided to use the premises as a day centre for homeless people. In October 1980 The Passage, under the leadership of Sister Eileen O'Mahoney and in collaboration with the Cathedral, opened its doors with a single paid employee and a few volunteers.

During the 1980s sections of the building were totally restructured. The Passage expanded rapidly to provide multifaceted services and training for homeless people, becoming the largest in Europe. By 2000 it had a 49-bed hostel taking rough sleepers and in Montfort House 16 self-contained flats and support workers for people with complex needs. The first four Directors of The Passage were Sisters: Eileen O'Mahoney (1980–1984), Barbara Smith (1985–91), Bridie Dowd (1992–2000) and Ellen Flynn (2000–2008). Large-scale fund-raising was undertaken and state funding received for specific services. In 2004 when the Province could no longer finance the running of St Vincent's Centre it was purchased by The Passage. The Province continues to rent a section of the house for its own Sisters.

In 1989 another collaborative venture, the Depaul Trust, grew from The Passage with the support of Cardinal Hume and in collaboration with the SVP. Depaul UK became an independent charity dedicated to supporting homeless, vulnerable and disadvantaged young people.

Westminster Leicester Place Notre Dame de France	1865–1878 Father Charles Faure, Superior of the French Marist Fathers who headed the French mission in London at Notre Dame de France in Leicester Place, asked for Sisters to work with very poor French citizens living in the area around the church. Three separate residencies were occupied by the Sisters and used for their works of teaching, visiting, care of orphan girls, a nursery and a night shelter. In 1867 the administrators of the nearby French Hospital and pharmacy, which was close by, asked for three more Sisters to care for twenty patients. The works were supported by collections, bazaars and a generous allowance from the French Embassy. The ill-health of the Sister Servant, and 'several other causes', led superiors to recall her to France and it was decided to recall the other nine Sisters at the same time. This was the Sisters' first hospital and pharmacy in England.
Westminster Beaumont Street no. 15	1868–1870 The Sisters were invited by benefactor Lady Mary Petre of Thorndon Hall in Brentwood, Essex to run a crèche or day nursery for the infants of the 'milk women' who delivered to the West End. Lady Mary, who organised public subscriptions for the project and provided the house, was the wife of the 12th Baron of Writtle and mother of 12 children, one of whom became Sister Mary Winifred Petre, Daughter of Charity. The House was opened by Archbishop Manning. The Sisters visited about 100 families and added a small orphanage in 1869. The work outgrew the premises and transferred to Bulstrode Street.
Bulstrode Street no. 4	1870–1884 In addition to the crèche (officially Blessed Benedict Joseph Labre Day Nursery) and the small orphanage for girls, the Sisters ran evening classes for working girls (Class of Perseverance) and a day school. Visiting in St James' parish continued, while Children of Mary, soup kitchen for men and dinners for 150 children were added. The work outgrew the premises and the fund-raising was largely undertaken by Sister Costello, the Sister Servant. Canon Barry, Rector of Spanish Place, gave large sums of money that came to him from anonymous donors to support the Sisters' works. In 1873 with further subscriptions via Canon Barry and others Lady Petre bought the freehold of a large property, nos 9 and 11 Lower Seymour Street. Some work moved to no. 9 and in 1884, with the purchase of the leasehold on no. 11, the entire work transferred.
Lower Seymour Street nos. 9 and 11 (renamed Wigmore St)	1884–1938 This House had the same works as Bulstrode Street but it also opened a hostel for young working women and included a chapel. The work expanded and nos. 13 and 15 were bought in 1893. Funds were donated from rented properties in the Howard de Walden Trust. In the late 1930s the property (which Lady Petre had left in trust to the Diocese to

be managed by Trustees) was sold to Selfridges department store. The Sisters and works transferred to a new purpose-built building at Blandford Street.

Blandford Street nos. 14–26	1938–2005 The new House was a large property. The nursery, St Vincent's primary school, a hostel for 80 young women and the orphanage continued, although the orphanage was discontinued after 1945 because of new government child care policies. The nursery was one of three in the borough. The hostel (Loreto Club) housed young working women, students and Sisters undertaking training for teaching and nursing in London institutions. A national Marian Centre operated from here from 1938–1974 distributing Miraculous Medals and Green Scapulars. In 1965 the House became the Juniorate for Young Sisters, most of whom were studying for professional qualifications. The nursery closed in 1971. Sisters visiting Holloway Prison lived here (1970). A Day Care Centre for elderly people (1972) was opened. In 1974 the Dympna Centre, started by Father Louis Marteau of the Westminster Diocese in 1971 as a counselling service for clergy and religious, took some of the space no longer needed by the Marian Centre. The National Office for the SVP and offices for Depaul Trust were later also based here. The Sisters continued their hot meal and breakfast service for about 80 people, seven days a week (considered by the agencies to be among the best in London for people on the streets). Meeting rooms were also provided, seven days a week, for numerous addiction support group meetings. Reduction in the number of Sisters meant that the House was closed in 2005. St Vincent's Primary School continues.
Bloomsbury Queen Square nos 40–41	1884–1923 and 1926–1941 Italian Hospital. Daughters were invited by Commendatore Giovanni Ortelli, a businessman, who founded the hospital in 1884 for poor members of the Italian community. The Sisters were employed by the hospital's Administrative Committee. The hospital had male and female wards, surgical ward and pharmacy, each with a Sister in charge as did the kitchen and laundry. In 1901 there were 52 beds and an operating theatre managed by nine Sisters, including three from Italy. In 1911 the hospital expanded further into Devonshire Street. Some funding came into the hospital via the King Edward's Hospital Fund grant. The Province withdrew because the conditions laid down by the managers for a new Agreement were not ones it could contract to comply with (guarantee of six Italian Sisters at all times). The hospital continued until 1990. The building is now part of Great Ormond Street Hospital.
Gower Street	1931–1933 St John the Baptist Home was bought by Lady Cadogan, a benefactress of the Italian Hospital, as an annexe to the hospital but given to the Sisters for a nurses' home and a hospice for six patients. The hospice work transferred to Edmonton in 1933 (see below, Middlesex).
Westminster Medway Street no. 33	1933–1975 St Louise's Hostel. Cardinal Bourne asked the Daughters and London Ladies of Charity to work together to create a hostel and night shelter for young women who came to London, mostly from Ireland, and had no family or contacts. It was to be a mix of working women who could pay and those who were destitute and the Sisters were to act as an employment agency to link women looking for work with prospective employers. It was run by a joint committee of the Ladies and Daughters and produced an annual report. In 1938 there were 166 working women and 25 homeless women resident. The joint committee was dissolved at the request of the Sisters who found difficulties with the Ladies over management and control. After the war it became more international with a significant number of residents from Africa and the Commonwealth. The property was gradually added to until it was seven storeys high and could accommodate 290. The Sisters added bedsits for 30 single homeless women aged sixteen to twenty-five with low to medium support needs. In 1969 the ground floor was given to the Legion of Mary for the care of people who had dropped out of society. The Sisters withdrew in 1975 and sold the property to the Irish Centre Housing Association, which continues to host hostel accommodation for women in 94 single rooms. The Sisters transferred to a house they already owned in Horseferry Road (backing onto the garden of 33 Medway Street) and very close to Arneway Street where they also worked (see below).
Horseferry Road no. 94a	1948 continuing. This property, known as St Mary's House, backs onto 33 Medway Street. It had been the site of St John's chapel, run by the Jesuits as a mission from Farm Street and known to have been the chapel frequented by Daniel O'Connell. (The ground between this House and the main hostel was the actual site of the former church.) The church was closed in 1902 when the Cathedral opened and was then left to become derelict until bought by the Sisters in 1948 to provide additional accommodation for 20 women. St Mary's was retained when St Louise's was sold. From 1976 it has been a residential house for Sisters continuing to work in the local area, initially at St Louise's and then at The Passage, in local parishes and hospitals and, more recently, 'Vincentian Care Plus', the Province's personal care visiting service for older people.

The foundation of the Cardinal Hume Centre (CHC) in 3–7 Arneway Street involved Daughters of Charity from the Horseferry Road community between 1985 and 1991. CHC was a new project, housed in the former Sacred Heart Convent attached to the Sacred Heart Church on Horseferry Road, to meet the needs of homeless young people identified by The Passage. Sister Eileen O'Mahoney inspired Cardinal Hume to initiate and put his name to a project. The Cardinal appealed to the religious congregations for funds and volunteers. The core team consisted of a Daughter of Charity as Director assisted by a Marist Priest Chaplain and another Daughter as Research and Service Development Officer. Sisters from six different congregations joined the core team to open the first phase of the work in 1986: a medical surgery and day centre for homeless young families in bed and breakfast accommodation. A hostel for newly homeless young people opened the following year, followed by an Educational and Skills Training Centre and move-on accommodation for substance abusers.

Bloomsbury Gower Street no. 111	1936/7–1966 St Teresa's Hostel for young women arriving in London to work or study was opened at the request of Bishop Butt who wanted a hostel near Euston Station 'on account of the great number of Catholic girls who come from Ireland and Scotland to find work and have no friends or family in the city'. It was one of several such hostels opened by the Province for this purpose in the period from c.1925 to the 1950s. The property was bought by the Province and accommodated 75–80 young women. It was always full. In 1941 one Sister began visiting in the parish of St Charles, Ogle Street. In 1960 the Sisters were approached by University College Hospital Medical School about an exchange of property as the school wanted to expand in Gower Street. After six years of searching for a suitable arrangement an exchange was about to be completed when the Archdiocese of Westminster, through Monsignor Bruce Kent, was alerted to it. Monsignor Kent identified the Daughters' property as the ideal solution to the diocesan plan for a university chaplaincy. With Cardinal Heenan's keen support for this proposal, and his canonical capacity to withhold consent for the Sisters to sell to the University, the Sisters sold to the Archdiocese. 111 Gower Street continues still as Newman House, Catholic Chaplaincy for the Universities and Other Higher Education Institutions in the Diocese of Westminster.
Notting Hill Ladbroke Grove	1941–1977 St Vincent's Nursing Clinic opened with some of the staff who had worked in the Italian Hospital (closed 1941 – see Bloomsbury above). It was owned by the Province. Discussions had begun before the war to open a hospital for poor patients who would be subsidised by admitting those who could pay: this was how the clinic operated. A ministry with Travellers who had a site close by was undertaken in the 1970s. The hospital and House were closed during the re-evaluation of the Province's works in the 1970s.
Notting Hill St Charles Square	1963-1976 St William's nursery was transferred from Feltham to St Charles Square, the headquarters of the Westminster Catholic Rescue Society, and the Sisters moved with it. A nursery and nursery nurse training facility were opened here in 1967. (See West London, Feltham.)
East End and East London	The Province had six or seven small community houses in the area at various times between the 1880s and 1960s, many of them on Commercial Road close to Limehouse Basin. In the mid-1960s the Province amalgamated the small houses and built De Paul House on Commercial Road as the 'core' House for all the Sisters in that part of the East End of London.
Hatton Garden Clerkenwell Road no.134	1883–1966 Daughters were invited by Rev. Dr Kirner, the Rector of the Italian Church of St Peter's, to open a House of Charity for visiting Sisters, parish work and to establish clubs and confraternities. The Ladies of Charity paid for one visiting Sister in Moorfields. The church was built for the growing Italian community, although it had a mixed congregation in its early decades, including many Irish. Founded in 1846 it was consecrated in 1863, had a capacity of 2,000 and became the heart of 'Little Italy'. The Sisters took over running the schools in 1884. 'Nothing could have been less promising than the struggle for the schools of the Italian Mission at Hatton Garden. The pressure of the authorities, the old School Board, the later County Council, and especially the present Board of Education...could not have pressed more heavily than on St. Peter's School, in a mission where the church was a heavy burden, the mission poor, the children numerous, and building space in a busy commercial neighbourhood exceptionally costly, even for the metropolis.' (*The Tablet*, 30 January 1915) The Sisters visited in the parishes of St Peter's, Moorfields and Bun Hill and taught in the school for more than 80 years.

Stepney Commercial Road nos 713–15	1890–1892 St Joseph's Home for Boys opened in Rose Lane in 1887 by Father William Barry who was appointed by Cardinal Manning as Crusade of Rescue Administrator. Barry accepted girls and infants and the home was soon too small. The Sisters, who worked closely with Manning on provision for destitute boys in Westminster and Leyton, seem to have been involved in Stepney from 1890. As the work expanded Barry took other houses in Commercial Road (713, 713a and 715). Some sources suggest that the Sisters remained at the girls' home at Commercial Road when St Joseph's Boys' Home removed to Enfield where the new institution was to be run by them, although the houses in Rose Lane and Commercial Road were sold at this time (see North London, Enfield).
Bow Common Devons Road no. 189	1907–1943 House of Charity for visiting, elementary school, confraternities, support of destitute callers. The Sisters were invited by Father James Casey, the parish priest of Holy Name and Our Lady of the Sacred Heart. Sister Feilding gave £200 to improve the building before they moved in and a Mrs Lyall donated £400 for them to develop a kitchen. The Sisters ran a dining centre for children serving breakfasts and dinners, provided by the London County Council (LCC) under the policy introduced in 1906. This house was bombed in 1943 and closed.
Limehouse Commercial Road no. 642	1909–1915 St Mary's House of Charity founded by Mrs Juliet Rush of Brackley in Northamptonshire, a member of the Ladies of Charity at Carlisle Place, for the parish of Our Lady Immaculate at Limehouse. Three visiting Sisters were sent to this parish that had been opened in 1881 to serve the largely Irish population of Limehouse. Father Frederick Higley, parish priest for 40 years, who built the church (literally) had a devotion to St Vincent and was keen to have Daughters of Charity for visiting. The presbytery of Our Lady Immaculate was very close to the Sisters' houses in Commercial Road and Island Row. In 1915 Mrs Rush decided she would 'give up the sisters at Limehouse' and asked for them to be removed. They moved to St Cecilia's and to the Wapping parish (see below). Father Higley secured the future of Daughters of Charity in Limehouse through the establishment of the Alice Jane Kitchen Fund of £10,000 yielding £200 a year for Sisters' stipends, to be activated when they could provide Sisters. He called the Sisters 'the living stones of the Church'. Father Higley died in 1934 and the Sisters arrived in 1938 supported by the Trust and living at 632 Commercial Road, 'Stella Maris' (see below). The parish church of Our Lady Immaculate and St Frederick now houses the nineteenth-century marble statue of Our Lady Immaculate that had formerly been in the Provincial House at Mill Hill alongside its own statues of SS Vincent and Louise. One of the church bells is named 'Joseph' for Sister Joseph Briody who was one of the early Sisters at Limehouse.
Limehouse Commercial Road nos 531–5	1911–1934 St Cecilia's. The Sisters ran a House of Charity and a clinic under the London County Council in a property which was owned by benefactor Lady Caroline [Edmund] Talbot (Viscountess Fitzalan Howard), sister-in-law to Sister Etheldreda Howard. This work was undertaken in collaboration with St Cecilia's Settlement which had been established in 1900 by Lady Talbot and was supported by several Ladies of Charity. The clinic was mainly for minor childhood ailments. An LCC nurse worked with the Sisters who also undertook visiting and sacramental preparation. When the Ladies withdrew from the Settlement in 1920 the evening classes and clubs they had run were taken on for the next two years by the Sisters. Visiting Sisters lived here and worked in Poplar and Limehouse, their stipends being paid by the Rector of St Mary and St Michael's in Poplar and Sister Ethel Pickwood respectively. Viscountess Fitzalan asked for the Sisters to be withdrawn in 1934 because she felt that they were no longer serving St Cecilia's as they had done in the past, but rather the parishes and schools. Seven Sisters were in the House at this time. Sister Provincial pointed out to her, in justice, that the Sisters' teaching salaries had been supporting St Cecilia's for many years. When the Sisters withdrew this work was taken on by the Little Company of Mary until 1944.
Wapping Pier Head	1915–1982 A House of Charity was opened after Father Sims of St Patrick's-in-the-East invited the Sisters to take charge of the girls' public elementary school and to visit in the parish. Evening classes, a girls' choir, mothers' meetings and women's confraternities were established. Many callers in need came to the house. The area had people from many nationalities, but there was a strong core of London Irish. 'Wapping was an island, then, surrounded by the river and dock water. Really like a village, properly-so-called, with all the advantages and disadvantages of a village – an Irish Cockney village'. (London Museum of Childhood website) The Sisters were part of this 'village' for many decades before the House was merged with other work in this part of London. Sister Pat O'Sullivan (1923–1987), for example, arrived in the East End in 1934 and served there for 60 years in the various houses. She was famously known in Poplar where she was placed for many

years, even being sent a bouquet of flowers by the Kray brothers when she was ill. This house transferred to De Paul House, Commercial Road.

Millwall Westferry Road no. 285	1918–1941 A House of Charity in St Edmund's parish. The Sisters were invited by a Miss Mary Ulcoq, described in the 1911 Census as 'a lady of charity of independent means' living at 285 Westferry Road. She created a foundation yielding £200–£300 a year. Their work was parish visiting, charge of the elementary school, confraternities and support of destitute callers. The property was leased and the House closed because of bombing but Sisters conducted visits from the Limehouse House.
Mile End Road no. 401 and Rhondda Grove no. 17	1931–1967 A House of Charity in Guardian Angels parish and linked to St Philip's Settlement House in Tredegar Square, Mile End. St Philip's House was the first Roman Catholic Settlement House (1894) in the East End of London and had been started by Lady Margaret Howard, sister of Sister Etheldreda Howard, as part of the Catholic Social Union initiative to the East End encouraged by Cardinal Vaughan. Lady Margaret Howard lived here with other Catholic women, including Lady Clare Feilding whose sister Edith was another Daughter of Charity. Lady Margaret was deeply involved with the parish, loaning £6,000 to extend the school and endowing this money in her will. She died aged 40 in 1899. Guardian Angels Church was re-built in her memory by another Howard sister, Lady Mary. The new church opened in 1927. Sisters undertook visiting and general work associated with St Philip's Settlement in Whitechapel, Mile End and Bow Common from their house, which was at Mile End Road and Rhondda Grove at different times. They taught in Guardian Angels school. Their stipends were supported by the Ladies of Charity. The works of this House and the Sisters became part of De Paul House, Commercial Road, the 'central house' for the East End.
Poplar Montague Place no. 7	1932–1967 St Catherine's House of Charity for visiting, charge of the elementary school, running confraternities and a range of clubs and support of destitute callers.
Limehouse Commercial Road no. 632	1938–1963 'Stella Maris' House of Charity for teaching in the elementary school and parish visiting. Sisters were moved here from the earlier Commercial Road house. The original property was demolished in 1963 and De Paul House was ready in 1967.
Commercial Road nos 628–32	1967–1999 De Paul House built by the Province to be a social and welfare centre for the East End of London with Sisters transferred from Tredegar Square, Rhondda Grove and Poplar. The Sisters living here were engaged in parish visiting (six parishes), teaching in local primary and secondary schools, care of destitute men (meals and drop-in centre), sacristy work, Children of Mary Association, social work with various authorities and agencies including the Catholic Children's Society (formerly Catholic Rescue), with whom a Family Centre was established, and district nursing. There was a nursery school and a small hostel as part of the House. Twenty three Sisters were living here at the point the House was closed.
Limehouse Island Row nos 63–64	1999–2009 The Province rented two flats in a housing development at the renovated dock from which Sisters undertook a range of ministries that included St Joseph's Hospice chaplaincy; a mission to the Travelling community; teaching; nursing; social work training; and visiting.

North London

Enfield Holtwhite's Hill	1892–1981 St Joseph's Boys' Home which was moved here from its first location in Stepney (see East London). The Sisters who had started to work there with Father Barry moved with the 138 boys aged between seven and twelve and continued to manage the Home. This large house at Holtwhite's Hill in two acres of land was bought by the Westminster Crusade of Rescue for £4000. Once boys reached the age of twelve they transferred to St Vincent's Home in Harrow Road, the original Crusade of Rescue home which had relocated from Hammersmith in 1876. In 1926 the buildings were extended to accommodate more boys: there were 180 by 1939. Until 1939 the boys were taught by the Sisters in a certified Catholic Poor Law school in the grounds of St Joseph's. In that year 100 of them transferred to the newly-built St George's Mixed Primary School in Enfield to join with other Enfield Catholic children, an important change that was part of a slow process of de-institutionalisation. In 1963 as part of child-care de-institutionalisation, six family group homes were built in the grounds of the two acres of land and two homes across the main Enfield Road, accommodating the children from the large Enfield institution and also the two institutions in Feltham. The Sisters continued here until 1981.

Edmonton Church Street nos 13, 15, 19 and 21	1909–1994 The Daughters were invited by Teresa Weld-Blundell (aunt of Sister Muriel Fraser) to establish either a crèche for babies of working mothers or a hostel for young working women in a house she had bought in Church Street. St Joseph's Hostel for young working women and servants out of employment was opened in December 1909. Between 1910 and 1920 there were between 30 and 40 residents but the numbers then declined. Sisters also visited in the parish of The Most Precious Blood and St Edmund. The Sisters noted that 'Miss Weld Blundell has formed several projects...each being as impractical as the others.' In 1925 they decided to take matters in hand and the work of the House was changed to a residential home and hospital for children with physical disabilities, most commonly as a result of polio. This work expanded to 100 children and the home occupied nos 13, 15, 19 and 21 Church Street with two of the houses being registered as a nursing home in 1932. By 1930 the House was 'very busy' because parish visiting and teaching in the parish school were also undertaken. A chapel was built in 1932. By the mid 1930s the property was in need of modernising and an appeal was headed by Lady Jean Bertie of Rothesay, Isle of Bute to raise the £40,000 target. This project was suspended during the war and was slow to re-start in the austerity that followed. However, a new block was built in 1963 for the nurses, staff and Sisters and a physiotherapy department and other facilities were developed over the years. By 1985 St Joseph's had 86 beds, mostly under contract to Haringey Health Authority. Sisters served as nurses or to support the social and spiritual welfare of patients, staff and visitors. One Sister visited in St Edmund's parish and another at St Francis de Sales parish Tottenham and the Sisters undertook hospital chaplaincy at North Middlesex Hospital. Sisters withdrew from the nursing home in 1985, continuing with other works until 1994 when the House, which was now too large, was sold. The Sisters transferred to St Alphege Road.
St Alphege Road no. 31	1994–2001 Sisters who lived here undertook pastoral ministry in St Edmund's, Edmonton and the Church of Mary Mother of God, Ponders End; chaplaincy in North Middlesex Hospital (Sister Clare Costello was a chaplain here for over 22 years) and work with homeless people in partnership with the SVP at 'Manna Centre', London Bridge.
Willesden St Paul's Avenue no. 60	1928–1940. At the request of Father Arendzen a Sister began visiting in the parish of St Mary Magdalen in 1923. In 1928 Cardinal Bourne bought the property for a hostel and the Sisters opened Our Lady's Hostel for Working Girls. It was a residence for visiting Sisters in this and neighbouring parishes. In 1940 the property suffered bomb damage and was uninhabitable. In 1942 the work here was transferred to a larger property owned by the Province at 247 Willesden Lane.
Willesden Lane no. 247	1942–1990 An approved probation hostel for girls aged fourteen to seventeen referred by the courts was opened by the Province at the request of Cardinal Hinsley: it accommodated 22 young women. Parish visiting continued in the parishes of Our Lady of Willesden and St Mary Magdalen, Willesden Green. The probation hostel work continued until 1969 when the premises were converted into ten flatlets offered to single pregnant women as an alternative to abortion following the passage of the 1976 Abortion Act. Between 1970 and 1990 the property comprised supported flatlets for homeless single mothers and babies. An annexe at Brondesbury Park, North Kilburn was used between 1982 and 1984. More than 400 mothers and their babies were accommodated in the flats over the 20-year period. The Sisters also supported Travellers through preparation for the sacraments, basic literacy classes and distribution of meals. In 1990 the Sisters withdrew from the work of supporting single mothers and this became the first house of the newly formed Depaul Trust, working with young, homeless individuals. The Sisters transferred to Victoria Road.
Kilburn Victoria Road no. 119	1990–2013 The Sisters who lived here had a range of ministries which included: visiting, social work, pastoral care of deaf people, retreat facilitation, hospital chaplaincy and involvement in the work of the Province's London-based and national initiatives – The Passage; Vincentian Volunteers; St Vincent's Family Project; Vincentian Care Plus.
Kilburn Compayne Gardens no. 88	1932–1965 House of Charity opened for teaching in the parish school, visiting and parish works. The Sisters ran a small private school which they inherited from another Community and closed in 1959.
Kilburn West End Lane	1947–1974 St Catherine's Hostel for Working Women. It was the Province's decision to start this work and it owned the property. This work transferred to Anson Road where it gradually became more focused on homeless women.
Cricklewood Anson Road nos 72 and 74	1974–1988 A hostel to support girls leaving care. In 1980 it became a hostel for homeless young women aged sixteen to twenty, providing bedsit accommodation. This work was funded by the GLC and Brent Housing. The hostel closed in 1988 because of the overlap

with the Willesden House (above) at a time when the Sisters could not support both. The Province sold the Cricklewood property and upgraded the Willesden property.

Kensal Green Mortimer Road no. 21	1990–1993 A rented house from which Sisters taught at St Mary of the Angels Primary School, worked at The Passage Day Centre Carlisle Place as Housing Adviser for the Homeless, served on the staff of Westminster Cathedral Night Shelter and as first director of the Depaul Trust.
North Brent Wrentham Avenue	2005- continuing. A house bought by the Province as residency for Sisters involved in a range of local ministries: parish visiting, hospital chaplaincy, administration and retreat work.

South London

Eltham, Mottingham	1903–1926 St Vincent's House. The Province was invited by Cardinal Bourne, then Bishop of Southwark, to take charge of a Catholic Poor Law school and orphanage for 75 boys under the Southwark Rescue Society. When it outgrew the accommodation it moved to Gravesend in Kent and became known as St Mary's (see South-East).
Walworth New Kent Road	1905–1941 House of Charity established by six French Daughters who were sent out of France by the superiors at the time of France's secularisation legislation of 1904–1906. They went first to Mill Hill to learn English and were then supported financially by the Duke and Duchess of Norfolk and a Mrs O'Brien for 12 years after which the Sisters used their own resources and donations. They spent one year in Clapham before deciding that it was too middle class for their works. The priest of English Martyrs parish Walworth asked for them for visiting and catechism classes. They established confraternities, extensive mothers' meetings and sewing classes. Visiting was extended to Bermondsey and in 1919 an Infant Welfare Clinic was taken on. In 1921 they were visiting more than 2,500 families distributing food and items to the value of around £500 annually. When the French Sisters were recalled to France that year the local people begged for them to stay. The works were continued by the Province until the House was closed in 1941 because of bombing locally.
Clapham Park Thornton Road	1907–1912 Daughters were invited by Cardinal Bourne and Mr Hugh Potter, who ran St Hugh's, a Catholic boys' home in Thornton Road, to manage and nurse boys' with physical disabilities that had resulted mostly from polio and TB. The work with disabled boys had started around 1900 but by 1906 funds had almost run out and the future was in jeopardy. In 1907 it was in an annexe to St Hugh's which was named St Vincent's with facilities for 25 boys but had an acute shortage of funds and space. Expansion took place in a new building at Clarence Road in Clapham Park managed as a separate charity with its own management committee. St Vincent's was certified as a Special Industrial School in 1910 and used the new 'open air' wards approach. In 1910, the home was visited by an orthopaedic surgeon, Mr McCrae Aitken, who treated 19 of the children very successfully, demonstrating what could be achieved with modern orthopaedics. The Sisters and their Board of Management wished to develop St Vincent's separately from Hugh Potter's activities and in a new location (there were tensions between the different ways of working). After many alternatives had been inspected it was decided to move out to Pinner in Middlesex in 1912. Forty boys were transferred. (See below Outer London, Middlesex, Pinner)
Blackheath	1932–1939/40 St Agnes Girls' Home for the Southwark Diocese Rescue Society under Canon Crea formerly of Blackheath parish. For vulnerable girls and young women. Closed as a consequence of the war.
Deptford New Cross Road no. 438	1977–2004 Sisters were requested by Father Flood who became parish priest at Our Lady of the Assumption in 1975. Initially four Sisters rented a house in Brockley before opening this House bought by the Province. The primary purpose was visiting. Their front room was known as 'the Parish Room' as they held meetings of various sodalities there such as the Marian Association and were involved in SVP and Union of Catholic Mothers. Some Sisters worked with the Travelling community who moved onto an empty site at Deptford in 1978, others worked with homeless people at the Shaftesbury Centre, taught in the parish school, undertook parish visiting, and took charge of the sacristy. There was a youth ministry in collaboration with the Young Catholic Workers Association in the wake of the 1981 Brixton Riot.
Abbey Wood St Bride's Close no. 7 Erith	2013- continuing. Three Sisters work as a team in the four parishes of Thamesmead and Abbey Wood: St Benet's, St David's, St John Fisher and St Paul's. They work in collaborating

with four Vincentian priests from the Nigerian Province serving the largely Black and minority ethnic (BME) population of the area. Sisters offer pastoral care to the six care homes in the area; are volunteer chaplains in the 15-bed hospice for the terminally ill; respond to families in need in collaboration with the Foodbank at the Baptist Church; and are in the process of establishing an SVP Conference. One Sister is a pastoral worker with Depaul Trust for young people who live in hostels.

West London

North Hyde Southall	1889–1903 The Province was invited to manage the Infirmary at St Mary's Orphanage for boys run by the Brothers of Mercy in a former army barracks that had been constructed during the Napoleonic War. In the 1880s the orphanage was criticised by inspectors for overcrowding and defective sanitary arrangements leading to outbreaks of contagious diseases among the boys. Sisters of the Poor Servants of the Mother of God had care of the Infirmary until they were withdrawn in 1888. The 1891 Census shows 5 Sisters present, 3 of whom were nurses, with 598 boys and 20 Brothers from the religious community.
Ealing Castlebar Hill no. 12	1920–2002 The Trustees of St David's Nursing Home for Disabled Soldiers invited the Daughters to manage the home which was established by Lady Anne Kerr in 1920 in memory of her son, David, who was killed in the First World War. Anne Kerr was the niece of Sister Etheldreda Howard and it was Sister Howard who was appointed as first Sister Servant at St David's, although she was only at Ealing a short time before her final illness (died 1926). Cecily Passmore, a friend of the Fitzalan Howard sisters, was secretary to the Trustees for many years. St David's opened with 50 beds. A chapel was built with funds raised by the Catholic Women's League and the first additional ward, St Mary's, converted from the gatehouse, was funded almost entirely by national collections made by the Children of Mary, although the home was never exclusively Catholic. The Ministry of Pensions provided financial support for some of the patients. Nursing was undertaken by the Sisters assisted by male orderlies. At the advent of the NHS the home was disclaimed (exempt) from the conditions of the Act. Funds were donated by the British Legion, the United Services Fund and many donors. It required a good deal of fund-raising to keep the home operating. The Board of Trustees gradually took over until in 2002 the Sisters closed their House on site and withdrew altogether. St David's continues to provide physiotherapy, occupational therapy, rehabilitation, long-, medium- and short-term care as well as respite and day care for people over the age of eighteen. It has 68 beds and also looks after people with multiple complex conditions including brain trauma.
West Hounslow Feltham/Hatton	1923–1962 St Anthony's Girls' Home run under the auspices of the Westminster Crusade of Rescue in a former country house called Temple Hatton. The Crusade had acquired the leasehold on the property in 1897 and in 1905 opened St Anthony's Home for Boys under the care of the Sisters of Good Hope. Crusade of Rescue provision was re-organised in 1923 and 170 girls were transferred to St Anthony's and St Vincent's which were thereafter run by the Daughters as homes for boys and girls. During 1924 there were extensive building works and Cardinal Bourne opened the modernised site in June. In 1939 a toddlers' department was added to St Anthony's and later a nursery (St Teresa's) with a training school for nursery nurses. St Anthony's itself was closed in 1960 because of the noise from Heathrow Airport. St Teresa's moved to St Charles Square (see above Central London) in 1962 when St Anthony's closed.
West Hounslow Victoria Road	1933–1985 St Louise's. The Sisters had the headship and teaching in the newly opened St Lawrence parish school which the St Anthony's girls attended. They ran a small private girls' school and also undertook parish visiting, sodalities, sacristy and liturgy, clubs and societies. The Sisters continued with parish visiting after they ceased to teach in the school.
West Hounslow Hatton	1949–1958 St Vincent's boys' home became a separate House with its own Sister Servant. The Sisters ran St Anthony's for girls, St Vincent's for boys and St Teresa's for infants on the same site but St Teresa's was part of St Anthony's House. St Vincent's was closed because of its proximity to Heathrow Airport and the increase in noise from air traffic. Some boys transferred to St Anthony's Feltham and to St Joseph's Enfield (see North London above).
West Shepherd's Bush	1925–1927 Elementary school and parish visiting. Established by the Province at the time of Visitatrice Hannezo but closed by the next Visitatrice: 'Owing to the headmaster's attitude towards our teaching Sister in the elementary school, the Council considers that she is prevented from having any influence for good among the children and that her

position is unbearable, therefore as the House depends for its support mainly on her salary, [we] withdraw the Sisters.'

Outer London – Middlesex

Mill Hill Hendon The Ridgeway Provincial House	1885–2007 St Vincent's Provincial House. Opened as the Central House when the Province of the British Isles was erected. It was the residency of the Visitatrice (Provincial) and Provincial Officers and the location of the Seminary for the formation of Sisters. The Paris Superiors purchased 'Littleberries', a seventeenth-century house with later additions and 46 acres of farm and grazing land, for £10,000, a debt then incurred by the new Province which was paid off a few years later in its entirety by Sister Brown Younger, a widow who had entered the community in her forties. The land was farmed to provide food or rented out to herdsmen to raise an income. The new Province built an orphanage and day school (see below), a large chapel (dedicated to the Sacred Heart of Jesus) to serve as the Provincial chapel for major liturgies and for retreats, a retreat block and a cemetery where many of the Sisters would be buried. A legacy from the Duchess of Norfolk helped with the Central House extensions. Many of the Sisters contributed to the adornment of the chapel through specific donations (altar, statues, Stations of the Cross) and this chapel served local Catholics as a parish church until 1923 when the church of the Sacred Heart and Mary Immaculate was opened in Mill Hill Broadway. Both the Sisters' chapel and the new parish were served by priests of the Congregation of the Mission who lived in a presbytery next to St Vincent's School (see St Vincent's House below). The Seminary housed 18 Seminary Sisters in 1890 and 24 at the time of the 1911 Census when there were also 28 Sisters either living at Central House or visiting. Sisters' retreats were held here and sick Sisters came to rest or convalesce. During the First World War Central House was used as a 'safe house' by the Paris Mother House: all the financial papers, valuables, vestments and sacristy vessels were taken from Paris to be stored at St Vincent's in a specially adapted secure cellar. The Mother House bursary office was based at Mill Hill until the end of the war. Over the decades Provincial House was periodically adapted and re-modelled as needs changed. In 2007 it was vacated and sold to a developer. A new Provincial House was created at The Priory on the other side of The Ridgeway, already in the ownership of the Sisters (see below). The Province has access rights to the community cemetery but has sold all the land that was purchased from the Littleberries Estate in 1885.
Mill Hill Hendon The Ridgeway St Vincent's Residential School	1887–1998 St Vincent's Orphanage (certified Catholic Poor Law school) for boys was built on the land owned by the Province at The Ridgeway. The foundation stone was blessed by Cardinal Manning in 1885 and the home opened in 1887 with its own Sister Servant and community. It comprised a crèche for infant boys and home for 210 boys under six who came from across the London Poor Law Unions and from the overcrowded orphanage at Leyton. In 1900 older boys began to be admitted and a school was built for them on the premises. A bakery and laundry were added in 1920. In 1932 in a rationalisation of provision, older boys were sent to Wiseman House in Walthamstow and younger boys from the North Hyde home were moved to St Vincent's. Girls were admitted with their brothers from 1953. Residential home numbers gradually reduced in the 1950s and group housing was introduced (there were 60 children resident in 1969), moving in 1975 to purpose-built housing at The Ridgemount (see below). From 1934–1971 there was a Nursery Training College in its own building. In 1971 the nursery building was re-named Langdale House and used until group housing was phased out. In 1972 the main building (former orphanage) was re-named and a new purpose found for it – Damascus House Retreat and Conference Centre run by the Congregation of the Mission in collaboration with the Daughters. In 1984 the former Langdale House temporarily housed the first course run by the St Anselm Institute, an international initiative of the Mill Hill Fathers to form leaders and formators from all parts of the world. This moved to a permanent home in Kent, and the building was then used for youth retreats. The whole complex was closed in 1998 because of shortage of Vincentian personnel and funding. The site and buildings were sold for housing re-development and refurbished as Millfield luxury flats.
Mill Hill Hendon The Ridgeway St Vincent's House	1888 continuing. St Vincent's House opened as the presbytery for the confrères of the Congregation of the Mission (Vincentians), including the Director of the British Province of the Daughters, who is always a member of the Irish Vincentian Province. The property, which was newly built in 1888, was across a small lane beside Central House. For a short period after 1993–1997 when the Vincentians left it was used as a house of formation for the Daughters and is now the residency for the members of the Provincial Council.

Mill Hill Hendon The Ridgeway St Vincent's School	1896–1986. St Vincent's elementary, later primary school. The school, which was built beside Provincial House and in front of the boys' home, was originally called Mary Immaculate School. It was later re-sited on the opposite side of The Ridgeway and in recent years has been entirely re-built to a very high standard. The last Daughter left the school in 1988 but the Province remained as Trustees until 2008 when the school was passed to the Archdiocese of Westminster. The school continues. A Sister is a Foundation Governor.
Mill Hill Hendon The Ridgeway The Priory	1926–2005 The Priory. A large house dating back to around 1754 opposite Provincial House was bought as a potential seminary but used from the outset for the care of sick and elderly Sisters. The House was extended and adapted over time. In 2000 the Care Standards Act removed the exemption from the 1984 Registered Homes Act which religious sisters had previously enjoyed and there was a reassessment of provision for elderly and ill Sisters at a time when the Province was thinking about selling Provincial House. The decision was made to use The Priory as the Provincial House. Other arrangements were made for the elderly Sisters of the Province, depending on their individual needs. 2008- continuing. Following a major refurbishment programme The Priory became the new Provincial House and Ridgemount became the offices for the Province.
Mill Hill Hendon The Ridgeway Wentworth Hall	1939 St Catherine's at Wentworth Hall was opened as a house for ladies of reduced means but existed only a few months because the building was requisitioned by the War Office for the duration of the war. In 1953 it was about to be taken over by the Parish of Mill Hill (in the charge of the Vincentians) as a chapel of ease when it was burnt down.
Mill Hill Hendon The Ridgeway Ridgemount	1975–1984 This property was built in the grounds of The Priory for use as a group home for teenagers who were transferred here from St Vincent's Residential School (see above). In 1984 it became a house for active older Sisters who in 2005 moved to 'Farmside' in Pinner. This building later became part of The Priory complex, now Provincial House (see above).
Pinner Eastcote House Wiltshire Road	1912–2003 St Vincent's Special Industrial School renamed St Vincent's Orthopaedic Hospital in 1923. St Vincent's moved from Clapham to a large house and grounds, built in 1893, which were bought by the Trustees and Management Board. The Industrial School certification was renewed and extended for 105 boys who 'but for their physical defect' (Children's Act 1908) would have been sent to an ordinary industrial school. St Vincent's became a leading orthopaedic treatment centre through a collaboration between Sister Joseph Fraser (Lady Muriel Fraser 1884–1989) who had entered the Community in 1913 with an orthopaedic nursing qualification, Sir Robert Jones (First President of the International Society of Orthopaedic Surgeons) who became Honorary Surgeon of St Vincent's, and David McCrae Aitken who had trained under Sir Robert and was appointed as Assistant Surgeon at St Vincent's. These three experts, who shared a passion for the development of treatment, had professional links even before they worked together at St Vincent's. Benefactions made by Sister Fraser's family (13th Lord and Lady Lovat of Beauly Castle in Inverness) enabled some of the necessary investment. By 1914 there were beds for 114 boys and an operating theatre. Boys learned a wide range of skills and trades so that they could be independent and some were employed on the staff. Girls were admitted in 1925. During the Second World War the hospital was part of emergency medical services. The hospital did not join the NHS in 1948 but most of its work was under contract with the NHS. A nursing school opened in 1947. Towards the end of the twentieth century orthopaedic surgery was being phased out and the emphasis at St Vincent's moved to providing nursing care for the young chronically disabled, patients with multiple sclerosis, brain injuries or stroke, out-patients rehabilitation and occupational therapy. In 1996 the name was changed to St Vincent's Hospital to reflect this wider community role. A specialist unit day centre for Alzheimer's patients opened in 1997 in collaboration with the Alzheimer's Trust. The impact of new government policies for health organisation led the Trustees to close the hospital in 2000 and to redevelop it as a Nursing Home. St Vincent's Nursing Home opened in 2006 with 60 beds. A number of older Sisters from The Priory needing nursing care live here and others visit to provide pastoral care to all residents.
Pinner High Street no. 43	2005- continuing. 'Farmside', a house for Sisters transferred from Ridgemount (above). This is a House for retired Sisters.
Pinner Northwood Hills Norwich Road no. 32	2005- continuing. Rendu House was bought by the Province as a residence for the Sisters active in a range of ministries in the area: parish visiting; administration and archives; pastoral care for St Vincent's Nursing Home in Pinner and Retreat Ministry. The Sisters in Rendu House and St Vincent's Nursing Home form one House.

398

In this region the Province has historically had Houses only in **Birmingham**. The Houses in Birmingham are organised chronologically as far as possible.

Birmingham
Bath Street and
Shadwell Street

1895–1924 The Sisters were invited by the Birmingham Catholic Girls' Aid Society (CGAS) chaired by Canon Greavey, administrator of St Chad's Cathedral. (CGAS became part of the Catholic Women's League in 1912.) In 1895 a group of Sisters began work from small houses in Bath Street (nos 58–59) and the adjacent Shadwell Street (variously at nos 1, 3, and 4). Two contracts were signed between the CGAS and the Sisters. The first (1895), which was also signed by the Bishop, was to establish a House of Charity with a night shelter, evening classes and visiting. A second contract in 1909 specified St Anthony's Working Girls' Hostel (which had opened in 1897), a workroom, a night shelter and an employment bureau for domestic servants known as St Chad's Register which generated income for the House. In this contract the Sisters' stipends were underwritten by Miss Weld Blundell. Although the exact chronology is not clear, it is known that by 1900 the Sisters were engaged in a web of connected activities concerned with vulnerable young women: daily visiting of the police lock-up and fortnightly visits to the HM Prison Winson Green were linked to their work at St Anthony's which accepted young women from the criminal justice system (a role the Home Office had asked the Province to take in a number of large cities). The night shelter work (used by 200 women in 1900) also linked to St Anthony's. In 1906 the workroom and police work were removed by the CGAS to St John's Gravelly Hill (see below) and in 1908 St Anthony's and the Servants' Home were moved to Vicarage Road in Edgbaston because the CGAS thought a more suburban environment would be better for them and for the night shelter (see below). In addition there were Visiting Sisters who undertook a large amount of parish visiting (7,000 home visits in 1900), working closely with the CGAS and senior priests at St Chad's to co-ordinate this ministry and share the costs between parishes. In 1900 four parishes were visited (St Chad, St Joseph, the Oratory District and St Patrick). Other parishes were added: St Catherine; St Peter; St Francis Xavier; St Michael and parishes in Bilston; West Bromwich; and Witton. It is unclear when the Sisters occupied different houses but they were all operated as one House with a single Sister Servant. Sisters transferred to Princip Street in 1924.

Birmingham Edgbaston
Vicarage Road no. 22

1908–1917 St Anthony's Girls Hostel was moved here from Bath Street/Shadwell Street (above) by the Management Committee which had come to think of the inner-city location as undesirable. However, the new suburban location was not a convenient one for young working women and the Committee decided to move the work back to Bath Street (see above). The Sisters remained until 1919 when they were transferred to join the work at Monument Road (see below).

Bath Street no. 59

1917–1924 St Joseph's Hostel for young women took over the work of St Anthony's and the earlier night shelter and came under a diocesan management committee. St Joseph's was both a continuation of the previous work with women who were sleeping rough and a response to the significant number of Irish women who migrated to work in local factories. Between 1917 and 1920 more than 500 women had used the facilities. In 1920 there were 72 residents of whom only 21 were able to pay the full cost. When the work outgrew this property there was a real effort in the Diocese and city to support an expanded facility. The Sisters transferred to Princip Street which became a significant centre for the Sisters' ministries.

Princip Street no. 33

1924–1983 St Joseph's Hostel continuing and enlarged. An anonymous benefactor gave an annual endowment of £100 and the Archbishop provided an interest-free loan of £4,000 for the Province to convert a former button factory for this purpose (the conversion was a major project in the financially straitened inter-war years). There was also a ten-bed night shelter attached to the hostel which itself accommodated 125. St Joseph's was opened by the Lord Mayor of Birmingham who supported the work personally. A significant number of Sisters continued the diocesan co-ordinated visiting across ten parishes; some Sisters were engaged in district nursing, others as social workers, visiting of Winson Green Prison and special needs catechesis across the diocese. In 1964 a new residential block was built for the Sisters (at this time 14 in number) after Father Patrick O'Mahoney (St Chad's Cathedral) wrote to the Management Committee to comment on the very poor accommodation it was providing for the Sisters. In 1971/72 the Sisters carried out modernisation of the cubicle accommodation in the hostel to create 52 single rooms with self-catering. The Sisters and the hostel transferred to Aston in 1983 because the district around Princip Street was developing light industries and costs were consequently rising.

Phillips Street no. 98
Aston

1983–1988 St Joseph's Hostel, night shelter for women and Sisters' House for visiting. Twelve Sisters lived here, most of whom were involved in visiting. The women's hostel had 19 individual rooms with facilities plus a night shelter for five women, converted by the

City Council from an existing block of flats. The hostel continued when the Sisters withdrew from the work in 1988 and transferred to Pitsford Street.

Pitsford Street no. 166	1988-2005 A range of parish and pastoral ministries which included: Diocesan RE Advisory Service; Birmingham City Council's occupational therapy disability team; prison visiting; volunteering at the Fireside Day Centre; and befriending asylum seekers and refugees. In addition there was a continuing ministry in St Patrick's parish and school and hospital chaplaincy in the Dudley Road Hospital. St Wilfrid's parish, Castle Bromwich, was also visited. A sister from the Irish Province lived in this community to work with the Irish community via the Irish Centre.
Birmingham Erdington Gravelly Hill	1906-1974 St John's Girls' Home and an elementary school for St Mary's and St John's parish. The property and three acres of land were given to the Province. In 1935 the Home was certified as a Home Office Approved School for Senior Girls (aged fifteen and sixteen). It had a laundry, workroom for residents with disabilities, and hostel for residents prior to release. When the Approved School closed in 1974 Birmingham Social Services used the buildings for St John's Residential Resource Centre (1976-2005) for young people on remand and for a secure unit. St Mary and St John Junior and Infant School continues.
Birmingham Monument Road	1918-1942 St Philip's. The Sisters were invited by the Oratory Fathers to manage St Philip Neri Orphanage, a boarding home for boys at the Oratory School, a girls' school and to undertake visiting in three parishes in the care of Oratorians. The Sisters stipends were paid from the Emma Poncia Endowment which had been left to found the orphanage. Sisters formerly at Edgbaston transferred here. This work was transferred to Westbourne Road.
Westbourne Road no. 17	1942-1968. Sisters continued in the boys' home, the school and with the visiting until 1968. The Sisters went to live in Princip Street from where they continued visiting and teaching.
Birmingham Deritend High St no. 172	1917-1929 St Brigid's Hostel for female munitions workers, many of them Irish, was opened at the request of the government as part of the war effort. A great deal of work had to be undertaken to turn these loaned premises into good quality accommodation. Over 200 women lived here to work in munitions factories between 1916 and the Armistice and the Sisters worked to make it a cheerful home for them. Concerts, dances, whist drives and other entertainments were run in the Hostel and residents' guests were welcomed. A number of the women who were residents became Daughters of Charity, several as nursing Sisters. After the war it was judged that the need for hostel accommodation was acute and St Brigid's continued as a hostel for working women. £4,000 was raised to improve it further. It was closed when there was no further need for the provision.
Birmingham Jenkin Street Hawthorne Court no. 1	1982-1985 Sisters took on the roles of Warden and Relief Warden responsible for sheltered accommodation for the elderly under the Mercian Housing Society.

NORTH-EAST

Co. Durham, Middlesbrough and Newcastle.

Co. Durham
Darlington

The first three Sisters arrived in 1880 and the last left in 2013. There were three main sets of activities during this period: parish visiting; the establishment of a number of schools, including a secondary school and a girls' industrial school; and an orphanage. At different times there were one, two and three separate Sisters' Houses in Darlington each with its own Sister Servant.

Darlington Coniscliffe Road no. 30	1880-1975 St Augustine's. The Daughters first came to St Augustine's parish at the request of the Bishop of Hexham and Father (later Canon) J. Rooney. Rooney became the Vicar General and the Diocesan Inspector of Schools. He and Sister Catherine Cullen, Sister Servant at St Augustine's (1881-1924), with the support of Sister Mary Petre, worked together to create a range of schools (see below), initially against considerable public opposition to the presence of the Sisters. Initially they found the local shops unwilling to serve them, even for cash. When they opened a dispensary and a soup kitchen opinions mellowed. Darlington was the only location where mainstream education became so central to the Daughters' local mission. St Augustine's elementary school had opened in 1871 and the Sisters took charge from 1880. They offered evening classes, clubs and societies, a meal service for children through the school and in 1882 opened a Pupil Teacher Centre from which the secondary school developed. In 1900 a house, 'Larchfields', opposite the elementary school, was bought and opened in 1904 as St Augustine's High School for older

	children and as a practice school. In 1905 the opening of Immaculate Conception School fulfilled this requirement (below). St Augustine's Primary School continued in its old building until a new school was built in the grounds of the former Immaculate Conception School (opened in 1985). Much visiting was done from St Augustine's. The Sisters left here in 1975 (compulsory purchase order) and moved to Milton Street.
Milton Street no. 9	1975–1992 The Province bought the former Methodist Manse and renovated it with the help of volunteers. The main work of the House was visiting and teaching in St Teresa's parish, in Carmel Secondary School and St Augustine's primary school. Sisters also undertook sacristy work and pastoral ministry. In 1992 they moved to a smaller house at Carmel Road North.
St Clare's Abbey Carmel Road North	1992–2003 This accommodation, adjacent to the Abbey and owned by the Poor Clare nuns, was made available to the Sisters by them. The Sisters moved to North Road in 2003.
St Thomas Aquinas Presbytery, North Road	2003–2013 St Thomas Aquinas presbytery had become vacant and the Sisters were invited to take on parish administration and pastoral work in the absence of a resident priest. Their ministries were: hospital chaplaincy, parish visiting and a wide range of pastoral work in the parish and the adjoining parish. The Vincentian Millennium Partnership was managed from the House. When this House closed it marked the withdrawal of the Sisters from Darlington after 133 years.
Darlington Carmel Road	1892–1969 St Vincent's later known as St Joseph's Industrial School. The school was opened to relieve pressure on another Catholic home in Gosforth in Newcastle which had become overcrowded. It was registered for 60 girls in 1893. The building had formerly been a boys' boarding school and was adapted for its new use before the Sisters, staff and girls moved in. It was re-certified for 120 girls in 1898 and for 140 in 1911. The school was an annexe of St Augustine's House until 1920 when it became a House in its own right. In 1926 it became a Poor Law school and after that a home which eventually took both boys and girls. When the home closed in 1969 some children transferred to the small house in Cleveland Terrace. St Joseph's Home was demolished in 1972.
Darlington 'Southend'	1905–1975 Immaculate Conception School developed out of the work of St Augustine's and moved to 'Southend', a house formerly belonging to a prominent Quaker family. It was purchased with legacies Sister Cullen and Canon Rooney had each inherited in 1904. As it was one of the few secondary school foundations (day and boarding) made by the Province it provided an opportunity for Sisters with appropriate qualifications to teach at this level. In 1910 the families of girls who had been awarded a County Council scholarship fought for and won the right to use their daughters' scholarships in Immaculate Conception, although one-tenth of the scholarship was deducted. In 1948 Aided status was granted. 1968 saw the first comprehensive intake following a decision to develop the school in this new direction. In 1974 Immaculate Conception amalgamated with St Mary's Boys' School and the merged school was re-named Carmel RC Aided Secondary School, later Carmel College Catholic Academy. In 1975 the Sisters moved to Stanhope Road and some of the Southend buildings were demolished under compulsory purchase order for road schemes.
Stanhope Road no. 46	1975–1990 Twelve Sisters moved here from Southend and were involved in teaching in Carmel Secondary School and parish visiting, the number being gradually reduced over time as Sisters were placed elsewhere or retired from these ministries. Some Sisters moved to the remaining house in Darlington when the Stanhope Road House closed in 1990 (see above).
Gainford	1900–1939 St Peter's Home and Poor Law School for Boys. The Daughters came to Gainford (which was not far from their houses in Darlington) at the invitation of Canon Rooney. He asked them to manage St Peter's (300 boys), regarded as model provision at the time. The boys were sent by 21 different Boards of Guardians and the funding from the Boards was supplemented by the SVP. In 1937 the home took in 120 Spanish children fleeing Civil War. At the start of the Second World War (1939) the Sisters and boys moved to Tudhoe and the Sisters had no further involvement with St Peter's which was re-opened in 1947 as an RC Approved Boys' School run by lay staff under the diocese.
Tudhoe Spennymoor	1894–1966 St Mary's Poor Law School and Girls' Home. The Province was invited by the Bishop to take over this home founded in 1867 by the diocese and previously run by an order of French nuns. In 1894 there were 19 resident children. The Sisters opened a school in the home and ran confraternities and guilds for boys and girls in the parish. By 1921 there were 186 children in the home. In 1939 the boys from St Peter's Gainford were moved here and the girls who lived here were transferred to St Joseph's Home in Darlington. Like St Peter's this home took in Spanish Civil War refugees. The home closed in 1966 and was demolished later.

Middlesbrough

Middlesbrough various addresses Park Road South no. 21 (from 1919)	1906–1988 St Philomena's House of Charity. The Sisters were invited by Bishop Lacy of Middlesbrough to visit, to establish and lead guilds, confraternities, and clubs and to take charge of Sacred Heart parish school. Sisters visited in the parishes of St Patrick's, St Francis of Assisi and Sacred Heart and distributed food to the needy from the House. They were renowned for their visiting in the parish and in the city, carrying quantities of food discreetly in their capacious sleeves and pockets. This was a large House of Charity which opened with seven Sisters and continued to be sustained at this size; in the 1970s there were eight visiting Sisters. The property belonged to the community. When it was closed the Sisters moved to Grange Close in Grangetown (see below).
Grangetown Robert Street then Granville Road no. 6	1921–1971 St Vincent's House for visiting in the parish of St Mary's and Corpus Christi and teaching in the primary school. The visiting was extended to include the hospital and the parishes of St Anne's Eston, St Gabriel's Ormesby and Corpus Christi in Middlesbrough. The Sisters lived in a small terraced house in Robert Street and moved to a small corner house in Grange Close before transferring to a newly built house in Grange Close in 1971.
Grangetown Grange Close no. 18	1971–1997 The Sisters continued with the existing parish visiting. In the 1970s the parish church was demolished and the Sisters' house became the centre for daily Mass for a period. The House closed in Grangetown and was re-opened in Marske-on-Sea. When it closed the Head of Corpus Christi Primary School, a former pupil, noted that 'Theirs has been such a valuable, personal involvement within the Catholic community of Grangetown'.
Marske-on-Sea Redcar Cleveland	1997–2003 The Sisters were engaged in many kinds of pastoral work in St Bede's parish and the parishes of St Mary's, Corpus Christi, Our Lady of Perpetual Help and Sacred Heart in the Middlesbrough district and chaplaincy at Middlesbrough Hospital. This House was also used by the Province as a holiday home for Sisters.

Newcastle

Newcastle Ashburton Gosforth Road	1885–1906 St Elizabeth's Industrial School, certified for 100 girls at Ashburton House, a former farmhouse in 12 acres acquired by the diocese for a school and orphanage. The land proved to be swampy and unhealthy and the school was closed after 20 years. Girls were transferred to Darlington.
Newcastle Elswick Brunel Terrace	1892–1950 St Vincent's Industrial School for Boys, later St Vincent's Home for Boys. The home was opened in two large semi-detached houses with stable and coach house in grounds of 2 acres. It was certified for 60 boys in 1894 and re-certified for 70 in 1904. Only younger boys were sent here and so little industrial training or work was undertaken. In 1900 there were five Sisters, two lay female teachers, a male tailor and a drill-master on the staff. It ceased to be a certified Industrial School in 1915 and continued as a boys' home and Poor Law school. The school was closed in 1950 because of policy changes. The Sisters transferred to Roman Way.
Newcastle West Denton Roman Way	1950–1983 St Vincent's Children's Home in smaller family units transferred from Brunel Terrace. When the home was closed the Sisters were transferred to Summerhill Grove to the work taking place there.
Newcastle Heaton Summerhill Grove no. 1	1983–1988 St Louise's. This House was established in support of Our Lady of Lourdes Deaf Club in Summerhill Grove and began as an annexe of St Mary's below. The Sisters lived in the flat next door and managed the club, training volunteers who would be able to take on the future management and sustain the club. They also ran a new project with Manpower Services, working with unemployed people and collaborating with the local SVP which had bought four houses to assist in the rehabilitation of some patients from St Nicholas Psychiatric Hospital in Gosforth. The Sisters who lived here moved to Simonside Terrace in 1988 when the House closed.
Newcastle Heaton Simonside Terrace no. 58	1966–1995 A number of houses were bought and collectively they were named St Mary's Family Group Homes, financed by the Hexham and Newcastle Rescue Society, to work with vulnerable young women who had left care. Groups were small and individual care was at the core of the work. Some houses were in Lesbury Road and Jesmond Park West. The Sisters moved to a small house in Cheltenham Terrace in 1995/96. The work with young women was continued through the diocese.
Newcastle Cheltenham Terrace no. 33	1996–2000 Residential house for Sisters who were involved in hospital chaplaincy, parish visiting and psychiatric care in the community.

Lancashire

Preston Fulwood Garstang Road	1896–1956 St Vincent's Boys' Home and Poor Law School built in 17.5 acres of land as a result of large-scale public collections from local people. £8000 was raised in one week in 1891 in response to appeals and bazaars for the support of destitute boys. The Sisters were invited by Bishop O'Reilly of Liverpool for this diocesan work. The school was certified in 1896 for 250 boys and a further wing added in 1901 for another 50 boys. Trades were taught. There was a strong emphasis on physical fitness and exercise, football and other sports as well as the St Vincent's brass band. A working boys' hostel was opened in 1926 for those leaving care but having no home (see below). The orphanage closed in 1956 and the remaining boys and Sisters transferred to Ashton-on-Ribble.
Ashton-on-Ribble	1956–1966 St Vincent's Boys' Home, a small group home where children lived in groups of about 12 with their own carers. Provision closed 1966.
Preston Deepdale Road Stephenson Terrace no. 98	1926–1954 Working Boys' Hostel, an annexe to St Vincent's, Fulwood had been opened in 1908 as a transitional home for boys who had left care to start work but who remained vulnerable. It became a separate House in 1948 and was handed over to a diocesan group in 1954.
Preston St George's Road	1916–1922 This House developed from the initiative of a Sister who lived at the orphanage in Fulwood and began to visit in the parish of the English Martyrs, a very populous working-class parish, to look after the sick poor in their homes. The work increased and another sister was asked for. It was supported financially by the local Ladies of Charity and the Jesuits of Preston. The Sisters lived in a small house until 1923 when a larger house, previously owned by the President of the Ladies of Charity, Mrs Hull, was bought at Moor Park Road.
Moor Park Road	1923–1990 Visiting continued for almost 70 years from this House. The Sisters transferred to a smaller house in Kenmure Road in 1990.
Kenmure Place no. 31	1990–1998 Chaplaincy at Royal Preston Hospital and visiting in St Maria Goretti's parish. When the Sisters withdrew from this House they had been in Preston for over 100 years.
Skelmersdale Walthew Park	1920–1930 St Joseph's Seminary (known as 'Upholland'). The Archbishop invited the Sisters to take charge of the seminarians' infirmary and the domestic service of the seminary. The Sisters' contract gave the Province the right to hold Provincial retreats at St Joseph's. Provincial officers accepted the invitation because they believed it was 'morally impossible' to refuse this request but the short duration reflects their lack of conviction, expressed in other parallel instances in Ireland and England, about the work being congruent with the Company's core purposes.

Liverpool

Liverpool Beacon Lane	1862–1965 Paris superiors contracted with the Liverpool Diocese to manage St Gonzaga's, an existing boys' orphanage for which they had failed to find any community of brothers to undertake the management. Renamed St Vincent's, the home was certified first as an Industrial School then as an Approved School for 240 boys aged from eight to fourteen, with a workshop for older boys. The school was the first boys' institution managed by the Sisters in Britain. The Bishop had had doubts about their capability to run it effectively but their success opened the way for other invitations to manage homes and institutions for boys. The Daughters in Britain developed a significant work in an area not normally undertaken by religious sisters in Britain or by the Daughters elsewhere. Sister Marianne Middleton of the recusant family of Stockeld Park in West Yorkshire was the first Sister Servant. During her 20 years as Sister Servant she used a good deal of her own money to improve the school. The Sisters and the male teachers they employed taught a range of skills from shoe-making to joinery. In 1895 St Vincent's developed a working boy's hostel in Everton for after-care of those who had left the home but remained vulnerable. In 1939 the Home was evacuated to Capel Curig and did not re-open at Beacon Lane after the war. It relocated to Market Harborough between 1947 and 1949 then moved to Formby and closed.
Liverpool West Derby Brunswick Road no. 59	1871–1972 The Managers of the Catholic Blind Asylum (founded in 1841 by Revd Dr Youens and John Rosson) invited the Sisters to take charge of the institution. The home was overseen by a lay committee and funded by subscribers. In 1871 it had 35 residents,

male and female, adult and children. This work involved managing a specialised residential home, training in Braille, a school and a home farm. In 1901–1902 some of the children's provision transferred to Yew Tree Lane (see below) but some remained at Brunswick Lane until 1929 when the asylum became a residential home for adults only. In 1930 this House became a canonically erected House with its own Sister Servant. The home was renamed the Catholic Blind Institute in 1954 and the male trainee hostel was closed in 1955. In 1972 the adult provision moved to purpose-built accommodation at Christopher Grange in Youens Way.

Liverpool Youens Way	1972 continuing. Christopher Grange purpose-built centre for visually impaired adults replaced the original Brunswick Road provision. This is a registered care home and visual rehabilitation centre for the region. Other works from this House included pastoral work at Christopher Grange, head of care St Vincent's Specialist School, classroom assistant, prison chaplaincy, parish visiting, hospital chaplaincy, secondary teaching, co-ordinator of Vincentian Volunteers, occupational therapy and craftwork. Sisters continue to live at Christopher Grange. A Sister is a Trustee on the Catholic Blind Institute Board (CBI).
Liverpool West Derby Rice House Yew Tree Lane	1901–1999 St Vincent's School for the Blind (residential) for children. Rice Farm, comprising 26 acres and ample space for future development, was bought by the managers in 1896 so that they could separate the adults and children at Brunswick Road (see above) and create a home and school for children. This took time because of financial constraints. The first accommodation block was completed in 1901/02 and was opened by Cardinal Vaughan. A chapel was built in 1911 and a second accommodation block opened in 1927. All the children were on site together from 1929. A partially sighted department was running from 1948 and a nursery opened in 1955. The first full inspection by the Ministry of Education took place in 1953. During the 1950s and 1960s there was an expansion programme; in the 1960s and 1970s the Sisters were actively involved in research projects with universities. They organised outreach educational conferences for parents as well as being involved with other professionals. The institute changed its name to St Vincent's Specialist School for Sensory Impairment and Other Needs and included a non-residential primary school. It was rated 'outstanding' by Ofsted 2010/11. The Sisters moved off-site in 1999 transferring to Cathedral Precinct Mount Pleasant (see below) but continued some involvement beyond this date.
Liverpool Mason Street	1867–1886 St Anne's Industrial School for Girls. Sister Voisin, one of the French Daughters missioned to Britain, was the first Sister Servant. The school was certified as an Industrial School in 1867 and there were six Sisters here by 1868. In the mid 1880s the Inspectors condemned the building and would have withdrawn the Home Office certification if better accommodation had not been found. At the time the Sister Servant was Agnes Robinson who raised the money necessary to move, including a large donation from Sister Dymock and from other Sisters and from many people in Liverpool who supported the Sisters' fund-raising enterprises. Sister Robinson was able to pay off the Diocesan loan that had been used to help build the new school on land provided by Mr Weld Blundell of Ince Blundell, Little Crosby (see below), one of the major landowners in the area who had several relatives in the community. He conveyed land at Freshfield to the Bishop of Liverpool. Once the new school was built the Sisters and girls transferred to Freshfield (see Merseyside, Formby, below).
Liverpool Old Swan May Place	1876–1880 The Lancashire Reformatory for RC Girls which had been founded in 1869 and opened at Blackbrook House in St Helens moved to May Place in 1876 where it was managed by the Sisters. Little is known about the short period that the Sisters worked here apart from the fact that they did so and that they handed over the home to a religious congregation when they withdrew. In 1901 the Sisters were invited back to Old Swan by Bishop Whiteside and the Liverpool Catholic Reformatory Association to resume this work. 1901–1922 St Vincent's Senior Home Office School for Girls (Approved School) for the Liverpool Catholic Reformatory Association. A Sister from May Place visited in St Oswald's parish, paid for by the parish priest and the local SVP conference. In 1922 the Home Office withdrew registration as part of a national re-organisation of remand provision. The property was owned by the diocese but the Sisters had invested in it heavily. The Sisters consulted the archdiocese about a new purpose for the building and the Sisters' House, out of which Sister Billing, the Sister Servant, and Archbishop Keating agreed to develop a hospice. A committee was formed to administer St Vincent's Hospice. 1922–1990 St Vincent's Hospice under the trusteeship of the archdiocese. No charge was made to patients other than voluntary donations: many were unable to pay anything

towards costs. Major fund-raising activities were undertaken but the Hospice always struggled to cover costs. In 1947 the Management Committee persuaded the Ministry of Health to allow it to remain independent. In the mid 1950s the Liverpool Regional Hospital Board contracted 32 beds. An appeal made by Matt Busby (manager of Manchester United Football Club) raised a significant sum of money and a League of Friends played an active part in supporting the work. The Sisters withdrew in 1990 when it became clear that the archdiocese lacked the funds to bring the building up to the required standard.

Liverpool Everton Everton Brow	1889–1942 St Mary's Hostel for working girls and young women on probation started at nos. 13 and 15, moving to 17 and 19 in 1894. The Sisters took on probation and court work at this time to prevent young women being sent to Protestant institutions. The Sisters added a Servants' Home, St Vincent's Night Shelter for destitute girls (1892), were visiting in five parishes by 1919, opened a day nursery in 1919, and worked with deaf people throughout diocese (1920). The House transferred to Shaw Street in the war and the Province closed the hostel for young women.
Shaw Street	1942–1946 War-time temporary move. Transferred to Prospect Vale after the war.
Liverpool Prospect Vale	1946–1955 St Joseph's Welfare Clinic and visiting. It was intended that this House would develop into a hostel to take the place of St Mary's closed in the war, but this did not come to fruition. Transferred to Ullet Road.
Liverpool Ullet Road	1955–1973 St Joseph's Mother and Baby Clinic. House closed.
Liverpool Leyfield, West Derby	1894–1956 The Sisters were invited by Bishop O'Reilly to take charge of a Liverpool Poor Law school for 350 boys and girls to prevent them being sent to Protestant institutions. The Bishop aimed to provide accommodation for 1200 Catholic workhouse children across the diocese and had bought the 25-acre Leyfield property for £5,800 to help achieve this aim. A lengthy piece about the opening of the school, describing all its modern facilities (of which the diocese was very proud) and with much praise of the work of the Sisters of Charity, was carried in *The Tablet* on 22 December 1894. There was a considerable debt on the house, with interest of £1,000 per annum being paid. The House notes state that Sister Hadfield, the Sister Servant, had innumerable difficulties at the outset because one Board of Guardians 'were principally bigoted Protestants and Freemasons' but also that the situation changed within three years. The Sisters ran the school under the direction of a Diocesan Board of Administrators. Transferred to Druid's Cross at the time when family group provision was introduced in 1956.
Liverpool Druid's Cross	1956–1974 Children's home for boys and girls in family groups.
Liverpool Eldon Place	1921–1928 House of Charity for parish visiting and general welfare work.
Liverpool Fairfield Holly Road no. 11	1925–1928 Guardian Angel's (renamed) Our Lady's Home for babies and infants and nursery nurse training. The Sisters opened a crèche and college in Holly Road under the Liverpool Catholic Children's Protection Society (LCCPS) in June 1925. The Sister Servant and the priest Secretary of the LCCPS, Father Bennett, did not develop a good working relationship with the former finding that promises about the building and funding were not being kept and the latter frustrated that superiors did not provide enough Sisters with the qualifications needed by the Ministry of Health for government recognition of the Home. In 1927 the Sisters gained recognition by the Ministry of Health and the Royal Society of Nursery Nurses for their training work at the home. However, after three years of hard work by the team of Sisters, superiors concluded that they would never be able to satisfy the standards required by Father Bennett or be left to manage the work as they saw best and they gave notice to withdraw from the work.
Liverpool Seaforth Crescent Road no. 9	1926–1995 St Patrick's House of Charity. St Patrick's was situated on the edge of the dockland area where there was much poverty. The Sisters were invited by Father Kehoe, parish priest of Our Lady Star of the Sea, who suggested that they buy a small house that was for sale close to the church from which they could visit in the neighbourhood. Their first House was in Lyme Grove where they lived until the mid 1950s. Sisters taught in the next parish of St John's Bootle. In the 1980s work in the area declined and the Sisters were involved with supporting families experiencing unemployment and financial hardship. The Sisters sold the house as the area changed and the work was no longer needed.
Liverpool Gateacre Grange	1939–1969 Virgo Potens Hospital and Convalescence Home at the Grange was opened at an inauspicious time given the onset of war. The Grange, a large and well-appointed house in 15 acres of land in a semi-rural location, had been built in 1863 by Lord

Wavertree. In 1924 it was bought by the Irish Province of the Vincentians as a house of studies for philosophy students at a time when accommodation was very tight at their seminary in Blackrock near Dublin. No further students were sent after 1928 and the house proved to be an expensive white elephant that was a drain on the Vincentian Provincial finances. After an attempt at running a fee-paying boys' school the Vincentians despaired of finding a buyer but Joseph Sheedy, Director of the Province, advised them that the Daughters were looking for an additional Liverpool House and would buy it. The Province paid £10,000 for the house and opened Virgo Potens Hospital with five Sister-nurses. A further house was bought as a nurses' home in 1945 and tennis courts built for the nurses. This was a general hospital and nursing of the chronic sick with 46 beds, a fully equipped operating theatre and X-ray department that was used extensively by the Daughters for their own Sisters and by other religious communities and priests. Sisters who worked in difficult settings used it as a place of recuperation. Exemption from the NHS was claimed in 1947. Although the hospital and nursing home had a strong reputation for its care of patients by the mid 1960s the Province was finding it difficult to sustain the hospital financially and to provide theatre nurses. The Province sold the property to the Apostleship of the Sea, the Catholic mission to seafarers, who 'snapped it up' as they were looking to open a home for retired seamen.

Liverpool Netherley Rathbone Road	1990 A decision was made following the 1990 Provincial Assembly to open a mission in Netherley. A council flat was acquired. As this proved unsuitable it was decided to merge two ministries, outreach to the people of the area and nurturing vocations. It was temporarily housed in 11a Rathbone Road until a suitable property was found (see below).
Liverpool Netherley Dosen Brow no. 66	1991–1995 The ministry to the people of Netherley was continued here. The Sisters eventually moved into St Gregory's Presbytery when the Parish was left without a resident priest (see below). 1995–2011 The house was used for the Vincentian Volunteer project.
St Gregory's Presbytery Damson Road no. 41	1995–2011 The Province rented this former presbytery from the Archdiocese of Liverpool when priests were withdrawn from living in the parish. They played a major role in supporting lay people in revitalising the parish and refurbishing the parish hall which was also used as a church and for provision of breakfasts for school children every school morning by the Sisters. Sisters were involved in parish visiting, school and hospital chaplaincy, youth work and teaching.
Liverpool Mount Pleasant Cathedral Precinct	1999–2014. Sisters from West Derby (above) moved here and opened this new House at the heart of Liverpool Metropolitan Cathedral at the request of the Archbishop and Chapter. Their ministries included: sacristan offices at the cathedral; hospice work at St Joseph's Hospice; part of the ecumenical chaplaincy team at the Royal Infirmary; bereavement counselling; parish ministry at St Christopher's parish in Speke; chiropody for the elderly; and hospital chaplaincy at Alder Hey Children's Hospital.

Merseyside and Cheshire

Little Crosby	1859–1970 An invitation was received in Paris from the Blundell family of Ince Blundell for Sisters to teach in St Mary's Elementary School and for parish visiting on the Blundell estate which had remained in Catholic hands since the Reformation. Several Blundell women entered the Company in the nineteenth century and there were strong links between them and the Daughters. This was always a small House which maintained its original work of teaching and visiting. Sisters were withdrawn in the Province's Vatican II review of its works.
Liscard Wirral	1863–1871 The Sisters ran the elementary school and small orphanage at the invitation of the parish priest, Canon Lennon. It was one of the Sisters' early works that closed because of inadequate finances but more particularly because Canon Lennon decided to raise funds by mounting a series of entertainments in the school, including dancing. Paris superiors disapproved of the Sisters being maintained by public dances and decided to withdraw them, to the regret of the Sisters concerned.
Formby Freshfield	1886–1922 (continuation of Liverpool Mason Street, above) St Anne's Industrial School for Girls was re-certified for 150 girls when it transferred in 1886. By 1901 there were 10 Sisters, 8 employed staff and 163 resident girls. St Anne's was closed in 1922 as part of the changes made by the Home Office to rationalise and change its system for juvenile crime. The remaining girls were moved to Blackbrook House in St Helens run by another

community. In 1933 the Home Office invited the Daughters to manage Blackbrook at a time of further re-organisation of provision (see St Helen's below). St Anne's was used by the Archdiocese of Liverpool to accommodate St George's Boys' Industrial School although at the time Father Byrne (Director of the Province) and Sister Petre (Sister Servant) made representation to the diocese about the amount of money the Sisters had put into the property over the years and the fact that they had undertaken most of the fund-raising (see Liverpool Mason Street above). 'Certain facts would seem to make them almost Co-Proprietors with the Archdiocese of St Anne's, if not in law, at any rate, in equity and truth' noted Father Byrne CM. No compensation was given after the Sisters withdrew.

Formby	1918–1920 Stella Maris Hostel, holiday home. The SVP asked the Sisters to take on running this house which was agreed to on a trial basis only and then discontinued.
Formby Raven Meols Lane	1949–1965 St Vincent's Approved School, transferred here from Beacon Lane Liverpool after the war (see above). House closed.
Bebington	1920–1984 St Edmund's Home for Boys for the Diocese of Shrewsbury Rescue Society, managed by a Diocesan Board. Between 1913 and 1920 the home had been run by the Sisters of the Immaculate Conception, a French teaching congregation whose English novitiate was nearby at Rock Ferry on the Wirral. They seem to have struggled with the very difficult financial situation. Eight Daughters were sent to work in the home, which they too found needed very tight financial management because there was no public financial assistance before the 1960s. Funding per child came from the diocese, which was not a well-endowed one, and from fund-raising. Sisters did all the cleaning and cooking to keep costs down and ran a large vegetable garden. The home had room for 120 boys. In 1948 Canon Hugh McHugh took over responsibility for the Rescue Society and re-negotiated the weekly allowance for each boy, but it was still low. In 1959 St Edmund's began to accept sibling sisters who were previously sent to the girls' home at Pantasaph and small group housing was introduced, halving the number of children accepted. In 1969 the Province made the decision to withdraw from St Edmund's because of the shortage of younger fully social work trained Sisters but was persuaded by McHugh and the Bishop to continue as St Edmund's was the only provision in the diocese. They did so on the condition that there was full collaboration with the new Commission for Social Welfare in order to solve a number of problems about status, funding and recognition. As a consequence the Shrewsbury Diocesan Rescue Society was formally linked with Liverpool Children's Society to achieve Assisted Status for St Edmund's and thus increase the income of the Home. The number of children gradually decreased in line with policies for fostering children in need and providing greater family support. The home was closed in 1984 and with it the chapel which had been a local Mass centre for more than 40 years.
St Helens Blackbrook Road	1933–1990 Blackbrook House Approved School for Girls. Blackbrook was opened in 1869 as the Lancashire Reformatory for RC Girls. It moved to May Place in Liverpool in 1876 where it continued under the Liverpool Catholic Reformatory Association, managed by the Sisters, until closure in 1922. It seems that Blackbrook House was re-instated as reformatory provision for the Salford Diocese at some time and was managed by another community of Sisters. In 1933 when the Home Office reduced the number of places and closed St Joseph's in Sheffield run by the Sisters it asked them to transfer their residents to Blackbrook and take on the management. Blackbrook had a school teaching life skills, school-leaving examinations and vocational subjects. There were good sporting and exercise facilities and a strong emphasis on educational development. A secure unit provided support in a secure setting for girls subject to a Secure Accommodation Order. The Sisters continued this taxing social work for almost 60 years and even after withdrawing from managing the school some Sisters continued to work with the residents. Other ministries from this house were: social work with the Rescue Society and Wigan Council; rehabilitation and after care; and teaching, nursing and parish visiting in St Mary's parish.
Blundellsands Warren Road no. 21	1980–1995 Our Lady's House for retired and active Sisters and a house for rest and recuperation. Sisters from Blundellsands and Seaforth transferred to the new community house of St Vincent's Leicester Street in Southport.
Southport Leicester Street	1995 continuing. St Vincent's residential care home for elderly Sisters.
Southport Leyland Road no. 99	2005 continuing. Santa Barbara residency for elderly Sisters.
Latham Road no. 28	2011 continuing. St Louise's residency for elderly Sisters.

Warrington Kestrel Lane nos 10–12	1979–1987 The Sisters went to the Birchwood district of Warrington because this was an entirely new estate with a need to build community and because the parishes (St Oliver Plunkett, St Stephen's in Orford and St Bridget's) were served by Vincentians. The Province gave a Sister for each parish for visiting and parish ministries. There was no church and the new school hall became the Mass centre and social centre. The Sisters helped to build up a wide range of groups: liturgy group; Naomi Circle for widows and widowers; Sunday crèche; youth group; baptism preparation for parents; senior citizens; play group; and St Justin's for Ethiopian mission. House closed in 1987.

Manchester and Salford

Salford Church Street	1847–1849 **This was the first Daughters of Charity House in Britain.** House of Charity for visiting in St John's parish and neighbourhood. A local wealthy cotton merchant, Joseph Lee, wrote to the Mother House in Paris and asked for Sisters to be sent to visit in the working-class district around the new church of St John's (later Salford Cathedral). As a result of harassment and bigotry they were withdrawn after less than two years and the Company did not return to England until 1857 when it went to Sheffield.
Manchester Chorlton-on-Medlock Stockport Road until 1884 then Victoria Park Longsight	1877–1971 St Joseph's Industrial School for Girls and an orphanage at the invitation of Bishop Herbert Vaughan. This Industrial School had been certified in 1871 at Grindlow House in Stockport Road, run by a Matron under the supervision of Father Thomas Quick. The Sisters took charge in 1877. In 1884 the school was moved by the Sisters to a larger house with grounds at Victoria Park. A public laundry was opened in 1887 to provide training and generate income for the school. In 1891 the Sisters built an auxiliary home for young women over sixteen who had no families to return to. Parish visiting in St Augustine's was undertaken from 1912 and a Sunday school in Denton parish was run from 1922. When the Home Office reduced the number of industrial schools in 1922 the remaining residents of St Joseph's Ancoats were transferred to St Joseph's Sheffield. The Province changed the use of the Victoria Park property to create St Joseph's Technical High School for Girls in 1923, a central (continuation) school which was part of the new post-elementary system in Manchester. The orphanage closed in 1927 and the technical school became the major commitment. The Sisters withdrew from living in St Joseph's in 1971 but continued working in the school until 1980. The school continued as Vincent de Paul Technical High School until 1999 when it was closed. The Sisters from Victoria Park transferred to Hathersage Road (below).
	The works of the Sisters' Houses in Ancoats and Chorlton-on-Medlock were distinct but mutually supporting. All were involved in visiting in very poor districts and focused additionally on work with destitute young women or those who had been charged with petty crimes or prostitution. This work was usually known as 'rescue' activity.
Manchester Ancoats Goulden Street	1887–1898 Bishop (later Cardinal) Vaughan asked for Sisters to open a House of Charity in this district which had many Irish and Italian residents (it was known as 'Ancoats Little Italy'). The Sisters visited in St Joseph parish and St Michael's mission. They ran a girls' night home which was a refuge for destitute young women, a crèche for working mothers, Sunday schools and night schools. The Sisters moved to St Vincent's parish (below).
Manchester Ancoats St Vincent's Street	1898–1938 St Vincent's House of Charity was opened and owned by the Province for parish visiting in St Vincent's and teaching in the elementary school. A major undertaking of this House was its night shelter for destitute girls and young women and probationary work of accompanying young women to court (from 1911) and subsequently placing them in work or hostels. A night school was opened between 1900 and 1912. A good deal of visiting was undertaken from the house, in prison, in the Manchester workhouse at Crumpsall and at Ancoats hospital. The annual Festa procession for the Madonna of the Rosario first organised by the Italian community in 1890 had its start point at St Vincent's. A child welfare centre and mother and baby home were opened in 1920. In the 1930s there was a major programme of slum clearance in Ancoats and Hulme when the Sisters living here moved to Rumford Street to amalgamate some of their work with that of the House that had been founded in 1893.
Manchester Chorlton-on-Medlock Rumford Street no. 85	1893–1961 Bishop Bilsborrow and Father Bernard Vaughan with the support of Miss Weld Blundell had opened a boys' trade school. It did not succeed and the Sisters were invited to take on the property as a training home for girls. Lady de Trafford and one or two other benefactors paid for one Sister between 1893 and 1918. The Sisters ran a girls' mutual aid

home (St Philomena's Hostel) for aftercare of young women from prison and for girls who were unemployed. This meant there was a link between the work of St Vincent's above and the Rumford Street House. In *c.*1905 a Local Government Certified Home for children from the various Boards of Guardians was opened by the Sisters. Visiting Sisters worked in two parishes. In 1917 the Holy Name Child Welfare Centre and Health Clinic was opened. In time the works spread into Upper Brook Street (nos 132–136), property that was owned by the diocese. The work of St Vincent's in Ancoats was moved here in 1938, the night shelter was renamed Seton Night Shelter. During the 1940s at the invitation of Bishop Marshall the Sisters set up a project, initially funded by the government, to support girls and women who became pregnant out of marriage during the war. The House was closed when Manchester University obtained a compulsory purchase order to clear the land for its own development but the support activities for pregnant single women continued temporarily at their Victoria Park House before moving to Hathersage Road when it opened in 1965.

Salford Broom Lane no. 61	1932–1975 St Teresa's. The Province bought two large houses in extensive grounds to create a maternity home for married women (deliveries and maternal care). At the request of Bishop Marshall the work was extended to single mothers. Gradually this latter work took over. Some mothers decided to keep their babies but most were adopted. St Teresa's had a training school for nursery nurses 1941–1945. Between 1948 and 1969 each parish priest in the Salford Diocese contributed towards the upkeep of the maternity home and was able to refer women to it. In 1965 the nursery was extended but the need then ceased quite rapidly with wider social changes including the development of oral contraception and the passage of the 1967 Abortion Act. Many of those who came were from Ireland where greater shame continued to be attached to unmarried motherhood. In 1975 the Sisters moved to Waterpark Road and the Province demolished the original houses and sold the land to build St Vincent's Housing Association, creating nine flats for the elderly. St Teresa's was officially closed in 1984 although its numbers had been very small in the previous decade. Sisters at St Teresa's visited in the parishes of St Thomas of Canterbury and Corpus Christi Miles Platting for many years.
Waterpark Road no. 62	1975–1979 A Sisters' residency for those who continued to work in the nursery at St Teresa's. In 1979 Waterpark Road was sold and the Sisters bought a vacant house in Broom Lane.
Broom Lane no. 58	1979–1988 Parish work at St Thomas of Canterbury and Corpus Christi Miles Platting.
Manchester Longsight Hathersage Road and Anson Road	1965–1992 St Vincent's Hall, purpose-built accommodation for 78 female students and young working women, was opened by the Province as one of its own initiatives. The community increased when Sisters from St Joseph's Victoria Park moved here in 1971. Some Sisters worked in Seton Night Shelter, others undertook parish pastoral ministries in various parishes or visiting at St Anne's Hospice; some were teachers. In 1979 Seton House (Anson Road) was leased to the Salford Catholic Children's Rescue Society for work with unmarried mothers. The Sisters also ran The Ephesus Centre Youth Centre from St Vincent's Hall. Beginning in 1989 the St Vincent's Liturgy Centre was established by Sister Ellen Flynn. It was located in the Diocese of Salford and worked with dioceses and religious orders throughout the country. Another initiative, Vincentian Volunteers, was also overseen from this House for a period. In 1992 the House was closed because of the reduction in the number of Sisters and a smaller property was bought in Swinton.
Swinton/Pendlebury Sefton Road no. 16	1991–1996. This House was not open very long but because the Sisters worked in a collaborative way with lay people and with religious communities, much that was started continued. Sisters lived in Swinton and undertook ministries in other locations, for example St Vincent's Liturgy Centre (which moved to St Boniface's Presbytery in Lower Broughton). Other ministries from the House included: parish youth ministry, parish visiting, catechesis, evangelisation and bereavement counselling, and occupational therapy in a local hospital.
Manchester Ancoats Victoria Square no. 143	1982–1990 The Sisters returned to Ancoats in 1982 to visit in St Michael's parish whose priest Father Ron Jeffers had asked them to develop the visiting that was already being undertaken in the parish by Sister Pauline Gaughan from Hathersage Road. Manchester City Council allocated her a council flat. At this time the former school next to the church was being converted into a hostel for men who had formerly lived in the 'Morning Star' hostel in Nelson Street run by the Legion of Mary. Pauline Gaughan was moved to work full-time in the new hostel ('Mary and Joseph House') where she recruited and trained a team of voluntary hostel workers. In 1983 a Marian Centre was established for the distribution of Miraculous Medals and Green Scapulars. Another Sister arrived in 1984 to visit in a number of local parishes and to prepare Catholics for the sacraments. Women helpers and volunteers with the hostel were given another flat in Anita Street. The Sisters' House was closed in 1990 but in 1993 a

new purpose-built Mary and Joseph House was opened for 41 men coping with alcohol dependency and related mental health issues. Vincentian Volunteers supported the House during their Vincentian formation and training, thus continuing the Sisters' work.

Manchester Chorlton-on-Medlock Milnrow Close no. 6	1990–2006 A House for Sisters in parish and pastoral ministry in local parishes. The Cornerstone Day Centre established by Sister Gaughan and Canon Kevin O'Connor at St Augustine's Hulme was supported from here. The House transferred to Birchvale Close in Hulme in 2006. Cornerstone continues as a day centre under the aegis of Caritas Diocese of Salford.
Hulme Birchvale Close no. 4	2006 continuing. The Province founded a project called 'Out There' to support families of prisoners. Other works include National Spiritual Adviser to the SVP, hospital chaplaincy, parish visiting and supporting Vincentian Volunteers.
Salford Little Hulton Our Lady's Presbytery Hallstead Avenue	1998–2014. The main ministry of this House was in the parish of Our Lady and the Lancashire Martyrs to administer the parish and undertake pastoral work in the absence of a resident priest. In addition the Sisters worked with the Catholic Welfare Society visiting elderly people to support them in their own homes and with the Brothers of Charity in their work for people with learning disabilities. Some Sisters support prisoners' families through the Sisters' 'Out There' project (see Hulme above).

SOUTH-EAST

Bedfordshire, Cambridgeshire, Essex, Hertfordshire, Kent, Sussex.

Bedfordshire

Dunstable Houghton Regis Elm Park Close no. 43	1973–1992 Daughters arrived in Bedfordshire in the early 1970s to assist Vincentian confrères who served two parishes, St Mary's in Dunstable and St Vincent de Paul at Houghton Regis. Both parishes had grown rapidly since the 1920s because of the motor industry and migration from the East End of London and Paddington. There was no church in Houghton Regis until the later 1970s and the informal arrangements, often based at the Sisters' House, helped to forge community. The Sisters began with visiting and other ministries were developed from this starting point: mother and toddler group; over-60s' club; teaching in St Mary's School Caddington and St Vincent's School; help with the existing SVP and starting a new Junior SVP group; and youth work. Other groups included the Prayer Group, Marriage Encounter, Rosary Link, Marian Group and Young Christian Workers, as well as a Christian Unity Group.
Linked to Luton	In 1987 Sister Eileen O'Mahoney, based at Houghton Regis, worked in Luton with young Irish emigrants. She was involved in establishing the Luton and Dunstable Irish Care and Advice Association based in Luton which in 1989 became The Luton Irish Advice Bureau. The Committee were persuaded to open a day centre for Irish emigrants who had 'lost their footing'. It opened in 1993 and went on to be a very active centre with many referrals from other agencies, working with the most entrenched of rough sleepers. When the Sisters withdrew from Luton in 1992 Sister Eileen continued to operate the day centre until she retired in 2000. The centre was renamed NOAH (New Opportunities and Horizons) in 1999 to express the way it had developed to offer hope through skills-training and personal relationships. NOAH continues to develop under Vincentian-inspired lay leadership and with the support of the Irish government and grants from other sources. In 2008 NOAH won the Day Centre of the Year Award.
Luton Abigail Close no. 7	2002–2007 Visiting and general pastoral ministry as part of NOAH. Closed 2007.

Cambridgeshire

The Sisters worked in Peterborough and its immediate environs for more than 100 years, their only centre in East Anglia or the East of England. Eastern England had a relatively small Catholic community until the late twentieth century and very few religious Sisters or Brothers. The Daughters' presence was a result of family connections.

Peterborough Manor House Street	1901–1966 Canon W. Moser, parish priest of All Souls, invited the Sisters to open a House of Charity for parish visiting and to have charge of the elementary school. He was the brother of Sister Agnes Moser (entered 1874 and became Sister Servant at St John's Boston Spa). The family had moved to Oxburgh in Norfolk when their parents had converted to Catholicism and their father had lost his partnership in the family firm in London as a

consequence. The Sisters were well looked after in the parish in the early years and never had any financial difficulties; all building works were undertaken by the parish or private individuals and the Sisters' stipends were paid promptly. During the Second World War Belgian refugees were housed here and a Daughter was appointed to support them. Sisters transferred to Park Road.

Park Road no. 237	1967–1982 House of Charity for parish visiting and teaching in the parish primary school and the secondary school. In the 1970s and early 1980s Sisters held the role of Diocesan RE Organiser for Northampton and then East Anglia dioceses and were responsible for organising catechetics in All Souls, and pastoral work for deaf adults and children.
Peterborough, Bretton Cleatham no. 29	1975–77 The Sisters rented a council house on a large new estate for visiting, social work and teaching as members of a wider inter-agency team (Bretton Community Work Team) providing services to newcomers. This House was run as an annexe to Park Road. At the wish of the local council they welcomed new residents to the estate and provided information on local services. House closed because of lack of personnel.
Peterborough, Bretton Kirkmeadow	1998–2005 Sisters returned to Peterborough for visiting and general parish works. They undertook voluntary work in the family centre and the parish school, provided hospital and hospice chaplaincy and ran a mother and toddler group. One Sister worked in a parish which had no resident priest. This was a House where older Sisters who were active could continue to undertake ministries.

Essex

Leyton Park House	1870–1902 St Agnes' Boys' Orphanage and Poor Law School for Westminster Diocese was established at the urgent request of Archbishop Manning at the time when he gained magistrates' authorisation to move Catholic children from workhouses in London. Boys here were aged between two and seven. St Agnes' began life in Etloe House (which had been Cardinal Wiseman's country house) but when this was sold in 1874 the orphanage moved to Leyton House, a grand country house which was re-named Park House. There were 150 children at the school in 1882 when Sister Mary Burns was the Sister Servant. The School choir sang at the parish church in Warley. The orphanage closed in 1902 when Cardinal Vaughan decided to re-organise the certified boys' schools in the diocese; younger boys were transferred to an existing home, St Charles at Brentwood and the Sisters were asked to take charge of St Charles.
Brentwood Weald Road	1902–1938 St Charles' Orphanage and Poor Law School for boys over the age of nine. St Charles' had been founded in 1886 by the Brothers of Mercy as part of Cardinal Manning's Westminster Crusade of Rescue project for Catholic children in workhouses and Protestant orphanages. Manning bought an 18-acre site at Brentwood where he decided to build an orphanage for 200 older boys. When Cardinal Vaughan re-organised provision for boys in certified schools St Charles' became a Poor Law school for younger boys under the charge of the Sisters with older boys being moved to other existing provision. The whole building was brought up to date at their request and the diocese leased the property to the Sisters for 20 years asking them to manage it themselves. It re-opened in 1902 as a Poor Law school managed by the Sisters. The Sisters withdrew in 1938 because they believed that the Bishop, on behalf of Cardinal Archbishop Hinsley (who became Archbishop in 1935), had set new conditions that they could not meet in order to force them to leave and enable their replacement by the Christian Brothers, whom he judged more suitable for boys.
Great Warley Warley House	1921–1963 Marillac House Sanatorium opened by the Province. The property was bought by Sister Ethel Pickwood for £4000 and given to the Province for a sanatorium – its location 400 feet above sea level being considered very favourable for this purpose. It was the first House in the Province to be named after Louise de Marillac, who had been beatified in 1920. The naming was part of the wider 'recovery' of the co-foundress in the Company at this time which preceded her canonisation in 1934. Marillac House was primarily for children and religious Sisters in the early stages of TB (there was also a small private school here that closed in 1958). A veranda was constructed in 1922 for open-air sleeping. In 1927 the home was approved by the Ministry of Health. The Sanatorium became well-known in Catholic circles through Scots-born Margaret Anne Sinclair, a Poor Clare nun of the Notting Hill Poor Clare Convent, whose community placed her at Marillac House when she was dying of TB of the throat in 1925. Margaret Sinclair was nursed by the Sisters until her death that same year. Before long she was being regarded as a saint by many Catholics, particularly those in her native Scotland, being declared Venerable in 1978. Sister Edith

Burd, Matron at the Marillac at the time, compiled reflections about her life, *The Spirit of Margaret Sinclair*, published in 1932. As treatment for TB changed and its prevalence declined Marillac House was changed into a hospital for the chronically sick. In 1956 the local hospital board asked the Daughters to take young chronically sick patients. It was to cater for these patients that the Province bought the building that had been the Officers' Mess of the Essex Regiment before it moved to Chelmsford. The building was adapted and opened in September 1963.

Eagle Way
1963 continuing. The Marillac continued as a registered charity with facilities for 50 chronically sick younger women under a contractual arrangement with the North East Thames Regional Health Authority. The Sisters and staff were supported by a large team of volunteers (League of Friends) whose presence was seen as vital in providing the homely atmosphere, extra services and events. A well-appointed chapel is used for Mass and Anglican Eucharist. The position of matron was held by a Sister and many of those nursing and providing pastoral care were also Sisters. In 1994 the whole building underwent refurbishment and became a nursing home for 50 men and women with physical disabilities needing 24-hour care, for example following a road accident. Between 2011 and 2013 the whole building was upgraded and work was completed on a rehabilitation unit to aid independent living with the aim of being 'a centre of excellence for helping adults with neurological and complex physical disabilities'. Warley is a not-for-profit independent care home registered with the Care Quality Commission. One part of the main complex is used as a care home for Sisters and other elderly clients. A separate house for the Sisters' community was built in the grounds and named after Sister Margaret Donworth who led the change of location in 1963. Active Sisters who live in the community are involved in pastoral care, administration, nursing, occupational therapy, social work, pastoral care of residents and fundraising.

Leigh-on-Sea
Hillside Crescent no. 18
Woodside
1922–1991 St Edith's holiday and convalescent home. The property was given to the Province by Arthur Moore of County Tipperary whose daughter Edith had been accepted as an aspirant in 1915 but died unexpectedly before she could enter. Edith had undertaken visiting in the East End of London and her mother decided to establish a holiday home for mothers and children from the Holy Child Settlement in Poplar in memory of her vocation. Father Gilbert of the parish of Our Lady of Lourdes in Leigh heard of her interest and collaborated to establish St Edith's which the Daughters were asked to run. Later the Province bought the house next door for a kindergarten. Woodside went on being used after the Second World War and in the years before its closure was used for residential care of the elderly, and long-term and respite care for 45 female patients. Sisters also visited in the parish of Our Lady of Lourdes. The house was sold and demolished and in 1991 a new building opened for the Anchor Housing Association called St Edith's Court.

Hertfordshire

Ware
St Edmund's Seminary
1927–1933 Senior clergy pressed the Provincial leaders to take responsibility for the student infirmary and supervision of domestic staff. The Province always doubted that this work was in keeping with the Vincentian calling and withdrew within six years.

Kent

Dover
Eastbrook Place nos 6–8
and Maison Dieu Road
1883–2005 Holiday home and 'open-air' school for delicate children from London children's homes. The House was given to the community by a relative of Sister Robinson. Many inner-city children were brought from London on holidays and for convalescence over the years. The Sisters visited soldiers' families. In 1889 they helped to form an Association of Ladies of Charity and in 1908 a boys' orphanage was begun under the auspices of the Southwark Rescue Society and Workhouse; this closed in 1917 and was replaced by an open-air school which then transferred to St Leonards-on-Sea in 1934, as the Sisters were advised that the strong winds at Dover were not helpful for some of the children's medical conditions (see below). While the holiday work for children continued, in 1934 the work of the House was expanded to teaching in St Paul's elementary school which continued through evacuation to Ebbw Vale during the war and until the school closed in the 1960s. After the war the Sisters developed a convalescent home for women in the House and this gradually changed to residential care of the elderly, which was very successful and much in demand. In 1981 the home was re-registered as St Mary's Residential Home. Sisters withdrew from St Mary's in 2005, which still continues as a private residential care home.

Gravesend Parrock Road	1926–1972 St Mary's Home for Boys transferred from Mottingham (South London) to Gravesend. Southwark Diocese bought Milton Mount College, a former boarding school for the daughters of Congregational ministers and pioneer for girls' education, for use by the Southwark Rescue Society as St Mary's Home. The Sisters were invited to run the home for 200 boys with Father Baker as Head. During the Second World War the home was evacuated to Ugbrooke Park, Chudleigh in Devon, the home of Catholics Lord and Lady Clifford, returning in 1945. After the war, like many other former orphanages, it struggled to reach the new standards in straitened times and its single-sex provision which separated siblings was not seen as best practice. Adaptations took place through purchase of family houses in Glen View, a road that backed onto Parrock Road (below). Milton Mount (St Mary's) was closed and was sold for development, being demolished in 1972.
Glen View nos 7 and 9	1956–1989 In 1956 the Southwark Rescue Society working with the Sisters opened family group homes in Glen View, a residential road that backed onto Parrock Road. This was the Province's first family group home and comprised two groups of 12 children each with their own carers. The group home approach gradually took over from St Mary's provision during the 1960s until it replaced it altogether. During the 1980s the Sisters managed four units for long- or short-term children's care, taking children in emergency situations. The Province withdrew in 1989 when it could no longer provide Sisters.

Sussex

St Leonards-on-Sea St Saviour's Road	1934–1995 St Vincent's Residential Open Air School for Girls transferred here from Dover. Sisters O'Hare and Moylan of Dover combed the south coast before finding this house which was bought by the Province. Children suffering from asthma, heart complaints and other health problems came from as far away as Huddersfield as well as from London and its adjacent counties. They stayed for varying lengths of time, according to medical recommendations. The London County Council sent about 20 children a month from the East End. With additional dormitory extensions there was capacity for about 90 children in the House. During the Second World War the House was evacuated for six years to Liphook in Hampshire while St Vincent's was requisitioned for troops. After 1946 further new buildings were added including a gym and hall. By the 1970s the demand for this work was decreasing and the role of the House was reviewed. The decision was taken to establish provision for older girls with social and emotional difficulties who were taught the normal full school curriculum. In the final years the residents were in family group houses in nearby streets. Closed as a result of educational reforms (Warnock Report) and sold.

WEST

Bristol, Devon, Herefordshire, Wiltshire.

Bristol

Bristol City Stapleton Road no. 61	1916–1971 House of Charity opened by the Province for the parish of St Joseph's and St Patrick's. The Sisters established confraternities and guilds, visited the prison and workhouse and taught in the elementary school. After many years the ministry was handed over to Anglican Sisters of Charity who had been founded in Bristol in 1869 using the Vincentian Rule. The Daughters transferred to Pennywell Road.
Pennywell Road	1971–2005 The Sisters also ran a day centre for the elderly and worked with the SVP on a homelessness project (1988). They undertook chaplaincy to RAF Lyneham; were part of the diocesan care of the deaf; and of an ecumenical team run by the Methodists working with and for young people. When they moved to Chesterfield Road in 2005 this work continued.
Bristol Chesterfield Road no. 135	2005–2011 The Sisters worked with street women in a day centre and undertook social work/counselling outreach, including tracing families of adopted children at their request. Other Sisters were involved in individual language teaching to migrants and refugees; support of parish groups.

Devon

Buckfastleigh	1901–1914 The Sisters were invited by the Prior of St Mary's Abbey (Benedictine) for teaching in the local elementary school, for working among female factory workers in the local wool mills including evening classes, to establish guilds and confraternities and for

parish visiting. The Prior provided a cottage close to the Abbey and stipends. The school that the monks opened caused a significant controversy for being 'sectarian' and a Board School was opened in opposition to it. The records do not state why the Sisters withdrew in 1914 but they were replaced by another community of Sisters.

Plymouth Gasking Street nos 20–22	1875–1931 The work with girl orphans at 20 Gasking Street had been started by a French woman who later entered the Company. When she left Plymouth, Bishop Vaughan invited the Daughters to take it on. As there was no funding, Sisters Burke and O'Farrell gave £90 per annum to pay the stipends of three visiting Sisters to get the project started. A workroom was opened in 1875 to raise money for support of the poor and the first orphan was received in the same year; the start of St Teresa's Home for Girls. The house next door was bought with subscriptions and another by Canon Charles Graham for a boys' orphanage in 1880. In 1883 the Sister Servant (Sister Etheldreda Howard) received permission to receive boys from the Poor Law Unions and workhouses and the home was certificated for 150 boys. It was decided to move the boys so that they would have more space. A property could not be found locally so when one was found in Torquay (former private school Torre College) it became a separate House (see below). The Sisters ran a workroom for fine sewing (which did not pay) and a laundry, built with a loan of £500 from the Duke of Norfolk, which did pay. In 1904 Bishop Graham bought a house at Gascoyne Place for the Sisters to open a hostel for working girls and a social centre for domestic servants to gather on their day off. The orphanage expanded greatly with the Sisters raising money through subscriptions and bazaars to pay for extensions. In 1909 another house was bought (9 Higher Street) where they ran a soup-kitchen and a mothers' meeting on a large scale. Sisters undertook prison visiting and opened a nursery in Saltash which was also a country house for the children (1914). In 1919 the Bishop hired rooms in Stonehouse and then bought a house (Durnford Street) so that the Sisters could run mothers' meetings and girls clubs there, which were very popular. The Sisters withdrew in 1931 because the building needed extensive improvement and neither they nor the diocese had the funds. The new Bishop replaced the Daughters with the Sisters of Nazareth who bought a fresh property for the orphanage and the diocese later sold St Teresa's. The Province had invested between £15,000 and £17,000 and felt that there had been an injustice.
Torquay Teignmouth Road	1889–1982 St Vincent's Home for boys moved here from Plymouth (see above) into a former private college. Several local benefactors (Hugh Liam, Miss Hallian and Miss Tilt) each gave £1,000 to buy the property. The home opened with 150 boys. New boys were referred largely by the Plymouth Rescue Society, parents and guardians. In their contract with the Bishop the Sisters were to visit and to establish guilds and confraternities in the parish of Our Lady of the Assumption. The first Sister Servant was Sister Sybilla Plowden who won a great deal of local support for St Vincent's after initial opposition. St Vincent's was rather far from the church and a chapel was built on site with funds donated by Mr Vernon Benbow in 1897. St Vincent's chapel became a well-attended local Mass centre. The home had its own (non-resident) chaplain – from 1928 it was served by the Marists from their college at Paignton who proved popular with the boys. In 1903, Sister Hilda Plater became Sister Servant (her brother was Charles Plater SJ) and her family donated £1250 in 1919 to develop St Philip's Working Boys' Home for aftercare. St Philip's Working Boys' Home was built in the grounds (1905/07) for about 20 boys leaving St Vincent's to qualify as teachers or learn trades. It later became a holiday home used to take children out of town orphanages for holidays. Fund-raising was constant because the school was voluntary and received no state funding. Until 1943 the boys were taught at St Vincent's which employed lay teachers as well as Sisters. The years from 1931 to the closure of the Home are sensitively and engagingly written about by Sister Monica Cowman who was for a long time Sister Servant and developed great wisdom about children in care (Footsteps: A History of St Vincent's Torquay). She was later Chair of the Irish National Committee on childcare. For many years Sister Cowman was a key figure of the Old Vincentians' Association that thrived after the closure of the Home.
Yelverton	1926–1941 The Province established a nursery nurses' training college registered and recognised by the Royal Society of Day Nurseries which awarded the qualifying certificate. This House was founded by the Province at a time when it was expanding in the field of trained nursery nursing and following changes to legislation about professional training requirements. Sisters studied here along with other women who wished to train. Specialist topics were formula food, health care and organised play. The building had accommodation for 50 children with 23 students in training at a time. Each group of children occupied a section of the house with its own nursery, night nursery and other facilities. Requisitioned August 1941 and closed.

Herefordshire

Lower Bullingham

1861–1939 The Company was invited to establish a House of Charity by the de la Barr Bodenhams of Rotherwas. Mrs Bodenham was Countess Irene Dzierzykraj-Morawska whose sister was a Daughter of Charity in Poland. The first Sister Servant was Sister Gabrielle Chatelain, sister of Henriette Chatelain, Sister Servant of Carlisle Place Westminster and the House was called St Elizabeth's. The Sisters ran an elementary mixed school, small orphanages for girls and boys, and boarding schools for boys and girls. The orphanages were closed down for lack of funding and the boarding schools expanded, taking non-Catholics as well as Catholics. Sister Cecily Arundell who was placed here for many years helped the House considerably by buying up all the premises that the Sisters rented and the houses adjoining (almshouses, the Post Office and forge) and an amount of land when the Rotherwas estate was sold in 1912. The schools were evacuated to Croft Castle at the outbreak of the Second World War.

Croft Castle Yarpole

1939–1946 For the duration of the war when the fee-paying school also took boys to the age of 12. After the war the school transferred to Broxwood Court in Herefordshire.

Broxwood Court

1946–54 Temporary home for St Elizabeth's fee-paying school which transferred to Lugwardine in Herefordshire in 1954.

Lugwardine

1954–1984 St Elizabeth's private school was developed at secondary level and became mixed in 1966. It continued until 1973 when the Province applied for it to be re-designated as a comprehensive school within the national secondary school re-organisation undertaken at that time. It became St Mary's Comprehensive School serving Herefordshire in 1973. The Province withdrew in 1984 but the school continues as St Mary's High School, with house names Marillac, De Paul, Labouré, Thouret and Virgo. It has a very strong reputation.

**Hereford
Berrington Street**

1875–1969 St Vincent's House of Charity at the invitation of Mrs Gillow, a wealthy local widow and benefactor, who provided a house for the Sisters to care for the orphans she had been looking after in her own home, and by the parish priest, Canon Dolman OSB. The orphanage was registered in 1879 for 30 children. The Sisters were asked by Canon Dolman, the parish priest of St Francis Xavier's church, to visit in the parish and teach in the girls' school. Teaching gave them access to a wide range of parishioners and they developed a close relationship with the parish. In due course their various works spread down a stretch of Berrington Street. Children were evacuated here during the Second World War. A new school was built in 1970. When the house needed radical updating the Sisters moved to the new parish in Hereford, Our Lady Queen of the Universe (later Queen of Martyrs) which had been established in 1954. The House transferred to Belmont Road in 1969.

Belmont Road no. 74

1969–1989 The House continued to run the children's home; teaching in girls' school; pastoral care. They added hospital visiting, an over-60s' club and a home help service. Some of the community from St Mary's Lugwardine moved here and the Sisters remained active in Hereford despite their age. At the death of the Sister Servant the house was closed.

Wiltshire

**Salisbury
Exeter Street no. 131**

1868–1972 St Elizabeth's Orphanage for Girls', Industrial School and House of Charity. The Sisters were invited to Salisbury by Baroness Elizabeth Herbert of Lea, writer, philanthropist and widow of politician Sidney Herbert who was Secretary of State during the Crimean War and a great friend of Florence Nightingale. The family seat was Wilton House Salisbury. Elizabeth Herbert had been received into the Catholic Church in 1866 and was in Henry Manning's circle but she is best known for her support of Cardinal Vaughan's St Joseph's Foreign Missionary College which was located close to where the Sisters opened their Provincial House in 1885. Although the Herbert family were not Catholics, Salisbury itself had a strong recusant history and A.W. Pugin was received into the Church here. Initially the Sisters lived in De Vaux Place, moving to a property in Exeter Street close to St Osmund's church, bought by Lady Herbert for St Elizabeth's Industrial School and made over to the Province. The property was described as 'a comfortable old-fashioned house with a garden running down to the river, with gardener's cottage, good stables and a coach house'. All of these were converted for the industrial school and orphanage with Poor Law school. The Sisters visited in St Osmund's parish and taught in the parish elementary school (see below). In 1870 St Elizabeth's Industrial School was certified for 50 girls, increasing to 125. A chapel was built in 1888, a new school with additional dormitories in 1898, and a public laundry in 1915. Baroness von Hugel, Lady Herbert's daughter, sent and financially supported many girls in the school.

A holiday house in Boscombe was bought for the children of the school. In 1923 with the educational re-organisation of industrial schools it was closed and the small number of remaining residents were moved to St Joseph's Home in Sheffield run by the Sisters. The parish school expanded into part of the vacated building. The Province orphanage continued until 1960 when it too was closed and a term-time-only remand hostel for 24 girls under the inspection of the Home Office was conducted by the Sisters. The Province gave up this work in 1972 when it could no longer afford to maintain the building adequately. Sisters moved to Fowler's Hill (below) and 131 Exeter Street became the property of St Osmund's parish.

1868–1980 St Osmund's Elementary School with approximately 140 children transferred to 131 Exeter Street when St Elizabeth's Industrial School closed. It became an elementary extended school with pupils to secondary age on four sites and had 400 pupils at the end of the Second World War. In the early 1960s provision was re-organised with separate provision at St Joseph's Catholic Secondary School at Laverstock for secondary aged children. The last Sister to teach in St Osmund's left in 1980 but the former dormitory is still in use, divided into two classrooms for Years 5 and 6 in St Osmund's Catholic Primary School.

| Fowler's Hill | 1972–1982 The Sisters moved here from 131 Exeter Street to continue parish work and teaching in St Osmund's School. Sisters left Salisbury in 1982. |

| Wardour | 1887–1965 Sisters were invited to open a small House of Charity by Baroness Arundell of Wardour (New Wardour Castle) whose daughter Cecily Mary was a Daughter of Charity in England. Wardour had a strongly recusant history and had had a Catholic parish and a Catholic school since 1780, originally for children of families working on the family estate. Sisters taught in the school, which had become a 'continuation school' with pupils to the age of 15, until 1964. Wardour Catholic Primary School continues. |

YORKSHIRE

Bradford and Leeds, Hull, Sheffield and York.

Bradford and Leeds

| Boston Spa Wetherby | 1874–1998 St John's Catholic Institution for the Deaf and Dumb (name changed to St John's Catholic School for the Deaf in 1953) is known as 'Boston Spa' in British Sign Language. This institution was transferred from Handsworth, Woodhouse near Sheffield where it had begun in 1870. It had been founded by Belgian priest and pioneer deaf educationalist Désiré de Haerne as the only residential provision for Catholic deaf children in England. In 1871 the Sisters were invited to manage St John's, which they did for 128 years. From the outset it was a national Catholic charity overseen by a board of trustees. Its earliest Secretary was the renowned Sheffield architect Matthew Hadfield, father of two Daughters of Charity. Pupils came from all over the country, Ireland and overseas. By 1900 it was the third largest residential specialist provision in the country with 110 boys, 87 girls, 8 Sisters and 13 auxiliary teachers. In the early decades a mixed-method of oralism and manualism was used, not least because de Haerne advocated the mixed approach. The first Sisters were sent to Belgium and Italy to learn something of the pedagogy used. They also visited other institutes in England. Before the 1950s the emphasis was on providing care and training rather than education. In his published life story, Kevin Fitzgerald, who lived at St John's between 1943 and 1951, was critical of the lack of educational aspiration of the school and of the domination of the oralist method of learning which had been introduced after the war at the demand of parents. From the 1950s many changes in approach and emphasis took place. By the 1960s Sisters regularly won awards for their teaching and Boston Spa developed an international reputation. A St Vincent's Unit was set up for children who could not cope in the main school. Because the Sisters also ran Tollcross Institute in Scotland, another specialist institution, and were involved in similar provision in Ireland, the work with deaf children and adults became a very significant dimension of the Province's ministry. The Sisters withdrew in 1998. The school continues as St John's Catholic School for the Deaf, a day and boarding school for hearing impaired pupils aged three to nineteen with specialist school status and rated 'outstanding' by Ofsted. |

| Leeds Southwaite Lane no. 15 | 1986–1995 The Sisters were in two addresses in the Seacroft district. The first was a tower block flat at 22 Parkway Court which proved too small and they transferred to 15 Southwaite Lane. A wide range of ministries were carried out: visiting, hospital chaplaincy at St James Hospital, adult education, confraternities and Vincentian formation, and classroom assistant in Yorkshire Martyrs Secondary School in Bradford. The parishes involved were Our Lady of Perpetual Succour and St Columba's. The Province had made |

416

a commitment to this mission for six years which was extended to nine. They had an offer of a council house in Holmewood Bradford and agreed that the rented house in Seacroft should close. The House was transferred to Bradford.

Bradford Holmewood Road no. 61	1995–1999 The Sisters were granted a council house to live and work with people in need in St Columba's parish which is largely made up of two council estates: Holmewood and Bierley. Work included ministries in Catholic children's homes; visiting and parish pastoral ministries; hospital chaplaincy at the psycho-geriatric hospital; deaf awareness and signing courses; and support work in Catholic secondary school.

Hull

Hull Wright Street nos. 10, 71, 72	1890–1909 St Vincent's Boys' Home. The Sisters were invited by Canon Sullivan of St Charles parish who gave the house in Wright Street for Sisters and 30 boys. At the time this was the only boys' Catholic orphanage in the Middlesbrough Diocese and soon proved to be inadequate in size. It also provided a home for those who had started work. Canon Sullivan set about raising funds for a purpose-built home but died in 1900 before this was completed. Fund-raising was undertaken by the local Catholic Men's Committee which kept St Vincent's open and enabled developments. It was a considerable achievement when the boys' home was transferred to new premises in Queen's Road in 1909 (see below).
	The Sisters also took charge of the girls' elementary school and infant school in 1893. In 1904 they opened a working girls' hostel and night shelter (transferred to 10 Wright Street 1910); established the Children of Mary; and ran weekly mothers' meetings. In 1911 71 Wright Street was bought for the Sisters by convert Catholic Lady Jessica Sykes, wife of Lord Sykes of Sledmere House, landowner and baronet in the East Riding. They opened a clinic which ran until it had to be closed during the First World War. The Province bought no 72 Wright Street in 1923. The Sisters left Wright Street when it was badly bombed in 1941.
Queen's Road	1909–1971 St Vincent's Home transferred from Wright Street. The Sisters also took charge of the elementary boys' school at St Vincent's parish in Queen's Road and visited in the parish. A working boys' hostel for aftercare also opened in 1909 (closed 1934). St Vincent's was requisitioned and the boys evacuated to Scarborough during the war. When it closed in 1971 the Sisters transferred to Westbourne Avenue, with two nearby family group homes.
Westbourne Avenue no. 41	1971–1992 Resident House for Sisters working in the parish and school. Subsidence in the property and a re-orientation of mission led the Sisters to transfer to Bransholme.
Bransholme Cosford Garth no. 36	1993–2006 The Sisters' House was a five-bedroomed council house in a deprived area of Bransholme, where they undertook pastoral ministries and visiting in the parish of St Mary Queen of Martyrs. The Sisters moved from this part of Hull to be part of a new mission and evangelisation team with local priests and people (see below).
Boulevard no. 200	2007 continuing. Sisters live in the former presbytery of St Wilfrid's parish and are involved in parish ministry, evangelisation and teaching English to refugees.
Annandale Road no. 96	2014 continuing. A group of Sisters was missioned to St Stephen's parish when the Congregation of Jesus withdrew, partly to ministry through the St Stephen's Neighbourhood Centre set up by the CJs in 2002 to meet the social and other neds of people in the Greatfield area and partly to form an evangelisation team with the DCs at St Wilfrid's and with clergy in the area.

Sheffield

Sheffield Solly Street nos 151 and 222 then Red Hill	1857–1938 House of Charity. **This was the Daughters' first House in Britain after the closure of the House in Salford in 1849.** The Sisters were missioned to collaborate with the Vincentians who had charge of St Vincent's mission to the Irish community in Sheffield. The chief benefactors in Sheffield were the Duke of Norfolk's family, the architectural Hadfield family and the Gainsfords of Darnall Hall. The ministry of the Sisters at Solly Street was to visit in the White Croft district, workhouse and hospital. The Sisters began the Children of Mary and other confraternities for women and evening schools open to all. In 1864 No 151 Solly Street was outgrown and the Sisters moved to 222 close to the north end of Red Hill. In 1878 they moved again to a larger house in Red Hill which had been the former Vincentian presbytery. From here they ran a hostel for working young women as well as the schools (1000 children by 1896) and visiting in the district. Between

1913–1925 a Catholic working boys' hostel for homeless boys run by the Sisters and offering training in trades was run in Solly Street in several houses.

Sheffield Howard Hill	1861–1886 St Joseph's Girls' Reformatory founded by committee of leading Yorkshire laity and the Bishop of Beverley with support of other northern bishops. It was their wish to have Home Office reformatory provision for Catholic girls from across the north of England to prevent them having to be sent to other reformatories. RJ Gainsford of Darnall Hall played a leading role in funding St Joseph's at Howard Hill, supported by the Duke of Norfolk. The Management Committee was chaired by Hon Charles Langdale MP, a leading Catholic layman of Houghton Hall in East Yorkshire whose sister, Mary, was a Daughter of Charity and later a member of the Province's Council. St Joseph's Reformatory was certified in July 1861 and re-certified in 1875 for 120 girls, mostly between the ages of nine and sixteen. In 1887 Sister Elizabeth Crawford who was Sister Servant here for many years obtained the Committee's agreement to close St Joseph's as a Reformatory and have it re-certified as an Industrial School because this classification gave more scope for educational work with the younger end of the age range. As a reformatory St Joseph's was regarded as a model of good practice by the state Inspectors for its educational work, order and what they called 'good sense' in responding to the girls. Its chapel, St Joseph's, served Catholics in the Walkley area as a Mass centre for 130 years before it was closed. The elementary school conducted on the site was also used by local people. When population growth meant it became too small the Sisters built a new St Joseph's School on land purchased by Sister Monica Weld who succeeded Sister Crawford as Sister Servant in 1897. It served Catholic children in the Walkley and Crookes areas. Sister Weld was Sister Servant for 23 years and in her time 15 young women from the school became nuns and sisters in other communities. In 1925 the Industrial School was recertified for 100 girls but changes in government policies meant that the Home Office asked the Sisters to transfer the 38 remaining residents to Blackbrook House in St Helens and, at the same time, to take on responsibility for Blackbrook House from another religious community (see North-West, St Helens).

1935–1974 St Joseph's Howard Hill became a certified home for 50 girls with severe mental and intellectual disability. In 1974 the facilities were turned over to the local Hospital Management Committee and the Sisters transferred to Ashdell Road.

Ashdell Road	1974–1989 Sisters continued to teach at St Joseph's Primary School in Howard Hill until 1981 when falling rolls closed the school and children transferred to St Vincent's in Solly Street. Sisters moved to St Ronan's Road.
Queen's Road no. 524	1989–2013 The focus of the work of this House was St Wilfrid's Drop-in Centre (now St Wilfrid's Centre) in Queen's Road, established to work with homeless, vulnerable and socially excluded people. The centre was the idea of Monsignor William Kilgannon of St Wilfrid's parish who invited the Sisters into partnership. It opened in 1991 with Sister Evelyn Warnock as first Director, succeeded by Sister Kathleen Page. The Centre expanded rapidly, extending into the old semi-derelict church within a couple of years. St Wilfrid's met a need and its facilities and services grew until it occupied three floors with a spacious recreation hall, interview rooms, kitchens, café, showers, and workrooms for skills development. The centre has always been inclusive and has reached a wide range of individuals, the majority of whom will not or cannot engage with other providers and many of whom have mental health needs. Three-quarters of clients are men. The Sisters led and fashioned the approach at St Wilfrid's, building up a strong team of volunteers who have identified with it over a long period. In 2005 the Province was no longer able to provide a Sister for the role of Director and Mr Kevin Bradley, who had worked with both Sisters, became Director. Under his leadership the centre continues to grow and adapt. Sisters resident in Sheffield continued to be involved at the centre, only withdrawing when they left Sheffield altogether. Other works from this House included working for the SVP furniture store and parish visiting. The Province withdrew from Sheffield on 20 September 2013 after 166 years' presence.
Sheffield Kirk Edge	1871–1887 Industrial School/Home. The Vincentians in Sheffield wanted an industrial school for boys to parallel provision for girls at St Joseph's Howard Hill. They gained support from the Duke of Norfolk to convert two houses at Kirk Edge and asked the Sisters to take charge. It was never a good location because of remoteness and problems with the water but the Sisters kept it open for 16 years before the decision was made to close on grounds of unsuitability. There is scant information about this House and some contradictory evidence about its status but the 1881 Census shows that there were six

Sisters living there with a female teacher, two dressmakers, a farm labourer, two servants and 76 girls, almost all aged between ten and fifteen. When it closed the remaining girls were transferred to the Daughters' Industrial School at Howard's Hill in Sheffield. The buildings, which belonged to the diocese, were used for various purposes and were then left empty. In 1911 they were taken over by the Carmelites from Notting Hill Carmel who founded the Monastery of the Holy Spirit and continue to live here.

Sheffield Woodhouse	1870–75 Catholic School for the Deaf at Woodhouse. The founder, Canon de Hearne, met the Sisters in Sheffield and invited them to take over the School which transferred to Boston Spa in 1875 (see Yorkshire, Boston Spa p. 30).

York

York George Street no. 14	1886–1903 House of Charity. Daughters were invited by Lord and Lady Kerr who worked with Canon Brady of St George's parish. Lady Anne Kerr was sister of Sister Etheldreda Howard. Her husband, Major-General Lord Ralph Kerr, was stationed in York at this time. Many Irish migrants lived in the area of St George's parish; the Sisters were asked to visit in the parish and in 1888 to take charge of the school in Margaret Street. Here they gave dinners to about 200 pupils each week. The Sisters established evening classes for adults and clubs for boys and girls as well as a social club for mothers. The school took over a former Wesley Chapel in Chapel Row in 1897. The Sisters transferred to a larger house in Fishergate when these works outgrew this small terraced house.
Fishergate Villa Fishergate no. 29	1903–1972 House of Charity. Fishergate Villa is a large detached early nineteenth-century house which afforded ample room to develop the Sisters' works in York. It was bought by Lady Gwendolyn Mary Herries who married Henry Fitzalan Howard, 14th Duke of Norfolk, brother of Sister Etheldreda Howard and Lady Anne Kerr. The Sisters opened a crèche and nursery school for children of working women and continued their other activities. By 1900 there were 500 children on the roll of St George's and the Sisters had added Children of Mary and other sodalities, a boys' club and gym, and a football team. In 1921 the schools had grown to 750 children. The Sisters continued to teach in the schools and to visit in the parish but their numbers and the range of their work gradually contracted. In 1972 they moved to a smaller house in Lawrence Street.
Lawrence Street no. 102	1972–1992 Sisters living here continued with parish work and St George's Catholic Primary School until they withdrew in 1992. A plaque in the church commemorates their 106 years of service in York. The school continues.

SCOTLAND

Arrangement of the information about Houses in Scotland

Scotland has been divided into regions as follows:
- Ayrshire, Dumfries and Galloway
- Edinburgh, Fife and Lothian
- Glasgow, Lanarkshire and Renfrewshire
- Highlands

Within this regional arrangement the information is organised by place and chronology.

AYRSHIRE, DUMFRIES AND GALLOWAY

Ayrshire
(in chronological order)

Dumfries Shakespeare Street	1892–1968 The Sisters were invited by Dean Turner (later Bishop Turner) and Lady Herries (Angela Fitzalan Howard) of Caerlaverock Castle, Dumfries and of Everingham in the East Riding of Yorkshire who was sister-in-law to two Constable-Maxwell Daughters of Charity and cousin of Sister Etheldreda Howard. Lord Herries built the cathedral church of St Andrew at Dumfries and the family paid for the Daughters of Charity to visit, prepare adults for the sacraments, run sodalities, instruct converts and to teach in St Andrew's parish elementary school. This school was built in 1842 (first Catholic school opened in Scotland since the Reformation) by the Maxwells of Terregles. The Sisters' house was next door to the cathedral and was owned by the parish. Five Sisters arrived in July 1892 and at one time all five were teaching in the secondary and primary schools, reduced to three in 1921 after the incorporation of Catholic schools under the Education Department. By 1950 the Sisters were running the Guild of the Immaculate Conception, Angels Guild, Children of Mary, Union of Catholic Mothers' Guild and the Needlework Guild which made clothing for those in need. Visiting formed a very large part of their work. The parish of St Andrew's was divided to form a new parish of St Teresa's, Lochside, and a Sister was appointed as Parish Visiting Sister there. The Sisters' house was damaged by the fire which completely destroyed St Andrew's cathedral in 1961. Sisters transferred to Brook Street to a property owned by the Province.
Brook Street no. 31	1968–2007 The Sisters continued their work of teaching, parish visiting and feeding the needy from their new House. In 1979 the last Sister finished in St Andrew's school and in the same year a Sister was appointed as Sister Chaplain to the newly-built General Hospital and to the psychiatric hospital. When the Sisters withdrew from Dumfries they had been an active presence in the community continuously for 115 years. More than 200 people attended the farewell Mass celebrated by the Bishop with the Bishop Emeritus and 16 priests of the Diocese who had served the local parishes.
Ayrshire Troon	1915–1962 The Sisters were invited by Rev Thomas Aquinas Hayes to open a House of Charity and undertake the running of the elementary school, visiting in the parish, catechesis and sodalities. Hayes had completed his training for the priesthood at All Hallows College in Dublin, a Vincentian College, and arrived in Troon in 1909. There was a Catholic school-chapel (1886) but no church. The Church of Our Lady of the Assumption and St Madden was consecrated in 1911, the money having been left to the parish by the 3rd Marquis of Bute in 1900, a convert to Catholicism. His wife, Gwendolen Fitzalan-Howard was sister to Angela Fitzalan Howard (Lady Herries who invited the Daughters to Dumfries in 1892) and she was Sister Etheldreda Howard's niece. In Troon the Sisters established a thriving Children of Mary sodality, a Boys' Guild and various evening classes. They lived in a semi-detached house which was owned by the parish.
Girvan	1999–2004 A holiday house for Sisters and relatives.
Mossblown St Anne's Presbytery	2000–2006 This House was originally opened as an annexe of the Dumfries House but was erected in its own right in 2002. The Sisters' main ministry was the pastoral administration and spiritual animation of this rural parish in the absence of a resident priest. In addition

they were involved in the work of SPRED (Special Religious Education) an international Catholic initiative developed in the Archdiocese of Chicago to integrate individuals with learning difficulties into the liturgy and parish community through catechesis and formation. Subsequently SPRED leaders trained in the SPRED method and became directors of programmes within their own diocese. It became embedded in five Scottish dioceses. When the Sisters withdrew from St Anne's parish they transferred to Ayr.

Ayr Fotheringham Road no. 26	2006 The Sisters continue with the ministries they had developed in Mossblown, working with the SVP.

EDINBURGH, FIFE
AND LOTHIAN

Edinburgh, Dundee, Dunfermline, Midlothian, Inveresk, Perth.

Edinburgh

The early years of the Daughter's history in Edinburgh are not altogether clear in terms of locations. This is partly because there was at first some difficulty in their relations with a senior priest to which they did not wish to draw attention in writing their records, and partly because, like many of their contemporaries, they moved between nearby houses until they found their preferred location. It was also the case that they had several houses and works at the same time which are not clearly demarcated in the remaining records.

Edinburgh
Albany Street

1894–1898 House of Charity in response to request from Canon Donlevy, parish priest of St Mary's cathedral, for Sisters for visiting in the parish, teaching in the elementary school, and to establish an academy for girls. Because in 1893 Pope Leo XIII had asked the Superioress General of the Company to assist in rekindling the faith in Scotland, she accepted Canon Donlevy's invitation. Their work included visiting, a pharmacy with a female doctor in attendance, sodalities, prison visiting and the parochial school. Clashes with Canon Donlevy about the internal management of the Sisters' House led him to dismiss and replace them. The Sisters left Edinburgh for a short period but soon returned first to Windmill Street (1898), which was unsuitable, and then to St John Street.

Edinburgh
St John Street no. 11

1898–1911 House of Charity St Patrick's. This foundation commenced in 1898 at the request of Archbishop Angus McDonald who invited the Sisters to visit the poor and take charge of the dispensary. St Patrick's was the oldest parish in Edinburgh, in the heart of Old Edinburgh, and was the centre for Irish migrants in the Cowgate area of the city. The pharmacy, which operated until 1911, had a woman doctor in attendance. In 1903 the Sisters opened St Anne's Girls' Home at this address with the Archbishop and Monsignor Grady as Patrons. It was for 20 young women who were working in the city's shops, factories and laundries as well as those temporarily out of work. This later became a separate House with its own Sister Servant (see below). The House moved to George Square which was quieter.

George Square no. 26

1911–1971 In this new location there were changes and adaptations to the Sisters' work. Between 1916 and 1928 the George Square Sisters took on probation work in the police courts working to prevent Catholic young women arrested for prostitution or drunkenness being imprisoned by finding them alternative housing and work under the auspices of the Edinburgh Catholic Women's Rescue Work. In 1928 'owing to various difficulties encountered by our Sisters in the efficient discharge of their duties in connection with the Edinburgh Women's Rescue Work, on account of undue interference by certain ladies, it is considered best to withdraw the Sister.' In 1918 the Sisters took over teaching at St Patrick's boys' school which had been previously run by the Sisters of Mercy. Four Sisters taught here. By 1921 a small hostel for young working women was in operation and in 1928 Monsignor Morris offered a plot of land for the Sisters to build another house. In 1940 the Sisters were asked to give temporary accommodation to women who had been bombed in London. They took 12 who remained until the end of the war. The hostel remained the main work until 1971 when the Sisters moved to Ferry Road, Muirhouse and the hostel closed. The Province owned the property.

There is some confusion in the archival record about the relationship between the house that had been opened in St John Street and that in George Square. There may have been more than one property in George Square over time. Transferred to Ferry Road.

Ferry Road nos 629 and 631

1971–2006 St Vincent's transferred from George Square. Four Sisters lived here in the 1980s. The main ministries from this House were parish visiting (St Paul's, St Margaret Mary's and St Patrick's), social work, hospital chaplaincy and the organisation of diocesan services for people with learning disabilities. Playgroup work was undertaken for four years and then handed over to parents. In 1992 the Sisters moved out of 631. The House at 629 later transferred to Muirhouse Avenue.

Muirhouse Avenue no. 4 St Paul's Presbytery	2003–2014 The Sisters lived in St Paul's Presbytery and continued parish ministry at St Paul's, along with parish ministry at Holy Cross. Sisters' ministries included: Directorship of SPRED (Special Religious Education); special education at Rosewell; ministry to deaf children; ministry to homeless people in Edinburgh; and engagement in community forums and neighbourhood partnership action groups.
Edinburgh Minto Street no. 48 and Upper Gray Street no. 9	1903–1921 St Vincent's boys' and St Mary's girls' orphanages taken on at the request of Archbishop James Smith and a number of priests. The children were accommodated between two houses in Minto Street and Upper Gray Street, neither of which had much land for expansion or garden for the children. There is a lack of precision about the houses and dates for each. The girls' and boys' homes started as mixed but were separated by 1904. Another orphanage, St Teresa's, was managed for the diocese nearby by another community of sisters. There were six Sisters living in Minto Street in 1909 one of whom visited in St Columba's parish. The House received income from Canon Mulland and Father Gray. In 1913 a Mr Wilson inherited the large mansion of Restalrig beside St Ninian's church and offered it to the Archbishop on lease at half the market rate for the Edinburgh orphanages and the work of the Sisters. The Sisters decided to accept the house for the girls' orphanage and refuge but to retain Minto Street and Upper Gray Street for the boys' home and for visiting work in the parish. They drew up a new contract with the Archbishop for Restalrig and moved the St Mary's and St Teresa's girls there in 1913. The boys remained until 1921 when they were moved to a larger house with gardens at Blacket Avenue (see below). 9 Upper Gray Street was sold.
Restalrig Edinburgh	1913–1933/34 (see above) St Mary's Children's Home for 40 girls at the request of the Archbishop. The children were supported by the Bell Trust Fund with a supplement for three years by Lady Anne Kerr, sister of Sister Etheldreda Howard and wife of Robert Kerr, 10th Marquis of Lothian and by the Archbishop from his personal wealth. The home lacked public funding and had been supported with £520 a year from the Bell Trust which could no longer support the work by 1920. The Sisters had to find other ways to support themselves. In 1921 they opened a home for mothers and babies and in the same year a Sister was appointed to teach in the parish school which provided a regular income for the House. The number of girls was reduced but the Sisters continued to try to make ends meet. The new Archbishop (Andrew McDonald, appointed in 1929) seems to have decided to try to find a religious community willing to undertake running a girls' orphanage at less cost. In 1931 he informed the Sisters that he would not need their services but for various reasons it was a further two years before the transfer to the Sisters of Nazareth was made and the home at Restalrig closed.
Blacket Avenue	1921–1931 St Vincent's Boys' Home. The Province bought two houses when St Vincent's moved here helped by a loan of £1500 from the Mother House in Paris and £500 from Provincial House and two £200 legacies from local benefactors. The Sisters also ran a boys' school at Blacket Avenue but lost this work when the diocese appointed a man as head teacher (at this time the Company did not allow Sisters to work under a head who was not a Sister) and it was clear to the Sisters that the rector of the parish preferred lay teachers. Closure of this home was part of the same change of diocesan policy as for the girls' homes. There were 27 boys resident at the time of closure. The property was sold by the Province in 1936.
Edinburgh Morningside Falcon Gardens	1910–1966 House of Charity in St Peter's parish for visiting and teaching in the parish school. The Sisters were invited by Father John Gray, parish priest of the mission which had been opened only the year before. Originally the Sisters were paid a stipend and given accommodation by the parish but from 1918 when all Catholic school teachers' salaries were paid by the local education authority they paid rent to the parish for the house. Three Sisters taught in the school. The Sisters established the Children of Mary, Girl Guides, and Boy Scouts. They withdrew in 1966 because of the fall in vocations and a change of works, although one Sister continued to teach at St Peter's from the George Square House.
Dundee Overgate Street no. 51	1905–1974. The Sisters were invited by Monsignor Turner, Vicar General of the diocese in association with the local Conference of the SVP. They wanted the Sisters to work among the working-class community particularly with women mill workers, many of whom were Irish migrants. The Sisters opened St Vincent's Hostel for working women; visited in the parish; established guilds and sodalities; and undertook other work given to them by the priests. Transferred to Magdalen Yard Road in 1908.
Magdalen Yard Road no. 26	1908–1974 In 1908 the Sisters added a day nursery at 14 Park Place for the children of women mill workers and were visiting in four large parishes. In 1917 they ran a refuge for destitute children that was financially supported by the SVP. Over time the refuge replaced St Vincent's

Hostel because the need was judged greater. Around 1920 the Sisters undertook prison visiting and were involved in court and probation work (the Police Court Rescue Scheme for younger women who might be re-housed away from their home district or 'placed' in work, including in England). A Girls' Club was established in 1938. The first house was rented but the Province bought the property in Magdalen Yard. Both were close to the docks.

Midlothian Rosewell	1924–1999 St Joseph's Hospital and Home. In 1924 the Province bought Whitehill House close to the village of Rosewell, ten miles from Edinburgh. It was a large Jacobean revival-style country house built by Colonel Ramsay, owner of local mines and brickworks. It had been used as a Red Cross hospital during the First World War and was then empty. The Sisters' put in a bid for the house for the purpose of developing a hospital and home for children with profound learning difficulties, often combined with physical disabilities, for example children with cerebral palsy. St Joseph's was licensed by the Board of Control and run by a Management Board. Many building and facilities were added over time until it became a large complex. By default, as some patients with no alternative homes stayed on beyond childhood, St Joseph's became a provision for adults as well as children. As the number of residents grew the facilities expanded and included: accommodation for 100 males (1932); chapel and recreation rooms (1940); nurses' home and concert hall (1964); St Joseph's Special School (1969); children's unit (1971); and swimming pool (1981). Referrals were made from all over Scotland. At its peak Rosewell (as it was usually known by the Sisters) cared for 300 residents. In 1942 the Province established St Joseph's Training School for Nurses for the Mental Handicapped Register and was approved for the Enrolled Nurses' Course in 1962 which continued into the 1970s. The resident doctor, Sister Price, was a Daughter. There were many adaptations to the social and health care provided as standards changed and new approaches to people with physical and learning disabilities developed away from a medicalised model towards supported independent living in the community. Since the 1970s St Joseph's Rosewell has earned an international reputation for the care provided e.g. in 1995 it housed the first Nordoff-Robbins music therapy unit in Scotland. Pope John Paul II went to Rosewell in June 1982 as part of his visit to Britain. The home closed altogether in 1998, a new development of flats and small houses having been built in the village of Rosewell for former residents and new clients. The Province established St Joseph's Services, a licensed agency to co-ordinate care in the community for people with learning disabilities. The new centre was opened by the Scottish Health Minister. With the closure of the home, the Sisters' residence for this and other works moved to Delta Place in Inveresk in 1999, convenient for Rosewell and for Edinburgh. Whitehill House itself was sold for development as residential accommodation.
Inveresk, East Lothian Delta Place no. 6	1999–2014 The Sisters continued to serve at St Joseph's Rosewell as Director of Services and in pastoral care service. Other Sisters in this house were involved in pastoral care for homeless people, hospital chaplaincy and as Vocations Director and National Catechetical Advisor for Deaf Children. St Joseph's Services is based at 70–72 Carnethie Street, Rosewell.
Rosewell, Midlothian Carnethie Street	2014 continuing. The Sisters transferred to Carnethie Street from Inveresk to continue their work in association with St Joseph's Service.
Dunfermline Abbey Gardens	1898–1991 A House of Charity founded against a background of anti-Papal agitation at the opening of the first permanent Catholic church in Dunfermline in 1896. Dunfermline is the location of the shrine of St Margaret of Scotland and therefore a place of significance for all Scots, as for Catholics. The Sisters' House was next to St Margaret's tomb in the grounds of Dunfermline Abbey (a Benedictine foundation). The Sisters were invited by Canon Mullan to manage the school, for general works and parish visiting. They established the Children of Mary, and working boys' night schools. The house was rented from the parish and paid for by the Sisters from their teachers' stipends. Mathilde Hallé (the daughter of Sir Charles Hallé, conductor and founder of the Hallé orchestra in Manchester) who was Sister Servant in the early twentieth century (d.1926) is buried locally at the request of the people. From the 1950s the Sisters became more focused on the parish and less on the school.
Viewfield Terrace no. 24	The Sisters moved to Viewfield Terrace in 1957 at the time of the opening of the mission of Our Lady of Lourdes church in Aberdour Road which became a parish in 1964. They lived here until transferring to a smaller house at Arthur Street in 1991.
Arthur Street	1991–2000 This was a Sisters' residence for those involved in parish ministries such as sacramental preparation, liturgy and bereavement support; hospital chaplaincy at Queen Margaret Hospital; and parish groups including the SVP.
Perth Stormont Street	1925–1935 St Joseph's House of Charity was opened for the purpose of teaching in St John the Baptist parish school and visiting in the parishes at the request of Bishop Toner of

Dundee to replace the Sisters of Mercy. The House was provided by the parish. Sisters ran sodalities and confraternities and a girls' club. In 1935 the Sisters moved to the next street, Melville Street, next to the parish church and school.

Perth Melville Street no. 16	1935–1982 St Louise's. This House had been the former chapel-house and had been the residence of the parish priest who offered it to the Sisters. One Sister visited in St John's parish, two taught in St John's elementary school. They ran the Catholic Needlework Guild, a club for Irish domestic servants 'who felt lonely in a strange land', a mothers' meeting, Children of Mary, Holy Angels Guild, and senior and junior girls' clubs. The Sisters added visiting to two new parishes, St Mary Magdalen's and Our Lady's, and visiting in the maternity unit of Perth Royal Infirmary. The parishioners were strong supporters of the Sisters' works in Ethiopia. The House was closed and the Sisters withdrawn as a result of the Province-wide re-assessment of works that took place in 1980/81 due to the contracting number of Sisters.

GLASGOW, LANARKSHIRE AND RENFREWSHIRE

Glasgow Whitevale Street no. 21	1887–1912 The Daughters were invited by Archbishop Charles Eyre to run a children's refuge and temporary night shelter for destitute and street children. It was managed by a committee of priests and laymen and was supported by the St Patrick's Kilsyth Conference of the SVP. For its first eight years the Conference gave 20 per cent of funds to support the refuge. There were also regular parish collections to support this work. In 1912 the refuge was transferred to a new building called Bellevue at Rutherglen in Glasgow.
Greenhill Road no. 62 Bellevue Rutherglen	1912–1961 At Bellevue the Sisters continued to run the refuge for boys and girls in acute need and for emergency destitution cases. The property was owned by the diocese and the work was under diocesan and SVP management. Families placed their children at Bellevue when they could not cope and removed them when their circumstances changed. There were many benefactors (SVP, crib collections, charitable collections and parental contributions in some cases) but there was always insufficient funding, and at times the there were large debts owed by the archdiocese. In the 1940s the Sister Servant reported paying off £3,300 of the £6,000 outstanding debt and being in a position to improve the building with the help of many individuals. In 1950s there was accommodation for 130 children with 10 Sisters but more children were accepted because of the policy of not refusing Catholic children. In 1959 there were still 97 girls and 89 boys. By 1961 Bellevue was judged not to meet required building standards and was closed. The chapel furnishings, including the altar, passed to Langbank Junior Seminary (see below).
Glasgow Tollcross	1911–1986 St Vincent's Deaf and Blind Institute (later re-named School for Blind and Deaf Children) was built and managed by the Sisters throughout its entire existence. Mr Smith-Sligo of Inzievar gave eight acres of land and Thomas Tiernan of Glasgow left £4000 to Sister Anne Farrell for the purpose of building a specialist institute for children with special needs in blind and deaf education who had been living in Smyllum Park orphanage (see below). Four Sisters were transferred from Smyllum Park with the children. An adult female department opened in 1913 and a workshop for adult blind men in 1914 in Partick, both of these involving the transfer of adults from Smyllum who had grown up in the orphanage but had no other home to go to. The Sisters opened workshops for the adult men in the Parkhead area. Sisters took over managing and teaching in the parish elementary school in 1916 and added parish visiting in 1919. The School came under the Education Board in 1925. Extensions and equipment were developed with loans from Paris and from Mill Hill central funds. St Vincent's, which was highly regarded, was visited by Helen Keller, the famous American deaf-blind author and radical political activist, in 1932. The hostel for adult blind women was closed c.1945 when most of the women had dispersed to live independent lives, leaving only those who preferred to stay with the Sisters. In 1965 the Strathclyde Authority extended the residential school for teaching of deaf children with a specially constructed building that included wall and floor features to minimise sound and enhance hearing. In 1970 a Sister was trained in social work for blind people and worked in the Archdiocese of Glasgow. When the residential school building was demolished in 1986 the teaching of deaf children and blind children continued in the school and one Sister continued teaching there until 1997. At this point the remaining blind pupils were transferred to units in mainstream schools. Sister Ailish Massey played a leading part in the development of a resource (Contact) for staff working with children who are deaf-blind. St Vincent's School for the Deaf continued until 2010 when pupil numbers were no longer viable and the school closed.

Glasgow Wilton Crescent (then Street) nos 67, 71–75, 79, 85	1913–1991 The Sisters ran a domestic training home for young Highland women and a home for working professional women at the request of Lady Encombe and Mrs Calder, whose project this was and who were financially responsible for it. Rents from the working women were intended to cover the costs of trainees who kept house and cooked for them. However, the arrangement never worked financially. When Lady Encombe ceased paying the Sisters' stipends (1917) the Sisters adapted to other works and remained. Five Sisters visited St Columba's, St Roch's, Garngad and St Patrick's, Partick parishes (1921); two of the Sisters ran dispensaries and nursed poor people in their own homes and meals were provided for homeless men. The Province bought two more houses in Wilton Street in 1919 and there was development into new activities, including teaching at St Columba's (1921). In 1922 the domestic trainees were transferred to Whitevale Street, Glasgow and a private nursing home was opened (see below). It seems not to have prospered and in 1930 was closed and the hostel training scheme was re-started. By 1938 the Wilton Street House actually comprised six houses and had become one of the Province's main houses in Britain for parish visiting – at one time nine parishes were visited. Services for the deaf were begun in 1942, developing into a Deaf Club in 1951. In 1967 part of the property in Wilton Street was separated to form a hostel for young women coming out of care in children's homes as a transition to full independence. The Sisters had some expertise in this field and a Sister worked as a Training Officer with the Scottish Catholic Child Care Office. The main hostel closed in 1971 and two houses (79 and 85) were sold. The Sisters lived in 71 and 75; 67 was adapted to create bedsitting accommodation for 12 homeless teenagers. In 1983 a Marian Centre was opened at 71 to spread devotions through the Miraculous Medal and Green Scapular. When the House was closed Sisters transferred to Maryhill Road.
Maryhill Road no. 139	1991–1997 St Columba's parish and St Bernard's parish, Nitshill. The Sisters were involved in a range of pastoral ministries in the parish and beyond. These included: prison visiting at Low Moss Prison, home visiting, sacristy, teaching at St Vincent's School, Tollcross, food and company for homeless men, and social activities for older people. The Sisters who lived and ministered here were themselves 'active retired'.
Glasgow Marham House Broomhill Partick (known as Whiteinch)	1916–1926 St Charles's Institute for children with cognitive disabilities opened at Marham House, Broomhill Partick under the administration of a Committee of Managers appointed by the Archbishop of Glasgow. The Daughters were invited to run the home which accepted up to 63 children from within the area of the Glasgow Archdiocese, funded by the parish and school boards in Ayrshire, Dumbartonshire, Lanarkshire, Renfrewshire and Stirlingshire. The Sisters were never comfortable with the requirement that boys and girls up to the age of sixteen were accommodated in one home with no male to oversee the boys. In 1924 Carstairs House, the former family house of the Monteiths, was bought by the Archdiocese of Glasgow and St Charles's Institute moved here in 1925/26 taking girls only.
Lanarkshire Carstairs	1926–1936 St Charles's Institute for girls with cognitive disabilities. In 1936 the Provincial went to Carstairs to look into reports from the Sisters of interference with the domestic management of the House by the parish priest and then to meet the Archbishop following which the Sisters were withdrawn. The work was taken over by the Sisters of St Joseph of Peace.
Glasgow Whitevale Street no. 21	1922–c.1930 This house, which belonged to the SVP and which had been used for several different purposes since the Sisters last lived here, was re-rented to the Province so that some of the young women from Wilton Crescent hostel (see above) could be re-housed here and space freed up at Wilton Crescent for the nursing home that was being developed there. The women remained at Whitevale Street until they were transferred back into Wilton Crescent. Parish visiting and teaching were also undertaken from Whitevale Street.
Glasgow Pollokshields Albert Drive no. 347 and St Andrew's Drive no. 53	1972 continuing. Children came from Smyllum orphanage (see below) to live in smaller group homes that were closer to the children's own families, in keeping with good practice in childcare. The Province bought two houses close to one another. Family groups always remained small, with siblings kept together. When childcare policies changed in favour of fostering rather than using small group homes, the work of this House in St Andrew's Drive was changed to a home for adults with mild to severe intellectual disabilities in 1983. A Sister provided pastoral ministry to members of the Catholic deaf community. By 1974 the House was residence for three Sisters who visited in St Albert's locally, St Luke's in the Gorbals, Holy Cross parish and two hospitals in the Gorbals district. This visiting team's ministry was extended further to include Our Lady of Consolation parish, the full-time chaplaincy role at South General Hospital and the respite co-ordinator role at the Hospice. The Houses regularly had student Sisters resident for a year. The house in St Andrew's

Drive was sold; Albert Drive continued with parish visiting, teaching, nursing, hospital and hospice chaplaincy, Directorship of the Glasgow club for Catholic deaf adults and residential care of adults with learning difficulties. Louise's Women Centre in the East End of Glasgow, for women in prostitution, was opened in 2001 as a collaboration of the archdiocese, SVP, several orders of sisters and volunteers. DCs were involved over seven years from this House and the House in Paisley. The Sisters in this House now run The Space, a community drop-in centre for residents of Govanhill who include a high percentage of Roma people, asylum seekers and migrants from Slovakia.

Glasgow Easterhouse Kildermorie Rd no. 25 Lochdochart Path	1986–1988 Sisters were missioned here for parish work. Because of the very high level of vandalism in the areas where they were renting, the Sisters were transferred to Lochdochart Path.
Lochdochart Path no. 4	1988–2009 From this residence the Sisters undertook chaplaincy in Belvedere Hospital; parish visiting in St Clare's and St Mark's parishes; visiting elderly people in their homes and in sheltered housing and care homes; adult literacy; and support of deaf people through St Vincent's Centre in Bridgeton. They trained and supported lay people in the setting up of a credit union and co-operative shop in a collaboration with Salesian Fathers and Sisters who were based at St Benedict's parish.
Glasgow Ruchill Bilsland Drive no. 701	1991–1995 Parish work was undertaken from this housing association flat. Visiting in Our Lady of Assumption Ruchill, Ruchill Hospital and St Mark's Carntyne was undertaken, as was working with homeless young people.
Glasgow Barrowfield Dalserf Street	1989–2000 Sisters were missioned here to take on wardenship of a block of flatlets owned by the District Council, who agreed to support the Sisters' proposal for a clustered housing provision for deaf-blind persons. Support for each tenant varied according to need and age. The project was administered by the Archdiocese of Glasgow which employed the Sister-warden. One Sister visited in St Michael's parish where many parishioners were elderly and housebound.
Glasgow Tollcross Park Drumover Drive	2003 continuing. Works from this house have included district nursing and the Govanhill project The Space. The Sisters who at present live in this house are engaged in parish visiting, hospice chaplaincy.
Lanark St Catherine's	1860–2002 St Mary's parish. **The Sisters' first house in Scotland**, originally called St Mary's and then re-named St Catherine's in 1872. Vincentian confrères arrived in Lanark from Ireland to take charge of the parish and new church of St Mary's, which had been built by convert benefactors Mr Bowie and Robert Monteith of Carstairs. Monteith wanted to have Daughters of Charity in the parish and was willing to pay the costs to support a House of three or four Sisters. The Sisters ran the school, visited in the parish and opened a small hospital. In 1860 several houses adjacent to the church (St Vincent's Place) were used as the hospital. A new hospital (St Mary's) was built in 1872 with the financial support of Sister Alice Blundell, and formally opened by Archbishop Charles Eyre in 1874. St Mary's Hospital, open to all, gradually extended: two women's blocks were added (1908), then a children's block and operating theatre (1909), a steam laundry (1916), outpatients and doctor's surgery (1921). In 1919 St Joseph's children's home was started. The Province owned the hospital, the children's home and laundry, and several tenements.
St Mary's	In 1949 the Church made the decision not to integrate the hospital into the state system and a second separate Sisters' House was established to manage the hospital. In 1972 a new building was constructed, overseen by one of the Sisters, the first in Britain to use the terrapin component method. It had 80 beds, 70 of which were contracted to the Health Board. The hospital placed a strong emphasis on an all-round therapeutic approach to well-being and recovery: there was a chapel, occupational therapy, social events, a library, shop, art and handicraft, lounges and gardens. St Mary's was closed in 2002 during NHS re-organisation and was later demolished.
Lanark Bannatyne Street no. 68 and Gavel Lane no. 8	2008 continuing. St Catherine's Registered Care Home. Opposite St Catherine's is Ozanam House which is on the second floor of the converted presbytery of the church, and which is used for retired, active Sisters. Gavel Lane, a short distance from St Catherine's, is also for retired, active Sisters.
Lanark Smyllum Park	1864–1981 Smyllum Park estate was bought by Robert Monteith of Carstairs, John Hope-Scott of Abbotsford and Rt Rev. J. Murdock for a large orphanage to serve across Scotland, as an alternative to Catholic destitute children being placed in Protestant orphanages. The

Sisters were contracted to run it from its opening, under the management of trustees who originally included the Archbishops of Edinburgh and Glasgow and the Provincial of the Vincentian Fathers. It seems to have been the policy of the Scottish hierarchy to concentrate provision for children in care, and Smyllum (as it was always known) grew to be very large as a consequence. At its peak the orphanage housed 700 children. Children came from across dioceses and Poor Law Boards and these Boards expressed great confidence in the home. From 1874 Catholic children in poverty with special needs such as deafness and blindness were referred to Smyllum. The developments and the fund-raising that were necessary to run the orphanage were led by Sister Anne Farrell of County Meath (1832–1913), whose life's work this was. She developed the property and the farm very extensively, showing considerable management skills. The complex at Smyllum had a boys' elementary school (1872); a Piers Pugin chapel (1883); 59 acres of farmland bequeathed by Lady Gray of Kilfauns Castle, Perth (1895); a girls' elementary school (1898); a nursery (1899); and an isolation hospital (1900). A deaf and blind school (1882) was built and operated until a special residential school opened in Tollcross in 1911 (see below). After the war the Sister Servant noted that the home had a high proportion of older girls with intellectual disabilities who were given training in either domestic or commercial skills until they reached the age of sixteen, despite the normal age of leaving being fourteen (later fifteen). During the late 1950s the numbers of children reduced and the house was gradually organised into six family groups with greater numbers of trained lay staff being employed. In 1971 the Provincial informed the Archbishop that, as children left, they would be gradually closing the orphanage because it did not meet modern good practice for small family care homes. The Province bought two large houses in Pollokshields to transfer children to group homes, but at the request of the Archdiocese some children continued at Smyllum until it was closed in 1981. The Archdiocese sought an alternative use for the extensive buildings and land which were eventually sold for housing development.

Lanarkshire Coatbridge	1867–1870 The Sisters were invited by Father Michael O'Keeffe of St Patrick's parish to teach and visit among the predominantly Irish community of St Patrick's and Coatbridge. They established three day schools, two night schools and three Sunday schools and built one school themselves on land donated by Father O'Keeffe and gave it to the parish. It is not altogether clear why, after such an investment and such a strong beginning, the Sisters were withdrawn. The main record notes that 'after a few years, difficulties arose which could not be smoothed away...'. This seems to refer to anxiety on the part of the hierarchy that the school might lose its Privy Council grant because the sisters were not certificated teachers and were, therefore, open to criticism by the education Board. The series of decisions leading to withdrawal was managed through the Paris superiors in consultation with the Sister Servant and the Vincentians at Lanark because it took place before the Province was established. When Canon O'Keeffe died in 1893 Sisters from Smyllum attended his funeral.
Lanarkshire Coatbridge Mitchell Street no. 79	1982–1992 Closed then re-erected 1994–1997. At the closure of Smyllum the Province consulted the Bishop of Motherwell to identify needs they might meet in the Glasgow area. Coatbridge with its very large working-class Catholic population was given priority. The Sisters applied for a council house and from there undertook pastoral work for St Monica's and St James's parishes. They had some involvement with a project initiated by Cardinal Winning providing aftercare of young mothers and babies, running a crèche and organising holidays for single parents and deprived families. Hospital visiting at Monklands and Bellshill hospitals was undertaken. In the 1980s there was an emphasis on placing younger Sisters here. In the late 1980s Sisters were involved in the Renew programme to encourage lay pastoral and liturgical leadership.
Mitchell Street	1994–1997 A different small council house was taken as a Sisters' residence to undertake parish visiting.
Renfrewshire Langbank	1920–1994 The Sisters were invited by the local Conference of the SVP to run a new children's holiday home for children living in deprived environments. The house was originally known as The Hollies and later Langbank. Funds to support a holiday home for 100 children were collected in Glasgow and the West. Trustees were appointed by the Archbishop of Glasgow to manage the home, which overlooked the Clyde and was within easy reach of Glasgow, and the Sisters were appointed to run it. During the 1920s and 1930s the demand was great and money was raised from local benefactors to extend the building with two new wings and a chapel designed by Donald J. Cameron. The Hollies was closed for six years during the war when a land-mine damaged the chapel. When it re-opened it was found that the need and demand had declined, partly because local authorities had taken on responsibility for holiday provision. Between 1920 and 1961 75,000 children had

enjoyed a fortnight's holiday at Langbank. The building was considered as possible replacement for Bellevue Refuge in Rutherglen (see above) but the public authorities refused this change of use. In 1961 the SVP handed the property over to the Bishops of Scotland who were seeking an extension of Blairs College Junior Seminary in Aberdeen. The building was adapted for 120 boys and the Sisters stayed on to run the infirmary and support services. The Junior Seminary closed in 1977 and the property reverted to the SVP which used it for retreats, meeting and conferences for a wide range of groups in need (such as Alcoholics Anonymous, one-parent families and disability groups). The Sisters continued to manage what was then known as St Vincent's College and Conference Centre. In 1989 the Province began 'Vincentian Volunteers', a one-year experimental volunteering programme for young people aged eighteen to thirty-five which ran from St Vincent's in collaboration with the National Council of SVP in Scotland. (Volunteers commit a year to the service of vulnerable people in the spirit of Vincent de Paul in a programme co-ordinated by Daughters of Charity.) The SVP decided to close the house in 1994 because it could no longer meet the costs of repairing the property. Vincentian Volunteers continues in several different locations in Britain.

Renfrewshire Johnstone North Road	1987–1991 St Vincent's Hospice run by the SVP Conference of Holy Redeemer church in Elderslie. This was a collaborative project between the Province and the SVP, making use of a large property. The Province sent three Sisters to nurse and care for terminally ill patients but prior to the opening of the Hospice two Sisters lived at Langbank while helping to decorate and furnish the building and to buy the necessary nursing equipment to transform the house into a fully equipped hospice. The Sisters lived on site for a period but then rented a flat nearby in Gibson Crescent to form their House. One Sister was Matron and another Administrator of the Hospice, which was (and continues to be) open to people of all creeds and none. A third Sister visited in local parishes. The decline in the number of qualified nursing Sisters available made it necessary for the Sisters to withdraw from Johnstone at the end of 1991, although some links were maintained for a period. (In 1993 the Hospice moved to new purpose-built premise in the country with room for 12 patients and many facilities for visitors.)
Paisley St James' Presbytery	1997–2009 The Sisters were invited by Bishop Mone to administer the parish for the non-residential priest. This involved the full range of pastoral, catechetical and non-Eucharistic liturgical provision for the parishioners of St James'. District nursing and involvement with women working in prostitution were also undertaken from this House.

HIGHLANDS

Kingussie Gynack Road	1934–1986 St Vincent's Sanatorium and Hospital. This was the most northerly House of the Daughters in Britain, not far from the ski resort of Aviemore. The sanatorium was built in 1901 and run by a German doctor using a treatment for TB observed in the Black Forest in Germany. On retiring he sold the property to Dr Felix Savy who ran the sanatorium until 1934 when the Province bought it, retaining Dr Savy as Medical Superintendent. The creation of new drugs to treat TB in 1948 rendered sanatorium treatment redundant and during the 1950s the hospital was adapted for geriatric nursing with a new wing and chapel being added. There was always a resident chaplain (one of whom was Father Thomson, brother of Visitatrice Anne Thomson and another Father Heslin, brother of Sister Bernadette Heslin). One of the features of this work was the continuity and stability of the House: for example, Sister Teresa Diamond was placed in St Vincent's for 41 years (d.1982) and Anne Thomson, who was placed here after she ceased to be Visitatrice (1946), remained here until she died. When the Sisters withdrew in 1986 the hospital was taken on by the Highland Primary Care NHS Trust as a residential nursing care facility.
Fort William	1926–1942 Bishop Oban asked for the Sisters to take over teaching in St Columba's elementary school. The Sisters added a hostel for young women with little income, who were intending to be teachers, undertook parish visiting and established sodalities. By 1942 the new Bishop wanted to open a secondary school and invited the Sisters of Notre Dame de Namur to run this together with the elementary school. He asked the Daughters to resign and to leave in the interests of what was best for the diocese. They did so and sold their house to the Notre Dame congregation.

WALES

The Sisters did not open any Houses in Wales until 1932. The number of Houses has remained small with transfers from one location to another but since the first House was opened the Province has given priority to maintaining a presence in Wales because there were relatively few other religious communities present.

The information is arranged primarily by chronology.

Pwllypant	1932–1935 The Sisters' first House in Wales. They were invited by the parish priest of St Helen's for visiting and parish work. The House soon transferred to Caerphilly where a new Mass Centre had been erected a mile from Pwllypant to meet the needs of the growing Catholic population.
Caerphilly Nantgarw Road	1935–2001 House of Charity. A church and presbytery were built here with a gift from the Marquis of Bute. The Province bought a house close by. As there was no Catholic school the Sisters undertook catechetical work over a wide area and the children came for religious instruction for 30 minutes before school each morning. The Sisters' House was extended in 1960 to accommodate this work which continued until Cardinal Newman Comprehensive School opened in Pontypridd in 1966. Sister Philomena Nicholson was appointed to the staff of the school in 1967 and was the first Daughter of Charity to teach in South Wales. Two Sisters were missioned to collaborate with the Apostolate to the Travelling People in Britain and provide support for Travellers in the Cardiff area. The Sisters' other ministries included pastoral care of deaf children and adults, SVP, sacramental preparation and sacristy of the parish church. When the House closed Sisters moved to Ely, Cardiff.
Cardiff Ely Grand Avenue no. 200	2001 continuing. Over the years, Sisters who lived here have cared for the elderly at home and undertaken prison chaplaincy. They currently work with the people in Ely; and support refugees and asylum seekers in Cardiff.
Cardiff Cathedral Road nos 41–43	1949–1976 Our Lady's Hostel. The Sisters were invited by Archbishop McGrath to take over a property that had been a maternity home. The Province bought the house (41) to be run as a hostel for Catholic young women, many from Ireland, who had migrated to work in local firms. A local business man, John Curran, was a major benefactor for the running costs in the first 15 years. The adjoining house (43) was bought in 1950. The hostel was opened in 1951. The Sisters were supported by a group of local women who volunteered to help with practical support such as food preparation. The hostel had many residents who were not Catholics and there was a steady flow of receptions into the Church. The Province opened a House of the Miraculous Medal to promote knowledge and distribution of the Medal and also a hostel for young working women. Two Sisters went weekly to Abertillery, a mining parish in the valleys, to provide catechesis. Another ministry was among the Travelling community across all their sites in and around Cardiff. By the 1970s, when eight Sisters were living there, the hostel was catering primarily for international higher education students and demand decreased as students sought greater independence. At this point during the major re-assessment of the works undertaken in the post-Vatican II era, the Province decided this work was not a priority. The property was donated to the archdiocese and is currently being used as the Archbishop's House and Curial Offices. The Sisters were transferred to Pentwyn.
Cardiff Pentwyn Bryn Pinwydden no. 106	1976–1991 Pentwyn was chosen so that the Sisters could work closely with people living on this council estate where more than half of the tenants were on Supplementary and Housing Benefit. Sisters undertook a range of ministries: hospital chaplaincy; RE teaching; infant school teaching; Family Centre and Diocesan social work; adoption and fostering with the Catholic Children's Society; visiting and Holy Communion to the sick; and work with prisoners' families. Initially there was no church in the area and Mass was said in the Sisters' House. After almost 15 years the Sisters moved from here because large estates of higher-quality, more costly houses were built in the area, thus making it less well situated for their work. The community initially moved to Caerphilly and then to Ely in Cardiff (see above).
Newport	1985–1987 Sisters with specialist knowledge of deaf communication were invited to minister to deaf people in the diocese.

429

Ammanford Brynderwen Road no. 1	1991–2004 With the withdrawal of Sisters from Pentwyn the Province wanted to open another mission in South Wales. At Ammanford they bought a four-bedroomed house which began as an annexe to the House in Cardiff and then became independent. The aim was for the Sisters to work with the very poorest in the local community and in the Parish of Our Lady of the Rosary alongside Father Haydn Blackley. They were involved in parish visiting, sacramental preparation, visiting residential homes and hospitals, meals on wheels and respite care in their house (one room in their House was registered). School and pastoral work with families in the valleys as well as the town was undertaken. Work began on a new church in 2003 (the original church having been demolished in 2001) and the Sisters returned for the celebration when it was consecrated in 2004.
St Davids Maes-Yr Hedydd no. 19	2001–2011 Annexed to Cardiff. The Sisters were invited to administer the parish for the non-resident parish priest and to provide pastoral support for parishioners.

Sources

MS Minutes of the Provincial Council since 1885 DCMH
MS House information compiled in 1921 DCMH
MS House Archives DCMH
'Survey of the works in 1970' DCMH
History of the Province – timeline compiled for the centenary in 1985 DCMH
History of the Province compiled in 2007 for 150-year anniversary DCMH
'The Development of the British Province' Chronological List DCMH

Meetings with a small group of Sisters with knowledge of the past 50 years in the Province.

Webpages for: St John's School for the Deaf and Hard of Hearing; Christopher Grange and St Vincent's Special School, Liverpool; The Passage, Carlisle Place, London; the Depaul Trust; St George's Catholic Primary School, York; St Vincent's Nursing Home, Pinner; St Wilfrid's Drop-In Centre, Sheffield; Wardour Catholic Primary School; and for many of the parishes.

Appendix II

Provincials and Province Directors

Visitatrices/Provincials

(The title Provincial was adopted in the Province of Great Britain in 1970)

Term of office	Name	Born	Age	Entered	Previous office
1885–1890	Juliette Minart	France	63	1848	Senior Sister Levant
1890–1919	Eugénie de Marcellus	France	50	1867	Company Bursar Visitatrice Portugal
1919–1926	Louise Hannezo	France	68	1878	Directress, Paris
1926–1928	Mary Boyle	Ulster	64	1883	Sister Servant
1928–1946	Anne Thomson	Scotland	49	1903	Assistant; Bursar
1946–1947	Barbara Burke	England	50	1923	Provincial Secretary
1947–1952	Mary McGee	Ireland	63	1920	Sister Servant
1952–1966	Anne Whalen	England	49	1924	Directress; Assistant
1966–1978	Gertrude Andrew	England	55	1936	Directress; Councillor
1978–1987	Joan Dwyer	England	55	1942	Assistant
1987–1996	Margaret Barrett	Scotland	44	1965	Directress
1996–2002	Mary (Zoe) O'Neill	Ireland	58	1959	Councillor
2002–2008	Sarah King-Turner	England	62	1980	Paris Secretariat
2008–2015	Marie Raw	England	66	1966	Councillor
2015–	Ellen Flynn	England	62	1972	Councillor

Provincial Directors

(all were priests of the Congregation of the Mission, Irish Province)

Term of office	Name
1885–1898	William Gavin
1898–1909	Joseph Walshe
1909–1922	William Byrne
1923–1938	John O'Connell
1938–1961	Joseph Sheedy
1955–1960	Patrick Travers (substitute for Sheedy)
1961–1967	James Cahalan
1967–1969	Felix McArtsney
1980–1986	Matthew Barry
1986–1995	Dermot O'Dowd
1995–2001	Michael McCullagh
2001–2012	Fergus Kelly
2013–	Paul Roche

Appendix III

Survey of Daughters of Charity in the British Province 2005

The Survey was conducted on the occasion of a Provincial Meeting, held at Ushaw College, Co. Durham, to which all Sisters had been invited.

1.0   **Participants were asked to state whether they were:**
a) 51 and over years of vocation (entered in 1955 or earlier)
b) Between 31 and 50 years of vocation (entered between 1956 and 1975)
c) Between 21 and 30 years of vocation (entered between 1976 and 1985)
d) 20 years and under of vocation (entered since 1986)

Participants were invited to answer the following questions and given space to reflect at some length.

2.0   *What attracted you to the Daughters of Charity when you were discerning your vocation?* (Please mention any guidance or direction you received).

3.0   *Did you know that the Company was different from other active religious congregations?* (canonically, the annual vows etc).

4.0   *What image of the Daughters did you have before entering and where had you got this image from?*

5.0   *What was most important to your formation before you made your Vows?*

6.0   *What has been most important since?*

7.0   *What was your first reaction to the changes brought about in the Company after the Second Vatican Council?* (for Sisters who were in the Company at this time)

8.0   *Reflecting on the changes, what do you think are the most important aspects of renewal to have come about?*

Index